'Rodric B
age just in time since its dangers are c   _gence. Our
leaders must take the lessons in this meticulous and revelatory
narrative.' Strobe Talbott, Brookings Institution

'Personal experience plus careful study have given him a remarkable
platform from which he brilliantly dissects the ethical dilemmas.'
Guardian

'A timely and sober book ... a trenchant and stimulating analysis of
nuclear deterrence' *Observer*

'[A]n extraordinary inquiry into the nuclear age, Braithwaite
examines not only the danger of these terrible weapons, but also
the mindset of scientists, soldiers and politicians who held the fate
of the world in their hands. For any reader who has ever wondered,
'what were they thinking?', Braithwaite has provided a history that
is brilliant and deeply disturbing.' David E. Hoffman, author of *The
Dead Hand*

'Highly urgent ... As Braithwaite explains very well, the capacity
to put yourself inside the mind of someone like Kim Jong-un is
of supreme importance ... Bluster about destroying a country is
no substitute for cool diplomacy. Braithwaite's book reminds us of
that.' *Evening Standard*

'[A] timely reminder that the threat of nuclear Armageddon did
not end when the Cold War did.' Jack F. Matlock, Jr., author
of *Reagan and Gorbachev: How the Cold War Ended*

'A fresh and invigorating take on the Cold War' *History Today*

'Rodric Braithwaite's new book is, like his other works, well
and clearly written, informed by careful research and a thought-
provoking read.' *International Relations*

'An even-handed, nuanced and often chilling account of the nuclear
confrontation between the USA and the USSR.' *Literary Review*

'Scintillating.' *The Times*

RODRIC BRAITHWAITE was British ambassador in Moscow at the time of the Soviet collapse in 1991. He was foreign policy adviser to the Prime Minister and Chairman of the Joint Intelligence Committee until the end of 1993. His books include *Across the Moscow River* (2002), *Moscow 1941* (2006) and *Afgantsy* (2010).

ARMAGEDDON AND PARANOIA

ALSO BY RODRIC BRAITHWAITE

Across the Moscow River

Moscow 1941

Afgantsy

ARMAGEDDON AND PARANOIA

THE NUCLEAR CONFRONTATION

RODRIC BRAITHWAITE

P

PROFILE BOOKS

This paperback edition published in 2019

First published in Great Britain in 2017 by
Profile Books Ltd
3 Holford Yard
Bevin Way
London WC1X 9HD
www.profilebooks.com

Copyright © Rodric Braithwaite, 2017, 2019

1 3 5 7 9 10 8 6 4 2

Typeset in Garamond by MacGuru Ltd

Printed and bound in Great Britain by CPI Group (UK) Ltd, Croydon CR0 4YY

The moral right of the author has been asserted.

All rights reserved. Without limiting the rights under copyright reserved above,
no part of this publication may be reproduced, stored or introduced into a
retrieval system, or transmitted, in any form or by any means (electronic,
mechanical, photocopying, recording or otherwise), without the prior written
permission of both the copyright owner and the publisher of this book.

A CIP catalogue record for this book is available from the British Library.

ISBN 978 1 78125 721 0
eISBN 978 1 78283 291 1

LONDON BOROUGH OF SUTTON LIBRARY SERVICE (WAL)	
30119 028 471 31 8	
Askews & Holts	Jan-2019
909.825	

For Jill.
Unchanged.
Everywhere.

'Is there either logic or morality in believing that if one side threatens to kill tens of millions of our people our only recourse is to threaten killing tens of millions of theirs?'

Ronald Reagan, Second Inaugural Address, January 1985

'I too was involved in the remarkable scientific and engineering achievements which enabled humanity to master a practically inexhaustible source of energy. But I am no longer certain that humanity has matured enough to manage that energy.'

Yuli Khariton, Director of the Soviet weapons programme, 1995

CONTENTS

THE SWORD OF DAMOCLES

'Every man, woman and child lives under a nuclear sword of Damocles, hanging by the slenderest of threads, capable of being cut at any moment by accident, or miscalculation, or by madness. The weapons of war must be abolished before they abolish us.'

John F. Kennedy, 1961[1]

NATE: How can you live like that? I mean, what if you found out you were going to die tomorrow?

BRENDA: I've been prepared to die tomorrow since I was six years old.

NATE: Well, why since you were six?

BRENDA: 'Cause I read a report on the effect nuclear war would have on the world and it was pretty clear to me at that point that this was definitely going to happen.

NATE: When you were six?

BRENDA: And I wake up every day pretty much surprised that, um, everything's still here.

NATE: Well, I don't understand how you can live like that.

BRENDA: Well, I thought we all did.

Six Feet Under, American TV comedy, 2001–5

On 8 August 1945 I was travelling on a train with my parents to our summer holiday when I read in the *Times* newspaper that Hiroshima had been wiped out by an atomic bomb two days earlier: 'Official reconnaissance photographs of Hiroshima show clearly that four and one-tenth square miles of the city, of a total area of almost seven square miles, were completely destroyed by one atomic bomb,' said the report. '"Destroyed" is the word used officially, but it appears that "obliterated" might be a better word.'

Three days later, a second bomb destroyed another Japanese city. Sitting in the Conservative Party's leather-upholstered Carlton Club, John Watson wrote to the editor of *The Times*: 'Now that the dust that was Hiroshima and Nagasaki is subsiding, there must be countless men and women [able to] observe in its stark reality the unparalleled horror that is being perpetrated in their name ... Two great cities and all who lived within them have been deliberately seared from the earth.' Posterity would condemn those who had first used atomic power for such a purpose. It was 'the most dreadful precedent in the history of mankind'.

Germany was as comprehensively destroyed by war as Japan. The Soviet Union lost far more people, Poland and Yugoslavia a far larger proportion of their people.

Yet the nuclear destruction of Hiroshima and Nagasaki did usher in a new era, despite the lingering feeling among some that the atomic bomb was just another weapon, different in degree but not in kind from the weapons of war that mankind had used throughout history. From that moment politicians and ordinary people alike – even in the nominally atheistic Soviet Union – began to use an old-fashioned language to speak about the new world. They talked of God and the Devil, of Apocalypse and Armageddon, and of the final confrontation between Good and Evil. Statesmen and commentators around the world hurried to agree that the atomic weapon would have to be banned if humanity were not to destroy itself. Some kind of world government would have to be set up to enforce the ban.

It did not happen, of course. The paranoia, the poisonous ideological fervour, the mutual demonisation with which the Soviet Union and its Western allies regarded one another, had been masked by the need to preserve a common front against Hitler. Now it broke out into the open. Neither the Americans, nor the British, still less the Russians, were prepared to be blackmailed by an opponent brandishing a bomb. Within the three governments, intelligent, decent and honourable men (there were very few women) planned the weapons and the systems that would enable them to wipe one another out at a blow. It was hard to argue that what they were doing was either rational or moral.

It was not that the politicians were unaware of their appalling responsibility. They hoped to deter war by making it clear to their adversary that any nuclear attack would inevitably be met by an equally destructive counterstroke. They called it 'deterrence', a policy of Mutually Assured Destruction, or MAD. Their critics sneered at the acronym.

There was not much that ordinary people could do about it. Some protested, without much effect. Others agreed with their governments that if the other fellow had the bomb they had to have it too. Most got on with their lives, like the inhabitants of Pompeii, and hoped the volcano would never blow up. As Fred Iklé put it before he became a hawkish Under Secretary in Ronald Reagan's Pentagon: 'We all turn away ... from the thought that nuclear war may be as inescapable as death, and may end our lives and our society within this generation or the next.'[2]

From time to time governments skirted catastrophe; but when it came to the crunch, they always stepped back. Despite their mutual suspicion, they tried to reach out to their adversaries to find ways of taming the monster. Mikhail Gorbachev and Ronald Reagan eventually found the political courage and the imagination to end the confrontation. In 1994 Presidents Clinton and Yeltsin agreed that their missiles would no longer be targeted against one another: a symbolic gesture to mark the formal end of nearly fifty years of hair-trigger confrontation.[3] The prospect of Armageddon receded. But it did not disappear.

At the height of the Cuban missile crisis in October 1962 I went into the Foreign Office each morning wondering if I would see Jill and my children again. Some people were more phlegmatic. When a BBC reporter asked one woman arriving at Charing Cross station what she thought of the crisis, she replied, 'I'm sorry, dear, I don't know. I'm only up in London for the day.'

My daughter Kate, like Brenda in the American sitcom, grew up dully aware that her existence might be blotted out in a flash. In Moscow, on the other side of the Iron Curtain, ten-year-old Vlad Zubok had nightmares when a school friend told him what a nuclear bomb could do. But he was an optimist and imagined that he would survive with his grandparents in the country even when Moscow was incinerated.

The atom bomb did not, as some had hoped, force the human race to abandon warfare altogether. Nuclear weapons proliferated; but those who had them were terrified to use them. Tens of millions of people went on dying in what now came to be called 'conventional' wars.

Throughout the decades after that train journey in 1945 I wondered what the scientists, the weapons designers, the military men, the officials, and the politicians thought they were doing. I decided to try to work it out for myself while I still had time.

Hence this book.

PART I

PROMETHEAN FIRE

ONE

THE DESTRUCTION OF JAPAN

'All belligerents in all conflicts are morally compromised, but this does not render all causes equally worthless.'

Max Hastings[1]

There was never much doubt about it: when it came to the crunch, the first atomic bomb would be dropped without warning on a city.

On 7 December 1941 Japanese aircraft attacked the American Pacific Fleet in Pearl Harbor without warning, sank three American battleships, damaged three more, and left 2,500 Americans dead. It was a stunning military operation, the culmination of decades of growing hostility between Japan and the West.

The Western imagination had long been filled with images of barbarian hordes from the East: Attila and his Huns, the Mongols 'like demons loose from Tartarus', fanatical oriental despots 'educated to be inscrutable and false ... like us in practically nothing'. But it was Kaiser Wilhelm II, the German emperor, who first talked of 'The Yellow Peril'. In America, prejudice was fed by Chinese and Japanese immigration into California. One populist politician declared immigration would 'soon convert the fairest State in the Union into a Japanese colony'. A series of excitable novels prophesied war.[2]

Meanwhile the Japanese reinvented themselves as a modern power. They conquered Korea, defeated the Russian Empire, and fought alongside the British and the Americans in the First World War. They sought their reward at the Versailles peace negotiations: equal treatment in the fledgling League of Nations. The British and the Americans rejected their plea. American politicians warned of serious consequences for the white race. The British feared the precedent for their Indian subjects.[3]

The Japanese did not forget. They believed themselves descended from the gods, distinct from all other races, innately superior, purer. They saw Westerners as overbearing, oversexed, malodorous, decadent, racist and determined on world domination. Their politics dominated by soldiers, they decided to gamble on war in order, they claimed, to liberate the oppressed peoples of the East from Western imperialism. In 1931 they invaded Manchuria and then China. Western powers with Far Eastern interests – America, Britain, Australia, the Netherlands – reacted by slapping an embargo on Japanese imports of iron ore, steel, and above all, oil.

To the Japanese, the attack on Pearl Harbor seemed a justified if desperate response.

Demonising the Enemy

In wartime you unite your people by persuading them that their enemy threatens their very existence. Atrocity propaganda multiplies: wives and mothers violated, children spitted, men tortured, prisoners executed wholesale, sacred buildings burned to the ground. Differences of race, religion, and political ideology inflame passions still further.

For the Americans it was a war of revenge from the start. At first they and the British were contemptuous of the new enemy: Japanese pilots were short-sighted, their aircraft frail, their warships top-heavy, their soldiers without initiative, their generals incapable of planning a complex campaign. 'You can take it from me,' said one British general on the eve of the Japanese attack, 'that we have nothing to fear from them.'[4]

Within days the British and Americans were suffering one defeat after another. The Japanese treated civilians and prisoners of war with great brutality: evidence, said General George Marshall, the US Army Chief of Staff, of 'the shallow advance from savagery which the Japanese people have made ... the future of the Japanese race itself depends entirely and irrevocably upon their capacity to progress beyond their aboriginal barbaric instincts'.[5] The Australian General Thomas Blamey told his soldiers, 'Your enemy is a cross between the human being and the ape. You know that we have to exterminate these vermin if we and our families are to live. We must go on to the end if civilization is to survive.'

Back home in America comic strips showed clean-limbed

young American soldiers rescuing American girls from their stunted, myopic, bucktoothed, barely human Japanese captors. In May 1944 *Life* magazine published its Photo of the Week: Natalie Nickerson is writing to her boyfriend, a naval lieutenant in the Pacific, to thank him for his gift. The gift – on the table as she writes – is the skull of a Japanese soldier.[6]

In November 1944 the American Office of Public Opinion Research conducted a nationwide poll in which they asked, 'What do you think we should do with Japan as a country after the war?' Thirteen per cent of those asked answered, 'Kill all Japanese.'[7]

Trial by Fire

Only a few years earlier both Britain and America had emphatically condemned the Japanese and the Germans for bombing cities. It was, the Americans said, 'a violation of the most elementary principles of humane conduct which have been developed as an essential part of modern civilization'.[8]

But, when it came to the crunch, none of the belligerents restrained themselves. All pleaded military necessity or the right to retaliate. British and American airmen had always believed passionately in the ability of strategic air power to win wars. Now they could put theory into practice. The Royal Air Force bombed Germany by night, deliberately targeting working-class areas in German industrial cities, a process described by a charming euphemism as 'de-housing the workforce'. The American Air Force in Europe tried bombing their targets accurately by day. In practice their bombs often fell wide and their targeting became increasingly indiscriminate. Even before Pearl Harbor American airmen were planning for 'general incendiary attacks to burn up the wood and paper structures of the densely populated Japanese cities'.*

---

* Some of their military and naval colleagues were unhappy. Brigadier General Bonner Fellers, an aide to General MacArthur, the American commander in the Pacific, thought that the air campaign against Japan was 'one of the most ruthless and barbaric killings of non-combatants in all history'. Admiral Leahy, then the most senior officer in the American military, thought that the strategic bombing of civilians was 'barbarism not worthy of Christian man' (J. Dower, *War without*

At first the Americans had no satisfactory airbases within range of Japan. In 1942 they asked the Russians for bases around Vladivostok. The Russian were unenthusiastic.[9] After their defeat by the Japanese in 1905, they had had to surrender their imperial possessions in the Far East. 'This defeat of the Russian troops,' Stalin said later, 'left a bitter memory in the minds of our people. Our people waited and believed that this blot would some day be erased.'[10]

But now was not the moment. That winter the Russians were fighting for their lives outside Moscow after six bitter months of retreat before the Germans. To throw them back, they had pulled in their reserves from the Far East. Stalin had a treaty of neutrality with Japan, and he had no intention of denouncing it until he was quite sure that German power was broken. Not surprisingly, when the Americans turned to him for help, he prevaricated.

By the summer of 1944, however, both the Germans and the Japanese were in retreat. The Americans began to plan the invasion of Japan itself. Russian armies, they hoped, could pin down the large Japanese force in Manchuria. Russian airfields could support American bombers in the final assault. The Chiefs of Staff told Roosevelt that 'Russia's entry at as early a date as possible is necessary to provide maximum assistance to our Pacific operations'.[11] When they met in Yalta in February 1945, Stalin promised Roosevelt that he would join the war in the East three months after he had beaten the Germans in Europe. In return he wanted the territories Russia had lost after 1905. Roosevelt agreed.[12]

Meanwhile the Americans tried other ways of bombing the Japanese mainland. In April 1942 General James Doolittle raided Tokyo with aircraft from the carrier USS *Hornet*. American bombers flew from India through China to reach their targets. The military results were negligible. In December 1943 the Americans decided on a new tack. They would capture an island base in the Pacific from which to bomb Japan direct with their revolutionary new B-29 bomber, the

Mercy, New York, 1986, p. 40). Similar moral objections were later also voiced by British admirals. They ceased abruptly when both countries sent a main part of their deterrent to sea in submarines under naval command.

Superfortress, the most powerful and sophisticated bomber of the war.

By the middle of 1944 one Pacific island after another was falling to the Americans as they advanced relentlessly towards the Japanese homeland. The Japanese fought back with suicidal bravery, dying in their tens of thousands and inflicting heavy losses on their attackers. In the summer of 1944 nearly 3,000 Americans died on the island of Saipan in the Mariana archipelago. So did almost the whole garrison of 30,000; more than 1,000 Japanese civilians – whole families – committed suicide. The battle of Okinawa began the following April and lasted eighty-two days. Over 12,500 Americans were killed, nearly 80,000 Japanese soldiers, and perhaps as many as 150,000 civilians. It was the first Japanese island to fall, and a terrifying foretaste of what the Americans might expect if they invaded the Japanese homeland.

By the autumn of 1944 the Americans' island bases in the Marianas were ready. The Superfortresses were now well within range of Japan. It was the beginning of a crucial new phase in the war.

The first attacks were launched at the high altitudes for which the Superfortresses had been designed, and they were aimed at industrial facilities. In November 1944 the bombers attacked Tokyo. Other raids followed in rapid succession. But they did little significant damage and the results were far below expectation. Then General Curtis LeMay arrived to command the campaign.

LeMay was a blunt, sarcastic, quiet-voiced, uncommunicative man, with very few social graces and a damp cigar permanently stuck in his mouth. He possessed a bull-like obstinacy, determined ruthlessness, and undoubted courage. He flew with the Flying Fortresses in the early months of the American bombing campaign in Europe, when the losses were tremendous. He was relentlessly demanding of his men. In return they feared but trusted him. By 1943 he had become the youngest general in the US Army.

LeMay's military philosophy was simple enough: 'I'll tell you what war is about,' he once said. 'You've got to kill people, and when you kill enough of them they stop fighting.' Many were unnerved by this brutal logic. During the Vietnam War he is supposed to have said that the Vietnamese should be bombed back into the Stone Age.

It was not quite true, but the accusation stuck. He was said to be the original for General Buck Turgidson in the film *Dr Strangelove or: How I Learned to Stop Worrying and Love the Bomb.*[13]

But whatever else he was, LeMay was a formidable military commander. He decided to abandon the ineffective high-level attacks. Much Japanese manufacturing was carried on in small workshops and private homes rather than in large-scale factories. So from now on the bombers would deliberately go in low and at night, raining incendiary bombs down upon the wood and paper houses in which most Japanese city dwellers lived.

On the night of 9–10 March 1945 the Superfortresses struck Tokyo again. The centre of the city was levelled by fire. Some 100,000 people – perhaps many more – were killed. Crews in the last aircraft over the target reported that they could smell burnt human flesh.[14] It was the most deadly raid of the Second World War: even more deadly than the bombing of Hiroshima and Nagasaki. In the campaign that followed, sixty-six Japanese cities were largely destroyed. Somewhere between 220,000 and 500,000 people were killed. Industrial production plummeted. Japan's cities were being destroyed in a rain of fire which continued until the very last days of the war.[15]

By the summer of 1945 Japan was assailed on all sides. The Japanese Air Force had virtually ceased to exist. American bombers roamed Japanese skies almost at will. The navy had been decimated in a series of epic sea battles, its remaining ships now mostly disabled or out of fuel. The coastal traffic that linked the Japanese islands and supplied the Japanese armies in China, Manchuria, and South-East Asia had ground to a halt. The economy was in ruins. Japan had gone to war to secure its oil supplies. Then it had more than 12 million barrels in reserve; now it had only 200,000.[16] Defeat was simply a matter of time.

But the Japanese generals were determined to go down fighting and to take as many Americans with them as they could. They armed tens of thousands of civilians with bamboo lances, and trained them to die in a forlorn last stand and share the honour of a glorious defeat. If enough Americans died in the assault, the generals hoped, they might abandon their policy of unconditional surrender and agree on terms that would allow the Japanese Army to preserve its honour.

The Most Terrible Weapon

This was fantasy, even if the Americans had not had a terrifying card up their sleeves.

The atom bomb was originally intended for the Germans: the British and Americans began work on it in 1940–41 lest Hitler get it first. But by the autumn of 1944 it was clear that the German nuclear project had failed and that Germany was nearing defeat. By then the Americans' massive Manhattan Project was ten months away from testing a bomb. When Winston Churchill and Franklin Roosevelt met that September, they decided that, when it was ready, the bomb 'might perhaps, after mature consideration, be used against the Japanese, who should be warned that this bombardment will be repeated until they surrender.'[17]*

When Roosevelt died in April 1945, Harry Truman, his Vice President and successor, knew nothing about the Manhattan Project. Now he learned from Henry Stimson, Secretary of War, that within four months 'we shall in all probability have completed the most terrible weapon ever known in human history, one bomb of which could destroy a whole city. With its aid even a very powerful unsuspecting nation might be conquered within a very few days by a much smaller one. Modern civilization might be completely destroyed.'[18]

In May 1945 Stimson set up an Interim Committee to discuss how the bomb should be used. Its members included James Byrnes, a former senator who became Secretary of State, and a number of distinguished academics. Attached to it was a Scientific Panel, which consisted of Robert Oppenheimer, Enrico Fermi, Arthur Compton, and Ernest Lawrence, all of whom had been involved in the Manhattan Project. After some agonised discussion, they had little doubt that the bomb would have to be dropped on a city.[19]

The thinking of Truman and his military advisors was heavily coloured by the shadow of the Okinawa battle, now in its final bloody days. Some argued that conventional aerial bombardment and economic strangulation would force the Japanese to give in, without using the bomb and without an invasion. The Japanese were

---

* This is an amendment to the fiercer language originally drafted, which said that 'when a "bomb" is finally available, it should be used against the Japanese.'

already trying to negotiate a settlement through the Soviets: when the Soviets invaded Manchuria, as they had promised, even the Japanese generals might be shocked into accepting that further resistance was useless. General Marshall, the US Army Chief of Staff, believed that the Russian attack 'might well be the decisive action'.[20]

Some countered that Russian help no longer looked necessary or even desirable: might the Russians not simply exploit victory in the Far East to impose their control there, as they had done in Eastern Europe? Why should the Russians have a share in the spoils of victory which America had earned throughout the long Pacific campaign?

Others believed that the Japanese would give up if the Americans modified their policy of unconditional surrender and allowed them to keep their Emperor. Without the Emperor's authority, indeed, the more fanatical Japanese soldiers might be impossible to control.[21] But, some said, this was an uncertain course. Even if some Japanese civilians were putting out peace feelers, the Japanese military were determined to fight to the death.

All agreed that Operation Downfall, the proposed invasion of Japan, could be a very bloody affair. The initial assault on the southernmost island of Kyushu was due in November. The final battle on the Tokyo plain would take place five months later. There was wide disagreement about the likely cost in American casualties: pessimists put it at between 1.7 and 4 million, including 400,000–800,000 dead.[22] For Truman the exact figures were unimportant. He was anxious above all to keep American casualties down to a minimum at this, the very last stage of the war.

Many involved in the discussions worried about the moral implications of using the new weapon and revisited ideas that had been discussed in the Interim Committee. Japanese observers should be invited to witness a demonstration explosion. Or a bomb should be dropped on a purely military target, far from civilian habitation. Or it should be dropped on a city, but only after the Japanese had been given time to evacuate the people. General Marshall feared 'the opprobrium which might follow from an ill-considered employment of such force'. Henry Stimson 'did not want to have the United States get the reputation of outdoing Hitler in atrocities'.

But these ideas were rejected. For General Groves, the head of the

Manhattan Project, the matter was simple enough. Some $2 billion had been spent on the bomb. If it was not used the American taxpayer would wonder why. However destructive it might be, it was just another weapon: it should be used in whatever way made military sense. If the Japanese were invited to a demonstration, they might not be impressed; and suppose the thing failed to go off? If they were warned to move people from target cities, they might simply replace them with American prisoners. The meeting concluded that there was no alternative to hitting a city, one with a large war industry, and without any warning.

Truman himself grappled inconclusively with the moral dilemma. He consoled himself in advance with the hopeful thought that the bomb would be used 'so that military objectives and soldiers and sailors are the target and not women and children. Even if the Japs are savages, ruthless, merciless and fanatic, we as the leaders of the world for the common welfare [are not]. The target will be a purely military one.'[23] That was, of course, a fantasy: no such target existed. On the day Nagasaki was bombed he spoke in a broadcast of the 'tragic significance' of the bomb.[24] And when the possibility of dropping further bombs was mooted, he told his advisers 'that the thought of wiping out another 100,000 people was too horrible'; he didn't like the idea of killing 'all those kids'.[25] But in later life he maintained that he never doubted that the bomb would have to be used.

The discussion then became specific: which city should be hit? Kyoto, Japan's ancient capital and a major cultural centre, was on the generals' list: they held that its destruction would have exactly the shattering effect on Japanese morale that was intended. Stimson insisted that it be struck off.

The Americans successfully tested their nuclear device on 16 July. Nine days later the order was given to deliver the first special bomb 'as soon as weather will permit visual bombing after about 3 August 1945 on one of the targets Hiroshima, Kokura, Niigata, and Nagasaki'. The military were authorised to drop further bombs as they became available.[26]

The 509th Composite Group, under the command of Captain Paul Tibbets, a veteran of the American bombing campaign in

Europe, had been specially trained to drop the atomic bomb. In June they moved to Tinian, by then the largest airbase in the world. They were joined at the beginning of August by a uranium bomb, coyly named 'Little Boy', and a plutonium bomb, 'Fat Man'.*

On Saturday 4 August Tibbets briefed his men. 'The moment has arrived,' he told them. 'This is what we have all been working toward. Very recently the weapon we are about to deliver was successfully tested in the States. We have received orders to drop it on the enemy.' This one bomb, the men were told, 'is the most destructive weapon ever produced. We think it will knock out everything within a three-mile area.' They listened in 'shocked disbelief'. The next day Tibbets ordered his plane to be named after his mother, *Enola Gay*. That night the crews were blessed at a service for Catholics at ten o'clock and for Protestants at ten thirty. One airman is said to have asked for absolution.[27]

On Monday 6 August 1945 the *Enola Gay* took off for the twelve-hour flight to Hiroshima and back. At 8.15 a.m. Hiroshima time 'Little Boy' exploded 600 metres above the city centre with a blinding flash. A mushroom cloud of radioactive dust rose eight miles into the sky. Tibbets told his men, 'Fellows, you have just dropped the first atomic bomb in history.' Robert Lewis, Tibbets' co-pilot, had kept a diary throughout the flight. Now he wrote, 'My God, what have we done?'[†]

President Truman heard the news as he was crossing the Atlantic on his way home from meeting Stalin at Potsdam. He issued a statement: 'Sixteen hours ago an American airplane dropped one bomb on Hiroshima, an important Japanese Army base. That bomb had

---

* The heavy cruiser *Indianapolis*, which had brought some of the components, was sunk soon after she left Tinian by a Japanese submarine, with heavy loss of life. It was an entirely legitimate act of war. But when the news got through – to Truman, and to the men on Tinian itself – their determination to punish the Japanese became even more incandescent.

† Lewis kept the diary at the request of William Laurence, the science correspondent of the *New York Times*, who had been refused permission to fly at the last minute. Laurence was, however, allowed to go with one of the bombers which attacked Nagasaki.

more power than 20,000 tons of TNT ... The force from which the sun draws its power has been loosed against those who brought war to the Far East.' He went on to warn the Japanese: 'We shall destroy their docks, their factories, and their communications. Let there be no mistake ... If they do not now accept our terms they may expect a rain of ruin from the air, the like of which has never been seen on this earth.'[28]

Churchill was more sober. 'This revelation of the secrets of nature, long mercifully withheld from man,' he declared, 'should arouse the most solemn reflections in the mind and conscience of every human being capable of comprehension.'[29]

Since they had been given carte blanche, the American commanders did not consult the politicians before dropping 'Fat Man', the plutonium bomb, on Nagasaki on 9 August.

Truman's announcement was followed by some unpleasant stuff in the press about the 'whining, whimpering, complaining' Japanese, who had got what they deserved for the treachery of Pearl Harbor and for all the wartime atrocities they had committed.

But many Americans foresaw that the horrible weapon they had used might eventually be turned against them. That first evening, NBC radio news said, 'We must assume that with the passage of only a little time, an improved form of the new weapon we use today can be turned against us.' The *Milwaukee Journal* speculated about 'a self-perpetuating chain of atomic destruction' that could obliterate the entire planet. The *New York Times* commented, 'Much of our bombing throughout this war – like the enemy's – has been directed against cities and hence against civilians. Because our bombing has been more devastating, Americans have become a synonym for destruction. We may yet reap the whirlwind.' An appalled reader of *Time* magazine wrote, 'The United States of America has this day become the new master of brutality, infamy, atrocity ... No peacetime applications of this Frankenstein monster can ever erase the crime we have committed.'[30]

These gloomy thoughts were offset by more pleasing ideas. The ability to unlock the power of the atom, some commentators said, would mean that energy would in future be as good as free – power for industry and transport, heating and lighting for cities and homes. People would fly in aeroplanes, sail on ships, travel on trains powered by nuclear engines. They would drive around in nuclear-fuelled cars for nothing. 'Atomic' became an advertising aid for everything that was fashionable in clothing. In less than a year, a new kind of skimpy swimming costume was named after the first American nuclear test on the Bikini Atoll.

At first there was little hard information from the Japanese cities themselves. Japanese radio reported that 'the impact of the bomb was so terrific that practically all living things, human and animal, were literally seared to death by the tremendous heat and pressure engendered by the blast'. The bomb exploded directly above a hospital in the centre of the city. It killed all the patients, doctors and nurses, and all the teachers and children in a nearby school. The troops of the garrison were on their morning parade: 3,000 died.

Teams began to arrive from outside, first Japanese, later American, British, and Russian. They found that blast and fire had destroyed nearly five square miles of the city.* One concrete building close to ground zero† survived almost intact; others were severely damaged. Brick buildings were completely destroyed within a radius of a mile; wooden buildings – the vast majority – were swept away.[31] American scientists measured the shadows of people burned into buildings and into the ground by the bomb's flash. Using a mathematical formula called 'the standardised casualty rate', they estimated that the bomb had killed and wounded people 6,500 times more efficiently per pound of explosive force delivered than a conventional bomb.[32]

Decades later it was still impossible to fix a final figure for the casualties, for those killed and wounded by the initial flash, blast, fire, radiation, fallout, and subsequent cancers. First reports broadcast

---

* The explosion raised the temperature briefly to 4,000 degrees Celsius. Iron melts at 1,535 degrees.
† 'Ground zero' was originally a technical term to signify the point on the ground directly below a nuclear explosion. It was later used as the name for an American anti-nuclear movement, before describing the site of the Twin Towers in New York destroyed in the terrorist attack of 11 September 2001.

from Japan said the corpses 'were too numerous to count'. At least 70,000–80,000 people were initially killed in Hiroshima and 35,000–40,000 in Nagasaki. Towards the end of August, the death rate started to rise again as the effects of radiation made themselves felt. No certainty was ever reached.

It took time for the voices of the survivors themselves – the *hikabusha* – to be heard. The survivors were reluctant to talk about their experiences and others to listen. At first the American occupying authority censored journalists' reports. The first substantial account, by the veteran reporter John Hersey, was published in August 1946 by the *New Yorker*. It immediately became a classic.

Hersey began with a vivid detail: 'At exactly fifteen minutes past eight in the morning on August 6, 1945, Japanese time, at the moment when the atomic bomb flashed above Hiroshima, Miss Toshiko Sasaki, a clerk in the personnel department of the East Asia Tin Works, had just sat down at her place in the plant office and was turning her head to speak to the girl at the next desk.'

After the bomb had fallen, 'Mr Tanimoto ... was the only person making his way into the city; he met hundreds and hundreds who were fleeing, and every one of them seemed to be hurt in some way. The eyebrows of some were burned off and skin hung from their faces and hands. Others, because of pain, held up their arms as if carrying something in both hands. Some were vomiting as they walked. Many were naked or in shreds of clothing. On some undressed bodies, the burns had made patterns – of undershirt straps and suspenders and, on the skin of some women (since white repelled the heat from the bomb and dark clothes absorbed it and conducted it to the skin), the shapes of flowers they had had on their kimonos.'*

Hersey's piece sold out on the newsstands within hours. It was

---

*Ten years later Kiyoshi Tanimoto, a Christian priest, brought a party of girls disfigured by the explosion to America for cosmetic surgery. To raise money he appeared on the TV chat show *This is Your Life*. Here, to their mutual surprise, he was introduced to Captain Robert Lewis, the co-pilot of the *Enola Gay*. Students of the grotesque can watch the episode on YouTube at https://youtu.be/ KPFXa2vTErc.

read in its entirety on the radio, distributed free by the Book of the Month Club, and published in book form in America and Britain. It was still in print seven decades later.[33]

The Russians Take a Hand

Churchill and Truman were in Potsdam when they heard that the bomb had been successfully tested in the New Mexican desert. They decided 'to tell the Russians at least that we were working on that subject, and intended to use it if and when it was successfully finished'.[34] But they were determined to give the Russians no details. They clung to the illusion that an American monopoly of the bomb would make the Russians more amenable.

In the margins of a meeting on 24 July Truman mentioned to Stalin, as casually as he could, that the United States had discovered 'a weapon of unusual destructive force'. 'Glad to hear it,' Stalin replied.

Churchill was sure that Stalin had no idea of the significance of what he had been told. 'Evidently in his intense toils and stresses the atomic bomb had played no part,' he wrote in his memoirs. '[H]is face remained gay and genial. "How did it go?" I asked [Truman]. "He never asked a question," he replied. I was certain therefore that at that date Stalin had no special knowledge of the vast process of research upon which the United States and Britain had been engaged for so long.'[35] Truman was under the same impression: 'He didn't realise what I was talking about.'[36]

It was a stunning misjudgement by both men. Stalin knew perfectly well what Truman was talking about, thanks to the Soviet agents who had comprehensively penetrated the Manhattan Project. At the beginning of July they reported that on about 10 July the Americans were going to test an atomic device, of which they gave a brief description. This information was available to Stalin by the time he left for Potsdam on 16 July. His allies' attempt to keep him in the dark smacked to him of double dealing and a desire to intimidate. He had no intention of being bullied. That evening he ordered that the rather modest Soviet nuclear programme be drastically accelerated.[37]

On 26 July Truman, Churchill, and the Chinese Nationalist government issued a declaration in Potsdam, calling on the Japanese to surrender unconditionally or suffer 'prompt and utter destruction'. The Soviet Union was not yet at war with Japan, so Stalin was neither consulted about the wording of the declaration nor asked to sign it.

On 28 July the Japanese government rejected the declaration. It was bitterly split. The politicians saw no point in continuing a war that could only result in Japan's utter destruction: by the end of the year, they feared, the country could face uncontrollable civil unrest. But General Anami, the War Minister, and many of his military colleagues still believed that it was their sacred duty – and that of the wretched civilians who would get caught in the crossfire – to die an honourable death.

The Russians now took a hand. Furious at being cut out of the Potsdam Declaration, Stalin suspected that the Americans intended to deny him the territories he had been promised at Yalta. The Americans' bombs were intended not to end one war, but to demonstrate that they would win the next.

Despite the ravages of the war in Europe Stalin had already amassed, in another triumph of Russian logistical genius, a force of more than 1.5 million men in the Far East, under the command of a favourite marshal, Alexander Vasilevsky. Now he was going to use it.

The attack was planned for 11 August. But now the bomb had been dropped on Hiroshima the war might end before the Russians could get into it. Stalin ordered Vasilevsky to attack two days early, at midnight on 8–9 August. That evening the Japanese ambassador in Moscow, Naotake Sato, finally got to see Molotov to make yet another futile attempt to persuade the Russians to mediate a peace. He received only a declaration of war.[38]

The Russians swept forward relentlessly. Facing them in Manchuria was the Army of Guandong: a far smaller force, hopelessly outmatched in guns, tanks, and aircraft, their best troops already drawn off to face the Americans elsewhere. Here and there they resisted bravely. But there was none of the fanaticism that the Americans had encountered in their island-hopping campaign. Within ten days the Japanese were surrendering in droves. They lost over 80,000 dead and 640,000 prisoners. Russian losses were 12,000 dead and 24,000 wounded.[39]

The Japanese Surrender

Despite the devastation in Hiroshima, the Japanese were still unwilling to surrender unconditionally. On 8 August Truman repeated that the Japanese could 'Expect a rain of ruin from the air, the like of which has never been seen on this earth'. The next day, a second bomb was dropped on Nagasaki.

By then the options for the Japanese had already narrowed dramatically. The hope that the Russians might mediate in a negotiation was ruled out: the Russians were triumphing in Manchuria and would soon be poised to invade the Northern island of Hokkaido.[40] After a tortured discussion on 10 August in which the Emperor intervened personally, the government finally accepted the Potsdam Declaration, provided that the Emperor's position was not prejudiced. Evasive language by the Americans seemed to offer that hope. The Emperor recorded a broadcast to the nation.

It was still not quite the end of the story. The next day Anami called on the people to 'fight to the bitter end, ever firm in our faith that we shall find life in death'.[41] A rebellious faction in the military stormed the imperial palace in the hope of laying hold of the Emperor's recording before it was broadcast, killed two senior officers, and attempted to assassinate the Prime Minister. The rebellion fizzled out and its leaders committed suicide. So did Anami, though he had opposed it. The Emperor's convoluted message went out on 15 August: 'The war situation has developed not necessarily to Japan's advantage ... We have ordered our government to inform the governments of the United States, Britain, China, and the Soviet Union that our empire accepts the provisions of their joint declaration.'

The massive American bombing campaign was brought to an end that day. But it was not until 17 August that the Emperor finally ordered his soldiers to lay down their arms. He chose to put the emphasis on the Soviet victory in Manchuria: 'Now that the Soviet Union has entered the war, to continue under the present conditions at home and abroad would only result in further useless damage.'[42]

Enola Gay: The Apotheosis

In 1993 the Smithsonian Air and Space Museum in Washington decided to mark the fiftieth anniversary of the bombing of Hiroshima with a major exhibition to be called 'The Crossroads: The End of World War II, the Atomic Bomb, and the Origins of the Cold War'. The centrepiece was to be the *Enola Gay*. The exhibition would clear away the myths and tell the whole tangled story as objectively as possible.[43] It would show the destruction at ground zero, with life-sized pictures of Japanese dead and wounded. It would conclude by focusing on the nuclear arms race 'to get people to think about [its] origins'.

The curators knew they were treading on sensitive ground, but they were unprepared for the storm of protest that broke out. American veterans charged that the Smithsonian's plan focused too much attention on the Japanese victims. One veteran called the proposed exhibition 'an insult to every soldier, sailor, marine, and airman who fought in the war against Japan'. Paul Tibbets, who had piloted the *Enola Gay* over Hiroshima, thought the proposals 'a damn big insult', and called on the Smithsonian to display the bomber 'proudly and patriotically'. Some argued that, by ending the war, the bombing had saved the lives of many Japanese as well. 'For all of our faults we have been a kind and just people,' one wrote to the press. 'We don't boil captives live as the Japanese did. We don't hold inquisitions like the Spanish, nor holocausts like the Germans. We were the first victors not to rape and pillage.' Another wrote that the curators at the Smithsonian were missing a great opportunity 'to show that American compassion is unique among nations'. America had displayed to the defeated Germans and Japanese 'the finest example of reconciliation and magnanimity'.

Congress supported the veterans against the Smithsonian's 'foggy revisionism'. One congressman called the proposed exhibit 'anti-American'. Eighty members of Congress demanded that the Director be dismissed and the exhibition cancelled. They threatened to cut funding. The Director prudently resigned and the curators caved in.

They had lost both ways. They had hoped that potential Japanese critics would feel the issues had been fairly covered. One Japanese resident in Washington was unimpressed and wrote to the mayor of Hiroshima that the *Enola Gay* belonged in the Holocaust Museum, not in the Air and Space Museum.

The *Enola Gay* eventually went on display in June 1995, with no historical context. It had to be protected against vandals by special surveillance cameras.

Was the Bomb Decisive?

It was almost universally accepted that the bombing of Hiroshima and Nagasaki ended the war in the Pacific. But historians continued to debate whether the Japanese decision to surrender was most influenced by the Soviet invasion, by the bombing of Hiroshima and Nagasaki, or by the realisation that Japan's ability to wage war had already been destroyed by the relentless American campaign. Some shared Stalin's suspicion that the bombing of Hiroshima was the first shot in the Cold War. Others thought that Truman and his advisers had been blinded by racial hatred of the Japanese.

The Japanese Army might have fought as fanatically as Anami hoped and the Americans feared; or their morale might have collapsed, as it did in the battles against the Russians. Japanese civilians might have fought to the death with their bamboo spears; or they might have turned to the Communists, as their own government half expected. Perhaps the Soviet attack did have a greater influence than the atomic bomb on the Japanese decision, as some serious historians argued.

By the second week of August, the Japanese government was beset by hostile circumstance: its navy destroyed, its air force practically out of action, its people increasingly hungry, the Russians triumphant in the north and about to invade. The situation, as the Emperor finally admitted, was indeed developing 'not necessarily to Japan's advantage'. The US Strategic Bombing Survey argued in its report the following year that 'even without the atomic bombing attacks, air supremacy over Japan could have exerted sufficient pressure to bring about unconditional surrender and obviate the need for invasion'.

The survey's use of the evidence has been challenged. But it concluded sensibly enough: 'There is little point in attempting precisely to impute Japan's unconditional surrender to any one of the numerous causes which jointly and cumulatively were responsible for Japan's disaster.'

Henry Stimson remained uneasy. In 1947 he published a painfully honest article which he hoped would satisfy the doubts of future historians. He believed that the nuclear shock had jolted the Japanese into surrender and thus avoided a bloody final battle. He concluded on a note of tortured optimism: 'In this last great action of the Second World War we were given final proof that war is death. War in the twentieth century has grown steadily more barbarous, more destructive, more debased in all its aspects. Now, with the release of atomic energy, man's ability to destroy himself is very nearly complete. The bombs dropped on Hiroshima and Nagasaki ended a war. They also made it wholly clear that we must never have another war. This is the lesson men and leaders everywhere must learn, and I believe that when they learn it they will find a way to lasting peace. There is no other choice.'[44]

Truman himself sincerely believed that the bombing had saved hundreds of thousands of American soldiers from dying at the hands of the fanatical Japanese military determined to commit national suicide. There are no solid grounds for such figures, but they are barely relevant. Truman's responsibility above all was to his soldiers. He was bound to do whatever he thought necessary to limit their casualties. His decision to drop the bomb was understandable and probably inevitable, whether or not it was necessary.

General LeMay never had any doubts. He saw little difference between systematically pulverising a city with thousands of conventional bombs and wiping it out in a flash with one atomic bomb: 'We scorched and boiled and baked to death more people in Tokyo on that night of 9–10 March than went up in vapour at Hiroshima and Nagasaki.'[45]

Paul Fussell, the cultural historian, had seen the horrors of war face to face, and he despised people who romanticised war without experiencing it. Wounded as an infantryman in France after D-Day, he had not fully recovered when, along with hundreds of thousands of other soldiers, he was earmarked for the invasion of Japan.

Nearly forty years later he tried to strike a balance: 'When the atom bombs were dropped and news began to circulate that "Operation Olympic" would not, after all, be necessary, when we learned to our astonishment that we would not be obliged in a few months to rush up the beaches near Tokyo assault-firing while being machine-gunned, mortared, and shelled, for all the practiced phlegm of our tough facades we broke down and cried with relief and joy. We were going to live. We were going to grow to adulthood after all.'

But Fussell did not attempt to evade the moral issue. And so he went on: 'All this is not to deny that, like the Russian Revolution, the atom-bombing of Japan was a vast historical tragedy, and every passing year magnifies the dilemma into which it has lodged the contemporary world. As with the Russian Revolution, there are two sides – that's why it's a tragedy instead of a disaster – and unless we are … simple-mindedly unimaginative and cruel, we will be painfully aware of both sides at once. To observe that from the viewpoint of the war's victims-to-be the bomb seemed precisely the right thing to drop is to purchase no immunity from horror.'[46]

TWO

TOUCHING INFINITY

'The reward is sheer beauty, and new eyes with which to see the world.'

Carlo Rovelli[1]

'As the light turned green and I crossed the street, it suddenly occurred to me that it might be possible to set up a nuclear chain reaction, liberate energy on an industrial scale, and construct atomic bombs.'

Leo Szilard, 1933[2]

The events and controversies surrounding the bombing of Hiroshima set the themes, political, military, and moral, for half a century to come. But the story began long before, when brilliant and dedicated men and women began to unlock some of the most intimate secrets of the physical world. Even in those early days, some were appalled at the use that might eventually be made of their discoveries.

The Intoxication of the Infinite

In the first decades of the twentieth century, scientists still thought of themselves as an international brotherhood.* The exploration of

---

* 'Brotherhood' was still the common term even though some of the leading physicists were women: Marie Curie and her daughter Irene, who got Nobel Prizes; Lise Meitner, who probably should have done; Ida Noddack, who was nominated for the Nobel Prize three times but didn't get it. In a different field Rosalind Franklin failed to get adequate recognition for her post-war work on the double helix. There were no women among the most senior scientists working on the American, Soviet, or British bombs. The Americans used teams of women to do mathematical calculations which much later would be done by computers. The Russians did recruit women mathematicians, weapons engineers, and others into medium and some fairly senior jobs.

the atom and its properties aroused a ferment of intellectual intoxication among them, and they saw an infinite beauty in the complex relationships that they uncovered. Their gift, like the gift of music, is something that the innumerate can only admire and wonder at.

Like their peripatetic forebears in the Middle Ages, these men and women travelled from one university and research establishment to another, experimenting, theorising, arguing, teaching. They came from Poland, Germany, France, Denmark, Britain, Italy, Hungary, and increasingly from America and Russia.

It was an article of faith among them that no one should try to monopolise the secrets of nature. One kept one's ideas and discoveries secret only long enough to write one's paper, publish it in a universally available scientific journal, and thus establish one's intellectual primacy: the Hungarian physicist Leo Szilard got into trouble with his mentor Ernest Rutherford when he tried to patent some of his more practical ideas. Although individual discoveries were associated with individual scientists, the steady growth of knowledge about the workings of the atom was the collective product of many people, working together in ways which are not always easy to disentangle.

But in 1939 the curtain came down, and the international brotherhood of science was all but shattered.

Relativity and Quantum Theory

In the search to understand the atom, theory and practical experiment were equally important. Central to the process were two theoretical breakthroughs. Revolutionary though they were, these theories built on and supplemented, but did not supersede, the work of predecessors such as Isaac Newton, whose ideas had dominated science for two centuries. In 1905 Albert Einstein outlined his special theory of relativity, complemented in 1915 by his general theory. In 1913 Niels Bohr followed suit with his first papers on quantum theory.

Einstein's theories of relativity enter an area where matters of common sense cease to be true, where the still mysterious effects of gravity combine with speeds approaching the speed of light to cause time to move at different rates for different observers, where parallel lines meet and the angles of a triangle no longer add up to 180 degrees.[3] These unlikely propositions were subsequently verified by experiment. A simple equation, $E=mc^2$, became the central symbol of Einstein's theory: even a non-mathematician can appreciate its elegance. It summarises the relationship between energy and mass: the amount of energy in a given mass is equal to the mass multiplied by the square of a constant equal to the speed of light, which is just under 300,000,000 metres a second. The implication of Einstein's proposition is that you can convert mass into energy, and so produce an immense explosion.

Quantum theory studies the apparently erratic behaviour of the very smallest particles of matter that make up the atom, and the electromagnetic and nuclear forces that govern them.* The theory is famously obscure. Indeed, the exuberant American physicist Richard Feynman, who worked on the American bomb, said 'I think I can safely say that no one understands quantum mechanics'.[4] Even Einstein was unsettled. Quantum theory seemed to make a virtue of the random, in violation of his belief that scientific theories should be elegant and consistent, that 'God does not play dice with the world'.[5] Eventually he generously conceded that Bohr's theory exemplified 'the highest form of musicality in the sphere of thought', a great compliment from someone who was himself a passionate musician.[6]

The theories of relativity and quantum physics are, intriguingly, incompatible in ways that are still not understood. But despite their obscurity, both theories work, and are central to modern everyday life: for example, satellite navigation devices could not function accurately without the insights that come from general relativity, and the transistors inside all computers could not function without quantum physics. Between them they were the background to the theoretical and practical work which led to the atom bomb.

The Pioneers

Among the early experimenters were Marie Skłodowska and her husband, Pierre Curie. They worked in France and discovered

---

* A central symbol here is another equation formulated by the British scientist and Nobel Prize winner Paul Dirac (1902–84). It is carved on his memorial stone in Westminster Abbey and reads $(i - m)\psi = 0$. It too seems elegantly succinct, though unlike Einstein's formula it conveys nothing to the non-mathematician.

radium and polonium, which Marie named after her native country, Poland. Both were awarded the Nobel Prize in 1903; in 1911 Marie was awarded a second Nobel Prize. Their daughter Irène married Frédéric Joliot. They too won the Nobel Prize and helped to make France a leading centre of nuclear research in the 1930s. Joliot remained in France during the war, and joined the resistance against the Germans. He became France's first High Commissioner for Atomic Energy and built France's first atomic reactor in 1948. A convinced Communist, he was sacked from his government post in 1950 because of his close connections with the Soviet Union. In 1945 Beria, the head of the Soviet secret police and responsible for the Soviet nuclear programme, suggested to Stalin that the Joliot-Curies be invited to work in the USSR 'on a permanent or long-term (3–5 year) basis without the right to leave'. Fortunately perhaps for them, Stalin turned the idea down.[7]

British writers were among the earliest to fantasise about a world dominated by nuclear weapons. British scientists and politicians were the first to take the practical decisions that eventually turned fantasy into reality. A galaxy of British and one New Zealand Nobel Prize winner helped identify and develop the basic principles of atomic science: J. J. Thomson, Ernest Rutherford, Frederick Soddy, James Chadwick, John Cockcroft, Paul Dirac, Ernest Walton. Many of them worked at the Cavendish Laboratory in Cambridge, where Thomson discovered the electron, the New Zealander Rutherford worked on the disintegration of the elements, Chadwick discovered the neutron, and Cockcroft and Walton split a lithium nucleus.

On the Continent, Enrico Fermi was professor of theoretical physics in the University of Rome in the 1920s. His powerful team included Emilio Segrè and Bruno Pontecorvo. Fermi was as distinguished for his experimental as for his theoretical work, and made notable contributions to the development of quantum theory and nuclear and particle physics. His wife was Jewish: they and Segrè emigrated to America in 1938 to escape Mussolini's anti-Semitic laws. In America Fermi led the team that designed and built the atomic pile in Chicago which in December 1942 demonstrated that it was possible to sustain a nuclear chain reaction: a major step towards a bomb. Pontecorvo moved to Paris in 1936 to work with Frédéric and Irène Joliot-Curie. He fled to the United States when Paris fell to the

Germans, and was employed on the bomb project in Canada during the war and then at the British Atomic Energy Research Establishment at Harwell. A Communist but not a Soviet agent, he defected to the Soviet Union in 1950 and worked there for the rest of his life.

Another remarkable group of scientists – John von Neumann, Eugene Wigner, Edward Teller, and Leo Szilard – were Jewish expatriates from anti-Semitic Hungary. They were collectively known as 'the Martians'. When asked if extraterritorial beings existed, Fermi is supposed to have answered, 'Of course, they are already here among us: they just call themselves Hungarians.' They too migrated across the Atlantic in the 1930s to escape Hitler, thus considerably reinforcing the scientific potential of the United States at the moment when science became the driving force of modern war.

Albert Einstein, the glory of the German school, was already in America when Hitler took power and remained there. But other German scientists also made highly significant contributions to nuclear physics. Max Planck was the first to contemplate the idea of quantum physics, even though he later found it hard to accept Bohr's more elaborate ideas. Werner Heisenberg was a key pioneer of quantum mechanics, best known to the layman for his formulation of the 'uncertainty principle', by which it is not possible to establish both the location and the movement of an object simultaneously. Otto Hahn was the first to demonstrate that uranium nuclei could be split by bombarding them with neutrons, an important step towards making the atomic bomb.

The Laggards Catch Up

Compared with what was going on in Europe at the beginning of the twentieth century, Russian and American physics got off to a comparatively slow start.

For the first two decades of the twentieth century, America lacked an indigenous school of theoretical physics. At that time Europe, not America, was the place to study postgraduate physics. So ambitious young American physicists served their apprenticeship in Cambridge, in the German universities, in Italy, the Netherlands, France and Denmark, where pioneering work on nuclear physics was being pushed forward at an increasingly dizzy rate. Isidor Rabi,

Robert Oppenheimer's colleague on the Manhattan Project, said that in those days, 'American physics was not really very much, certainly not consonant with the great size and wealth of the country. We were very much concerned with raising the level of American physics. We were sick and tired of going to Europe as learners. We wanted to be independent. I must say I think that our generation … did that job, and that ten years later we were at the top of the heap, and it wasn't just because certain refugees came out of Germany, but because of what we did here. This was a conscious motivation. Oppenheimer set up this school of theoretical physics which was a tremendous contribution. In fact, I don't know how we could have carried out the scientific part of the war without the contributions of the people who worked with Oppenheimer.'[8]

Brilliant, charming, erudite, Oppenheimer came from a cultured and prosperous New York family. Few would have predicted that he would become a brilliant manager of the Manhattan Project: that, and the sensational way in which he was brought down by a security witch-hunt after the war was over, made him internationally famous, forever associated with the building of the bomb and for some a kind of martyr.

Oppenheimer graduated from Harvard University in 1923. Percy Bridgman, his physics teacher at Harvard, recommended him to Rutherford at Cambridge thus: 'As appears from his name, Oppenheimer is a Jew, but … I think you need have no hesitation whatever for any reason of this sort from considering his application.' Rutherford turned him down, but J. J. Thomson agreed to supervise him.

By the time Oppenheimer left for Europe in September 1925 the revolution in physics was in full flood. Many American physicists were still oblivious of it. 'I didn't learn about quantum mechanics until I got to Europe,' Oppenheimer later wrote. 'I don't believe they were actually known … in America, anyway.'[9] He was not happy at Cambridge: he disliked the laboratory work and his private life was miserable. But it was in Cambridge that he met Dirac and Niels Bohr, whom he called his God, and some of the younger physicists later involved in the British nuclear weapons project, like Chadwick and Patrick Blackett, another future Nobel Prize winner and a committed socialist.

By now Oppenheimer had decided that his vocation was to be a theoretical physicist. So he moved to Göttingen in Germany, which was then the centre of theoretical physics as Cambridge was the centre of experimental physics. There he was taught by Max Born, another future Nobel Prize winner, who had nurtured the talents of Heisenberg, Fermi, Hahn, and two of the Martians, Wigner and Von Neumann. After visiting the universities at Leiden and Zurich, Oppenheimer returned to the United States in 1928 to take up a professorship at the University of California, Berkeley. There he gained a remarkable reputation as a teacher: versatile, concerned, critical, but brilliantly able to inspire his graduate and postdoctoral students.*

Ernest Lawrence was more orthodox and a very different kind of scientist from Oppenheimer. He never studied outside America, and was interested in practical research and in the management of large scientific projects. His invention of the cyclotron particle accelerator in 1932 brought him the Nobel Prize. The cyclotron became a basic instrument for exploring the composition of the atom and an essential tool for the construction of an atom bomb. An effective lobbyist who raised very large sums of money for his expensive devices, Lawrence tried but eventually failed to steer clear of politics. When the Russians made him an honorary member of the Soviet Academy of Sciences in 1942 he was presented with his membership booklet by Andrei Gromyko, then chargé d'affaires at the Soviet Embassy in Washington.[10] In 1952, with the support of Edward Teller, he set up the Lawrence Livermore Laboratory for the design of nuclear weapons. Though he had been a good friend of Robert Oppenheimer at Berkeley, he contributed damaging evidence to the security hearing which destroyed Oppenheimer's official career in 1954.

Richard Feynman was a New Yorker like Oppenheimer, but from a more modest family, a practical joker, a jazz drummer, and an

---

* Hans Bethe, a colleague on the Manhattan Project, wrote of him,
'Oppenheimer created the greatest school of theoretical physics that the United States has ever known. Before him, theoretical physics in America was a fairly modest enterprise, although there were a few outstanding representatives'
('J. Robert Oppenheimer: April 22, 1904–February 18, 1967', National Academy of Sciences of the United States of America *Biographical Memoirs*, p. 71, 1997).

enthusiastic lover of women. A 1999 poll of 130 leading physicists by the British journal *Physics World* ranked him as one of the ten greatest physicists of all time: the only American on the list. The others were Albert Einstein, Isaac Newton, James Clerk Maxwell, Niels Bohr, Werner Heisenberg, Galileo Galilei, Paul Dirac, Erwin Schrödinger, and Ernest Rutherford.[11] Columbia University refused to admit him as a student because they already had too many Jews, so he went instead to the Massachusetts Institute of Technology, and then to Princeton University, where he attained a perfect score for mathematics and physics in the entrance exams, an unprecedented feat. He got his PhD in 1942 and joined the Manhattan Project in 1943 as one of its youngest scientists. He returned to academic work after the war at Cornell University and then California Institute of Technology (Caltech). In his last years he became internationally famous for discovering why the space shuttle *Challenger* had blown up.

Hanging in the Institute of Physics in Moscow, now a museum, is a colourful portrait by the painter Boris Kustodiev, who had made a career of painting prominent Russians, including the great Russian bass Chaliapin. The picture shows two young men in their early twenties. The bright colours emphasise the rather arrogant expression on their faces. Their names are Piotr Kapitsa and Nikolai Semenov.

The story of the picture, as told seventy years later by Kapitsa's widow, was this.[12] The two young men were both brilliant physicists who had only recently completed their studies. They called on Kustodiev and said, 'You've spent your career painting people who are already famous. We're not famous yet, but we're going to be. Why don't you paint *our* portrait?' As payment they offered him a chicken and a bag of wheat. At that time of revolution, civil war, and famine it was enough. Kustodiev accepted the commission. Both young men went on to win the Nobel Prize. Both were involved in the Soviet nuclear weapons programme.

An impenetrable blanket of security, barely lifted by the Soviet leader Nikita Khrushchev in the late 1950s, obscured the brilliance of the scientists who developed the Soviet bomb. Igor Kurchatov and Yuli Khariton, the eventual scientific leaders of the Soviet nuclear weapons project, are barely known in the West. Lev Landau was one of the greatest scientists of the century. But only Andrei Sakharov became a household name to compare with Oppenheimer, and that for reasons only loosely connected with his science.

Like the Americans, the Russians were slow to develop an indigenous school of physics: at the beginning of the twentieth century, theoretical physics as a branch of science did not exist anywhere in Russia.[13] The Russians did have one venerable scientific institution, the Institute of Physics, which traced its origins back to the 'Cabinet' which Peter the Great set up in his newly founded Russian Academy of Sciences in St Petersburg. But it was not until 1912 that the 'Cabinet' became first a fully fledged laboratory and then, in 1921, the Institute of Physical Mathematics. In 1934 its Physics Department was moved to Moscow and became the Institute of Physics, named after the nineteenth-century physicist Peter Lebedev.[14] The Ukrainian Institute of Physics and Technology was established in Kharkov in 1931. The following year its scientists repeated the experiments that had just been done by Cockcroft and Walton in Cambridge to split the lithium nucleus. Among the Institute's alumni were Lev Landau, Evgeny Lifshits, and Igor Kurchatov, all of them subsequently involved with the Soviet bomb project.

Seven devastating years of war and civil war had left Russia in ruins as the 1920s began. But Soviet physics nevertheless began to gather momentum. The Institute of Physics rapidly became associated with a number of major scientific breakthroughs. Among those who worked there were seven men who eventually won the Nobel Prize: Igor Tamm, Pavel Cherenkov, Ilya Frank, Alexander Prokhorov, Vitali Ginzburg, Andrei Sakharov, and Nikolai Basov. Other Soviet scientists made important contributions to mathematics, population genetics, psychology, animal and plant ecology, and physics.[15]

Two distinguished men from the older generation had a major influence over these new developments. Vladimir Vernadsky gained a worldwide reputation as a crystallographer, mineralogist, and geochemist, and was one of the pioneers of modern ecological thinking. He was born in St Petersburg, studied in the Faculty of Physics and Mathematics there, and later in Paris, Munich, and Italy. In 1898 he became a professor at Moscow University, and then moved to direct the Museum of Geology and Mineralogy in St Petersburg. He led expeditions to map the country's resources of radioactive minerals, a search set back by war and civil strife; an anti-Bolshevik, he was briefly arrested for espionage in 1921.

The next year Vernadsky set up the Radium Institute in St Petersburg. He had spoken even before the war of 'the possibility of sources of atomic energy exceeding all sources of power hitherto imagined by mankind'. The task of his new institute was to master the problem. He was away for four years lecturing in Paris, so that most of the responsibility for running the new institute fell on Vitaly Khlopin, after whom it was eventually named.[16] By then Vernadsky's son George had emigrated to America, where he founded the Russian Faculty at Yale University. The connection between father and son played its own small but significant part in the development of the Soviet bomb.

Abram Ioffe studied at the Technological Institute in St Petersburg and then in Munich, where he got his doctorate under Wilhelm Roentgen, the Nobel Prize winner and discoverer of X-rays. From 1906 he worked in the Polytechnic Institute in St Petersburg. In 1918 he set up the Institute of Physics and Technology in St Petersburg which now bears his name. His students included Piotr Kapitsa, Nikolai Semenov, Lev Landau, Yakov Zeldovich, Igor Kurchatov, Igor Tamm, Yakov Frenkel, and Yuli Khariton, all of whom played a major part in the Soviet bomb project. By the mid-1930s Ioffe's Institute had become the leading Soviet centre for nuclear physics. He remained in charge of it until 1950, when he fell foul of the anti-Semitic campaign unleashed by Stalin.

The head of the Department for Nuclear Physics in Ioffe's Institute was Igor Kurchatov, the future head of the Soviet atom project. Born in Siberia, he studied naval engineering in Leningrad before moving to Ioffe's Institute. In the 1930s he helped Khlopin's Leningrad Radium Institute design and install Europe's first cyclotron. Unlike some of his colleagues, Kurchatov did not study abroad. A plan for him to spend time with Edward Lawrence in Berkeley fell through, perhaps for political reasons. After he was appointed to direct the nuclear programme, he swore he would not shave until the programme succeeded, and was known to his colleagues for the remainder of his life as 'The Beard'.

Kurchatov had an invaluable ability to get things done in the fraught world of the Soviet bureaucracy The secret police described him to Stalin as the leading atomic scientist in the Soviet Union. 'He is energetic and has great organisational skills. By nature he is closed, cautious, cunning, and a great diplomat.' Kapitsa's wife Anna remembered him as 'a very fine scientist, a remarkable diplomat and tactician. He was able to make our leaders respect and listen to him. He could approach them in a way which made them feel that, far from despising them, he was one of them ... Kurchatov had a sense of diplomatic tact which enabled him to get through to these people ... and get them to do what was needed ... he was a very courageous man.'[17] Khrushchev thought him 'an attractive and witty man as well as a brilliant scientist', and took him along on his trip to London in 1956.[18]

Of equal importance to the success of the Soviet atom project was Yuli Khariton. Khariton studied under Nikolai Semenov in the early 1920s and then spent some time under Rutherford in Cambridge. On his return he became head of the Explosion Laboratory in the Leningrad Institute of Chemical Physics. He remained with the Soviet nuclear weapons project for the rest of his long life: he died in 1996. No one from Yeltsin's government came to his funeral.[19] Almost nothing in his background qualified him to rise to the top of his profession at the very heart of Stalin's secret state. For a start, he was Jewish. So were many of his most brilliant fellow scientists, but it was not a recommendation in Stalin's last, anti-Semitic years. His family background was equally unpromising. He was born in 1904 into a family of intellectuals. His father was a journalist and was exiled after the Revolution with other 'ideologically alien' members of the intelligentsia. He settled in Riga, was arrested when the Soviet Union took over Latvia in 1940s, and died in a camp. His mother was an actress in the Moscow Art Theatre. She divorced in 1907, married again, left for Germany, and in 1933 emigrated to Palestine. One sister lived in Kharkov under German occupation, another barely survived the siege of Leningrad, and his mother-in-law died in the Riga ghetto. Any one of these details could have led to his disgrace or worse in the Stalin years.

Igor Tamm came from a part-German, part-Cossack family. One of his colleagues later called him a typical example of the solid, middle-class, professional Russian intelligentsia which produced committed revolutionaries, poets, and engineers. He was born in Vladivostok and grew up in Ukraine. To distract him from the local Marxist politics, his parents sent him to study in Edinburgh. At the outbreak of war, he returned to study physics in Moscow. In 1917 he went down to Ukraine to assist the Social Democrats make a revolution. There he was caught by the Bolsheviks crossing the lines without papers. They threatened to shoot him as a White spy. He explained that he was not a politician but an academic mathematician. One of his captors asked him what error would be made by cutting off a Maclaurin series at the nth term. Tamm struggled with the correct answer, but his interrogator confessed that he too had forgotten most of his maths, and Tamm was spared.[20] In 1928 he visited Britain, where he met Paul Dirac, who became a frequent visitor to the Soviet Union. Tamm remained a Marxist, but spoke out in favour of genetics at a time when it was under vicious attack by Stalin, and would discuss with Sakharov the most sensitive questions of all: the purges, the Gulag, anti-Semitism, collectivisation, the difference between Communism in theory and Communism in practice. But his independence of mind was matched by sufficient circumspection to keep him out of trouble.[21]

Circumspection was not the prime characteristic of Piotr Kapitsa, the subject of Kustodiev's portrait. After briefly serving as an ambulance driver at the front, he joined Ioffe's St Petersburg Polytechnic Institute in 1916. He got married that year. Three years later his wife and her two children died from Spanish flu and his father-in-law was shot. To help Kapitsa get over the tragedy, Ioffe arranged a post for him at the Cavendish Laboratory in Cambridge under Rutherford. He remained there for the next thirteen years, telling his mother, 'The opportunities for work here are such as I never dreamed of ... I have only now come into my own. I find success exhilarating and my work inspiring. This is all I have left after the death of my family.' He became a member of the Royal Society in 1929. The Mond Laboratory was specially set up for him in Cambridge in 1933. His friend Eric Gill, the sculptor, carved a crocodile (the nickname for Rutherford) on the entrance to the laboratory which is still there. He founded an informal seminar, a rumbustious Russian-style *kruzhok* known as the Kapitsa Club, which continued to exist until 1958. The house in Cambridge where he lived with his second wife, Anna, whom he married in 1927, continued for decades to be used as a base by visiting Russian scientists.

In 1929 Kapitsa was elected to the Soviet Academy of Sciences as a corresponding member. He returned home every year for the summer vacation. But the tolerance of the Soviet government towards the free movement of scientists was diminishing fast. In 1934 Stalin stopped Kapitsa from returning to Cambridge: 'Kapitsa may not be arrested officially, but he must be retained in the Soviet Union and not let return to England,' Stalin wrote. 'This will be a sort of house arrest. After that, we will see.'[22] The Soviet government bought his Cambridge equipment, which they reinstalled in a laboratory which they built for him in Moscow, the Institute of Physical Problems.

Kapitsa now began to bombard the Soviet leaders, from Stalin downwards, with letters. He managed to combine remarkable frankness with a sufficient degree of tactical skill to gain the respect of the leadership. He was thus able to help fellow scientists who fell foul of the system, and to survive the storms which lay ahead for him personally. He began with a firm admonishment to Vyacheslav Molotov, Stalin's Prime Minister: 'You had better accept me as I am: a bit impudent, a lover of freedom, independence in my scientific work, unable to wag my tail, even if I had one, but certainly committed to the Union and to the work for socialist construction, to which you are also committed.'[23] In defence of a mathematician who had been attacked in *Pravda* he told Molotov, 'We have not so far succeeded in producing new scientists from among our young people. I explain this by a very wrong attitude on your part towards science – much too narrowly utilitarian and insignificantly supported.'

He believed that the Soviet Union was settling down, and wrote to Niels Bohr in 1935 that the regime treated its scientists like 'a child with a pet animal which is tormented and tortured by him with the best intentions. But indeed the child grows up and learns to look properly after his pets, and make of them useful domestic animals. I hope it will not be long to happen here.'[24]

He was far too optimistic. It was the eve of the purges, which swept some of his most brilliant colleagues away.

Intimations of Armageddon

The implications of the new physics aroused fears and doubts right from the beginning. In 1904, five years after the Curies discovered radium, Rutherford's collaborator, the British physicist Frederick Soddy, speculated that 'the man who put his hand' on the energy locked up in radium and other heavy matter 'would possess a weapon by which he could destroy the earth if he chose'.[25]

The imagination of writers had already been gripped. In 1900 the eminent American astronomer Simon Newcomb wrote a novel, *His Wisdom the Defender*, in which Professor Campbell discovers a new kind of energy capable of producing a weapon of unseen destructive power: the scene is set in 1941. Newcomb's reliability as a prophet was somewhat dented when he asserted in 1903, the year the Wright Brothers made their first flight, that 'aerial flight is one of the great class of problems with which man can never cope'.[26]

In 1908 the French writer Anatole France published *Penguin Island*, in which a group of terrorists design a radium-based bomb. It looks like 'an egg made of white metal and provided with a capsule at each end' and it can be detonated from a distance. The terrorists use the bombs to destroy many public buildings in Paris, with huge loss of life. Capitalist society is brought to its knees.[27] In 1927 a Soviet writer, Vadim Nikolsky, wrote *In a Thousand Years' Time*, a science fiction novel in which the first atomic explosion takes place in Paris in 1945 and destroys two-thirds of Europe.[28] In an elegantly light-hearted novel by the British diplomat and writer Harold Nicolson, *Public Faces*, published in 1932, the British acquire a monopoly of nuclear weapons and the rocket planes to deliver them. The bellicose Minister for Air insists on dropping a nuclear bomb off the coast of America to demonstrate its power: a large part of Carolina is inundated and thousands of Americans killed. In 1938 J. B. Priestley, a popular British left-wing writer and broadcaster, published *The Doomsday Men*, about a sinister group in California which is barely prevented from blowing the world to pieces.[29]

But the most influential novel was H. G. Wells's *The World Set Free*, published in 1914 and dedicated to Soddy. Wells envisages that the 'problem of tapping the internal energy of atoms ... is solved by a wonderful combination of induction, intuition, and luck ... so soon as the year 1933'. 'The power to destroy was continually increasing,' Wells observed. 'Destruction was becoming so facile that any little body of malcontents could use it … It was a matter of common knowledge that a man could carry about in a handbag an amount of latent energy sufficient to wreck half a city.' Wells imagines a devastating European war in which Paris and Berlin are both destroyed by atomic bombs. A British expeditionary force in the Netherlands is inundated when the Germans use atomic bombs to destroy the dykes. The war ends when a group of enlightened statesmen set up a world government to replace the murderous rivalry of nation states. Ominously, the story did not end there: 'the battle-fields and bomb fields of that frantic time in human history are sprinkled with radiant matter, and so centres of inconvenient rays.'[30]

Winston Churchill was deeply impressed by the vision of his friend Wells and took up these themes in his journalistic writing. In 1924 he published *Shall We All Commit Suicide?* Explosives of hitherto unknown power, he feared, could eventually be delivered to their targets by unmanned aircraft: 'Mankind has never been in this position before. Without having improved appreciably in virtue or enjoying wiser guidance, it has got into its hand for the first time the tools by which it can unfailingly accomplish its own extermination.' In 1931 he warned that 'while men are gathering knowledge and power with ever-increasing and measureless speed, their virtues and their wisdom have not shown any notable improvement as the centuries have rolled … Under sufficient stress, starvation, terror, warlike passion, or even cold intellectual frenzy, the modern man we know so well will do the most horrible deeds.'

Despite such doomsday language, many qualified people remained sceptical that a nuclear weapon was feasible. Rutherford said a few weeks after Wells's book was published, 'The suggestions of Mr Wells must be considered as a dream of the future.' There was 'not the slightest evidence that radioactive energy could be released quickly enough to make explosives'. In 1933, by which time Chadwick had isolated the neutron, a crucial step towards harnessing the power of the atom, Rutherford asserted that, 'Anyone who looked for a source of power in the transformation of … atoms was talking moonshine.' *The Times* added, with its customary authority, that even if the existence of the neutron was confirmed, for 'humanity in general' the results of this and other nuclear experiments 'would make no difference'.

Other eminent scientists followed suit. Albert Einstein said in 1934 that he was no prophet, but doubted if it would ever be possible to exploit nuclear energy: 'I feel absolutely sure, nearly sure, that it will not be possible ... It will be like shooting birds in the dark, in a country where there are few birds.'[31]

The scepticism was reflected in British official circles. Henry Tizard, the Rector of Imperial College, told the Air Ministry's Air Defence Committee that there was a 10,000 to one chance against nuclear energy having military applications. Churchill's scientific adviser Frederick Lindemann (later Lord Cherwell) told him, 'There is no danger that this discovery, however great its scientific interest, and perhaps ultimately its practical importance, will lead to results capable of being put into operation on a large scale for several years.'

Churchill thought Lindemann was probably right for now. But he was not sanguine for the future. In November 1939 he wrote, 'With these immense resources of power available, it seems likely that means will ultimately be found to tap them. If this were achieved, man's control over nature would take a step forward greater than any since in Palaeolithic times when he discovered how to make fire.' He envisaged a future battle in which the fighting was done by faceless puppet masters drinking coffee at their desks, when 'some spectacled "brass hat" ... extinguished some London or Paris, some Tokyo or San Francisco, by pressing a button'.[32]

The idea that civilian populations were a legitimate object of air attack did not, of course, have to await the arrival of the nuclear weapon. In January 1915 the Kaiser authorised a bombing campaign against Britain whose purpose would 'lie not only in the injury which will be caused to the enemy, but also in the significant effect it [would] have in diminishing the enemy's determination to prosecute the war'. For the next three years German Zeppelins and Gotha bombers attacked British towns, killing 1,413 people in all, over 1,100 of them civilians. The Prime Minister, David Lloyd George, recalled that as the raids on London grew in intensity there was by the middle of 1917 'grave and growing panic amongst the population in the East End'. He asked General Smuts, a Cabinet colleague, to draw up a report. Smuts concluded that 'the day may not be far distant when aerial operations with their devastation of enemy lands and destruction of industrial and populous centres on a vast scale may become the principal operations of war'. It was a vision enthusiastically taken up by the commanders of the new Royal Air Force, which was born on 1 April 1918.[33]

Fear grew in the remaining years of peace. The British military writer General J. F. C. Fuller warned in 1923 that an air attack would transform London into a 'vast raving Bedlam'; the government 'would be swept away by an avalanche of terror'.[34] In 1934 Churchill predicted in the House that if London were bombed, 30,000 or 40,000 people would be killed or maimed and 3 or 4 million people driven out of the city.[35] H. G. Wells's novel *The Shape of Things to Come* (1933) and the film version (1936) begin with the destruction of 'Everytown' from the air. In 1939 another military strategist, Basil Liddell Hart, thought that a quarter of a million people might be killed and injured in Britain in the first week of war.[36] The Home Office predicted in 1939 that air attacks on London would result in 2.5 million casualties in ten weeks.[37] The fears seemed to be confirmed by the effects of Japanese bombing in China and German bombing in Spain. The destruction of the Basque town of Guernica by German bombers in 1938 seemed a foretaste of what was to come. It is not surprising that, as Harold Macmillan, Prime Minister at the time of the Cuban missile crisis in 1962, later said, 'We thought of air warfare in 1938 rather as people think of nuclear warfare today.'[38]

Headed for Grief

When asked by American radio, on the eve of the war, Enrico Fermi said that an atomic bomb might be twenty or twenty-five years away. Niels Bohr thought it inconceivable that any nation could muster the industrial effort which would be needed to build a bomb. An American scientific journal, *Weekly Science News Letter*, said firmly that 'scientists are anxious that there be no public alarm'. The 'wild speculations' of H. G. Wells and J. B. Priestley should be ignored. The world was not about to be blown to bits.

They were already behind the times. In December 1938 Otto Hahn and Fritz Strassmann of the Kaiser Wilhelm Institute for Chemistry in Berlin succeeded in splitting uranium by bombarding it with neutrons. They published their findings in the German scientific journal *Naturwissenschaften*, which Joliot-Curie and his team in Paris confirmed by experiment. Hahn's long-term colleague, the Austrian physicist Lise Meitner, had taken refuge in Sweden from Hitler's anti-Semitic laws. It fell to her and her nephew Otto Frisch to give a theoretical explanation of Hahn's findings, estimated the energy released, and give a name to the phenomenon – fission. They set out their findings in the British journal *Nature*. By June 1939 *Naturwissenschaften* was already discussing the potential military applications.[39]

Leo Szilard, the irrepressible Hungarian 'Martian' who had moved to America to escape the Nazis, had not forgotten the nuclear vision that had come upon him as the light turned green on that road crossing in London. Now he and others began to look more closely into what happened during nuclear fission. On 3 March 1939 their experiments confirmed that the neutrons released could start a chain reaction: an atomic bomb was feasible. That night, he later remembered, he could not sleep: '[T]here was little doubt in my mind that the world was headed for grief'.[40]

As scientists and governments understood that a bomb was a real possibility, the international brotherhood of science began to fray. Some scientists tried to keep up a free exchange of views about the common secrets of nature. But under the growing pressure of war, governments offered the scientists a Faustian bargain: they would provide the scientists with resources that they could never have dreamed of; but the price was that all such things would henceforth be covered with a thick blanket of security. Most scientists accepted that it was their patriotic duty to comply. From then on the circulation of scientific papers bearing on the problem began to dry up. Only the Russians continued to publish for a few months until they and their government also realised that there were some things best kept secret.[41]

As the Second World War began, C. P. Snow, the British scientist, administrator, and novelist, warned that 'Some physicists think that, within a few months, science will have produced for military use an explosive a million times more violent than dynamite ... Such an invention will never be kept secret. For a short time, perhaps, the U.S. Government may have this power entrusted to it; but soon after it will be in less civilized hands. If it is not made in America this year, it may be made next year in Germany.'[42]

Now the scientists themselves began to discuss what would be needed to turn theory into a practical weapon. German scientists met in Berlin in September 1939 and concluded, 'If there is the slightest chance that it is possible – it must be done.' They got nowhere, above all because the wartime resources in Germany were insufficient. At the end of the war some of the most eminent, Hahn and Heisenberg among them, were comfortably interned by the British at Farm Hall near Cambridge. When they heard about Hiroshima, they tried to work out why the Americans had succeeded where they had failed. The British, who were eavesdropping, heard some claim that, at least once they realised the extent of Hitler's crimes, they had deliberately failed to make the necessary effort.[43] The record is ambiguous. The moral ambiguities are brilliantly explored by Michael Frayn in his play *Copenhagen* about the visit which Heisenberg made to Niels Bohr in German-occupied Copenhagen in 1941, perhaps in an unsuccessful attempt to find out what Bohr knew about the Anglo-American bomb project.[44] The elderly Max Planck was not one of those detained. A pioneer of quantum theory, he opposed the Nazis discreetly. But although his son was arrested after the July 1944 plot against Hitler and tortured to death, he was one of the few German scientists to accept that he too shared responsibility for the crimes of the Third Reich.

Japanese scientists had kept well abreast of the developments in nuclear physics between the wars, and in 1934 one of them pointed to the possibility that the power of the atom could be harnessed for the production of weapons. By March 1943 they had concluded that a bomb was feasible, but had achieved nothing significant. The Americans tipped their nuclear cyclotrons into Tokyo Bay in November 1945.[45]

Only the Americans had the financial and industrial resources to produce a practical bomb by 1945. British, Russian, and German scientists possessed much of the scientific knowledge. But their countries were fighting for their lives and none were able to muster the necessary resources during the war.

All that changed when the fighting stopped. The underlying scientific principles were available to all who cared to look. The engineering remained difficult, but determined governments reasoned that what others had done they could do too. The Russians mounted a massive effort to match the Americans. They let off their first fission device in 1949, and they drew level with the Americans when they exploded their first sophisticated fusion device in 1955. The British were only a few years behind. The French, the Chinese, and others followed.

Democrats like to believe that the arts and the sciences thrive only in a free society. The arts did indeed wilt in Hitler's Germany: but he failed to get a bomb not because he had expelled some of his best scientists but because wartime Germany lacked the resources. Stalin did get his bomb. And under Stalin, Shostakovich and Prokofiev, Akhmatova and Pasternak, Bulgakov and Solzhenitsyn, all produced creative work that has entered the canon. Nothing is simple.[46]

THREE

BRIGHTER THAN A
THOUSAND SUNS

'Now I am become death, the destroyer of worlds.'

Bhagavad Gita[1]

'The basic principle of an atomic bomb is extremely simple: it's incorporating it into a practical design that is exceptionally difficult.'

Vladimir Belugin, Director of Arzamas-16, 1987–96[2]

There are two ways of causing a nuclear explosion. The first is nuclear fission, the process behind the bombs dropped on Hiroshima and Nagasaki. You bombard a sufficient amount of fissile heavy metal – uranium 235 or plutonium, for example – with neutrons so that each neutron splits off another two or more. Each new neutron then splits off others in its turn, thus producing a chain reaction. If you bring enough pieces of subcritical uranium 235 or plutonium together into a critical mass and contain them in a very small time and space, they will split spontaneously and generate a massive explosion. The bomb dropped on Hiroshima had an explosive power equivalent to some 15,000 tons (15–20 kilotons) of conventional explosive – and yet that was little more than 1 per cent of the energy locked inside the 64 kilograms of enriched uranium it contained.

This was a comprehensible figure: Curtis LeMay's bombers had been dropping a comparable amount each time they raided one of Japan's cities.[3] A single atomic bomb could not obliterate a large modern city which, unlike Hiroshima, was properly braced for atomic attack. Some people therefore argued that the atomic bomb could be regarded as just another weapon, the latest stage in a process that had started with the club, the spear, and the bow and arrow.

But the power of the atomic bomb was limited. It relied on nuclear fission, and could not easily be made to yield more than about a megaton – a million tons of conventional explosive power.[4] These constraints would fade if fusion, rather than fission, were used to generate the nuclear explosion. The trick was to use a fission trigger to generate temperatures and pressures similar to those in the sun to force together – fuse – the atoms of some substance much lighter than uranium, such as hydrogen or one of its derivatives. That gave you your explosion. Weapons based on this principle were colloquially called hydrogen or H-bombs, or thermonuclear bombs.

The arrival of the thermonuclear bomb signalled a revolution in military affairs almost as great as the revolution brought about by the atom bomb. There is no theoretical limit to the size of the explosion you can produce with a fusion bomb. The Soviet 'Tsar Bomba' generated fifty megatons when it was tested in 1961, and it was capable of twice that. In the 1960s the Americans deployed a bomb yielding 25 megatons. Throughout the 1970s the Russians deployed some two hundred 20 megaton warheads. Yields came down as missiles became more accurate and carried multiple warheads. But a handful even of the smaller weapons – delivered by rocket – could destroy the largest city.[5] Properly deployed, a larger number could cripple or destroy a whole country. A strategic nuclear exchange between two nuclear superpowers could, it was generally believed, kill tens or hundreds of millions of people, or, in the worst case, the whole of humanity.

Few could now seriously deny that this was a step change from the process that had started with the club. Some people still maintained that the destructive power of nuclear weapons was grossly exaggerated. On the whole, those who were actually responsible for handling the things disagreed with them.

The First Steps

Leo Szilard had hoped in vain to persuade his colleagues to keep secret the dangerous facts about the physical world that were emerging. Fearful that Hitler's Germany would get the bomb first, he and his fellow 'Martian', the brilliant, fiery, opinionated, and difficult Edward Teller, now prevailed on Einstein to write to President Roosevelt warning him that a bomb might be constructed of unprecedented destructive power. Alexander Sachs, a banking adviser to the President, delivered their letter in October 1939. Roosevelt remarked, 'What you are after is to see that the Nazis don't blow us up.' 'Precisely,' said Sachs. Roosevelt set up an Advisory Committee on Uranium under Lyman Briggs, the head of the National Bureau of Standards. In November 1939 Briggs reported that a bomb was possible.[6] But Briggs was not a dynamic man, many doubted that building a bomb was worth the expenditure of time and resources, and it took time to sort out an effective administrative machine. In the summer of 1941 the project was taken out of Briggs' hands, and handed over to the far more effective Vannevar Bush, the Chairman of the National Defense Research Committee and later of the Office of Scientific Research and Development.

The British Take Action
Meanwhile the British had already begun to tackle the matter seriously.

At first it was believed that several tons of uranium would be required to generate a nuclear explosion: an impractical condition for a usable weapon. But in the summer of 1939 Rudolf Peierls, a physicist from Berlin who had fled to Britain, began calculating the mass more exactly,[7] and the following year, in March 1940, he and Lise Meitner's nephew Otto Frisch, now also a refugee in England, sent a short memorandum to the British government entitled 'On the Construction of a "Superbomb" Based on a Nuclear Chain Reaction in Uranium'. No one, they said, had yet looked at the possibility of using fissile uranium-235 as the basis for a bomb. One would need a mechanism which kept two or more subcritical bits of uranium-235 apart until the explosion was needed. One kilogram of uranium might be enough. A five-kilogram bomb would produce an explosion equivalent to several thousand tons of dynamite. The radiation from the explosion would kill people several miles downwind for days afterwards. The main problem in producing a bomb would be to separate sufficient uranium-235 from uranium-238, in which it occurs only in small quantities.

The paper was examined by a committee known, for reasons which became a matter of dispute among historians, as the MAUD

Committee.* Four of its members went on to work on the nuclear project: James Chadwick, John Cockcroft, Patrick Blackett, and Mark (Marcus) Oliphant, a distinguished Australian physicist. It got to work in June 1940 as France was falling and the British feared invasion. As 'enemy aliens', Frisch and Peierls were excluded from its first meetings on security grounds, though the ban was lifted after four months.

In July 1942 the MAUD Committee reported to the British government that it would be possible to make an effective bomb by firing two subcritical pieces of uranium at one another down the barrel of a gun. Such a device would weigh no more than a ton and could be dropped by parachute from a bomber: 'the destructive effect, both material and moral, is so great that every effort should be made to produce bombs of this kind.' Work should therefore go ahead 'on the highest priority and on the increasing scale necessary to obtain the weapon in the shortest possible time'. Foreshadowing the post-war nuclear arms race, the report concluded: 'Even if the war should end before the bombs are ready the effort would not be wasted, except in the unlikely event of complete disarmament, since no nation would care to risk being caught without a weapon of such decisive possibilities.'[8]

But there were two difficulties. The British were fighting for their lives. Did they have the resources to build the massive industrial plants that would be needed, and could they secure them against German aerial bombardment? If not, could they negotiate a cooperative arrangement with the Americans which would preserve their ability to pursue an independent programme for the later use of nuclear power in war and peace?

---

* Some believe that MAUD stood for Military Application of Uranium Detonation. Others think that it came from the misreading of a message from Lise Meitner about Niels Bohr, then safe but unhappy in Denmark. The message read '*MET NIELS AND MARGRETHE RECENTLY BOTH WELL BUT UNHAPPY ABOUT EVENTS PLEASE INFORM COCKCROFT AND MAUD RAY KENT.*' Maud Ray was formerly governess to Bohr's children, then living in Kent. The message meant no more than it said. (G. Farmelo, *Churchill's Bomb*, London, 2013, p. 161).

Churchill's adviser Lindemann was quite clear: 'We must go forward. It would be unforgivable if we let the Germans develop a process ahead of us by means of which they could defeat us.' He was not convinced that the Americans were fully up to the job: 'Physicists and engineers in the US would be competent to develop this project, [but] it would seem undesirable to depend on them. In general, the Americans [are] slow starters.' He wondered if the Americans could keep their mouths shut: an irony, given the number of British scientists and officials already recruited by Soviet intelligence.

But Lindemann's most substantial point was a strategic one, though illusory: 'Whoever possesses such a plant should be able to dictate terms to the rest of the world … However much I trust my neighbour and depend on him, I am very much averse to putting myself completely at his mercy and I would, therefore, not press the Americans to undertake this work.' The Chiefs of Staff agreed: 'The development should proceed in this country and not abroad', even if tests had to be 'carried out, if necessary, on some lonely, uninhabited island'.

Churchill was inclined to agree. On 30 August 1941 he sent a minute to General Ismay, the Chief of the Imperial General Staff, saying, 'Although personally I am quite content with the existing explosives, I feel we must not stand in the path of improvement, and I therefore think that action should be taken in the sense proposed by [Lindemann] and that the Cabinet Minister responsible should be Sir John Anderson.'*

Others were more realistic. Tizard thought it would be 'absurd' to try to make nuclear bombs in Britain during wartime. Others thought that the idea of setting up a nuclear bomb factory in Britain was impracticable, even deplorable.[9] An idea gained force that the plant should be built in Canada with the Americans as consultants. But for the time being the British project went ahead as the Prime Minister directed.

---

* Sir John Anderson was a former civil servant who became Home Secretary under Churchill. 'Anderson shelters' were named after him. They were simple devices of corrugated iron and were distributed to the population during the war. We had one in the garage, though we rarely bothered to use it.

The British had already shared a copy of the MAUD Report with Lyman Briggs, who sat on it. Vannevar Bush eventually put it to Roosevelt in the late autumn of 1941, and that only after the Americans had been lobbied by Mark Oliphant. Roosevelt then proposed to Churchill that 'any extended efforts may be coordinated or even jointly conducted'. Churchill's lukewarm reply was delayed for a further two months. British historians suggest that Churchill had thus missed a major opportunity. Had he replied to Roosevelt more quickly, they argue, the British would have been able to negotiate more equal terms.[10] But the British negotiating position was intrinsically weak. The eventual success of the project depended above all on American industrial and financial power and engineering skill. The Americans would have had no great reason to be generous even if Churchill had responded to Roosevelt more rapidly.

The Americans Take Over

By the end of 1941 the Americans finally began to bring a formidable energy to bear on the project. It was soon clear to the British that the Americans were forging ahead and that their pioneer work was a dwindling asset.[11]

Churchill agreed with Roosevelt in Washington in June 1942 that the research plants should be constructed in America. He believed that the two countries would 'at once pool all our information, work together on equal terms, and share the results, if any, equally between us'.[12]

He was probably deluding himself. The Americans were determined to run the show their way and to limit the information they shared with the British about the work they were doing.[13] Draconian security measures increasingly kept British scientists away from the American project. At the beginning of 1943 Vannevar Bush concluded that it would be best to end the exchange with the British altogether; though a restricted exchange might have to continue. Roosevelt agreed.[14]

Sir John Anderson was incensed and immediately wrote to Churchill: 'This development has come as a bombshell and is quite intolerable.' Churchill asked how much a purely British project would cost. His people told him that it would require a massive diversion of resources and skilled manpower from other military projects. Anderson reluctantly concluded that 'it would be far more efficient to work closely with the Americans and, if they refused to share the weapons, use the experience of working on the project to build a bomb after the war'.[15] Churchill had another go at Roosevelt when he visited Washington that May. Roosevelt was charmingly reassuring, but the Americans remained uncommunicative. The prospects seemed increasingly gloomy.

Matters were smoothed over when Churchill and Roosevelt met in Quebec in August 1943 and in the President's country estate at Hyde Park on the Hudson in September. British and American brains and resources should be pooled. Neither would use the weapon against the other. Nor, without the consent of the other, would either use the weapon against third parties or convey any information about it to outsiders. Since the costs would mostly fall on the Americans, Churchill accepted that after the war Britain would exploit any commercial or industrial opportunities deriving from the joint project only 'on terms to be specified by the President of the United States to the Prime Minister of Great Britain'.[16]

For the British the most important provision of all was that their collaboration with the Americans should continue even after the war unless it was terminated by joint agreement. Unfortunately the agreement was informal, personal between the two leaders, not legally binding. In later years politicians on both sides of the Atlantic attacked it as a sell-out of the national interest: the British resented the constraints on their ability to exploit the commercial opportunities; the Americans resented the notion that they could not use their nuclear weapons without British agreement. The Americans repudiated the Quebec agreement as soon as the war was over.

Meanwhile, however, the agreement made it possible for the British and the Americans to resume their collaboration. Chadwick, Peierls, and Oliphant joined the Manhattan Project immediately. They left from Liverpool on board the RMS *Andes*. For lack of more appropriate transport, they and their luggage were delivered to the ship in a fleet of funeral hearses.[17] They were followed eventually by about two dozen more British scientists.

In later years there was some dispute about how important the British contribution to the nuclear project had been. In his memoirs, Harold Macmillan wrote, 'Britain had been first in the field and might be said, up to the end of the War, to have had an equal share in the equity with America.' He, Churchill, and other senior British politicians used this as an argument to persuade the Americans to continue sharing their nuclear expertise after the war.

Needless to say, the Americans saw it differently. General Groves, the head of the Manhattan Project, was lukewarm: 'On the whole, the contribution of the British was helpful but not vital. Their work at Los Alamos was of high quality but the numbers were too small to enable them to play a major role.' President Kennedy's adviser McGeorge Bundy was judicious but more generous. The British contributed very little to the large-scale engineering and industrial enterprise, but one American scientist judged that the MAUD Report and the British intellectual input 'certainly shortened by a year the time which would otherwise have been required'. Even if you cut that time by half, said Bundy, 'there would have been no bomb in 1945 without the British'.[18]

As was inevitable, the Americans' sense of gratitude in their dealings with the British on nuclear affairs was carefully calibrated to what they saw as their interests, as the British were soon to discover.

The Manhattan Project

In October 1941 Roosevelt approved a crash programme to develop a bomb. Lawrence continued to develop his cyclotrons at Berkeley, which could provide the basis for one method of uranium enrichment. The 'Metallurgical Laboratory' was set up under the Nobel Prize winner Arthur Compton at the University of Chicago to oversee research into the atomic chain reaction. The team from Columbia, including Enrico Fermi, was brought in to focus the effort.[19] They built their reactor in an improvised building under a squash court in Stagg Field, the university's football ground. It was here, on 2 December 1942, that they initiated the first self-sustaining nuclear chain reaction. Exactly twenty-five years later *Nuclear Energy*, a sculpture by Henry Moore, was erected on the site to commemorate the event.

Robert Oppenheimer was one of those who had been alerted by Hahn's discovery of fission in 1939 to the possibility of a nuclear weapon. He had already begun calculating the size of the necessary critical mass.[20] In May 1942 Ernest Lawrence persuaded the Chairman of the National Defence Research Committee, James Conant, to appoint Oppenheimer as the project's director for fast neutron research, with the title Coordinator of Rapid Rupture.[21]

That summer Oppenheimer held a series of meetings in Chicago and Berkeley to discuss what direction the research should take. The participants included Robert Serber, Hans Bethe, and Edward Teller. They agreed that a fission bomb was possible, if you had enough fissile material. They first settled on the gun-type design suggested in the MAUD Report. The science was comparatively simple. To bring the two pieces of subcritical uranium together at a sufficient speed was primarily a problem of engineering.

But there was a more sophisticated alternative: an 'implosion' weapon, in which a lump of plutonium would be compressed until it reached critical mass. Plutonium would be cheaper to produce than uranium-235 and the resulting bomb would be more powerful. But bringing plutonium into a critical mass was a more complicated piece of engineering than firing two bits of uranium together in a gun. The trick was to surround the plutonium with specially shaped conventional explosive, wired to explode simultaneously and specially shaped to focus the force inwards. If this could be achieved with sufficient speed and accuracy, the plutonium would be compressed to twice its density and it would explode. Otherwise it would merely fizzle.

For Edward Teller that was still not enough. He insisted on turning the discussion towards fusion, the idea first suggested to him by Enrico Fermi that a much bigger explosion – a thermonuclear explosion – could be triggered by using a fission bomb to set off a nuclear explosive by raising its temperature to something close to the temperature of the sun. The nuclear explosive would be not uranium but deuterium, a comparatively common isotope of hydrogen. Such a bomb could be made to explode with a force of 80,000–100,000, or even 1 million tons of TNT (the figure was a gross underestimate: the Russians' 'Tsar Bomba' exploded with a force of fifty megatons in 1961).*

---

*Teller briefly distracted everyone by wondering if a nuclear bomb might ignite the earth's atmosphere. Hans Bethe rapidly demonstrated that his calculations were wrong.

Teller's listeners 'forgot about the A-bomb, as if it were old hat, something settled, no problem, and turned with enthusiasm to something new'.[22] But Oppenheimer insisted on putting first things first. The priority was to produce a workable fission bomb, in time for it to be used in the war. The hydrogen bomb could be left until later.[23] Most of the others thought this was right, but Teller resented the decision deeply. The 'Super' became his obsession. A difficult and opinionated man, he became almost unmanageable when the Manhattan Project got under way. Oppenheimer had to allow him to pursue his own research into the 'Super'. The resulting tensions were to have a fateful impact on Oppenheimer's own career a decade later.

There were many daunting problems to be solved before a bomb could be built. Apart from designing the weapons themselves, there was a shortage of uranium-235 and plutonium. Uranium-235 could be provided by gaseous diffusion and electromagnetic separation. Plutonium was produced in a reactor. But even by December 1943 only two milligrams of plutonium were available.[24]

It was clear that the time had come to move the project out of the university and transform it into a major military-industrial undertaking. In June 1942 Roosevelt agreed expenditure of $54 million for construction, $31 million for research and development, and $5 million for contingencies: by the time the project was completed in 1945 it had cost $2 billion, or about $27 billion in the dollars of 2016.*

The project now came under the army's Corps of Engineers. They formally named it 'The Manhattan Project' in August 1942 for arcane military reasons of their own. Such a massive project required exceptional people to drive it. In September 1942 an army engineer, Colonel Leslie Groves, was appointed on promotion to brigadier general. He had successfully completed many large projects, and had built the Pentagon in less than eighteen months. He was difficult, decisive, and a good judge of men. His deputy, Colonel Kenneth Nicholl, said of him, 'General Groves is the biggest S.O.B. I have ever

---

* The 2016 figure is calculated on the basis of historical US inflation data, using Calculator.net.

worked for ... He is always a driver, never a praiser. He is abrasive and sarcastic ... He has the guts to make difficult, timely decisions. He is the most egotistical man I know. He knows he is right and so sticks by his decision. He abounds with energy and expects everyone to work as hard or even harder than he does ... If I had to do my part of the atomic bomb project over again and had the privilege of picking my boss I would pick General Groves.'[25]

Two dedicated industrial sites were built for the production of uranium and plutonium: Oak Ridge in Tennessee, where uranium was enriched; and Hanford in Washington State, where uranium was transformed into plutonium.

Oak Ridge was fairly isolated and secure, but accessible by road and rail. The population of the new settlement grew from about 3,000 in 1942 to 75,000 in 1945. It had ten schools, seven theatres, a library, a symphony orchestra, restaurants, cafeterias, supermarkets, and its own hospital run by the military. One of the uranium-separating buildings was the largest building in the world at the time.

Hanford, which was set on the Columbia river amid desert scrub, began to produce plutonium in November 1944, and delivered the explosive for the Trinity test and for 'Fat Man', the bomb dropped on Nagasaki. By the end of the Cold War Hanford had produced enough plutonium for more than 60,000 weapons. The reactors were then decommissioned, but despite a vigorous clean-up Hanford remained the most contaminated nuclear site in America. A new town, Richland, was built nearby. Richland High School's sports teams were called the Bombers. Their logo was a mushroom cloud.

One of Groves's first problems was to find a director for the group that would actually design and build the bomb. As he explored his new empire, and met the scientists already working on the nuclear matter, he naturally came across Robert Oppenheimer, and was impressed. There were good arguments against giving Oppenheimer the job. He had little administrative experience and lacked a Nobel Prize, which might undermine his authority with some of the scientists in his team. More worrying, he had been involved on the fringe of radical politics throughout the 1930s. He had raised money for the

Republican cause in the Spanish Civil War and for social issues in California. His brother Frank, his wife, his mistress Jean Tatlock, and many of his pre-war associates were Communists or far to the left. He was still contributing money to left-wing causes in April 1942.[26]

Groves later wrote, 'No one with whom I talked showed any great enthusiasm about Oppenheimer as a possible director.' But Groves was confident that Oppenheimer was the right man to run the scientific side of the bomb project.[27] His judgement was vindicated. Oppenheimer turned out to be a brilliant leader, capable of finding practical as well as theoretical answers to the problem of building the bomb. Isidor Rabi, who had known Oppenheimer since 1929, said that the appointment was 'a real stroke of genius on the part of General Groves, who was not generally considered to be a genius'.[28]

Even after he began working as the director of the project, Oppenheimer still had no security clearance. Soviet agents were already trying to recruit agents among the scientific community in Berkeley and in March 1941 the FBI opened their first file on Oppenheimer after he attended a party for two known Communists organised by his friend Haakon Chevalier. In January 1942 the San Francisco office of the FBI reported to J. Edgar Hoover, the head of the organisation, that Oppenheimer, Chevalier, and two other men were 'inimical to the welfare of this country', and recommended that they be placed under surveillance and their telephones bugged. Hoover gave permission to bug Chevalier but no more.

Groves cut the Gordian knot. In July 1943 he ordered that clearance be issued 'without delay, irrespective of the information you have concerning Mr Oppenheimer. He is absolutely essential to the project.'[29]

The security authorities remained unhappy. In August 1943 Oppenheimer was interviewed by Boris Pash, the local head of army intelligence, to whom he told a complicated story. Some months earlier he had been asked by an 'intermediary' for information about military scientific work which could be passed on to the Soviet Consulate. He had of course refused. But he knew that the 'intermediary' had also approached others. When Pash asked for a name, he demurred, on the grounds that the man was a friend. That, and his failure to contact the security authorities immediately, were two more black marks against him.

Worried by Oppenheimer's evasiveness, in December 1943 Groves ordered him to reveal the name of the 'intermediary'. He named Chevalier. Groves then demanded the names of the other people Chevalier had approached. Oppenheimer asked that Groves should undertake not to pass the names on to the FBI. He then admitted that there had not been three people, but only one: his brother Frank.

Groves honoured his word not to pass on what Oppenheimer had said. In so doing he was committing much the same crime as Oppenheimer himself: lying to a federal official and withholding vital information about an espionage contact. Ten years later Lewis Strauss, the head of the US Atomic Energy Commission, used that lapse to induce Groves to testify against Oppenheimer at the security hearing which destroyed his official career. But Groves never changed his view that he had taken the right decision and that no one else could have done the job as well as Oppenheimer.[30]

Los Alamos

In November 1942 Oppenheimer and Groves went to inspect a site for the laboratory in the mountainous deserts of northern New Mexico. Oppenheimer knew the area well: he and his brother Frank had long rented a hut there. High in the mountains lay the Los Alamos Ranch School, founded in 1917, run on the principles of the Boy Scouts movement, and attended in their time by the well-known (indeed notorious) authors Gore Vidal and William Burroughs. For Groves it was almost ideal: isolated, with only a single road and one telephone line to the outside world. Within days the school had been compulsorily purchased, the boys evicted, and work begun on building a sophisticated laboratory from scratch, the offices and homes of those who would work there, and barracks for the soldiers who would protect it.

Los Alamos opened for business in March 1943. By the summer 4,000 people had moved there. By the end of the war there were 8,750 people, of whom 1,750 were dependants. Today the population is 11,200.[31] Oppenheimer, his wife and their baby son lived in the cottage built for the school's matron. It was one of six cottages in what came to be called 'Bathtub Row', because for a while they were the only houses to have baths.

Los Alamos came under the general supervision of the military, who were therefore responsible for security. This meant that Los Alamos, like Oak Ridge and Hanford, was subject to the attentions of the army's Counter Intelligence Corps, which employed 300 agents under the command of the able and perceptive Captain John Lansdale.[32]

The whole area was surrounded with a security fence. Entrance and exit were controlled by military police. Inside Los Alamos there were no banks and no post office. Mail was censored. Cameras were confiscated. The inhabitants were occasionally allowed into nearby Santa Fe or to visit the local Indian ruins. Wives were not supposed to know what their husbands were doing – an impossible restriction to enforce.

The scientific work was segregated in a secure 'Technical Area', which contained a foundry, a library, and dozens of laboratories.[33] Groves's initial idea was that the scientists should be recruited into the military: they would thus be subject to military discipline and it would be easier to enforce security. Their activities would be strictly compartmentalised: those engaged in one aspect of the project should not know what the others were up to.

Surprisingly, Oppenheimer was at first agreeable, and hankered after a commission as lieutenant colonel. But he soon discovered that the scientists he hoped to recruit for the project were flatly opposed. They were not prepared to don uniform, and they were firmly convinced that scientific research could only prosper if it was shared and discussed within the scientific community. That was the way science had made progress through the ages.

Groves retreated. The scientists would retain their civilian status. They would be under the authority not of the military but of Oppenheimer as 'Scientific Director'. Within the 'Technical Area' they would be free to exchange views. Groves was nevertheless disconcerted to learn that this involved, among other things, a weekly session attended by all the scientists, at which Oppenheimer's pupil Robert Serber delivered comprehensive lectures on what would be required to build a bomb.[34]

Oppenheimer optimistically hoped that 'we shall all be one large family doing work inside the wire', but Enrico Fermi's wife, Laura, said that many of the European-born wives were reminded of concentration camps.[35] The scientists found Groves irritating, clumsy, and ignorant. They joked about his attempts to prove himself their intellectual equal.

Richard Feynman, brilliant, irreverent, and young, made systematic fun of Groves's security measures. He discovered that the local workers had made a convenient hole through the fence, slipped through it repeatedly, and bamboozled the guards by repeatedly checking in at the gate without, apparently, ever having left. He learned to crack the official safes and left provocative messages inside them. When the censors said that he should tell his young wife, Arline, then still in New York, not to mention censorship in her letters, he pointed out that he had no way of doing that, since he wasn't meant to mention censorship in his letters either.

By the time Arline came to join him, she was terminally ill with tuberculosis. Feynman lodged her in a hospital in the nearby town of Albuquerque. To visit her, he used to borrow a car from his friend Klaus Fuchs. It was the car Fuchs was using to smuggle secret documents out of the camp to his Soviet spymaster.*

Groves was able to apply the 'need to know' principle at Oak Ridge and Hanford in a way he had failed to do in Los Alamos. Those who worked there were mostly engineers and supporting staff, not scientists. They had no hifalutin ideas about the necessity of interaction, discussion, and debate. Most of them only discovered that they had been helping to build a bomb when they heard the news of Hiroshima.

Trinity: The American Test

The scientists and engineers were confident that 'Little Boy', the uranium bomb, would work, so they decided not to waste scarce nuclear materials by testing it. Because the plutonium 'Fat Man' was much trickier, Oppenheimer decided to go for a full test, which he code-named Trinity. A test site was constructed in the desert near

---

* There is an account of Soviet operations against the Manhattan Project, and the contribution it made to the Russians' own weapons project, in Chapter 9: Know your enemy. Feynman mentions his use of Fuchs's car in *Surely You're Joking Mr Feynman!*, New York, 1997, p. 129.

a military base at Alamagordo, close to an old route taken by the Spanish conquistadors called the Jornada del Muerto, the Road of the Dead. The test was fixed for 4.00 a.m. on 16 July.

The test device – they called it 'the gadget' – was assembled on Friday 13 July. The date was chosen with black humour by George Kistiakowsky, a Harvard chemist who had been born in Kiev and was responsible for the bomb's complex trigger mechanism. He had fixed on that day in order, he said, to bring good luck.

At first the luck looked poor. To begin with, the trigger mechanism refused to fit together properly. Then bad weather – thunder, lightning, and hail – delayed the test for two days. The night before the test Oppenheimer and Groves spent sleeplessly in the control dugout, 'South 10,000', which was 10,000 yards from ground zero. The weather was still unsettled when Oppenheimer decided to risk it. The countdown started with twenty minutes to go. Popular music from a local radio station was still seeping through the loudspeakers in the control room. At 5.25 a.m. a rocket was fired; and another when only a minute was left. 'I never realised seconds could be so long,' James Conant whispered to Groves. Everyone else was silent. As the last seconds ticked away Oppenheimer held on to a post to steady himself.

Then everything was lit by the brilliance of the explosion. It lasted so long that Conant thought at first that something had gone terribly wrong and the whole world had gone up in flames. 'Good God, I believe the long-haired boys have lost control,' one officer shouted.

But then came the roar of the explosion. Oppenheimer's face relaxed into an expression of tremendous relief. Some of the observers stood rooted to the spot. Others did a little dance, or shouted in triumph. Then came the reaction. For many it was a glimpse of the end of the world: Oppenheimer remembered a passage from the Hindu scripture, the *Bhagavad Gita*: 'Now I am become death, the destroyer of worlds.'* Kistiakowsky said, 'It was as if God himself

---

* Or so Oppenheimer claimed many years later. In the Penguin Classics edition, the line is given as: 'I am all-powerful Time, which destroys all things.' Oppenheimer, however, remembered the translation of his Sanskrit teacher, Arthur Ryder: 'Death am I, and my present task destruction.'

had appeared among us.' Chadwick called it 'a vision from the Book of Revelation'. Rabi was thrilled to start with, but then 'I had goose flesh all over me when I realised what this meant for the future of humanity.' It was left to Ken Bainbridge, an experimental physicist from Harvard, to say, 'Now we're all sons of bitches.' His words have become almost as well known as Oppenheimer's.[36]

Enrico Fermi used to say to colleagues troubled about the morality of building the bomb, 'Don't worry me with your conscientious scruples. After all, the thing's superb physics.' But the explosion shook him so much he had to be driven home. His wife remembered that when he arrived, 'He seemed shrunken and aged, made of old parchment, so entirely dried out and browned was he by the desert sun and exhausted by the ordeal.'

Brigadier Thomas Farrell, Groves's assistant, shared the sense of apocalypse. He walked over to Groves and said, 'The war is over.' 'Yes,' replied Groves, 'after we drop two bombs on Japan.'

Henry Stimson, the US Secretary of War, was with Truman for his meeting with Churchill and Stalin in Potsdam (Berlin) when the test took place. Groves telegraphed Farrell's description of the 'awesome roar' of the blast, which 'warned of doomsday and made us feel that we puny things were blasphemous to dare tamper with the forces heretofore reserved to the Almighty. Words are inadequate tools for the job of acquainting those not present with the physical, mental, and psychological effects.' Churchill called it 'The Second Coming in wrath'.[37]

That was when people started to talk about Armageddon.

The scientists had cast bets to see who could guess the size of the explosion. Most were considerable underestimates: in the event, the explosion was equivalent to about 21,000 tons of TNT. The prize went to Rabi, who guessed 18,000 tons.[38] The heat of the explosion was felt twenty miles away and the light was seen more than a hundred miles away. The army put it about that the blast was due to an accidental explosion in an ammunition dump.

A Quantum Leap: The Super Bomb
For all its horror, the fission bomb dropped on Hiroshima was a

comparatively small affair. It was followed within less than a decade by the far more destructive thermonuclear or hydrogen bomb.

In autumn 1941 Enrico Fermi first discussed the idea of a hydrogen or 'super' bomb with Edward Teller, who picked it up and ran with it. But Oppenheimer, too, incorporated provision for the 'Super' in his initial plans for Los Alamos. In August 1944, he recommended that once the war was over, 'the subject of initiating violent thermonuclear reactions be pursued with vigor and diligence, and promptly'. In July 1945, just before the fission bomb was dropped on Hiroshima, Groves told Stimson that a thermonuclear bomb might be feasible. The possibility needed to be studied very carefully: 'Such a bomb might introduce the possibility of world destruction if some scientists are correct that the explosion could ignite the entire world's atmosphere.'

The euphoria which Oppenheimer had experienced after the Trinity test faded rapidly. His FBI watchers reported that he was a 'nervous wreck'. His mood began to shift against the idea of the 'Super', and he became an erratic critic, sometimes vehemently opposed, sometimes reluctantly in favour. In September 1945 he called a meeting of the Scientific Panel – the body which had advised Stimson on the use of the bomb – to finalise a report on future research. One brief section dealt with the 'Super'. After the meeting Alfred Compton wrote to the Commerce Secretary, Henry Wallace, who had been Roosevelt's Vice President. In his letter he went so far as to say, 'We feel that this development [the 'Super'] should <u>not</u> be undertaken, primarily because we should prefer defeat in war to victory obtained at the expense of the enormous human disaster that would be caused by its determined use.' It was not a well-judged move. Compton believed that Wallace had been influential in getting the atom bomb developed, and evidently hoped that he might be equally helpful in killing the 'Super'. But Roosevelt had replaced Wallace with Harry Truman at the beginning of 1945, and by the autumn Wallace was already being widely criticised for being so soft on Russia.[39]

Edward Teller dismissed the moral argument as irrelevant: 'If the development is possible, it is out of our powers to prevent it.' Now he set out to build a team at Los Alamos to pursue his obsession. He formed the idea that, behind his back, Oppenheimer was discouraging scientists from joining. He added one more to his list of grievances against his former boss. In April 1946 he held a three-day seminar on the 'Super' at Los Alamos. One of those present was Klaus Fuchs. On his return to London, Fuchs gave his Soviet handler the drawing of an advanced design for a 'Super' based in part on an idea he and Von Neumann had put forward earlier.[40]

Oppenheimer left Los Alamos in November 1945. In 1947 he became the Director of the Institute of Advanced Studies at Princeton, where Albert Einstein was still a Fellow. He was also appointed Chairman of the General Advisory Committee which provided scientific advice to the Atomic Energy Commission, which was set up in 1947 to manage nuclear affairs.

At the end of October 1949 – a month after news of the successful Soviet fission test had broken – Oppenheimer called a meeting of the Committee to discuss the 'Super'. The Joint Chiefs of Staff were present. George Kennan, the State Department's most eminent Soviet expert, Hans Bethe, and Robert Serber were brought in as outside advisers. Teller was not invited. Opinion crystallised against the 'Super' on practical and moral grounds: even the military were unenthusiastic. A hydrogen bomb project would use up scarce resources. Even if it were feasible, it would take at least five years to produce a weapon. In the Committee's final report Oppenheimer and five others wrote, 'We recommend strongly against [developing the hydrogen bomb]. We base our recommendation on our belief that the extreme dangers to mankind inherent in the proposal wholly outweigh any military advantage that could come from this development. If super bombs will work at all, there is no inherent limit in the destructive power that may be attained with them. Therefore, a super bomb might become a weapon of genocide. We believe a super bomb should never be produced.'

Fermi and Rabi expressed themselves even more strongly in their minority report: 'The use of such a weapon cannot be justified on any ethical ground. Its use would put the United States in a bad moral position relative to the peoples of the world. Any postwar situation resulting from such a weapon would leave unresolvable enmities for generations. It is necessarily an evil thing considered in any light.'

The Committee concluded with the hope that 'the development

of these weapons can be avoided. We are all reluctant to see the United States take the initiative in precipitating this development.' They believed that even if the Russians developed a hydrogen bomb, the Americans could retaliate adequately with their existing stocks of atomic weapons. Even more desperately, they tried to persuade themselves and others that 'In determining not to proceed to develop the super bomb, we see a unique opportunity of providing by example some limitations on the totality of war and thus of limiting the fear and arousing the hope of mankind.'[41]

Glenn Seaborg, who had worked with Fermi in Chicago on the Manhattan Project, was unable to attend the meeting. But he injected a note of caution in a letter to Oppenheimer: 'Although I deplore the prospects of our country putting a tremendous effort into this, I must confess that I have been unable to come to the conclusion that we should not. My present feeling could perhaps be best summarized by saying that I would have to hear some good arguments before I could take on sufficient courage to recommend not going toward such a program.'[42]

Seaborg's was the voice of realism There was no likelihood that unilateral action by the Americans would shame others into following suit: Andrei Sakharov later commented sarcastically that any show of American restraint would simply have been seen by the Russians 'either as a cunning and deceitful maneuver, or as evidence of stupidity or weakness'.[43] The Russians were already working on the weapon. Their scientists shared some of the misgivings of their American opposite numbers. But few of them wavered in the conviction that it was their patriotic duty to give their country whatever weapons it needed to match or outmatch the United States.

The General Advisory Committee forwarded its high-minded conclusions to David Lilienthal, the Chairman of the Atomic Energy Commission. In November 1949 the Commission voted three to two to recommend against the development of the hydrogen bomb.

But by then the train had left the station. Now the Russians had tested their own fission device, the political and military pressures on Truman to go ahead were irresistible. Even a man of high principle like Hans Bethe swallowed his opposition to building a hydrogen bomb when he contemplated the possibility that the Russians might get one first. Senator Brien McMahon went further, and warned in apocalyptic language that a failure to go ahead might mean 'unconditional surrender ... to alien forces of evil.'[44]

Truman asked for advice from a small group consisting of Dean Acheson, the Secretary of State, Louis Johnson, the Secretary of Defense, who supported the idea, and Lilienthal, who was still against. When they met the President, he summarily rejected Lilienthal's arguments: 'It was like saying no to a steamroller', Lilienthal ruefully noted in his diary.[45]

On 31 January 1950 Truman announced that he had directed the Atomic Energy Commission 'to continue its work on all forms of atomic weapons, including the so-called hydrogen or super-bomb'. The news of Fuchs's treachery came through at the beginning of February. The Pentagon speculated in panic that a Soviet Super 'may be in actual production'. Truman ordered that the programme be given the highest priority, with the aim of producing up to ten hydrogen bombs a year. He instructed Johnson and Acheson to 'undertake a re-examination of our objectives in peace and war and of the effect of these objectives on our strategic plans, in the light of the probable fission bomb capability and possible thermo-nuclear bomb capacity of the Soviet Union'.[46] This study was to become National Security Council Paper 68, 'United States Objectives and Programs for National Security', or NSC-68, a defining document in the evolution of American strategy.

Lilienthal resigned as Chairman of the AEC shortly afterwards. In his place Truman appointed another member of the Commission, Gordon Dean, who served until Lewis Strauss replaced him in 1953. Thomas Murray, an industrialist with strong but muddled religious convictions, was appointed to fill the gap amongst the Commissioners. Teller lost no time in lobbying him. But Murray was not the best target for Teller's ideas. He thought that waging nuclear war against the Soviet Union was 'something we are morally permitted to do; it may be something we are morally obliged to do'. But he also thought that Superbombs, which could destroy whole cities, violated the Christian principle of proportionality, and in January 1954 he was one of the first to advocate a test ban.[47]

Teller's original idea, the 'Classical Super', proved a dead end.

But a major breakthrough was made in January 1951 by Stanislaw Ulam, a Polish émigré physicist who had been brought into the Manhattan Project by Bethe. Ulam suggested an ingenious way of linking the fission trigger with the thermonuclear explosive. Though he later downplayed Ulam's contribution, Teller built on this insight to devise a practical mechanism.

'From then on,' said Ulam, 'pessimism gave way to hope.' Bethe was impressed. Even Oppenheimer's unhappiness about the project now began to diminish. Revealingly, he justified the change thus: 'When you see something that is technically sweet, you go ahead and do it.'[48] Once again, the intellectual intoxication of the nuclear project overcame the doubts of those involved.

The Crushing of Robert Oppenheimer

But Oppenheimer's ambiguous attitude towards the 'Super' project contributed materially to his later undoing.[49] No one ever succeeded in diminishing his overwhelming contribution to the success of the Manhattan Project. After the war he became a national hero, on the front cover of *Time* magazine as the inventor of the atom bomb, in demand all over the world to give talks to scientists and to the public.

But the army's security service and the FBI remained uneasy. And Oppenheimer had attracted powerful enemies. Edward Teller had not forgiven him for the slights he believed he had suffered at Los Alamos. He set out systematically to undermine him. In May 1952 he told the FBI that Oppenheimer had 'delayed or attempted to delay or hinder the development of the H-bomb'. He mixed claims that he did not personally believe Oppenheimer to be disloyal with comments that 'a lot of people believe Oppenheimer opposed the development of the H-bomb on direct orders from Moscow'. He would, he said, 'do most anything' to get Oppenheimer off the General Advisory Committee.

Meanwhile Ernest Lawrence, a natural empire-builder, had been campaigning for a new laboratory, a rival to Los Alamos, which would concentrate on weapons design and work on the 'Super'. He suspected Oppenheimer of opposing the idea; but he was a master lobbyist and got his way. The new Lawrence Livermore Laboratory opened in September 1952 in the countryside outside San Francisco. It eventually had about 8,000 employees, of whom 3,000 were scientists, and an annual budget of over $1 billion. Until the end of the Cold War, two-thirds of its work was on nuclear weapons, including the neutron bomb and the warheads for the MX, Minuteman and Poseidon missiles, and later on X-ray lasers and Brilliant Pebbles, technologies associated with Reagan's Star Wars project, the Strategic Defense Initiative. The laboratory also worked on new energy technologies, environmental clean-up, and the Human Genome Project.[50]

Oppenheimer now managed to acquire an even more formidable enemy. Lewis Strauss had been a naval intelligence officer in the naval reserve; during the war he worked on the Navy's Bureau of Ordnance, eventually rising to admiral. Through his financial contributions to cancer research, he had got to know a number of scientists, including Lawrence and Szilard. He joined the Atomic Energy Commission when it was set up in 1947. It was he who had offered Oppenheimer the directorship of the Institute of Advanced Studies at Princeton. But he was suspicious of Oppenheimer's opposition to the hydrogen bomb, and he had seen a copy of Compton's imprudent letter to Henry Wallace which apparently preferred defeat to victory won by the thermonuclear weapon.

Oppenheimer, for his part, dismissed Strauss as someone who was 'not greatly cultivated but will not obstruct things'. It was a massive misjudgement.[51] In June 1949 Strauss testified to a congressional committee about the dangers, as he saw them, of sending isotopes abroad to friendly countries. In his own testimony, Oppenheimer ridiculed Strauss publicly. 'No one,' he said, 'can force me to say that you cannot use these isotopes for atomic energy. You can use a shovel for atomic energy; in fact you do.' Strauss was outvoted, and never forgave Oppenheimer: one observer later remembered that at the end of Oppenheimer's testimony there 'was a look of hatred there that you don't see very often in a man's face'. When Eisenhower offered him the chairmanship of the Atomic Energy Commission in 1953, Strauss replied that he 'could not do the job at AEC if Oppenheimer was connected in any way with the programme'. He persuaded Edgar Hoover of the FBI to put Oppenheimer under close surveillance, including tapping his phones. The surviving files of the FBI apparently record what amounts to a conspiracy to oust Oppenheimer from public office.

Senior military officers had their own worries about Oppenheimer's loyalties. The views he held on the desirability or otherwise of thermonuclear weapons, strategic bombardment, and other contentious matters were shared by several of his scientific colleagues. But his more extreme enemies saw his opinions as part of a 'pattern of behaviour' that showed he was working actively against US interests.[52]

In 1953 Oppenheimer's membership of the General Advisory Committee was not renewed, though he was retained as a consultant and kept his security clearance for the time being.

By then the Americans were still reeling from the shock of hearing that the Russians had successfully exploded a nuclear device. They had also discovered that the Russians had comprehensively spied on the Manhattan Project. In 1945 the members of a Soviet spy ring in Canada were arrested: they included the British physicist Alan Nunn May, who had worked on the Manhattan Project and passed details to the Russians. In 1948 a senior State Department official, Alger Hiss, was accused of being a Soviet agent: he denied it, and was convicted of perjury in January 1950. Klaus Fuchs was arrested in Britain in February 1950. A week later, Senator Joe McCarthy announced that he had a list of more than 200 Communists inside the State Department and began his campaign against the real and imagined activities of those he accused of 'un-American activities' and Soviet-inspired subversion. The Soviet intelligence success was seized on by those who thought it impossible that the Russians were capable of building a bomb on their own. In 1953 Judge Kaufman sentenced Julius and Ethel Rosenberg to death for their involvement in what he called 'this diabolical conspiracy to destroy a God-fearing nation'.[53]

Emotions were fanned by a spate of Hollywood films, featuring John Wayne and other stars, with names like *I Married a Communist* (1949), *I Was a Communist for the FBI* (1951), and *My Son John* (1952), which showed Communists as violent and cynical thugs, ruining decent families, plotting revolution, ordering the killing of informers, stirring up violent industrial unrest and ethnic rioting, all under the direct orders of Moscow.

This atmosphere encouraged those who could not accept that some scientists might have genuine concerns about the 'Super' bomb. They saw not sincerely held moral scruples, but some kind of sinister intent. In December 1953 William Borden, formerly the staff director of the Congressional Joint Atomic Energy Committee, wrote to Strauss that he believed that thermonuclear weapons could be used to 'cauterize Soviet global aggression'. He concluded that 'more probably than not' Oppenheimer was an agent of the Soviet Union.* Strauss took the opportunity to suspend Oppenheimer's security clearance.

In April 1954 the Atomic Energy Commission held hearings on whether the clearance should be definitively revoked. The hearing was chaired by Gordon Gray, a conservative Democrat who was President of the University of North Carolina. The other members of the board of enquiry were Thomas Morgan, a Republican businessman, and Ward Evans, a scientist who had the additional qualification, in Strauss's eyes, of having regularly voted against clearance in previous security hearings. The case against Oppenheimer was conducted by a brilliant trial lawyer, Roger Robb. He was defended by the distinguished, gentlemanly, but inadequate Lloyd K. Garrison, whose task was rendered harder when Strauss denied him access on security grounds to the documents on which Robb based his case.

A string of sympathetic witnesses testified in support of Oppenheimer: George Kennan, Hans Bethe, James Conant, Enrico Fermi, David Lilienthal, Vannevar Bush, John Lansdale, the army security officer at Los Alamos, and others.

Vannevar Bush and Isidor Rabi were particularly vigorous. Bush attacked the Atomic Energy Commission for 'placing a man on trial because of his convictions'. Rabi was unintimidated by Robb or by the circumstances. 'I think Dr Oppenheimer is a man of upstanding character, that he is a loyal individual, not only to the United States, which of course goes without saying in my mind, but also to his friends and his organizations to which he is attached,' he said. 'To tell you frankly, I have very grave misgivings as to the nature of this charge, still have, and the general public discussion which it has aroused.' And he added sarcastically, 'We have an A bomb and

---

* Ironically, a security lapse at the Atomic Energy Commission so infuriated Eisenhower that he wondered if it was perhaps Borden himself who was the second Fuchs (G. Herken, *Brotherhood of the Bomb*, New York, 2002, p. 242). See also S. Schweber, *In the Shadow of the Bomb*, Princeton, 2000, p. 130.

a whole series of it, and we have a whole series of Super bombs and what more do you want, mermaids?'[54]

But Oppenheimer's fate was sealed by his inability, under cross-examination from Robb, to explain why he had lied about his relationship with Haakon Chevalier, about which he had been questioned in 1943 by General Groves. And two key witnesses, whom Oppenheimer might have expected to support him, failed to do so.

The first was General Groves himself. Groves had dismissed concerns about Oppenheimer's security credentials during the time of the Manhattan Project. He was now asked whether, in the light of his present knowledge, he would still give Oppenheimer security clearance. He replied, 'I would not clear Dr Oppenheimer today if I were a member of the Commission.' Grove may have been referring to the altered circumstances of the day. The evidence that the Russians had indeed been spying on the Manhattan Project perhaps justified the adoption of more stringent security criteria. But it also seems that in the run-up to the hearing Strauss may have effectively blackmailed Groves by hinting that his earlier role in covering up the Chevalier affair had left him vulnerable.[55]

Edward Teller was equally shifty, with less excuse. He told the board that he believed Oppenheimer was loyal, but that he had often found Oppenheimer's actions hard to understand. He would prefer to see the vital interests of the country in other hands: 'If it is a question of wisdom and judgment, as demonstrated by actions since 1945, then I would say one would be wiser not to grant clearance.'[56] He had been coached in advance by Robb.

In the end, Oppenheimer's equivocation over the Chevalier affair determined the verdict. The board accepted that he was a loyal citizen of the United States, but they wrote in their conclusion, 'Being loyal to one's friends is one of the noblest of qualities. Being loyal to one's friends above reasonable obligations to the country ... however, is not clearly consistent with the interests of security.'

To Strauss's surprise and fury, Ward Evans disagreed with the verdict. Evans pointed out that no new information about Oppenheimer's left-wing associations had come to light since he had been cleared to work on the Manhattan Project: 'There is not the slightest vestige of information before this Board that Dr Oppenheimer is not a loyal citizen … I personally think that our failure to clear Dr Oppenheimer will be a black mark on the escutcheon of our country.'[57]

Strauss manoeuvred to ensure that the Atomic Energy Commission ignored Evans's minority view. Oppenheimer's security clearance was revoked and he was debarred from further government business. He returned to the Institute for Advanced Study in Princeton, continued to speak in public on a wide variety of subjects, and especially in Europe he was regarded as something of a martyr. The full transcript of the hearing against him was not declassified until 2014.

In 1958 Gordon Dean, Lewis Strauss's successor as Chairman of the Atomic Energy Commission, called for a re-evaluation of the case. The conclusion was that the original inquiry had been an abuse of the judicial system. Strauss was unreconciled. When President Johnson awarded Oppenheimer the Fermi Medal in 1963 (ironically, the previous recipient was Edward Teller), Strauss wrote furiously to *Life* magazine that the award had 'dealt a severe blow to the security system which protects our country'.[58]

Oppenheimer died in 1967. Edward Teller outlived him by more than three decades. His personal reputation among his fellow scientists never recovered. But he remained to the last a hardline and vocal participant in matters of national security. He was in his late eighties when he became an adviser and supporter of Ronald Reagan's impractical proposal for missile defence, the Strategic Defense Initiative.

FOUR

A FLASH OF LIGHTNING

'Fire came down from God out of heaven and devoured them.'
Book of Revelation 20:9

The Russian people heard the news of Hiroshima on the day the bomb fell on Nagasaki. The veteran British war correspondent Alexander Werth, himself of Russian origin, felt the reaction on the street: 'the significance of Hiroshima was not lost on the Russian people ... [who] clearly realised that this was a New Fact in the world's power politics, that the bomb constituted a threat to Russia, and some Russian pessimists I talked to that day dismally remarked that Russia's desperately hard victory over Germany was now "as good as wasted".'[1] One man from Chelyabinsk in Siberia said in a fury, 'We did not do well, having taken Berlin, not to destroy our allies too. We should have pushed them into the English Channel. America would not now be rattling its weapons.'

The British Embassy immediately picked up the prevailing sentiment: 'At the very moment that the Russians had delivered the final crushing blow to Germany, after they had suffered terrible losses and national security seemed achievable for the first time in the life of a whole generation, the bomb fell upon their heads. When they realised that their comrades in arms had no intention of sharing the secret of the atom bomb with them, but that they planned in reality to use it as an instrument of pressure, their disbelief brought all their old suspicions back to the surface and forced them to recognise that once again they faced the prospect of national humiliation.'

A week after the bomb fell the US government published 'A General Account of the Development of Methods of Using Atomic Energy for Military Purposes' by Henry DeWolf Smyth, a physicist involved in the Manhattan Project. It described in remarkable detail the bombs and the physics behind them, though it said nothing about their design, or the crucial engineering, industrial and military processes which had made them practically possible. It concluded with prophetic words: 'A weapon has been developed that is potentially destructive beyond the wildest nightmares of the imagination; a weapon so ideally suited to sudden unannounced attack that a country's major cities might be destroyed overnight by an ostensibly friendly power.' In future, it warned, 'civilization would have the means to commit suicide at will … these are not technical questions; they are political and social questions, and the answers given to them may affect all mankind for generations.'[2]

Smyth's report was translated into forty languages. *Britanski Soyuznik* (British Ally), the British journal which appeared in the Soviet Union during the war, carried the full text. Andrei Sakharov, a brilliant young Russian physicist who became crucial to the development of the Soviet hydrogen bomb, read it avidly. It 'contained an abundance of declassified information and a general description of the structure of the atom bomb. I would snatch up each new issue and scrutinise it with an interest that was purely scientific.' Alexander Solzhenitsyn claimed that he managed to get hold of a copy of the Smyth report in the Gulag, and gave a lecture on it to his fellow prisoners.[3]

Stalin shared the popular mood of dismay. He had picked up the aggressive rhetoric which was already emerging from some parts of the American body politic. He saw the bombing of Hiroshima as 'atomic blackmail against the USSR, as a threat to unleash a new, even more terrible and devastating war'. Having barely survived the German surprise attack in 1941, he was not going to let himself be caught again. He would ensure the Soviet Union's defences at whatever cost to the Soviet people.

The burden would be very considerable indeed.* Twenty-seven

---

*Vladislav Zubok quotes a figure of 44.5 billion roubles for the cost of the Soviet programme between 1947 and 1949. It is not quite clear how this compares with the American expenditure of $2 billion on the Manhattan Project, since dollar/rouble exchange rate calculations for that period are meaningless. ('Stalin', in J. Gaddis (ed.), *Cold War Statesmen Confront the Bomb*, Oxford, 1999, p. 45, million Soviet citizens had died and the country had been devastated in four years of the most brutal fighting. Stalin feared that discipline had slackened during the war. Now he launched a new wave of repression: there were some 2.5 million prisoners in the Gulag when he died in 1953. Once again the peasants were forced to surrender their produce to fuel the reconstruction of industry. In villages where none of the men had survived, the women had to do the work, drawing the ploughs because the draught animals were dead. The government raised prices on essential products. Famine loomed again. One terrified woman wrote, 'Our children are living like animals – constantly angry and hungry.' Another said that she would have to steal to feed her children: at least in prison you would get fed. Once again there was cannibalism. Workers went on strike in Siberia and the Urals. One and a half million people died of hunger and disease between 1946 and 1948.[4]

The Americans Lose Their Monopoly

Stalin's overwhelming objective was to break the American nuclear monopoly. American scientists knew it was only a matter of time. Others were contemptuous. In October 1945 Truman told Oppenheimer that the Russians would never get the bomb.[5] In 1948 General Groves wrote in the *Saturday Evening Post* that the Soviet Union 'simply does not have enough precision industry, technical skill or scientific numerical strength to come even close to duplicating the magnificent achievement of the American industrialists, skilled labor, engineers and scientists who made the Manhattan Project a success. Industrially Russia is, primarily, a heavy-industry nation; she uses axle grease where we use fine lubricating oils. It is an oxcart-versus-automobile situation.'[6]

The Russians exploded their first nuclear device a year later. But in a sense Groves was right. The Americans began with a very substantial lead. They had been the first to test a bomb. They had been the only ones to use an atom bomb in war. They also had a far wider and more sophisticated range of engineering skills, a far richer, far

quoting N. Simonov, *The Military Industrial Complex of the USSR in the 1920s–1950s*, Moscow, 1996, pp. 241–2.)

more enterprising and far more flexible economic system. Russia was well behind America in areas of engineering, technology, and industrial organisation crucial to the design and construction of a nuclear weapon.

But Russia had strengths which Groves failed to see: world-class scientists, inventive engineers, dedicated managers, almost unlimited resources of labour, much of it forced; a brilliant espionage operation through which the Russians acquired a knowledge of the American programme; and a leader with the will and the authority to drive a hugely expensive crash programme against all odds.

And the Russians were capable of prodigies of improvisation. If industry was incapable of producing sophisticated measuring equipment, the scientists got stuff at home and abroad, cannibalised it, and made what they needed. Their computer technology was far behind the Americans; so they relied on their brilliant mathematicians to calculate by hand. When they ran out of mercury, the State Planning Committee allocated them the country's entire supply; everyone else did without thermometers for years.[7] Forced by circumstance to be more imaginative and inventive than the Americans, by an effort of determined organisation allied to a marked carelessness for health and safety, they overcame their disadvantages.

Their fear that the Americans would attack them was genuine and widespread. The Soviet elite – the scientists, the officials, the generals – believed it was their patriotic duty, at whatever cost, to protect their country from the threat apparently posed by the American nuclear monopoly.

Ordinary people felt the same. After Churchill's speech in Fulton in March 1946 about an Iron Curtain descending across Europe, people in Siberia 'expected English and American military moves against the USSR at any time'. A Moscow factory worker thought that the British and Americans were already fighting in Greece and China: 'Any day now they will attack the Soviet Union.'[8] Fear turned close to panic at the beginning of the Korean War in 1950, when people began to stockpile matches, salt, soap, kerosene: their traditional reaction in times of tension. The popular 1961 song 'Do Russians Want War?' (to which the answer was of course an emphatic 'No!') was seen in the

West as a piece of Soviet propaganda. It was no more than an accurate expression of the popular mood.

And so, despite extremities of hardship and oppression, people were prepared, however reluctantly, to endure, to do what was necessary to rebuild the country's industry and its armed forces, if that would prevent another war. They persuaded themselves that Stalin knew what he was doing. They said, 'There's no other way.'

Paranoia, the Purges, and Soviet Science
Fear of the outsider had deep roots in Russian history and in the brief history of the Soviet state.

After the initial success of their revolution in 1917, the Bolsheviks were convinced that the capitalists would stop at nothing to eliminate them. These were not idle fears: the infant Soviet state was indeed surrounded by real or potential enemies, beset by small and determined, if not very effectual, domestic conspirators, and invaded from all points of the compass by foreign armies, American, French, British, Polish, German, and Japanese. They were not confident they could survive.

To consolidate the new regime Lenin created and used the instruments of terror without compunction. The political environment deteriorated further in the late 1920s as Stalin fixed his growing authoritarian power on the country. Understandable fear became unreasonable paranoia. Stalin unleashed a reign of terror to root out the subversive, the unorthodox, or the simply inconvenient. The purges swept millions of people away, including, perversely, people in the military, in government service and industry, whom Stalin needed to build and defend his new state. In 1937 and 1938 about 2.5 million people were arrested. Around 800,000 were executed for alleged, usually fabricated, political offences. Many more were killed without a hearing or died under interrogation or in prison, in the camps, and as a result of the forced collectivisation of agriculture. Despite the best efforts of scholars both in Russia and abroad, it may never be possible to establish the exact numbers.

Science was not spared. Genetics and modern biology, computer science (then known as cybernetics), all fell under a murderous ban. Distinguished scientists died because their ideas were incompatible with the primitive dogmatism of the ideologues and of Stalin himself. Stalin had strong and destructive views about any kind of sociological or economic theory which seemed to compete with his own version of Marxism–Leninism. Some branches of science were set back for decades: the inadequacy of Soviet computers compounded the halting manner in which the Soviet economy adapted to the technological age. Genetics were a particular target. Stalin favoured the views of Trofim Lysenko, who believed the characteristics of living organisms could be manipulated, a reflection of Stalin's own belief that human society was infinitely malleable. Lysenko's ideas were proclaimed the only correct theory. Many orthodox geneticists were imprisoned and some were executed. Only under Khrushchev was the ban lifted in the mid-1960s.

Physics escaped the mayhem by the narrowest margin. Communist ideologues found the theories of relativity and quantum mechanics particularly objectionable because they seemed to replace the immutable laws of the solid Newtonian world in which Marx had done his thinking with a fanciful universe where nothing was what it seemed, where electrons could be in two places at once, where space and time, as normal people understood them, had been overthrown. Such 'bourgeois idealism' seemed to contribute nothing to the building of the new state. The authorities demanded that the physicists should gear their work more adequately to the short-term objectives of successive Five Year Plans.

The physicists could not bend if they were to continue with their life's work, even though those who deviated too far from the orthodoxy could find themselves before the secret police interrogators, in the Gulag, or in an unmarked grave. Some managed to hide the extent of their disagreement. Some could not, or disdained to do so. Some spoke with remarkable courage. Yakov Frenkel, back from a year as visiting professor at the University of Minnesota, was quite uncompromising. 'What I have read in Engels and Lenin does not delight me at all. Neither Lenin nor Engels is an authority for physicists,' he said in 1931. 'As a Soviet person I personally cannot sympathise with an opinion that is harmful to science. There cannot be proletarian mathematics, proletarian physics etc.'[9] That was blasphemy in Stalin's Russia.

Frenkel nevertheless died in his bed in 1952. Others were less lucky. Boris Hessen, the Dean of the Faculty of Physics of Moscow University and a distinguished Marxist philosopher of science, was arrested and later shot. The internationally respected Ukrainian Institute of Physics and Technology in Kharkov became a particular target. In 1936 eleven members of the Institute were arrested, including the Director, Alexander Leipunsky.* Five were shot, including the outstanding physicist Lev Shubnikov. The Institute ceased to exist as a centre for international scientific research. It became instead a closed institute for military research.

The career of Lev Landau illustrates the extraordinary life a world-class scientist could live in Stalin's Russia – precarious, nerve-racking, yet holding the possibility of great professional achievement.[10]

One of the most brilliant physicists of the twentieth century, comparable, some said, with Richard Feynman or even with Einstein himself, Landau was born in Baku, an infant prodigy who never really grew up. By the age of thirteen he had learned calculus, contemplated suicide, and was nearly expelled from school. After studying in Leningrad, he worked in Ioffe's Institute of Physics and Technology, in Germany with Heisenberg, in Denmark with Niels Bohr, and briefly in Cambridge. He then moved to the Ukrainian Institute of Physics and Technology, but decamped to Kapitsa's Institute of Physical Problems in Moscow in 1938 to escape the purges.[11]

That summer he and two other former members of the Kharkov Institute circulated an inflammatory leaflet around Moscow University. It read: 'Comrades! The great cause of the October Revolution is being despicably betrayed. The country is inundated with torrents of blood and filth. Millions of innocent people are being thrown into prisons and no one can tell when his own turn will come ... Stalin is no different from Hitler and Mussolini ... The only way out for the working class and for all toilers of our country is a struggle against Stalinism and Hitlerist fascism, a struggle for socialism.'

Not surprisingly the three men were arrested. Landau's colleagues were tortured and sent to the Gulag. Landau himself was kept

---

* Leipunsky was later released and became a major figure in the Soviet nuclear project.

in prison. Kapitsa wrote to Stalin on his behalf. Only another physicist, he said, could appreciate that Landau was one of the two finest physicists in the Soviet Union. Landau was 'provocative and cantankerous, likes to find errors in others, and when he does, especially in important senior people, such as our academicians, he irritates them with irreverence. This way he has acquired lots of enemies.' But he asked that Landau be handled with 'especial care'. Perhaps for that reason Landau was not beaten.

But he was not released either. A year later Kapitsa wrote again, this time to Lavrenti Beria, the head of the secret police, the NKVD.* He proposed that 'Landau [should] be released from arrest under my personal guarantee. I guarantee to the NKVD that Landau will not engage in revolutionary activity in my Institute ... Should I observe Landau making any comments directed against the Soviet authorities, I shall immediately inform the organs of the NKVD.'

Two days later the NKVD let Landau go. His anti-Soviet activities had been sufficiently proved, said the tortuously worded order for his release. 'However, taking into account that: 1) Landau L. D. is an outstanding physicist in theoretical physics and may in the future be useful for Soviet science; 2) Academician Kapitsa P. L. expressed willingness to undertake guarantee for Landau L. D.; 3) the Minister of Internal Affairs of the Soviet Union, Commissar of State Security of the first rank, Comrade L. P. Beria, has ordered Landau to be freed against a guarantee from Academician Kapitsa; IT IS RESOLVED: The prisoner Landau L. D. is to be freed, there is to be no further action in his case, and his file is to be deposited in the archives.'[12]

In 1943, as he was collecting his team for the initial work on a Soviet bomb, Igor Kurchatov needed someone to calculate one of the central processes of a nuclear explosion. 'This difficult task,' he recommended, 'might be entrusted to Professor L. D. Landau, the well-known theoretical physicist, specialist, who has a particularly intimate knowledge of such matters.'

---

* The Soviet secret police was known at various times as the Cheka (Extraordinary Committee), the NKVD (National Commissariat of Internal Affairs), the MGB (Ministry of State Security), and the KGB (Committee of State Security). In Russia today it is called the FSB (Federal Security Service).

Kurchatov fought to get his man. In 1946 he eventually succeeded: Landau returned to the centre of affairs. He had still not learned to keep his head down. While he was working on the bomb project in 1947 he said, 'Our science has been entirely prostituted, even more than abroad, where scientists do have some freedom.' He left the project after Stalin's death in 1953 and severely criticised the Soviet invasion of Hungary in 1956: 'We should salute the heroism of the Hungarian people. Our own are up to their waists in blood.' The secret police produced a background note for the Politburo. Landau's 'political views over many years are those of a man who is markedly anti-Soviet, hostile to all aspects of Soviet reality', it said. He had gone as far as to say that 'Our system, as I have known it since 1937, is a completely fascist system. It's clear that Lenin was the first fascist.' In the Soviet Union, that was sacrilege. And yet they left him alone.[13]

Landau was seriously injured in a car crash in 1962 and never returned to creative scientific work. He died in 1968.

Kapitsa had his own difficulties with Beria. When Stalin put Beria in charge of the Special Committee to run the nuclear weapons project in August 1945, Kapitsa was appointed as one of the scientific advisers. The two men had never liked one another and neither made much attempt to hide his feelings. Now a colleague denounced Kapitsa to Stalin for mismanaging the work on the production of liquid oxygen for which he had been awarded the title of 'Hero of Socialist Labour'. Beria backed the colleague, and proposed he be appointed as Kapitsa's deputy.

Furious, Kapitsa wrote to Stalin in October, complaining of Beria's behaviour in this particular case, and more widely of his ignorant and discourteous attitude towards science and scientists in general. In Soviet circumstances it was, said Kapitsa, impossible for scientists and politicians to collaborate effectively.* He asked to be released from his government posts, including the Special Committee.

---

* Kapitsa told Stalin that scientists in the Soviet Union should occupy much the same position as 'intellectual leaders', and receive the same respect from the government, as senior churchmen had received before the Revolution: an odd argument to use with a committed atheist and former seminarist.

Nothing happened, so in November Kapitsa wrote Stalin another lengthy and sarcastic letter. The Special Committee, he said, was functioning badly. not least because Beria and the other senior officials heading it were behaving like supermen. 'It's true [Beria] waves the conductor's baton. There's nothing wrong with that, but the first fiddle should come next, and he should be a scientist. After all, it's he who gives the tone to the whole orchestra. Comrade Beria's weakness is that the conductor should not only wave the stick: he should understand the score too ... Our exchanges are not very friendly. I suggested he should come to my institute, so I could teach him some physics.' Kapitsa repeated his request to be released from the Special Committee. 'Comrade Beria will no doubt be pleased to see me go.' He added a postscript: 'This letter is constructive criticism, not a secret denunciation. I would like Comrade Beria to see it.'

A few months after writing so scathingly about Beria, it is said, Kapitsa received a letter from Stalin himself, the only reply he ever had. It read, 'Comrade Kapitsa. I have read all of your letters. They are very instructive. I hope we can meet and talk about them.' The meeting never took place.[14]

Stalin did indeed show the correspondence to Beria, who asked him for permission to arrest Kapitsa. Stalin told Beria to leave him alone. But Kapitsa was soon released from the Special Committee. Over the next eighteen months he lost most of his official posts and the institute he headed. He spent the next few years effectively under house arrest in his dacha outside Moscow, though he was still able to do small scale research and occasionally to publish. His name disappeared from public view (his friends in the West thought this meant he was working on a Soviet bomb). He found all this deeply depressing. But like Landau and later like Sakharov, his intellectual gifts and his moral compass saved him from the fate which overtook so many lesser people in the Soviet system. He was rehabilitated after the death of Beria.

Ten years later Kapitsa wrote to Khrushchev that his criticism of the management of the Soviet bomb project was intended to be constructive. 'There is no foundation for the criticisms which had been directed against me that I am a pacifist, and that that is why I refused to work on the atom bomb'; and he pointed out that he had taken an active part in defence work during the war. 'Although', he went on to say, 'I personally do not see why a person should be blamed for refusing on grounds of conviction to make weapons designed to destroy and kill.' Even under Khrushchev, that was not a sentiment a patriotic Soviet citizen was expected to voice.

The Wartime Project

When C. P. Snow warned in 1939 that scientists in the United States, Germany, France, and England were working on the military use of nuclear fission, he did not mention the Russians. Almost nobody did at that time.

Despite their troubles under Stalin, Soviet physicists managed to follow the development of international scientific thinking in the years before the war. They were quick to realise the significance of Hahn's successful splitting of the uranium atom. Kurchatov replicated Hahn's experiment. Khlopin and Zeldovich worked on the chain reaction in 1939. Two of Kurchatov's PhD students, Georgi Flerov and Konstantin Petrzak, demonstrated the spontaneous fission of uranium. Their results were published on 1 July 1940 in the American journal *Physical Review*. Soviet scientists went on publishing their results right up to 1941: unlike their British and German colleagues, they were not yet at war.[15]

On hearing of the work being done by Khlopin and Zeldovich, Igor Tamm apparently remarked that 'a bomb can be built that will destroy a city out to a radius of maybe ten kilometres'. Ioffe and Kapitsa remained sceptical.[16] Kurchatov said that research had shown that, though fission was possible, its practical application still faced enormous difficulties. At that stage the Soviet scientists did not report to their government on the military potentialities.

But on 5 May 1940, William Laurence, the science writer of the *New York Times*, wrote that scientists, especially in Germany, were now working on the explosive properties of uranium. He warned of the colossal impact that this could have for the course of the war in Europe.* Vladimir Vernadsky was tipped off about the article by

---

* Laurence was born in Lithuania and shared the concerns of émigré physicists about German nuclear plans. He was the only journalist present at the Trinity

his son George, who was living in America.[17] A memorandum he and Khlopin prepared for the government in July 1940 recognised that much research remained to be done, and that there were many practical obstacles to be overcome; but these were not matters of principle. Germany, Britain, and America were devoting considerable resources to the problem. They recommended that the Soviet Union follow suit. As a first step the Soviet Union needed to build up its very meagre stock of uranium. The government set up a Commission on the Uranium Problem under the Academy of Sciences in July 1940, and charged it with coordinating further work on the subject. A few weeks later Ioffe told the Academy that in Kurchatov, Khariton, Zeldovich, and Petrzak the Soviet Union already possessed the right men to carry the practical business forward. But no active programme of practical research was launched for the time being.

In October 1940 V. A. Maslov and V. Shpinel, two PhD students* from the reconstituted Kharkov Institute of Physics and Technology, applied for a patent 'On the use of uranium as an explosive and toxic agent'. Drawing on the work of Zeldovich and Khariton, the two men set out, in terms uncannily close to those in the Frisch–Peierls memorandum to the British government of March 1940, the requirements for an atom bomb. This was a coincidence: it was not until September 1941 that the first intelligence material reached Moscow from Klaus Fuchs, the Soviet agent inside the British bomb project. Maslov and Shpinel proposed in addition that conventional explosive be used to compress the uranium into a critical mass: the implosion mechanism later devised at Los Alamos for the plutonium bomb. But Khlopin commented that the proposal as yet had no basis in reality: 'it is essentially a fantasy.' Maslov tried again at the beginning of February 1941, writing this time to the Minister of Defence, Marshal Timoshenko. The document was filed away with a note,

---

test and flew with one of the aircraft escorting the B-29 that bombed Nagasaki. He won the Pulitzer Prize in 1946. Nearly twenty years after his death in 1977 he was accused of participating in the official cover-up of the effects of radiation.

* The Russian term is 'Candidate in Physical Mathematical Studies'. It is a formal postgraduate title, the first step towards a doctorate. It does not exist in British universities, where the nearest equivalent is perhaps the Research MSc.

'Not confirmed by experiment. Experimental data to be presented.'[18] Less than nine months later Kharkov fell to the German invaders.

The Germans attacked the Soviet Union on 22 June 1941 and at first carried all before them. Two weeks later the Soviet government set up a Scientific-Technical Council to harness science to the war effort. The members included Ioffe, Kapitsa, and Semenov. For the time being, most nuclear scientists abandoned their research for work more directly related to weapons production. Vernadsky's Uranium Commission ceased to function. Kurchatov's department was evacuated from Leningrad to Kazan. Kurchatov himself embarked on a project to protect Soviet ships from German magnetic mines.

But the subject was firmly in the air. At a meeting of scientists in October 1941 held to denounce the German invasion, Kapitsa told his audience that an atomic bomb was possible in principle. The technological obstacles were huge, but so were the opportunities. Flerov had been called up as an aircraft engineer. But he maintained his interest in his subject and deduced from the sudden silence in the international scientific journals that the American, British, and German governments were all now working on the nuclear weapon. In December 1941 he set out his proposal for an experimental bomb in which the explosion would be initiated by bringing together two subcritical pieces of uranium in a gun barrel: the solution proposed by Peierls and Frisch. To dramatise his argument, he said that the country that first built an atom bomb would be able to dictate its terms to the rest of the world: exactly the point that so worried Stalin after the bombing of Hiroshima in 1945. His note reached Sergei Kaftanov, the government's 'plenipotentiary for science', who took an immediate interest.* Flerov was demobilised and from then on played a full role in the project.[19]

By August 1942 the Germans had swept through Ukraine and were fighting on the outskirts of Stalingrad. Until they won that crucial battle in February 1943, the Russians had little time or energy to organise themselves seriously for work on a nuclear weapon. Even so,

---

* There is a story that Flerov also wrote directly to Stalin, but there is no evidence that Stalin actually saw his letter.

in September 1942 the State Committee for Defence (GKO)* ordered the Academy of Science to set up a special laboratory in Kazan on the Volga to investigate ways of producing uranium and to report by 1 April 1943 on the feasibility of using uranium for a bomb or for fuel.[20]

Kurchatov did not think this was enough. That winter he was shown some of the intelligence and prepared an analysis for Molotov. He was particularly good at adapting his style to his audience. The people he most needed to persuade, Beria and Stalin, were highly intelligent but wholly ignorant of science: the technical explanations which he wrote for them are a pleasure for the lay reader.† In his note he said that the British scientists – many of whom he knew by reputation – seemed convinced that a bomb was feasible: they were talking of producing three bombs a month by 1943, though that was probably too optimistic. The Soviet Union was lagging behind. Kurchatov recommended that a committee should be set up under Molotov's chairmanship. Its members would include Kapitsa, Ioffe, and Semenov. Khariton, Zeldovich, and others should be brought into the project.[21]

Molotov passed the note to Stalin. Kurchatov's recommendations were approved, his proposed committee was set up, and in February 1943 he was appointed to direct the new laboratory. He was now given full access to the intelligence reports, his department was renamed Laboratory No. 2, and its work immediately became top secret.[22]

Khariton originally resisted Kurchatov's attempt to recruit him for the new project. But Kurchatov was already looking beyond the end of the war: 'We mustn't lose time. We will win this war, but we must look beyond that to the future security of the country.' Khariton agreed to cooperate.[23]

At that point Stalin still appears to have seen little urgency. He followed the 'atom project', as it was later called, in the closest detail, as he followed everything: the smallest matters were referred to him

---

* The GKO was chaired by Stalin and was the highest decision-making body in the country.

† The Soviet industrialists found the jargon of the scientists incomprehensible: it was as if they were talking different languages. Kurchatov organised seminars to bring them together and intervened tactfully when things looked like going off the rails (A. Pervushin, *Atomny Proekt*, Moscow, 2015, p. 405).

for a decision. But even though Kurchatov's programme was still a comparatively small-scale affair, Stalin evidently concluded that there was little point in diverting valuable resources to build a bomb which would be too late for use against Germany. When Laboratory No. 2 moved into new accommodation on the north-east outskirts of Moscow in April 1944, it still employed only eighty-three people, of whom only twenty-five were scientists.

The news that the American programme had succeeded changed all that. On 20 August 1945, a month after Stalin's brief exchange with Truman in Potsdam, the Soviet government set up a Special Committee to complete a bomb project by 1948. Its chairman was Lavrenti Beria, the head of the NKVD. The other members were the head of the Central Committee Secretariat Georgi Malenkov, the head of the State Planning Bureau Nikolai Voznesensky, the Minister of Armaments Boris Vannikov, and two deputy ministers of the NKVD, Avraamy Zaveniagin and Viktor Makhnev. There were two scientists, Kurchatov and Kapitsa.* A 'First Main Directorate' was set up under the Special Committee. It was chaired by Vannikov, reported direct to the Politburo, and was given unlimited access to resources and personnel. This committee became in effect the General Staff of the Soviet project, responsible for all its major decisions.[24]

Igor Kurchatov was named as the overall administrator of the research project, and Yuli Khariton as its 'chief designer'. Between them the two men covered roughly the responsibilities exercised at Los Alamos by Robert Oppenheimer.

Stalin knew he needed the physicists if he was to get his bomb. He accepted that they needed some freedom to exchange their professional ideas, ideas which he did not understand, but knew were essential to his purpose. Even though he seems to have suspected that some had moral doubts about the project, he and Beria handled the physicists with what was for them a remarkable degree of restraint.[25] Beria put their personal files under lock and key in his own secretariat, with strict instructions that he alone was to have access to them.

---

* This was the Committee from which Kapitsa soon sought to resign.

In Stalin's paranoid last years the ideological pressure neverthe-less increased. Ioffe and Tamm, amongst others, were criticised for spreading cosmopolitism (a shorthand phrase which usually meant that those targeted were Jewish), and idealism (meaning that they believed in relativity and quantum physics). Beria asked Kurchatov whether it was true that relativity and quantum mechanics were 'idealist'. Kurchatov replied that if the theories were rejected, it would not be possible to go ahead with the bomb project. According to his son, it was Beria who protected his people from anti-Semitism and frustrated the party hacks who wanted to anathematise the two theo-ries. After he fell from power, Beria was accused among other things of having contaminated the Academy of Sciences by failing to weed out the Jewish scientists there.[26]

Despite his baleful reputation, Beria was an outstanding admin-istrator. Crudely speaking, his function in the Soviet nuclear project was similar to that exercised over the Manhattan Project by General Groves. But his overall power and responsibilities were much wider – and much more sinister. He had managed the Gulag ruthlessly but effectively. He now called on nearly 300,000 of its prisoners for the rougher tasks – the mining of uranium and the construction of the necessary industrial and test facilities.[27]

But Beria was also capable of thinking unSoviet thoughts. Sakharov once asked him: 'Why are our new projects moving so slowly? Why do we always lag behind the USA and other countries, why are we losing the technological race?' Beria's reply was simple and revealing: 'Because we lack R & D and a manufacturing base. Everything relies on a single supplier, Elektrosila. The Americans have hundreds of companies with large manufacturing facilities'.* The uneasy sense that they lagged behind, that they had to prove themselves, that they needed to strain every nerve merely to catch up with the Americans, remained prevalent in Soviet thinking and the Soviet weapons programme.[28]

Beria did not long survive the struggle for power which broke

---

* *Elektrosila* was a massive factory in Leningrad, which produced heavy electrical equipment and enjoyed something close to a monopoly in the Soviet Union. It later gave its name to a metro station, a football club, and a pop group.

out after Stalin's death in March 1953. He proposed a number of measures of relaxation in domestic and international affairs. His colleagues feared he was bidding for popularity. They arrested and tried him that summer, and had him shot in December.

The nuclear organisations were brought together under the Ministry of Medium Machine Building, a non-committal name seen in the West as a duplicitous attempt to hide its true purpose. The Minister, effectively Beria's successor, was Vyacheslav Malyshev, another of Stalin's effective administrators. The Ministry not only developed, produced, and serviced weapons. Initially it was also responsible for storing them without detonators and other devices needed to activate them. The whole could be delivered to the military and mated with their launchers only on the direct order of the government. This function was taken over by the Ministry of Defence in 1959.[29]

The necessary work fell into three categories: mining, refining and processing uranium and building a reactor to produce plutonium; doing the basic scientific research on nuclear fission and fusion; and designing and testing a weapon.

The first of these – the production of uranium in sufficient quantities – was for a while the most crucial. The Russians had barely explored the resources of their own country: they now found uranium in Russia, Central Asia, the North Caucasus, and Ukraine. They struck agreements with Czechoslovakia and East Germany, in whose existing mines uranium was extracted at a murderously hectic pace by convicts and political prisoners. In 1943 they even managed to buy some uranium from the Americans: General Groves decided that an outright refusal might make the Russians think something was up, so they were allowed a meagre amount.[30] The first batch of plutonium was produced in the closed city of Chelyabinsk-40 in February 1949.[31]

The second task was to create the necessary scientific facilities. Existing research institutions in Leningrad and Moscow were expanded. So was the Ukrainian Institute of Physics and Technology, which had been so badly hit during the purges. Others were built from scratch.

Kurchatov began building F-1, the first experimental nuclear reactor, in the summer of 1946 on the territory of Laboratory No. 2 on the outskirts of Moscow. On 25 December it went critical, four years after Fermi's reactor in Chicago. As Beria and Kurchatov reported to Stalin, 'We are now in a position to solve the most important problems of the industrial production and use of atomic energy, which up till now were only surmises based on theoretical calculation.' This was a breakthrough, in recognition of which Stalin received Kurchatov and the members of his team: the only such occasion in the history of the Soviet atomic project. More than sixty years later the facility was still being used for experimental purposes. Muscovites wondered from time to time how safe it was to live with a nuclear reactor in their midst.[32]

The next task was to develop a bomb. An offshoot of Laboratory No. 2 – Design Bureau No. II – was set up for the purpose under Khariton. He now needed a secret and safe place to conduct the work.

The Closed Cities

In April 1946 a site for Khariton's operations was found near the small town of Sarov, about 500 kilometres east of Moscow. The location first of a Tartar fort and then of a small monastic community, Sarov was home to a fashionable nineteenth-century saint, St Serafim, and a favourite place of pilgrimage of the last Tsar, Nicholas II. After the Revolution the monastery was closed and many of the monks shot (their cells were used for the first laboratories of Design Bureau No. II). Sarov became little more than another camp in the Gulag. A few years before the scientists moved in, some prisoners hit a guard over the head with a shovel, grabbed his machine gun, and shot their way out of the camp to hide in the surrounding forests. The NKVD brought in the army and the fugitives were destroyed by artillery.

The code name for the new research centre was Arzamas-16: the real Arzamas lay sixty kilometres to the north. The name Sarov disappeared from the maps and the town was surrounded with a draconian security perimeter. Its inhabitants were not exactly prisoners, but they lived restricted lives in conditions of the utmost secrecy, able to come and go only under strict control.

Some of the Soviet Union's most distinguished scientists worked there. They were painfully aware that the facilities they used had been built by those they called 'Beria's slaves'. 'Every morning long grey lines of men in quilted jackets, guard dogs at their heels, passed by our curtained windows,' Andrei Sakharov remembered. 'It was some consolation, of course, that the zeks [prisoners] were not dying of hunger ... We could help the prisoners (or least the trusties) in small ways, with old clothes, a little money, something to eat ... After the 1953 Amnesty that followed Stalin's death, the zeks were replaced by army construction battalions (another form of conscript labour, but at least they weren't prisoners).'

The younger scientists were often recruited straight from university and told only that they would be doing work of great national importance somewhere in the provinces. Many spent the rest of their careers – perhaps four or more decades – in the restricted world of Arzamas-16: Khariton was still there at the age of ninety-one. The restrictions could be daunting. When the 23-year-old Ludmila Fomicheva, an explosives expert, arrived there in the mid-1950s, she found the town surrounded by barbed wire and guarded by soldiers and dogs. Her documents were checked at excruciating length before she was allowed in. The scientific research facilities and the testing areas – the *Promzona* (production zone), the equivalent of the Technical Area at Los Alamos – were separated from the town by another barbed-wire fence, controlled in the same way; and the zone was further split up into separate facilities. At each barrier she underwent the same checks. People were, of course, allowed to leave for Moscow, Dnepropetrovsk in Ukraine, where most missiles were designed or built, or anywhere else that official business might take them. But only their closest relatives were allowed to visit them, and then only after weeks of getting the necessary permissions.[33]

The senior scientists were accompanied night and day by security officers, sometimes under the name of 'secretaries', carrying barely concealed pistols. The scientists called them 'ghosts' and had different ways of dealing with them. Kurchatov took no notice of them. Others found their presence a continual strain and a humiliation. Sakharov and some colleagues were briefly arrested in the surrounding forest when they strayed too near to the barbed wire. He later wrote ironically, 'We were encouraged to throw ourselves into our work by the fierce concentration on a single goal, and perhaps also by the proximity of the labour camp and a strict regimentation.' Stories multiplied. A baffled Beria was once supposed to have asked Stalin what to do with some recalcitrant scientists. Stalin's answer was simple and practical: 'Leave them in peace. We can always shoot them later.'[34]

Despite the constraints, there were also great advantages to be had from working in Arzamas-16. There was little in the way of entertainment: a theatre, a couple of cinemas, a youth club. But the inhabitants were privileged, well housed, well paid, and well fed by Soviet standards. Life there was much easier than life 'on the Mainland', as they called the whole of the Soviet Union outside their small world, where the standard of housing and food had recovered little since the war. Their offices and homes were bugged. But they felt able to discuss politics with much more freedom than would have been prudent elsewhere. For the scientists freedom of discussion was essential to their creative work. But it inevitably led to a lack of the high standard of political discipline expected of Soviet citizens. General Groves had been defeated by a similar problem at Los Alamos.

Above all, there was great professional satisfaction. The young scientists worked among senior colleagues of the greatest distinction, operating at the outer fringe of physical and technical knowledge in an atmosphere of intellectual excitement. Work on the bomb gave them the opportunity to do what Enrico Fermi had called 'superb physics'. As Sakharov wrote in his memoir, 'The physics of atomic and thermonuclear explosions is a genuine theoretician's paradise … A thermonuclear reaction – the mysterious source of the energy of the sun and stars, the sustenance of life on earth but also the potential instrument of its destruction – was within my grasp. It was taking place at my very desk.'[35] Oppenheimer had described Los Alamos as 'a remarkable community, inspired by a high sense of mission, of duty and of destiny, coherent, dedicated, and remarkably selfless'.[36] The same was true of Arzamas-16. When those who had worked in both places were able to meet after the Cold War, they found they had much in common.

Another closed town, code-named Chelyabinsk-40, was founded in 1945 to service what became the Mayak plant for the production of plutonium. It was sited amid forests and lakes: the presence of substantial supplies of water for cooling purposes was key. It too was built by prisoners – some 40,000 of them. The first task was to construct a much more powerful reactor, A-1 (or 'Annushka', 'Annie'), based on Kurchatov's F-1. Next came a plant for separating plutonium from the uranium produced in the reactor and another for processing the plutonium into metal for bombs.

In March 1948, when the reactor was finally being assembled, Kurchatov came to speak to the staff. He assured them that they were building not for a year or two, but for centuries. He quoted Pushkin's *Bronze Horseman* about the building of St Petersburg: 'Here we will found a city to spite our arrogant neighbour', to help defend the country against its enemies. Chelyabinsk-40 would become a peaceful city, with schools, shops, a theatre, and a symphony orchestra. 'And if over that time not a single uranium bomb has burst over our heads,' said Kurchatov, 'we and you can be happy. And our city will become a monument to peace.'

There were serious hiccups. Some were the inevitable product of inexperience. Others were the consequence of inadequate safety procedures, complicated by excessive secrecy. Radioactive cooling water from the reactors was dumped into a nearby lake. Nuclear waste escaped into the wider river system. In 1957 an explosion in a reprocessing plant resulted in the third most serious nuclear accident after Chernobyl and the accident at Fukushima in Japan. About 10,000 people were evacuated from the villages affected by this accident. The number of fatalities is disputed: the figures range from around fifty to over 8,000, with 200 as the most commonly quoted. All this was kept secret for decades. The CIA apparently heard of it in 1959 but is said to have suppressed the details for fear of the effect on the American nuclear industry. Fuller details emerged after Gorbachev came to power.[37]

In 1957 another weapons establishment was set up to mirror Arzamas-16. It too had a code name, Chelyabinsk-70. It was based not in a historic town, but in a former sanatorium set on an isthmus between two lakes deep in the picturesque forests of Siberia. One reason for the decision was that Arzamas-16 was within range of American bombers; it was simple insurance to build an equivalent elsewhere. Another was that competition between the two laboratories would spur the creative work of each. There was a third thought, not much spoken about: there were too many Jews at Arzamas-16. But any attempt to set up a 'purely Russian' centre was bound to fail and the idea was forgotten.[38]

Ten closed cities were set up in all. One was installed in a former sanatorium in Sukhumi on the Black Sea and was staffed by Germans. In 1945 the Russians, like the Americans, sent teams of scientists and intelligence officers – they included Khariton, Flerov and Zeldovich, all suitably disguised as lieutenant colonels – to scour Germany for equipment, materials, documents, and people who had been involved in the German nuclear project. General Groves's Alsos teams of scientists, soldiers, and intelligence officers got there first, and swept up many of the prizes.* But the Russians nevertheless came back with 300 tons of uranium oxide, the apparatus from the Kaiser William Institute, where Hahn had first split the uranium atom, and 122 German scientists. Another 135 specialists were fished out of prisoner of war camps. Some worked in Sukhumi. But Professor Nikolaus Riehl was privileged. An engineer who was born and studied in St Petersburg, he was put in charge of the munitions factory at Elektrostal, seventy kilometres east of Moscow. Using German equipment which had survived the bombing of Berlin, he was given the task of producing uranium metal for Laboratory No. 2. Some of the Germans were awarded the Stalin Prize for their work. Some were given financial bonuses. Riehl was made a Hero of Socialist Labour, given the Stalin Prize and the Order of Lenin, 350,000 roubles, a car, and a dacha outside Moscow. It is said that when he returned to Germany in 1955 Riehl sold his dacha to the cellist Mstislav Rostropovich. It was there, in a neat irony, that Solzhenitsyn wrote much of the *Gulag Archipelago*.[39]

The closed cities opened up with the collapse of the Soviet Union. Arzamas-16 was twinned with Los Alamos: its inhabitants ironically called it 'Los Arzamas'. By 2010 it had 94,000 inhabitants. The Federal Russian Nuclear Centre (All-Russian Scientific Research Institute for

---

* The Alsos teams were commanded by Colonel Boris Pash, the security officer who had earlier cross-examined Robert Oppenheimer. Alsos is the Greek word for 'grove' – General Groves was not pleased by the reference.

Experimental Physics) continued to work there on nuclear weapons for the new Russian state. It was still surrounded by a security fence, and all its inhabitants had to have electronic passes to get in and out. The atomic museum, with examples of all the nuclear weapons developed at Arzamas-16, was rarely visited by the locals; and outsiders had to get special permission. The monastery of St Serafim was restored and returned to the Orthodox Church. Serafim himself was named the patron saint of atomic workers in 2007.[40]

Chelyabinsk-70 was renamed Snezhinsk and twinned with Livermore in California. In 1993 the 86-year-old Edward Teller, one of the founders of the Lawrence Livermore Laboratory, came to visit, lively and opinionated, his intellectual curiosity as sharp as ever, still scarred by the alienation from his fellow scientists which followed his testimony against Oppenheimer. In Russian eyes he had always been 'the symbol of American imperialism', 'the atomic devil'. Now he and his Russian opposite numbers found much in common: patriotism, professional commitment, and a belief that nuclear explosions were still essential – at least for peaceful purposes, such as warding off asteroids about to hit the earth.[41]

Chelyabinsk-65, which had begun life as Chelyabinsk-40, was now renamed Ozersk, but continued to process and recycle nuclear waste. Like Sarov and Snezhinsk, it remained closed. But the inhabitants of all three cities were rather happy that restrictions continued. They helped to keep the towns free of crime.

The Russians Catch Up: The First Soviet Test

The first Soviet atomic device was called RDS-1, an acronym for *reaktivny dvigatel* or 'jet engines', the official code name for the device. The acronym was variously interpreted as 'Stalin's jet engine' or 'Russia can make it'.

RDS-1 was designed and built at Arzamas-16 under the overall direction of Khariton and Kurchatov. It was a plutonium implosion device, with a yield of twenty-two kilotons, similar in size and shape to 'Fat Man', the bomb dropped on Nagasaki. This was not a coincidence, since the Russians had taken the deliberate decision to follow the route successfully pioneered by the Americans, of which their intelligence had given them an ample account. Suggestions for a simpler and cheaper approach, put forward among others by Kapitsa, were rejected by Stalin on the grounds that there was no certainty they would work.

RDS-1 was tested on 29 August 1949 in the desert in Kazakhstan. It was four years almost to the day after Stalin had launched his crash programme. The test had no official codename: the documents called it simply 'test of the first exemplar of an atomic bomb'. No one knows who decided to remedy the omission – perhaps a historian or an official who thought something more catchy was needed. But it was not until the 1980s that the first Soviet test became firmly known in Russia and abroad alike as 'First Lightning'.* As in the Americans' Trinity test, the device was mounted on a tower over 100 feet high. Military fortifications and civilian buildings were constructed around it. Tanks, aircraft, vehicles, and other military and civilian equipment were placed at various distances from the tower. So were over 1,500 animals, which were tethered in the open and under cover. Kurchatov and others were there to observe. Beria insisted on being present too, and Kurchatov had to use all his diplomatic skills to make sure that he did not get in the way.

Twenty minutes after the explosion two tanks, specially shielded with lead, were driven to inspect the results. The tower had been completely destroyed. So had most of the civilian housing, though more robustly constructed industrial buildings had survived. Military equipment had been severely damaged. Civilian vehicles had been wrecked. One fifth of the animals – dogs, sheep, goats, pigs, rabbits, rats – had been killed outright. Soldiers evacuated the rest. One soldier found a bar of chocolate and ate it. He was buzzing with radiation when they got him back and they had to pump him out. He survived.[42]

Stalin immediately awarded generous prizes to those who had taken part. The most senior were made Heroes of the Soviet Union. Their children were offered free places in the higher educational

---

*I am greatly indebted to Pavel Podvig for pointing this out. The arguments are spelled out at 'First Soviet nuclear test: RDS-1 *vs.* Joe-1, Stalin's Rocket Engine, and First Lightning' http://russianforces.org/blog/2017/05/first_soviet_nuclear_test_rds-.shtml).

institution of their choice. Their families were given the right to travel free anywhere in the country. Kurchatov was given a villa in the Crimea.

According to one story, Beria drafted the list of prize-winners on the basis of a simple principle. If the test had failed Kurchatov and the others would have been shot; Stalin and Beria had already lined up their successors. Lesser figures would merely have been sent off to the camps. The story was not particularly plausible. Beria and Stalin thoroughly understood that they could not afford to waste such a scarce resource if they were to catch up with America. Throughout the project, none of the leading scientists, not even Landau, was arrested and none was shot.[43]

An American reconnaissance aircraft picked up samples of the fallout from the test a few days later. On 23 September Truman announced, 'We have evidence that within recent weeks an atomic explosion occurred in the USSR.' He again called for 'that truly effective and enforceable international control of atomic energy which this government and the large majority of the members of the United Nations support'.[44] This was a sideswipe at the Russians, who had already turned down the American 'Baruch Plan', which they believed was biased against them.* Two days later the Russians, still unwilling to come completely clean, issued a tortuous announcement 'concerning the statement by US President Truman about the carrying out of an atomic explosion in the USSR'.

The Americans were in shock: they had believed that the Russians would be unable to build a nuclear device before 1952 at the earliest. When they learned of the Soviet intelligence operation against the Manhattan Project, many concluded that it was treachery, not the skills of Soviet scientists and engineers, which had enabled the Russians to catch up. They vented their fury in the anti-Communist witch-hunt which followed.

The Soviet success did not mean that the Russians were able quickly to build up a workable nuclear arsenal. By the end of 1949 two more RDS-1 devices had been built, and by the end of 1951 there were twenty-nine of them. A modernised version was delivered to

---

* The Baruch Plan is more fully described in Chapter 13.

the air force in 1953. Meanwhile the scientists in Arzamas-16 pressed ahead with the development of smaller, lighter but more powerful warheads. In 1954 they began to design and produce nuclear warheads for the battlefield.[45]

The Russians Build a Super

The possibility of building bombs far more powerful than those dropped on Japan had already seeped into the public domain. Mark Oliphant, the Australian physicist involved in the Manhattan Project, spoke publicly as early as October 1945 about the possibility of making a bomb a hundred, even a thousand, times more powerful than the Hiroshima bomb. In July 1948 an article, 'The Superbomb is Possible', in *Science News Letter* argued that 'any competent chemist' could work out the basic principles.[46]

Russian scientists were already doing so. In September 1945 Frenkel suggested to Kurchatov that a fission bomb might be used to trigger a fusion explosion: the first documented suggestion of the kind in the Soviet files.[47] That month Kurchatov saw a detailed intelligence report on American thinking. Niels Bohr was now back in Denmark. In what was almost an action replay of Heisenberg's famous visit to Copenhagen in 1941, Beria sent a scientist on his team, Yakov Terletsky, to pump Bohr for what he knew in November 1945. Bohr was entirely non-committal, as he had been with Heisenberg. That did not prevent the KGB general responsible, Pavel Sudoplatov, from later claiming that Bohr had been a Soviet agent.

Kurchatov's overwhelming priority was still to produce a fission bomb. But he could not ignore the new information. He reported to Beria in December 1945 that the thing was possible in principle. In June 1946 the government set up a team under Igor Tamm to study whether it was feasible in practice. That autumn Klaus Fuchs, now back in Britain, told his case officer at the Soviet Embassy that Fermi and Teller were doing theoretical work on the Super at Chicago, though he did not know if practical work had yet begun. In March 1948 he handed over a detailed theoretical study of the superbomb. It lacked some of the calculations on which work would have to be based. Nevertheless it was judged sufficiently important to be submitted immediately to Stalin and Beria.[48]

A month after Truman ordered the American superbomb programme to go ahead in January 1950, Beria's Special Committee gave
the green light for a device, code-named RDS-6, to be produced in time
for a full-scale test in June 1952. Khariton and Zeldovich were instructed
to do the basic calculations and were given access to the intelligence.

Andrei Sakharov was now invited to join the new project.
Towards the end of 1946 he was summoned to the ornate Peking
hotel in Moscow, a bizarre architectural fantasy of chinoiserie and
Stalinist neo-Gothic: an invitation of the kind Soviet citizens were
too prudent to refuse. There a man calling himself General Zverev
told him that 'we' were following his progress, and invited him to
work on 'state projects of the greatest importance'. He would have
access to the best scientific literature and equipment. And he would
get somewhere decent to live in Moscow. Sakharov turned the offer
down.

He was motivated by principles on which he was never to compromise. When he started his secret work, a senior security officer
pressed him to join the Party. It was the conventional, even the man-
datory thing for someone who was engaged on work of national
importance. He refused: he could not join the Party 'because a
number of its past actions seemed wrong to me and I feared that I
might have additional misgivings at some future time'. He referred
specifically to the purges and the collectivisation campaign of the
1930s. He got away with it.

In June 1948 Tamm told Sakharov that he was setting up a special
group to work on the hydrogen bomb. He had been ordered to recruit
Sakharov and two other young scientists, Vitali Ginzburg and Yuri
Romanov. This time Sakharov did not refuse. He was indeed given
housing: one room for his wife, his mother-in-law, his daughter and
himself.[49] Less than two years later he was ordered to Arzamas-16.
Tamm thought his theoretical talents would be wasted on the practical work of building a bomb, but there was nothing to be done.
Sakharov spent the next eighteen years at Arzamas-16, more or less
cut off from the rest of the world.

He soon came up with an idea for a fission-fusion bomb, a
hydrogen bomb of sorts. Alternating layers of fissile material and deuterium would be compressed into a critical mass using conventional

explosives. The Russians called it the Sloika, after a Russian word for a layer cake, and they came to know it as 'Sakharov's First Idea'. Ginzburg suggested that lithium deuteride should be used instead of deuterium. This was the 'Second Idea'. Since lithium deuteride was a solid, the Soviet device would not need the massive cooling arrangements which had made the Americans' first effort so unwieldy.

The original deadline of 1952 was unrealistic, but in August 1953 the Russians successfully tested a device based on Sakharov's ideas. There was a last-minute panic when the test team realised that no one had worked out how far the fallout from the explosion would spread. They made the necessary calculations on the basis of an American manual, since they had none of their own. Seven hundred army trucks had to be mobilised to evacuate those at risk. During the test Vyacheslav Malyshev, the minister who took over after Beria was executed, was exposed to a dose of radiation which killed him four years later.

In a sense the 'First Idea' turned out to be a dead end, in Sakharov's own later words, neither original nor successful.[50] The Sloika was not yet a fully developed bomb: it yielded 'only' 400 kilotons, compared with the fifteen kilotons yielded by the Hiroshima bomb, and could not be scaled up. But unlike the ungainly monster the Americans had tested on Bikini Atoll, the Soviet device was small enough to carry by air.

Sakharov now returned to an idea he had first suggested in 1949: a two-stage bomb in which deuterium would be triggered by a fission explosion. The government ordered that a thermonuclear warhead and a missile to carry it be developed by 1955 on the basis of this 'Third Idea'. Spurred by the successful American test at Bikini Atoll in March 1954, the Russian team went into overdrive. In June 1954 they reported that it was in principle feasible to create 'transportable, extremely powerful, and exceptionally economical devices'. In June 1955 Zeldovich and Sakharov formally reported that they had completed the basic design for an experimental device code-named RDS-37, thanks to 'an impressive example of creative team work'.[51]

In November 1955 the Russians tested RDS-37 by dropping it from an aircraft at the site near Semipalatinsk in Kazakhstan known as the Polygon. In principle capable of yielding three megatons, it was scaled down for the test to 1.6. The Russians had created a usable thermonuclear weapon. They had more than drawn level with the Americans, who did not test an air-dropped fusion weapon until the following year.

After the test Marshal Nedelin, the Deputy Minister of Defence in charge, held a dinner in celebration. He asked Sakharov to propose the toast. 'May all our devices explode as successfully as today's, but always over test sites and never over cities,' said Sakharov. Everyone fell silent. Nedelin made an obscene joke, to make it quite clear that it wasn't the business of the scientists to have views about when and how their inventions should be used.

Sakharov and his colleagues were nevertheless showered with honours. Sakharov was elected unanimously to the Academy of Sciences, even though he was only thirty-three and had only just earned his doctorate. At the end of 1953 he and Tamm were made Heroes of Socialist Labour and were awarded Stalin Prizes worth a great deal of money. In the Soviet system, this was the height of achievement. But it was all hidden from the general public until Khrushchev brought the scientists out of the shadows and paraded them to the world as well as to the Soviet people.

Doubts and Fears

Sakharov and his colleagues saw themselves as soldiers in what had become a scientific war with the United States. They were inflamed by a sense of drama, of the monstrous destructive force of the weapons they were building, the scale of their enterprise, and the price paid for it by their poor, hungry, war-torn country. Sakharov remained a believer in deterrence long after he went into political opposition in the Soviet Union.[52]

Like their opposite numbers in the West, some of the Soviet scientists worried about the moral justification for what they were doing. They understood, said Sakharov, the 'terrifying, inhuman nature of the weapons we were building'. Kurchatov himself returned from a thermonuclear test in a state of deep depression. He told one of his colleagues, 'Now I see what a fearful thing we have done. Our only concern should be to prohibit the whole thing and rule out the possibility of nuclear war.' One Russian observer later remarked that the triumphant discovery of the bomb was not a miracle but a monstrosity.[53] But it seemed obvious to them that if the Americans had the bomb, their country had to have one too. '[W]e thought of just one thing,' one of them said, 'what we should do to complete the work as soon as possible – before the American atom bomb fell on us.' They consoled themselves with the belief that nuclear weapons could successfully deter a nuclear war: as one of them said, they forced national leaders to be more cautious. Sakharov believed that Stalin shared the goal of making his country strong enough to ensure peace. He too mourned Stalin's death in March 1953 – something for which he later blushed. Evgeny Avrorin, the second scientific director of Chelyabinsk-70, accepted that the weapons could wipe out the whole of humanity. A substitute should be found. But what? The ideal was universal trust and disarmament properly controlled. But those, alas, did not exist.[54]

Perhaps it was only the out-and-out maverick Landau who articulated a different view. And even he stayed on board as long as Stalin was alive.[55]

PART II

FORGING A SYSTEM

FIVE

THE CHARM OF STRATEGY

'All roads in the strategic equation lead to MAD.'

anonymous American strategist[1]

'It is a long-cherished tradition among a certain type of military thinker that huge casualties are the main thing. If they are on the other side then this is a valuable bonus.'

Terry Pratchett[2]

The word 'strategy', in peace as in war, calls up the idea of a coherent body of thought offering a sure guide to the solution of wide-ranging and complex problems.

The confidence is misplaced. Helmut von Moltke, the great German strategist of the nineteenth century, said, 'No plan survives contact with the enemy.'[3] For him strategy was no more than a system of expedients. You tried to establish some basic principles of action. You familiarised your commanders and their men with your ideas. You made detailed plans for battle. But you were acutely aware that things might turn out quite differently in practice: the future was unknowable and the unexpected was almost certain to happen. The most elaborate strategic theories were frequently knocked off course by gritty reality, technological change, political expediency, and the sheer difficulty of the subject.

Setting the Stage: The Red and the Black

The nuclear confrontation may be said to have started on that day in Potsdam when a furious Stalin concluded that he had been double-crossed. The Cold War lacked the racial undertone of the Pacific War. But emotions ran as strongly. Each side demonised the other in extravagantly ideological and sometimes deeply unpleasant language, reminiscent of the passionate religious conflicts of an earlier age. Each mounted wide-ranging and expensive subversive propaganda campaigns against the other. Even as Gorbachev's reforms were beginning to take hold in the mid-1980s the Soviets were still fabricating and disseminating unpleasantly mendacious accusations that the Americans were behind the spread of AIDS.[4]

Throughout the nineteenth century, Western attitudes to Russia alternated between the idea of Russia as an exotic despotism; Russia as an international threat; Russia as a major ally; and Russia as an indispensable contributor to European culture.

The publication of the *Communist Manifesto* by Marx and Engels in 1848 marked a qualitative change. In his encyclical Quanta Cura of 1864, Pope Pius IX condemned Communism and Socialism as a 'most fatal error'.[5] Later popes condemned the 'evil growth of socialism', and 'atheistic communism'. After the Russian Revolution, the relationship between America and 'the world's first socialist state' was dominated on both sides by the language of Holy War, a contest between good and evil.

Most Americans were Christians when the evangelist Billy Graham proclaimed in 1949 that 'Communism is a religion inspired, directed, and motivated by the Devil himself, who has declared war against Almighty God.'* Long before Ronald Reagan called the Soviet Union an evil empire, President Truman promised, 'We shall firmly adhere to what we believe to be right; and we shall not give our approval to any compromise with evil.' He believed that 'All who cherish Christian and democratic institutions should unite against the common enemy. That enemy is the Soviet Union, which would substitute the Marxian doctrine of atheistic communism for Revelation.'[6] Senator Edward Martin proclaimed that 'America must move forward with the atomic bomb in one hand and the cross in

---

* In 1948 91 per cent of the population of America were Christians and 4 per cent were Jews. These proportions began declining in the 1980s, and the number of people with other religions rose from practically nothing to 5 per cent; and the number of people with no religion increased from 2 per cent to 13 per cent (https://en.wikipedia.org/wiki/Historical_religious_demographics_of_the_United_States, accessed 4 January 2016).

the other.'[7] Senator Joseph McCarthy spoke of a 'final, all-out battle between communistic atheism and Christianity'. J. Edgar Hoover, the crusading head of the FBI, personally endorsed a comic book for Catholic children about the consequences of a Communist takeover of the United States.[8]

Americans sometimes underestimated what the Russians were capable of achieving. Their black-and-white rhetoric was often extreme. But it was also a reaction to Soviet reality: the massive brutalities of civil war, collectivisation, and the Gulag; the purges and shootings of the 1930s; the ruthless expansion of Soviet power in Eastern Europe after the war; the repression of dissidence in the 1960s and 1970s.

The Russian attitude to the West was just as hostile. Separated by geography, by the choice of Orthodox instead of Catholic Christianity, and by the Tartar invasion in the thirteenth century, in the eighteenth century Russia became a power which the other Europeans could not ignore. In the nineteenth and twentieth centuries Russian literature, music, and art became an inescapable part of European high culture. The Russians won great victories over their enemies. But they also suffered devastating defeats. Their attempts to reform and modernise their political system collapsed time and again.

By way of compensation, Russia's nineteenth-century thinkers claimed exceptional virtues – courage, truth, justice, loyalty, friendship, warmth, what they thought of as the great Russian soul – and contrasted them starkly with what they saw as the decadent mentality of the rest of Europe: formalistic, inhuman, cold, bourgeois, and hypocritical. Russia, they convinced themselves, had a mission to deliver a unique message to the rest of the world.*

Lenin and his fellow Bolsheviks inherited the sense of mission.

---

* There was an element of compensation here. The American scholar-diplomat George Kennan wrote of 'the suspicion, equally latent in every Russian soul, that the hand of failure lies heavily over all Russian undertaking, that the term "Russia" does not really signify a national society destined to know power and majesty, but only a vast unconquerable expanse of misery, poverty, inefficiency, and mud' (*Memoirs*, Vol. I, Boston, 1967, p. 505).

The message was somewhat different. Marxism was a creed of universal application, but it would fall to Russia – the Soviet Union – to lead mankind to a shining future. The language the Bolsheviks directed against Party rivals, domestic enemies, and foreigners was unusually violent. They called their enemies harmful insects, lice, and bloodsuckers. Suspecting the possibility of a rising in Nizhni Novgorod, Lenin gave his local representatives orders to 'organise immediately mass terror, shoot and deport the hundreds of prostitutes who are making drunkards of the soldiers, former officers and the like'.[9] Andrei Vyshinsky, the chief prosecutor during the Moscow show trials in the 1930s, demanded that the accused – 'these miserable hybrids of foxes and pigs, these stinking corpses' – be shot like mad dogs. Foreign enemies – Hitler, Churchill, Wall Street bankers – were depicted in cartoons as spiders, octopuses, and monkeys. Particular targets were the 'aggressive plans of American Imperialism' and 'the idiocy of modern-day American bourgeois culture and morals'.[10]

The uneasy relationship between the Soviet Union and its wartime allies began to deteriorate well before the war ended.

Britain had gone to war to defend Poland. Now the Red Army was clamping Soviet rule all over Eastern Europe. Churchill ordered the British Chiefs of Staff to suggest ways of ejecting them. In May 1945 they produced a plan for Operation Unthinkable, whose aim was to force Russia to give a 'square deal' to Poland. The plan envisaged that hostilities would start on 1 July 1945 – before the war against Japan was over – with an attack on the Soviet forces in Eastern Europe by forty-five British and American divisions, backed by Polish divisions and 100,000 rearmed Germans.[11] The Chiefs, presumably with their tongues in their cheeks, described this scheme as 'hazardous' and Churchill did not pursue it. The Chiefs were nevertheless in no doubt that now the war with Germany was over the Russians were the only major threat Britain faced. Ministers and the Foreign Office discouraged them from planning on that basis too obviously. But by the end of 1947 the relationship with the Soviet Union had deteriorated to the point where the British military were given the green light to plan on the basis that the Russians were the main threat.[12] The Russians were rapidly informed of such plans thanks to their spies within the

British establishment – Kim Philby, Donald Maclean, Guy Burgess. Their paranoia was not assuaged.

The Russians and the Americans now began to set out their mutual suspicions in a series of planning documents and intelligence estimates. In February 1946 George Kennan, a diplomat and one of America's most distinguished Russian experts, sent a telegram from the US Embassy in Moscow which, at some 10,000 words, became known as 'The Long Telegram'.* Kennan believed that the 'Kremlin's neurotic view of world affairs', its unjustified belief that the capitalist world was irredeemably hostile to the Soviet system and out to destroy it, derived from a 'traditional and instinctive Russian sense of insecurity'. He thus placed himself from the beginning on the dovish side of those who were inclined to believe that Soviet policy was primarily defensive, in contrast to the hawks in Washington, who believed (mirroring their opposite numbers in Moscow) that the unrelenting aim of Soviet Communism was to gain world domination.

But even Kennan was not reassured by this Russian instinct for defence: the Russians sought their security 'only in patient but deadly struggle for total destruction of rival power, never in compacts and compromises with it'. Kennan believed that the Soviets were 'committed fanatically to the belief that with us there can be no permanent modus vivendi, that it is desirable and necessary that the internal harmony of our society be disrupted, our traditional way of life be destroyed, the international authority of our state be broken, if Soviet power is to be secure'. The outcome depended 'on degree of cohesion, firmness and vigor which Western World can muster'.

After returning to Washington, Kennan set out his thoughts on policy in an article in the June 1947 issue of the magazine *Foreign Affairs*, 'The Sources of Soviet Conduct'. Anonymously signed, it became known as 'The X Article'. Kennan argued that 'the main element of any United States policy toward the Soviet Union must be that of a long-term patient but firm and vigilant containment of Russian expansive tendencies'. The response should be political and economic.

---

* In those days telegrams were deciphered by hand. Telegrams from Kennan were unusually long. The cryptographers in the State Department learned to dread their arrival (private information).

Kennan argued against a military response, which risked 'emphasizing a danger which did not actually exist but which might indeed be brought into existence by too much discussion of the military balance and by the ostentatious stimulation of a military rivalry'.[13] He made no mention of nuclear weapons. But to his dismay his idea was transformed into a policy of military confrontation. That was unnecessary in his view, since the problem would eventually be solved by the inevitable process of history. As he wrote prophetically in 1951, 'When Soviet power has run its course, or when its personalities and spirit begin to change (for the ultimate outcome could be one or the other) let us not hover nervously over the people who come after, applying litmus papers daily to their political complexions to find out whether they answer to our concept of "democrats". Give them time; let them be Russians; let them work out their internal problems in their own manner. The ways by which people advance toward dignity and enlightenment in government are things that constitute the deepest and most intimate processes of national life. There is nothing less understandable to foreigners, nothing in which foreign influence can do less good.'[14]

But by then Kennan had long been overtaken by the evolution of thinking in Washington. The Japanese war had barely ended before James Conant, one of those intimately involved in the Manhattan Project, was advising the War Department to prepare for nuclear war against Russia. Lest the American people resist the new weapon, their fears should be managed, distilled, and drip-fed back to them, rather like a doctor treating a man with diabetes. It would be a delicate matter. The physician, wrote Conant, 'had to frighten the patient sufficiently in order to make him obey the dietary rules; but if he frightened him too much, despondency might set in – hysteria if you will – and the patient might overindulge in a mood of despair, with probably fatal consequences.'[15]

The Soviet view of American policy was equally gloomy, though less publicly expressed. In the autumn of 1946 the Soviet ambassador in Washington, Nikolai Novikov, wrote a paper for Stalin's foreign minister, Vyacheslav Molotov.[16] He lamented that Roosevelt's policy of cooperation with the Soviet Union had been replaced by Truman's policy of confrontation, which was 'characterized ... by a striving for world supremacy [and a belief] that the United States has the right to lead the world'. The Americans were rebuilding their armed forces, constructing a network of bases many thousands of miles from their borders, and creating 'ever newer types of weapons'. They were expanding their influence in Europe and the Middle East, in China and the Far East. They were aiming to transform the United Nations into 'an Anglo-Saxon domain in which the United States would play the leading role'. All this was a deliberate reinforcement of the hard-line policy recently announced by President Truman's Secretary of State, James Byrnes. Novikov believed that the aim of the policymaking elite in Washington was to impose its will on the Soviet Union. Moscow shared his views entirely.

Stumbling Towards a Strategy

All this set the stage for more than four decades of nuclear confrontation. The most urgent task for both sides was to devise a strategy for handling it which enabled them to pursue their national ambitions and fend off unacceptable pressures without letting the whole thing run dangerously out of control. They more or less succeeded, at the cost of very frayed nerves.

The broad idea which dominated most thinking about nuclear strategy was deterrence. A British Prime Minister, Stanley Baldwin, told the House of Commons in 1932, 'I think it is well also for the man in the street to realise that there is no power on earth that can protect him from being bombed. Whatever people may tell him, the bomber will always get through. The only defence is in offence, which means that you have to kill more women and children more quickly than the enemy if you want to save yourselves.' This was not quite the idea of deterrence which later took root, and which was intended to prevent war by threatening a potential aggressor with a devastating response. But it contained the germ.[17]

British airmen had studied the effects of the German air raids on London in 1916 and 1917. They concluded that civilian morale would quickly crumble under air attack. Targeting civilian populations was therefore the best (perhaps the most moral and humane) way to win wars in future. They convinced themselves that this was compatible with the laws of war, provided that the primary aim was not to kill civilians but to destroy (or, in a later euphemism, 'degrade') the enemy's capacity to wage war. The Royal Air Force argued that it should be able to operate 'unhampered by the inevitable fact that there is bound to be incidental loss, and possibly heavy loss of civilian life'. By 1943 it was measuring the success of its bombing campaign against Germany in terms of 'acres of devastation per acre of built-up areas attacked'.

David Lloyd George pointed out that, on the contrary, the moral effect of the German air raids on London was short-lived: 'the undoubted terror inspired by the death-dealing skies did not swell by a single murmur the demand for peace. It had quite the contrary effect. It angered the population of the stricken towns and led to a fierce demand for reprisals.'[18] Defence by fighter aircraft and anti-aircraft guns in sufficient numbers could defeat an enemy bomber force, as the British defeated the Germans in 1940. Later experts never agreed on whether, and by how much, the ruthless bombing campaign shortened the Second World War against Germany.

But Baldwin was right. Even if the defenders shot down an improbably high proportion of incoming bombers, some would always get through. Even a handful of aircraft armed with thermo-nuclear bombs could inflict unimaginable damage. The idea that the only defence is offence – or the deterrent threat of it – became a fundamental principle of strategic planning for nuclear war.

Conundrums

Robert Oppenheimer warned in 1952 that the superpowers would soon be like 'two scorpions in a bottle, each capable of killing the other, but only at the risk of his own life'.[19] That situation had, to all intents and purposes, arrived by the early 1960s, as the Russians and the Americans became increasingly able to make warheads of convenient size and almost unlimited power, and missiles which would eventually be able to deliver them with pinpoint accuracy a continent away. From then onwards they both knew that each could destroy the other, almost regardless of any countermeasure they might devise.

There developed an intense debate around a complex tangle of conceptual, strategic, and organisational conundrums. The problems were simple to define, but hard to resolve. In what circumstances would you use nuclear weapons, and to what purpose? What kind of target did you need to hit to achieve that purpose, and how did you find it? How would your hardware – the warheads, the missiles, the communications systems which had never been tested in battle – actually work when the time came? Would the politicians and generals be able to manage effectively under the stress of a nuclear exchange? Would the survivors be able to cope with the devastating aftermath? How long might the fighting go on after the initial nuclear exchange? How useful would a conventional force then be, and how large a force would you need?

And how did you manage the conflicting demands of politics, strategy, and economics? Did you need at all costs to maintain superiority over your opponent in the sheer numbers of nuclear weapons you piled up? What was the point of having such a powerful military force that it bankrupted you? The Russians and the Americans never managed to answer these questions adequately, though here the Americans had the clear advantage of a prospering and resilient economy.

The British, of course, were too poor to be seriously tempted.*

The Russians were traumatised by memories of the way they had been caught out by the Germans in June 1941; the Americans had equally bad memories of Pearl Harbor six months later. Both were obsessed by the need to avoid another surprise attack, a 'bolt from the blue'.

But this central problem gave rise to a further set of unanswerable questions. If you thought your enemy might have plans to attack you, was it safer to cut the Gordian knot and launch a preventive war against him? If your intelligence showed he was actually on the verge of attacking you, should you launch a 'first strike' in an attempt to destroy his weapons before he could use them in a pre-emptive or first strike? To protect yourself against a sudden attack designed to kill (decapitate) your political leadership and destroy your capacity to retaliate, should you plan to 'launch on warning', and get your own missiles off in the few minutes before they were destroyed by

---

* The British did deploy, for a number of years, tactical nuclear bombers and artillery. But they never had a convincing doctrine for using them.

your enemy's incoming missiles? Could you ensure that your own strategic force could survive (or ride out) an attack – by putting it underground, or into submarines, or into a mass of bombers – so that you could then retaliate in a second strike?

More generally, should you aim to hit your enemy's weapons ('counterforce') or his cities ('countervalue')? Was a strategy of 'limited nuclear war' possible, whereby you would direct your strikes only at your enemy's military establishments and factories, rather than his cities? How would he know the difference, especially when, as in Russia, military establishments and cities were often close together? Was a strategy of 'controlled escalation' nevertheless feasible, whereby you would launch your weapons in packets, until your enemy decided that the thing was no longer worthwhile and agreed to terminate the conflict short of a full-scale nuclear exchange? Would such war termination even be physically possible, given that the means of communication between the contending parties might well have been destroyed in the first exchanges? Could you safely launch limited or regional strikes ('limited nuclear options', in the jargon),without risking escalation to something more serious?[20]

Every proposed course of action had obvious political or practical disadvantages. Each required impeccable intelligence and early warning systems of improbable reliability. In the age of the bomber, both sides might hope for some hours of warning while they considered whether to launch their own bombers. But once the attack could be delivered by missile, the decision-makers might have no more than ten minutes before the incoming missiles struck.

Both sides maintained that they had no intention of striking first or taking pre-emptive action, though individuals on both sides sometimes muddied the waters with extravagant and irresponsible remarks.* Some American experts nevertheless interpreted Soviet talk about launch on warning as cover for acquiring a first-strike capacity. Soviet experts were equally suspicious of similar talk on the American side. Each side interpreted the other's preparations for fighting and winning a limited nuclear war as evidence of aggressive intention.

---

* Less so on the Russian side, where individuals and the press were far less free to air their prejudices.

Though the language differed in Washington, Moscow, and London, the issues were the same. They were never satisfactorily resolved. In response to the 9/11 terrorist attack on New York, the administration of George W. Bush adopted a new National Strategy of the United States in 2002. It stated that 'To forestall or prevent ... hostile acts by our adversaries, the United States will, if necessary, act preemptively in exercising our inherent right of self-defense'. Like its US and Soviet predecessors, this proposition depended on the uncertain availability of reliable intelligence.[21]

Since no one had experience of nuclear war, no one could know the answers: all was theory. Laurence Freedman, a sober writer on the subject, wondered if the concept of 'nuclear strategy' was a contraction in terms.[22]

Mutually Assured Destruction

There was no reason to doubt the repeated assertions by leaders on both sides that they had no intention of firing the first shot. But each was driven by the belief that the other was out to destroy his dearest values and his cherished institutions. It was a threat which they believed had to be resisted at all costs, even at the risk of unbearable destruction to both sides. The old rules still applied. You had to stand up to the bully; it was better to hit him before he hit you; a glorious defeat was better than an ignominious submission. So if the other guy had the bomb, you had to have it too. And your threat to use it had to be sufficiently credible to convince him that he would certainly be destroyed if he attempted to use his bomb first.

This was the essence of Mutually Assured Destruction or MAD, a strategy which was much criticised and ruthlessly satirised. Herman Kahn, the American strategic theorist, commented that MAD was 'so uncomplicated, inexpensive, convenient, and politically and emotionally acceptable that it seems practical and even moral. In fact it is gravely defective – politically and militarily, and especially morally.'[23]

But despite the acronym, MAD was not irrational. Nuclear weapons existed, and there was always a risk that they would be used. So each side aimed to take the other's people hostage, and each was frightened into good behaviour. Of course there was always the possibility of accident. So both sides had the strongest incentive to make sure that their systems of political, military, and technical control were robust enough to avoid misjudgement, accident, or a deliberate act by a rogue player.

MAD was simple, easy to understand, and durable, unlike many of the convoluted theories which emerged over the years. It was adopted not only by theorists, but by politicians and the military on both sides of the Iron Curtain as the defining, comprehensible, and oddly comforting principle of the nuclear confrontation. Many ordinary people agreed with them. The minority of those who did not were never able to change the policy.

Strictly speaking, MAD was different from common or garden deterrence. The theorists believed that it meant that each side should leave itself just a bit open to attack, to reassure the other that his deterrent would work too. It was not an idea that appealed much to the military on either side, who believed that one should not rule out any useful device for defending oneself, and that it was their professional duty to maintain superiority over the enemy by all means possible. Under pressure from President Kennedy and President Nixon the American military went along, grumbling, with the arms control arrangements of the 1960s and 1970s. But they kept their options open, and at the end of the 1970s, when the Soviet nuclear forces appeared to have overtaken them by a substantial margin, they set out energetically and effectively to catch up. The Russians too incorporated the idea of arms control into their doctrinal thinking. But they too continued their massive nuclear build-up.

In practice the distinction was not very important. Each side was determined to maintain the capacity to wipe out his opponent after he had already been struck, come what may. It was not until the confrontation was almost over that the military were prepared to accept that they had provided themselves with an arsenal far larger than they could use, a situation for which the term 'overkill' was coined. As Stanislav Voronin, a Russian weapon designer, said, 'The fact that we all piled up so many nuclear weapons was crazy ... At first we didn't quite realise that the nuclear weapon is not appropriate for use on the battlefield. But now it's clear – it is political, a weapon of deterrence.'[24]

Those who supported deterrence used to say that if, contrary to all probability, a nuclear exchange occurred, it would mean that the policy had failed. It was never quite clear how this would console those who survived.

The Constraint of Geography

For more than a decade the Americans' bombs and their aircraft greatly outmatched the Russians'. The technological gap narrowed in the 1970s and the 1980s until the Russians had more or less caught up.

But technical parity was not the same as strategic symmetry. Geography greatly complicated the calculations of both sides. The Russians were a European continental power. Their ground forces were always a threat to Western Europe. They themselves regarded massive ground forces as a necessary insurance: they could never forget the numerous times they had been invaded from the West, most recently when they were disastrously surprised by the Germans in June 1941.

The threat to America was different. The Americans had been protected from invasion by the oceans. They had no need to fear a Soviet attack on the ground, and at first they felt invulnerable from the air as well. In the first decade after the war they moved rapidly to ring the Soviet Union with bases from which they could hit Soviet targets with medium-range bombers and missiles. By the early 1950s these bases were becoming vulnerable to Soviet attack. So the Americans moved their strategic forces to safer bases in America itself or sent them to sea in submarines.

The Russians had no foreign bases within range of America: their attempt to acquire one in Cuba ended in humiliation. They were unable to threaten America effectively until well into the 1960s. But once they too could strike America with missiles from Soviet bases or from the oceans, the protection which geography had given the Americans all but disappeared. The two sides arrived at strategic deadlock.

Technological Instability

By the late 1960s the main technological outlines of the confrontation were in place. The Americans and the Russians each had bombers, land-based missiles, and submarines with which they could strike the other. The Americans had a balanced, technically mature, and very numerous force – a triad. The Russians' bomber force was inadequate and their submarine fleet was noisy and unreliable. They relied overwhelmingly on powerful land-based missiles. Over the years their missiles became more accurate; they introduced new and more exotic kinds of bomber; their submarines became quieter and harder to detect. But they never quite caught up. If the Americans had a strategic triad, balanced between bombers, submarines, and intercontinental rockets, the Russians had 'a tricycle, a single big wheel, the … Strategic Missile Force, and two smaller wheels, the submarine force and the strategic bombers'.[25]

Both sides worked incessantly to improve their military technology. A welter of accusations and counter-accusations broke out each time one side made a technological breakthrough that the other feared would disrupt the fragile, unstable, and always contested nuclear balance and leave him vulnerable.

By the late 1960s both Russian and Americans missiles were becoming so accurate that they could destroy even the most heavily protected missile in its silo: theoretically an invitation to both sides to strike before their missiles were destroyed.*

One defensive solution was to take the missiles out of their silos and to move them about by road and rail so that the enemy would never quite know where they were. Both sides expended much ingenuity on the problem, and further muddied the waters of the strategic debate. An offensive answer was to arm missiles with Multiple Independently Targetable Reentry Vehicles (MIRVs). In theory the MIRVs from one missile could destroy several missiles on the other side, thus overwhelming the opponent's missile force by sheer weight of numbers.

---

* Both sides continued to develop new missiles until the end of the confrontation. The American MX missile, the Peacemaker, which could carry as many warheads as the SS-18, came into service in 1986, but was decommissioned in 2005. The Russian answer to the MX was the Molodets (SS-24), which was first deployed in 1987 and withdrawn from service by 2008. The American Midgetman, a small mobile intercontinental missile, was cancelled in 1992. Topol (SS-25), its Russian equivalent, remained part of Russia's strategic arsenal in the new century.

The Americans were the first to develop MIRVs. In 1970, to the dismay of those who hoped that the arms race could be brought under control, they put MIRVs on a new generation of Minuteman, enabling each missile to carry several warheads able to hit different targets. They could now, at least in optimistic theory, destroy the Russian land-based nuclear force in a single surprise attack.

It was a self-inflicted wound. American analysts had long estimated that the Russians would eventually have enough MIRVed missiles of their own to stand a good chance of wiping out America's land-based missiles. The analysts were right. By 1974 the Russians were already deploying MIRVed missiles (the SS-17 and SS-19), and bringing into service their powerful and increasingly accurate SS-18 missile, which could carry up to ten independently targetable warheads.[26] With these the Russians were now, in theory, also in a position to destroy their enemies' land-based strategic nuclear force. The fears were grossly overblown. But the Americans had indeed opened another Pandora's box and given a dangerous further twist to the arms race.*

The SS-18s became an obsession in Washington politics. The issue of Minuteman vulnerability was born, and dominated the American strategic debate into the 1980s, the third great and misplaced scare after the scares over the Bomber Gap, which was used by conservatives to attack Eisenhower in the mid-1950s, and the Missile Gap, which Kennedy exploited to get himself elected in 1959.[27]

Limited Nuclear War

Both sides worried away incessantly at another conundrum. If a strategic exchange made little sense, could 'tactical' nuclear weapons be used effectively on a smaller battlefield? Could they be employed in Europe, where the superpowers were face to face on the ground? Robert Oppenheimer for one hoped that small nuclear weapons would make it possible to escape the genocidal implications of strategic bombardment, and 'bring the battle back to the battleground'. One of the first studies was Project Vista, which concluded in 1961

---

* The controversy in Washington over 'Minuteman vulnerability' is described on page 346.

that the Russians could be stopped in Europe by conventional and small nuclear weapons.[28]

But there were fundamental problems which resurfaced every time the experts looked into the idea. How did your opponent know that your limited use of small nuclear weapons was not the prelude to an all-out attack? How did you know whether he would respond in an equally limited way? Could you be sure of controlling the exchange in the stress of battle? How did you end the confrontation?

There was also the perennial problem of definition. For the Americans, long-range missiles that could hit the United States were 'strategic'. Short-range missiles that could hit only the Europeans were merely 'tactical'. For the Russians there was little difference. American short-range missiles based in Europe could hit the Russian heartland almost as destructively as American long-range missiles. For the Russians both were equally 'strategic'. Once the two sides started talks on limiting the size of their strategic force, the Russians tried to insist that all American 'forward-based systems' capable of hitting the Soviet Union – missiles based in Europe, missiles on submarines and aircraft carriers – should be included. For good measure they demanded that the British and French systems be included too.

This was a reasonable position: after all, the Americans regarded the medium-range missiles which Khrushchev attempted to insert into Cuba in 1962 as a strategic threat. But then and later, the Americans simply refused to discuss the matter. The French and the British rejected the idea that anyone else should negotiate away their national deterrent. Their armouries, they said, were a small fraction – less than 2 per cent – of those held by the superpowers (though not too small, they hoped, to inflict 'unacceptable damage' on the Russians*). They said that they would reduce their arsenals only when the superpowers had drastically reduced theirs.

But however reasonable their position may have seemed to them, the Russians were unable to make their arguments prevail even in their first talks with the Americans about the limitation of strategic

---

* I examine the concept of 'unacceptable damage' in Chapter 8.

arms. Gorbachev eventually abandoned the position in order to clinch agreement with Reagan. In the background his generals muttered 'treachery'.

By now both sides were developing 'battlefield weapons' to use in an otherwise conventional war in Europe, and were training their soldiers to fight and survive on the nuclear battlefield. For the Americans and their allies, the primary purpose was to stop an attack by the Russians' overwhelming conventional forces in Europe. For the Russians, battlefield weapons were a natural complement to their conventional forces whether in attack or defence.

The Americans proclaimed, not always consistently, that a limited nuclear war in Europe could be contained and controlled. The Russians were less sure. At best the first nuclear explosion might shock both sides into getting things back under control. But the destruction, confusion, and desperation that would accompany even a limited nuclear exchange might produce just the opposite result: panic, loss of control, and a determination to avoid defeat by firing off still more nuclear weapons.

By the late 1960s the Americans had some 7,000 nuclear warheads in Europe, but no doctrine for their rational employment in a limited war. They had nuclear shells that could be fired from conventional artillery, battlefield rocket launchers, minuscule Davy Crockett missiles that could be carried on a jeep,* and Atomic Demolition Munitions (ADMs) – nuclear landmines placed along the border with East Germany, to be blown up if the Russians advanced. Though a cumbersome NATO doctrine for using these things was eventually worked out, soldiers on the ground evidently thought that much of the logic chopping was eyewash. When one British official, Michael Alexander, asked the US commander on NATO's Central Front how he would use his tactical nuclear weapons, he replied, 'If I see those bastards coming over that hill, I'll nuke them.'[29]

In the 1970s both introduced highly mobile, shorter-range

---

* It was popularly believed that these devices had such a short range that they would inevitably kill the men who fired them. They nevertheless remained in service for nearly a decade.

missiles into Europe. The Russians made the first move in 1976 by deploying their medium-range mobile missile, the SS-20, as a replacement for less capable missiles which were already there. They appear to have given no serious consideration to the wider political consequences or to the interpretation that the West was likely to put on their action. The SS-20s were no threat to the American homeland, but could hit any capital city in Europe. The Americans and NATO countered in December 1979 with the so-called Dual Track Decision: the Americans would deploy cruise missiles and Pershing II mobile missiles in Western Europe, but were willing to reach an agreement for the elimination of all such missiles on both sides. The Russians argued that the Pershings could hit targets well inside the Soviet Union with very little warning and perhaps wipe out the Soviet leadership in a surprise attack: they were therefore strategic weapons. The Americans denied that they had the necessary range and accused the Russians of deliberately muddying the waters. In fact the range of the Pershing II was 1,500 miles, well above the 900 miles publicly claimed for it.[30] Widespread protests against the NATO decision in Europe and America were naturally fanned by the Russians.

All this left America's European allies in a desperate position. They believed that American tactical nuclear weapons were necessary to deter an overwhelming Soviet attack. This was called 'extended deterrence': America would use its nuclear weapons in defence of its allies as well as itself. But in the late 1950s the Europeans had already begun to fear that American determination would not hold if it risked provoking a strategic attack on America itself.[31] The other side of the coin was that for the Europeans a 'limited' war with tactical nuclear weapons was likely to be as destructive as a strategic exchange would be for the Americans and the Russians. An Anglo-American military study concluded in August 1963 that 'in constrained warfare in Central Europe casualties may well exceed five million; in unconstrained warfare casualties may well exceed fifty million.'[32] The British planners were sceptical that the two sides would observe constraints in the heat of battle. The more sanguine Americans accepted that the allies might have to abandon constraints to avoid defeat. One NATO exercise, in which only the Alliance used tactical nuclear weapons, left nearly 2 million Germans dead, even without allowing for the effects of radiation. As one senior German politician put it, 'The shorter the range, the deader the Germans.'[33]

Caught between the alternatives of Soviet invasion and nuclear destruction, the Europeans never escaped the horns of this very unpleasant dilemma.

The Voice of the Military

It is not easy for civilians to think their way into the military mind. That is because professional military officers have a different relationship with society from the rest of us. It is their task to send men to die for their country, and if necessary to die themselves. Even in democracies ruled by civilians they live in a closed culture, permeated with ideas of duty, gallantry, glory, and ultimate sacrifice. Since they are the ones who get sacked, court-martialled, or shot if they lose a battle, they have a professional bias in favour of planning for the worst case, restrained from time to time by politicians who tell them there is not enough money for their favourite schemes. They need that mindset to do their job. It does not matter much whether they are British, American, or Russian.

Politicians, commentators, anti-nuclear activists, and historians tended to see the military as hopelessly conservative, intellectually limited, narrow-minded, and opposed to sensible schemes for escaping from the nuclear dilemma. This was unfair. Most officers – Soviet as well as Western – understood the futility of an all-out nuclear exchange, and the devastating impact it would have on their own countries, their compatriots, their families, and themselves. They were never much impressed with the more exotic ideas of the nuclear theorists. It was their job to work out how to use the lethal gadgets which were available to them. On both sides they therefore planned for a wide range of contingencies, for local and all-out war, for the offence as well as the defence. Since they could never be sure of their opponents' intentions, they inevitably assumed that they were irremediably malign.

And by definition they planned for victory. In 1980 the Americans' military manual read: 'The US army must be prepared to fight and win when nuclear weapons are used.' There was much logic chopping among American experts about whether 'win' or the less ambitious word 'prevail' was appropriate. Reagan's Secretary of Defense, Caspar Weinberger, swept the distinctions aside: 'You show me a Secretary of Defense who is not planning to prevail, and I'll show you a Secretary of Defense who ought to be impeached.'[34]

Marshal Nikolai Ogarkov, the intelligent and clear-sighted Soviet Chief of the General Staff from 1977 to 1984, summed it up admirably. When the veteran arms negotiator Oleg Grinevsky asked whether he really believed in Soviet plans for an offensive in Europe using nuclear weapons, he replied, 'Personally I don't believe it. But I have to prepare for it, whatever form it takes. Especially when the Americans talk about such a war.' And he added, 'I do not have the right to command soldiers and send them into battle, unless I myself believe in victory and prepare for it.'[35]

Once the Cold War was over, some of the military plans began to emerge from the archives. Some historians confused planning with intention and concluded too quickly that this meant that the military on one or perhaps both sides intended a nuclear war. There is no evidence that this was true. The military knew it made no sense, and in Washington, London, and Moscow they were kept firmly under civilian control, whether because that was the traditional arrangement, as in Britain, or because it was the way the constitution worked, as in America, or because it was a matter of profound political and ideological conviction, as it was in the Soviet Union.

The fear that a rogue commander could initiate a nuclear war was much exaggerated in the popular mind. But to drive home a point, Stanley Kubrick made *Dr Strangelove or: How I Learned to Stop Worrying and Love the Bomb*. It was a black comedy, perhaps the most influential film ever made about the nuclear confrontation, in which a maverick commander launches a nuclear attack against the Soviet Union without political authority. The US Air Force was sufficiently upset to insist on inserting a disclaimer: 'It is the stated position of the U.S. Air Force that their safeguards would prevent the occurrence of such events as are depicted in this film.' For Kubrick himself, black comedy was the only sensible response to what he saw as the absurdities of nuclear strategic thinking: 'In the context of impending world destruction, hypocrisy, misunderstanding, lechery, paranoia, euphemism, patriotism, heroism and even reasonableness can only provoke a grisly laugh.'[36]

Calculating the national interest and the means to secure it was not in the least simple. Perceptions, definitions, and understandings of what was needed were shifting, elusive, and subject to unending argument. It was for the military to devise their plans and the weapons to implement them, and to recommend accordingly to the politicians: there was no one else professionally qualified to do so. But that did not mean that their judgements were necessarily correct, or that their plans were feasible, affordable, or politically acceptable. Their attempts to forge a coherent strategic doctrine were regularly knocked off course by inter-service rivalries which prevented them from reaching a conclusion except at the lowest denominator. Such matters of national importance were, in the end, for the politicians to decide. But it was a rare politician who felt able to challenge military judgement. In America, the Soviet Union, and Britain the military always bowed to the politicians' decisions in the end. But that did not stop them from intriguing against their political masters, who were, they often grumbled, ignorant, feckless, parsimonious, and playing fast and loose with the nation's security.

The generals of the nuclear age suffered one immense handicap. They lacked even their predecessors' dubious advantage of being able to plan (often wrongly) on the basis of what they thought they had learned in the previous war. Despite their superior expertise in the management of conventional warfare, their answers to the whole oppressive mass of unprecedented problems associated with the planning of nuclear war were often as tentative, short-lived, and wrong-headed as those of the civilians.

Command and Control

All strategic nuclear theories had to cope with an almost insoluble practical dilemma. No nuclear strategy made sense unless the decision to use nuclear weapons was kept under absolute political control: you needed to be quite sure no one could fire your weapons without proper authority. But you also had to be able to respond to the slightest apparent threat in the shortest possible time, under the most adverse circumstances. Even if your adversary succeeded in killing your leadership in a surprise attack, he had to believe that he would still face retaliation.

All the nuclear powers tried to resolve this dilemma, but it became increasingly hard. The Americans had plenty of time for discussion before they dropped the bomb on Hiroshima. The Cuban missile crisis in 1962 was spread over thirteen days or more: the decision-makers on both sides had time to consider their moves, to send messages, to draw back from the brink. But a decision in the thermonuclear wars which loomed in the 1970s and 1980s might have had to be taken in as little as five minutes. The planners could only hope that their elaborate procedures would hold up under the unprecedented stress and destruction of a nuclear exchange. Until the end both sides desperately dug deeper shelters. They multiplied ever more exotic methods of communication between their civil and military leaders and the men manning the weapons. They kept specially equipped aircraft to act as aerial control centres if the civil and military leadership was wiped out on the ground. But their efforts had an abstract air about them. Governments found it hard to convince even themselves that their systems would work.

The difficulty under such circumstances of putting together a coherent strategic doctrine was crisply analysed by Henry Kissinger in his book – first published in 1957 – *Nuclear Weapons and Foreign Policy*.[37] It applies to all countries at all times. The British suffered from a particularly bad attack of the problem in the first two decades of the twenty-first century, when they found it impossible to put together a recognisable strategic doctrine at all.

The President was the ultimate authority in the American system. In theory, no nuclear attack could be launched without his decision. But in practice the American command system was not easy to police, and it evolved over time. The American military kept their weapons on a hair-trigger alert, to a degree of which their political bosses were not always wholly aware. They pressed for delegated authority ('predelegation', in the jargon) to fire their weapons if the system began disintegrating under attack: if, that is, the President and his deputies were killed or incapacitated. Their master target plan, the Single Integrated Operational Plan, was initially designed to be simple, comprehensive, overriding, and inflexible, so that American strategic weapons could be fired purposefully even in the chaos of nuclear battle, even if the command system was disrupted by Soviet bombardment.

This focus on the need to hit targets almost regardless of other considerations generated tension with the politicians. Successive presidents regularly demanded greater flexibility to allow for pauses in the fighting to communicate with the enemy and find ways to end the violence. Under pressure from Nixon the plans were modified to offer a bewildering variety of options. But the detailed targeting plans for nuclear war were still closely guarded by the military. They were arcane and highly technical. Most politicians had neither the time nor the intellectual and moral self-confidence to challenge them. It was not until the mid-1980s that a more rigorous order was imposed. By then the confrontation was practically over (see Chapter 15).

In February 1961 Robert McNamara, President Kennedy's Defense Secretary, told him, 'The chain of command from the President down to our strategic offensive and defensive weapon systems is highly vulnerable in almost every link.'[38] Five months later Kennedy learned that 'a subordinate commander faced with a substantial Russian military action could start the thermonuclear holocaust on his own initiative if he could not reach you.'[39] During the Cuban missile crisis in October 1962, General LeMay's successor as Commander of the Strategic Air Command, General Thomas Power, ordered his aircraft on to heightened alert (DEFCON 2) without informing Kennedy. One of his military subordinates, General Wade, worried that Power was 'not stable' and could launch the force on his own initiative.[40] It was General Power who famously said, 'Why do you want us to restrain ourselves? ... The whole idea is to kill the bastards! ... At the end of the war if there are two Americans and one Russian left alive, we win!' His interlocutor replied, 'Well, you'd better make sure they're a man and a woman.'[41]

In the 1960s the Americans began to introduce Permissive Action Links (PALs), technical devices intended to ensure that weapons could not explode accidentally or be fired without proper authority. The US military resisted them at first: the devices might go wrong and put weapons out of action just when they were needed. There is a story, which the airmen dispute, that the Strategic Air Command set the codes for their Minuteman force to 00000000 to ensure that nothing could prevent them being fired in a crisis. Sophisticated electronic devices eventually replaced the mechanical locks, but it was not until 1987 that they had been fitted to all US nuclear weapons.[42]

Soviet leaders were equally concerned to maintain tight political control over their nuclear forces: one qualified American observer thought their system was more reliable and under tighter political control than the American one.* Like the Americans, the Russians worried about how far it was safe to delegate authority to launch the weapons. They were more prepared to sacrifice hair-trigger readiness for a rigidly centralised political control. They kept their aircraft and submarines (though not their missile force) on a comparatively low level of readiness. At first they stored their warheads separately, not least because they had to be kept in a controlled environment. Warheads were later mated with their missiles when they were loaded onto submarines or into silos. But Soviet bombers, unlike American bombers, never flew with nuclear weapons on board for reasons of safety. These measures partly reflected the Russians' comparative lack of technical sophistication. But they also reduced their ability to react immediately to an American attack, or to launch their own 'bolt from the blue'.

An elaborate system of electronic communications in theory kept senior Soviet commanders in constant touch with their subordinates. Overall command was not concentrated in a single person, as it was in the United States, where the President had ultimate authority as Commander-in-Chief. Under what was known as the 'Kazbek' system, the General Secretary of the Party, the Minister of

---

*The Soviet system was described in detail by Valeri Yarynich, a former officer in the Soviet rocket forces who spent much of his career helping to design and build it (V. Yarynich, *C3*, Washington, DC, 2003). Bruce Blair, a former Minuteman officer, judged that '[A] long-standing and deep-seated obsession with controlling nuclear weapons led the Soviets to go to extraordinary lengths to ensure tight central control on nuclear weapons. Their safeguards were even more stringent than those of any other nuclear power, including the United States' (B. Blair, *The Logic of Accidental War*, Washington, DC, 1993, p. 107).

Defence, and the Chief of the General Staff travelled everywhere with a 'nuclear football', which tied them into the early warning system. Reserve 'footballs' could be allocated to their designated successors if they were incapacitated.

To launch their nuclear weapons, the military and the political leadership each had to issue a 'permission command' which was electronically combined into a single command for the next level down. This system of dual validation continued at every level down to the crews in the submarines, the bombers, and the missile sites. A separate electronic command switched on the launch equipment and documentation. Modern Soviet Intercontinental Ballistic Missiles (ICBMs), like the SS-18, could not be fired without key codes transmitted from the General Staff, who could countermand orders issued by maverick missile crews. Lower commanders could resist orders they thought improper. There were devices to prevent the warheads on some missiles from being armed if they behaved erratically, and others to destroy missiles in flight if they went off course. The reliability of these admirable technical devices – like their equivalent, the Americans PALs – could never, of course, be wholly guaranteed.

Like the British and the Americans, the Russians tried to ensure that their leadership would survive a nuclear exchange. They built an elaborate network of command bunkers deep under Moscow, with a metro network leading out of the city to enable them to escape if necessary. Bunker No. 42, several hundred metres underground in the city centre, was designed to enable nearly 3,000 people to survive a nuclear attack for up to two days. In post-Communist Russia it became a tourist attraction, complete with computer games enabling you to fire a salvo of missiles at New York. None of this would have been much use in the aftermath of a determined nuclear attack on Moscow, especially in the last two decades of the Cold War, as Western missiles improved dramatically in accuracy. Any survivors who managed to escape from their shelters would have emerged into an utterly ruined city.

The Russians gave sustained attention to developing secure systems to ensure that the leadership could communicate even in the worst circumstances with those directly in charge of the weapons. At the time of the Cuban missile crisis in 1962 the system was called

Monolit. If the General Staff decided to launch a nuclear strike, they transmitted a code word to the missile commanders by radio and cable. The recipient would then open his sealed orders and launch his weapons. This system was slow and the orders could not be recalled. In 1967 a new system was implemented, called Signal. It could quickly issue orders directly to the troops and the orders could be recalled. But it was the men on the ground who actually launched the weapons and, as with Monolit, it depended on their discipline and self-control. In the mid-1970s another system was introduced, Signal-M. This enabled the General Staff to fire the missiles by remote control, using communications rockets capable of transmitting the launch codes to the missile sites. It was tested in 1984.

The final and most sophisticated system was called Perimetr. Even if the Soviet leadership had been wiped out, the ultimate decision could still be taken by officers buried deep underground. The Russians hollowed out a command post inside a granite mountain in the Urals – they called it the Grotto – from which the surviving commanders could issue an electronic order to retaliate direct to the weapons themselves. It went into service in 1985. It was a partial equivalent of the American programme for Enduring National Leadership, which was designed to preserve a semblance of authority if the President was killed.

A surreal improvement to Perimetr enabled retaliation to be automatically triggered by a computer even if everyone, high and low, was already dead. This system, which was called the Dead Hand by those in the know, resembled the system described by the fictional Soviet leader in *Dr Strangelove*. It was never actually installed. Marshal Akhromeyev, the Soviet Chief of the General Staff at the time, is said to have opposed it on the grounds that the ultimate decision could only properly be taken by a human being.[43]

The American and the Soviet systems of command and control depended on the absolute discipline and discretion of those charged with operating the systems and manning the weapons, as well as the impeccable functioning of their sophisticated technical safeguards. As a number of incidents demonstrated over the years, neither could be guaranteed. Mobile intercontinental missiles could not be so strictly controlled as those in fixed silos. It was hard to communicate with a submarine underwater: the decision to launch its missiles could, in the end, be taken by its crew.[44]

From time to time there were worrying stories about low morale, drug and alcohol abuse, and poor security procedures on American missile sites. Such stories did not emerge on the Russian side, but there was no good reason to think that the situation was much better there.

All this could work in either direction. It was perhaps in theory possible – though not very likely – for a rogue commander to launch his weapons on his own initiative. But it was also possible for people far down the line to ignore orders they considered wrong. In the mid-1970s a malfunction occurred in the Soviet system and alert orders were automatically transmitted to the command posts. Instead of observing them, the recipients asked their superiors if they were genuine: the country was not, after all, at war.[45]

In *Crimson Tide*, an American film made as late as 1996, a Russian submarine shadowing a US missile submarine too closely tears away its trailing underwater aerial. The American commander is cut off from Washington in the middle of receiving an apparent order to fire his missiles at Vladivostok. His number two persuades him not to fire until he has re-established communication, and all ends well. But the US Navy found it necessary to insert a disingenuous disclaimer into the film: 'As of January 1996, primary authority and ability to fire nuclear missiles will no longer rest with U.S. submarine commanders ... Principal control will reside with the President of the United States.' The story in the film was not implausible: something similar happened during the Cuban missile crisis, when a Soviet submarine commander lost contact with Moscow and had to be dissuaded by his senior colleagues on board from launching a nuclear torpedo at the American carrier battle group that was pursuing him. This story is expanded in Chapter 13: Skirting the Brink.

Though the evidence was not firm, it was likely that American submarines carried on board all that they needed to fire their missiles without authority from their headquarters.[46] British submarine commanders, too, were apparently authorised to fire their missiles on their own initiative if they lost contact with their headquarters in a crisis and had reason to believe that government in Britain had been wiped out in a nuclear strike. The options were set out for them in a personal 'Letter of Last Resort' from the Prime Minister which was only to be opened in extremis.[47]

The implication was discouraging for those who believed that the final decision had always rested with the supreme political officer, whether it was the President, the General Secretary of the Soviet Union, the Prime Minister of Great Britain, or the President of France. Such complexities and uncertainties helped to generate paranoia and anxiety on both sides, and made the confrontation more difficult to manage.

These were the considerations which governed the way in which the Americans and the Russians worked out their national strategies. Each introduced their own nuances, and each accused the other of ignorance, misunderstanding, deception, and aggressive intent. But neither could escape reality.

Exposed and vulnerable on their little island, the British added their own nuances, which were sometimes illuminating. But if their strategic thinking seemed less complicated than the debates in Moscow and Washington, that was primarily because their limited resources forced them towards a greater simplicity.

In all three capitals the debates were shot through with confusion and contradiction.

SIX

THINKING ABOUT THE UNTHINKABLE

'Welcome to the world of strategic analysis, where we program weapons that don't work to meet threats that don't exist.'

official, US Department of Defense[1]

'If 180 million dead is too high a price to pay for punishing the Soviets for their aggression, what price would we be willing to pay?'

Herman Kahn[2]

'Peace is our Profession'

motto of the US Strategic Air Command

Playing Games

Henry Kissinger was still a young academic at Harvard when he defined it thus: 'the crucial object of strategy ... is to establish a reasonable relationship between power and the willingness to use it, between the physical and psychological components of national policy.'[3]

It was the Americans who made the largest and most ingenious contribution, in public as well as in secret, to the development of a body of strategy for deploying, threatening, or actually using the nuclear weapon. The strategic debate in America was more imaginative, far-reaching, and original than any other. The arguments that were bandied around were often wrong, but rarely boring. It was the Americans who determined what was orthodox and what was not, and it was they who invented the jargon, a necessary but bewildering array of concepts, terminology, and acronyms which were not easily deciphered by the outsider.

The public debate was initially dominated by a remarkable group of civilian theoreticians, people with little military experience but immensely subtle and ingenious minds. Their writing was clear, elegant, and persuasive. Their arcane and intricate ideas were intellectually stimulating, deeply serious, and profoundly well informed. But they often resembled the fine-spun theories of theologians in the medieval University of Paris, logical and fluent, but far removed from common sense or practicality.*

Many of these people were associated with the RAND Corporation, the think tank set up by the US Air Force in 1945 – economists, mathematicians, psychologists, sociologists, anthropologists, political scientists. They helped pioneer systems analysis, game theory, linear programming, and computing. Thirty of them won the Nobel Prize.†

They were not unduly modest. An observer called them a 'new priesthood, unique to this country and this time, of American action intellectuals ... Husky, wiry, physically attractive men, who by and large are married to exceptionally pretty women ... Their ideas are the drive wheels of the Great Society, shaping our defense, guiding our foreign policy.' In language not best calculated to please the military, one of them declared that Cold War questions 'require an analytical approach, an ability to think in abstract or conceptual terms. This is the sort of thing an intellectual, by virtue of his training, and mental discipline, can do better than a military professional who is not an intellectual.'[4]

These people reduced unprecedented problems to manageable proportions, sometimes by oversimplifying their assumptions and placing them within an unrealistic political framework. Not everyone was impressed. Solly Zuckerman, the British government's scientific adviser, was devastating: their approach, he said, was 'based upon assumptions about human behaviour which seem totally unreal. It

---

* In *Flawed Logics*, Baltimore, 2013, James Lebovic dissects and demolishes the logic of the nuclear strategists with delicate ruthlessness.
† One was the Hungarian Martian, John von Neumann, who had worked on the Manhattan Project. He hoped to generate 'a complete set of rules of behavior in all conceivable situations' (P. Erickson et al., *How Reason Almost Lost Its Mind*, Chicago, 2013, p. 29).

neither constitutes scientific analysis nor scientific theorising, but is a non-science of untestable speculations about Western and Soviet bloc behaviour.'[5]

The man widely credited with laying the foundations of Western thinking about nuclear deterrence was Bernard Brodie, a scholar from Yale University who had served on the naval staff during the war. He immediately realised the far-reaching implications of the nuclear bombing of Japan, and edited and contributed to a pioneering book, *The Absolute Weapon: Atomic Power and World Order*. As early as February 1946 General (not yet President) Dwight Eisenhower received an advance copy in typescript. In the first chapter, 'War in the Atomic Age', Brodie wrote, 'Thus far the chief purpose of our military establishment has been to win wars. From now on its chief purpose must be to avert them. It can have almost no other useful purpose.'[6] Those words have been much cited since. Thomas Schelling used game theory to study how governments might bargain before and even during a nuclear exchange. In his influential 1958 article 'The Delicate Balance of Terror', Albert Wohlstetter started from the premise that a Soviet nuclear attack was a real, perhaps an imminent possibility.[7] He and his equally formidable wife, Roberta, were awarded the Presidential Medal of Freedom by Ronald Reagan in 1985. Henry Kissinger, who wrote *Nuclear Weapons and Foreign Policy* in 1957, had the most distinguished career of all, and went on to become President Nixon's National Security Advisor and Secretary of State.

For the public, the image of the American strategic theorist was Dr Strangelove, the terrifying hero of Stanley Kubrick's film, the German scientist who cheerfully contemplates a doomsday in which a political and military elite – and the women from whom they would breed a new humanity – would survive nuclear holocaust in deep impregnable mines, while the rest of the world's population perished.

No one is quite sure who the model was for Dr Strangelove. Some said it was Edward Teller, the enthusiast for the hydrogen bomb. Others thought it might be Kissinger, or Wernher von Braun, the German rocket scientist. But the most favoured candidate was a man from RAND, Herman Kahn.

Kahn believed that one should think coldly and analytically

about the various ways in which a nuclear war might be started, conducted, and brought to an end. He began from two premises, one obvious, the other highly controversial. First, nuclear war was feasible, since the United States and the Soviet Union had massive nuclear arsenals aimed at each other. Second, like any other war, it was winnable.

Kahn was a brilliant, if interminable, speaker. In his writings he drove logic to some unattractive conclusions.* Whether hundreds of millions died or 'merely' a few major cities were destroyed, he argued, life would go on, as it had after the Black Death in four-teenth-century Europe. However horrible a nuclear war might be, those who proclaimed that the survivors would envy the dead were simply wrong. America needed to make it clear that it would if neces-sary repel a Soviet conventional attack with nuclear weapons: all else would be mere bluff. Further aggression should be countered by esca-lation, a larger nuclear response up a ladder of graduated rungs until the enemy folded or the final strategic exchange took place. Kahn's ladder had forty-four rungs, ranging from 'ostensible crisis' to 'spasm or insensate war'.[8]

Critics were appalled. They accused Kahn of lowering the emo-tional and intellectual barriers to nuclear war, creating the illusion that it could be successfully fought, and so making it more likely. One critic wrote in a review of Kahn's *On Thermonuclear War*, 'This is a moral tract on mass murder: how to plan it, how to commit it, how to get away with it, how to justify it.'[9] The critics were particularly scathing of Kahn's use of the term 'megadeath' as a convenient unit to signify 1 million casualties in a nuclear war.

That is not reasonable. The weapons existed and Kahn was justi-fied in trying to think through the consequences. Whether he and his fellows had as much influence as they have been credited with is another matter. Fred Kaplan concluded that the efforts of the games

---

* Kahn's steamroller style of argument resembles that of Stalin and Tolstoy. Kahn, too, starts from an often arbitrary premise and drives relentlessly to an appalling conclusion. Like theirs, his conclusions were not always wrong. He had a puckish sense of humour. Stalin, too, had a sense of humour, but it was terrifying. Tolstoy had no sense of humour at all.

players, 'these war planners who never saw war', were futile. 'It was, after all, only rational to try to keep a nuclear war limited if one ever broke out, to devise plans and options ahead of time that might end the war quickly and favorably, to keep the scope of its damage not too far out of tune with the importance of the political objectives over which the war was declared to begin with. Yet over the years, despite endless studies, nobody could find any options that seemed practical or made sense … The nuclear strategists had come to impose order – but in the end, chaos still prevailed.'[10]

Neither the official nor the academic world in America devoted much attention to Russian or Soviet studies before the Second World War: as one scholar said, never before 'did so many know so little about so much'.[11] During the war Russian studies expanded. But even in 1947, as the Cold War got under way, the fledgling CIA was still employing fewer than forty Soviet analysts, of whom only twelve spoke any Russian. The Americans set out to rectify the situation with characteristic energy, and for the next four decades devoted generous resources to the study of the Russian language and culture, and the Soviet political, economic, and social systems. Universities set up interdisciplinary departments of Soviet studies. Government and the military set up their own language schools and expert analytical groups. For a while people thought social science held the answer: a new generation of social scientists were convinced that their discipline could have 'consequences as revolutionary as those of atomic energy'. A group of social scientists had done a wartime study on the Japanese character, though they did not speak the language and knew little of Japan's history and culture. They believed their work had helped shorten the Pacific War. They proposed to apply the same techniques to the Soviet Union. Among them was the British sociologist Geoffrey Gorer: he detected in Russians an endemic mixture of aggression and submission, which he believed stemmed from their having been swaddled as babies.

With the tentative thaw which followed Stalin's death, limited exchanges began between American and Soviet scholars. A 'combination of broad interests and deep pockets' produced over the years a formidable body of work of the highest intellectual distinction, full of new information and insights into the way the Soviet Union worked. Economists, historians, and political scientists moved with increasing ease and frequency between academia and the official world in order to shape a considered response to the new threat. Some of them – Henry Kissinger, Zbigniew Brzezinski, Condoleezza Rice – ended up in the highest reaches of the American government.

There were of course differing opinions and an infinity of nuance among scholars about the relationship between Russian history and the Soviet system, and about how the United States should cope with it. But there were two broad schools of thought. One held that the Soviet system was intrinsically weak, ill-adapted to the demands of the modern industrial era, and that in the long run America's superior political institutions and its military and economic power would prevail as the Soviet system collapsed under its own weight. The other believed that the Soviet system was built upon an unchanging Russian political and imperial tradition: the Soviets' strength of purpose was implacable, they would always prefer guns to butter, and their drive for world domination could only be stopped by firm American action.

The differences became more emotional with the passionate disagreements over Nixon's policy of détente in the 1970s, Reagan's harsh anti-Soviet rhetoric in the early 1980s, and Gorbachev's revolutionary changes after 1985. They continued even after the Soviet Union had ceased to exist. Scholars fought new and inconclusive battles over the reasons for its collapse, a question to which there could never be a single or agreed answer.

The Shaping of American Strategy

Meanwhile successive presidents commissioned a series of policy documents which estimated the threat from the Soviet Union, recommended the means and doctrines to counter it, and set the tone for American strategic thinking throughout the Cold War.

These documents drew on the work of the games players and the scholars. But they were shaped above all by the attitudes of senior civilian and military officials, men of strong opinions, well versed in the art of getting their way in the Washington jungle. They were not always interested in the nuanced ideas presented to them by the experts and relied instead, according to the French sociologist Raymond Aron, on a 'shockingly primitive level of public information'. They inclined to the view that it was always safer to exaggerate Soviet strengths rather than play them down, to plan on the basis of the worst case. The Soviets, they confidently believed, were prepared to use every kind of political and military pressure, subversion, economic bribery, or blackmail to achieve their aim: the worldwide victory of their version of socialism, without war if they could, but through war if they must. The huge Soviet military establishment went far beyond anything the Russians could possibly need for their defence. No scenario for Soviet aggression seemed too extreme.

Few of the policymakers had direct experience of the Russians and, as Solly Zuckerman had charged, made little attempt to understand how the Russians thought about managing their side of the conflict.[12] In these documents the Russians themselves figured as an abstraction, cardboard cut-outs shaped to fit the argument, their real intentions, ambitions, capabilities, and weaknesses ignored. The analyses looked at no alternative explanation of the Soviet military posture, the fears as well as the ambitions of the Soviet leadership, the difficult choices they faced, or the alternative courses they might follow. They dismissed as irrelevant, exaggerated, or simply fraudulent Russian fears of the US bases that surrounded them, the powerful nuclear armed submarines and aircraft carriers which patrolled the nearby oceans and seas, the nuclear bombers and missiles based in America which were aimed at their most sensitive targets.

Though they were written over four decades, these influential policy documents resembled one another in style and logic. Indeed they were often written by the same people: Paul Nitze, for example, was involved in the drafting of NSC-68 for President Truman in 1950 and of Presidential Directive 59, 'Nuclear Weapons Employment Policy', or PD-59, for President Carter thirty years later. He left his hawkish imprint on both.*

---

*Paul Nitze was Vice Chairman of the Strategic Bombing Survey and visited Japan to assess the effect of the atomic bombing. He succeeded George Kennan as Director of the State Department's Policy Planning Staff.

Presidents Try to Define Strategy

Truman: Bombing Cities, Winning Wars

In the first few years after 1945 the strategic problem seemed simple enough. The Americans had gone home at the end of the war. But, people believed, the Soviets had failed to demobilise and thus retained an overwhelming advantage.

The figures were a bit more complicated than that. In 1945 the Russians had 11.5 million men under arms. The Americans had just over 12 million. Both sides then demobilised massively. By 1948 the Americans had 1.5 million men under arms and the Russians 2.8 million.[13] The crucial advantage for the Russians was not the figures, but the geography. Their soldiers were on the right side of the Atlantic and the Americans were not.

The Americans therefore initially planned to deter or reverse any Soviet adventure in Europe by bombarding the Soviet Union with nuclear weapons, a grander version of the wartime bombardment of Germany and Japan. The first plan was drawn up within months of Hiroshima. It suffered from a serious weakness: the air force had neither the bombs nor the bombers to mount such an attack.

Moreover the plan started from a false premise. The Russians may have had the numbers, but their weapons were worn out and increasingly obsolete. The devastated state of the Soviet economy was reason enough to prevent Stalin from attempting a full-scale invasion of Europe, even if his innate caution had not done so. No evidence has emerged that he ever had such plans.

Thanks to his excellent intelligence, Stalin did know that the American stock of atomic bombs was still too small to pose a serious threat. That reinforced his determination to demonstrate that he was not to be intimidated. He felt reasonably safe in challenging the Americans over Berlin in 1948 and supporting the North Korean invasion of South Korea in 1950. The Americans nevertheless successfully stared down both challenges by purely conventional means.

Churchill, insecure in his grasp of the facts and erratic as so often in his judgements, said in 1949, 'It is certain that Europe would have been communized and London under bombardment some time ago but for the deterrent of the atomic bomb in the hands of the United States.'[14] Such erroneous views left their mark on the public perception of the post-war Soviet threat for many years to come.

In June 1947 the US Joint Chiefs of Staff sent an 'Evaluation of the Atomic Bomb as a Military Weapon' to President Truman.[15] It was well argued, it eschewed ideology, and its conclusions were stark. Atomic bombs could 'not only nullify any nation's military effort but demolish its social and economic structures and prevent their reestablishment for long periods of time … In conjunction with other weapons of mass destruction as, for example, pathogenic bacteria, it is possible to depopulate vast areas of the earth's surface, leaving only vestigial remnants of man's material works.' Deep shelters could protect military facilities but, the Chiefs said bleakly, were 'impracticable for the defense of a city and its inhabitants'.

But until a reliable system of international control had been set up, said the Chiefs, the United States was open to a devastating surprise attack by a nuclear-armed enemy. They therefore recommended that the President should meanwhile be empowered to 'order atomic bomb retaliation … to prevent or frustrate an atomic weapon attack upon us'. They concluded, 'A peace enforced through fear is a poor substitute for a peace maintained through international cooperation.' But until then 'this nation can hope only that an effective deterrent to global war will be a universal fear of the atomic bomb as the ultimate horror of war'. Thus the Chiefs adopted the idea of deterrence little more than a year after the publication of Bernard Brodie's seminal chapter on 'War in the Atomic Age'.

A parallel military plan envisaged hitting seventy Soviet targets, killing nearly 3 million people and wounding another 4.5 million. 'Assuming a plentiful supply of atomic bombs and a war aim of complete subjugation of the enemy,' wrote the Air Staff, 'it would be feasible to risk an all-out atomic attack at the beginning of a war in an effort to stun the enemy into submission.'[16]

These tentative ideas were not backed by substance. For more than a decade after 1945 the United States had no coherent plan for using its nuclear weapons. Plan Totality, put together in the autumn of 1945, envisaged a nuclear attack on twenty cities in the Soviet Union. This was meaningless: a year later Americans still had only eleven atomic bombs and seventeen B-29 bombers capable of delivering them.[17] Press reports during the 1948 Berlin crisis that nuclear-capable B-29 bombers had been sent to Britain were a bluff. By then the Americans had about fifty bombs, but none of the aircraft sent to Britain was appropriately modified.

At first the air force, the navy, and the army all went their mutually competitive ways, developing their own weapons, devising their own operational plans, working out their own lists of Soviet targets. The result was confusion: more weapons of more types than America needed, and competing plans that would have resulted in the same target being hit several times over.

The initial instrument of a more coherent strategy was the Strategic Air Command, which was set up in 1946. At first it was a shambles, perhaps the result of complacency: one of its Deputy Commanders declared that 'No major strategic threat or requirement now exists in the opinion of our country's best strategists nor will such a requirement exist for the next three to five years.'[18] To get to their targets, its bombers would have first to fly to Texas to collect their bombs, then to England or Newfoundland to refuel. On one exercise, more than half the planes could not get off the ground.

Once again Curtis LeMay, the man who had got a grip on the bombing of Japan, was called to sort things out. He took over the Strategic Air Command in October 1948, and was disgusted with what he found. 'I should go on record and say this flatly: we didn't have one crew, not one crew in the entire command, who could do a professional job.'[19] He sorted things out with his accustomed ruthless efficiency and relentless energy. Within five years the Strategic Air Command looked entirely different. It had 500 bombers, 500 aerial tankers, and a global network of bases from which to strike the Soviet Union direct. Its official motto was 'Peace is our Profession'. Under LeMay there was an unofficial motto too: 'To err is human; to forgive is not SAC policy'.

In June 1948 Stalin launched his abortive blockade of West Berlin. The judicious caution which Kennan had expressed a year earlier in his X Article in *Foreign Affairs* was overtaken. The Defense Secretary, James Forrestal, commissioned a 'comprehensive statement of national policy' from the State Department's Policy Planning Staff, which Kennan now headed. The resulting documents went well beyond the limited objectives to which Kennan had originally subscribed.

The first of these, NSC-20/1, 'U.S. Objectives with Respect to Russia', reflected Kennan's hand. It spoke at philosophical length of the enduring determination of the Soviet Union, and before it the Russian Empire, to expand 'beyond its legitimate limits' (the phrase 'legitimate' was often used later, but rarely defined). America should push back to change the Russian approach to international affairs, ensure that Russia ceased to be a strong military power, and make it a dependent part of the world economy. War was not inevitable. But if it came, the United States would win. It should not then occupy a defeated Russia, nor try to impose democracy upon it. But it should open up Russia to the outside world, and limit the Russians' authority over their national minorities, perhaps through a federal arrangement which would benefit Ukraine.

NSC-20/4, 'U.S. Objectives with Respect to the USSR to Counter Soviet Threats to U.S.', followed in November. It stated bluntly that the Soviet Union's ultimate objective was to dominate the world. This was 'the greatest single danger to the United States for the foreseeable future'. The Soviet leaders would resort to war with little hesitation to achieve their ends, a judgement based, the authors admitted, on no intelligence about Soviet military capabilities and intentions. They recommended that America should build up its military capability to counter Soviet ambition.[20]

The NSC-20 papers were released in 1978. The Russians read them as evidence of enduring and implacable American hostility and quoted them ever afterwards.[21]

Conventional Rearmament: NSC-68

President Truman was not initially impressed by this call for an arms build-up: he had just promised defence cuts in his re-election campaign. His mind was changed by events.[22] Stalin's adventure failed in Berlin, but 1949 brought a menacing change. The Russians were clamping their rule on Eastern Europe. Communists were insurgent in Greece. In August the Russians detonated their first nuclear device. And in the autumn of 1949 Mao Tse Tung proclaimed the People's

Republic of China. America's position in the world seemed to be threatened as never before.

Truman called for a new study of American strategic objectives. He received it in April 1950. It was drafted by the State Department's Policy Planning Staff, now under Paul Nitze, and it was called NSC-68, 'United States Objectives and Programs for National Security'.

Verbose, repetitive, and muddled, this was nevertheless a defining document in the evolution of official American strategic thinking.[23] In a flurry of rhetoric drawn in part from the Declaration of Independence of 1776, it contrasted the 'Fundamental Purpose' of the United States with the 'Fundamental Design' of the Soviet Union.* The 'purposes' of the United States promoted 'the marvelous diversity, the deep tolerance, the lawfulness of the free society'. The 'designs' of the Soviet Union were directed to 'the complete subversion or forcible destruction of the machinery of government and structure of society in the countries of the non-Soviet world and their replacement by an apparatus and structure subservient to and controlled from the Kremlin … The United States, as the principal center of power in the non-Soviet world and the bulwark of opposition to Soviet expansion, is the principal enemy whose integrity and vitality must be subverted or destroyed by one means or another if the Kremlin is to achieve its fundamental design.' This was the Manichaean language of 'Godless Communism'. It was hardly appropriate to a policy document.

NSC-68 argued that the Kremlin would go to war should it 'become convinced that it could cause our downfall by one decisive blow'. The Soviet Union's armed forces were 'far in excess of those necessary to defend its national territory'. By 1950 the Soviet Union would be able to overrun Western Europe, attack the British Isles, and assault the sea lanes in the Atlantic and the Pacific. By then the Russians would have up to twenty atomic bombs, with which they could hit Alaska, Canada, and the United States. By 1954 they would have at least 200 bombs and the aircraft to deliver them. If it came to war they would doubtless use them. An inadequately armed America

---

* The Declaration of Independence spoke of the British 'design to reduce [free men] under absolute Despotism'.

could find itself at war with the Soviet Union within a year. Indeed, one of the drafting officials said that America was already 'in a war worse than any we have ever experienced'.[24]

To counter the Soviet 'design', to block the expansion of Soviet power by all means short of war, the United States should use its economic strength to maintain a clear superiority in nuclear weapons, and to build up the military strength of its allies to offset Soviet conventional superiority. It should make clear that the United States would use its nuclear weapons first, if that were necessary to prevent victory by overwhelming Soviet conventional forces.

Such measures combined would make nuclear war less likely. The longer aim should be to block the expansion of Soviet power, push back Soviet influence, and 'foster the seeds of destruction within the Soviet system'. There were risks. Once both sides had substantial nuclear forces, each might miscalculate the risk of war. '[T]hese are risks we will invite by making ourselves strong, but they are lesser risks than those we seek to avoid.'[25]

Thus the paper's ambitious aim was political, not military. American measures against Russia, it argued, must not be 'so excessive or misdirected as to make us enemies of the people instead of the evil men who have enslaved them'. If America could go beyond that and 'make the Russian people our allies in the enterprise we will obviously have made our task easier and victory more certain'.

The paper's analysis of Soviet capacities and intentions, like that of its NSC-20 predecessors, was based neither on hard intelligence nor on a sophisticated evaluation of how the Russians saw their own strengths, weaknesses, and fears. It did not explain why the Russians should risk all by an invasion of Western Europe. It ignored a CIA finding that the Russians lacked the strength to occupy the Continent and hold it down. And it grossly overestimated the size of the Soviet atomic arsenal.

However out of place it looked in a policy document, the inflated rhetoric of NSC-68 was not accidental: it was intended as a spur to action. As Dean Acheson wrote later, 'The purpose of NSC-68 was to so bludgeon the mass mind of "top government" that not only could the President make a decision, but that the decision would be carried out.' The arguments were deliberately stripped down to be 'understandable and clear' to the average American citizen. 'If we made our points clearer than the truth, we did not differ from most other educators and could hardly do otherwise.'

The paper put no figures on the costs for the military build-up it proposed. That was deliberate: the authors feared that once considerations of cost entered the argument, it would never be brought to a conclusion. But they calculated that the military budget would have to go up to $50 billion a year: the existing ceiling was $13.5 billion.[26] The Secretary for Defense, Louis Johnson, a fiscal conservative, initially opposed its recommendations on economic grounds, though he eventually put his signature to it. George Kennan thought the whole thing was exaggerated.[27]

Truman did not endorse NSC-68 immediately: he was inclined to agree that the proposals would overstrain the economy. But in July 1950 the North Koreans invaded the South: conclusive evidence, it seemed, that the Soviet Union was implacably aggressive. Truman gave the green light to a massive rearmament programme. American defence expenditure nearly doubled between 1951 and 1952. Whether this was a direct consequence of the arguments in NSC-68, or whether it would have happened anyway, is unknowable.

NSC-68 was declassified in 1975. The veteran Soviet diplomat Georgi Kornienko later wrote that it helped to ensure that the relationship between the United States and the Soviet Union was more confrontational than it need have been. The Soviet Union never had a similar 'Cold War catechism'. But the concepts which underlay Soviet foreign policy were nevertheless almost a mirror image. While firmly convinced that they themselves had no aggressive intentions, Soviet policymakers too believed that their opponents were aiming at world domination. The result was a vicious circle, which ratcheted up the arms race and increased the risk of military confrontation.[28]

Eisenhower: Conventional Defence versus Massive Retaliation

While the American monopoly lasted, some people managed to persuade themselves that atom bombs were merely another weapon in a chain that led from the stone axe through the bow and arrow to the machine gun and the conventional heavy bomber. As late as 1954 Eisenhower could still say, 'Where these things are used on strictly military targets and for strictly military purposes, I see no reason why they shouldn't be used just exactly as you would use a bullet or anything else.'[29]

But by then the Americans and the Russians had both successfully tested thermonuclear devices capable of unlimited destruction. And soon the Americans could no longer plan on the assumption that their cities were beyond Soviet reach. Soviet bombers still had little chance of hitting American targets. But in August 1957 the Russians tested the R-7 rocket, capable of flying nearly 4,000 miles, a design which was still being used sixty years later to launch Russian spacecraft. In October this rocket launched the world's first artificial satellite, the Sputnik, which orbited the earth sending out a tiny *beep*, visible and audible proof that here at least Soviet technology had overtaken the Americans. The Russian leaders and the Russian people were jubilant.

Sputnik left the Americans correspondingly dismayed. What James Killian, who was to become Eisenhower's science adviser, 'felt most keenly was the affront to my national pride', and the violence done 'to a belief so fundamental that it was almost heresy to question it: a belief I shared that the United States was so far advanced in its technological capacity that it had in fact no serious rival'.[30]

In December 1959 the Russians created the Strategic Rocket Forces, and a couple of months later Khrushchev told his colleagues that the arrival of the intercontinental missile made it possible to negotiate agreements with the Americans, because 'main-street Americans have begun to shake from fear for the first time in their lives'.[31] Four years later, in April 1961, the Russians stole another march, when Yuri Gagarin became the first human being to journey into space.

Despite the blow to their self-confidence, the Americans did not take long to catch up. In 1958 they launched their own intercontinental rocket, the Atlas. In 1969 they placed the first man on the moon. For all their ingenuity the Russians lacked the resources to maintain the competition.

Each side was now, in theory, capable of subjecting the other to the most destructive bombardment. From now on both were deterred from nuclear war not by the complexity of their doctrines or the size and sophistication of their arsenals, but by their common fear of even a limited nuclear exchange. At the time of the Cuban missile crisis in 1962 the Americans still had a formidable nuclear superiority over the Russians. Yet President Kennedy chose not to use it, for fear of the damage that would be caused if even a few Soviet rockets hit American cities.

Dwight Eisenhower hoped, like Truman, to resist unnecessary defence expenditure. Two weeks after assuming office in January 1953 he ordered the National Security Council to 'figure out a pre-paredness program that will give us a respectable position without bankrupting the nation'. He brought teams of experts together in Operation Solarium to consider alternative scenarios for dealing with the Soviet Union.[32]

But his political opponents increasingly accused him of weakness. When the Federal Civil Defense Agency demanded a massive five-year $32 billion shelter programme, he set up a panel under H. Rowan Gaither, a founder of RAND, in April 1957 to investigate 'various active and passive measures to protect the civil population in case of nuclear attack and its aftermath'. It was an apparently limited task. But Paul Nitze once again led the drafting, and by the time Gaither delivered the final report in November 1957 it had gone well beyond its original mandate.

The report was called 'Deterrence and Survival in the Nuclear Age'. Like NSC-68, it judged that the Russians' effort to 'build military power far beyond any concepts of Soviet defense' demonstrated their expansionist intentions. In a decade their 'annual military expenditure may be double ours'.* By 1959 or 1960, it warned, 'the USSR may be able to launch an attack with ICBMs carrying megaton weapons against which SAC [Strategic Air Command] will be almost completely vulnerable under present programs ... If we fail to act at once, the risk, in our opinion, will be unacceptable.'

The report claimed that the Russians had fissionable material for at least 1,500 nuclear weapons, a long-range bomber force of 1,500

---

* This judgement was mildly absurd. The Soviet economy was tiny by comparison with the American. The Russians themselves found it almost impossible to work out accurately how much they spent on defence.

aircraft, and a short range force of 300 jet bombers. They were probably ahead in developing intercontinental missiles, they had cruise missiles, up to 500 submarines, and a sophisticated air defence system which included 10,000 fighter planes. And they had created all this while maintaining a ground force of 175 divisions and supplying large quantities of military equipment to the Chinese and their other allies.

Gaither recommended that the American population be protected by better air defences and a fallout shelter programme. The power and reach of US deterrent forces should be increased, and the Strategic Air Command put on continual alert. If this were done soon, 'the U.S. will be able to carry out a decisive attack even if surprised. This could be the best time to negotiate from strength since the U.S. military position vis-à-vis Russian might never be as strong again.'

Thereafter things would get worse. By the 1970s a small technological advance on either side might enable it to destroy the other. This, the panel concluded soberly enough, suggested 'the great importance of a continuing attempt to arrive at a dependable agreement on the limitation of armaments and the strengthening of other measures for the preservation of peace'.

The report went to President Eisenhower in November 1957. Neither he nor his Secretary of State, John Foster Dulles, was impressed. The President said he was not prepared to turn America into a garrison state. Dulles objected in particular to the civil defence proposals. Nitze retorted that without a vigorous civil defence programme, the Soviets could 'destroy the fabric of our society and our nation'. He then leaked the report to the press. Implying insultingly that Dulles was not up to the job, he wondered 'whether there is not some other Republican disposed to exercise the responsibility of the office of Secretary of State'.[33]

Many of Gaither's figures about Soviet strength were fantasy. The report admitted that 'by the very nature of the sources of intelligence information, none of the specific numbers cited above can be precisely known'. In 1976 a Senate committee declassified the report and subjected it to a withering criticism. It was nevertheless such figures, and Khrushchev's attempt to bluff the Americans by falsely claiming that the Soviet Union was turning out missiles 'like sausages', that gave rise to the perception of a Missile Gap between the United States and the Soviet Union which was exploited by John Kennedy in his campaign to become President in 1959.

Gaither recommended that America's allies should build up their own conventional forces to match the Russians on the ground. The idea was not new; indeed it had already failed. The NATO Lisbon Conference in February 1952 had called for the Alliance to raise ninety-six divisions, an absurdly overambitious target. At a time when NATO only had about twenty-five divisions available, there was never a chance that the Europeans would achieve it. The following year the target was more than halved to some thirty-five divisions. Even this number was never attained. By 1965 American analysts had in any case concluded that, if you used qualitative as well as quantitative criteria, 'NATO and the Warsaw Pact had approximate equality on the ground.'[34] But whatever the truth, NATO thinking continued to be dominated until the last years of the Cold War by fear of a massive Soviet conventional attack.

The failure to build up NATO's conventional forces inevitably led the Americans to look again at their nuclear strategy. They hit on a policy known as 'massive retaliation'. In an article for *Life* magazine in May 1952, John Foster Dulles called for a 'Policy of Boldness'. The free world needed, he said, 'to develop the will and organize the means to retaliate instantly against open aggression by Red armies, so that if it occurred anywhere, we could and would strike back where it hurts, by means of our choosing'.[35] For these ideas Dulles suffered much criticism and some ridicule.

The doctrine was refined in another National Security Council paper, NSC-162/2 of October 1953, on 'Basic National Security Policy'. It judged, like its predecessors, that the Russians were determined eventually to dominate the non-Communist world. Their capacity to launch a nuclear attack on America was growing. No positive gesture from the Russians was to be trusted. America still had the means to inflict 'massive retaliatory damage' on the Russians without much fear of a counterstrike. It should counter Soviet – and Chinese – conventional aggression wherever it occurred. 'In the event of hostilities, the United States will consider nuclear weapons to be as available for use as other munitions.'

The implication that the Americans might use nuclear weapons in regional wars was bolstered by Vice President Nixon, who wrote in the *New York Times*: 'Rather than let the Communists nibble us to death all over the world in little wars, we would rely in the future primarily on our massive mobile retaliatory power which we could use in our discretion against the major source of aggression at times and places that we choose.'

The conclusions of NSC-162/2 were nevertheless rather sober. The paper recognised that the Russians would eventually catch up and that a threat to use nuclear weapons in regional wars would then become less credible. Dulles emphasised that America did not intend to 'rely wholly on large-scale strategic bombing as the sole means to deter and counter aggression'.[36] Eisenhower himself added that the policy of massive retaliation should be reconsidered if it looked like working to America's disadvantage.

LeMay had by now refashioned the Strategic Air Command into an effective instrument. But there was still no good plan for its employment. Eisenhower insisted that the military put together a Single Integrated Operational Plan (SIOP) to combine the capabilities of American strategic bombers, intercontinental missiles, and missile submarines, so that the Soviet Union could be bombarded in a coherent manner. To the great displeasure of the army and the navy, SIOP remained under the effective control of the air force. The plan was completed in December 1960 and put into effect in April 1961: confusingly it was called SIOP-62. It provided for 3,200 warheads to be used against the USSR and its allies and against China – all at once. It contained no easy way of confining strikes to the Soviet Union if the other countries were not involved. It was all or nothing.

The Joint Chiefs of Staff calculated that under this plan between 360 and 450 million people would die in the Sino-Soviet bloc in a matter of hours. Eisenhower was appalled: the plan, he said, frightened the devil out of him. He insisted the planners devise ways of using the nuclear weapon with greater discrimination and control. But it was too late to do anything before he handed over office to John Kennedy.[37]

Kennedy and Johnson: Strategy by Numbers

Kennedy was unwilling to accept that there really was no choice but what Herman Kahn charmingly called a 'wargasm', a devastating all-out strike against the Soviet Union which risked inviting the destruction of the United States. To sort things out, he appointed the brilliant Robert McNamara as his Defense Secretary. McNamara had served in the air force during the war as a statistician calculating the effectiveness of its bombing campaign against Japan. Afterwards he joined the failing Ford Motor Company, helped to turn it round, and became its President in 1960. He remained as Defense Secretary under Kennedy's successor, Lyndon Johnson, and was reviled ever afterwards for escalating the war in Vietnam.

McNamara's first need was to impose order and method on the sprawling Pentagon. He centralised the hitherto independent intelligence functions of the separate armed forces, and took the budgeting function under his own control. He demanded an immense abundance of facts from his subordinates, in an attempt to put figures on things that were not easily quantifiable. He applied the latest techniques of systems analysis to set out alternative courses of action, in the belief that he could make rational choices untrammelled by the experience and traditions or, as he saw them, the conservative prejudices and tribal loyalties of the military.[38]

His aim was to create a strategic force 'of a character which will permit its use, in event of attack, in a cool and deliberate fashion and always under the complete control of the constituted authority'. The principal military objectives of this force 'should be the destruction of the enemy's military forces, not of his civilian population ... We are giving a possible opponent the strongest imaginable incentive to refrain from striking our own cities.'[39] To assist him, he recruited some of the brightest analysts from RAND into his own office. He employed Thomas Schelling as a consultant and maintained close links with Albert Wohlstetter. Some of the simplifying assumptions that they had used to underpin their theories now became a basis for policy.

His ideas were reflected in the next SIOP, SIOP-63, which contained an array of options intended to 'permit controlled response and negotiating pauses in the event of thermonuclear war'. The plan provided for the possibility of a pre-emptive strike in response to unequivocal strategic warning of Soviet attack. It allowed the option of striking industrial capacity while sparing cities. And it omitted Moscow from the first wave of attacks to allow a pause for negotiation, what was called 'intrawar bargaining'.[40]

At one end of the targeting plans was 'assured destruction', the ability to inflict unacceptable damage on the Russians even after the United States or its allies had been struck first, by destroying up to a third of the Soviet population and half of Soviet industry.* At the other was 'damage limitation'. Only military targets would be struck, those from which the Russians could hit America. The necessary but unfortunate corollary was that the Americans would have to strike first – before the Soviets could fire their weapons. Somewhere in between were 'limited nuclear options', the idea that the Americans should be able to use nuclear weapons to deter or repel limited or regional Russian aggression.

These options depended on some optimistic assumptions. Would the Russians be able to distinguish between a limited and an all-out strike? Would they too be willing to confine their attacks only to military targets? Was there in practice much possibility of distinguishing between civilian and military targets, given that in the Soviet Union the two were often close together?

McNamara himself came to realise that the American arsenal, for all its growing sophistication, could not guarantee the destruction of all Soviet weapons in a first strike. He began to edge back towards a strategy of deterring attack by threatening to destroy cities.[41] He thus sent a confusingly mixed message. The Russians concluded, perhaps inevitably, that he was preparing for military victory in a first strike. Kennedy's Deputy National Security Advisor, Walt Rostow, told the Soviet Deputy Foreign Minister, Vasili Kuznetsov, that 'any Kennedy rearmament would be designed to improve the stability of the deterrent, and the Soviet Union should recognise this as in the interests of peace'. Kuznetsov was not impressed. As McNamara came to recognise, the Russians 'could not read our intentions with any greater accuracy than we could read theirs'.[42]

---

* By 1968 the Americans had, they believed, the capacity to destroy nearly 50 per cent of the Soviet population and 80 per cent of the industry.

McNamara eventually concluded that there was little point in continuing tit-for-tat competition with the Russians. There was a limit beyond which an increase in the sheer numbers of weapons gave no extra security. For as long as he could promise them increased budgets, the military just about put up with him. But the hostility of the military became increasingly evident as the money began to run out. Congress was not prepared to subordinate its interests, views, and prejudices to McNamara's simplifying rationality. Even with the President's backing, he often had to compromise his objectives to keep the politicians on board.

Despite his formidable intellectual credentials, McNamara proved in the end no more capable than anyone else of devising a fully coherent and satisfactory nuclear strategy.

Nixon: Back from the Brink

In 1970 Richard Nixon reformulated the basic problem in a speech to Congress: 'Should a President, in the event of a nuclear attack, be left with the single option of ordering the mass destruction of enemy civilians in the face of the certainty that it would be followed by the mass slaughter of Americans?'[43]

The moment that Robert Oppenheimer had long predicted, when the two superpowers would find themselves like scorpions in a bottle, came in October 1962 with the frightening experience of the Cuba missile crisis. Thereafter the two sides began to look for ways of lowering the tension between them. In December 1967 NATO adopted a report on 'The Future Tasks of the Alliance', which recommended that the Alliance should adopt a two-track policy.* It should continue to deter Soviet adventurism. But it should also seek a dialogue with the Russians about ways of reducing tension, lowering the level of the conventional confrontation in Europe, and tackling the underlying political problems which divided it. The pursuit of détente, intermittent and with many setbacks, remained a major theme of the nuclear confrontation until the end of the Cold War.

---

* It was known as the Harmel Report after the Belgian Foreign Minister Pierre Harmel, who had called for a new look at NATO strategy a year earlier.

The Americans continued to seek a more flexible nuclear strategy. Richard Nixon's Defense Secretary, James Schlesinger, refined McNamara's ideas in an attempt to increase the President's options. For example, if the Russians attacked Western Europe, they would be countered with selective strikes against Soviet military targets. Attacks on Soviet cities would meanwhile be withheld. With their military capacity degraded and their cities still open to bombardment, the Russians would have a strong reason to avoid attacking American cities and to end their aggression.

This was not intended as a first-strike policy. But the Russians did not believe American statements to the contrary. Anatoli Dobrynin was the highly competent and well-informed Soviet ambassador in Washington at the time.* He believed that Schlesinger's new doctrine was a deliberate attempt 'to legitimize a strategic nuclear war and, indeed, to increase the strategic nuclear threat to the Soviet Union, since the United States had more MIRVed missiles'.[44]

If any mutual understanding were to be reached, therefore, it would have to be explicitly negotiated, rather than assumed or implied. In February 1967 President Lyndon Johnson offered the Russians talks on the limitation of strategic arms. The idea was taken up by President Nixon and his Secretary of State, Henry Kissinger, who found a ready interlocutor in the Soviet leader, Leonid Brezhnev. The agreements they negotiated included the SALT I agreement, the Anti-Ballistic Missile Treaty of 1972, and the Helsinki Accords of 1975, which settled a number of outstanding European problems (the negotiations are briefly described in Chapter 13). For a while the level of tension between the two superpowers diminished significantly.

---

* Dobrynin was ambassador in Washington from 1962 to 1968. He found his way deep into Washington politics and his memoirs are an invaluable source of information on American as well as Soviet attitudes. Inevitably he has been accused of presenting a self-serving and partial view: that is the fate of all political memoirs. The introduction to his book has one of the most sensible descriptions of what an ambassador is for that I know.

Carter and the End of Détente

But conservative opposition to détente began to grow in the second half of the 1970s. The United States was still suffering from the aftermath of defeat in Vietnam, Portugal underwent a left-wing revolution, and the Communists seemed poised to enter government in Italy. Conservatives increasingly accused the Russians of using détente as cover for the aggressive expansion of their influence in the Third World. Alfred Wohlstetter and Paul Nitze publicly accused the Russians of building up an arsenal sufficient to fight and win a nuclear war. The critics charged Nixon and Kissinger with creating 'a myth of détente', and claimed that Kissinger and the CIA had systematically underestimated Soviet aggressive intentions. They manoeuvred President Ford, who succeeded Nixon in 1974, into setting up a group of experts to make an independent assessment of the Soviet threat. The team was led by Professor Richard Pipes, a respected writer on Russian history from Harvard. Once again, Paul Nitze was a member. They were known as Team B; Team A were the CIA analysts whose assessments they rubbished.

Team B concluded that the Russians were planning to fight and win a limited nuclear war. Their report was leaked in December 1978.* Despite sustained and justified criticism, it became the intellectual basis for a massive arms build-up under presidents Carter and Reagan. It helped define the mood in the early Reagan years, and made it harder for Washington to appreciate underlying Soviet weaknesses and the revolutionary impact of Gorbachev's reforms. As late as 1990, Frank Gaffney, a senior Reagan defence official, claimed that the Team B analysis had been justified by events, and wrote, 'Now is the time for a new Team B and a clear-eyed assessment of the abiding Soviet (and other) challenges that dictate a continued, robust US defense posture.'[45]

Three days after Carter won the election in November 1976, Eugene Rostow, a former Under Secretary in the State Department, revived the Committee on the Present Danger – originally set up during the Korean War – whose central thesis was that 'The principal threat to our nation, to world peace, and to the cause of human

---

*Team B's deliberations are described in more detail in Chapter 9.

freedom is the Soviet drive for dominance based upon an unparalleled military buildup'.[46] Its members included Nitze, former Defense Secretary James Schlesinger, George Shultz, who became Reagan's Secretary of State, and Ronald Reagan himself, then still Governor of California. Their aim was to avert the risk that 'the United States will celebrate its two-hundredth birthday by betraying the heritage of liberty which has earned it the wonder and envy of the world from the moment of its founding to this, and by helping to make that world safe for the most determined and ferocious and barbarous enemies of liberty ever to have appeared on the earth'.[47] Such inflamed language did not make for sober analysis.

Jimmy Carter was by no means the feeble dove his opponents pilloried. In 1978 he issued a directive which instructed that 'U.S. missiles and bombers must be able to destroy about 70 percent of the Soviet Union's so-called recovery resources, meaning the economic, political, and military facilities critical to the functioning of society'.[48]* The following year his Defense Secretary, Harold Brown, wrote in his annual report for 1979, 'It is essential that we retain the capability at all times to inflict an unacceptable level of damage on the Soviet Union, including destruction of a minimum of 200 major cities.'[49]

In July 1980 Carter approved a new Presidential Directive, PD-59. This recommended that, if deterrence failed, the United States should 'be capable of fighting successfully so that the adversary would not achieve his war aims and would suffer costs that are unacceptable'. PD-59 therefore set out options for using nuclear weapons not only to deter, to retaliate, or to pre-empt an enemy attack, but to fight a protracted war. Once war started, they could also be used selectively to add to the pressure for 'war termination'.[50] It was not clear what this vague formula might mean in practice, nor whether in the stress of even a limited nuclear war either side would be able to negotiate coherently.

---

* A review at this time found that a major nuclear war between the Soviet Union and the United States would result in minimum of 140 million dead in America, 113 million dead in the Soviet Union, and the destruction of three-quarters of each economy (D. Ball and J. Richelson (eds), *Strategic Nuclear Targeting*, Ithaca, 1986, p. 75).

There was in any case nothing new in the idea that America should be able to fight and win a nuclear war. It had long been firmly embedded in American military thinking, though even inside the Pentagon there were sceptics. Alain Enthoven, an Assistant Secretary there, had already written in 1975 that 'Tactical nuclear weapons cannot defend Europe: they can only destroy it ... Twenty years of effort by many military experts have failed to produce a believable doctrine for tactical nuclear warfare'.[51]

By now US targeting options included industries and institutions which the Soviet Union would need in order to recover from an attack. The thought was briefly mooted that the Soviet Empire could be dissolved and the captive peoples – Ukrainians, Balts, Caucasians, and Central Asians – liberated by targeting the physical transport and industrial links between them and Russia, destroying Soviet military establishments on their territory, and killing as many ethnic Russians as possible. The idea collapsed under its own weight when it was realised that Russians lived indistinguishably among the non-Russian people of the Union, so that it would be impossible to discriminate.[52]

Another idea found its way more permanently into the targeting plans. Harold Brown testified to the Senate that the Soviet leadership were more concerned to preserve their power structure than their own lives or the lives of millions of their fellow citizens, a proposition for which he offered no concrete evidence.[53] So PD-59 contained the further thought that deterrence would be enhanced if the Soviet leaders and their government machine could be specifically targeted by very powerful bunker-busting missiles. The idea of targeting the Soviet leadership had been around at least since British strategists first started to talk about the 'Moscow criterion' in 1962. PD-59 left unanswered the question: how would you negotiate an end to nuclear war if there was nobody left to negotiate with?

The Russians of course also did their best to equip themselves to fight on the nuclear battlefield. They too interpreted their opponents' plans for conducting nuclear war as evidence of aggressive intention. Yuri Andropov, who had taken over as Soviet leader from Brezhnev two months earlier, told Warsaw Pact leaders in January 1983 that the Americans were no longer talking about deterrence: 'now, by creating the improved missile systems, they are not trying to conceal the fact that those are realistically designed for a future war. This is where the doctrines of a "rational" or "limited" nuclear war come from, this is the source of the arguments about the possibility to survive and to win in a protracted nuclear conflict. It is difficult to say which part of it is nuclear blackmail and which part represents readiness for a fatal step.'[54]

The generals on both sides naturally planned to win rather than lose the nuclear battle if it began. But, as always, one needs to distinguish between plans and intentions. There is no evidence that either side intended to launch a war in Europe, whether conventional or nuclear.

Victory without Strategy?

In the end the fine-spun concepts of the games players from RAND and elsewhere were ignored by the generals and hijacked by politicians, and the competing interests of government departments, the armed services, and industrial companies, as weapons in their complex intrigues and rivalries. Practice was invariably cruder than theory, and often bore little resemblance to it.

Senior veterans of the confrontation came together in 1994 at an American resort in Musgrove Plantation, Georgia, to try to make sense of it all. Admiral Stansfield Turner, a former Director of the CIA, remarked ruefully on that occasion that neither side seemed to have understood the fears, perceptions, and motivations of the other. The apparently endless cranking out of ever more exotic weapons, the tortured arguments about missile throw-weight, warhead numbers, missile vulnerability, and all the other technicalities which had so engaged both sides, had been without practical meaning. Neither side was ever able to destroy the other beyond risk of retaliation. The years of theological discussion, Turner concluded, had been totally irrelevant.[55]

American grand strategy proceeded from the premise that the Soviet Union was essentially evil, that it was unremittingly aggressive and expansionist, and that it aimed to impose its philosophy on the rest of the world by peaceful means if possible, but by force if necessary. These propositions were unsupported by real evidence. America was economically and technologically stronger than the Soviet Union. So American grand strategy was, often by inadvertence, magnificently simple. By putting all possible political and economic pressure on the Russians, always backed by the possibility of war, it could eventually force their retreat.

If success is the only criterion, American strategy worked: at the end of the confrontation the United States was standing, the Soviet Union was not. But this was hardly thanks to the clarity of US strategic thinking, which remained muddled until the end. Nor did it have much to do with the balance of nuclear power between the two. The Soviet Union was brought down above all by the declining viability of its political system, and its inability to compete economically.

SEVEN

UPDATING THE ART OF VICTORY

'Theory without practice is dead.'

Marshal Alexander Suvorov*

'Andrei Antonovich, are you sure this is just an exercise?'

Leonid Brezhnev to Marshal Grechko, 1972[1]

The Soviet Strategic Debate

The public pronouncements of Soviet politicians and senior officers on international affairs, like those of their American opposite
numbers, were suffused with ideology. The Russians proclaimed that
it was the final destiny of mankind to live under socialism; the Americans proclaimed that its natural state was to live under democracy.
Khrushchev may have been the last Soviet leader actually to believe
in the ideology more or less literally, though there are strong traces
of it even in the thinking of Mikhail Gorbachev, with whom the line
ended. But by inescapable convention, the ideology seeped into and
coloured official documents, including those about nuclear strategy.
This could lead to incoherence. In the mid-1970s the Soviet General
Staff Academy taught its students that 'in a nuclear war there will be
no winner or loser. However, Soviet strategy policy is that the victory
will belong to socialist countries because their aim in the war is just,
the morale of their population is higher, their national economic
system is better, and at the head of socialist governments are hard-
working people who are members of the Marxist–Leninist Party.'[2]

In the Soviet Union there was of course no proper public

---

* The Russian general Alexander Suvorov (1730–1800) never lost a battle. His brief
manual 'The Art of Victory' remains a classic. The thought in the epigraph is also
attributed to others, such as Karl Marx.

discussion to compare with the debate in America. The Soviet military were serious and responsible when they looked at the implications of nuclear war. But they conducted much of their discussion behind a thick veil of secrecy. Leaking was not a recognised tool of government in the Soviet Union. We do not have a series of high-level Soviet policy papers to match Truman's NSC-68 and Carter's PD-59; nor do we have the intelligence analyses on which they would have been based. Moreover, according to Sergei Tarasenko, an adviser to Gorbachev's Foreign Minister, Eduard Shevardnadze, the military kept their professional analysis to themselves: the diplomats 'had no conscious line about what kind of configuration of forces we wanted to have – the relative mix of various kinds of forces, or various kinds of weapons systems'.[3]

That made it harder to draw a comparison between the way the Russians and the Americans thought about nuclear war. But despite the secrecy, the debate occasionally broke cover.[4] In March 1960 Nikita Khrushchev triggered a discussion about the extent to which nuclear weapons had transformed the nature of war. There were lively theoretical exchanges in the open military press and more discreetly in the secret journal *Voennaya Mysl* (Military Thought). In 1963 the former Soviet Chief of the General Staff Marshal Vasili Sokolovsky produced a substantial volume on *Military Strategy: Soviet Doctrine and Concepts*, which represented an uneasy compromise between the conflicting views then being expressed among the military. Khrushchev caused it to be published: it was, he thought, a sobering reminder to American hotheads.[5]

In the 1960s Brezhnev set up a number of academic think tanks to broaden the debate, drawing on outside thinking in Russia and in America. Soviet doctors published their worries about radiation in 1962. In the 1970s and 1980s the cardiologist Evgeny Chazov, who was close to the leadership, investigated the medical and biological effects of nuclear war, drawing on American research.[6]

Among the most influential think tanks was the Institute of Canada and the USA, set up in 1967 by Georgi Arbatov. He was a fluent English speaker and a regular visitor to the United States, where he was unpopular among conservatives, who regarded him as no more than an agent of the KGB.[7] At home Arbatov had to put up with vicious attacks from the military, who resented his refusal to take them at their own estimation and his belief that the military-industrial complex was pursuing its own narrow interests at the expense of those of the country as a whole.

Although Arbatov had fought with distinction in the Second World War, the formidable Marshal Andrei Grechko dismissed him with ponderous sarcasm: 'Since Comrade Arbatov is not at all a military man, I do not think that he should take it upon himself to give advice and make proposals about military matters ... We who have spent our whole lives in the army sometimes know better how to resolve this or that problem in the military sphere.' Arbatov made himself equally unpopular with the KGB.[8]

Arbatov later admitted, 'In addition to our mistakes, and our inability to break away sufficiently quickly from our stereotyped ideas and even language, we were also thrown off balance by an elementary lack of knowledge which rendered even the most perceptive researcher impotent.'[9] His son Aleksei was one of the most distinguished and sober-minded commentators on Russian military affairs in the twenty-first century, and provided a necessary counterpoint to some of the noisy rhetoric of the new generation of Russian nationalists.

Stripped of Marxist–Leninist jargon and the sterile formulae about imperialist aggression, public statements by Soviet leaders, Soviet military writing, and the testimony of senior officials and generals once the Cold War was over gave a reasonable idea of what the Russians thought about the complicated tangle of political and military problems they faced.

In the West there was often an assumption that the authoritarian Soviet system was purposeful, disciplined, and single-minded, capable of effectively coordinating its military, political, and industrial policies to a single end. That was not so: the Soviet system was no more coherent than governmental systems in the West. Even under Stalin it was riven by inter-service rivalry, industrial and political intrigue, jockeying for position, and personal ambition. It was worse under his successors. Such things affected the evolution of strategy in the Soviet Union, just as they did in the West. General Andrian Danilevich, who was involved in the planning of Soviet strategy for much of his career, made the point with force: 'if you look for some rational reason, you will be lost. When I first came to the General Staff in 1963, I thought that every decision was thoroughly worked out and researched until they got the right answer. Later I understood this was not so.' It was necessary to make military plans for all possible eventualities. But even though you could plan for 1,000 scenarios, he liked to say, it would be the 1,001st that hit you. It was, he said, 'a very slippery situation'.[10] Those who have served in Western military or official organisations will recognise the problem from personal experience.

Some Western analysts nevertheless condescendingly accused the Russians of failing to understand the subtleties and recommended sending teams of experts to the Soviet Union to enlighten them. Paul Warnke, the head of the US Arms Control and Disarmament Agency, said in 1977 that the Soviet idea that you could fight and win a nuclear war was 'on a level of abstraction which is unrealistic. It seems to me that … we ought to be trying to educate them into the real world of strategic nuclear weapons, which is that nobody could possibly win.' As one American rightly commented, American strategists tended to forget 'that ours is not the universal language and that an apparent stupidity can mask a fully developed opinion of an altogether different kind'.[11]

Although they kept abreast of it, the Russians thought that American strategic theorising and the peculiar jargon that went with it were overelaborate. Theoretical constructs such as 'strategic stability', 'nuclear sufficiency', 'massive retaliation', 'counterforce strategy', 'controlled escalation' – all that was unlikely to be relevant under the stress of nuclear war.[12]

The Russians proceeded in effect from four comparatively simple principles. First, the Soviet Union had to match or outmatch the Americans in every category of weapon if it was to avoid nuclear blackmail or nuclear destruction. Second, even nuclear weapons were there to be used in an extremity, so they had to be incorporated into Soviet war-fighting plans. Third, the working assumption of the Soviet military was that the object even of a nuclear war was victory, even though Soviet politicians were well aware that 'victory' in this context had little meaning. Fourth, attacks on cities for their own sake made little sense because of the risk of retaliation: the Russians eschewed 'countervalue' targeting, though they would have been as likely as the Americans to hit cities if it had come to an exchange. All this was little different in essence from the assumptions which underlay American thinking. Both sides talked about 'victory' in nuclear war from time to time in order to show determination and thus enhance deterrence. That was not surprising, since the laws which governed nuclear weapons were the same everywhere.

Russian thinking was, however, coloured by the humiliation, as they saw it, of the 1962 Cuban missile crisis, when superior American power forced Khrushchev to abandon his bid to equalise the stakes by placing Soviet missiles within range of Washington. Thereafter the Russians were determined to level the playing field by developing a full panoply of nuclear weapons and their launchers – bombers, submarines, and missiles.[13]

All Russians vividly remembered the German surprise attack of June 1941 which had nearly destroyed their country. The Soviet military believed that it was now their primary task to do all they could to prevent or counter a similar surprise attack by the Americans. A key figure in the later military debates was Marshal Sergei Akhromeyev, the Chief of the General Staff. Highly intelligent, with an ironic sense of humour, he was a distinguished veteran of the Second World War who later served in Afghanistan, a man much respected by the Americans who negotiated with him.* Asked by Anatoli Dobrynin, the Soviet ambassador in Washington, whether he believed the Americans might attack the Soviet Union, he replied, 'It is not my mission to believe, or not to believe … We proceed from the worst possible scenario of having to fight the United States, its

---

* Paul Nitze, the American hawk who later became a flexible negotiator, first dealt with Akhromeyev at the Reykjavik summit in October 1986. He found Akhromeyev a man of great courage and character, a first-class negotiator in a bad cause. When Akhromeyev quoted Fenimore Cooper to George Shultz, Reagan's Secretary of State at Reykjavik, he was perhaps unduly impressed by Akhromeyev's grasp of American culture, not knowing that *The Last of the Mohicans* was something every Soviet child read at school (G. Shultz, *Turmoil and Triumph*, New York, 1993, p. 763).

European allies, and probably Japan. We must be prepared for any kind of war with any kind of weapon. Soviet military doctrine can be summed up as follows: 1941 shall never be repeated.'[14]

His attitude was shared by his military colleagues. General Viktor Starodubov, a principal adviser to the Soviet General Staff on arms control, said in 1994, 'We were afraid that the US could just wipe out the small number of strategic forces that we had, and then dictate their conditions to us. That is why we considered the possibility of a launch under attack, or a strike immediately after we got a signal about a nuclear attack from the United States. Later, when we had achieved relative parity, we considered only the option of a retaliatory strike. The idea behind it was deterrence, even though on our side this term – "deterrence" – was not used at all for a long time. But in fact the concept of deterrence existed from the very beginning of the existence of the Soviet strategic forces.'[15]

Worst-case planning was as deeply lodged in Soviet military thinking as it was in American.

General Secretaries Contemplate Nuclear War

Stalin: Nuclear Strategy from a Position of Weakness
Stalin's first priorities after the war were domestic: to secure his own rule, to restore the discipline that had been relaxed during the war, and to stamp down on any new-fangled ideas that the returning soldiers might have brought back with them from Europe.

He needed of course to rebuild the Soviet Union's war-shattered economy. But he needed also to maintain sufficient armed strength to keep order at home, impose it on the countries of Eastern Europe, dominate the Soviet half of defeated Germany, and ward off any adventures that might tempt his former Western allies. He had rapidly demobilised the Soviet armed forces at the end of the war, and there was no margin for the assault on Western Europe which so many Western observers feared at the time. George Kennan, the clear-sighted American ambassador in Moscow, concluded in September 1952 that 'the Kremlin leaders had no desire … to become involved in another foreign war for the foreseeable future, and this – in terms of Soviet policy determination – meant anything up to fifteen or twenty years.'[16]

Stalin stuck with the combination of strategic and ideological principles that had shaped his policies before the war. The first priority had to be to strengthen the Soviet Union. If the Soviet Union was overwhelmed by its enemies, world socialism could not survive.

But Soviet ideology insisted that Communism was bound to triumph: that was the Mandate of History. Hence it followed that the Soviet Union could survive even a nuclear war. While the Soviet Union was relatively weak, it needed to be cautious day by day. But it could not abandon promising opportunities to spread the revolution further. If, for example, revolution occurred in Western Europe – perhaps in France or Italy, where the Communist Parties were very large – Soviet forces in Eastern Germany and Central Europe should be able to intervene in support, or at least deter a counter-revolution.

In 1942 Stalin had listed certain 'permanently operating factors' which determined victory or defeat in war: the stability of the home front (the 'rear' in Soviet parlance), the morale and size of the army, the quantity and quality of its weapons, and the ability of its commanders. These remained the conditions of victory. Russia had been thoroughly surprised by Hitler's attack on the Soviet Union in June 1941, but had nevertheless emerged victorious. Now Stalin argued that a surprise attack, even with nuclear weapons, could not in itself determine the outcome. The Soviet system would ultimately prevail in war or in 'peaceful competition' with the capitalist world. Surprise, thought Stalin, might win battles. But it could not win wars.

Stalin's contention was not simply a bluff or a failure of imagination. He knew that the Americans had neither the bombs nor the bombers to deliver a serious strike against the Soviet Union until the end of the 1940s. But the American monopoly nevertheless had a political impact, which he was determined to minimise. He publicly downplayed the significance of nuclear weapons to compensate for the Soviet Union's lack of them. But until his scientists had broken the American monopoly, he needed to play for time.

Khrushchev Recognises the Dangers
The Soviet military initially shared Stalin's view that the next war would resemble the last. An attack by a foreign enemy – this time the Anglo-Americans, not the Germans – would be repelled in a

protracted war. They hoped at first that their country's vast expanse could serve them as it had done in Russia's earlier wars. Industry could be dispersed, people could be evacuated or sheltered, and the country could weather even a nuclear attack. In February 1954 Marshal Vasilevsky, the man who had routed the Japanese in Manchuria in 1945, was still arguing that 'the outcome of war is determined not by the collateral factors but by the permanently operating factors'.[17]

Marshal Andrei Grechko, another war veteran, was Warsaw Pact commander, Chief of Staff, and then Minister of Defence from 1960. He too remembered how the Soviet Union had been caught napping in 1941, and he was determined it should not happen again. He had little patience with the idea that the Soviet Union should be able to survive a first strike and then retaliate, and little interest in the development of the smaller, more accurate, and better-protected missiles that would be needed for a second strike. For him, nuclear weapons were no different in essence from any others. The war, he thought, would be won by the side that had the largest number of powerful missiles and used them first. The Soviet Union should retaliate with a full-scale nuclear strike against any Western use of nuclear weapons, even in symbolic numbers against subsidiary targets. He effectively resisted attempts to change Soviet strategy and force structures in a more sophisticated direction. Younger staff officers thought him 'a saber-waving horse soldier of limited intellect'. He remained an obstacle to arms control agreements with the Americans until his death in 1976.[18]

Soviet military thinking nevertheless evolved as the Soviet Union tested its first atomic bomb in 1949, its first usable hydrogen bomb in 1955, and its first two-stage ballistic missile in 1957.[19] Since their bomber programme could not match the Americans', the Russians concentrated instead on developing more advanced intercontinental missiles and a submarine missile system as an answer to the American Polaris. By 1965 they had taken the decisions which would enable them to achieve not strategic superiority, but a kind of parity.

Over the next decade the Soviet military discussed how to ward off a surprise attack with great intensity. In 1955 Marshal Rotmistrov and General Talensky argued in *Voennaya Mysl* that the 'permanently operating factors' were neither a law of war nor a guarantee of Soviet victory. Economic, political, and military strength would no doubt be the deciding factors in an extended war. But a surprise attack with nuclear weapons could bring immediate victory to the attacker. The Russians needed to have the option of striking first if they thought the Americans were about to attack. But Rotmistrov emphasised that 'Striving to seize and hold the strategic initiative must not be understood as intention to start a preventive war against the enemies of the USSR who are preparing to attack us.' This remained the Soviet position in public and in private until the end of the Cold War.[20]

Soviet military and civilian leaders continued to pay lip service to their ideological belief in the ultimate victory of Communism. But reality inevitably pressed in on ideology and eventually prevailed. Even those who were nowhere near the centre of the Soviet policy-making machine could see the contradictions in the official policy: Mikhail Botvinnik, the reigning world chess champion, wrote to the Party leadership in 1954 to ask how one was 'supposed to match the danger of nuclear annihilation with the official ideological thesis that wars were begun by the imperialist "warmongers"'.[21]

The discussion continued to centre first on the vexed question of surprise attack. Could a country's political and military leadership, its forces in the field, its economic capacity, much of its population – Stalin's 'permanently operating factors' – be destroyed by nuclear weapons at a single blow? Or was it still possible to wage a protracted war, perhaps because both sides decided to refrain from using nuclear weapons, or because they voluntarily limited their use by some process of agreed or implied mutual restraint?

But the Russians inevitably became more interested in the idea of deterrence rather than war-fighting, and of nuclear weapons as an essential, if not sufficient, instrument for preventing war. The core of the debate began to shift. In March 1954 Georgi Malenkov, the Prime Minister, was the first Soviet leader to say publicly that a world war in the nuclear age 'would mean the end of world civilisation'. Since the capitalists now understood that the Soviet Union had the capacity to destroy their cities, disagreements with them could be settled by compromise. Resources could then be switched from defence to the consumer.[22]

In April 1954 Vyacheslav Malyshev and Igor Kurchatov presented a remarkable paper to the First Party Secretary Nikita Khrushchev, who was to take effective power from Malenkov a year later. The paper was entitled 'The Dangers of Atomic War and President Eisenhower's Proposal' and was a commentary on ideas which Eisenhower had introduced the previous December in the United Nations. Eisenhower had warned of 'the probability of civilization destroyed – the annihilation of the irreplaceable heritage of mankind handed down to us generation from generation' if an international regime were not set in place to halt the nuclear arms race.[23] Picking up on these ideas, Malyshev and Kurchatov told the leaders in no uncertain terms that 'Today's atomic technology, based on the exploitation of thermonuclear reaction, makes it possible to increase the explosive energy contained in a bomb practically without limit … Since there is no practical defence against such a bomb, it is clear that the use of atomic weapons on a mass scale will lead to the devastation of the warring countries … And so one is forced to recognise that an immense threat hangs over humanity which could end all life on Earth.'[24]

One leading Soviet weapons scientist, Viktor Adamsky, believed that this letter awakened the Soviet leadership to the full danger of the thermonuclear weapon and fundamentally changed their attitude to nuclear war.[25] But the change did not happen overnight. Malenkov launched his ideas about nuclear war in the middle of the sharp competition for power which followed Stalin's death. Khrushchev attacked him for defeatism at a Central Committee meeting in April 1954. The Americans might fear the destruction of world civilisation, but American behaviour could be dangerously irrational, he warned. The Soviet Union needed to increase its military strength to deter them effectively.

Once he had forced Malenkov out of office in February 1955, Khrushchev stole his clothing. After meeting Eisenhower in Geneva in July 1955 he concluded that 'our enemies were afraid of us in the same way as we were of them'.[26] At the 20th Party Congress in March 1956 – the occasion on which he denounced Stalin in his 'Secret Speech' – he pushed through a resolution which asserted that the Soviet Union and its allies had the means to rein in the warlike ambitions of the capitalists: 'there is no fatal inevitability of war.' He suggested that there could be no victor in a nuclear war, though he wriggled a bit by adding the qualification that thermonuclear war was disastrous but possible; and that if it occurred capitalism would perish but civilisation would not. Western leaders, too, were still arguing that their society and values would survive nuclear war. There was not much logic on either side.

Some of Khrushchev's colleagues, such as Molotov, were unhappy that he was abandoning Stalin's ideological legacy.[27] But on the whole his ideas prevailed. In 1960 the Soviet Party journal *Kommunist* rubbished the idea that nuclear war could further the triumph of socialism. On the contrary, it would be a catastrophe which would 'in no way be a factor that would accelerate the revolution and bring nearer the victory of socialism'.[28] An international Communist meeting spoke of a 'serious threat to all mankind', the possibility that hundreds of millions would die in a nuclear war. It was the 'historic mission' of Communists 'to save mankind from the nightmare of a new world war'.[29]

Khrushchev was an unlikely man to grapple with the intellectual, moral, and political complexities of the nuclear age. A peasant from the Ukrainian border who had connived at some of Stalin's worst crimes, he nevertheless, in the view of one seasoned but admiring foreign observer, had 'a breadth of understanding and a depth of vision unusual in politicians of any stamp ... rough, domineering, violent, sometimes vindictive, boastful, filled with a peasant cunning, quite uneducated in the conventional sense, and with a mind that was never fully trained, [who] nevertheless embodied certain qualities of character, imagination, perhaps even humility, which set him apart from his colleagues'.[30]

This man now began to move towards a more sophisticated idea of nuclear military power, closer to 'Mutually Assured Destruction'. He somewhat lifted the inhibition on public discussion, as part of his policy of allowing a bit more openness in public life. Despite objections from his security people, he took Kurchatov on his visit to Britain in spring 1956. His aim was threefold: to show that, unlike Stalin, he trusted the Soviet intelligentsia; to demonstrate his pride in Soviet science; and to make the point that Western domination of the nuclear weapon was over. In Downing Street he introduced Kurchatov to Churchill as 'Academician Kurchatov, the man who makes our hydrogen bomb'. Kurchatov lectured to the British Atomic Energy Research Establishment at Harwell on the latest Soviet research on controlled fusion, a degree of technical openness which went beyond what was then current on either side of the Atlantic. Even Edward Teller was impressed by the substance of the report.[31]

Since Khrushchev no longer believed in the possibility of a protracted war he argued that missiles would be the dominant weapon in future. Conventional weapons, navies, and large land forces were becoming obsolescent. Like Eisenhower, he concluded that this would make it possible to cut back on conventional military expenditure and spend the money elsewhere. In January 1960 he announced that the armed forces would be reduced by 1.2 million men in three years. A quarter of a million officers were retired, many without compensation or provision for adequate housing.[32] Cuts were made in plans to procure tanks, bombers, and surface naval vessels. In January 1961 Khrushchev told the Supreme Soviet that the Soviet Union should be able to survive a first strike by virtue of its size, and then retaliate; but the aim was to deter a war, not to fight it.[33]

The military were not best pleased. Several senior Soviet officers pointed out in *Voennaya Mysl* that Khrushchev's overwhelming emphasis on strategic weapons would reduce the Soviet Union's ability to wage conventional war – the only sort of war that was, in practice, likely to occur in the nuclear age. With an inadequate conventional force the country could end up with a choice between surrender and a potentially suicidal nuclear exchange. In October 1964 the generals joined those who overthrew Khrushchev.

The Brezhnev Years: Détente and Its Demise

As the 1960s wore on, the Russians became more confident of the efficacy of their weapons and turned further towards the idea of mutual deterrence. In 1967 the commander of the Strategic Rocket Forces argued that efficient early warning and alert systems would prevent 'the aggressor from hitting the missiles on the opponent's territory before they can be launched. Even in the most unfavourable case when some of the missiles fail to launch before the aggressor's attack, they will still survive thanks to the high protection of the launchers against a nuclear explosion, and they will still be able to carry out their combat mission.' Thus even after a first strike each side would retain the capacity to devastate the other.[34]

As the discussion broadened out the Russians had to ask themselves some immediate questions which required practical and early answers. Should the Soviet Union build on its existing missiles, liquid-fuelled, cumbersome, unprotected by hardened silos, effectively the first strike force favoured by Marshal Grechko? Or should it go for highly accurate multiple-warhead missiles in hardened silos, which would enable the country to ride out a first strike and retaliate?

Rather surprisingly, perhaps, the debate was carried into its next stage by Leonid Brezhnev, who was Secretary General from 1964 until his death in 1982. Brezhnev was not one of the most distinguished or imaginative Soviet leaders. The physical decline of his later years cast a retrospective shadow over his reputation. But he was an effective politician: he would not otherwise have gained high office or retained it for so long. His personal physician, Evgeny Chazov, later wrote in his memoirs, at a time when Brezhnev was regarded among the Moscow intelligentsia as a figure of fun, that he was 'impressive and smart in appearance, with a military bearing, a pleasant smile, a way of encouraging you to open up in conversation, a sense of humour … and he knew his stuff.'[35] He was nevertheless poorly educated, had little grasp of economics, was mild in manner but vain and corrupt. After his first stroke in 1974 he was increasingly unable to run the country. And yet his colleagues allowed him to remain in office until his death, a measure of how dysfunctional the Soviet political system had already become.

Brezhnev's domestic purpose was simple: to stabilise the system after the upheavals of Khrushchev's time. That led him to resist reform, crack down sharply on opposition and dissidence, retain the conservative old guard – and thus inadvertently to push the Soviet Union further along the road to collapse. He made a number of gestures towards ordinary Soviet people which were much appreciated at the time: a five-day week, pension reform, a better deal for collective farmers, a modest improvement in the supply of consumer goods. But the trial in 1966 of the writers Andrei Sinyavsky and Yuri Daniel, who had published satirical works in the West, was the first such move against intellectuals since Stalin's day. It marked the beginning of a new – though by earlier Soviet standards comparatively modest – wave of repression.

Brezhnev also remained determined, like his predecessors, to continue the policy of expanding Soviet power and influence abroad. There was a key ideological principle at stake: the 'international class struggle', which cast the capitalist world – and especially the United States – as the unrelenting enemy, and bound the Soviet Union to support the 'national liberation movements' in Central America, the Horn of Africa, and in Angola with economic aid, political support, weapons, and military advice in increasing volumes throughout the 1970s.

Until the ill-fated invasion of Afghanistan in December 1979, these adventures led to few casualties: only 145 Soviet personnel died in the Third World between 1962 and 1979.[36] But they inevitably aroused the suspicion and hostility of the American government, undermined Brezhnev's desire to reach an accommodation with the United States on the nuclear matter, and thus, as Georgi Arbatov said, 'played into the hands of the extreme rightwingers in the United States'.[37] Anatoli Chernyaev, one of his advisers, saw Brezhnev as a Faust-like figure, torn between two angels: the angel of realism and common sense, and the angel of ideological and imperial ambition.[38]

But Brezhnev did feel deeply about one thing: his responsibility as leader of the other nuclear superpower. He was of course associated with the Soviet invasion of Czechoslovakia in 1968, and this left a deep shadow over his pretensions to be a peacemaker. But demonstrating to his conservative colleagues that he was prepared to stick up for Soviet interests in the old-fashioned way may paradoxically have strengthened his hand when he came to pursue his policy of détente: the arms agreements with the Americans, the settlement on Berlin of 1972, the Helsinki agreements of 1975.[39] He stuck firmly to the view that nuclear war of any kind would be catastrophic and that the idea of 'victory' in a nuclear war made no sense. '[W]orld war with the employment of nuclear missile weapons,' he said in 1967, 'would lead to the death of hundreds of millions of people, to the annihilation of entire countries, to the contamination of the atmosphere and surface of the Earth.'[40]

In 1972 he and his Prime Minister, Aleksei Kosygin, took part in an exercise to model the consequences of a nuclear first strike against the Soviet Union. The soldiers explained that, according to their calculations, the Soviet armed forces would be reduced to a mere 1,000th of their previous strength; 80 million citizens would be dead; 85 per cent of Soviet industry would be destroyed; the European part of the USSR would be lethally contaminated by radiation. The Soviet retaliatory strike would be even more destructive. 'When the time came to push the button,' General Danilevich remembered, 'Brezhnev was visibly shaken and pale and his hand trembled and he asked Grechko several times for assurances that the action would not have any real-world consequences. "Andrei Antonovich, are you sure this is just an exercise?"'*

Georgi Arbatov later wrote, 'No one doubted that Brezhnev was weak on the theory, especially the theory of international relations. But he stood with his feet on the ground, especially in that first period of his leadership of the country, and understood very well, in the manner of the man in the street, that the highest priority for the nation was the preservation of peace. And he saw clearly that openly pushing towards that goal was a reliable way of securing the popularity of his policy and of himself. And I am sure that he was sincere in that objective, since he had fought in the war.'[41]

Brezhnev was nevertheless under continual pressure from conservatives in the Party and government, who were determined to stick to the path of orthodoxy. 'I genuinely want peace and will never back down,' he once said. 'Some people, however, dislike this policy ... [They] are inside the Kremlin. They are people like me. Only they think differently!'[42] To bolster him against his conservative colleagues, Brezhnev recruited a group of comparatively liberal advisers, many of whom had emerged during Khrushchev's 'thaw' in the 1960s. These spoke for his 'good angel', people such as Arbatov, Nikolai Inozemtsev of the Institute of World Economy and International Relations (IMEMO), Vadim Zagladin of the International Department of the Central Committee, and others who were able to think new thoughts and offset the pressures from the old guard.[43]

---

* In subsequent exercises involving Soviet politicians, the military ensured that the scenarios were less menacing (J. Hines et al., *Soviet Intentions 1965–1985, Vol. II*, Washington, DC, 1995, pp. 27–8).

The debate within Brezhnev's entourage was real. The conservatives, too, were aware of the dangers of nuclear war and conscious of the growing dysfunction of the Soviet state. Andrei Sakharov warned Brezhnev directly in 1970 that 'dislocation and stagnation' in the economy would continue to grow unless something was done about the 'anti-democratic norms of public life' set by Stalin. The head of the State Planning Commission, Nikolai Baibakov, reinforced the message when he told the Politburo in 1974 that the economy was in serious trouble. Morale declined among the Party's own officials as they realised the extent and nature of the crisis. Among ordinary people discontent grew as the volume and variety of goods in the shops declined. Boris Yeltsin, then First Party Secretary of the Sverdlovsk Region, told his people in 1981 that food rationing would continue: families could expect no more than a kilo of meat products per person on holiday occasions – that is, twice a year on May Day and Revolution Day. In per capita consumption the Soviet Union was, by the late 1980s, in seventy-seventh place in the world; 44 per cent of Soviet pensioners received less than the official subsistence minimum.[44]

But there was no agreement over what should be done: the failure of Khrushchev's ham-fisted reforms in the 1960s had left people disinclined to repeat his mistakes. The liberals were nevertheless convinced that the country could no longer sustain the economic burden of imperial expansion and the arms race. The solution was to abandon the international class struggle, expand the accommodations of détente, and relax the rigid political controls at home which stifled economic initiative and enterprise. Only thus could the Soviet Union prosper – or even survive. When Brezhnev, during his visit to America in 1973, said, 'Humanity has outgrown the straitjacket of the Cold War, it wants to breathe freely and spontaneously,' he seemed to be saying what the liberals wanted to hear.[45]

Such ideas were anathema to the 'conservatives', those who spoke for Brezhnev's 'bad angel', elderly men such as the influential Second Party Secretary responsible for ideological orthodoxy, Mikhail Suslov, who wielded almost as much authority as Brezhnev himself; Andrei Gromyko, the Foreign Minister; Yuri Andropov, the Chairman of the KGB; Andrei Grechko and his successor as Defence Minister, Dmitri

Ustinov, a powerful veteran of the defence industry. These were able and intelligent men, and they were convinced that success abroad and stability at home were based on military power and ideological orthodoxy. The military and the defence industry, who were still receiving the lion's share of the Soviet budget, naturally agreed. The biggest arms build-up in Soviet history took place under Brezhnev.[46]

Much as they disliked the intellectual and political inadequacy and blatant careerism of the Soviet leadership, Anatoli Chernyaev and his fellows were grateful for the ambiguities of Brezhnev's inconsistent mixture of common sense and ideological orthodoxy. The success of Brezhnev's visit to America, the ending of twenty years of mutual abuse, the signature of unprecedented strategic and political agreements between the two superpowers, represented a remarkable reversal of events – 'provided,' Chernyaev prudently noted in his diary, 'there is no restoration of the old ways, as there was after the Twentieth Party Congress', which marked the beginning of Khrushchev's short-lived policy of de-Stalinisation. '[H]owever paradoxical it may seem,' Chernyaev later wrote, 'the confirmation of Brezhnev as sole leader guaranteed international détente for a while (at least until the beginning of his final psychological and intellectual collapse),'[47]

But by the middle of the decade Brezhnev's health – and with it détente – were entering a steep decline. With the deployment of SS-20 missiles in the Western Soviet Union in 1978, the invasion of Afghanistan in December 1979, and the Polish crisis in 1980, détente came to an end. Ronald Reagan became President and the 'Second Cold War' began.

The Threat to Europe

For each side, Europe was both a hostage and a possible prize. There is no evidence that the Russians ever hoped to incorporate Western Europe by military means. But Stalin and Khrushchev had some hope that political pressure and blackmail might at least enable them to neutralise West Germany. And over the years the Russians built up a formidable concentration of aircraft, tanks, guns, and soldiers in East Germany and Eastern Europe, supported by the armies of their allies in the Warsaw Pact, which Soviet generals claimed to believe would be reliable in the event of war. Western military planners were bound to consider them as a potential invasion force. By the 1980s, Chernyaev sourly noted, 'the noisy language in the West about the Soviet threat was based on facts'. It was a thought echoed by Anatoli Dobrynin, the Soviet ambassador, who commented in his diary that the Russians were 'feverishly building up our nuclear and conventional arms in Europe beyond any reasonable measure'.[48]

Because of the Russians' conventional superiority, it was NATO's proclaimed policy to use nuclear weapons first to stop them if they attacked in Europe. Russian proposals that the two sides should pledge not to be the first to use nuclear weapons were, NATO believed, merely intended to make it safe for the Russians to launch a conventional attack.[49] So they dismissed the Russian proposals as propaganda, as perhaps they largely were. They were in any case meaningless, since such a pledge would have little force in a serious crisis.

After the end of the Cold War the situation was reversed. Russia's conventional forces all but collapsed. The Russians proclaimed that they would use their nuclear forces first to defend themselves or their allies against aggression. Now it was the turn of the West to accuse the Russians of playing irresponsibly with nuclear fire.

The Russians did indeed devise plans to advance to the German border and on to the English Channel. At first they believed that nuclear strikes against NATO airfields and other targets would clear the way for them to reach their objectives in a matter of days.* But in the 1970s further research showed that the chaos caused by the strikes would halt all serious movement for days. The resulting fallout would contaminate Eastern Europe and parts of the Soviet Union.

---

* Material discovered in the East German archives after the Cold War indicated that in the late 1970s and early 1980s the Warsaw Pact planned and trained to use nuclear weapons first in a surprise attack on Europe. Assertions that this meant the Warsaw Pact actually intended to attack are a classic confusion between plans and intentions (*Military Planning of the Warsaw Pact in Central Europe: A Study, Based on Records from the East German National People's Army (NVA)*, Federal German Ministry of Defence: see *International History Project Bulletin*, Issue 2, Fall 1992. An account of the debate surrounding the report is given in J. Hines et al., *Soviet Intentions 1965–1985, Vol. II*, Washington, DC, 1995, pp. 41–4).

The Soviet planners concluded that the use of nuclear weapons in a European campaign would probably defeat its own object: 'short-range land-based nuclear weapons are the most inconvenient and dangerous for all countries in the deterrence arsenal.'[50]

They did, however, think that the Warsaw Pact would have the advantage if the war remained conventional. So in the mid-1970s, under the energetic and intelligent leadership of Marshal Nikolai Ogarkov, who was Chief of the General Staff from 1977 to 1984, they turned their attention to ways of conducting and winning a purely conventional war. These were encapsulated in the three-volume *Strategy of Deep Operations* produced between 1977 and 1988 by a team on the General Staff under General Danilevich. This envisaged an overwhelming attack by massive ground and air forces to reach the Rhine in five to seven days, and remained the Russians' basic strategic document for the remainder of the Cold War.* The advance would be covered by highly powerful, accurate, and mobile SS-20 missiles, which could hit all the major cities of Western Europe, and which the Russians began to deploy from 1976. These formidable weapons would, the General Staff believed or hoped, deter NATO from any nuclear response to a Soviet conventional offensive. To maximise the surprise, the attack would be launched under cover of preparations for a military exercise. The Soviet armies would move with such devastating speed that NATO would be unable to organise a coherent defence. These ambitious plans were tested in a major exercise, Operation Zapad (West) in 1981. They had already been picked up by Western intelligence and helped to stoke an answering American arms build-up.[51] But they suffered from a fundamental flaw. By the mid-1980s Ogarkov himself was arguing that the Soviet Union had neither the technology nor the economic resources to implement them.

Yuri Andropov argued that the SS-20s were no more than a modernisation of tactical weapons the Russians already had in Europe. But Georgi Arbatov pointed out that the deployment of the SS-20s would

---

* By 1985 NATO had developed a matching strategy, 'Follow on Forces Attack'. This broke with NATO's previous defensive strategy design to stop Soviet forces reaching the Rhine, in favour of deep lunges into Eastern Europe with highly sophisticated new weapons.

be hugely expensive, unite NATO, and give NATO every excuse to deploy similar missiles themselves.[52] Arbatov was right. America and its allies saw the SS-20s as a deliberate attempt to blackmail the Europeans. Tempers flared on both sides. The Russians eventually recognised that, whatever the military rationale, they had made a serious political error by deploying the SS-20s in the first place.

What would actually have happened if fighting had begun in Europe, and who if anyone would have used nuclear weapons first, is of course unknowable.

Radical Thinking among the Generals

As détente failed and East–West tension grew in the early 1980s with the arrival on the scene of Ronald Reagan, some Soviet generals began once again to write about the possibility of victory in an all-out confrontation. The Second World War had left them, like everyone else in the country, determined to avoid another war at all costs. But the decision did not rest with the Russians alone. Their potential enemies had made it clear that if necessary they would not hesitate to use their tactical nuclear weapons first. The Soviet Union had no option but to match them. If it were attacked, they argued, it needed to be able immediately to launch a massive counterattack into enemy territory, if necessary with nuclear weapons.

But these generals did not have the deciding view. Defence Minister Dmitri Ustinov said firmly that 'the USSR does not count on achieving military victory in nuclear war'.[53] The 1983 edition of the *Soviet Military Encyclopedia*, reflecting what was becoming an orthodoxy, said that Soviet military theory rejected the idea of limited nuclear war because it could not be contained.

The worries of ordinary people were increasingly reflected in the press. In 1982 the cultural-political weekly *Literaturnaya Gazeta* wrote, 'The danger today ... lies in the fact that casual statements [in the West] about first and pre-emptive strikes, about demonstrative detonations, and about the acceptability of either limited or protracted nuclear war depending on the circumstances, create a nervous atmosphere and increase the danger of the accidental outbreak of war. When people are nervous, things can go wrong ... If events get out of control no "hotline" is going to be of any help.'[54]

In 1985 Marshal Ogarkov, who as Chief of the General Staff had driven the planning for the *Strategy of Deep Operations* in the 1970s, broke publicly with the old argument that, even in the nuclear age, war made sense as a continuation of policy by other means: 'Only if one lost one's common sense entirely could one try to find arguments and set goals that could justify unleashing world war and thus risking the complete annihilation of the human race. Thus it is an indisputable conclusion that it is criminal to consider thermonuclear war as a rational and seemingly "legal" means of continuing policy.'[55] General Chervov, who had helped to negotiate the arms agreements with the Americans, added that humanity was going through an exceptionally dangerous period. The prevention of nuclear war was now the most imperative task it faced. General Volkogonov, the head of the Army's Political Administration, whose unorthodox ideas later embroiled him with his military colleagues, wrote in *Pravda* in August 1985 that 'the issue is no longer victory or defeat, but existence or annihilation … True security now consists not in achieving victory in war, but in preventing a nuclear cataclysm.'[56]

Disillusion
The Soviet civilian experts had already begun to chime in publicly. In 1983 Professor Vitali Zhurkin strongly criticised Western theories that an limited nuclear exchange could be followed by successful attempts to bring the conflict under control. Such misconceptions were highly dangerous. Any use of nuclear weapons would cross the Rubicon and trigger a chain of irreversible developments. It would endanger the vital interests of the other side and provoke a retaliatory strike. Nuclear war was not a 'joint venture', not a game with known rules and restrictions, but the most serious catastrophe in human history. Academician Yevgeni Velikhov, the distinguished physicist who advised the Soviet government on disarmament matters, added that even a 'limited' nuclear war in Europe would mean the destruction of European civilisation.[57]

By the end of the decade the civilian commentators were becoming ever more outspoken. They launched the idea of 'reasonable sufficiency' (which the Russians had rejected when it was first formulated by Nixon) and 'non-offensive defence' to demand cuts in the bloated Soviet military inventory. In 1990 Sergei Blagovolin of the Institute of National Security and Strategic Studies wrote that 'an analysis of the events of recent years leads to the conclusion that the scale of our military preparations, whether one likes it or not, has exceeded all reasonable parameters'.[58]

These ripening ideas entered a new phase when the Politburo elected Mikhail Gorbachev as General Secretary of the Soviet Communist Party in March 1985. By then an increasing number of people had begun to realise that 'the danger of war came not from imperialism but from the very existence of adversarial confrontation and deterrence based on alert nuclear weapons'.[59] Gorbachev made it clear that he too believed that Soviet society and the Soviet economy had been undermined by the excessive proportion of the national wealth devoted to armed forces that had been inflated beyond any utility.

Marshal Akhromeyev admitted that it was difficult for the generals to revise their thinking in the direction Gorbachev wanted. Throughout their careers, he and his colleagues had been dominated by ideas they had inherited from the great Soviet generals of the Second World War. But they recognised that their task was no longer to think in simple military terms. Military policy had to work hand-in-hand with foreign policy. Its main aim was now to prevent a war rather than fight one. In order to give politics a chance to bring the fighting to an end, the military now envisaged that the Soviet Union would initially confine itself to fighting a defensive battle. They would counterattack only if negotiation failed. Akhromeyev persuaded himself that 'the new Soviet foreign policy ... led to a lowering of military tensions, to a lessening of the military danger for the Soviet Union, and that was achieved not by military but by political means.'

But it was a hard time for some of his colleagues, 'a time of great shocks'.[60] The normally cool General Danilevich said with unusual passion that arms control agreements negotiated with the Americans 'were strongly opposed by the military because the concessions that we made outweighed the benefits by two, three, four times, but we were forced into these concessions because we saw that not to concede would not solve the main problem. The picture at these negotiations was very complicated and very dramatic. If it were described factually and in detail, showing what effect it had on our hearts and minds, it would be a tragedy, in the spirit of Shakespeare. We were forced to sign something that our hearts were against.'[61]

EIGHT

STRATEGY FOR A SMALL ISLAND

'Short of sacrificing our vital interests or principles, we must do everything possible to prevent global war which would inevitably entail the exposure of the United Kingdom to a devastating nuclear bombardment.'

British Chiefs of Staff, 1954[1]

When John Major, the British Prime Minister, told the Russian President in January 1992 that the British nuclear deterrent consisted of four ballistic missile submarines, of which only one was on patrol at any given moment, Boris Yeltsin at first seemed surprised. But he soon recovered his composure, and indicated generously that he didn't think he needed to worry too much about such a small force.[2]

British thinking about nuclear affairs was less histrionic than the American, and rather more open than the Russian. For the two superpowers the British deterrent was a comparatively minor affair – little more, though in different ways, than an irritation on the fringe of more pressing concerns. Yet partly because Britain was so small and vulnerable, and its deterrent so comparatively simple, the ideas of the British were sometimes clearer, and often more grimly sober, than those of their partners and adversaries.

Britain's Strategic Dilemma

The British were determined from the beginning to get their own bomb. For the first three decades of the twentieth century they were in the forefront of scientific research and strategic thinking. They pioneered work on the nuclear weapon. After the bombing of Hiroshima, they decided that in a dangerous world, where you could not rely even on an ally as staunch as America, you needed your own ultimate weapon under your own independent control. They made valiant and – for a time – successful efforts to construct their own system.

But they recognised that their strategic reasoning had to overcome a fundamental difficulty. The Americans and the Russians persuaded themselves for a while that their countries were so large that their people and their social, political, and economic systems might, at a pinch, survive a nuclear exchange. The British never had that illusion. A nuclear exchange would leave their small island devastated, perhaps beyond recovery. British strategic thinking always had about it an air of desperation.

In 1941 the MAUD Committee had looked forward to a British post-war programme: 'no nation would care to risk being caught without a weapon of such decisive possibilities.'[3] By 1943 Frederick Lindemann was wondering, 'Can England afford to neglect so potent an arm while Russia develops it?' A year later the Chiefs of Staff decided that the Soviet Union was the most likely threat to British post-war security, and British scientists recommended a post-war programme which would rapidly 'produce in the United Kingdom after the war a militarily significant number of bombs, say ten'.[4]

By spring 1945 the Americans were moving their troops from Europe to the Far East to finish off the Japanese. Churchill worried that the Russians might take the opportunity to attack in Europe. The Chiefs sent a soothing reply: 'It is only by the use of rockets and other new weapons that the Russians could develop any serious threat to the security of this country.' The Russians did not then have any rockets; but the Germans had already shown the way to the future in the last year of the war, when hundreds of their V-2 rockets landed on south-east England.[5]

The Americans were almost as much of a worry as the Russians. After their wartime rows, the British could not rely on American support for their post-war nuclear ambitions. Indeed, the collaboration formally ceased with the passage of the Atomic Energy Act in August 1946, the 'McMahon Act'. This was named after Brien McMahon, its original sponsor in the Senate, who called the successful nuclear test in Alamagordo 'the most important thing in history since the birth of Jesus Christ'. The act banned any exchange of classified nuclear information with other nations until effective international safeguards against nuclear weapons had been put in place.[6] The British invoked Churchill's Hyde Park Agreement with Roosevelt. The Americans denied its existence. It later turned out that it had been misfiled among Roosevelt's personal papers.

The British were thus pushed towards developing a nuclear weapon of their own, a means of delivering it, and a strategy for its use. The reasons were threefold. They wanted an independent deterrent to discourage a Russian attack. They feared that America might be unwilling to defend Europe once America too became vulnerable to Soviet nuclear weapons. And they believed that if they developed their own weapons, the Americans would be more willing to collaborate. British policymakers never abandoned the aspiration or illusion that by remaining close to the Americans they could persuade them to draw back from a dangerous course of action.

The process was initially driven by Clement Attlee, Churchill's underestimated wartime deputy.* Attlee had known nothing about the Manhattan Project before defeating Churchill at the election and becoming Prime Minister in July 1945. But the day after the bomb fell on Hiroshima, he called a meeting of senior ministers – it was to become a Standing Committee called GEN 75 – to discuss atomic policy, and within three weeks he had written a clear-sighted memorandum, calling for an early 'decision on major policy with regard to the atomic weapon'.[7]

His premise was uncompromising: 'the modern conception of war to which in my lifetime we have become accustomed is now completely out of date.' The defensive measures which had worked during the war – dispersal of industry, air raid shelters, foreign bases – would be 'futile in face of the atomic bomb'. Britain's geographical position made its great cities vulnerable to a continental power. Britain and America could try to impose a worldwide regulation and inspection of all laboratories and plants before others unravelled the secrets of atomic power. But that was neither desirable nor practicable. A year

---

*Told that Attlee was a modest man, Churchill replied that he had much to be modest about. Mrs Thatcher, on the other hand, thought Attlee was 'All substance and no show.'

before Churchill used the analogy, he wrote, 'We would not be able to penetrate the curtain that conceals the vast space of Russia. To attempt this would be to invite a world war leading to the destruction of civilisation in a dozen years or so.'

Attlee's attempt to find a broader solution was less hard-headed. The only sensible way forward, he argued, was for Britain, America, and the Soviet Union to banish 'the whole conception of war ... from people's minds and the calculations of governments ... All nations must give up their dreams of realising some historic expansion at the expense of their neighbours. They must look to a peaceful future instead of a warlike past. This sort of thing has in the past been considered a Utopian dream. It has become today the essential condition of the survival of civilisation and possibly of life in this planet.' Such ideas were widely shared. They were never more than dreams. In September Henry Stimson, Truman's Secretary of War, outlined similar, but more concrete, ideas in a memorandum to the President on the need for 'a satisfactory international arrangement respecting the control of this new force'.[8] He recommended that America and Britain should discreetly propose to the Russians an understanding to refrain from manufacturing nuclear weapons. Meanwhile the idea should not be aired more widely, since the Russians would react badly to anything that looked like ganging up.

Truman rejected Stimson's ideas as politically impractical. In November 1945 he, Attlee, and William Mackenzie King, the Canadian Prime Minister, publicly proposed the creation of a UN Atomic Energy Commission without consulting the Russians.[9] The Americans put forward their Baruch Plan for the elimination of atomic weapons under the inspection and control of the United Nations. The Russians did indeed react badly and the idea got nowhere.*

Attlee's paper did however spell out or imply a number of more practical issues that were to puzzle British policymakers for the rest of the Cold War.

What kind of nuclear strategy could make sense for a very small island that was almost uniquely vulnerable to nuclear attack? Patrick

---

* The story is set out more fully in Chapter 13.

Blackett, one of the scientists involved in the wartime project, argued that it made no sense for the UK to build or acquire nuclear weapons since, unlike the United States, Britain was within striking distance of Soviet aircraft.[10] Attlee's answer was deterrence. He had agreed with Stanley Baldwin before the war that the 'only defence is in offence'. Now he wrote that 'bombing could only be answered by counter-bombing. Both derive from Guernica. The answer to an atomic bomb on London is an atomic bomb on another great city.'

British officials had already begun a sophisticated strategic debate which remained hidden from the outside world. Asked by the Chiefs of Staff to look into the nature of future warfare, a group of distinguished scientists under Henry Tizard reported in July 1945 that Britain needed to design and produce atomic bombs and the aircraft to deliver them if they were to deter a potential aggressor similarly armed. That autumn the Admiralty warned that a determined atomic attack could obliterate Britain overnight, unless Britain had an adequate deterrent, which might best be provided by atomic bombs launched from submarines. But it concluded mournfully that 'the greatest hope for our children and grandchildren lies in the enlightenment of man's nature and an appreciation of the issues involved, rather than in developing the means of mutual destruction.' In October the Chiefs endorsed the idea of deterrence, and called on the government to start the production of nuclear weapons as soon as possible.

Thus the ideas of deterrence, missile submarines, and the enticing alternative of international control or general abolition (recognised as unattainable by most civilian and military officials) were present from the start of the British official debate. Bernard Brodie's theory of deterrence, and his belief that in the new age the only purpose of military power was to avert war, surfaced in the public domain a year later.[11]

But there was an obvious problem. How could Britain find the resources to develop a nuclear weapon when its economy had been strained to breaking point by total war?* The answer, unpopular with

---

* 'In 1946 Britain retained 18.7% of its manpower in military service compared with 10% in the USA. Expenditure on defence in that year was running at 18.8% of national income whereas in the United States it was 10.6%' (I. Clark and N. Wheeler, *The British Origins of Nuclear Strategy 1945–1955*, Oxford, 1989, p. 25).

soldiers, sailors, and airmen, was to cut back on conventional defence. The 1947 Defence White Paper admitted that 'developments in recent months have stressed the urgent need for restoring a balanced peace economy at the earliest moment, and by all possible measures. Defence policy must be compatible with this national need.'

But what did you do if deterrence failed, and you had to use your weapons in war? One answer was to destroy the bases from which the Russians could attack. Logically that meant that you should strike them before they struck you. And your attack had to be improbably accurate, comprehensive, and successful: what was the point if enough Russian bombers or missiles survived to wipe you out anyway? And even if nuclear weapons were cheaper, the Chiefs of Staff did not agree that they had altered the whole nature of warfare. Conventional forces were not obsolete: 'armies cannot,' they argued, 'be defeated by this form of [nuclear] attack alone.'[12]

Such puzzles about the feasibility of fighting an extended nuclear war, the role of conventional forces in the nuclear age, the advantages and disadvantages of pre-emptive attack, and above all the conundrum of nuclear warfare for a small and indefensible island were never properly resolved; nor could they be.

Building the British Bomb

The drive to build a British bomb now gathered pace. On 29 August 1945 Attlee set up a committee to consider the issues he had raised in his paper. It was chaired by John Anderson and its members included the Permanent Under Secretary at the Foreign Office; the Chief of the Imperial General Staff; a representative of the Treasury; and five physicists, Edward Appleton (Secretary of the Department of Scientific and Industrial Research), Henry Dale (President of the Royal Society), George Thomson, James Chadwick, and Patrick Blackett, all past or future winners of the Nobel Prize.[13]

The issues were clear enough. What was the scale of the threat? How many bombs did the British need to deter it? How would they deliver their bombs if deterrence failed? British analysts, like their American opposite numbers, had no secret intelligence about Soviet intentions: they could only make a guess. They did not seriously consider that the Russians would deliberately launch a nuclear war. But they feared that war might break out by accident or miscalculation, or by the unintended escalation of a dispute in a peripheral part of the world. Unlike some Americans in their brief period of nuclear monopoly, they did not believe that nuclear blackmail or preventive war could solve the Russian problem once and for all.

In September 1945 British officials forecast that 'an enemy' could build 500 bombs during 'ten years of peace'. If fifty of these were used on the United Kingdom, 'overnight the main base of the British Empire could be rendered ineffective'. A month later they recommended that 'we should undertake production of bombs on a large scale for our own defence as soon as possible'.[14]

The first requirement was for nuclear reactors to produce the necessary fissile material. When ministers discussed a programme in October 1946, Hugh Dalton, the Chancellor of the Exchequer, and Stafford Cripps, the President of the Board of Trade, argued forcefully that diverting resources from the civilian economy would soon lead to serious financial and economic trouble. But then Ernest Bevin, the Foreign Secretary, arrived late from an unsatisfactory meeting with James Byrnes, the American Secretary of State. He intervened with characteristic force. 'No, Prime Minister, that won't do at all. We've got to have this. I don't mind for myself, but I don't want any other Foreign Secretary of this country to be talked at, or to, by the Secretary of State in the United States as I just have in my discussions with Mr Byrnes. We've got to have this thing over here, whatever it costs. We've got to have the bloody Union Jack on top of it.'*

The balance between keeping the economy healthy and spending money on defence was difficult enough in America. In Britain the need to economise forced the British time and again to reduce their ambition to cut a dash on the world scene. But the formal decision to build a British bomb was nevertheless taken in January 1947. This

---

* Byrnes's arrogance had already irritated the Russians. When the Council of Foreign Ministers met in London in September 1945, his veiled references to America's nuclear monopoly provoked Molotov to say, 'You know we have the atomic bomb.' It was not yet true, but the Russians were closer to making a bomb than Byrnes gave them credit for (P. Hennessy, *Cabinets and the Bomb*, Oxford, 2007, p. 48).

time the doubters were excluded from the meeting. Bevin's clinching argument was that 'We could not afford to acquiesce in an American monopoly of this new development. Other countries also might well develop atomic weapons. Unless therefore an effective international system could be developed under which the production and use of the weapon would be prohibited, we must develop it ourselves.'[15]

The British Define Their Strategy

British nuclear strategy at the highest level was driven by three prime ministers – Attlee, Churchill, Macmillan – who provided both an intellectual and a political input. Their policies were discussed in the most profound secrecy, a tradition deep-rooted in the British governmental machine: Solly Zuckerman, the British government's first Chief Science Adviser, commented sourly that 'in this respect the UK is not an open society'.[16]

But nuclear strategy was, in the view of officials and senior ministers, something unique, quintessentially a matter for insiders. The issues were so complex, the need for secrecy so overriding, the politics so sensitive, that the discussion had to be confined to a small group. It could not safely be opened up even to a wider audience of political and official colleagues, let alone to the general public. Informed debate was much more narrowly based in Britain than in America.

That did not, of course, prevent public discussion between more or less well-informed outsiders. Every now and again a military or civilian official could not restrain his anger at the way policy was being handled and broke cover. But there was nothing to resemble the rumbustious debate in America.

The British refined their ideas on strategy as they got closer to obtaining their own weapon. But the central aim was to convince the Soviet leadership that – even without the Americans – the British could mount an unacceptably destructive blow against them. Wisps of the idea continued to hang about that a nuclear strike against Britain could be prevented, or its effects minimised, by striking the Russian bases from which it would be launched. But this was always beyond the British capability. More promising was the idea of destroying what the planners described as early as 1949 as 'Soviet state power'.[17]

This thought remained central to British strategic planning through to the end of the Cold War. Since state power was of course lodged in cities, notably Moscow, this made nonsense of claims that the British deterrent was primarily directed against military targets.

In the spring of 1952 the Chiefs of Staff took themselves off to the Royal Naval College in Greenwich for five days. The result was a 'Global Strategy Paper'. In language reminiscent of that being used in American strategic policy papers at the time – NSC-68 and the Gaither Report – it spoke of the 'implacable and unlimited aims of Soviet Russia', and said firmly that 'the ultimate goal of the leaders in the Kremlin was world domination'. Unlike the Americans, however, the Chiefs did not believe war was imminent and were uneasy about the talk they occasionally picked up in Washington about preventive war. But they remained firm in the conclusion that the British needed their own nuclear weapons to leave the Russians in no doubt that any aggression in Europe would be met with 'an instantaneous and overwhelming atomic air attack'. That would increase Britain's political influence, especially in Washington. And it would save money on conventional defence.[18]

The strategic problem was, however, already changing radically. It was no longer a question of an 'atomic air attack' but of attack by far more powerful hydrogen bombs. Churchill remarked to his private secretary, with characteristic hyperbole, that 'the difference between the hydrogen bomb and the atomic bomb is greater than that between the atomic bomb and the bow-and-arrow.'[19] The British now had to decide whether they should follow the Americans and Russians, and take the major step of developing thermonuclear weapons. The Chiefs had no doubts: 'If we did not develop megaton weapons we would sacrifice immediately and in perpetuity our position as a first-class power. We would have to rely on the whim of the United States for the effectiveness of the whole basis of our strategy.' They had no illusions about what a nuclear war would be like. But they concluded that, 'Short of sacrificing our vital interests or principles, we must do everything possible to prevent global war which would inevitably entail the exposure of the United Kingdom to a devastating nuclear bombardment.'[20]

Churchill agreed. If Britain had its own weapons it could hope to dissuade the Americans from undertaking a 'forestalling war' against the Soviet Union into which the country would be dragged willy-nilly. In Cabinet several ministers echoed Churchill's worries: 'the greatest risk was that the United States might plunge the world into war, either through a misjudged intervention in Asia or in order to forestall an attack by Russia. Our best chance of preventing this was to maintain our influence with the United States Government.' Ministers speculated hopefully that 'it was at least possible that the development of the hydrogen bomb would have the effect of reducing the risk of nuclear war.'

One unnamed minister wondered. 'Was it morally right that we should manufacture weapons with this vast destructive power? There was no doubt that a decision to make hydrogen bombs would offend the conscience of substantial numbers of people in this country.' Someone, perhaps Churchill, replied that there was no difference in kind between atomic and thermonuclear weapons: 'In so far as any moral principle was involved, it has already been breached by the decision of the Labour Government to make the atomic bomb ... the moral issue would arise, not so much from the possession of these weapons, but on the decision to use them ... if we were prepared to accept the protection offered by the United States use of thermonuclear weapons, no greater moral wrong was involved in making them ourselves.'

No one seems to have commented on the obvious question: what meaningful 'vital interests and principles' would survive if the country had been devastated?[21]

The Defence White Paper of 1957 brought these ideas together for the benefit of the public, which had hitherto remained largely ignorant of official thinking. The Defence Minister, Duncan Sandys, told the House of Commons, 'In present circumstances, it is impossible effectively to defend this country against an attack with hydrogen bombs', a remarkably frank admission. Instead, he said, 'the available resources of the nation should be concentrated not upon preparations to wage war so much as upon trying to prevent that catastrophe from ever happening'. Since 'the only means which the free world possesses to protect itself against Communist aggression and domination is the power to threaten retaliation with nuclear weapons ... it is desirable that Britain should possess some element of nuclear deterrent power of her own, rather than relying exclusively on the Americans.'[22]

This apparently coherent view still left many issues hanging in the air. Should the British aim, after all, to mount a pre-emptive strike against Soviet bases? Or should they concentrate on threatening Russia's great cities with hydrogen bombs, since that would surely deter the Russians from any foolish adventure? Should the army be given atomic mines and artillery to support the conventional battle on the ground? Should, indeed, resources be after all diverted from the nuclear arm to enable Britain and its allies to halt the Russians with conventional forces before either side used its nuclear weapons? Was that remotely credible, since both sides would surely use their nuclear weapons rather than let themselves be defeated?

The navy advanced the moral argument. It was quite wrong to let the RAF kill civilians massively with hydrogen bombs. Instead the navy's aircraft carriers should be used to deliver atomic bombs accurately on military targets. This special pleading got nowhere.

The strategic conundrums could not in the end be resolved. To try to pursue them to a conclusion would have made it impossible to devise a nuclear policy at all. So the government set them aside. Henry Tizard, who had always been a sceptic, believed that the whole thing was misconceived. 'We are not a Great Power,' he said, 'and never will be again. We are a great nation, but if we continue to behave like a Great Power we shall soon cease to be a great nation. Let us take warning from the fate of the Great Powers of the past and not burst ourselves with pride.' It was sufficient, he thought, to rely on the American nuclear shield.[23]

But the views of Tizard and others like him were firmly ignored. With the broad principles of strategy apparently settled, the government could now concentrate on producing the weapons with which to put the strategy into effect.

Once again the initial ideas were vague. In January 1946 the Chiefs of Staff reported that 'it is not possible now to assess the precise number [of bombs] which we might require but we are convinced we should aim to have as soon as possible the stock in the order of hundreds rather than scores.'[24] The following summer the Chief of Air Staff drafted the specification for a long-range bomber 'capable of carrying one 10,000 lb bomb to target 2000 nautical miles from a base', and placed a formal requisition for an atomic bomb with the Ministry of Supply, the responsible government department. These early ideas were formulated at a time when the British were still years away from having nuclear bombs or the V-bombers by which they intended to deliver them.[25]

Over the next decade the British tested a range of atomic and then thermonuclear devices and warheads. They detonated their first nuclear device in October 1952 in Australia, and deployed their first bomb, the Blue Danube, a year later. This was a fission bomb with a yield similar to the Hiroshima bomb. By now the Russians and the Americans were already testing their first thermonuclear devices. The British paused only briefly before deciding that they too needed a thermonuclear weapon. The first test, Operation Grapple in 1957, was disappointing. But it showed the Americans that the British were capable of developing their own sophisticated nuclear systems, and the Anglo-American cooperation that had been so brutally terminated at the end of the war was resumed under the 1958 Mutual Defence Agreement. With some assistance from the Americans, the British rapidly developed a thermonuclear warhead, Yellow Sun, which they deployed in 1958.

Planning for War
The British had by now made plans for action in the event of nuclear war. They had already more or less abandoned hope of protecting the mass of the population (see Chapter 12). But they did hope to preserve the core of central government – politicians, military leaders, senior officials, intelligence officers, and their support staffs. In 1961 they opened a bunker at Corsham in the Cotswolds to shelter up to 4,000 people in the event of nuclear war. It was successively known by the code names Burlington, Turnstile, and others. Up to 100 feet underground, it covered thirty-five acres and contained an infirmary, a bakery, a laundry, two large kitchens, a telephone exchange, office space, and living accommodation. Some planners doubted that all those designated to go there in an emergency would do what they

were told: some might prefer to join their families to face Armageddon together.

Since no one could be sure that the Russians had not worked out the location of Burlington, the government devised supplementary arrangements. They set up fourteen Regional Seats of Government, each with its own bunker, on the assumption that it would not be possible to run the country as a unity for some time after a nuclear attack. They drafted an Emergency Powers (Defence) Bill, to be enacted in the event of war. It put all powers of law and order, including life and death, into the hands of Regional Commissioners.

A 'War Book', regularly updated, set out measures for the conduct of nuclear war. It provided that the Prime Minister should appoint two deputies in case he was incapacitated or unavailable. When asked for names in November 1961, Harold Macmillan wearily scribbled, 'I agree the following: First Gravedigger: Mr Butler [his Deputy]; Second Gravedigger: Mr Lloyd [Selwyn Lloyd, the Foreign Secretary].'[26]

In case neither the Prime Minister nor his deputies could be contacted to authorise nuclear retaliation, the officer commanding the V-bombers was to 'order all bombers to become airborne under positive control'. They should fly towards their Soviet targets, but should not attack without a further specific order. The British commander should 'confer with the nominated United States commander to ascertain what instructions he has received'. If all else failed, he should 'authorise on his own responsibility retaliation by all means at his disposal'.[27]

An Elegant Dependency

The British policy of nuclear independence from the Americans was not easy to sustain, and there was an essential ambiguity at its heart, since the British could hardly confront the Russians effectively except in concert with the Americans. At first the British had a lever, but it was a wasting one. In the immediate aftermath of the war the Americans had neither the aircraft nor the missiles to reach the Soviet Union from the continental United States. The short-term answer was to acquire air bases close to their targets. In 1946 the British Chief of the Air Staff – apparently without seeking the agreement of ministers – agreed informally with his American opposite number that American aircraft might use RAF bases in Britain. American atomic weapons were based there from 1952.

This arrangement was never formalised, nor were the Americans willing to divulge their plans for using the bases in the event of war. They refused to share targeting information on which the British could make their own plans. They made it clear that they would decide for themselves whether to go to nuclear war or not, despite the agreement which Churchill thought he had extracted from Roosevelt at Quebec in 1943. Understandings were reached in the late 1950s which helped to mitigate these frictions. But the limits of the 'special relationship' were clear.

The policy of independence became increasingly compromised as the rate of technical change accelerated. By the time of the Cuban missile crisis in 1962 it was effectively over. The British never had enough V-bombers to hit all the Soviet bases that threatened them.* They hoped, but did not know, that the Americans would deal with the rest. General LeMay and his colleagues in the Strategic Air Command were reluctant enough to share their targeting plans with their own government, let alone with the British. Nor, despite the competence of their intelligence agencies, did the British have an adequate capacity to identify the right targets. As the Americans developed ever more sophisticated devices for monitoring the Soviet Union – U-2 reconnaissance planes and then reconnaissance satellites – the British fell ever more behind. They consoled themselves with the knowledge that they could hope to hit Moscow and that would be enough to deter the Russians. The 'Moscow criterion' became central to their nuclear strategy.

The British had prided themselves on their technical edge over the Russians, and even the Americans. But when they tried to develop a liquid-fuelled ballistic rocket, Blue Streak, they found it too expensive, too vulnerable, and already obsolete by the time it was cancelled

---

* The Russians had more than 190 air bases and the V-bombers could attack only forty of them. Of the thirty-six Blue Streak missiles available in 1963, only fourteen could actually be launched and only eleven were likely to reach their targets (J. Baylis, *Ambiguity and Deterrence*, Oxford, 1995, pp. 218, 356).

in 1960.[28] Their V-bombers looked impressively modern; but within a couple of years of entering service they were already becoming vulnerable to Soviet air defences. To extend their useful life, work began in 1956 on the Blue Steel missile, which the bombers could launch while they were still beyond the range of the Soviet defences. But Blue Steel was never up to standard, although it remained in service until the end of 1970.

Faced with the failure of both Blue Streak and Blue Steel, Macmillan persuaded Eisenhower in 1960 to let Britain have Skybolt, an air-launched missile the Americans were developing for their own purposes. In parallel, though not as a formal condition, Macmillan agreed that the Americans might base their Polaris nuclear missile submarines in Holy Loch, some thirty miles from Glasgow. Macmillan soon had second thoughts: an American nuclear base so near to Britain's third-largest city would be a domestic political nightmare once people realised that it had become a prime target for Soviet attack. He proposed putting the base in Loch Linnhe, 100 miles to the north. But Eisenhower was adamant: for overwhelming practical reasons the base needed to be near a major port and airport.

The British had taken a calculated gamble: their 'independent' deterrent would have to rely on an untried bit of American equipment. All was upended when John Kennedy came to power. His Defense Secretary, Robert McNamara, thought that bombers were an anachronism in a world of intercontinental missiles and nuclear submarines. Skybolt was dogged with technical problems and by the time it made its first successful test flight, in December 1962, the Americans had already brought their first Polaris submarines into service. The trouble with Polaris was that it was not accurate enough to use against Soviet missile sites – it was of use chiefly against cities. But the Americans eventually solved that problem, first with the Poseidon missile in the 1970s and then with Trident. Meanwhile they were well on the way to developing the accurate and solid-fuelled Minuteman. They no longer needed Skybolt and cancelled it in November 1962.

The British were left high and dry, a painful and public demonstration of the extent to which their nuclear independence had been eroded. An acrimonious debate followed in the House of Commons: the Liberal leader, Jo Grimond, asked Harold Macmillan, 'Does not this mark the absolute failure of the policy of the independent deterrent?'[29]

The Nassau Agreement

The Americans had never been very keen on the idea of an independent British deterrent anyway. As early as 1952 the American Joint Chiefs of Staff suspected that the British were using it to wriggle out of their commitment to increase their conventional forces to NATO. McNamara and Kennedy feared that further support for the British deterrent would infuriate the French and the Germans, and undermine prospects for the united Europe they wanted to encourage. McNamara told NATO ministers in June 1962 that 'limited nuclear capabilities, operating independently, are dangerous, expensive, prone to obsolescence and lacking in credibility as a deterrent.' Worse, they might simply invite a pre-emptive strike on their possessor. All in all, the Americans thought it would be better if the British dropped their independent deterrent altogether.[30]

Macmillan now swung into action with impressive speed and energy. In December 1962, supported by his Foreign Secretary, Alec Douglas-Home, and his Defence Secretary, Peter Thorneycroft, he met Kennedy at Nassau in the Bahamas to negotiate a new basis for a British nuclear force capable of deterring the Russians. Like his predecessors, he too was motivated by the thought that the British also needed 'to have enough nuclear power to prevent some foolish decisions being made to our detriment on the other side of the Atlantic'.

The British believed they had an implied bargain with Eisenhower: if the Americans could not supply Skybolt, they were morally bound to supply its equivalent. The alternative would be a serious breach in the Anglo-American relationship. At Nassau Macmillan pulled out all the stops, threatening at one point to walk away from the negotiations and to 'make a reappraisal of [British] defence policies throughout the world'. His Private Secretary recalled, 'He made a most moving and emotional speech, about the great losses and the great struggles for freedom and so on, and Britain was a resolute and a determined ally, who was going to stand firm, and that it was very unreasonable for the United States not to assist her to do so ... And it was very well done indeed and very effective, and there wasn't a dry eye in the house.'[31]

It worked. Kennedy agreed to provide the British with Polaris missiles. The British would provide their own warheads and the submarines to carry them. They had been tinkering with nuclear propulsion since 1946 and already had a nuclear submarine, HMS *Dreadnought*, due to enter service in April 1963. To save time they persuaded the Americans to supply one of their latest propulsion systems, over the strong objections of Admiral Hyman Rickover, who was in charge of the expanding American nuclear fleet. Subsequent British nuclear submarines were fitted with British propulsion systems. In the decades which followed the British built two more generations of missile submarines of increasing sophistication. These carried the Polaris missile until the mid-1990s.

The Americans hoped to limit any damage to their other European relationships by binding the British Polaris force unequivocally into NATO. Macmillan secured a let-out. The force would be used for 'the international defence of the Western Alliance in all circumstances except where Her Majesty's Government may decide that the supreme national interests are at stake'. Kennedy suggested that the Anglo-French invasion of Suez in 1956, when the Russians had threatened to bombard Britain and France if they did not withdraw, was just that kind of situation.

Macmillan asked his Cabinet to agree that 'these words could be publicly defended as maintaining an independent United Kingdom contribution to the nuclear deterrent ... a virtually indestructible second-strike deterrent weapon of proven capability, and with prospects of a long life'. He admitted that the new reliance on American technology left Britain somewhat less independent than before. But he argued that the Western Alliance would cease to be a free association if one member had a technical and scientific monopoly. Britain needed to be able to counter a Soviet nuclear threat even in the absence of American support. Without an independent deterrent, Britain would lose its ability to influence disarmament negotiations. The deal which he had negotiated represented 'a realistic compromise, in present circumstances, between independence and interdependence'.

His colleagues worried that until the British submarines were operational the Americans could threaten to cancel the deal. Some of them were beginning to wonder whether it was worth continuing with the independent deterrent at all. But in the end they agreed that he had done a good job. Subject to some improvement in the language of the agreement, he got their full support.[32]

In private Macmillan had his own doubts. He asked Home and Thorneycroft whether, 'if we were driven into a corner, we could either as a bluff or as a reality, make a Polaris missile perhaps of a simpler kind ourselves from our own designs'. But the arithmetic was overwhelmingly unattractive.

When Macmillan presented the Nassau Agreement to the House of Commons, Harold Wilson, the Labour Leader of the Opposition, was scathing. 'How can one pretend to have an independent deterrent when one is dependent on another nation – a reluctant one at that – to supply one with the means of delivery?'* Cynics clung to one useful thought. No one would know whether or not a missile emerging from the depths of the ocean was British or American. That would help to keep everyone on their toes, the Russians as well as the Americans.[33]

Despite the tortured arguments of Macmillan and his successors, the Nassau Agreement marked the end of any serious British pretension to nuclear independence. Maintaining the 'independent deterrent', and the 'special' Anglo-American relationship that underpinned it, became a priority for successive British governments and determined the shape of British foreign policy for the next five decades and more, sometimes to the detriment of other British interests. Experience showed that the Anglo-American relationship was not only special. It was very one-sided.

The Resolution-class submarines the British designed and built for themselves were elegant and capable, in British eyes at least as

---

* Once he became Prime Minister in 1964, Wilson and his Defence Minister, Denis Healey, inevitably took a different view. Healey thought that Macmillan had got a good deal, a cheap system for the capability it offered, useful in a dangerous world. Wilson thought it would be a way of restraining the Americans (P. Hennessy, *The Secret State*, London, 2010, p. 76).

good as their American equivalents. Thanks to the close relationship between the British and American navies and intelligence agencies, the British had the information they needed to hit Soviet targets. And it was indeed true that the British were free to press their own nuclear button if they saw the need to do so.

But the submarines' missiles – powerful, accurate, and capable of penetrating the Russian defensive screen – were supplied by the Americans, and had to be tested and serviced regularly in America. The missile compartments on the British boats were necessarily modelled on their American counterparts. Their warheads, though British-designed, were based on American concepts. All this American technology was subject to draconian American security regulations. Part of it could only be serviced by American technicians and over time an increasing amount of it was buried deep inside systems that were therefore no longer wholly British. If, for any reason and at any time, the Americans decided they would no longer support the British deterrent, they could switch off the facilities on which it depended. Its operational effectiveness would then inevitably fall away after two or three years.[34]

During the Suez Crisis of 1956 the British had no nuclear weapons. Some saw the Falklands crisis of 1982 as no less a test of Britain's 'supreme national interests'. But the British made no move to threaten or use nuclear weapons against Argentina in that war: the government recognised that the political effect on Britain's international position, as well as on its relationship with Washington, would be disastrous.[35] Outsiders never ceased to wonder in what circumstances, if any, the British might decide that their 'supreme national interests' would so differ from those of the Alliance in general or the Americans in particular that they would decide to fire their nuclear missiles all on their own.

The Coming of Trident

After 1972 the Americans began to replace the Polaris missiles on their submarines with Poseidon, a MIRVed missile which was more powerful, more accurate, and better able to get past the Soviet defences. They also began to develop a new and even more capable missile, the Trident. For a variety of political, technical, and financial reasons the British decided not to ask for Poseidon. Instead, they developed Chevaline, a new multiple warhead to go on their Polaris missiles, which was supposed to have a better chance of penetrating the defences around Moscow. It was a clumsy device and cost so much more than the estimate that the discussions were kept secret from the Chancellor of the Exchequer, Denis Healey, even though he had recently been a most distinguished Defence Secretary himself.[36]

The British were now having to look forward to a time in the 1990s when they would have to replace their Resolution-class submarines. In December 1978 British officials led by Antony Duff, the senior Foreign Office expert (himself a wartime submariner), and Ronald Mason, the Chief Scientific Adviser at the Ministry of Defence, prepared in the utmost secrecy a key paper for the Prime Minister, James Callaghan, entitled 'Factors Relating to Further Consideration of the Future of the United Kingdom Nuclear Deterrent'.[37] When Callaghan lost the election in May 1979 he arranged for the papers to be passed to his successor, Margaret Thatcher. It was the basis for her agreement in 1980 with President Carter that a new generation of British submarines should be equipped with Trident missiles.

The Duff–Mason paper was a major document, sober, lucid, and brutal. It was in three parts: the case for and against a British deterrent; the degree of 'unacceptable damage' any deterrent would need to inflict on the Soviet Union; and the various technical options for meeting this requirement.

Duff and Mason began by recognising an important truth about the nature of deterrence: 'There can be no absolute certainty that, following a massive nuclear attack on the United Kingdom, a Government would take a deliberate decision to order a retaliatory strike by the British deterrent. But the essential thing is that the Soviet Government should believe that there is a real possibility of their doing so. Provided our deterrent was perceived to have the capability, the Russians could not rule out this possibility. This is sufficient for deterrence.'

They then listed four reasons – they were not new – for retaining a British nuclear force. It would enable the British to defend their national interests independently of the Americans if need be; it would provide 'a second centre of decision-making' within NATO: Russian decision-making would be complicated because they would have to calculate British reactions well as American ones; it would be a modest addition to the American nuclear contribution to NATO; and (a reason which the government was reluctant to admit in public) it would give the British added political status and influence.

Duff and Mason went on to define 'unacceptable damage', a concept that the Russians and the Americans used as well.* One way of deterring the Russians was to threaten to destroy their cities. In 1959 the military planners suggested that demolishing forty cities would do the job. In 1962 they concluded that it would be enough to destroy the five largest Soviet cities, so that they could no longer function as major administrative, economic, and military centres.[38]

Duff and Mason came up with three options. All took it for granted that there would be millions of civilian casualties. The first option, and the most effective, would be to destroy Moscow together with its government and military centres. Since these were protected in deep bunkers, they could only be destroyed effectively if the weapons were exploded at ground level to increase lethal fallout. 'Option 1 would,' Duff and Mason wrote, 'inflict a greater penalty than the others, involving as it would both large-scale civilian destruction and very severe damage to the government capability; and it would there-fore provide greater certainty of deterrence.'

The second option would be to destroy Moscow, Leningrad, and two other large cities. 'A capability on this scale,' Duff and Mason commented, 'could threaten damage beyond repair to nearly half the buildings in four major cities of the Soviet Union and the possibil-ity that more than 5 million people might be killed and a further 4 million injured. It would involve the destruction of the Soviet capital and the centre of the Soviet bloc, of cities which are major centres

---

* The Americans considered that the destruction of one-quarter to one-third of their population and two-thirds to three-quarters of their industry would be unacceptable to the Russians. The Russians calculated that 40–45 per cent destruction of the US GDP would be enough (J. Lebovic, *Flawed Logics*, Baltimore, 2013, p. 68).

of military research, development, and production ... and of areas within these cities which are of major importance for Russian history and culture.'

The third option – to leave out Moscow and aim instead to inflict grave damage on Leningrad, other large cities, and a number of other targets – would be cheaper, easier, but less devastating.

The last part of the paper dealt with alternative weapons systems. The choice was between ballistic missiles – Polaris, and, in future, Trident – supplied by the Americans; or submarine-launched cruise missiles, bought off the shelf from the Americans or designed and built in Britain. Duff and Mason argued that cruise missiles would in the end be expensive and ill-adapted to penetrate the defences around Moscow. They therefore came down in favour of a new generation of submarines armed with Trident, which they believed could deliver destruction on the necessary scale.

David Owen, the Foreign Secretary, disagreed. 'I am not convinced that the Soviet leadership would be willing to risk even a single major Soviet city for the sake of an attack on Britain alone,' he wrote to the Prime Minister. A cruise missile force would be cheaper and more flexible, but still capable of killing a million Russians, which they would surely find an unacceptable price for destroying the United Kingdom. The anti-missile system defending Moscow was not as effective as the British military feared: it was rarely tested and was less capable than the Nike Zeus system, which the Americans had dismantled because it was technically inadequate.* Since the Russians could not rely on their defence system, 'it was quite legitimate to pose the fundamental deterrence not in terms of "can we be absolutely sure that our missiles would reach their targets", but rather in terms of "could the Russians be absolutely sure that they would not"'.[39]

Michael Quinlan, the widely respected Ministry of Defence expert on nuclear policy, articulated the general opposition to Owen's ideas from civilian and military officials alike.[40] Cruise missiles, he

---

* Owen may well have been right. There is no good reason to believe that the Soviet system was superior to the American system (there is a discussion of a modest later Soviet effort at http://russianforces.org/blog/2012/10/very_modest_expectations_sovie.shtml).

said, would be too vulnerable to Soviet countermeasures. Owen's idea of mounting them on hunter-killer submarines was unworkable. Moreover, '[i]n this field nothing is provable but it is far from clear that [the Russians] would regard less than half of 1% of their population as an unthinkable price for contemplating a conquest of western Europe.' The Soviet Union had a higher 'threshold of horror' than Britain, he wrote, because it had lost more than 20 million people in the Second World War. An effective deterrent against the Russians required up to 10 million dead.[41]

This argument was common on both sides of the Atlantic among military planners and theoreticians such as Albert Wohlstetter and Richard Pipes.[42] Whether the prospect of 1 million or 20 million dead would deter the Russians is unknowable. They repeated often enough in public that they had no desire to repeat their appalling wartime experience, though Western governments dismissed that as propaganda. After 1945, unlike the Americans, they fought on a major scale only in Afghanistan. Public intolerance for their comparatively limited losses there helped to push the Soviet government into ending that war. The terrible losses that the French and British suffered in the First World War left them unwilling to fight in the 1930s; but the Germans, who had suffered equally, were left yearning for revenge. Such complex matters need to be analysed and demonstrated rather than simply asserted.

The Thatcher government adopted the Duff–Mason report. But the idea that British nuclear strategy inevitably involved the killing of millions of civilians made people uneasy. The government tried to allay the worries in a paper about the Trident decision which the Ministry of Defence issued in July 1980. This said that the government's 'concept of deterrence is concerned essentially with posing a potential threat to key aspects of Soviet state power. There might with changing conditions be more than one way of doing this, and some flexibility in contingency planning is appropriate. It would not be helpful to deterrence to define particular options.'[43]

This tortuous language was devised by Michael Quinlan, who explained separately that it 'was intended to imply targeting concepts which, while still countervalue [targeting of cities and civilian populations] and not promising to exempt cities or in particular Moscow, would not be exclusively or primarily directed at the destruction of cities. The impulse behind this was ethical, and reflected in some degree vigorous public debate in Britain on the moral tolerability of striking at populations.'[44]

Quinlan was in no doubt, as he wrote to the Catholic journal *The Tablet* in 1981, that 'any extensive strategic nuclear attack will kill great numbers of non-combatants even if this is not its direct intent'.[45] But his underlying thought was that the latest missiles were far more accurate, which meant you could strike military targets precisely, thus minimising civilian casualties. He did not go into further detail in his public debates because of his duty to preserve official secrets. One interlocutor remarked that if he could not produce the facts, he was in no position to conduct the argument.[46] The more modern Trident II (D5) missile, which Mrs Thatcher persuaded the Americans to supply in 1982, was indeed significantly more accurate than its predecessor. But it would still have killed very large numbers of civilians living and working close to many 'military' targets in the Soviet Union. A study concluded in 2013 that a British attack on Moscow would result in 5.4 million deaths, 4.5 million inside the city and a further 870,000 in the Moscow region.[47]

Not everyone was convinced that – provided this was not your prime objective – it was morally acceptable to pursue a policy which unavoidably involved killing millions of civilians. The planners themselves either did not notice, or were not concerned, that wiping out Moscow at the outset of a nuclear war would negate any American plans (unconvincing though these were) to escalate their nuclear exchanges with the Russians in a sufficiently orderly way to terminate the war by mutual understanding when both had had enough.

It was yet another example of the incoherence of strategic thinking and planning on all sides.

Suite Française

Apart from the British, the French were the only other Europeans who had the capacity, the will, and the sense of national greatness to become a nuclear power. The Germans certainly had the capacity, but the other Europeans, the Russians, and the Germans themselves were aghast at the possibility that they might acquire nuclear weapons, and a number of international agreements were put into place to ensure that they did not.

By the time the Nassau Agreement was signed the French had already created an independent nuclear force which left the British distinctly worried. Would it be any good? Would it simplify or complicate relationships inside NATO, whose military organisation France had left in 1966? Could the British afford to cooperate with the French without antagonising the Americans – or vice versa? Were the Americans likely to collaborate with the French, and what effect would that have on the British special relationship with the Americans? If the British decided that the nuclear game was no longer worth the candle, could they pull out and leave the French as the sole nuclear power in Western Europe without fatally damaging their own prestige?*

The ink was hardly dry on the Nassau Agreement when Macmillan was told by the British Embassy in Paris that Kennedy had also offered Polaris missiles to the French.[48] Macmillan told the embassy to reassure the French that the Nassau Agreement fully preserved Britain's right to use or brandish its deterrent, and would not limit its ability to combine their nuclear efforts with the French if necessary.

But de Gaulle turned the American offer down. He did not believe that France could rely on 'extended deterrence': the proposition that America would use its nuclear weapons to defend its allies as well as itself. Supported by his countrymen, he was determined to follow a different and more independent path.

The French had started early. Their scientists were in the nuclear business from the beginning: Bertrand Goldschmidt, Marie Curie's last assistant, invented a method for extracting plutonium while working on the Manhattan Project, and was the prime force behind the design of the French bomb. The socialist government of Pierre Mendès France decided to set up a nuclear force against the background of France's humiliating defeat in Indochina. The decision was strongly endorsed by General de Gaulle when he returned to power in

---

* Michael Quinlan and others steadfastly denied in public that these matters of prestige figured in British thinking. They were, however, explicitly spelled out in the Duff–Mason memorandum of December 1978.

1958, since he believed that the Americans, bogged down in Vietnam and increasingly worried about the vulnerability of their own cities to Soviet nuclear attack, could not be relied upon to defend France against Soviet aggression.

The French tested their first fission bomb in 1960 and their first hydrogen bomb in 1968. In order to retain their freedom to develop their nuclear force, they refused to sign the Partial Test Ban Treaty, though they ratified the Comprehensive Test Ban Treaty in 1998. From 1971 to 1997 they deployed fixed and mobile land-based missiles. They introduced their first supersonic strategic bombers in 1964 and nuclear-capable fighter-bombers from 1973. Their most modern fighter-bomber, the Rafale, came into service in 2011: one version could operate from both French and American aircraft carriers. Their first ballistic missile submarine, the Redoutable, went to sea in 1971. It carried sixteen missiles similar to the American Polaris. From 1999 their submarine fleet consisted of four boats, of which one was to be at sea at any one time. The most modern were armed with missiles similar to the American Trident II. This was by any reckoning a formidable force.

French nuclear strategy was clear, logical, cold-blooded, and simple. France was far weaker than Russia, but deterrence would work if France could credibly threaten to inflict unacceptable damage. France could not afford to waste its effort on targeting the Soviet military, so it would concentrate on destroying Soviet cities. One influential French strategist, General Gallois, said, 'Making the most pessimistic assumptions, the French nuclear bombers could destroy ten Russian cities; and France is not a prize worthy of ten Russian cities.' As de Gaulle is said to have put it, 'Within ten years, we shall have the means to kill 80 million Russians. I truly believe that one does not light-heartedly attack people who are able to kill 80 million Russians, even if one can kill 800 million French, that is if there were 800 million French.' Although it lacked the tortuous complexities of American strategic thinking, this strategy was not much different from the theory of Mutually Assured Destruction.

Unlike the British, the French did not abandon their ability to drop nuclear weapons – whether strategic or tactical – from aircraft. But French strategy, too, had a desperate air to it. They assumed that their country would be destroyed whatever damage they managed to inflict on the Russians. It was a bee-sting strategy: the bee can inflict a wound, but does not survive. Despite the greater independence of the French nuclear force, it was difficult to imagine circumstances in which the French, any more than the British, would actually use their nuclear weapons except perhaps as part of a general war.

Though both sides kept it very quiet, France asked for American advice on its nuclear military programme in 1969. A method known as 'negative guidance' was devised to get round the prohibitions of the McMahon Act. The French would describe their research to the Americans, who would tell them whether they were on the right lines on such crucial matters as MIRVs, missile design, Soviet anti-missile defences, and advanced computer technology. In exchange the Americans benefited from French research, and the French developed a targeting plan coordinated with NATO as well as a purely national plan for the French deterrent.[49] The years of close collaboration on technical matters made it not unlikely that the French, as the British, were constrained by the Americans' draconian security provisions. But the French force was no less independent than the British force. The two were peers.

None of this made the British very happy. Prime Minister Heath suggested in the early 1970s that it would make sense for the two countries to pool their efforts. The Royal Navy successfully resisted. They feared arousing the ire of the crusty Admiral Rickover and compromising their own cooperation with the Americans. The French force, they regularly implied, might be independent, but without American expertise and intelligence it could not be relied on to hit its targets.

The British did not entirely ignore the possibility of collaborating with the French. When the government was considering Trident the Cabinet Secretary, Robert Armstrong, wrote to Mrs Thatcher, 'Our basic reason for not choosing the French alternative is that it would almost certainly give us a less effective weapon at greater cost. If we were convinced that we should base our long-term decisions on the hypothesis that the American connection was likely to decline, and the French connection to become our predominant international link, then we should arguably go into partnership with the French.

Politically and economically it would be a more evenly balanced partnership, but it would seriously worry the Germans, it would pose great problems with the Americans, on whom we remain dependent for keeping Polaris going through the 80s. And is France's long-term reliability inherently greater than the Americans?'[50]

After the end of the Cold War the French and the British did begin to move towards one another in a gingerly fashion. In 1996 President Chirac and Prime Minister Major agreed on some principles of nuclear collaboration. The British refused to discuss patrol patterns, for fear of possible American objections. Their caution was unfortunate: in 2009 HMS *Vanguard* and the French missile submarine *Le Triomphant* collided while on patrol in the Eastern Atlantic, an accident which regular discussion of patrol areas might have helped to avoid.[51]

Some constraints fell away after France rejoined the military organisation of NATO in 2009. In 2010 Prime Minister Cameron and President Sarkozy committed themselves to long-term Franco-British military cooperation, including the design and testing of nuclear weapons and joint development of technologies and systems for the next generation of nuclear submarines. The American government was mildly approving. The agreement soon began to fray at the edges, as Anglo-French agreements had so often done in the past. But it marked a considerable step forward from the days of Admiral Rickover.[52]

By 2015 the French nuclear force had outstripped the British and was the third largest in the world.

***

None of the strategists in any of the nuclear powers ever devised a wholly convincing theory, despite their intellect, their seriousness, their dedication, and their ingenuity. Perhaps the British and the French came closest, precisely because their choices were starker and simpler than those of the two superpowers.

Luckily none of them ever discovered whether their theories would work or not.

NINE

KNOW YOUR ENEMY

'Many intelligence reports in war are contradictory, even more are false, and most are uncertain.'

Carl von Clausewitz[1]

'Policymakers and private citizens who expect intelligence to foretell all sudden shifts are attributing to it qualities not yet shared by the deity with mere mortals.'

US House of Representatives, 1993[2]

'We didn't realise how f****** scared Soviet leaders were of us.'

Milt Bearden, CIA[3]

Strategy is useless in practice unless you know where your enemy is, what weapons he can bring against you, and – if possible – what he intends to do next. All governments, all organisations, and indeed all people need reliable information (for which 'intelligence' is only a grander name) if they are to plan their lives effectively. The trouble is that reliable intelligence, whether it is gathered openly or through secret agencies, is not easy to come by, to evaluate, or to act upon.

Some in the intelligence world make a distinction between 'secrets', factual information which your opponent wishes to hide from you; and 'mysteries', his emotions and worries, the mood of his people, and the likely political and economic developments in his country, all of which affect the way he manages his political, economic, and military situation and the way he intends to deal with you.

Somewhere between secrets and mysteries come 'plans'. Governments and generals draw up elaborate plans for future action. A competent intelligence agency can sometimes get hold of the relevant documents. But as the nineteenth-century German strategist

Helmuth von Moltke pointed out, plans do not always survive contact with reality. They may be unrealistic, they may not work, or the planner may change his mind. So you may have your opponent's plans but misjudge his intentions. It is good to get hold of your opponent's plans. But that still does not mean you will be able to predict what he does.

By the time the Cold War ended each side knew a very great deal – to an extent perhaps unprecedented in history – about the other's secrets: his weapons systems and the technology behind them, his military dispositions, his economic situation, and the layout of his territory should they wish to bomb or invade it. Much of this knowledge they gained by techniques which would have been perfectly familiar to Queen Elizabeth I's brilliant spymaster Walsingham: placing or recruiting agents in the opponent's military, political, bureaucratic, industrial, or scientific establishments, listening to his conversations, intercepting and deciphering his official communications. The Russians did this with great success in the decades before and after 1945. The Americans did not get going until after the war; then they too had some spectacular successes.

But the Cold War also saw a revolution in the technical means by which the contenders spied on each other, methods which had been pioneered in the two world wars. The Americans led the revolution, but the Russians followed close behind. Aerial reconnaissance became satellite photography, able to record events on the ground in the greatest detail. Each could record and analyse the mass of data thrown up by the weapons tests of the other, even when these took place thousands of miles away. Each could hoover up the other's wireless communications and telephone conversations, and make a stab at reading one another's heavily encrypted messages with their increasingly sophisticated machines. By the late 1960s much of the secrecy with which the military had always tried to cloak their activities had become futile.

As with the fashioning of strategy, geography initially favoured the Americans. Just as they could ring the Soviet Union with military bases, so they could surround it with electronic listening posts and operate sophisticated spy planes which for a while could fly across the Soviet Union with impunity.

Without bases near to America, the Russians could not equal them. But the advent of reconnaissance satellites in the 1960s greatly reduced their geographical disadvantage. Now both were able to form a good picture of one another's military dispositions and the characteristics of their weapons.

All this mass of information was analysed by both sides, and used to improve their weapons systems and modify their military dispositions to match or overmatch the other. But even the best Western analysts made serious errors about apparently verifiable Soviet 'secrets', such as the disposition of Soviet forces and the development and deployment of new Soviet weapons. Their exaggerated belief in the accuracy of the Soviet SS-18 missiles fed the myth of Minuteman vulnerability and helped to heighten emotions in the final stages of the nuclear confrontation. Though we know much less about the work of the Soviet analysts, they doubtless failed in similar ways.

But what the massive intelligence effort on each side could not do was to produce a sober, consistent, and reliable picture of their opponent's mysteries: all those intangible things on which he would base his decisions and take the actions which you wished to forestall. It is a common illusion that if you can only place good enough spies close enough to your opponent – to the Kremlin, to Saddam Hussein, or for that matter to Vladimir Putin – you can penetrate the mysteries and find out what he is going to do. But the solution to a mystery is not a matter of fact: it is a matter of judgement. And in the real world, judgement is always and inescapably distorted by prejudice, preconception, political passion, and institutional rivalry. So it was in London, Washington, and Moscow during the Cold War.

It was not that the agencies lacked competence. They did what they could to bring the tools that Clausewitz recommended – common sense and a knowledge of men and affairs – to bear on the mysteries they were trying to unravel.[4] But you cannot predict the future, whether you are talking about the affairs of foreigners or even about your own domestic affairs. Who could have expected the emergence of Gorbachev in the hidebound Soviet Union of 1985? Who could have expected the ultra-hawk Ronald Reagan to press for the end of nuclear weapons?

As the US Congress pointed out, it is no good expecting mortal men to exercise skills which are still reserved to the deity.

Despite the secrecy which surrounded it, the Americans' intelligence apparatus, like their strategic community, was far more open to public scrutiny than the Soviet or even the British equivalents. Its failures as well as its successes were far more widely trumpeted. But there was no reason to suppose that its overall performance was any better or worse than that of its competitors.

It was far bigger, better funded, and better equipped even than the organs of Soviet intelligence. But what looked like a huge advantage could turn out to be a something of a burden. An apparently unstoppable proliferation of sophisticated and expensive intelligence agencies fuelled rivalries and interfered with sober judgement.

By 2015 there were sixteen separate government intelligence agencies in the United States under the overall authority of the Director of National Intelligence.* They were the Central Intelligence Agency (CIA); eight agencies under the Department of Defense, including the Defense Intelligence Agency and the National Security Agency responsible for electronic eavesdropping; the Federal Bureau of Investigation (FBI) under the Department of Justice; and the Bureau of Intelligence and Research under the State Department. The Treasury and the Department of Homeland Security also had their own intelligence organisations. There were 854,000 people working on intelligence matters who held top-secret clearances. Not all of them were government employees: 29 per cent worked for private contractors. In the fiscal year 2012 this massive apparatus cost $53.9 billion, roughly the size of the economy of Bulgaria.[5]

Too many people and too many agencies generated too much information. The problem of collating it all, eliminating contradictions, and reducing the whole to usable proportions became next to impossible. As big an intelligence bang could have been got for a much lesser buck.

It did not begin on anything like that scale. At the beginning

---

* Before the terrorist attack on New York in September 2001, the role of 'Director of Central Intelligence' was exercised by the Director of the CIA.

of the Cold War the American capacity for collecting and evaluating intelligence on the Soviet Union was very limited. In 1947 the Chiefs of Staff decided that they needed 'an intelligence service with a far greater effectiveness than any such service this country has had in peace or war'.[6] In trying to work out whether war with Russia was likely in the immediate future, the CIA admitted in the same year that 'available intelligence … is too meager to support a conclusion that the USSR either will or will not resort to deliberate military action during 1948–49.'[7] Four years later the CIA was still lamenting that 'We have no reliable inside intelligence on thinking in the Kremlin … Reliable intelligence of the enemy's long-range plans and intentions is practically non-existent … In the event of a surprise attack, we could not hope to obtain any detailed information of the Soviet military intentions.'[8]

Spies

Because the Soviet Union was a closed society, running spies there was usually a matter of nightmarish difficulty.* The Americans and the British nevertheless recruited some very effective agents against the Russians. Most of these were people who for one reason or another – usually dissatisfaction or disgust with the system – offered their services voluntarily.

Piotr Popov, an officer in Soviet military intelligence, the GRU (Glavnoye Razvedyvatelnoye Upravlenie), became the CIA's first major source in the Soviet Union in 1953. He seems to have been motivated by anger at his government's treatment of the Soviet peasants, including his own family. He supplied valuable intelligence about Soviet military capabilities and espionage operations while he was serving in Vienna and later in Berlin. His employers eventually got on to him (he may have been betrayed by his own carelessness, or by the British double agent George Blake, at one time also in Berlin), and he was shot in 1960.[9]

Oleg Penkovsky was also an officer in the GRU. In 1961 he was recruited by the British, to whom he passed information about Soviet

---

* The difficulty of running an agent in Moscow is well documented by David Hoffman in *The Billion Dollar Spy*, London, 2015.

missile development which they shared with the Americans. This was useful (though perhaps not as decisive as some accounts would have it) in the run-up to the Cuban missile crisis. He was arrested just as the Cuban crisis was reaching its height, and executed.

Much invaluable information came from Adolf Tolkachev, a Soviet electronics expert working in a secret radar research institute. He eventually established his credentials with the Americans, and from 1978 to 1985 provided them with thousands of documents about Soviet military avionics. He was eventually betrayed by a disaffected CIA officer, arrested, and shot.[10]

Oleg Gordievsky, a middle-ranking KGB officer, worked for the British from 1974 to 1985. He was eventually unmasked by his employers, but before they could arrest him the British smuggled him out of the Soviet Union. Gordievsky did not produce the kind of hard technical intelligence provided by Penkovsky and Tolkachev, though he usefully identified a large number of Soviet agents working in the West and in the KGB's headquarters back home. His significant contribution was to improve the inadequate understanding in the British and American governments of Soviet concerns about the nuclear confrontation. He was not particularly well placed in the Soviet policymaking apparatus, but he was a trusted member of the Soviet official world and was thus well able to convey an authentic idea of the atmosphere in which the Soviet leaders took their decisions, and in particular their concern at the increasing belligerence of American policy under Ronald Reagan.

It was easier to run spies in the Warsaw Pact countries. The locals were not sympathetic to the aims of their Communist governments or their Soviet allies. Some East European military and intelligence officers concluded that the truly patriotic thing to do was to pass information to the West. Over the years they delivered a great deal of hard information about Soviet and Warsaw Pact weapons and military dispositions.

The Russians had always been good at spying. After the Revolution they identified Britain and later America as the main enemy and built up major networks in both.

Their most spectacular and elaborate success was the operation against the Manhattan Project. They rightly called it *ENORMOZ*, a Cyrillic transliteration of the English word, in deference to the magnitude of the project.* Unlike much information gathered by secret means, what the Russians wanted was concrete and verifiable. It was either information about the physical world, which was in principle available to any country that, like the Soviet Union, had qualified scientists. Or it was information about engineering processes, which either worked or didn't – something your agents could observe and you could test for yourself. None of these things were mysteries: they were secrets waiting to be revealed.

The Russians placed their agents at the heart of government in London and Washington. They recruited scientists – Klaus Fuchs, the German; Alan Nunn May, the Englishman; Ted Hall, the American – involved in the most intimate secrets of the atomic project. Some of those in Los Alamos were never identified. George Koval, an 'illegal' living under deep cover as an American citizen, was conscripted into the US Army, given a specialised training, and sent to work in Oak Ridge, the massive plant for enriching uranium, the only agent the Russians managed to place there. In 1948 he left quietly for Europe, and ended up in the Soviet Union.[11]

The first detailed intelligence about the British project came through in September 1941 from the NKVD's resident in London, Anatoli Gorsky. The British, he reported, had concluded that a bomb was feasible; it would take between two and five years to build; and the necessary enriched uranium would be isolated in a gaseous diffusion separation plant to be built in North America. Gorsky's source was probably John Cairncross, private secretary to Lord Hankey, the minister dealing with the MAUD Committee.[12] Cairncross's information was supplemented by Klaus Fuchs, a theoretical physicist who had been a Communist in Hitler's Germany, fled to Britain in the 1930s, and studied at Bristol and Edinburgh universities. Briefly interned as

---

*Whoever devised the code names for the Soviet operation had a sense of humour. Grigori Kheifets, who was running agents against the Manhattan Project in California, was called *Charon*, after the character who ferried souls into the underworld in Greek mythology.

an enemy alien, Fuchs became an assistant to Rudolf Peierls, who was by then working on the British atomic bomb project.* This valuable information had no immediate effect. It arrived at a time of panic as the Germans seemed to be on the verge of capturing Moscow. The Soviet intelligence authorities feared that it could be a plant by Western intelligence, intended to divert Soviet research into false channels.

It is hard to imagine that the Anglo-Americans would have had the time, energy, or interest to mount such an elaborate wrecking operation against their wartime ally. But Vitali Khlopin, the head of the Radium Institute who had done significant work on the physics of the chain reaction, thought the report might be genuine. Beria recommended to Stalin in March 1942 that the intelligence be taken seriously. It continued to flood in from London: 277 pages of documents in August 1942 alone. For security reasons its distribution was restricted. Kurchatov, the leader of the Soviet nuclear project, was first allowed to look at it that November.[13]

The Russians turned their attention to the United States when the main Allied effort moved there. The volume of intelligence began to increase rapidly. At first Kurchatov did not think that the stuff he was getting from America was as valuable as the material he had seen from Britain. That changed at the end of 1943, when Klaus Fuchs joined the Manhattan Project. The information he supplied included a detailed description of the design of the plutonium bomb that was dropped on Nagasaki and became the model for future weapons. In December 1944 Kurchatov was given a file containing 100 pages of typescript and some 800 photos. It was, he said, 'an excellent summary of the latest information on a number of matters of theory and principle', and he suggested questions to be followed up by the

---

* Cairncross went on to work at the code-breaking centre in Bletchley Park and then for the Secret Intelligence Service, whose secrets he also passed to the Russians. He was not unmasked until after the war and was never prosecuted. Fuchs returned to Britain at the end of the war, was arrested in 1950, served his term in prison, and returned to East Germany in 1959. The *ENORMOZ* operation was curtailed after the Soviet agents began to be rounded up in Canada, America, and London between 1945 and 1950.

Soviet agents. As the volume of material mounted it became hard to find enough translators with the necessary security clearance.[14]

By the beginning of 1945 the Russians knew that the Americans would test a nuclear device in a few months' time. With Stalin's demand that August for a crash programme, they began to develop their own thinking more urgently.

How important the intelligence was to the Soviet atom project remained a matter of controversy. Sceptical of Russian skills, many Americans initially concluded that information passed by the Soviet Union's atomic spies was the only possible explanation for their success in detonating a weapon a mere four years after the Trinity test. Edward Teller believed that Fuchs saved the Russians ten years. American fury at this treachery fuelled Senator McCarthy's campaign against alleged Communists in US government service in the years 1950 to 1954.

But there was controversy on the Russian side too. Some former Soviet intelligence officers asserted that the intelligence material was crucial, not the native brilliance of Soviet scientists and engineers.[15] A senior KGB officer, Pavel Sudoplatov, claimed in a sensational book that the KGB had received secret information about the bomb from Robert Oppenheimer, Leo Szilard, and Enrico Fermi; Niels Bohr, in particular, had given information 'essential to starting the Soviet reactor'. Sudoplatov's claims were roundly dismissed by another veteran Soviet intelligence officer, Vladimir Barkovsky. He came from military intelligence, the GRU, which never took the KGB's pretensions kindly. He himself had worked indirectly with Klaus Fuchs. 'Neither Kurchatov nor [Soviet] intelligence,' he said firmly, 'received any help from Bohr, Oppenheimer, or anyone else of that calibre. It is time we said farewell to the myths.' A former KGB colleague, Yuri Kobaladze, said in 1994 that Sudoplatov's claims 'do not correspond to reality'.*

---

* Secret agencies everywhere have a tendency to exaggerate their achievements. Graham Greene's *Our Man in Havana* is a satire, but like any good satire it reflects one aspect of reality. During the war the Americans, in what was called the Venona Project, intercepted heavily encrypted Soviet telegraph traffic between

Kurchatov had no doubt about the value of the intelligence, and he was generous about his American and British opposite numbers. He told Molotov in the summer of 1943, 'The material I have looked at contains an exceptionally important report on the start-up of a graphite moderated reactor in America – an event which one can only regard as an outstanding event in world science and technology.'[16] His progress reports are full of references to the ways in which the intelligence enabled him and his colleagues to avoid chasing will-o'-the-wisps.

Russian scientists were naturally incensed at the implication that their contribution was merely secondary. Yuli Khariton, the Director of Arzamas-16, pointed out that he and others were working on the basic science in 1939–40, and had even then pointed out its military potential. The intelligence led to the Soviet leadership's decision to base the Soviet fission bomb on the American model, which they knew would work, rather than risk losing time by trying out possibly superior Soviet alternatives, as Kapitsa had advised. But it was still necessary to check the intelligence in case it contained inaccuracies, and to solve many difficult engineering and production problems that it did not cover. Khariton and Barkovsky thought Fuchs's work so valuable that they tried but failed to get him a Soviet medal.

It was different with the thermonuclear fusion bomb. Here, said Khariton, the intelligence made no significant contribution. Fuchs had reported on Teller's attempt to design a superbomb. Teller's design was seriously flawed, but Fuchs was arrested before this became clear to the Americans themselves. Sakharov's 'First Idea' enabled the Russians to test a deliverable fusion device in 1953, ahead of the Americans.[17]

Even after their operation against the Manhattan Project had run out of steam, the Russians continued to have considerable success in recruiting well-placed agents. They could no longer rely on ideological

---

the United States and Moscow. This material not deciphered until 1946 and after. The information it contained then helped to unmask Klaus Fuchs and others. Identities were masked by code names. Some were clearly agents: *Captain* was Franklin Roosevelt and *Boar* was Winston Churchill. Others were never identified (https://en.wikipedia.org/wiki/Venona_project, accessed 9 April 2016).

commitment, but they were able to motivate their agents in other ways, through greed, resentment, or fear. In 1968 they recruited John Anthony Walker, a warrant officer in the US Navy who needed the money. Between 1968 and 1985 Walker, his son, and a colleague helped the Russians gain access to American naval communications and decipher over a million naval messages. This enabled them, it is said, to work out where American submarines were at all times, thus seriously compromising the American deterrent. The *New York Times* called it the most damaging Soviet spy ring in history.[18]

The Russians and their Warsaw Pact allies also penetrated NATO and its European member governments. In 1977 the East Germans successfully placed Rainer Rupp inside NATO headquarters, where he filched secret documents about NATO strategy, the disposition of NATO's cruise and Pershing II missiles, and NATO intelligence estimates of Warsaw Pact capabilities. Rupp was not identified until 1993, when he was tried and imprisoned. He claimed in 2008 – not very plausibly – that he had averted a nuclear exchange at the time of the Able Archer* exercise in autumn 1983.[19]

Spy Planes, Satellites, and Hearing Aids

It was in the collection of technical intelligence that the Americans' economic and financial resources and their technological prowess gave them a marked edge.

At first their geographical advantage enabled them to send their reconnaissance planes along the Soviet border and occasionally deep into Soviet airspace in what amounted to a systematic violation of international law. In the spring of 1956 there were apparently 156 such flights in seven weeks: a whole squadron of RB-47 aircraft is said to have flown hundreds of miles into Russia in broad daylight.[20] From time to time the Russians shot the intruders down: in all, 180 American airmen were killed. The Russians issued routine complaints and the Americans issued routine denials, but both sides avoided making a major issue of it. After 1956 the Americans flew their revolutionary U-2 aircraft over the Soviet Union twenty-four times, too high for Russian anti-aircraft weapons to hit them. By 1961 these missions had

---

*Able Archer is dealt with more fully in Chapter 14.

photographed about 15 per cent of the country.[21] On 1 May 1960 the CIA sent Gary Powers on a flight intended to take him from Peshawar in Pakistan to Norway – the first to cross the whole country. But by now the Russians were able to destroy aircraft at great heights. Powers was shot down over Sverdlovsk in the Urals, causing a major crisis in Soviet–American relations. U-2 flights over the Soviet Union were ended, though they continued in other parts of the world and revealed the Soviet move to install missiles in Cuba the following year.

The situation was transformed by the development of the reconnaissance satellite, which could operate with impunity, and enabled each side to pile up unprecedented amounts of accurate data about the characteristics and purposes of the other's weapons and the organisation and dispositions of his forces.

The Americans first flew a Corona reconnaissance satellite in 1959. The photos it took were dropped in capsules, whose parachutes opened once they entered the atmosphere, enabling them to be recovered by military aircraft as they fell. Later satellites were able to transmit their photographs direct to the ground. The resolution of satellite photographs – the detail they could show – increased from year to year. The first photographs could distinguish objects on the ground forty feet across. Soon that was down to three feet, which for technical reasons remained the optimum, though higher resolutions soon became technically possible.[22]

The Americans and the Russians eavesdropped on one another's radio transmissions from the very beginning. Once again the Americans exploited their geographical advantage by placing listening stations around the Soviet border, in Britain, Cyprus, and Iran (until the fall of the Shah).[23] These intercepted Soviet communications and monitored Soviet weapons tests and rocket launches. One of the reasons the KGB used to justify the Soviet invasion of Afghanistan in 1979 was that the Americans were proposing to set up stations there too.

Some of the other American technical operations were wildly imaginative and wildly expensive. Project Azorian attempted in 1974 to recover a sunken Soviet missile submarine from the bed of the Pacific Ocean: it was only partially successful, and cost $800 million. Operation Ivy Bells was equally ambitious. It began in 1971 and used a specially equipped submarine to place listening devices on a Soviet communications cable in the Sea of Okhotsk. After yielding much useful intelligence, Ivy Bells was eventually betrayed by an official from the National Security Agency, but the Americans continued to mount similar operations in other parts of the world.[24]

The Russians had been very good at the traditional skills of intercepting correspondence and breaking codes in the Tsarist time and that tradition continued. They were less ingenious in the conduct of technical intelligence operations, mainly for lack of resources. Although they were the first to put Sputnik into space, they lagged behind the Americans in their use of reconnaissance satellites. They launched their first Zenit satellite in 1961, two years after the Americans. From then until 1994 more Zenits were put into space than any other type of satellite of any nationality.[25]

Perhaps the most significant political and psychological consequence for the Russians of these technological advances was the realisation that they could no longer rely on the paranoid secrecy with which they had always surrounded themselves, what the Marquis de Custine, who visited Russia in 1832, had called 'secrecy useful and secrecy useless'. With the arrival of the reconnaissance satellite Russia could never again be so closed to the outside world. Arms control agreements with the Americans would earlier have been impossible because each side feared the other would cheat. Henceforward they could be checked by 'national technical means of verification'.

What Did It All Mean?

Assessment is the main challenge in the intelligence process. It is all very well to assemble the raw material from your agents' reports and your technical devices. But that is not much use until you have put the stuff together in the form of judgements on which your weapons designers, military commanders, and politicians can base policy.

Both sides amassed a pile of facts about the other's military capacity. The facts were not always accurate, and they were sometimes distorted by misinformation, deceit, or self-delusion. But from the early 1960s it was clear that each had the capacity to wipe out the other several times over.

However, the essential question was this: how likely was it that your enemy intended to do so? The orthodox principle is that even if you can form a reasonable picture of his military capacity you cannot establish his intentions with any certainty. Prudence therefore demands that your own planning should not worry too much about his intentions, but concentrate on matching his capabilities.

In practice it is different: governments and military commanders cannot be prevented from wanting to know what their opponent is going to do next. That is a matter of judgement, and on all sides of the Cold War judgement was distorted by ideological prejudice, interdepartmental rivalry, group thinking, and a desire (often unconscious) to say what your bosses expected. Though they rarely admitted it, even to themselves, a sober and reliable assessment of their opponents' intentions remained beyond both the Americans and the Russians, the British and others. All were trying to unravel mysteries which were essentially unknowable. All were hampered by their inability to put themselves in their opponents' place, to imagine the world as seen through the eyes of the other.

Once again there was an imbalance in the confrontation. This time it was a matter not of differing geographies, but of differing societies. The closed nature of Soviet society meant that the Americans had almost no secret intelligence about Kremlin decision-making and very little public information either. The Russians had far too much information about the American decision-making process: official pronouncements; leaks from government agencies; the contradictory statements of politicians, generals, bureaucrats, and think-tankers, sometimes reliable, often self-serving, frequently contradictory. Throwing out the chaff, sorting out the truth, trying to work out where all the conflicting information netted out was difficult for the Russians, as indeed it sometimes was for America's allies. Although it was rather common for Western commentators to describe the Soviet system as impenetrable or unpredictable, the vagaries of American politics, and the significant changes in style if not always in substance as one president succeeded another, meant that predicting what America was likely to do next was much more of an art than a science. As the Soviet Foreign Minister Andrei Gromyko once complained, American attitudes 'change as quickly as the weather in the North Atlantic'.[26]

Even the quantitative data generated by technical means, the reconnaissance satellites and the eavesdropping devices, were not always useful when it came to judging the quality of the opposing forces: which weapons would reliably work as designed, how many were serviceable at any given moment, how many military units were at the highest level of efficiency, and how many were badly led, badly manned, and badly equipped? The intelligencers on both sides therefore tended to assume, for simplicity's sake, that all equipment worked as advertised and that all their opponent's military formations were equally formidable. This helped to exaggerate the threat and distorted thinking about the appropriate response.[27]

The American assessment of Soviet intentions found its most influential expression in the series of strategic documents from Truman's NSC-20/1 in 1948 to Carter's PD-59 in 1980, as described in Chapter 6. All suffered from the weakness admitted in NSC-68 of 1950, that its descriptions of Soviet military capabilities 'do not represent an evaluated estimate of Soviet intentions to utilize these capabilities, do not take into account the effect of counteraction, and are based on the assumption of no important change in the territory under Soviet control or in the type of that control'.[28]

The assessments in the strategy documents suffered from two other less tangible weaknesses. The first was a profoundly ideological approach to the adversary. Lacking hard intelligence, American strategic assessments instead drew inferences from the public statements of Soviet generals and politicians and from the works of Marx, Lenin, Stalin, and others.[29] The relationship between these and the Soviet government's policies and intentions was obscure. In 1951 RAND published a brief book by Nathan Leites, *Operational Code of the Kremlin*. It was explicitly based on the writings of Lenin and Stalin, and drew on no other sources. Much cited in its time as an authority, the book is useless as an explanation of the way the Soviet government behaved. The public rhetoric of 'Godless Communism', the idea that the confrontation between America and the Soviet Union was a struggle between Good and Evil, seeped into American official papers and undermined their objectivity. Clausewitz's warning that all intelligence assessment should be tempered by common sense and the fruits of experience was not always applied with rigour. Marshall Shulman, an adviser on Soviet affairs in the State Department in the late 1970s, pointed out that the Russians would come to alarming conclusions about American policy if they based their assessments on the public statements of some American generals.[30]

The second weakness was a persistent inability or unwillingness to understand that the Russians were at least as afraid of the Americans as the Americans were of the Russians, and that this was bound to affect Soviet policy profoundly. This blindness to Russian fears found a dramatic expression in Reagan's realisation, at the end of 1983, that 'many Soviet officials fear us not only as adversaries but as potential aggressors who might hurl nuclear weapons at them in a first strike.'[31] As Dobrynin, the long-standing Soviet ambassador in Washington, once asked, 'Don't you realise that for us, too, this is an insecure world, an unsatisfactory world?'[32]

Not everyone thought that these were weaknesses. For them the strategic reviews were political documents, intended to sustain the determination of American leaders and the American public. They were meant to deliver the clear message that it was always safer to assume the worst case: the Soviets were irredeemably aggressive, they were stealing a significant strategic march over America, and they might well attack the United States if they thought they could get away with it. Paul Nitze, who helped write NSC-68, later admitted that nobody involved really thought the Russians were about to attack.[33] Dean Acheson, Truman's Secretary of State, thought that the purpose of such reviews went beyond analysis: they were meant to create the right climate for decision-making. Reagan's Defense Secretary, Caspar Weinberger, said three decades later, 'Yes, of course we used worst-case analysis. You should always use a worst-case analysis in this business. You can't afford to be wrong. If we won by too much, if it was overkill, so be it.'[34]

It may have been understandable politics; but it was disreputable intellectually.

As détente began to break down in the mid-1970s there was a return to the ideologically driven exaggerations of the earlier period. The report of Team B, whose genesis was described in Chapter 6, was rather less colourful in its language than some of its predecessors. But its relentless logic was just as schematic and just as ideological, and its conclusions about the thinking of the Soviet leadership just as scantily based on hard information.

Perhaps reflecting the interests of the Team leader, the historian Richard Pipes, much of the analysis rested on assumptions about the nature of Russian history, the importance of ideology in Soviet policymaking, and the extent to which ideological formulae represented genuine operational goals rather than mere posturing to the national or international audience.

Russian history, said the Team, was a record of continuous imperial expansion and aggression. Soviet leaders held that the universal victory of 'socialism' was inevitable, a clear statement of an essentially offensive objective. They believed that all means were legitimate in its pursuit: propaganda, deceit, subversion, violence, war. 'Détente' and 'coexistence' were mere tactics on the way to ultimate triumph.

The Russians, said the Team, were preparing for a Third World War 'as if it were unavoidable'. They still believed, with Clausewitz, that war was simply the pursuit of policy by other means, that war is otherwise 'a senseless thing without an object'.[35] For the Russians even nuclear weapons were not 'unique instruments to be used as a very last resort, but as elements of a whole range of mutually supporting means of persuasion and coercion available to the state in pursuit of its interests'. Within the next ten years 'the Soviets may well expect to achieve a degree of military superiority which would permit a dramatically more aggressive pursuit of their hegemonial objectives, including direct military challenges to Western vital interests, in the belief that such superior military force can pressure the West to acquiesce or, if not, can be used to win a military contest at any level.'

Team B thus oversimplified Clausewitz's formula that war is 'a continuation of politics with the admixture of other means'. Americans tended to believe that politicians have no business trying to influence the conduct of war; they come back into their own only when the generals have won the victory. Soviet ideologists (including Stalin) were reluctant to abandon the proposition that war could promote the world-wide victory of Socialism. On neither side of the Iron Curtain was there ever a consensus about whether nuclear weapons could sensibly be used to advance policy. On the whole the politicians on both sides were more sceptical than the generals. In real life both sides continued to use 'conventional' weapons to fight wars for political reasons. But whatever they may have said, neither ever acted as if they believed that nuclear weapons could ever serve a practical military purpose.[36]

The Team went on to insist that the Russians' civil defence plans were further evidence of their aggressive intentions, of their belief that they could fight and win a nuclear war. The proposition became a political football in Washington. The CIA said, sensibly enough, that the Russians would be 'unable to prevent massive casualties and the breakdown of essential structures'. There was no evidence that the Russians had ever practised evacuating their cities, something that would take them days to effect. Nor was there evidence that they had implemented plans to disperse or shelter their industry to any significant extent.[37]

The Team dismissed this as yet another example of CIA complacency. Despite the absence of evidence, Reagan claimed that the Russians had evacuated 20 million people from their cities in an exercise. Some officials said that the Russians were spending $2 billion a year on civil defence, while America was spending only $125 million. One claimed that the network of bunkers the Russians were building 'were costing a phenomenal 1–2% of Soviet GDP'. Conservatives called for America to match the Russian scheme with a massive civil defence programme of its own.[38] There was never any prospect of that happening.

The CIA seemed to think, said the Team, that the Russians were trying to create strategic forces which could absorb an American first strike and then retaliate. They were wrong. Soviet weapons programmes, the Team maintained, were not simply a response to American technical advances. The Russians sought strategic superiority in all branches of the military, including the nuclear: 'They think not in terms of nuclear stability, mutual assured destruction, or strategic sufficiency but of an effective nuclear war-fighting capability.' They had been caught napping by Hitler in 1941: next time they would strike first. And they believed they could absorb the consequences.

The Team showed no sense that these issues might be a matter of genuine debate among the Russians themselves.* They dismissed as mere propaganda the repeated assertions by Soviet leaders that a nuclear war would be unwinnable and a catastrophe for mankind. On the contrary, Pipes argued that in a nuclear exchange with America 'all of the USSR's multimillion cities could be destroyed without trace or survivors, and, provided that its essential cadres had been saved, it would emerge less hurt in terms of casualties than it was in 1945'.[39] This was an extreme version of a questionable proposition that ran throughout British and American official thinking about deterrence (see Chapter 8).

Assessments by American professional analysts were less coloured by the distortions which marred the strategic reviews. Their National Intelligence Estimates (NIEs) represented a judgement reached between the agencies, often after bitter disagreement. They were regularly criticised for reflecting merely the lowest common denominator of a wide range of opinion. They occasionally became the subject of vivid political controversy in Congress and, on being leaked by one or other interested party, in the press as well.

The record of the analysts at the working level was nevertheless comparatively good. Their judgements about the likelihood of Soviet Union military aggression, especially on a strategic scale, were usually sober. Their predictions were inevitably wrong from time to time, sometimes because they were too complacent, sometimes because they were too scary: up to the eve of the crisis in October 1962 they were predicting that the Russians would not risk placing missiles in Cuba.[40]

But all organisations suffer from groupthink and the American analysts were no exception. Many tried to understand the obsessions, ambitions, ignorance, and paranoidal fears of the Soviets. But in the atmosphere of Cold War conflict, understanding was often confused with sympathy, and could be hazardous. Ray Garthoff, one of the most perceptive of the American scholar-analysts, wrote in 1991, 'The principal fault of the process of assessing the adversary ... was the

---

* Solly Zuckerman wondered who in the Soviet government machine actually held the views attributed to 'the Soviet Union' (*Nuclear Illusion & Reality*, New York, 1982, pp. 73–4).

inability to empathize with the other side and visualize its interests in other than adversarial terms.' But, he added, an American official who departed from 'the implicit stereotypical cold war consensus' risked damage to his career and influence. Such inhibitions reached to the highest levels: during the Cuba crisis John Kennedy tried constantly to see events through Khrushchev's eyes. But he warned a journalist 'It isn't wise politically to understand Khrushchev's problem in quite this way'.[41]

This unenthusiastic description of the American assessment process is inevitably unfair. Even after the Cold War ended Soviet intelligence assessments, and the operational conclusions that the Soviet military and politicians drew from them, remained under lock and key. We have to extrapolate from partial documents, interviews, memoirs, and public statements. But what evidence there is shows that in Moscow, too, judgement was often distorted by politics, obsession, ambition, ignorance, paranoia, interdepartmental rivalry, and ideological prejudice.

The Russian machinery for collating, summarising, and drawing conclusions from a wide range of overt and secret information seems to have lacked the comparative organisational coherence of the British and American systems. Before he was appointed by Gorbachev after the 1991 coup to reform the KGB, Vadim Bakatin believed that it was distinguished by its intellectual and analytical skills. He was disappointed to discover that a proper Analytical Directorate had been set up only a year earlier. Analytical work in other departments and in the think tanks was not properly coordinated. Raw information piled up on the desk of the Chairman of the KGB, who selected whatever he thought worthy of the leadership's attention.

And in Moscow the views and prejudices of the leader were even more decisive than they were in London or Washington. Stalin was the most egregious example. His agencies produced a stream of accurate intelligence about Hitler's plans to attack the Soviet Union throughout 1940 and 1941. This was inconvenient, because he needed time to expand, train, and equip the Soviet armed forces with modern equipment. He shot two of his intelligence chiefs who warned of an imminent attack. Their replacement was determined not to go the same way and bent his assessments to fit Stalin's views. The result was a spectacular debacle when the Germans struck on 22 June 1941.

After the war the analytical functions of the civilian (KGB) and military intelligence (GRU) agencies were briefly combined into an Information Committee with Molotov as Chairman.[42] But over the years the attempt at coordination broke down. The KGB, the GRU, and the Secretariat of the Party produced their own assessments. The leaders themselves often preferred to make up their own minds. Khrushchev embarked on his adventures in Berlin and Cuba without seeking any preliminary advice or assessment from his intelligence agencies.[43]

After he became Chairman of the KGB in 1967, Yuri Andropov raised the prestige, career prospects, and numbers of his analysts.* But the KGB was responsible for the internal as well as the external security of the country and its leaders were not always able to distinguish between the two. When the dissident writer Solzhenitsyn was expelled to the West in 1974, the KGB told the Politburo that its 'humane action' had been widely and sympathetically understood by foreign diplomats and journalists. Either it was being deliberately misleading or it was hopelessly misinformed.[44]

Vladimir Kryuchkov, Bakatin's predecessor as head of the KGB, took a direct part in the country's internal politics. He fed distorted and manufactured information to Gorbachev and the public. In December 1991 and again in June he accused the CIA of being behind all the Soviet Union's domestic troubles.[45] He helped lead the abortive coup against Gorbachev in August 1991. But even he eventually accepted that the cause of the Soviet collapse lay within the country itself. One of his colleagues said more explicitly, 'The bitter truth is that not the US Central Intelligence Agency, and not its "agents of influence in the USSR", but we ourselves destroyed our great state, and all our highest party and state figures continued to pursue chimaeras, not wishing to distinguish myth from reality.'[46]

---

* The British double agent Oleg Gordievsky reckoned that the number of KGB analysts grew from fewer than seventy in the mid-1970s to more than 500 by the mid-1980s (R. Garthoff, *Soviet Leaders and Intelligence*, Washington, DC, 2015, p. 41).

But the myth that a great country had been destroyed by a lethal combination of secret foreign enemies and the domestic traitors they recruited nevertheless survived, took deep root, and flourished in Putin's Russia.

The British had fewer resources to devote to the production and assessment of intelligence than either the Americans or the Russians. In some ways this led to a more compact and more easily managed machine. Raw intelligence was competently produced by the Secret Intelligence Service (the British equivalent of the CIA) and the Government Communications Headquarters (GCHQ, the equivalent of the National Security Agency). Assessments were drafted by a small team of officials seconded from the intelligence agencies, the military, the Foreign Office, and the Treasury, and approved by the Joint Intelligence Committee, on which sat the heads of the bodies represented in the drafting. Reflecting the bias of British civil servants towards quiet consensus, the drafting process was usually less confrontational than the noisy dialectic which characterised the American equivalent. The product was often criticised as merely bland. The British assessments nevertheless stood up reasonably well in the glare of hindsight.

But everywhere it happened too often that, as Percy Cradock, the distinguished Chairman of the British Joint Intelligence Committee at the end of the Cold War, said, 'The analysts become courtiers, whereas their proper function is to report their findings, almost always unpalatable, without fear or favour.'[47]

In December 1988 Douglas MacEachin, a highly respected analyst from the CIA, found himself telling Congress that the Agency had 'never really looked at the Soviet Union as a political entity in which there were factors building which could lead to at least the initiation of political transformation ... Moreover, had [such a study] existed inside the government, we never would have been able to publish it ... had we done so, people would have been calling for my head.'[48] In April 1989 another National Intelligence Estimate noted, despite some dissenting voices, that 'for the foreseeable future the Soviet Union will remain the West's principal adversary'.[49]

The Soviet Union ceased to exist less than three years later.

Did Secret Intelligence Help Keep the Peace?

Markus Wolf, the last head of the East German secret police, the Stasi, believed that the spies helped to keep the peace in Europe: the danger of nuclear war was lessened because each side knew so much about what the other was up to. Vadim Bakatin liked the idea that trust between nations would flourish if the public statements of politicians were confirmed by secret intelligence.[50]

It may be true that the more each side knew of the capabilities and anxieties of the other, the less prone they might be to take ill-considered action. Perhaps that is the lesson to draw from Reagan's recognition at the end of 1983 that the Russians really were afraid of American aggression. But claims by intelligencers on both sides that their work substantially reduced the risk of surprise, and thus made a crucial contribution towards keeping the peace, are impossible to verify and hard to sustain.

In one sense, however, the intelligence relationship between the Soviet Union and the West was unprecedented and invaluable. The agreements between them on strategic arms control provided that each should rely on 'national technical means' to check up on the other's compliance.* This required a degree of mutual trust which was not easily available in the Cold War. But both sides were driven to the realisation that a world without such understandings would be altogether too dangerous.

Intelligence was in any case only ever one part of the picture, of varying importance in different cases. The judgements of individual political leaders were usually far more important.[†]

---

* The SALT II Agreement of 1979 included the remarkable condition that neither signatory should attempt to conceal the electronic data generated by its weapons tests by encryption. What could legitimately be encrypted was much debated: there were things that each side still wished to keep from the other. In the early 1980s some Americans accused the Russians of cheating, but the accusation was never established (M. Herman and G. Hughes (eds), *Intelligence in the Cold War*, Abingdon, 2013, p. 56).

† Politicians on both sides often found intelligence fascinating and failed to recognise its limitations. They hoped that it could give them the certainties they craved, but which by their nature were not available.

Michael Alexander, one of Mrs Thatcher's wisest aides, claimed that she paid little attention to intelligence when it came to taking decisions. In his view, 'the intelligence agencies and their product do not have a central impact on government decision-making in peacetime, even when the peace is a Cold War.' He put his finger on a different aspect of the problem: the Western allies' 'misplaced belief during much of the Cold War that the Russians would always triumph in negotiation, [which] helped to undermine Western self-confidence on a number of occasions'. The Russians were, in fact, at least as incompetent in negotiation as the West: their frequent obstructionism was a telltale sign that they too lacked self-confidence.

Thatcher and other leaders felt able to use exaggerated language in public, which was distorted by emotion and political self-interest. Leaders on both sides sometimes took risks which later seemed unconscionable: Khrushchev over Cuba, Nixon's irresponsible bluffing,* Reagan's aggressive posturing. Secret intelligence may have helped to stop them going too far. But it is too large an assertion to claim that its contribution was crucial. Michael Alexander believed that those responsible for everyday affairs proceeded on the working assumption that there would be no doomsday.[51] But the political leaders knew as much about doomsday as anyone: it was they who bore the responsibility, not their generals or intelligencers or officials. When it came to the crunch it was they who pulled back from the brink.

---

* Nixon's belief in the 'Mad President' tactic is described in Chapter 13.

TEN

NOW THRIVE THE ARMOURERS

'From that moment technology assumed command.'

Solly Zuckerman[1]

In January 1953, thousands of mice invaded an arsenal in Central Russia and ate the insulation on the missiles stored there.* Hundreds of cats were brought in to deal with them. Korolev, the Soviet rocket designer, was reduced to tears of laughter when he heard about it. General Volkodav ('Wolfhound'), the man in charge of the arsenal, was sacked for criminal negligence.[2]

The Charm of Technology

From Achilles' shield and Arthur's Excalibur to the humble Kalashnikov and the glittering intercontinental bomber, men have always loved their weapons. They radiate function and beauty, poetry and power. It is no accident that the film *Dr Strangelove or: How I Learned to Stop Worrying and Love the Bomb* begins with a B-52 bomber sinuously weaving its way towards its Soviet target to the sound of romantic music.

The arms race was driven not only by military rivalries, but also by the enthusiasm of the men and women who designed the weapons, who were as fascinated as the physicists by the problems their work threw up and the elegance of the solutions they found. Solly Zuckerman, the British government's scientific adviser in the 1960s, thought that 'A new future with its anxieties was shaped by technologists, not

---

* The story became legendary in the Soviet rocket industry. There seems to be something special about Soviet mice: they also ate the insulation in German tanks outside Stalingrad in 1942, immobilising nearly half the vehicles in the 22 Panzer Division (A. Beevor, *Stalingrad*, London, 1998, p. 231).

because they were concerned with any visionary picture of how the world would evolve, but because they were merely doing what they saw to be their job.'[3]

The Lawrence Livermore Laboratory was set up in 1952 to provide competition to the original laboratory at Los Alamos. The nuclear weapons designers there were convinced that their work was necessary. America's possession of modern and effective nuclear weapons, they believed, was the best way of restraining Soviet ambitions and preventing nuclear war. Those who did not agree with them, who campaigned against nuclear weapons and nuclear testing, were surely naive and misguided, perhaps even deliberately manipulated by America's enemies.

But the weapons designers were not simple-minded conservatives. Many were also concerned about the environment. Some campaigned for human rights. Others opposed the Vietnam War. Many preferred the atmosphere of intellectual freedom at the laboratory: unlike the university, it emphasised teamwork and there was not the relentless pressure to publish in order to advance your career. The disadvantage, of course, was the secrecy that surrounded the laboratory's activities, which made it hard for a scientist to establish his reputation if he wanted to move into the outside world.[4]

The Americans never devised an orderly way of providing the right number and mix of weapons to fit their nuclear strategy, which was itself always in a degree of flux. 'There was never a precise answer to the question of "How Much Is Enough?" with respect to nuclear weapons,' wrote the American authors of one substantial study of the US nuclear arsenal. 'No efficient analytical process was developed to determine how many ICBMs, missile submarines, nuclear artillery shells, or whatever delivery system should be built to serve the goal of deterrence, or if that failed, to fight a nuclear conflict. In fact the process was exceedingly arbitrary and capricious. The stockpile could easily have been twice as large or half as large as what it turned out to be if US military and civilian leaders made different decisions.' Henry Kissinger said that the attempts to reconcile clashing views between the army, the navy and the air force 'resulted in instruments more akin to an agreement between sovereign states than to a workable doctrine'.[5]

Robert McNamara made a determined effort to discipline the process. He was able to impose his will for a time. But in the end he was defeated, thanks to the competing pressures from the weapons designers and producers, the three armed services, different parts of the government, and ambitious individuals in Congress. Perhaps the only person to match McNamara in intellectual force and determination to get a grip on an unsatisfactory situation was Denis Healey, British Defence Secretary from 1964 to 1970. Healey's task was easier, because Britain's limited resources simplified the problems. But even he was unable to eliminate inter-service rivalry and reduce the country's system of military procurement to order. Four decades after Healey cancelled two proposed new aircraft carriers they were back, the largest vessels ever to be built for a much diminished Royal Navy.

Outsiders assumed that the authoritarian Soviet system managed better, that it was capable of far more coherent planning than the noisy and disunited West. This was an illusion.

In the Soviet system, the military industrial complex against which Eisenhower had warned was made literal flesh. The Military-Industrial Commission of the Soviet Union (Voenno-Promyshlennaya Kommissia, or VPK) was formally created in 1957. It was headed by a Deputy Prime Minister: for the first five years by Dmitri Ustinov, who later became a highly influential defence minister, then for more than twenty years by Leonid Smirnov, who was previously in charge of the missile factory in Dnepropetrovsk; and in the Gorbachev years by Yuri Masliukov, who was also the last head of the State Planning Bureau and later served in the government of Boris Yeltsin. Its members included the senior military commanders and the Chairman of the Academy of Science. Its task was to bring order to the proliferation of ministries, committees, enterprises, and research projects involved in the production of weapons which had sprung up during and after the war. In the last resort it was firmly under the central control of the Party and the government. But it was nevertheless a substantial player in the disorderly process of weapons procurement.[6]

The enthusiasms, ambitions, and concerns of the American weapons designers were mirrored on the Soviet side and had at least as great an impact on procurement decisions. There too a kind of competition operated. But it did not deliver the goods. The Soviet arms industry was riven by rivalries between powerful designers and producers of competing weapons. Unnecessary weapons were produced to satisfy the ambitions of industrial and military bosses, and to keep workers paid and employed. As Senior Designer Stanislav Voronin put it, 'our system of totalitarian, centralised management demanded endless changes, and so in effect we designed new prototypes every three or four, even every two or three years. That's why we ended up with so many weapons of so many different types, at such expense.'[7]

The so-called 'small civil war' between the rocket designers led to the notorious dispute between missile designer Vladimir Chelomey and his rival Mikhail Yangel. Chelomey was pushing his SS-19 rocket, which carried six warheads, but was in its initial configuration rather vulnerable to an American first strike. Yangel's SS-17 rocket carried only four warheads, but was comparatively well protected. The choice depended in part on the question of military doctrine which nagged Russians and Americans alike: should they aim to fire their missiles on being warned that their adversary's missiles were about to be fired or were already on their way ('launch on warning') or should they wait until the rockets were already under way ('launch under attack)? Or should their rockets be so well protected that some of them would survive and could be fired in retaliation even after their adversary's rockets had landed?

This was not a simple issue. In July 1969 the Soviet top brass met in Crimea to come up with an answer. Each designer had his supporters, but there was no agreement on the central issue of doctrine. In the interests of peace and quiet Brezhnev allowed both projects to go ahead: an expensive non-decision.[8] That did not settle the debate: the advantages and disadvantages of 'pre-emption', 'launch on warning', and 'launch under attack' continued to be debated in Moscow, as they were in Washington, until the end of the Cold War.

In such ways Soviet weapons producers often succeeded in foisting on the military large volumes of obsolescent stuff that they did not want and found it hard to man and deploy.* Dubious projects

---

* It was a characteristic weakness of the Soviet economic system that it turned out the goods that suited the producers, not the consumers.

were kept going so that skilled design teams should not be dispersed. The Ministry of Defence, commented Sakharov's colleague Yuri Romanov sourly, did not have the guts to turn the rocket engineers down.[9] The authorities could not even keep an accurate count of the number of weapons produced, as they discovered when they had to trade figures in their arms control negotiations with the Americans.[10]

The overproduction had many disadvantages. It reinforced the impression in the West that the Soviet Union was planning for war, and that it was positioning itself for victory at least in Europe. It weakened the Soviet economy, in the end fatally. And in spite of all their efforts, and many successes, the Russians never quite matched the Americans' technological prowess. Vitali Kataev, a senior missile designer and later a senior official in the Central Committee's Defence Department, believed that the low quality of Soviet technology and materials was a continual drag on the Soviet missile and space programmes.[11]

Delivering the Payload

There was little point in the brilliant scientists and engineers at Los Alamos, Livermore, Arzamas-16, and Chelyabinsk-70 producing sophisticated bombs and warheads unless some means could be found of delivering them to their targets. At first the only way was to drop the bomb from an aeroplane.

The Americans, with their wartime experience of strategic aerial bombardment, had a head start. They set up the Strategic Air Command in March 1946. Its mission was 'to conduct long-range offensive operations in any part of the world'. It was equipped with 180 B-29 bombers.

But the B-29 was vulnerable to modern jet fighters, and its range was limited. It was replaced first by the massive B-36, the largest piston-engined aircraft ever made, the Peacemaker,* and then by the Boeing B-47, the Stratojet. Both were flown by James Stewart,

---

*Among the weapons to which the Americans gave the name 'Peacemaker' were this bomber and a nuclear missile. This matched the motto of the Strategic Air Command: 'Peace is our profession'. No irony was involved.

himself a former bomber pilot, in dramatic movies sponsored by the US Air Force. The B-47 was small, fast, and elegant. But it lacked the range to reach targets inside the Soviet Union without refuelling. The Americans settled finally on the Boeing B-52 Stratofortress, one of the most successful aircraft of all time. It could fly fast and high, and it could reach the Soviet Union from bases in America without refuelling. When it first came out, Henry Kissinger thought that at the current rate of technological change it would probably be obsolete in five years.[12] Fifty years later it was still in service. Throughout the Cold War B-52s loitered on the fringes of the Soviet Union, poised to strike in case of nuclear war.[13] They fought in shooting wars too: in Vietnam, during the first Gulf War in 1991, the Kosovo war in 1999, the Afghanistan war in 2001, and the Iraq war in 2003. The B-52 became a star in its own right, a universally recognised symbol of American military and technological power.

In the late 1940s the American public was warned about the Soviet nuclear threat in a series of colourful and noisy films. In 1954 the US Air Force put out an animated film called *Let's Face It* which showed Soviet bombers coming unannounced and unprovoked over the North Pole to destroy cities all across America.

At that time, the menace was largely imaginary, and it was subsequently always exaggerated. Unlike the Anglo-Americans, the Russians had no experience of mounting a massive air campaign.[14] In 1945 they had no adequate long-range bomber. As a stopgap they reverse-engineered four American B-29s which had force-landed on Soviet territory during the war. The result was named the Tu-4 after the Design Bureau headed by Andrei Tupolev. Ten of these, modified to carry atomic bombs, entered service in autumn 1953. They posed a threat to Europe. But they did not have the range to hit America. Neither could the first Soviet long-range jet bomber, the Tu-16 (NATO gave it the name Badger), which began to reach Soviet units in 1954. A big four-engined jet, the Myasischev M-4 (NATO name Bison), came out in the mid-1950s. It too was a comparative failure.[15] But the Tu-95 Bear, which appeared at much the same time, was a surprising success. It had four old-fashioned propeller engines but it was almost as fast as the Bison and had a somewhat longer range. Like the B-52, it remained in service into the twenty-first century.

The Korean War triggered a massive arms build-up in the Soviet Union as it did in America.* Stalin ordered 100 bomber divisions to be deployed to bases on the Arctic ice from which to bombard the United States. The bases were to be secured by mammoth submarines which would carry soldiers, tanks, and aircraft. These 'preposterous' ideas got nowhere.[16]

But the Russians did eventually set up bases in remote parts of northern Russia. These were hard to supply and operate. Because the Russians were concerned about safety and determined to keep their aircraft under political control at all times they did not, unlike the Americans, fly them armed with bombs on alert patrols. But despite the difficulties the Russians had, by the end of the 1950s a small bomber force trained and capable of delivering transpolar attacks on America.[17]

Even before then these rather modest developments were generating something close to panic in America, exacerbated by inadequate intelligence and political opportunism. In February 1954 the American journal *Aviation Week* reported that the Russians had nuclear armed bombers capable of reaching the United States. In May 1955 a National Intelligence Estimate forecast that within three years the Russians would have 600 Bisons and Bears: nearly two-thirds could be expected to break through America's defences in a surprise attack.[18] In July 1955 another NIE estimated that the Russians were already capable of launching an attack with 250 aircraft with almost no warning. By 1958 they would have about 1,100.[19]

The CIA analysts had few hard facts on which to base such estimates. So they eked them out with shaky assumptions. They knew the size of the Moscow factory where the Bisons were built. They calculated how many aircraft an American company would produce in a similar factory, and assumed that the Russians would achieve

---

* The number of men under arms grew from 2.9 million in 1949 to 5.8 million by 1953. Investment in the military and in the defence industries grew by 60 per cent in 1951 and 40 per cent in 1952 (O. Khlevniuk, *Stalin: New Biography of a Dictator*, Yale, 2015, p. 197).

the same rate. In July 1955 ten Bisons flew over the reviewing stand at the Tushino Air Show in Moscow. Eighteen more flew over some time later. It looked like a great show; but the Russians had probably simply flown the same aircraft around twice. A year later an American U-2 reconnaissance aircraft photographed twenty Bisons on a base near Saratov. The CIA multiplied this figure by the number of Soviet bomber bases and concluded that the Russians could already deploy hundreds of the aircraft. In fact the U-2 had photographed the entire Bison fleet. By such means the CIA persuaded themselves that by the early 1960s the Russians would have 500 Bisons available. In reality they only ever built ninety-three.

These wild misestimates nevertheless generated a storm in the American press and in Congress. Senator Symington, a fierce critic of Eisenhower's attempts to limit defence expenditure, claimed that 'the United States and its allies may have lost control of the air' to the Russians. Hawkish officers and politicians trumpeted the idea of a growing Bomber Gap between the United States and the Soviet Union. They demanded more expenditure on the military. Sceptics were accused of being 'weak on defense'. Congress voted $980 million for additional B-52s to match the alleged Soviet build-up.[20]

The Russians did not, of course, abandon their attempt to match the Americans, but their efforts were not very successful. The Defense Intelligence Agency (DIA), backed by conservative lobbyists and publicists, maintained that the supersonic Tu-22M Backfire was a strategic bomber capable of reaching the United States. The Russians vehemently denied it. The dispute complicated arms control negotiations between the Russians and the Americans in the 1980s. Much later the DIA conceded that the Russians were right. The last Soviet bomber was the Tu-160, the Blackjack, which was introduced into service in 1987. It remained in the Russian air force after the Soviet collapse, along with the Tu-95MS, a descendent of the aircraft which had first entered service in the 1950s.

The Soviet bomber force was never a major threat to America: it had comparatively few aircraft and a limited prospect of penetrating the Americans' formidable air defences.[21] The Bomber Gap did indeed widen dramatically, but in favour of the Americans. By the end of the 1950s the Soviet Union had about 150 long-range bombers, as opposed to the 1,100 the CIA had predicted. The Strategic Air Command had almost 2,000. When the Cold War ended the Russians still had only 144 bombers.[22]

The Bomber Gap was a myth.

Even the fastest bombers took a long time to reach their targets. In the second half of the 1950s the Americans constructed a radar chain across the north of Canada which would give several hours' warning of the approach of Soviet bombers over the Arctic. The Strategic Air Command trained its crews to get their aircraft on the way towards their Soviet targets before they could be destroyed on the ground by the Russians.

But this was a makeshift. Within a few years both the Russians and the Americans would have intercontinental ballistic missiles. Warning times would then be reduced to half an hour or less. So that they would not get caught on the ground, the Strategic Air Command kept up to a third of its bombers on alert at the end of the runway, fuelled, loaded with bombs, ready to take off. Twelve bombers were always in the air, armed and ready to fly to their targets. An airborne command post flew continuously in case the Strategic Air Command's underground command post in Omaha was destroyed by a Soviet strike. This airborne alert ended in January 1968, after two bombers crashed in Spain and in Greenland with their bombs aboard. But the B-52s were not taken off ground alert until the end of the Cold War.

The bombers were always vulnerable to the air defences on both sides, despite the ingenious expedients their commanders devised to enable them to penetrate to their targets. Missiles were the obvious alternative, provided they could be made reliable and launched rapidly enough to escape an incoming attack; and had the range to fly thousands of miles to their targets, and then hit them accurately.

These were difficult tasks. Here the Russians began with a significant lead and the Americans once again perceived themselves to be on the wrong side of a gap.

Konstantin Tsiolkovsky was a provincial eccentric who nevertheless succeeded in working out some of the basic principles of rocket

When the report of the bombing of Hiroshima on 6 August 1945 reached America, the papers immediately speculated that America's cities, too, would soon be exposed to a similar destruction: America would reap the whirlwind that it had sown. The speculation died away for a few years thereafter, only to be renewed when the Russians demonstrated in 1949 that they too had mastered the nuclear secret.

NAGASAKI

'Fat Boy' was dropped on Nagasaki on 9 August 1945. It was based on the implosion device exploded during the *Trinity* test a month earlier. Nagasaki was shielded from some of the destructive effects by the surrounding mountains.

The Russians based their first bomb (the picture shows a replica of Fat Boy) on the same principles, which they had derived from their own research and from the intelligence supplied by Klaus Fuchs and others.

THE SOVIET TEST

The first Soviet nuclear test on 29 August 1949 took the Americans by surprise. American scientists respected their Russian colleagues, but more widely it was believed that the Russians lacked the necessary industrial and organisational skills: they could only have made such rapid progress because of their intelligence operation against the Manhattan project.

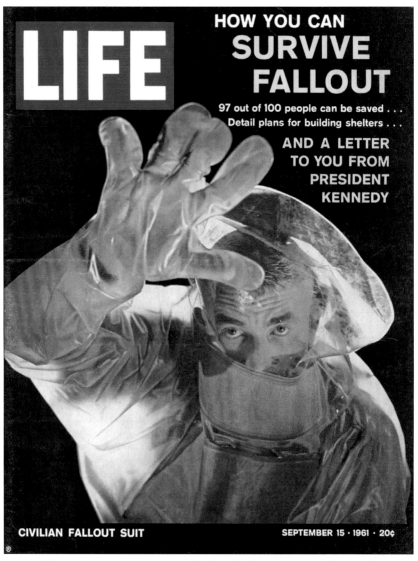

Now that their nuclear monopoly had been broken, the Americans' sense of vulnerability increased greatly. Ideas for sheltering the population against nuclear attack were put forward by government and business. None were plausible.

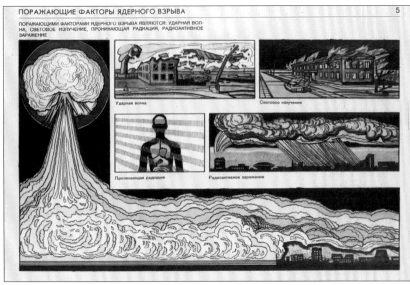

From *Grazhdanskaya Oborona* [Civil Defence] a handbook for Soviet university students first published in 1970 but still in use at the end of the Cold War.

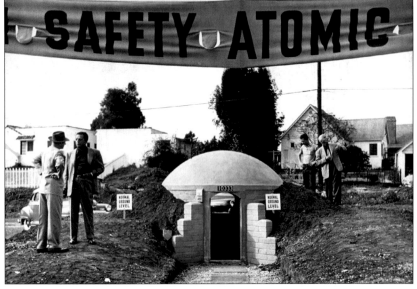

The US government encouraged private business to produce fallout shelters and the equipment to go with them. Here the stuff is being exhibited at a county fair.

LEADERS

[*Clockwise from top left*] Leonid Brezhnev whispering to Richard Nixon; Khrushchev expressing himself with characteristic force; British Prime Minister Harold MacMillan and President John F. Kennedy in Key West, Florida, 1961; Mikhail Gorbachev and Ronald Reagan enjoying their first meeting in Geneva in 1986.

SECRET SITES

For the site of their secret nuclear weapons laboratory, the Americans commandeered the Los Alamos Ranch School on a high plateau in New Mexico. The Russians took over the town and Monastery of Sarov in Central Russia, a favourite place of pilgrimage of Tsar Nicholas II, and renamed it Arzamas-16. Both sites were surrounded by barbed wire perimeters and heavy security, which in the case of Los Alamos proved inadequate.

WIZARDS OF ARMAGEDDON

Stanley Kubrick never revealed who was the model for the antihero of his great film *Dr Strangelove*. Some believe it was Herman Kahn, the strategic theorist who invented the idea of the megadeath, others that it was Edward Teller, the brilliant Hungarian physicist who insisted that the hydrogen bomb had to be built, pushed Reagan's Star Wars scheme, and helped to bring about the downfall of Robert Oppenheimer.

PROPAGANDA

This Godless Communism, a comic strip published by the Catholic Guild in 1961, showed how ordinary Americans would live under Communism. Hollywood made several anti-Communist films in the 1950s. The Soviet poster attacks the League of Nations and the Western bankers allegedly behind it. The cartoon, from 1986, shows an American scientist handing a phial of AIDS virus to an American general.

THE MEN BEHIND THE BOMB

[*From top left, clockwise*] Niels Bohr and Albert Einstein, whose revolutionary theories of relativity and quantum physics provided much of the theoretical basis for the nuclear weapon; General Groves and Robert Oppenheimer, who led the Manhattan Project; and Igor Kurchatov ('The Beard') and Yuli Khariton, who led the Soviet project.

SOVIET SCIENTISTS

Petr Kapitsa and Nikolai Semenov, two future Nobel prize winners, painted by Boris Kustodiev.

The secret police mugshot of Lev Landau, one of the most
brilliant scientists of the twentieth century.

WEAPONS

The US Strategic Air Command was by far the most powerful strategic bombing force in history. It was set up in 1947, but did not come into its own until the charismatic and ruthless Curtis LeMay reorganised it a year later. Its motto was 'To err is human: To forgive is not SAC policy.'

From 1966 the SAC was equipped with the Boeing B-52 bomber which starred in the film *Dr Strangelove*, remained in service into the twenty-first century, and became an icon in its own right. This colourful example was used by the US National Aeronautics and Space Administration for experimental purposes.

By the end of the 1990s, the British had come to rely for their deterrent solely on a small, but very competent, fleet of Vanguard class ballistic missile submarines. Highly competent vessels were British designed and built, but their Trident missiles were supplied by the Americans under the agreement negotiated at Nassau in the Bahamas by Kennedy and Macmillan at the end of 1962.

The Russians lagged behind the Americans in both the size and sophistication of their nuclear forces. But their SS-18 Satan rockets were more powerful than anything the Americans had.

PROTEST

The Russians organised massive 'Peace' campaigns in the West (The caption reads 'No room for them to land' on the banners marked 'Peace'.) The elderly Bertrand Russell (*left*) was arrested in Whitehall in 1961. Joseph Rotblat (*right*), a founder of the Pugwash Conferences, believed in quiet persuasion.

AFTERMATH

After Britain, the Soviet Union, and the United States signed the Partial Test Ban Treaty in the summer of 1963, they abandoned nuclear testing in the atmosphere. Their test sites – like this Soviet site – were abandoned. But much incidental pollution remained in the surrounding areas – in Australia, the Pacific, in mainland America and the Soviet Union. And France and China ignored the ban for several decades, as did other aspiring nuclear powers.

And the major nuclear powers went on testing their weapons underground for many more years. Most of them ratified the Comprehensive Test Ban Treaty in 1998, which banned underground testing. But the Americans refused to do so.

As the twenty-first century got into its stride, the major nuclear powers were all modernising their armouries, as newcomers struggled to catch up.

flight, including the 'Tsiolkovsky equation', which calculates how fast a rocket must go to break out of the earth's atmosphere into space.[23] He was an inspiration for Soviet rocket research, though he made no practical contribution towards it. In 1933 the Group for the Study of Reactive Motion was set up in Moscow. Its members included Sergei Korolev, who later became one of the Soviet Union's leading rocket designers. The group launched its first rocket in March 1933. It reached the modest height of 1,000 feet. That September the Reaction Research Institute was formed in Leningrad with the support of General Tukhachevsky, then nearing the height of his career as a military reformer.

The rocket engineers and their supporters suffered greatly during Stalin's purges. Tukhachevsky was shot in 1937. Korolev was sent to the Gulag, first to a labour camp and then to a *sharashka*, a design bureau manned by convicts and headed by the aircraft designer Tupolev. The same thing happened to Valentin Glushko, a pioneer designer of rocket engines who, like Korolev, later rose to eminence.[24]

The successful German V-2 missile attacks on London in 1944 revived Soviet interest in rockets.* Korolev and Glushko were fished out of their camps and sent to defeated Germany to find out what the Germans had been up to. Most of the senior German specialists had already fled to the West, and the Soviet team's haul of experts and information was rather modest. But by the middle of 1946 the Russians had collared enough German specialists to restart production of V-2s first in East Germany and then in Moscow, where the Germans remained until the mid-1950s. Korolev was appointed to head Special Design Bureau No. I. Another design bureau was set up under Vladimir Chelomey to explore the advantages of cruise missiles derived from the German V-1 'Doodlebug'.[25]

The Soviet military were not at first in favour of missiles, which

---

* Perhaps the first man to work out some of the practical principles of space flight was Hermann Oberth, who wrote a ground-breaking study in the early 1920s. He was the technical adviser to the great German film director Fritz Lang for his remarkable *Frau im Mond* (*Woman on the Moon*, 1929). One of Oberth's acolytes was the teenage Wernher von Braun. The story of the American and Soviet rocket programmes was told in a BBC docudrama, *Space Race* (2005).

they considered cumbersome, ineffective, and expensive. One general remarked that his troops would be able to storm any town if they were fuelled with as much alcohol as the rockets seemed to need. The first ballistic missile brigade was nevertheless formed in July 1946, and from 1950 Korolev's upgraded V-2s began to come into service. These were inaccurate, their range was limited, and they could not carry a nuclear warhead. Although their successor, the R-5, was specifically designed to carry a nuclear warhead, its range was only 750 miles: adequate to hit Europe, useless for hitting American bomber bases in the American heartland.

But Korolev's R-7 was a major step in the right direction. It could carry a five-megaton thermonuclear warhead for 5,000 miles, and came dramatically to the world's attention in October 1957, when it launched the Sputnik. Its descendants were still in use more than half a century later to deliver payloads into space.[26]

But the R-7 was far from an ideal strategic weapon. It was hugely expensive. At first it was hopelessly inaccurate. It took twenty hours to fuel before it could be launched and was thus vulnerable to an American pre-emptive strike. It could only hit the United States if it was based in northern Russia. A dedicated base was built in Plesetsk, near Archangel. But the climatic conditions there were atrocious, and there were never more than four R-7s on alert at Plesetsk at any one time. Moreover the Russians were slow to recognise that their success with Sputnik had also ushered in the age of reconnaissance satellites. They assumed that the Plesetsk base could be kept secret. But before it was even finished, the Americans had photographed it from their U-2 aircraft and their reconnaissance satellites. The Russian missiles were now exposed and vulnerable. The problems diminished as later variants of the R-7 had longer range and could be based further south.

A furious Khrushchev authorised Korolev's rival Yangel to begin work on two new missiles. These had storable fuels so that they could be launched within thirty minutes of an alert, and smaller warheads so that they were lighter and easier to manage. By the summer of 1960 Yangel's R-12 missiles had been deployed in the western Soviet Union, from where they could hit American air bases in western Europe.

But Yangel also got into trouble. His intercontinental R-16 – a monster over thirty metres long, three metres in diameter and weighing 141 tons – was due to be tested in late 1960. Despite a growing number of technical glitches, the commander of the Strategic Rocket Forces, Marshal Mitrofan Nedelin, insisted that the test should take place in time to celebrate the anniversary of the Revolution on 7 November. Only one courageous individual, Colonel Titov, spoke out against him. Under pressure to beat the deadline, the launch team short-cut the safety procedures and worked without sleep for three days to get things ready in time.

The result was a spectacular disaster. Nedelin and others who should have been at a safe distance were crowding round the rocket as testing began. A combination of malfunction and sloppy procedure caused the missile to blow up in an immense fireball. Those nearest to it were engulfed in the flames. Those further away were poisoned by vapour from the propellant. In all about 100 people died.[27] Yangel survived because he had gone off to have a smoke.

Leonid Brezhnev, then Khrushchev's Prime Minister, came to investigate. He sensibly told Yangel's designers, 'We understand that we are engaged in the most complex undertaking. It's impossible to do it without mistakes in such affairs. That's why we are not going to carry out any investigation. We must get rid of any technical shortcomings and continue the work.' Yangel accepted overall responsibility for the disaster. Only one person was sacked – a young woman design engineer. There was no witch-hunt.[28]

The affair was hushed up. Nedelin was officially reported to have died in an air accident. News leaked out to an Italian newspaper within weeks, though full details did not appear in the Soviet press until 1989.[29] Work on the R-16 went ahead nevertheless. It was successfully tested in February 1961, and four missile regiments became operational the following November. The missiles were still not based in silos, and they still took too long – three hours – to prepare for launching. But Yangel's R-16 continued to outperform Korolev's missile, and it became the first Soviet ICBM to be deployed in significant numbers.*

---

* Korolev was now working on a rival rocket, the R-9. It failed its first tests because Glushko's engines did not work. Relations between the two men deteriorated disastrously, despite Khrushchev's attempts to mediate. Glushko

From 1965 the Russians began to develop a second and militarily more useful generation of missiles with the range to strike across continents. They could be launched more rapidly than their predecessors, because they were permanently fuelled; and they were designed to be placed in underground silos. One of them, known to the Russians as the R-36M and to NATO as the SS-18 Satan, could carry a heavy payload of ten or more independently targetable warheads with great accuracy. When they got to know of it at the beginning of the 1970s, the Americans immediately saw it as a direct threat to their own missiles. It became a major bone of contention between the two countries.

Despite the blow to their self-esteem inflicted by Sputnik, the Americans were not all that far behind the Russians. Their first rockets, too, were based on the German V-2, and German experts were involved in the design.

Like the Russians, the Americans then moved to produce intermediate-range ballistic missiles, IRBMs. The US Air Force favoured classical names for their missiles, and the first two were called Thor and Jupiter. Like the earlier Russian missiles, the Thors had to be stored above ground, separately from their volatile liquid oxygen fuel, and it could take up to two days to prepare them for launching. That made them obvious targets for a Soviet attack. The Jupiters were equally unsatisfactory: they were more accurate than the Thor, but otherwise suffered from the same deficiencies. Since neither could hit the Soviet Union from the United States they had to be stationed on the territory of America's allies, the Jupiters in Italy and Turkey, the Thors in Britain, where they were under the joint control of the US Air Force and the Royal Air Force.*

What the Americans needed, like the Russians, was strategic missiles with intercontinental range. Four missiles became the backbone of their strategic force: Atlas, Titan I and II, and Minuteman.[30]

refused to work on Korolev's plans for a Soviet moon mission: one reason why the Russians lost the moon race to the Americans (S. Zaloga, *The Kremlin's Nuclear Sword*, Washington, DC, 2002, p. 89).

* These missiles figured in the Cuban missile crisis, discussed in Chapter 13.

Atlas was unreliable at first: out of ninety-five test firings, thirty-eight were failures. But in the panic following Sputnik, it had the attraction that it promised to be available before the other missile then being developed, the Titan. It nevertheless remained a problematic device. It was expensive to maintain, took too long to launch, and could not be placed in an underground silo. It was so inaccurate that General Powers, LeMay's successor as commander of the Strategic Air Command, who preferred bombers, thought it never had much chance of hitting its target.[31] It was phased out after 1962.

Titan II addressed some of the weaknesses suffered by its predecessors. It could be kept in a silo. Its thermonuclear warhead could yield nine megatons, three times as much as all the explosive dropped in the Second World War, including the bombs dropped on Japan. It could hit a target 6,000 miles away. And it could be launched rapidly enough in a crisis to make military sense. But it too was a tricky beast. The liquid fuel was hard to manage and there were a number of unpleasant accidents when it got out of control. It nevertheless remained in service until 1981.

The obvious answer was solid rather than liquid fuel. This was far easier to manage and the missiles could be ready for action at very short notice. Even as Titan was being deployed, the US Air Force was developing the Minuteman, small, solid-fuelled, and comparatively inexpensive. Later versions had greater payload, accuracy, and range. The military were so taken by it that they argued for a strategic missile force of 2,500. By the end of 1963 nearly 400 Minutemen had been deployed and the number had doubled two years later. By then the Americans had almost as many ICBMs as bombers.[32]

The atmosphere in a missile site was very special. Bruce Blair served in a Minuteman site in the 1970s and described what it was like to practise launching his missiles: 'It's nerve-racking because it's easy to make a critical mistake. If we decoded a message incorrectly and dialed a single wrong digit into the computer that targeted our missiles, we might attack and destroy cities instead of rural missile silos in Russia. We could have easily killed millions of civilians by mistake … There was no feeling of dread or guilt as we decoded the launch order … No more than two minutes elapsed between the time of the

launch order's arrival and our final key-turn. No little lights of conscience flickered in our minds. Launch officers in their early twenties,
like myself, rarely struggled with the moral question of following
orders that potentially could kill so many innocent civilians. It was
all rationalized in the name of "deterrence".'[33]

It was not very different in a Soviet missile site. The Russians
trained crews for the massive SS-18 missile at a base in a forest in
Balabanovo near Moscow.* An SS-18 was housed there for training
purposes. The walls of its silo were covered with what looked like
stalactites, insulation against the damp. The cover of the silo was
an immense steel shield, which could be opened in seven seconds
– beautifully made, like a Japanese camera, quite unlike the average
Soviet artefact. Since this was a training facility, the command post
was above ground.

The launch team consisted of two smart young officers. They
would give visitors a rather histrionic display of their launching
procedures, which were very similar to those described by Bruce Blair.
They called out and verified codes as they received them, punched
them into their computers, and 'launched' ten rockets against what
they too called the 'potential enemy'. Like their opposite numbers in
Britain and America, they had no doubt that they would do their duty
if it came to the real thing. Nor did they have any illusions about what
would then happen to their families who lived with them on the base.[34]

In his last State of the Union message in January 1961 the ever-scep-
tical Eisenhower said that 'The "Bomber Gap" of several years ago
was always a fiction, and the "Missile Gap" shows every sign of being
the same.'[35]

By mid-1961 the Americans had seventy-eight land-based missiles. The navy had eighty missiles which could be launched by their
five nuclear submarines while submerged. And the Strategic Air
Command had over 1,500 intercontinental bombers.[36]

American intelligence analysts were then calculating that the Russians had somewhere between fifty and 200 intercontinental ballistic
missiles. But there was no concrete evidence that the missiles had been

---

* It now houses the Museum of the Strategic Rocket Forces.

deployed. None had been identified by the U-2 reconnaissance aircraft flying across the Soviet Union. One theory assumed that this was because the U-2s could only cover a small area of the Soviet Union. More paranoid commentators argued that the absence of evidence merely showed that the Russians were very good at hiding things.

But in August 1960 the Americans' reconnaissance satellites systematically photographed the whole of the Soviet Union for the first time. They gathered enough material to show that Eisenhower was right: there was no Missile Gap, any more than there had been a Bomber Gap. The Russians' missiles would take six hours to launch, their missile submarines were in port, their air defence system had such holes in it that an American bomber force could get right through. The small Soviet bomber force might – perhaps – have been able to attack America; but they were not on alert. The Russians were in no shape to launch a surprise attack, and were themselves vulnerable to a first strike by the Americans.

The analysts climbed down, but their climb-down was tortuous. If you lumped together all Soviet strategic nuclear capabilities, they argued – missiles, bombers, and submarines – they might 'pose a grave threat to US urban areas, but a more limited threat during the months immediately ahead to our nuclear striking force'. The Strategic Air Command disputed even these more modest conclusions, and continued to demand thousands more bombers and 10,000 Minutemen.[37]

They did not get them. The government decided at the end of 1964 on a ceiling of 1,000. By then the gap which had apparently opened up by the launch of Sputnik had been decisively closed. The Americans now had three legs to their nuclear deterrent: bombers, land-based intercontinental ballistic missiles, and a burgeoning fleet of invisible submarines.

Even after the Second World War submarines used diesel engines to run on the surface. Underwater they used electric engines. They were cheap, quiet, and hard to detect when submerged. Their 'snorkels', the breathing tubes invented by the Germans shortly before the war ended, and new techniques of 'air independent propulsion' enabled them to remain underwater for longer periods. But sooner or later they had to surface to ventilate their interiors and recharge their batteries. And then they became very vulnerable to attack. Submarines would only become an effective strategic nuclear arm when they could live submerged and undetected for days or weeks at a time, and when their missiles could be fired underwater and still hit targets thousands of miles away.

Nuclear power was the answer. It could generate steam or electricity to run the submarine's engines, and purify the air and the water for its crew. The range and endurance of a nuclear-powered submarine would then be limited only by the amount of food it could carry and the stamina of the men aboard. In 1954 the Americans launched the *Nautilus*, the world's first nuclear submarine. *Nautilus* could remain underwater for up to four months and was the first submarine to navigate under the Pole. It opened an entirely new era in submarine warfare. No major navy could afford not to follow where the Americans had led.

At first the Americans armed their nuclear submarines with cruise missiles launched on the surface. But the obvious next step was to arm them with ballistic missiles which they could launch underwater. The first nuclear missile submarine, the *George Washington*, was designed to carry sixteen Polaris missiles. These were not large enough to carry the heaviest warheads, they were not very accurate, and their range was comparatively short. Firing a missile from a submerged submarine was much more complicated than firing it from an underground silo, and failures with the Polaris test programme nearly brought it to an end. But in mid-1960 the *George Washington* successfully fired two Polaris missiles underwater, and went on its first operational patrol that November.[38]

Eisenhower wanted to restrict the size of submarine force as part of his attempt to put limits on defence expenditure. But Kennedy authorised a rapid expansion of the fleet. By 1962, the year of the Cuban missile crisis, the Americans had twenty-six operational nuclear submarines. Under the relentless leadership of Admiral Rickover, by 1967 their ballistic missile fleet consisted of forty-one submarines carrying 656 missiles, which they nicknamed the '41 for Freedom'.*

---

* The SALT agreement of 1972 limited to 656 the number of submarine missile tubes permitted to the Americans. Conveniently this was the same as the number of tubes mounted by the forty-one submarines.

The weaknesses of the Polaris missile were gradually rectified. It was replaced by the much more powerful Poseidon missile in the early 1970s. The Trident I and II missiles followed, and the Ohio class of submarine was constructed to carry them.

The Russians were the first to fire a missile from a submarine, but their progress thereafter was slower than the Americans'. In 1954 they launched a version of the army's Scud missile, modified by Korolev, from the sail (conning tower) of a diesel submarine. These missiles had to be launched on the surface, they were inaccurate, their range was inadequate, and their fuel had an unpleasant tendency to leak and catch fire.

This first generation of missile submarines were diesel boats. They were noisy and easy to detect. Because their missiles had such inadequate ranges, they had to cross the Atlantic and close America to hit their targets. Communications between them and their bases were patchy, and the General Staff were fearful that one of the boats might escape their control. Nevertheless four submarines with somewhat improved missiles were deployed from 1959 with the Northern Fleet and two in the Pacific. Their missiles were primarily aimed at targets in Europe and Japan.

The first Soviet nuclear-powered submarine was launched in 1958, four years after the Nautilus. But in their hurry to catch up the Russians cut too many corners. The submarine reactors were unreliable, and the Russians could not mount regular standing patrols against the American continent until the second half of the 1960s.[39] Even then their submarines carried only three missiles each. By then Americans submarines were already carrying sixteen Polaris missiles.

Confusingly named Soviet submarines succeeded one another with bewildering frequency. The Russians gave them a project name, and sometimes the name of a fish – Murena (Eel), Kalmar (Squid). NATO, however, gave them code names: Echo and Golf for the first nuclear-powered submarines; Hotel, Yankee, Delta for their successors. Soviet submarines became quieter and thus harder for Western submarine-catchers to find. Their range and endurance increased. They were armed with far more potent missiles. By the time the Cold War had finished, the Russians had built 245 nuclear-powered attack and missile submarines, more than the rest of the world combined.

The last of the Soviet Cold War missile submarines was the hugely expensive Typhoon, the largest submarine ever built, whose missiles were powerful enough to hit America from the comparative safety of its bases in northern Russia. The Russian name for this massive vessel was Akula (Shark). NATO gave the same name to a completely different submarine, a hunter-killer, which the Russians called after a different predator, Shchuka (Pike). It was a further cause of muddle.

Both sides used their nuclear-powered submarines to monitor one another's naval activities. Once again the West had the geographical advantage, penetrating deep into the Russians' naval citadel north of Murmansk. There were apparently thirteen underwater collisions between Soviet submarines and their American opponents, and two involving the British.[40]

By the 1980s each side had strategic forces of overwhelming power. Americans bombers and intercontinental ballistic missiles could hit Soviet targets from a continent away. Their submarines, now armed with Trident missiles, were operating so close to the Soviet Union that the Soviet leaders might get no more than ten minutes' warning of an attack. Medium-range American missiles based in Europe would give an even shorter warning. The British and French were multiplying the number of warheads their submarines could deliver. The Soviet leaders feared they could be killed before they were able to take countermeasures.[41]

As the Soviet political leadership weakened under the ailing Brezhnev and his two elderly and short-lived successors, the Soviet military pushed ahead with a massive arms build-up: by the late 1970s the Russians were producing strategic missiles at about four times the rate of the Americans.[42] Carter, Reagan, and their advisers saw the Soviet build-up as an intolerable threat, even though they had a sufficiency of warheads and little reason to change their mature weapons systems, Minuteman, Trident, and the B-52 bomber, which remained effective well into the twenty-first century.

It was the Russians' nuclear forces that had enabled them to face up to their American adversary throughout the Cold War. The Russians hung on to them after the Soviet collapse as a symbol of fading power. In 1993 they published a new military doctrine, which said that they would consider using nuclear weapons first if there were no other way to defend Russia's national interests. Russia thus aligned itself with NATO's traditional position that its willingness to use nuclear weapons first was its only sure defence against the overwhelming strength of the Soviet armies in Europe.

The wheel had come full circle.

Accidents Will Happen

Human agency – misjudgement, miscommunication, ill-considered risk-taking – was not the only trigger of crisis (these are described in Chapter 13). There were many lesser near-crises, false alarms, and technical accidents associated with nuclear weapons and their systems of command and control. Some were rectified because of their inbuilt fail-safe systems; some by human intervention; some by good luck. None resulted in a nuclear explosion.

False Warnings

In November 1979 American military computers appeared to show that a massive Soviet nuclear strike was imminent, aimed at the US command system and nuclear forces. Minuteman control centres were warned to stand by, interceptors took off, and the President's 'doomsday plane' – the flying command post from which he could if necessary manage a nuclear war – was launched, though without the President on board. The alert was cancelled after six minutes when early warning satellites and radars showed no sign of an attack.

What had happened was that an exercise tape simulating an attack had accidentally been put into the Strategic Air Command's operational computer system. The air force took remedial measures which, Congress was told, would 'guarantee that [a similar incident] could never recur'. The General Accounting Office said, slightly less categorically, 'this type of false alert should not recur'.

The Russians picked it up. Leonid Brezhnev wrote secretly to President Carter that the erroneous alert was 'fraught with a tremendous danger ... I think you will agree with me that there should be no errors in such matters'. Carter replied that the accusations were 'inaccurate and unacceptable', language which Marshall Shulman, the State Department's adviser on Soviet affairs, thought 'snotty' and 'gratuitously insulting ... false alerts of this kind are not a rare occurrence'. There was a 'complacency about handling them that disturbs me'.[43]

Another false alert occurred within a year. On 3 June 1980 military computers again indicated a major missile attack. Bomber crews started their engines. Minuteman bases stood by. Once again the alert ended when radars showed no evidence of an attack.

Three days later it happened again. This time the warning went almost to the top. Carter's National Security Advisor, Zbigniew Brzezinski, was awakened at three in the morning by his military assistant, William Odom, who told him that some 250 Soviet missiles had been launched against the United States. The President had no more than ten minutes to order retaliation, but Brzezinski wanted confirmation before disturbing him. Odom rang back to say that the previous report was wrong: 2,200, not 250, missiles were on the way. Brzezinski was about to call the President, when Odom rang yet again. Other warning systems had shown no confirmation of a Soviet attack. Brzezinski had not bothered to wake his wife, reckoning that everyone would be dead in half an hour anyway.[44]

The post-mortem revealed that a computer chip had failed. The colonel who had called the alert was sacked. Thereafter his function was assigned to generals only, on the principle that colonels may make mistakes, but generals never do. Thirty years later, the US Air Force was still using the same computers.[45]

These incidents caused a flurry of press reports, numerous congressional investigations, and further remedial measures. They were also picked up by the Russians, who exploited the incidents in their propaganda to portray American policy as dangerous.

There was no reason to believe that such misadventures did not occur on the Soviet side as well, though few escaped into the public domain.* One unsettling incident occurred as a series of NATO

---

* One that did, though it did not involve the Soviet nuclear forces, was a mutiny aboard the Soviet frigate *Storozhevoy* in Riga in November 1975. The ship's commissar persuaded the crew to take it to sea in protest against the Brezhnev

exercises began in autumn 1983. On 26 September Colonel Stanislav Petrov was on duty at the command centre for the new and still error-prone Oko early warning system, when it generated an ambiguous signal that five American missiles were on the way. Petrov correctly concluded that it was a false alarm and decided not to inform his superiors. People in the West later speculated that his report might have triggered a nuclear exchange if it had gone forward. The Russians maintained that the system contained other safeguards: no decision to launch a nuclear counterstrike would have been taken on the basis of a single report. Petrov himself played the incident down. But he was showered with Western awards in his retirement, and a Hollywood film was released in 2015 about *The Man Who Saved the World*.[46]

Technical Mishaps

Apart from false alarms generated by the warning systems on both sides, the weapons themselves suffered many technical malfunctions over the years.

The American Defense Department classified such accidents according to code words, many whimsically drawn from Native American usage. 'Pinnacle' was an accident that resulted in military action, disturbed international relationships, or got into the press. 'Pinnacle-Nucflash' accidents involved the detonation or possible detonation of a nuclear weapon or the accidental or unauthorised launch of a missile or aircraft towards another nuclear state. Other incidents – the unauthorised launch or jettison of a weapon, a fire, an explosion, a release of energy, or a nuclear explosion which did not risk war – were called 'Broken Arrows'. In 2013 the Defense Department said that thirty-two 'Broken Arrow' incidents had occurred since 1950. The total may have been nearly twice that. In the course of the Cold War the Americans lost eleven nuclear bombs that were never recovered.[47]

Between 1950 and 1980 there were some twenty-five accidents involving American aircraft and nuclear weapons. Aircraft crashed,

---

regime. It was brought to heel by aircraft and naval vessels, and the commissar was shot.

blew up, or disappeared. One flew into a cloud and was never seen again. In January 1961 a B-52 broke up over North Carolina: by a narrow margin, its two nuclear bombs did not explode. A B-52 collided with an aerial tanker over Spain. The conventional explosives in two of its hydrogen bombs blew up when they hit the ground and a great deal of plutonium was scattered around. A third was found intact. The fourth fell into the sea. The Americans paid compensation and shipped tons of radioactive soil to America for decontamination. The Spanish government banned US aircraft from carrying nuclear weapons in its airspace. The Danish government followed suit when a loaded B-52 crashed in Greenland in 1968: the incident formed the climax of *Strategic Air Command*, a film starring James Stewart.

Rockets were also prone to accidents. They caught fire and blew up in their silos. Weapons fell off trolleys while they were being loaded, or got mislaid in store. Sensitive fusing devices malfunctioned or short-circuited, with potentially disastrous consequences.

By the late 1970s the United States arsenal contained fifty-four liquid-fuelled Titan II missiles. In August 1965 a launch site in Arkansas was being hardened to make it better able to survive a nuclear strike. The warhead had been removed from the missile, but its tanks were full. A fire broke out and the place filled with smoke. Fifty-three construction workers were asphyxiated. The missile itself was undamaged.[48]

In August 1978, at a missile base near Wichita, Kansas, two men died while a Titan II missile was being refuelled. A young technician was badly hurt. The official report saddled him with the blame.

In September 1980 an airman dropped a tool while he was working on a Titan II missile in Arkansas. The tool pierced the rocket's fuel tank. Fuel poured out and the next morning the rocket blew up. Its warhead landed a hundred yards away. The safety mechanisms worked: there was no explosion and no loss of radioactive material. But the rocket site was destroyed and one man was killed. An investigation concluded that the Titan II was 'potentially hazardous, [but] basically safe [and] supportable now and in the immediate future'. That was hardly a ringing endorsement.[49] The Defense Department eventually admitted to the Senate that the missile was inaccurate and accident-prone. Sixty-three Titan II missiles nevertheless remained in service until 1981. By then full details of its operational procedures had been passed to the Soviet Embassy in Washington by a Titan II officer.

Once the switch was made to solid-fuelled rockets the missile accident rate fell significantly. But in October 2010 a computer failure put fifty Minuteman missiles temporarily out of action. It emerged that a circuit board had been improperly installed during routine maintenance.[50]

Over the years there were a number of accidents involving American nuclear submarines. Most were comparatively minor, though several resulted in the release of radioactive substances. In 1963 the USS *Thresher* sank in the Atlantic 200 miles off Massachusetts: an inquiry blamed faults in its design and construction. In 1968 the USS *Scorpion*, carrying two nuclear torpedoes, sank in very deep water 400 miles off the Azores. The cause was never finally decided: theories include inadequate maintenance and the explosion of one of the submarine's own torpedoes. Conspiracy theorists attributed it to an attack by a Soviet submarine. The crews perished in both disasters.

Some American weapons were inadequately designed in the first place. The Snark was the Americans' first intercontinental missile. Named after the mysterious creature in Lewis Carroll's poem, it was descended from the Germans' wartime 'Doodlebug'. It had wings, a jet engine, a range of about 6,000 miles, and carried a four-megaton warhead. But like Carroll's original, it was distressingly wayward: it was reckoned to have a one in ten chance of hitting its target. One Snark on a test flight failed to stop when it was supposed to, eventually ran out of fuel, and crashed somewhere in Brazil. Thirty Snarks were nevertheless briefly deployed from 1959 until Kennedy declared them to be 'obsolete and of marginal military value'.[51]

Not much is publicly known about Soviet nuclear accidents. Russian scientists claimed that the Soviet safety record was substantially better than the American. The weapons were specifically designed, they argued, to resist fire and external explosion. Rigorous operating procedures ensured that weapons and fissile material could be safely transported. They were fully guarded against theft and terrorist attack. There was, the scientists maintained, no accident with Soviet weapons that resulted in the dispersal of nuclear explosive, like the American accident in Spain.[52]

That may have been true in a narrow sense. But it was not the whole story by a long chalk. Under Mikhail Gorbachev more began to emerge about Soviet nuclear accidents. There was the steady poisoning of the environment around the Mayak plant, the result of ignorance as well as accidents. There was the missile explosion which killed Marshal Nedelin in October 1960. And there was the reactor explosion in Chernobyl in 1986.

There were plenty of lesser incidents too. Soviet weapons builders admitted that their safety standards were low at first, partly because they were working at such speed to catch up with the Americans.[53] The detonators used in earlier warheads were unstable, and liable to explode and cause injury if mishandled or set off by static electricity. Large pieces of equipment dropped off the vehicles that were carrying them.[54]

A tragic consequence of the Russians' hurried submarine development programme was that their boats were prone to accident. Ten accidents involved reactor or other nuclear components. Twelve were the result of fires or equipment malfunctions. Six submarines were damaged or lost following collision with US vessels and three as a result of other collisions. One submarine lost a nuclear weapon which was recovered after a massive search. Over the years some 240 Soviet submariners died, perhaps more.[55]

In October 1960 the reactor cooling system of the November-class submarine K-8 started to leak while it was exercising in the Barents Sea. Three crew members were exposed to radiation as they attempted a repair. In April 1970 the K-8 suffered two fires while in the Bay of Biscay. It was taken in tow but sank with fifty-two sailors still on board.

In July 1961 the Hotel-class submarine K-19 was on its maiden voyage when its reactor cooling system started to leak. Eight sailors who tried to mend the leak died of radiation immediately, and fifteen more over the next two years. Another twenty-eight sailors died in a fire in 1972. Soviet sailors grimly nicknamed the submarine 'Hiroshima'. Four decades later the Americans made a film about the K-19's first accident. Called *K-19: The Widowmaker*, it won the qualified approval of the survivors.*

The accidents went on. In April 1977 submarine K-171 accidentally released a nuclear warhead off Vladivostok. The warhead was recovered after a search involving dozens of ships and aircraft. In August 1985 ten men were killed by a reactor explosion in the Echo-class submarine K-431. In October 1986 three men were killed by an explosion in a missile tube in K-290. The boat was about 500 miles east of Bermuda and later sank while under tow. Gorbachev privately informed Ronald Reagan before announcing the incident publicly.

In 2000 the Oscar II-class submarine *Kursk* sank in the Barents Sea. This was not a nuclear accident: it was caused by the explosion of a faulty torpedo. All 188 on board died, most immediately, some after surviving a few hours. Unlike the accident with the K-19, the affair was massively covered in the world's media.

***

Thus, despite the most rigorous procedures, accidents could still happen. Even the most sophisticated systems could go wrong. Neither side in the Cold War could claim a better record than the other.

---

*One of them, the ship's cook, Vladimir Romanov, got rich on retirement. He bought the Scottish football club Heart of Midlothian in 2005 and his old submarine in 2006 (R. Woodman and D. Conley, *Cold War Command*, Barnsley, 2014, p. 92; and https://en.wikipedia.org/wiki/Vladimir_Romanov).

PART III

COPING WITH THE CONSEQUENCES

ELEVEN

A VERY PLEASANT WAY TO DIE

'Death isn't cruel, merely terribly, terribly good at his job.'

Terry Pratchett[1]

In their memorandum to the British government of March 1940, Peierls and Fritsch had warned that 'the radiations would be fatal to living beings even a long time after the explosion'. Oppenheimer and Groves devised safety measures for the staff of the Manhattan Project: an accident at Los Alamos on 21 August 1945 nevertheless led to the death by radiation of a young physicist, Harry Daghlian. Another, on 21 May 1946, led to the death of a Canadian physicist, Louis Slotin. Oppenheimer predicted that radiation from an explosion would endanger life 'for a radius of at least two thirds of a mile'.[2] By the summer of 1942 the Americans were worrying that the Germans might start using dirty bombs within a matter of months. The Germans had no such capacity. But the Americans started to consider countermeasures. In May 1943 Oppenheimer wrote to Fermi about a scheme for using strontium to poison food. There were many practical difficulties, and Oppenheimer recommended that the scheme should not be attempted 'unless we can poison food sufficient to kill a half a million men, since there is no doubt that the actual number affected will, because of non-uniform distribution, be much smaller than this.'[3] The idea was not seriously pursued. But both the Americans and the British had good reason to be aware of the dangers of radiation.

Oppenheimer and Groves nevertheless ignored or played down what they knew. Groves told General Marshall just after the Trinity test, 'No damaging effects are anticipated on the ground from radioactive materials.' Ground troops would be able to move in immediately, 'preferably by motor but on foot if preferred'.[4] Even after the bombings, Oppenheimer said in August 1945, 'There is every reason to believe that there was no appreciable radioactivity on the ground at Hiroshima and what little there was decayed very rapidly.'[5]

Truman, Stimson, and the other politicians who took the final decision to drop the bomb knew nothing of the radiation risk, though it is unlikely that their decision would have been different had they been better informed.

Radiation: Lessons from Hiroshima

After the bombing, Radio Tokyo described Hiroshima as a city of death, 'peopled by [a] ghost parade, the living doomed to die of radioactive burns. So painful are these injuries that sufferers plead: "Please kill me". No one can ever completely recover.' The American occupation authorities in Japan nevertheless asserted at first that the effects of radiation and fallout were limited. In 1946 the US Strategic Bombing Survey estimated that about 70,000 to 80,000 people were killed in Hiroshima and 35,000 to 40,000 in Nagasaki, but said 'there are no indications that radio-activity continued after the explosion to a sufficient degree to harm human beings.'[6]

Groves was particularly irked by the Japanese accounts, which he dismissed as an attempt to elicit sympathy, even though they were supported by some 'idiotic' American scientists. Colonel Rea, a doctor at the Manhattan Project's special hospital at Oak Ridge, agreed with him. What the Japanese were talking about was perfectly consistent with the normal burns you would expect on the victims of an explosion. The Japanese were dishing out a 'good dose of propaganda'.[7]

Groves sent a team to investigate under his assistant Brigadier Farrell. It included Oppenheimer's protégé Robert Serber.[8] Shortly after arriving in Tokyo, Farrell told the press that there was no radioactivity left on the ground; no one had died from radiation sickness; all those who had died were killed by blast or fire.* He was challenged by the left-wing Australian journalist Wilfred Burchett, one of the

---

* Failure to take radiation casualties into account was a flaw of many later estimates by the US military of casualty rates following a nuclear strike.

first independent journalists to get to Hiroshima.* 'In Hiroshima', Burchett had written, 'thirty days after the first atomic bomb people are still dying, mysteriously and horribly – people who were uninjured in the cataclysm – from an unknown something which I can only describe as the atomic plague.' Farrell accused him of succumbing to 'Japanese propaganda', and he was relieved by the military of his notes, his camera, and his film.[9]

The Americans continued to suppress journalistic reports, confiscate Japanese film footage, and play down casualty figures. General MacArthur, the commander of the American occupying forces, banned an article on the effects of the bomb on Nagasaki by the *Chicago Tribune*'s George Weller. Farrell's team were not allowed to share their findings with Japanese doctors.[10] It was not until February 1952 that Japanese scientists and doctors were freely able to investigate atomic injuries for themselves. Masuji Ibuse's powerful novel *Black Rain*, about a young girl dying of radiation sickness, was not published in Japan until 1965.†

Groves was not, in the end, able to deny that something untoward was happening. But he seems to have been able to cheer up himself, and perhaps his audience as well, when he told a Senate Committee in November 1945 that 'as I understand it from the doctors, it is a very pleasant way to die'.[11]

The problem was to put a number on it all. No one knew exactly how many people had been in Hiroshima and Nagasaki at the time of the

---

* Burchett was a Communist sympathiser, later an uncritical supporter of the Communist regimes in North Vietnam, China, and the Soviet Union. He was accused by some of being a Soviet agent. His story appeared in the London *Daily Express* on 5 September 1945.

† *Black Rain* was based on diaries and interviews and describes the fate of a young woman at first apparently unaffected by the radioactive 'black rain' which fell on Hiroshima (later research has established no strong links between the rain and long-term health outcomes: http://www.rerf.jp/library/rr_e/rr1407full.pdf. Thanks to Alex Wellerstein for this information). *Black Rain* was first published in Japan in 1965 but did not appear in English until 2012. *Barefoot Gen*, by Keiji Nakazawa, based on the author's childhood experiences, was serialised as a manga cartoon from 1973 to 1985.

bombing. Many deaths went unreported, often because there were no immediate survivors left to report them. Medical services in the stricken cities were almost completely disrupted. One estimate was that between 90,000 and 166,000 people died in Hiroshima, while another suggested that 60,000 to 80,000 died in Nagasaki within the first few months after the bombing. But it was not clear how many of these deaths could be attributed to radiation rather than to the direct effects of blast and heat – perhaps somewhere between 5 and 15 per cent; nor how many deaths in later years were due to the long-term effects of the bombing and how many to other causes.[12]

But people went on dying all the same. Some died within the week. Others appeared to recover, but sickened again after ten to fifteen days, or weakened and died after months of agony. One Hiroshima schoolboy described what happened to his mother: '[Her] hair had almost all fallen out, her chest was festering, and from the two-inch hole in her back a lot of maggots were crawling in and out. The place was full of flies and mosquitoes and fleas, and an awfully bad smell hung over everything.'[13]

The Americans were right in one sense: levels of radiation in Hiroshima and Nagasaki fell rapidly. 'Practically all the radioactive products', as they said, had been 'carried upward in the ascending column of hot air and dispersed harmlessly over a wide area'.[14] Seventy years later the radiation level attributable to the bombings was so low that it could barely be distinguished from the natural level. It was not enough to affect human health. Both Hiroshima and Nagasaki were flourishing.

But despite much later research, radiation and fallout never entirely lost their mystery.

Joseph Rotblat, the campaigner for nuclear disarmament who had himself worked on the Manhattan Project, wrote in 1981 that even though fallout would produce heavy casualties, it was 'impossible to calculate accurately the extent of the loss in human lives and health, of present and future generations, which might result from the radiation effects of a nuclear war'.[15]

The Radiation Effects Research Foundation, a Japan–US organisation which continued to investigate the effects of radiation in the twenty-first century, conceded that it was an unsatisfactory business. There were too many unknown factors for scientists to come to a settled conclusion. But the broad facts were generally agreed. People directly exposed to the 'ionising' radiation released in a nuclear explosion suffered from vomiting, diarrhoea, severe blood disorder, and a greatly increased vulnerability to infection. If they were under cover, the effects would be much less. Buildings and the ground itself were also affected: people entering Hiroshima and Nagasaki in the first three days after the explosions received significant doses of radiation.

The radiation directly produced by a nuclear explosion was lethal but short-lived. But radiation was also produced by fallout: the fission products which fell to the ground over the following days, weeks or months. Over half the radioactive substances might fall to the ground within the first twenty-four hours. But if the wind and weather were right, debris sucked up by the mushroom cloud could be dispersed across the globe. It could take weeks, months, and years before they came back to earth.

By then many of them were no longer dangerous. But strontium-90 and caesium-137 could survive to get into the food chain, through plants and fish, though milk and meat, until they eventually entered people's bodies. Though the effects were hard to quantify, they could cause various cancers, damage to unborn children, and genetic mutation. Some effects could be delayed, perhaps for years. They were often statistically small (though a small proportion of a large population would mean a large number of additional deaths). It could be difficult to distinguish them from diseases that would have occurred naturally. The Foundation concluded that there was no safe lower limit, a conclusion that was not universally accepted.[16]

Testing

These uncertainties encouraged those opposed to nuclear weapons to exaggerate the effects of radiation and fallout; while those involved in their production and possible use tried to play them down.

Governments, military commanders, and scientists believed they had to test their new weapons to see how they worked. From 1945 to 1992 the Americans and the Russians, followed by the British, the French, and the Chinese, carried out a great many tests. The United

States conducted the largest number, but the Soviet tests produced the largest explosive yield.

Outside the continental United States, the American carried out their main tests in the Marshall Islands in the Pacific Ocean: sixty-seven between 1946 and 1958. The local inhabitants were evacuated beforehand, and returned when their homes were deemed safe again.

After trying out an experimental gadget in May 1951 (Operation Greenhouse), the Americans tested their first true thermonuclear device on Enewetak Atoll in 1952 (the 'Ivy-Mike' test). This was a massive mechanism weighing eighty tons, which had to be kept at the right temperature by a cumbersome cooling plant. There was no question of it being a usable weapon. But it had an explosive yield of more than ten megatons, or 400 times the power of the Hiroshima bomb. It vaporised the island of Elugelab, leaving behind a deep crater about one kilometre across.

On 1 March 1954, in a test code-named Castle Bravo, the Americans exploded a thermonuclear device on the island of Bikini sufficiently compact to be made into a bomb. It was expected to yield six megatons. But the calculations had gone wrong. The device yielded fifteen megatons, the largest the Americans ever tested. The Atomic Energy Commission claimed (though the scientists on the task force disagreed) that an unexpected shift of wind deposited fallout much further than expected. White flakes of vaporised coral blanketed the American task force out at sea. The crew had to be evacuated from a US weather station on an atoll 100 miles from the explosion. Two days later a destroyer evacuated the inhabitants of Rongelap Atoll. Most of them had burns; some were vomiting. Soon they began to suffer hair loss and internal bleeding. Many of the children eventually had to be operated on for thyroid problems. The islanders were allowed to return three years after the test, but twenty years later the northern islands of the atoll were still too radioactive to visit.

But it was the fate of the crew of a Japanese fishing boat, *Lucky Dragon*, that caught the world's attention. A few hours after the explosion, intensely radioactive fallout began to land on the vessel, which was outside the exclusion zone declared by the American authorities. The Americans attempted to slap a news blackout, because examination of the fallout debris could reveal how the new weapon was designed. Lewis Strauss, the head of the US Atomic Energy Commission, privately told President Eisenhower's press secretary that the *Lucky Dragon* was a Soviet spy ship.

But the news inevitably broke. Strauss tried to argue in public that the fishermen's injuries were not caused by radiation. He made things worse when he added that the weapon tested at Bikini could be made large enough to flatten any city, however large, including New York. The American press was filled with artists' impressions of Manhattan destroyed. The White House received more than a hundred letters of protest a day.

The biggest impact was of course in Japan. One Tokyo newspaper commented that the Japanese people were 'terror-stricken by the outrageous power of atomic weapons which they [had] witnessed for the third time'. When the *Lucky Dragon* returned to port, Yasushi Nishiwaki, a biophysicist at Osaka City University, examined the crew. He asked Strauss which elements were contained in the fallout and how the victims could best be decontaminated. He got no reply, but to calm things down the Americans offered immediate compensation. Joseph Rotblat concluded from Nishiwaki's meagre data that the Castle Bravo device was a fission-fusion-fission device which had generated far more fallout than expected, and that a future hydrogen war would be very contaminating indeed.[17]

Although radioactivity in the lagoon and the sea eventually disappeared, the coconuts on Bikini were still radioactive in 2001. In 2012 the United Nations reported that Bikini Island should not be permanently resettled because 'the effects of radiation have been exacerbated by near-irreversible environmental contamination'.[18]

Within America itself, the Americans conducted over 900 tests at a desert site in the state of Nevada.* It was about sixty miles from the city of Las Vegas, which supplied the test site with equipment and stores. Since Nevada had legalised prostitution, soldiers stationed for weeks or months in depressing surroundings were able to enjoy an

---

*Between 1951 and 1992 the Americans conducted 928 tests in the Nevada site, 828 of them underground.

additional comfort. The shock of the tests could be felt in the city, and the sight of the mushroom clouds became a regular tourist attraction until 1962, when tests in the atmosphere ceased. In 2005 the National Atomic Testing Museum opened in Las Vegas. Organised tours went around the test site every month.

A number of tests, code-named Desert Rock, explored the ways soldiers could survive and fight on an irradiated nuclear battlefield, and the effect on tanks and helicopters and other equipment. Private Curtis Sandefur and more than 2,000 of his fellow Marines took part in Desert Rock V in 1953. So did numerous pigs. The soldiers were protected from radioactive dust as far as the incomplete knowledge of the day allowed. The pigs were not. Sandefur and the others were told by their officers that radiation levels were minimal and perfectly safe. They were then placed in an open trench two miles from ground zero. The nuclear device, slightly more powerful than the bomb dropped on Hiroshima, exploded just after 4.30 a.m. It lit up Las Vegas, and was visible 300 miles away in Los Angeles. After the shock wave had passed, the Marines moved forward. Despite the precautions, a gust of wind exposed them to unexpected levels of radiation. Other tests exposed civilians as well as soldiers to radiation and fallout.[19]

A similar test was conducted by the Soviet army in 1954 at the village of Totskoe in the Urals. Like the Desert Rock exercises, it was designed to test the ability of soldiers and equipment to operate on the nuclear battlefield. A large contingent of troops, 45,000 officers and men – a motor rifle division, 320 planes, 600 tanks, and 600 armoured personnel carriers – was deployed under the command of the Soviet Union's most famous soldier, Marshal Zhukov. The exercise was observed by the two Soviet leaders, Khrushchev and Bulganin, and some of the most senior Soviet generals.

The peasant women who gave the soldiers food as they travelled east towards the test site assumed they were off to fight the Chinese. But the fortified battlefield the soldiers had to build when they got there was meant to resemble what they would find if they had to fight in Europe. For greater realism they did their digging in gas masks. To cheer them up, they were given special rations.

On 14 September an aircraft dropped a bomb twice as powerful as the Hiroshima bomb on the target, around which were parked military vehicles, tanks and aircraft, and tethered animals. Aircraft and artillery bombarded the target five minutes later, and three hours thereafter the troops were sent in. The soldiers went forward in special clothing carrying dosimeters: they were to withdraw if the dose went above 50 rem (a measure of exposure to radiation). As Nikolai Pyshnikov remembered fifty years later, 'Before the explosion the people in our unit, who were to lead the advance, were first given underwear, warm covering – the temperature was 36 degrees! Then we got special darkened inserts for our gas masks, through which you could barely see the sun, and capes made of material like paper soaked in kerosene, and thick synthetic knitted socks to go over our boots up to the knees They were green and smelled bitter.'[20]

At the last moment the wind changed, as it had done in Desert Rock V. The radioactive cloud was carried not towards uninhabited countryside, as had been planned, but towards the city of Orenburg and beyond.

Two days later *Pravda* carried an uninformative report that an atomic weapon test had been successfully carried out, designed to study the effect of an atomic explosion and the problems of defence against atomic attack.

The soldiers were made to sign confidentiality agreements valid for twenty-five years. When they began to feel ill – as many of them did – they were therefore unable to explain the circumstances to their doctors. They eventually received medical assistance for illnesses caused by nuclear testing. But they got no financial compensation. What happened to the local inhabitants remained unknown.

In September 1961 Khrushchev announced that the Russians had a bomb capable of yielding 100 megatons. They tested it two months later on their northern test site in the archipelago of Novaya Zemlya. The mushroom cloud rose over seven times the height of Mount Everest. Buildings more than thirty miles away were destroyed, and windowpanes were broken in Norway and Finland.

People eventually nicknamed the massive device 'Tsar Bomba', by analogy with the Tsar Bell and the Tsar Cannon on show in the

Kremlin. Unlike those two monstrous pieces of equipment, it worked exactly as designed.

'Tsar Bomba' was indeed capable of yielding 100 megatons, but Yuli Khariton and his team deliberately halved the yield for fear that fallout might spread into the Soviet mainland. By comparison, the largest American test, Castle Bravo, yielded only fifteen megatons, though it spread far more radioactivity. 'Tsar Bomba' was more than a thousand times as powerful as the two bombs that were dropped on Japan, or ten times the yield of all the conventional explosives used in the Second World War, or a quarter of the estimated yield of the eruption of Krakatoa in 1883. It was also comparatively clean, generating a low amount of fallout relative to its yield. Several ingenious schemes were put forward for its practical use. Academician Oleg Lavrentiev suggested using it to generate a tsunami and flood the American coast. Sakharov had the bright idea of putting it in a massive torpedo to fire against an American harbour. An admiral to whom he put the thought was shocked at the prospect of massive civilian casualties. Ashamed of himself, Sakharov abandoned the idea.[21]

The British and French, eventually followed by the Chinese and others, also tested their devices, though of course on a smaller scale.

The British tested in Australia and on islands in the Pacific from 1952, and set up a permanent testing ground at Maralinga in Western Australia in 1954. Between 1956 and 1958 they tested their first thermonuclear devices on Christmas Island in the Pacific in an operation code-named Grapple. Nine tests were conducted in the atmosphere. The largest device yielded three megatons.

The dangers of fallout were largely ignored. Servicemen on Christmas Island, who included 500 New Zealand sailors, were not warned against drinking local water, eating local fruits, bathing in the lagoons, and breathing in dust. At Maralinga about 16,000 Australian civilians and servicemen and 22,000 British servicemen were exposed to nuclear fallout. The indigenous people there were forcibly relocated, but some continued to use a traditional route which passed through the testing range.

The French conducted over 200 tests between 1960 and 1965, seventeen in Algeria and the remainder in uninhabited atolls in

French Polynesia, where they exploded their first thermonuclear device in 1968.

In 1984 an American judge ruled that the US government had conducted the tests in the Nevada desert without due care. In 1990 Congress passed the Radiation Exposure Compensation Act and in 1986 it set up a Nuclear Claims Trust Fund for the inhabitants of the Pacific islands where the Americans had conducted their earlier tests.

The consequences of the Soviet tests were not publicly admitted or investigated until the last years of the Soviet Union, when they were looked into by various international bodies. The results were contradictory and inconclusive. No one attempted to deny the ecological and human impact of the disasters associated with the Mayak plant in Siberia. But the Russian state had too few resources to do much in the way of compensation.

The British conduct of their tests in Australia were pilloried by an Australian Royal Commission in 1985. The British Ministry of Defence later admitted liability and paid compensation to British, Australian, and New Zealand servicemen and civilians and Aboriginal groups who had been affected.[22]

The French authorities maintained for many years that their tests had not had any bad effects, but after their last nuclear test in 1996 they asked the International Atomic Energy Agency for a study. In 2009 the French Ministry of Defence offered 10 million euros as compensation.[23]

Confusing the Argument

The US Chiefs of Staff *Evaluation of the Atomic Bomb as a Military Weapon* pulled no punches about the devastating effect of radiation on the survivors of a nuclear attack. But in the 1950s and 1960s the nuclear weapons states downplayed the damaging effects of radiation in order to deflect popular criticism from their test programmes. At that time the American military regarded enemy casualties caused by fallout as a 'bonus effect'. It was strontium that Oppenheimer had suggested in 1943 might be used to poison half a million people.[24] In 1950 the US government had already found that the strontium-90 generated in a nuclear explosion could persist for years, get into the food chain, and contaminate children's milk. They suppressed the information. The Foreign Office circulated a 'guidance telegram' to its staff which said that strontium-90 was practically risk-free.

Soviet officials were equally pragmatic, or cynical. Sakharov expressed his worries about testing to Nikolai Pavlov, a senior KGB officer in the administration of the Soviet project whom he respected. Pavlov replied, 'If our work and our testing are giving us strength for that battle [against the forces of imperialism] – and they certainly are – then the victims of that testing, or any other victims, don't matter.'[25]

As the debate spilled over into the public domain it became increasingly passionate and the arguments on both sides more extreme. The Nobel Prize winner Linus Pauling claimed that one teaspoonful of strontium-90, 'if distributed equally between all the people of the world, would kill all of them within a few years'. His sincerity was undeniable. Many of his facts were not.

Edward Teller counterattacked with equal extravagance: 'World-wide fallout is as dangerous as being an ounce overweight or smoking one cigarette every two months. It is not as apt to produce mutations as wearing trousers. It is, in other words, not worth worrying about.'[26]

Each side accused the other of lying. The scientist Joseph Rotblat, a measured critic of government policy, later commented judiciously that neither side knew what it was talking about: 'We did not know at that time very much about the effects of small doses of radiation and therefore the conclusions which were come to depended from what angle you came.'[27]

The Test Ban and Politics

Nevertheless the disconcerting facts continued to emerge. In May 1955 Joseph Rotblat publicly argued that a full-scale atomic war 'would have disastrous results for the whole world, partisans and neutrals alike, from the genetic point of view, quite apart from the immediate effects. But even without a war there is a probable risk of running into genetic trouble, if the tests of these weapons continue at the present rate.'[28]

Governments, too, were beginning to think that something had to be done. The obvious priority was to limit – preferably to ban entirely – the most immediately dangerous tests, those in the atmosphere. Some suggested pursuing the more ambitious aim of a comprehensive ban as a first step towards reducing or even eliminating nuclear weapons altogether. But for governments that was still a step too far: underground testing caused little immediate damage, but it enabled the nuclear weapons states to go on perfecting their arsenal.

In the Soviet Union the debate was launched by the paper which Kurchatov and Malyshev sent to Khrushchev in April 1954 on 'The Dangers of Atomic War'. In it they said, 'Even though no more than a few dozen test explosions have been conducted so far, the average radioactivity of the earth's surface has significantly increased. Reserves of water are also being poisoned.'[29] Andrei Sakharov took up the theme in 1958: 'The cessation of test explosions will preserve the lives of hundreds of thousands of people.'[30] A collection of articles by distinguished Soviet scientists published in English in 1962 argued that, though good data was lacking, it was clear that nuclear testing had already affected the environment. Even if the effects were small, they were cumulative and there was no lower limit. Several contributors criticised the United States for not taking up the Soviet Union's longstanding call for a test ban. Their arguments were, alas, undermined when Khrushchev unilaterally resumed testing that autumn.[31]

But the discussion continued. In April 1963, after negotiations for a Test Ban Treaty had stalled, Viktor Adamsky, a member of Sakharov's team, wrote to Khrushchev: 'reaching an agreement banning testing in the atmosphere and in space and limiting underground testing to low yield devices would put an end to radioactive contamination of the atmosphere, slow down the arms race, and, most likely, halt the further spread of atomic weapons to countries which do not already possess them ... without the ability to conduct atmospheric tests, a country which does not already have nuclear weapons will not be able to develop a sophisticated nuclear weapons system.' Khrushchev liked Adamsky's arguments and they influenced him when the Test Ban Treaty negotiations were resumed.[32]

Thinking in the West was evolving as well. In January 1954, Thomas Murray, the maverick of the Atomic Energy Commission, proposed a test ban and lobbied Eisenhower directly. His colleague Lewis

Strauss countered with a warning against seeking any agreement with a 'cynical and treacherous enemy'. To Strauss's fury, Murray took the argument to the Senate, where he argued that the targeting of Russian cities was morally unjustifiable.[33]

Eisenhower could see the political dangers of doing nothing. As he elegantly put it to a meeting of the National Security Council in May 1954, two months after the Castle Bravo test, 'Everybody seems to think that we're skunks, saber-rattlers and warmongers. We ought not miss any chance to make clear our peaceful objectives.' One way of doing that would be to propose a moratorium on testing. Dulles supported him. But Strauss and the military opposed the idea, and it hung fire.[34]

In February 1955 the scientists in the Atomic Energy Commission published a report on the Castle Bravo test despite opposition from Strauss and from the State Department, who feared it would discourage America's allies. They calculated that a similar bomb dropped on a city would kill half the population living up to 160 miles downwind. They emphasised the particular risk from strontium-90, especially to children. They nevertheless managed to draw some soothing conclusions. The amount of radiation in the atmosphere would have 'to be increased many thousand times before any effect on humans would be noticeable': the exposure from fallout was comparable to 'exposure from one X-ray'. The risks from testing were very small when set against the gains for 'the security of the nation and of the free world'.

In May 1956 the Americans tested a 'clean' bomb in Bikini, designed to minimise fallout. Eisenhower hoped that this might demonstrate that testing was not quite as dangerous as the critics claimed. But 'clean' was a relative term: the fallout was scattered over 17,000 square miles of the Pacific. And once again Strauss misspoke himself. He claimed that the test had demonstrated 'much of importance not only from a military point of view but from a humanitarian aspect.' People were outraged that he could use the word 'humanitarian' in connection with a thermonuclear explosion. Hostile letters again flooded into the White House.[35]

That June, General James Gavin, chief of research and equipment development for the US Army, inadvertently created a sensation when his secret testimony to the Senate was leaked to the press. A large-scale thermonuclear attack on the Soviet Union, said Gavin, could cause 'several hundred million deaths depending on which way the wind blew. If the wind blew to the south-east, they would mostly be in the USSR, although they would extend into the Japanese and perhaps down into the Philippine area. If the winds blew the other way they would extend well back up into Western Europe.' Gavin was a wartime hero who had parachuted into Normandy on D-Day and his words carried weight. In private he was supported by a Pentagon spokesman, who estimated that 500 million might be killed, including nearly half the population of the United Kingdom.[36]

In 1957 the British author Neville Shute published a novel, *On the Beach*, which immediately caught the public imagination.[37] The story is set in 1963. A nuclear world war has occurred. The combatants have deliberately used dirty bombs to generate large quantities of lethal fallout. Life in the northern hemisphere has been wiped out by a radioactive cloud. Now the cloud is slowly drifting south. One of the last surviving American submarines, the USS *Scorpion*, is based in Melbourne, Australia. Law and order still prevail there, but the authorities have provided everyone with suicide pills. The book ends as the civilians take their pills and the crew of *Scorpion* scuttle their ship. A film followed in 1959. The main roles were played by some of Hollywood's best-known stars – Gregory Peck, Ava Gardner, Fred Astaire. Both book and film were very successful around the world.*

But Strauss and many in the military remained bitterly opposed to the idea of a ban. It would be impossible to police: the Russians could cheat at any time by testing underground or in outer space. In any case, as Strauss told the press in 1956, the risk from fallout was 'vague and unproven' compared with the 'more immediate and infinitely greater dangers of defeat and perhaps obliteration' at the hands of the Russians.[38] In 1957 Teller and Lawrence testified to Congress that the fallout hazards from testing were negligible. Perhaps 50 million people could be saved in a nuclear war if 'clean' bombs were used

---

*In the film, the name of the submarine was changed to *Sawfish*, because there was already a real American nuclear submarine called *Scorpion*. Ironically, the *Scorpion* was later lost in the eastern Atlantic.

instead of the dirty bombs the Americans currently possessed. They repeated the arguments to Eisenhower a few days later. Eisenhower was seduced. He agreed to more research, and he publicly – and wrongly – claimed that American bombs were already 96 per cent fallout-free. His words were echoed by Dulles.

Khrushchev's dismissal of all the talk of 'clean' bombs was sarcastic. 'Mr. Dulles makes a statement which sounds as though he was making propaganda for the atom bomb, trying to make it palatable,' he told Roosevelt's widow, Eleanor. 'He talks of a clean bomb as if there were such a thing as a clean bomb. War is a dirty thing.'[39] Others joined in the criticism. Eisenhower began to feel that America was being 'crucified on the cross of Atoms'.[40] Moreover, he discovered that his experts were deeply split. Isidor Rabi, whom he trusted, told him forcefully that the views of Teller and Lawrence were wrong. Rabi favoured a test ban, and now Eisenhower began to swing back towards him. To ensure more balanced advice, he set up the President's Scientific Advisory Council (PSAC). The Council believed that a ban could be monitored effectively, but could not decide whether it would be to the military advantage of the United States or not.

The military were quite sure it would not. That October American opinion was shocked when the Russians put the Sputnik into space. General Groves had said the Russians could not even make a jeep. Now they seemed to be ahead in the military-technological race. Teller began to use his contacts in Congress and the press to mobilise opinion against a ban: the Russians were ahead, and America needed to catch up.

Eisenhower decided it was time to cut through the noise. In the middle of January 1958 he suggested to the Russians that scientists from the two countries should meet to discuss the technicalities. The Russians sensed a political opportunity. They unilaterally halted their own testing and proposed a general moratorium. The American and the British governments faced the prospect of a propaganda defeat.[41]

That April Dulles told his advisers that it was urgent to 'erase the picture which people abroad hold of the United States as a militaristic nation [which] hurts us and probably causes us to lose more than we gain from small technical military advances … Do we want further refinement of nuclear weapons at the cost of moral isolation of the United States?' Strauss argued that the danger to humanity lay in nuclear war, not nuclear testing. A freeze would leave the advantage with the Russians. The National Academy of Science and the British Medical Research Council, he claimed, said that fallout from tests was no danger to health. Dulles nevertheless carried the meeting with a proposal that America announce a unilateral moratorium, with provisions for a regime of inspections, provided the British came along.[42]

Khrushchev picked up Eisenhower's proposal for an experts' meeting. Scientists from America, Britain, France, Canada, the Soviet Union, Poland, Czechoslovakia, and Romania met in Geneva throughout the summer of 1958. They reported that a network of control posts in Eurasia and North America would be able to detect atmospheric tests down to one kiloton and 90 per cent of underground tests down to five kilotons. They did not say who would work in the control posts or how the process would be supervised.

The day after their report Eisenhower decided to join the moratorium. America, Britain, and the Soviet Union agreed to begin negotiations. All three hurried to hold last-minute tests while they still had the chance.

The negotiations began in Geneva in October 1958 and continued for nearly four years. The most knotty issue was the question of inspection. To ensure that the Russians did not cheat, the Americans demanded a rigorous and intrusive inspection regime. Ernest Lawrence calculated that tens of thousands of US and UN inspectors would be necessary, an all or nothing proposition which Dulles thought would make the Americans a laughing stock.[43] The Americans greatly scaled it down before they got to Geneva. Eisenhower was willing to settle for a less than perfect inspection system because it would discourage cheating. Conservative Republicans in the Senate disagreed.[44]

The Russians suspected, as Khrushchev told the British ambassador, that American inspectors would double as spies. Their fears were not entirely unjustified. The Americans did indeed see inspection as a way of opening up some of the secrets of the Soviet Union.[45] Khrushchev had another worry as well: he later wrote in his memoirs that if Moscow had admitted American inspectors, 'they would have discovered that we were in a relatively weak position, and that realization might have encouraged them to attack us.'[46]

Eisenhower nevertheless hoped to sort out the difficulties if he met Khrushchev at a summit. The meeting took place in Paris in May 1960. It ended in disaster almost before it had begun. The Americans had been sending their U-2s over the Soviet Union, believing that they flew too high for Russian anti-aircraft weapons to hit. They were unpleasantly surprised when the Russians shot down a U-2 over the Urals on the eve of the summit. Eisenhower did not at first know that the Russians had captured the pilot, Gary Powers, and attempted a denial, which the Russians saw as an outright lie. Khrushchev demanded an apology. Eisenhower refused. Macmillan failed to calm things down by pointing out that both sides conducted aerial espionage. Khrushchev was not mollified. The summit collapsed; in July the Russians shot down another American reconnaissance aircraft north of Murmansk; the Berlin Wall was built in August; Khrushchev decided to await the election of a new president before resuming his exchanges with the Americans.[47] Surprisingly, the test ban negotiations stumbled on.

On leaving office at the end of 1960, Eisenhower famously warned against 'the acquisition of unwarranted influence, whether sought or unsought, by the military-industrial complex'. Less remembered was his point that sweeping changes in America's industrial-military posture were being driven by the technological revolution: he spoke of the 'danger that public policy could itself become the captive of a scientific-technological elite'. Asked which scientists he had in mind, he answered: Edward Teller and Wernher von Braun, the rocket scientist.[48]

Harold Macmillan, the British Prime Minister, was a determined and consistent advocate of a limitation on nuclear weapons. Even before the collapse of the Paris summit, he had not been sanguine about its prospects. 'The Americans are divided, and with an administration on the way out the Pentagon and Atomic groups are gaining strength,' he noted in his diary in March 1960. He feared that the American military were keen 'to go on indefinitely with experiments (large and small) so as to keep refining upon and perfecting the art of nuclear weapons'. He found the collapse of the summit 'ignominious; tragic; almost incredible'.[49]

Macmillan had served in the trenches in the First World War and had seen enough of the Second: the avoidance of war was his overriding priority. He was also conflicted: like previous prime ministers he believed that Britain needed a minimal nuclear force to guard against the Russians and keep an eye on the Americans. But he had no illusions: he slashed expenditure on civil defence because he believed that it could not save sufficient people in a nuclear exchange.

He was, however, in a fix. On the one hand, his advisers told him that the British could not forgo testing until they had perfected their weapons. On the other, domestic opposition to nuclear testing was growing. It was fuelled in October 1957, when a fire broke out in the reactor at Windscale in Cumbria, part of the British weapons project. Contamination spread across England, Wales, and northern Europe. The accident was caused by misjudgement and faulty instrumentation – the same failings that lay behind the explosion in Chernobyl twenty-nine years later.

When John Kennedy was elected President in November 1960 Macmillan wrote him a lengthy letter (privately he called it his 'Grand Design') about the challenge of the Soviet threat – political and economic at least as much as military. He emphasised the importance of disarmament, especially a test ban. He lamented that he could not make out 'whether Khrushchev has misunderstood or misrepresented what we have been trying to say to him. Perhaps we may be able to make him realise that we really do want disarmament.'

Macmillan's elaborate circumlocutions left Kennedy unimpressed. But he nevertheless asked Macmillan to meet him for a talk about the deteriorating situation in Indochina. Macmillan accepted, with some apprehension because of the age gap between them. But it was an welcome opportunity to press his concerns on the new President.[50]

Khrushchev of course understood perfectly well what Macmillan and others were saying to him. But he too was under pressure from his military to resume testing. In July 1961 he told his scientists that he intended to break his self-imposed moratorium. Sakharov sent him a note: 'I am convinced that a resumption of testing at this time would only favor the USA. Prompted by the success of our Sputniks, they could use tests to improve their devices. They have underestimated us in the past, whereas our program has been based on a realistic appraisal of the situation. Don't you think that new tests will seriously jeopardize the test ban negotiations, the cause of disarmament, and world peace?'[51]

Khrushchev dismissed Sakharov's right to make such judgements. '[Sakharov] is poking his nose where it does not belong. Leave politics to us – we are the specialists. You make your bombs and test them. And we won't interfere with you; we'll help you. But don't try to tell us what to do or how to behave. We understand politics. I'd be a jellyfish and not Chairman of the Council of Ministers if I listened to people like Sakharov!'

In his memoirs Khrushchev omitted the colourful language and spoke of Sakharov with great respect, and with some sympathy for his arguments. But he never abandoned his view that, as the man responsible for the security of the state in a dangerous world, he had had no option but to go ahead with the tests.[52] At the end of August 1961 he announced that the Soviet Union would abandon the moratorium. The Russians exploded a bomb the next day. In response Kennedy ordered a resumption of underground testing, though he delayed testing in the atmosphere for a few more months.

The American military and their supporters, such as Edward Teller, had not lessened their opposition to a cessation of tests. The Joint Chiefs of Staff reiterated that nuclear testing was central to national security: 'only through an energetic test program in all environments can the United States achieve or maintain superiority in all areas of nuclear weapons technology.' Teller thought that the Russians would evade a ban by secretly testing underground.[53] General LeMay held a meeting with Teller and others which strongly recommended the resumption of testing in the atmosphere and, for good measure, in space as well. Almost as a throwaway, his meeting suggested that weapons with yields as high as 1,000 megatons 'should be reconsidered and re-evaluated for their possible military use'. A week later the Russians exploded the 'Tsar Bomba'. The device proposed at LeMay's meeting would have been twenty times as powerful, a doomsday weapon of no practical military value. Worthy of Dr Strangelove, the idea was not pursued.[54]

In December 1961 Kennedy and Macmillan met again, this time in Bermuda. Kennedy was now persuaded that a resumption of testing was unavoidable. He made the seductive proposal that the Americans should use the British test facility on Christmas Island, in return for valuable technical information and the use of the American test site in Nevada. Macmillan said passionately that the two of them 'could not sit in an ordinary little room four days before Christmas and talk about these terrible things without doing something about it'. He asked for time to consider Kennedy's request. But he could not long resist it.

Back home in England, Macmillan spent Christmas Day brooding. The nuclear arms race was 'at once so fantastic and retrograde, so sophisticated and so barbarous, as to be almost incredible'. Eventually, nuclear weapons would turn up in the hands of 'dictators, reactionaries, revolutionaries, madmen. Then, sooner or later, and certainly I think by the end of this century, either by error or folly or insanity, the great crime will be committed.'[55]

He now pushed the Americans to try once more to persuade Khrushchev to go for a test ban. The State Department commented sourly, 'We can't let Macmillan practice emotional blackmail on us.' But the attempt was made. Khrushchev turned it down.[56] The two sides tested more than 200 weapons during 1961 and 1962, to the accompaniment of noisy mutual accusations of bad faith, some justified. But the pressure within governments, from their peoples, and from international opinion continued to grow. It was brought into sharp focus by the Cuban missile crisis in October 1962.

The Russians and the Americans were both increasingly influenced by another fear: the prospect that third parties might acquire nuclear weapons. A ban might make it harder for them. The CIA wondered what would happen if a nuclear-armed China attacked an American ally in Asia. If the Americans then responded with force, the Soviet Union would have to choose between seeing China beaten and coming to its aid, then stumbling into an unwanted nuclear war with America. Some optimistic analysts thought, on the contrary, that the Russians might even join the Americans in military action to prevent the Chinese going nuclear. Needless to say, nothing came of this ambitious thought.

Whatever their worries about China, the Russians were certainly alarmed by the possibility of a nuclear West Germany. The Americans had canvassed a clumsy proposal for a multilateral force (MLF), in which European crews, including Germans, would help man American ships armed with nuclear weapons. Supported as usual by the British, this far-fetched idea got nowhere. In August 1962 Kennedy's Secretary of State, Dean Rusk, pleaded with the Soviet ambassador to Washington, Anatoli Dobrynin, to recognise that while the Americans and the Russians might differ about which nuclear-armed third countries posed the greater threat, 'surely we could agree that [they] would both be better off if none of them developed nuclear weapons'.[57]

Macmillan was determined to press ahead. During his meeting with Kennedy in December 1962 in the aftermath of the Cuban missile crisis, a message arrived from Khrushchev which said that the time had come 'to put an end once and for all to nuclear tests'. On the vexed issue of inspection, he offered two or three on-site inspections a year. Macmillan saw this as a real concession. Kennedy 'agreed that it marked a substantial advance'.[58]

On his return to Washington Kennedy ran into fierce opposition from his generals and in the Senate. But Macmillan continued to push. In mid-March he wrote to Kennedy: '[F]rom the man-in-the-street's point of view, the two sides have come a great deal nearer. Indeed to the layman, we would seem so near that it would be almost inconceivable that the gulf could not be bridged. I have a feeling that the Test Ban is the most important step that we can take towards unravelling this frightful tangle of fear and suspicions in East–West relations.' He proposed that Kennedy should send an emissary to Moscow to probe Khrushchev's thinking: Averell Harriman, who had been the American ambassador in Moscow during the war, or even his brother Robert.

Kennedy too was 'haunted by the feeling that by 1970, unless we are successful, there may be ten nuclear powers instead of four, and by 1975, fifteen or twenty. I regard that as the greatest possible danger.' Both he and Macmillan feared that Germany might demand control of nuclear weapons. Macmillan suggested a 'non-dissemination agreement', the germ of the Non-Proliferation Treaty signed in 1968 after both he and Kennedy had left the scene.

The two men wrote to Khrushchev in April 1963. Macmillan noted wryly: 'The State Department (after being sceptical, not to say hostile) have suddenly become enthusiastic about the joint approach to Khrushchev. I suppose this means that the President's Press boys are getting ready to represent it as an entirely American initiative, with the young New Frontiersman in the van and the old British PM being dragged reluctantly at his heels.'

Khrushchev's immediate reaction was harshly unhelpful. The joint letter was full of the same old stuff, he said irritably. Instead of accepting his proposal for two to three inspections, Kennedy and Macmillan were haggling, obviously still wanting to introduce their spies. But he offered a gleam of hope: he would be prepared to receive their representatives. They replied that they would send their men to Moscow in six weeks' time.

Kennedy now prepared the ground – brilliantly. On 10 June he spoke at American University in Washington. He reminded his audience how much the Russians had suffered in the last war. In the next, both countries would be destroyed in the first twenty-four hours. He spoke of the vicious and dangerous cycle of mutual suspicion in which new weapons begat counter-weapons, of the shared interest of Americans and Soviet peoples in peace, and of the need for them to live with their differences if they could not be resolved. 'For, in the final analysis, our most basic common link is that we all inhabit this small planet. We all breathe the same air. We all cherish our children's future. And we are all mortal.' He announced a moratorium on American tests as an earnest of good faith, provided that other states followed suit. And he concluded, 'Chairman Khrushchev, Prime Minister Macmillan, and I have agreed that high-level discussions will shortly begin in Moscow looking toward early agreement on a comprehensive test ban treaty. Our hope must be tempered with the caution of history; but with our hopes go the hopes of all mankind.'[59]

This speech was a far cry from the harsh simplicities of NSC-68 and other American policy documents. And it broke the ice. Khrushchev called it the best speech by any president since Roosevelt. He indicated that the Russians would drop some of their prior conditions. To ensure that political considerations dominated, the Americans were represented by Averell Harriman. The British were represented by Lord Hailsham, a somewhat eccentric Tory veteran, who was ably supported by the British ambassador, Humphrey Trevelyan, whom the Russians liked and respected.

Even so, the negotiations were tense and ill-tempered. The Russians wanted a broader agreement, a non-aggression treaty, and tried to make it a condition for the test ban. Harriman and Hailsham wiggled round them. The Chinese attacked the Russians for betraying the Communist cause by negotiating with capitalists (Khrushchev commented that the Chinese would be more restrained once they got their own bomb).[60] But on 25 July there was a breakthrough as both teams abandoned their sticking points.

To Macmillan's deep regret, the treaty left open the possibility of testing underground. All three established nuclear powers were to exploit that loophole for nearly three decades. Between 1945 and 1963 the Russians and the Americans had conducted an average of thirty tests a year; from then until the end of the Cold War in 1991 the average went up to forty-two.[61] The French and the Chinese, who had not yet got the bomb, refused to sign the treaty and ignored the ban for a decade or more.*

But when he heard that the text had been initialled, Macmillan gave the good news to his wife and then burst into tears. 'So was realised,' he later wrote, 'one of the great purposes I had set myself.'[62]

The Neutron Bomb

The Test Ban Treaty, however imperfect, was the first important step towards reining in the monster. But the fear of radiation which had driven it did not go away. It was reignited by the emergence, in the

---

*The Chinese carried out twenty-three atmospheric tests between 1964 and 1980. The French carried out fifty atmospheric tests from the mid-1960s to the mid-1970s.

late 1970s, of the so-called 'neutron bomb'. This was designed to emit about ten times the radiation produced by a 'conventional' nuclear bomb, and to be small enough to use in battlefield artillery and missiles. The aim was to destroy enemy troops while – if you were lucky – not killing too many civilians or causing too much damage to property. It seemed a good weapon to use against the overwhelming hordes of tanks that the Russians had assembled in Europe.

In June 1977 the *Washington Post* revealed that the Carter administration planned to deploy neutron warheads on its Lance missiles in Europe. The weapon, the article said, was the first explicitly designed to kill people through radiation rather than fire and blast. The popular reaction in Europe and America was so strong that the British, the West German, the Dutch, and the Danish governments refused to support its deployment. Zbigniew Brzezinski, Carter's National Security Advisor, told him that the Europeans 'are terrified by the political consequences of seeming to approve nuclear warfare on their territory and of endorsing a weapon which seems to have acquired a particularly odious image'. The feebleness of the Europeans infuriated Carter. But in April 1978 he bowed to political reality and cancelled plans to produce the new weapon.[63] Sam Cohen, its inventor, maintained that this was a 'shameful' error.

The Russians joined the Europeans in campaigning against the neutron bomb. Leonid Brezhnev, the Soviet leader, described it as a 'capitalist bomb', because it was designed to destroy people while preserving property. Ironically, so did Harold Brown, at that time the Director of the Lawrence Livermore Laboratory, where it had been devised. None of this stopped the Russians from testing their own neutron bomb in secret.

That was not the end of the story. Reagan resumed production in 1981. The Russians employed enhanced radiation warheads in their anti-missile defence system. The French tested their own neutron bomb in 1967, but stopped production in 1986 because of domestic and foreign pressure. In 1984 the Israelis were reported to be producing neutron bombs. The Chinese announced in 1999 that they had the relevant technology. In 2012 a former British minister suggested that they might be used to prevent terrorists infiltrating into Afghanistan from Pakistan.[64]

Nobody ever quite explained why killing a lot of people and destroying comparatively little property was so much worse than killing a lot of people and destroying a lot of property; nor why death by radiation, though certainly not 'very pleasant', was an order of magnitude worse than being burned alive, dismembered, or permanently incapacitated by high explosive. Perhaps it was an atavistic fear of the unseen killer that comes mysteriously and insidiously by night: the image of Death itself.

TWELVE

LIVING ON THE VOLCANO

'I will have to direct all our people to live like troglodytes underground as being the only hope of survival, and that by no means certain.'

Clement Attlee, 1945[1]

'When we first learned about civil defence in my primary school, I was so stressed that I kept on waking up after dreaming about that devilish mushroom cloud.'

anonymous Russian blogger*

'When one lives on Vesuvius, one takes little account of the risk of eruptions.'

Harold Macmillan[2]

After Hiroshima people learned that a new world war might kill them in their tens of millions. Governments knew that any defensive scheme would be grossly expensive and unlikely to work. But they could not afford to be accused of neglecting their responsibility.

The Americans had never been bombed, and they were rich. Steeped in their native tradition that you could solve any problem if you hurled enough money, enterprise, energy, and imagination at it, they initially threw themselves into the business of civil defence with

---

* The blogger was commenting on an incident in 2013 when a meteorite exploded about eighteen miles over Siberia near Chelyabinsk with a force equivalent to a 500-kiloton nuclear warhead. There were 1,500 people injured and 7,200 buildings damaged. People photographed the event from their cars, drove on, and posted the results on YouTube (see http://cccp-foto.livejournal.com/647397.html and https://en.wikipedia.org/wiki/Chelyabinsk_meteor).

noisy enthusiasm. Secret government plans leaked regularly, everything was debated publicly, and businessmen with an eye to profit offered neat little fallout shelters for the better-off.

It was different for the Russians and the British. They had survived aerial attack in a brutal war. They wearily began to put together civil defence schemes like those that had worked in the past – mass evacuation, shelter programmes, air defence – as if more of the same might just about do the trick. But civil defence had to compete with the need to rebuild economies shattered by war. Neither had the resources to do more than scratch the surface.

In theory there were four ways that you could try to protect yourself against a nuclear attack. You could shoot down the incoming bombers and missiles. You could evacuate key industries and vulnerable people to safer parts of the country. You could provide shelters against blast, fire, radiation, and fallout for those who remained. You could find ways to protect central and local government and the communications between them and the population at large, so that the authorities could maintain order while your country was under attack, and restore some kind of normal life thereafter.

Such schemes would all have been wildly unpopular, prohibitively expensive, and certainly inadequate. Even those they enabled to survive might be hard put to find food and shelter in what was left of the outside world. The thermonuclear bomb destroyed what plausibility they might have had.

By the end of the 1950s the British government had recognised that for their cramped little island there could be no meaningful protection. They continued to pay lip service to civil defence, but not much real money. The reality dawned more slowly on the Americans and the Russians, who hoped that their countries' vast extent would offer a degree of protection.

For some Americans a serious strategic argument was involved. A believable civil defence system, they thought, was essential to maintain popular support for deterrence. Nelson Rockefeller, the Chairman of Eisenhower's Psychological Warfare Panel, argued that 'will to resist' was central to the confrontation with the Russians: 'The side preserving its manpower resources and maintaining its will to resist would have a major advantage.'[3] The corollary of this was that any signs that the Russians were developing their civil defences was yet another indication of their aggressive intentions. Such arguments continued to surface from time to time until the last years of the Cold War.

It made no serious difference. The Russians and the Americans continued to devise new schemes until the end of the Cold War. None was any more plausible than the others.

Sheltering a Continent

Even before Hiroshima, some Americans began to think about how to protect civilians from atomic attack. Scientists on the Manhattan Project suggested that city dwellers would have to be permanently dispersed. Once the Russians tested their first bomb in 1949, the flood of fantastic proposals increased. One suggestion was that American cities should be rebuilt on entirely new lines so that the potential targets within them were too far apart to be destroyed by a single bomb. It would 'spell the end of the metropolis as we know it'. But properly done, the new cities might be more orderly and more attractive than the old.[4] In 1950 *Life* magazine published a plan by the Massachusetts Institute of Technology to build eight-lane 'Life Belts' around the nation's major cities, with campsites and prefabricated hospitals for the survivors of a nuclear attack.[5]

The first official proposal came in 1946, when the United States Strategic Bombing Survey suggested a large federal shelter programme based on a study of the effects of the bombing of Hiroshima and Nagasaki. They conceded that no government programme could shelter the whole population, and critics pointed out that those left out might be dangerously discontented.

An alternative was to leave it to private initiative. Enthusiasts thought that could have great psychological advantages. The homeowner would be proud to own a shelter he had built himself. That would counteract anxiety and 'contribute to the feeling that "I am really able to do something about it"'.[6] But there was a hitch here too. Not everybody would be able to afford to build their own shelters. There were obvious political risks in appearing to divide those who would be saved and those who would not.

Optimists thought it was mainly a matter of public education: a 'well-designed program of training and indoctrination [would] give the general public a more healthy attitude toward atomic warfare'. But psychiatrists worried about the psychological effects. After a nuclear attack there would be 'large numbers of individuals wandering about aimlessly, unable to help themselves or others, adding to the confusion and impeding rescue efforts'. Dale Cameron, the Assistant Director of the National Institute of Mental Health, proposed that people be organised into small therapy groups under leaders trained in psychiatry, who would 'assist the group in working through its fears and apprehensions'. After an attack, group members would seek each other out to provide mutual support. A study carried out at Cornell University concluded that 'the human susceptibility to crack up and panic' could be predicted by examining the behaviour of goats under stress. The news was good: a goat exposed to the Bikini test was filmed eating, moments after the blast, 'very much undisturbed. No collapse. No nervous breakdown'.[7]

Washington continued to come up with modest measures of its own. Truman set up the Federal Civil Defense Administration, which lasted in one form or another until long after the Cold War was over. His government published 'Survival under Atomic Attack', which opened with the comforting thought that 'You can live through an atom bomb raid and you won't have to have a Geiger counter, protective clothing, or special training in order to do it ... atom-splitting is just another way of causing an explosion.' The booklet aimed to kill a number of myths: that atomic weapons would destroy the earth, that radioactivity was the greatest threat, that radiation sickness was always fatal. And it suggested some simple precautions. You should hide underground if you had time; otherwise you should 'jump in any handy ditch or gutter'. You shouldn't leave rubbish around your home which could catch fire. You should close the windows and doors and draw the curtains. You shouldn't use the telephone except in a real emergency. And you shouldn't rush outside immediately after a bombing.[8]

The government campaign was backed by numerous films. The most famous was *Duck and Cover*, produced in 1951 for schools throughout the country.[9] Bert the Turtle walks down the road, while a chorus sings, 'Bert the turtle was very alert; when danger threatened him he never got hurt. He knew just what to do.' The children should 'duck and cover' like Bert, the film said, when they saw the flash of an atomic bomb: get under their desks, hide in a ditch or behind a wall. Millions of children practised the routine in their schools. Some were given dog tags so their bodies could be identified after an attack.[10] The song sold 3 million copies. The US Library of Congress decided the film was 'historically significant' and ordered it to be preserved in the National Film registry.

Much mocked, the film became a symbol of the futility of trying to defend yourself in a time of nuclear war. That was perhaps unfair. The recommendations in *Duck and Cover* and 'Survival under Atomic Attack' would have worked, more or less, against a few fission bombs. They would have been little use against a strategic bombardment by thermonuclear weapons.

American attitudes towards evacuation changed several times as the practical problems became clearer. In 1951 the Federal Civil Defense Administration sponsored a film called *Our Cities Must Fight*, which told city dwellers to remain in their cities even under nuclear attack, so as to keep industrial production going. In Europe in 1940, the film warned, refugees clogged the roads and got in the way of soldiers trying to fight the Germans. 'Running away would be desertion pure and simple. It would not only be treason but would be handing the enemy a victory. The question is, have Americans got the guts?'

Three years later, however, the US Air Force was warning – prematurely, since the Russians did not yet have that capability – that enemy aircraft could drop nuclear bombs anywhere in the United States. Evacuation became an accepted way of dealing with a nuclear attack. Another air force film called *Let's Face It* argued, 'The fate of your nation depends on what you do when enemy bombers head for our cities – take shelter or evacuate.' It concluded rather discouragingly that the government's evacuation plans could save many lives in the 'fringe areas' surrounding a city struck by a nuclear bomb.

In the mid-1950s a number of American cities put the government's ideas to practical test. In 1955 the city of Portland, Oregon, recruited volunteers for an exercise called Operation Greenlight. In just over half an hour more than 100,000 people were successfully moved out into the surrounding countryside. Two years later a TV docudrama, *A Day Called X*, was made to mark the event. Critics pointed out that in reality people would have panicked and order broken down. In 1955 Portland could expect three hours' warning of approaching bombers. But there would only be about fifteen minutes' warning of an attack by intercontinental ballistic missiles: too little to conduct an evacuation. In 1957 the formidable New York city planner, Robert Moses, commented sourly that any evacuation route could be clogged by one broken down vehicle. 'Any thought that you can evacuate a large population in a short time from any large city, even if you have a place to move them to, is so much moonshine'.[11]

One unconvincing idea succeeded another. In 1957 Eisenhower commissioned a study on 'measures to protect the civil population in case of nuclear attack and its aftermath'. This was the Gaither Report, which we have already discussed in Chapter 6. Its call for a massive rearmament programme had a major impact on policy. But its recommendations on civil defence were feeble: there should be a nationwide programme of fallout shelters, but blast shelters would be very expensive, and could protect only some of the population.[12]

Perhaps the answer – even in the age of the thermonuclear bomb, which had changed everything – was private money after all. The National Security Council looked at an eight-year plan to spend $32.4 billion on a massive shelter programme, to be financed partly by the government and partly by private money. Eisenhower's Vice President, Richard Nixon, was one of the sceptics. He put the argument with brutal clarity. Whether 30 million or 50 million Americans survived a nuclear war was beside the point: in either case 'there would be no hope of the United States surviving'. America's defence rested on the ability of its nuclear forces to deter war in the first place. To prevent popular support for deterrence from collapsing, Nixon believed, expenditure should be just enough to sustain the public illusion that a practical civil defence could be maintained.[13]

The Berlin crisis of 1960–61 reignited interest. As the crisis heated up, President Kennedy announced a nationwide fallout shelter programme costing $695 million. His brother Robert pressed for a scheme that would require everyone to practise evacuation and shelter drills once a week. The Pentagon drafted a pamphlet, 'Fallout Protection – What to Know About Nuclear Attack – What to Do About It', which again favoured leaving civil defence largely to private enterprise. The President asked his friend the economist Kenneth Galbraith to look at the draft. Galbraith was scathing. The division into haves and have-nots was immoral, he said. And it was impolitic too: 'a design for saving Republicans and sacrificing Democrats [which] in the main writes off those who voted for you'. The thing made no sense anyway, said Galbraith: those who survived in their shelters would emerge into a barren and hideous world, 'with no food, no transportation and full of stinking corpses'.[14]

Life magazine made its own contribution in September 1961 with a long article on 'How You Could Survive Fallout'. It told its readers 'How to build shelters … Where to hide in cities … What to do during an attack'. If they followed the advice, 97 per cent of them would survive. A shelter programme would create a new market, 'in keeping with the free enterprise way of meeting changing conditions in our lives'. The President was induced to send the magazine a letter of endorsement.*[15]

A kind of hysteria began to take over. The Reverend L. C. McHugh, a columnist for the Catholic magazine *America*, assured his readers that 'it was ethically permissible to shoot your neighbors if they tried to break into your fallout shelter'. Edward Teller lobbied Kennedy for a shelter programme costing $50 billion (in nominal terms, twenty-five times the cost of the Manhattan Project). It was not a difficult problem, he argued: the Russians might build more powerful bombs, but all you needed to do was to dig deeper shelters.

One of Kennedy's advisers grumbled that the whole thing was 'rapidly blossoming into our number one political headache'. But Congress was becoming increasingly unenthusiastic. By the summer of 1962 the proposed $695 million programme had been whittled back to $80 million.[16]

The issue waxed and waned with the rise and fall of international tension. As détente unravelled in the second half of the 1970s, the enthusiasm for fallout shelters revived, at least among the politicians

---

* The front cover of this issue of *Life* magazine is among the illustrations.

and think-tankers in Washington who believed that an effective civil defence programme would demonstrate American will and reinforce deterrence. President Carter cautiously agreed: such a programme would help to 'reduce the possibility that the US could be coerced in time of crisis [and] provide some increase in the number of surviving population and for greater continuity of government should deterrence fail and escalation control fail in order to provide an improved basis for dealing with the crisis and carrying out eventual national recovery'.[17]

This was hardly a clarion call. President Reagan attempted to better it when he came to power. In 1983 he proposed a seven-year Crisis Relocation Plan, which would ultimately cost $10 billion. The Federal Emergency Management Agency, the successor to the Federal Civil Defense Administration, said that 'A close look at the facts shows with fair certainty that with reasonable protective measures the United States could survive nuclear attack and go on to recovery within a relatively few years.'[18] The programme was meant to enable America to fight, survive, and win a nuclear war. It was designed to evacuate up to 80 per cent of the population from 400 probable target areas to rural 'host centres' over three days. Four million 'essential' workers would be provided with blast shelters at their places of work. Essential industrial equipment would be dismantled and buried in safety so that it could be reassembled and production restarted once the attack was over. Special bunkers would be constructed to protect the President and senior officials so that government could continue to function. The entire population was to be provided with fallout shelters or encouraged to build their own.

Thomas K. Jones, a senior official in Reagan's Defense Department, claimed that it was all quite simple: 'If there are enough shovels to go around, everybody's going to make it. Dig a hole, cover it with a couple of doors, and then throw three feet of dirt over it. It's the dirt that does it.' Do it right, said Jones, and America could recover from a nuclear war in two to four years.[19] He was much derided then and later. In fact his bland advice did not differ so very much from what the British and Soviet governments were telling their people. Reagan's grandiose civil defence programme got nowhere.

Right from the beginning there were critics who claimed that the official programmes were deliberately designed to increase fear of the Russians and so emasculate criticism of the policy of deterrence. In June 1955 twenty-eight protesters were arrested in New York for refusing to take part in a compulsory civil defence exercise. So was a shoeshine man who happened to be drinking at a nearby water fountain. The examining magistrate told the protesters that they were 'murderers' who 'by their conduct and behavior contributed to the utter destruction of these three million theoretically killed in our City'.[20] The protests nevertheless continued until in 1960 they generated so much negative publicity that civil defence exercises in New York were halted.*

The Reagan government were not perhaps as certain as they wished to seem that even a well-funded civil defence programme would work. In September 1982 Reagan approved a massive secret programme called 'Enduring National Leadership'. Costing hundreds of millions of dollars a year, this was intended to preserve effective government even if the President was killed. In the event of a mounting crisis, three potential successors would be dispatched to separate secure bunkers around the United States. Whichever successor survived a nuclear strike that killed the President would take over the job and do his best to run what remained of the country.

Some argued that the plan was a subversion of the provisions for presidential succession in the Constitution.[21] But whatever else it was, it was hardly a convincing scheme for protecting a substantial part of the population of the United States from nuclear catastrophe.

Games Adults Play: Civil Defence in the Soviet Union

Ordinary Russians knew well enough what a nuclear war would involve. The image of the mushroom cloud became as deeply lodged in the Soviet imagination as it was in the West.[22] Large numbers of young military conscripts learned the drills they needed to survive on

---

* The American public never recovered their earlier enthusiasm and belief in civil defence. When I asked an American farmer's wife in 1983 what she would do if she heard the nuclear alert, she said, 'I would stand in the porch of my house and watch.'

the nuclear battlefield. Information seeped through from the West from broadcasts. Soviet officials who served abroad had access to the voluminous literature and to films about nuclear war, and brought their knowledge home. Some people got hold of smuggled Western books and journals, and in later years of taped versions of films such as *Dr Strangelove*.

Igor Maskaev first learned about the nuclear threat when he was still at primary school and watched *Vybor Tseli* (Choosing the Target) on television with his parents. The film was made in 1975, at the time of Brezhnev. It was set in a secret weapons establishment, in a small town in Siberia with an old monastery and only a few streets surrounded by forest. It looked very like Arzamas-16, even though the place was officially still surrounded with the deepest secrecy. Mikhail Romm, the film's distinguished director, said that some of it was actually filmed there.*

The film set out to tackle the moral problem posed by nuclear weapons. It showed Oppenheimer's equivocations about the decision to bomb Hiroshima and the anguished discussions of the German scientists. But the central character was Igor Kurchatov, who half expects, he tells a friend, to be judged harshly by future generations for his role in designing the nuclear weapon. But his responsibility to the present generation of his fellow countrymen left him no choice. His bomb would enable the Soviet Union to deal with America as an equal. Then at last it would be possible to reach a peaceful settlement. By the end of the film Kurchatov is dying of radiation sickness. He had always refused to take sensible precautions, despite Beria's strict instructions, and it killed him in 1960, at the age of fifty-seven.

The young Igor was not interested in these weighty issues. He was fascinated by the film's colourful depiction of the mushroom cloud – a studio reconstruction, rather than the real thing, as he was

---

*Another film dealing with the moral issue, *Devyat Dnei Odnogo Goda* (Nine Days in One Year), was made fourteen years earlier under Khrushchev. It too was apparently set in Arzamas-16. It too came to the conclusion that Soviet scientists had no choice but to develop the nuclear weapon. As its hero put it, if he and his colleagues had not done so, their country would have already been reduced to a pile of rubble.

disappointed to learn years later. He was proud when his father told him: 'Your name is the same as his – Igor Vasilievich. I was thinking of him when we were choosing your name.' His mother, who worked in the local hospital, told him about radiation and what had happened to the people in Hiroshima. He never forgot those two evenings in front of the television.

At school Igor and his classmates were shown a film about what to do if there was a nuclear explosion. They were taken to see an air raid shelter. It was some distance away, but the children were assured that there would be transport to take them there in an emergency, and food available when they arrived. Although Igor and his friends doubted that they would survive a nuclear war, they were proud of their country's ability to give as good as it got if the Americans attacked. Back home, his father mumbled that it was best to do what the teachers said, even if it didn't make sense.

Like their opposite numbers in the West, the Soviet authorities believed that effective civil defence – or at least its appearance – would bolster the credibility of their deterrent. In order to cheer them up, they told people at their places of work, in universities, in schools, that war could not be ruled out as long as imperialism existed. But a good system of civil defence could protect them.

There were compulsory civil defence training programmes for all. School children learned the Soviet equivalent of 'duck and cover'. In 1962 the authorities put out a film, *Grazhdanskaya Oborona v Selskoi Mestnosti* (Civil Defence in the Countryside), which illustrated, in a series of rather leisurely dramatised episodes, how people could protect themselves through shelter-building, evacuation, and disciplined preparedness. A 1970 handbook for university students, *Grazhdanskaya Oborona** (Civil Defence) was illustrated in the popular style of the traditional peasant woodcut, the *lubok*. There were the usual maps with concentric circles imposed on them to show the range of the damage, and other maps to show the downwind extent of fallout. Such mildly optimistic publications closely

---

* Russians shortened the phrase to *Grob* – which conveniently enough is the Russian word for 'coffin'.

resembled their equivalents in the West. In the Soviet Union, as in Britain, people were exhorted to await instructions from the authorities. There too people were given no hint that the authorities might themselves be out of action.[23]

In theory, the Soviet authorities had the instruments to enforce their plans. This helped to mislead Western observers into taking plans for reality. But there was no reason to think that Soviet plans would work any better than Western ones. The Soviet authorities were very good at moving large numbers of people about in the most brutal manner – they had shifted millions of prisoners, troops, and evacuees all over the country in both peace and war. But it is unlikely that they could have emptied a city more quickly than Portland, Oregon, was emptied during Operation Greenlight in 1955.

If, as some American conservatives maintained, the Soviets were preparing for a surprise attack on America, emptying their cities would not be a good start. American intelligence would pick it up immediately. All element of military surprise would be lost. Soviet political and military leaders were surely able to work that out for themselves.*

Like their Western counterparts, the Soviet authorities complained about the lack of public enthusiasm for their policies. They lamented that 'the devastating force of nuclear weapons … makes some people feel that death is inevitable for all who are in the strike area'. Moscow University students in the 1980s treated the whole subject with unbecoming levity: they fooled around in their civil defence classes, throwing paper darts at the diagrams and maps on the walls which showed ground zero after a nuclear strike.

In the 1970s the Russians, like their Western colleagues, began to conclude that the problem was intractable. Civil defence almost faded away as a subject for study in the General Staff Academy.†

---

* In 1960 Leon Goure produced a much-quoted study (*Soviet Civil Defence*, Rand, 1960). It was sensible as far as it went, though it was inevitably based on Soviet public statements rather than observed facts.

† There was only one lecture on civil defence in the General Staff Academy course in the mid-1970s and the last article devoted to the subject in *Voennaya Mysl* appeared in 1974.

Doubts and criticism grew after the disastrous accident in the Chernobyl nuclear power station in 1986. The liberal journal *Twentieth Century and Peace* published an article, 'Games Adults Play', which was a devastating criticism of the effectiveness, competence, and even the purpose of civil defence. General Vladimir Govorov, who as head of the Civil Defence Service helped to clean up after the Chernobyl accident, was asked in an interview, 'We spend millions on civil defence. But we ourselves are now saying: There can be no survivors in a nuclear war. So what is the point of all this?' He replied, 'A reasonable question, and it does not befit a military man to evade a direct answer. But I would rather put it slightly differently: It is not a question of survival being impossible, rather it is victory that is impossible.' The government newspaper *Izvestia* published a poll showing that, at least in Moscow, an overwhelming majority thought that a world nuclear war would be an unmitigated disaster.* The United States and the Soviet Union would be completely annihilated, and human civilisation would perish. The Soviet Union would not use nuclear weapons first; but it was not clear that the United States would be equally restrained. To prevent an accidental nuclear war, nuclear weapons should be eliminated entirely. Not many of those polled thought this was very likely.[24]

All in all, people in the Soviet Union ended up knowing almost as much and feeling just as powerless as their opposite numbers in the West. The mixture of scepticism, patriotism, and fatalism which characterised Russian attitudes to nuclear war and the possibility of defence against it was not, in the end, all that different from the attitudes of people in Britain and America.

Pennies and Sixpences: The British Prepare to be Blown to Atomic Dust

The British began by assuming that, unlike the Americans, they would be 'highly resistive' to atomic attack because they had survived the German Blitz. It took some years to convince them that previous

---

* Opinion polls were first conducted in the Soviet Union in the 1960s, but the results were rarely published. The situation improved markedly under Gorbachev (B. Grushin, *Chetyre Zhizni Rossii*, Moscow, 2003).

experience was largely irrelevant to a small island with no space to shelter its people. British governments gradually abandoned the idea that a civil defence programme could save lives on any useful scale. They aimed instead to preserve some semblance of government to run what was left of the country after an attack. Even this was hard to turn into an affordable, practical, and politically acceptable plan. Governments never ceased to worry that the public would demand expensive and ineffective schemes that would cripple the national economy and undermine the national defences. Despite the lip service they paid to civil defence, it always came third in their priorities after preserving the economy and building the strategic deterrent.

In November 1945 a British delegation visited Hiroshima and Nagasaki: its members included Jacob Bronowski, the Polish-born mathematician and polymath, who later became one of the first scientific pundits on television. In their report to Attlee in January 1946 they concluded that 'bombing had changed its character and its scale beyond recognition'. British buildings were more robustly constructed and less vulnerable to fire than Japanese buildings. An atom bomb on a British city the size of Hiroshima might kill only 50,000 people. But the authors invited the reader to 'picture the destruction here set down as it would strike a city which he knows well, its people, its houses, its public buildings, its factories, and its public services'.[25]

Thereafter things moved slowly.[26] By the time of the Berlin crisis of 1948, there were still no up-to-date plans for civil defence. The old plans were dusted down. It then appeared that there were not enough air raid sirens. The Foreign Office was told to find some in occupied Germany. A Civil Defence Act was passed that December. But when North Korea invaded the South in July 1950 the Home Office had to admit that it would be unable to cope with an attack even on the scale of the wartime Blitz.

A passionate argument now began between the Home Office and the defence planners which lasted for many years, and which the Home Office eventually lost beyond recall. The Home Office used the argument already being deployed in America. Our deterrent posture depended on the general belief that we were prepared to use our nuclear weapons if necessary. It would be seriously undermined if our people felt that not enough was being done for them, and our soldiers felt that their families were not being properly protected. The deterrent, said James Chuter Ede, the Home Secretary, required a better-prepared civil defence programme.

Attlee disagreed. Ede's measures would create a 'Maginot attitude of mind' among the population. What we needed was to 'increase the active defence preparations which were designed to deter the enemy from attempting war'. Churchill was more cynical: like Richard Nixon, he believed the government should give the impression of pursuing an active civil defence policy, while taking care 'to avoid spending large sums of money on measures which would pay no dividends'. The Chiefs of Staff conceded only that civil defence could be useful if it concentrated on 'measures for carrying on essential activities during the initial intense phase of the war'.

The Ministry of Defence soon concluded that there was 'in the foreseeable future *no* effective defence against atomic attack'.[27] In 1953 a study group under Robert Hall of the Cabinet Office explained in homely language what would happen if the Russians bombed Britain. 'Take a half inch map of London,' they wrote, 'put down a sixpence with its centre over each ground zero; draw a circle around it, and let that represent the area (three quarters of a mile in radius) within which everybody is killed or seriously injured, and all the houses are completely destroyed or so badly damaged as to require demolition. Do the same thing with pennies, and you will have the ring (between three quarters of a mile and 2 miles from the burst) within which all the houses are uninhabitable, at least temporarily.'*

Four hundred thousand people would die in London, and 1.3 million in the country as a whole. Ten million would be homeless. And what about the survivors? 'What about John Smith of Laburnum Villa, Stoke Newington, just on the outer edge of a penny circle?' There would be no power, no fuel, and perhaps no water. John Smith would not be able to get to his job because 'there are five sixpenny rings between his house and it, with not a chance of getting through to it above ground, and the tubes have not started running again'.

---

* A sixpence was the size of a modern 5p coin; a penny was the size of a 2p coin.

Hall's conclusions were grim: 'The question is whether or not the barest mechanism of life can be maintained in the bombed areas for the first few days.' It would be uncertain how far 'Government, in the ordinary sense of the word, has survived'. There would be 'the nerve-racking effects of blast, the fires raging everywhere, the sight of the injured whom no help can reach – above all, perhaps, the dread of the unknown and the terror of radioactive effects'. It was 'a shattering prospect, and it is a bold man who would deny the probability of a mass flight, set off by the instinct of self-preservation, and the possibility of serious panic, especially in congested areas such as the East End of London'.[28]

The Home Defence Committee drew two main conclusions from Hall's report. The idea of fighting on after an atomic attack could be ruled out: the main effort would have to be devoted to national survival. And everything should be done to prevent such an attack ever taking place – and for that a powerful deterrent was essential.

In the House of Commons the report was heavily attacked. The MPs had assumed that the purpose of civil defence policy was to save lives. Now it appeared that civil defence was a façade, and that the policy of the government was primarily aimed at military and economic survival. In private the Cabinet Secretary, Norman Brook, agreed that 'façade' was the right word.

These conclusions were bad enough. But they were upended by the American test of a thermonuclear device at Bikini in March 1954. People sensed that this was a turning point: a few thermonuclear bombs could kill many more people than a large number of atom bombs. Harold Macmillan noted in his diary that 'it is obvious there is tremendous interest, almost panic, in many parts of the world, about the hydrogen bomb'. Nesta Payne, a BBC radio producer, told her boss, 'I think we ought to do a programme on the hydrogen bomb and its implications for the human race. Full stop. It seemed clear that in the war in which hydrogen bombs are used, England would quite clearly be finished ... Like many people, I have simply avoided thinking about these bombs and their implications during the last 10 years. Now that I have been obliged to do so, I feel very strongly indeed that ... [we] face dangers which might completely engulf the whole of the human race.' Her programme was never made.[29]

Coventry City Council decided at this time that its civil defence arrangements were a useless waste of money and closed them down. Other councils threatened to follow suit. They were viciously attacked as unpatriotic: the magazine *Civil Defence* suspected a conspiracy. The new Home Secretary, Sir David Maxwell Fyfe, tried to rally opinion with some words of common sense: 'We must not lose our nerve in the face of this fresh potential horror. To suppose that one such bomb could destroy the world or even kill everyone in this country is a sign of ignorance, hysteria and panic. What it can do is sufficiently horrible without indulging in unreasoning exaggeration.'[30]

In their major strategic document of July 1954, 'United Kingdom Defence Policy', the Chiefs of Staff estimated that a Soviet attack on ten cities would kill between 5 and 12 million people. But, they argued, if the British also had thermonuclear weapons they could deter aggression while cutting conventional forces. Ministers seized on the opportunity to save money, and persuaded themselves that war was relatively unlikely in the next five years.

But something still needed to be done about public morale. Maxwell Fyfe commented on the Chiefs' paper that 'the policy [of deterrence] outlined ... could not be sustained unless the British public were prepared to accept the risks which it involved. If these risks were to be run, public opinion must be carefully prepared.' So ministers ordered the expansion of existing plans for evacuation. The number of people to be evacuated rose from 4.6 to 12 million people. Mothers and children would have priority. Essential workers would be left in place. No one ever managed to define who these 'essential' workers might be.

Treasury officials attacked the new plans as hopelessly unrealistic. Richard Clarke was scathing: 'there is something faintly comical about dividing the population into classes, some of which are told by Home Office officials that they are to go and others to stay ... The standard work on the subject is by Mr H. G. Wells, written, I think in 1896 – "The War of the Worlds" – which is much better than any piece of Home Office paper that I have yet seen.'

In February 1955 the government admitted that life after a thermonuclear attack 'would be a struggle for survival of the grimmest kind'. There was no 'simple or immediate solution' to the problem of civil defence. But they were confident that the British people shared their determination 'to face the threat of physical devastation, even on the immense scale which must be foreseen' rather than adopt 'an attitude of subservience to militant Communism, with the national and individual humiliation that this would bring'. They offered no evidence for this belief.

William Strath, the head of the Cabinet Office Central War Plans Secretariat, was working on yet another report, which he delivered in March 1955. His findings were even more stark than Hall's. Ten ten-megaton bombs dropped on Britain would kill 9 million people from blast and heat, and 3 million from radiation. Another 4 million would be seriously injured or disabled. A single bomb would cause 4 million casualties in London alone. These figures ignored the genetic consequences of radiation. The survivors would be left struggling against disease, starvation, and psychological collapse. The military might have to take the most drastic steps to preserve order.

Any remedy, Strath considered, would require a radical overhaul of the country's wholly inadequate plans for civil defence. Since central government in London would probably break down, a system of regional government would have to be created. Such measures would leave the country with sufficient resources for a slow recovery. The implication was that Britain would otherwise collapse as an organised society.* Gwilym Lloyd George, who had replaced Maxwell Fyfe as Home Secretary, believed the shelters would have to be built. There was little point, he thought, in 'keeping forces for the "hot war" if the morale of this country is to collapse and we lose the will to fight'.[31]

But as always there was not enough money to finance a civil defence programme in which few believed. Forced to choose, the government continued to give priority to the deterrent. What had

---

*Gwilym Lloyd George pointed out that the key facts in the Strath Report were available to anyone in Britain who cared to look. Even so the report remained secret for decades.

seemed like a surprising admission when the Defence Secretary, Duncan Sandys, told the House of Commons in 1957 that there was no way of protecting the British people against nuclear attack had already come close to a truism. Even the normally critical *Manchester Guardian* said that 'it will only come as a shock to those who have been cherishing illusions dangerous to themselves'.

The 1957 White Paper thus marked the end of any serious attempt to construct a viable civil defence system. But the official studies continued. In 1958 the Joint Committee for the Study of All-Out War (JIGSAW) considered what a global nuclear war might look like. JIGSAW started with a definition of 'breakdown': the point at which a government could no longer ensure that its orders were carried out. This was a prospect that faced even the superpowers. Edgar Anstey, the Home Office representative on JIGSAW, believed that 'Neither the USA nor the Soviet Union stood the slightest chance of "winning" a global nuclear war in any meaningful sense'.[32] For Britain things would be worse. Only 15 million people would survive an all-out nuclear war. No civil defence arrangements could change that. But to keep up public support for its deterrent policy, the government needed 'to create the image of preparedness; to provide succour to the minds of those questioning the deterrent; and to influence those who, in the final emergency, might see the lack of government preparations and decide to protest against any possible British participation in a nuclear war'.[33]

Even if it could not protect the population at large, the government did not abandon the aim of preserving some system of authority that could give the devastated country a hope of recovery. It was after the Berlin crisis of 1961 and the Cuban missile crisis of 1962 that they built the secure bunker in the Cotswolds and the Regional Seats of Government described in Chapter 8.

It was an essay in futility. By the mid-1960s the Russians probably knew where the emergency centres were. Their existence was revealed to the public in 1963 by the so-called 'Spies for Peace', a maverick protest group. Assiduous journalists like Duncan Campbell managed to put together a surprisingly accurate picture of the government's supposedly secret arrangements.[34] In 1964 the new Labour government decided that no more regional centres should be built.

The following year the government effectively closed down its civil defence programme and concluded that even its plans to preserve a nucleus of government to run the country after an attack were impractical.

Successive governments nevertheless continued to worry about public morale and went on trying to create an 'image of preparedness'. There were no civil defence classes in British schools, as there were in Russian and American schools. But in 1963 the government did publish a pamphlet entitled 'Civil Defence Handbook No. 10: Advising the Housekeeper on Protection against Nuclear Attack'. It was sensible and clearly written, full of practical advice about how to make your house safe against fire, blast, and fallout. But it was ten years too late. It drew on the lessons of Hiroshima and might have been adequate for the atomic age. But it was totally inappropriate for the thermonuclear age. It was ruthlessly attacked in Parliament and by anti-nuclear campaigners, and lampooned by the satirical show *Beyond the Fringe*.*

In 1965 the BBC commissioned a film to mark the twentieth anniversary of Hiroshima: *The War Game*, by Peter Watkins. This showed the effect of a Soviet missile striking Rochester in Kent. Watkins drew on 'Civil Defence Handbook No. 10' to show how its injunctions would fail under the stress of nuclear attack. Those in the know thought that the reality would be even worse than the film. Norman Brook, by now the BBC's Chairman, thought that the film had been made with considerable restraint. But 'the subject is, necessarily, alarming; and the showing of the film might have had a significant effect on public attitudes to the nuclear deterrent'. The BBC decided it would be better if the film were not shown.[35]

Civil defence continued a ghostly existence until the end of the Cold War. The simple nostrums of 'Civil Defence Handbook No. 10' lived on. In May 1980 the government issued a new booklet. 'Protect and Survive' explained the effects of heat, blast, radiation, and fallout. It told people how to construct a fallout shelter in their home, using

---

* The show never lost its popularity and remains available on YouTube at https://www.youtube.com/watch?v=AobLKuLszXs.

doors, earth, and old mattresses. They would need a survival kit: food and water for fourteen days, two toilet buckets, books and magazines, toys for the children, a radio (with spare batteries) to listen to government instructions. If anyone died, the survivors should label the body and move it into the next room; but after five days they should bury it outside, if by then it was safe to do so. They would be told by radio when to emerge from their shelters and what to do next. The necessary but unspoken assumption was that the authorities and their communications would have survived the attack.

In November 1981 ministers rather desperately issued another piece of paper, 'Civil Defence: Why We Need It'. Honest people could disagree about the best means of preventing war, they said plaintively. 'But whatever view we take, we should surely all recognise the need – and indeed the duty – to protect our civil population if an attack were to be made upon us; and therefore to prepare accordingly … Even the strongest supporter of unilateral disarmament can consistently give equal support to civil defence, since its purpose and effect are essentially humane.' After all, the pamphlet argued, people wore safety belts in cars, even though they didn't expect to have a crash. Civil defence served a similar function: it was a matter of common prudence.[36]

The critics produced their own rebuttal, 'Protest and Survive', by E. P. Thompson. Anti-nuclear campaigners protested that the government were making nuclear war more likely by popularising the idea that it could be survived. They accused the government of gross and immoral cynicism, of building shelters for themselves to survive a war in which millions would die. That was unfair on the planners, who knew that, whatever defensive measures they took, most of them – and their families – were as likely to die as their fellow countrymen.

Meanwhile another generation of children was being introduced to the facts of nuclear life. Penny Daniel, in her early teens, was debating in school what she and her friends would do with the four-minute warning they would get of a nuclear attack, and reading a graphic novel (later a film) by Raymond Briggs called *When the Wind Blows*, about what would happen to an ordinary middle-aged couple if they tried to follow the government's advice. It did not leave an encouraging impression.

***

At the time of the Berlin crisis in 1961 the British Foreign Secretary, Alec Douglas-Home, suggested that the British people were 'quite ready to be blown to atomic dust' if that was the price for resisting the Russians.[37] He did not say where he got that idea from.

But even when anti-nuclear protest in Britain was at its height, no more than 30 per cent of the population wanted to abandon the country's nuclear weapons. The majority believed that they should be retained, at least as long as other nations kept theirs. They resigned themselves to living on a volcano that might explode at any moment.

The British government was under no illusion either. Their civil defence policy was a policy of despair. But like their opposite numbers in America and the Soviet Union, they could see no alternative.

THIRTEEN

SKIRTING THE BRINK

'Nuclear war could occur not through evil intent, but could happen through miscalculation. Then nothing could save mankind.'

Yuri Andropov, Soviet General Secretary, 1983[1]

Mutual deterrence is a delicate thing. It works because both sides terrify themselves and one another into avoiding war. Each side has two overriding but conflicting priorities: to impose the tightest possible political and technical controls on its systems and thus eliminate all possibility of war by technical accident or human error; and to ensure that they can nevertheless fire off their weapons against an attacker even when they have no more than a few minutes' warning.

Each side has to assume (but cannot know) that their opponent is equally meticulous, and that his systems, too, are robust against accident or miscalculation.

These conditions are hard to meet in the real world. The two superpowers blustered and took risks in at least three major crises – around Berlin in 1961–2, around Cuba in 1962, and during the troubled events of 1983, the 'Second Cold War'. Despite their best efforts, there was a steady stream of technical accidents and mishaps among the weapons systems. Accidents at civil nuclear plants – Three Mile Island in America in 1979, Chernobyl in the Soviet Union in 1986, Fukushima in Japan in 2011 – showed that even the best technology could go terribly wrong.

Taming the Monster?
In that knowledge, the American, Soviet, and British governments did indeed try to bring the monster under control. Viscerally hostile

to one another, trust between them seemed impossible. Yet they were forced to find common instruments to avoid mutual catastrophe. Sometimes responding to public opinion, sometimes defying it, politicians on both sides pressed the process forward. Slowly a messy cobweb of agreements was generated which introduced a modicum of order and predictability into the nuclear confrontation.

In May 1944 Bohr tried to persuade Churchill that it was futile to think that the secrets of the physical world could be hidden from the Russians or anyone else who was determined to acquire them. The only way forward was to bring the Russians into the picture, and reach a common agreement to keep the genie under control. Churchill roundly rejected his proposal. Roosevelt seemed more sympathetic at his meeting with Bohr in August. But when the two leaders met that September, they agree that the idea was untenable, and ordered their security people to keep an eye on him to ensure he kept his mouth shut.

But the thought would not go away. In September 1945 Henry Stimson, Truman's Secretary for War, sent a memorandum to the President on the need for 'a satisfactory international arrangement respecting the control of this new force'.[2] He recommended that America and Britain should sound out the Russians before going public: they would react badly to anything that looked like ganging up.

Truman thought this was politically naïve. Instead he, Attlee and Mackenzie King, the Canadian Prime Minister, publicly proposed the creation of a UN Atomic Energy Commission in November 1945. Truman then commissioned Dean Acheson, the future Secretary of State, and David Lilienthal, the Chairman of the US Atomic Energy Commission, to sketch out a draft UN treaty for an international agency to control the world's supply of fissile material capable of being used in weapons; it would release small amounts but only to countries genuinely developing atomic energy for peaceful purposes. Robert Oppenheimer played a major part in the drafting.

Acheson underlined that, though the Americans currently had the nuclear monopoly, it could not last. What was proposed was therefore 'a plan under which no nation would make atomic bombs or the materials for them. All dangerous activities would be carried on – not merely inspected – by a live, functioning international authority.' The historian David Holloway called the report 'a bold attempt to come to terms with the problem of international control'.

The report leaked even before it got to the United Nations in March 1946. By then it had already been fatally modified by Bernard Baruch, a financier and veteran adviser of presidents, whom Truman had appointed to present the proposal there.* Against Acheson's advice, Baruch insisted on two provisions. There should be sanctions against states which contravened the agreement. And permanent members of the Security Council should not be allowed to use their veto rights to evade sanctions if they transgressed. He may have been trying to introduce a necessary safeguard into what was otherwise too weak a test. But in practice this meant that the Americans could keep the weapons they had; but that anyone who tried to match them (understood: the Soviet Union) could be punished.

The Russians reacted as badly as Stimson had predicted. It was hardly surprising that they turned the American proposal down. They countered with a proposal to ban the production, stockpiling and use of atomic weapons. Existing bombs were to be destroyed immediately; punitive measures for non-compliance were to be enacted within six months. That was of course equally unacceptable to the Americans. The Russians were widely blamed, then and later, for refusing to accept the American proposal. But Baruch's amendment had already ensured that it would not be adopted.[3]

The near-death experience of the Cuban missile crisis in 1962 persuaded the nuclear powers that they had to do better than that. The Partial Test Ban Treaty of 1963 (whose genesis is described in Chapter 11) was the first important step towards reining in the monster. Its failure to cover testing underground was partially rectified by a general moratorium on testing underground which began in the early 1990s.

Another major agreement, the Nuclear Non-Proliferation Treaty signed in 1968, aimed to prevent the spread of nuclear weapons, to encourage nuclear disarmament, and to promote the peaceful use of nuclear energy. It was originally valid for twenty-five years, but in

---

*Dean Acheson believed that Baruch's reputation as a wise man 'was without foundation in fact and entirely self-propagated'.

1995 it was extended indefinitely. Nearly 200 countries had signed it by 2015. India, Pakistan and Israel had not. North Korea withdrew in 2003. The treaty was based on a central bargain. The five recognised nuclear weapons states – America, Russia, Britain, France, and China – agreed to eliminate their nuclear arsenals over time, and the others agreed never to acquire them. Some, such as South Africa, abandoned programmes they had already started. The nuclear weapons states were also obliged not to help others acquire or manufacture nuclear weapons, or to use their nuclear weapons against non-nuclear states.

The practical effect of the treaty is not easy to assess. It may have had some success in limiting an increase in the number of nuclear weapons states. In the 1960s it was predicted that there would be up to thirty nuclear weapons states within twenty years. Forty years later there were still only nine, the original five plus India, Pakistan, Israel, and North Korea. Strenuous efforts to ensure that Iran was not misusing its treaty right to develop the peaceful use of nuclear energy as a cover for a weapons programme seemed to have succeeded by 2015. Some countries that might have been expected to develop nuclear weapons never tried; others gave up after they had started.

But the original nuclear powers largely ignored their own obligations under the treaty. They did reduce their arsenals, and claimed credit accordingly. But that was because they had more obsolescent weapons than they could possibly need. There was a limit below which they were not prepared to go, and all retained viable arsenals. At Review Conferences held every five years they were regularly attacked for failing to disarm. In 2015 they again tried to explain why they were all modernising their armouries and still had 22,000 warheads between them. The non-weapons states remained unimpressed.

The Politicians Chance Their Luck

But at the same time as they were trying to get the monster under control, the leaders of the nuclear powers were engaged in a potentially lethal competition from which they found it almost impossible to extricate themselves.

Even though they still had a nuclear monopoly, the Americans did not use or seriously threaten to use the weapon during the confrontation around Berlin in 1948, during the Korean War in 1950, or to avert the Communist victory over the French in North Vietnam in 1954. John Foster Dulles, Eisenhower's Secretary of State, thought the apparent taboo unfortunate. Thomas Schelling, one of the most sober and durable of the American strategic theorists, thought it was just that taboo which prevented catastrophe.[4]

By the early 1960s the Strategic Air Command could reach deep into the Soviet Union from its bases in the continental United States and around the Soviet periphery. So could American Thor missiles based in Britain, and Jupiter missiles in Italy and Turkey. American submarines armed with Polaris missiles began operating out of Holy Loch on the west coast of Scotland from March 1961.* The Russians still had nothing comparable. They could hit targets in Europe with their medium-range missiles, but in 1961 they had only four, and a year later only twenty, capable of hitting the United States.[5] Their bomber force was far smaller than the Strategic Air Command. Its aircraft had little ability to penetrate the American air defences and lacked the range to return home. Their submarines could not launch their missiles underwater and had no bases close to the American heartland from which to operate.

Berlin 1961

But the American monopoly was already beginning to fray away. In the early 1960s Khrushchev challenged it with a series of gambles.

The first was around Berlin. Berlin was well inside the Soviet zone when Germany was divided at the end of the Second World War. Each of the four victorious powers had a sector there, to which the Western powers had access by road, rail, and air. In 1948 Stalin tried to force them out with a blockade which was defeated by a Western airlift.

In January 1961 Khrushchev warned that unless the Western powers dismantled the occupation regime in Berlin he would end

---

* The Americans agreed rather grumpily that the missiles in Britain could only be launched if a British and an American officer both turned a key on the controls. This dual key system was derived from an arrangement in the Bank of England which ensured that no one person could open the vaults on his own (J. Baylis, *Ambiguity and Deterrence*, Oxford, 1995, p. 257).

it unilaterally. By now the German Democratic Republic, as the Soviet occupation zone was called, was so unpopular with its own citizens that they were fleeing to the West in increasing numbers. In August 1961 the East German government walled off their half of Berlin to stem the flow. Soviet troops and aircraft began to harass the Western occupying powers on their lines of communication with the city. Khrushchev assumed that the Americans would not dare to use nuclear weapons to offset the Russians' overwhelming superiority in conventional forces around the city.

By then John Kennedy was President. He understood the risks of nuclear war perfectly well. As the crisis escalated, his National Security Advisor, McGeorge Bundy, warned that nuclear planning had become so dangerously rigid that it 'may leave you with very little choice as to how you face the moment of thermonuclear truth … In essence, the current plan calls for shooting off everything we have in one shot and it is so constructed as to make any more flexible course very difficult.'[6] Kennedy asked General LeMay and Harold Brown, his director of Defense Research, how many Americans would die in a nuclear exchange with the Russians.* LeMay said that if the Russians struck first there would be 60 million American dead. Brown said that even if the Americans struck first, 20 or 30 million Americans would still die in the Russian counterstrike. Kennedy saw no significant difference and concluded that there must never be a thermonuclear war.[7]

But Kennedy also thought that Khrushchev could not be allowed to get away with it. 'It is not that … we underestimate the dangers of war,' he said. 'But if we don't meet our commitments in Berlin, it will mean the destruction of NATO and a dangerous situation for the whole world. All Europe is at stake in Berlin.'[8] The US military had plans to force open the motorway to Berlin by sending down an armoured column, backed by the nuclear threat. Dean Acheson, the former State Secretary now acting as Kennedy's adviser, argued: 'Khrushchev will be deterred only by a US readiness to go to nuclear war rather than to abandon the status quo.'

---

* Harold Brown worked as a researcher and then Director of the Lawrence Livermore Laboratory, and became Secretary of Defense under President Carter.

It did not come to that. In July Kennedy said on TV, 'We cannot and will not let the Communists drive us out of Berlin.' But he warned that 'miscommunication could rain down more devastation in several hours than has been wrought in all the wars in human history'.[9] He did not specifically brandish the nuclear threat. That autumn a face-to-face confrontation between Soviet and American tanks on the boundary between East and West Berlin ended when the Russians withdrew. The American tanks withdrew immediately after.

The Americans considered that they had won. Khrushchev thought the opposite. He had not got all he wanted, but the Wall had not been effectively challenged. 'By refusing to back down in the face of intimidation by the West,' he wrote in his memoirs, 'we guaranteed the GDR's right to control its own territory and its own borders. We had good reason to celebrate this moral and material victory, for we had forced the West to recognise the GDR's unwritten rights.' And indeed the Wall remained in place for nearly three decades.[10]

Within a year Khrushchev was trying his luck elsewhere.

The Cuban Missile Crisis
In April 1961 the Americans backed a botched attempt by Cuban exiles to overthrow Fidel Castro's increasingly Communist government in Cuba by armed invasion. Khrushchev responded by provoking an even more dangerous crisis.

He had two main aims. One was to give the Castro government an effective military guarantee against further American attempts at invasion. The other was to make a short, sharp dash towards a makeshift nuclear parity by installing Soviet medium-range missiles on Cuba able to menace the American heartland and thus match in some measure the ring of American bases threatening the Soviet Union. As Khrushchev himself put it, '[T]he installation of our missiles in Cuba would, I thought, restrain the United States from precipitous military action against Castro's government. In addition to protecting Cuba, our missiles would have equalized what the West likes to call the "balance of power".' By these means, he hoped, he could force the Americans to deal with the Soviet Union on a more equal basis.[12]

In May 1962 Khrushchev agreed with Castro on a plan called Operation Anadyr, under which the Russians would secretly deploy to Cuba thirty-six R-12 intermediate-range ballistic missiles and forty-two Ilyushin Il-28 nuclear bombers, which could directly threaten major cities in the United States. Cuba itself would be defended by four mechanised infantry regiments, two regiments of FKR mobile cruise missiles with nuclear warheads, a dozen Luna tactical ballistic missiles with a range of thirty miles,[13] forty fighter aircraft, and a naval force including missile submarines.*

The success of the operation would depend on flawless planning, impeccable execution, and a security veil so impenetrable that the Americans would not discover what was going on until it was too late. These were hard conditions. But if it worked, it would be a gamble worth taking. Khrushchev was advised it could be done. Since he had no intention of launching a war, he assumed the Americans would acquiesce in a fait accompli.

Those were fatal misjudgements.

The Americans had wondered for some time whether the Russians might try to put missiles into Cuba. By August 1962 they were beginning to get reasonably good intelligence about Soviet military shipments, though as yet nothing concrete about missiles. On 4 September Kennedy publicly warned that 'grave issues' would arise if he found evidence of Soviet military bases or missiles on the island.

By the end of September the Americans had still not detected the full extent of the Soviet deployment. Over 30,000 Soviet troops under the command of General Issa Pliyev had already reached Cuba. His Luna battlefield missiles could, if it came to the point, destroy the American base at Guantanamo. The cruise missile regiments were on their way. The initial naval force was about to leave the Soviet Union. It consisted of four large modern diesel submarines (NATO code name Foxtrot) of the 69th Submarine Brigade based in Murmansk. Their task was to secure the area around the Cuban port of Mariel and prepare it for the arrival of the missile submarines. The

---

* These were diesel-powered submarines. By the summer of 1962 the Soviet nuclear-powered submarines were all in dry dock, having their reactors refitted following a number of incidents including, in the summer of 1961, the accident to the K-19 (see Chapter 10).

Foxtrots were not themselves missile boats, but each carried a nuclear T-5 torpedo capable of destroying an assemblage of enemy ships, such as a carrier battle group.*

But on 15 October U-2 spy planes brought back photographs from Cuba which showed beyond doubt that Soviet missiles sites were being prepared there. The photographs were on Kennedy's desk on 18 October when the Soviet Foreign Minister called on him. It was an awkward meeting. Kennedy read from his statement of 4 September. Gromyko equivocated. The Americans were furiously convinced he had blatantly lied. Indignant at the Russians' perfidy, Kennedy is supposed to have remarked to McGeorge Bundy at an early stage of the crisis: 'It's just as if we suddenly began to put a major number of MRBMs (Intermediate range missiles) in Turkey. Now that'd be goddamn dangerous, I would think.' Bundy is said to have replied: 'Well, we did, Mr President.' In Bundy's own account, the story is a bit more complicated. The American missiles, which had a longer range than the Soviet missiles, were sent to Turkey in 1959 as part of a NATO plan to counter new Soviet missile deployments. By 1962 everyone except LeMay believed they were obsolete. In August 1962, before the crisis broke, Kennedy asked what action could be taken to withdraw them. Nothing was done, not least because of the likely effect on Turkish and allied confidence. Fifteen missiles were still in Turkey at the height of the crisis and proved a useful negotiating chip in its resolution.[14†]

The first meeting of Kennedy's Executive Committee for managing the crisis – ExCom – took place four days later. The Joint Chiefs of Staff believed that missiles in Cuba would seriously affect the strategic balance. McNamara disagreed: the Americans had some 5,000 strategic warheads, while the Soviet Union only had 300. An extra

---

* The US Navy had nuclear torpedoes as well, the Mark 45 torpedo with an eleven-kiloton warhead. Six hundred were built and were in service from 1963 to 1976. Existing Mark 45 torpedoes were then reconfigured for conventional use, renamed the Freedom torpedo, and sold to foreign navies (https://en.wikipedia.org/wiki/Mark_45_torpedo).

† Gromyko later said that he had been asked no direct question and had therefore been able to avoid a direct answer. Diplomacy on all sides proceeds by such equivocation.

forty missiles in Cuba would make little strategic difference. But Kennedy considered that the *political* balance would be affected: this was not acceptable. General LeMay presented a plan to bomb the island. Kennedy turned it down: he hoped for a negotiated outcome. To shocked silence around the table, LeMay retorted, 'This is almost as bad as the appeasement at Munich,' and told the President, 'You're in a pretty bad fix.' Kennedy replied, to strained laughter from the others, 'Well, you're in there with me personally.' But to strengthen his arm, he agreed that American nuclear forces should be put on alert, and preparations made for an attack on Cuba.

The American military wanted to attack before the missiles became operational. Kennedy chose the less inflammatory alternative of a naval blockade (his lawyers advised him to call it a 'quarantine', a word which, unlike 'blockade', had no military connotations). On 22 October he announced that all ships bound for Cuba would be turned back if their cargoes contained offensive weapons.

By now the possibility of a nuclear confrontation had become quite real. By the third week in October the Soviet military were convinced that they were close to war. Pliyev's nuclear-tipped missiles were in place. His instructions for using them had been formulated with much difficulty by a Politburo divided on how much authority should be delegated to him: Anastas Mikoyan, one of its most senior members, pointed out that using them might start a thermonuclear war. Meanwhile the four Foxtrot submarines, with their nuclear-tipped torpedoes, were already well on their way.[15]

Soviet forces in Poland were ordered to stop all exercises, return to their command posts, and be ready for action.[16] The missile site in Nizhni Tagil received the code word Brontosavr (Brontosaurus), the order to open the sealed instructions for launching their rockets. One of those present remembered that the colonel in charge was shaking: 'It was strangely quiet. I cannot forget the mixture of nervousness, surprise, and pain on the faces of each operator without exception.'[17] The missiles at Plesetsk were made ready to strike New York, Washington, Chicago, and other American cities. Soviet strategic bombers were moved to their forward bases.[18]

The four Foxtrot submarines left Murmansk on 1 October,

commanded by Ryurik Ketov, Aleksei Dubivko, Nikolai Shumkov, and Valentin Savitsky.[19] The commander of the 69th Submarine Brigade, Captain Vitali Agafonov, sailed with Ketov; his Chief of Staff, Vasili Arkhipov, travelled with Savitsky.* The captains were briefed on the eve of their departure by Admiral Vitali Fokin, the First Deputy Head of the Soviet Navy, and Admiral Anatoli Rassokho, the Chief of Staff of the Northern Fleet. Rassokho apparently told them that the captains were authorised to use their nuclear torpedoes under three conditions: if they were attacked by depth charges and their boat was severely damaged; if they surfaced and were fired upon; and if they received specific orders from Moscow. The sealed orders the captains opened once they were at sea were more tightly drawn: the nuclear torpedoes were to be used only on direct orders from Moscow, and only if the orders were explicitly verified by the captain and his two most senior colleagues. The instructions failed to say what should happen if communications with Moscow broke down. But whatever the orders said, Moscow had no way of preventing a submarine commander and his colleagues from firing their nuclear torpedo if they so decided. The outcome, as with Pliyev's missiles, would depend on their judgement and their discipline.[†]

Each boat carried extra food, fuel, and equipment, together with a specialist intelligence team. These took up valuable space, needed special facilities, and were resented by the boats' regular crews. Because they were diesel-powered, the submarines could travel faster on the surface than submerged. But to avoid detection they had to spend much of the day underwater, coming up at night to recharge their batteries. To reach Cuba by their deadline, the captains had to hope that neither mechanical failure nor foul weather would hinder them.

---

* Arkhipov had distinguished himself during the accident to K-19 the previous year.

† There is a more dramatic version. Fokin is said to have told the captains, 'If they slap you on the left cheek, do not let them slap you on the right one.' Rassokho is supposed to have gone further: 'I suggest to you, commanders, that you use the nuclear weapons first, and then you will figure out what to do after that.' Although this version was attested by some of the participants many years later, it seems unlikely that the two admirals would have given orders so unclear and so irresponsible.

Their hopes were soon dashed. Storms forced them to reduce speed. The navigators could not see the sun or the stars to fix their positions. The compasses went wrong. The radio operators could barely get through to Moscow. One of Dubivko's officers got appendicitis and the boat had to dive so that he could be operated on in the calmer waters below.

The tropical waters were calmer, but now the American anti-submarine forces – three carrier battle groups and a horde of aircraft – forced the boats to stay submerged for days at a time. They had no air conditioning. The heat in the engine rooms rose above 140 degrees Fahrenheit. The refrigerators failed, the food began to rot, and the crews went on short rations. There was not enough water to wash, the men got ulcers, and the doctor's ointments turned their skin green. Anatoli Andreev, one of Dubivko's junior officers, wrote in the journal he was keeping for his wife: 'Today three sailors fainted from overheating again. Those who are off duty are sitting immobile, staring at one spot. They don't walk when they go on watch: they crawl.'

The despised intelligence teams now came into their own, tracking the movements of the American ships and listening to their conversations. The Soviet navigators were conveniently able to correct their errors when the Americans reported their positions.

The submariners began to understand the crisis they were sailing into. Moscow had told them little. But now they could listen to American domestic broadcasts, and learned that the Americans were blockading Cuba and might invade at any moment. They heard Kennedy announce on the radio that he was determined to drive off the Soviet submarines. They wondered whether they were at war.

They had good reason. Kennedy ordered his commanders to act cautiously: 'We don't want to have the first thing we attack as a Soviet submarine.'[20] On 24 October, well into the crisis, the Americans told Moscow that if they found a submarine, they would drop innocuous explosive grenades nearby as a signal that it should surface. It is not clear if the message reached the submarines. But the American ships were now harassing them not only with grenades, which to them sounded like depth charges, but by making as if to ram them, and in one case apparently launching a torpedo.[21]

One by one the submarines had to surface, their batteries flat, their engines incapacitated. Shumkov found himself in the middle of a carrier battle group, helpless, unable to move. Moscow sent a tug to bring him home. Dubivko came up when an American destroyer seemed about to ram him. He sent Anatoli Andreev up on deck, pallid, emaciated, filthy, green from the doctor's medicine, wearing only ragged underpants, defiantly waving the Soviet naval ensign on a stick at the American sailors photographing him. Dubivko refused the Americans' offer of help, dived deep, and made his escape. Ketov was the only captain to evade his pursuers successfully.

But Valentin Savitsky came close to destroying a carrier battle group with his nuclear torpedo on Saturday 27 October, the most dangerous day in the crisis: the day when an American U-2 was shot down over Cuba, Castro urged Khrushchev to threaten a nuclear strike against America, and Kennedy resigned himself to early military action if negotiation failed.[22]

When the carrier *Randolph* and its escorts started dropping grenades on him, Savitsky blew his top. As Vadim Orlov, one of the intelligence officers, remembered it, 'The Americans hit us with something stronger than grenades – apparently with a practice depth bomb. We thought – that's it – the end. After this attack, the totally exhausted Savitsky summoned the officer assigned to the nuclear torpedo, and ordered him to arm it: "Maybe the war has already started up there, while we are doing somersaults here. We're going to blast them now! We will die, but we will sink them all – we will not become the shame of the fleet."' Vasili Arkhipov, who as Chief of Staff of the Brigade outranked Savitsky, refused to endorse the order. Savitsky got a grip on himself and decided he had no option but to surface.

When they got back to Murmansk, the captains were criticised for letting the Americans force them up: they should have used their weapons or gone down with their boats. They defended themselves stoutly: they had been sent on a mission for which their boats were totally unsuited. Marshal Grechko, the Chief of the General Staff, was so furious that he smashed his glasses and stormed from the room. A soldier, not a sailor, he had thought that the Foxtrots were nuclear-powered and could remain underwater indefinitely. The official report admitted, 'It is natural that in the situation of such concentration of anti-submarine forces in a small area of the ocean, discovering the diesel submarines that had to surface to recharge their accumulator batteries was just a question of time.'[23]

The officers' careers survived.

It was a near-run thing on the American side too. The US Armed Forces had a system of alerts called DEFCON (Defense Readiness Condition), graduated in ascending order of seriousness from 5 to 1: DEFCON 3 put the air force on to fifteen-minute alert; DEFCON 2 was the next step to nuclear war. Alerts were supposed to be initiated by the President and the Defense Secretary through the Joint Chiefs of Staff.

On 22 October the US Armed Forces (except those in Europe) were put on to DEFCON 3. On 24 October General Thomas Powers, the Commander of Strategic Air Command, raised its alert level to DEFCON 2 without consulting the President. To make sure the Russians noticed, he sent the order unciphered to his bases around the world.[24] Twenty-three B-52s armed with nuclear bombs were sent to points within striking distance of the Soviet Union. The obsolescent B-47s were placed on fifteen minutes' notice. Over 500 nuclear-armed interceptors were positioned within an hour's range of Cuba. Their pilots were authorised to use their weapons only on the orders of their superiors. But there were no technical safeguards to prevent them dropping their bombs on their own initiative.

At midnight on 25 October a guard at an air base in Minnesota saw a saboteur climbing the security fence. He shot at the figure, and alarmed other bases nearby. Volk Field in Wisconsin accidentally sounded the wrong signal. Nuclear-armed F-106A interceptors began to taxi down the runway: a command car, flashing its lights, managed to stop them. The 'saboteur' turned out to be a bear.

The American early warning system picked up a missile apparently headed towards Florida and due to strike in two minutes. No explosion occurred: someone had chosen that moment to run a training tape simulating an attack. Meanwhile test launches from Cape Canaveral, a mere 375 miles from Havana, were continuing despite the crisis. On 26 October a Titan II was fired towards the South

Atlantic. After a moment of panic the operators of the early warning system realised that it was not heading towards the United States. The same day, the Vandenburg base in California went ahead with the long-prepared test launch of an Atlas missile into the Pacific.

The next day a U-2 reconnaissance plane strayed far into Siberia before it was escorted out by Soviet fighters. Khrushchev protested to Kennedy: 'How should we regard this? What is this, a provocation? One of your planes violates our frontier during this anxious time we are both experiencing, when everything has been put into combat readiness. Is it not a fact that an intruding American plane could easily be taken for a nuclear bomber, which might push us to a fateful step?'

A furious President Kennedy remarked, 'There's always some son of a bitch who doesn't get the word.'[25]

Savitsky's torpedo could have destroyed the American aircraft carrier, many of its escorting vessels, and his own boat as well. The crisis would then have taken a far more dangerous turn. The Soviet ballistic missiles on Cuba never became operational. Neither did the Ilyushin bombers. But if the Americans had invaded Cuba, General Pliyev could have used his nuclear missiles on his own initiative.[26] On both sides there were no effective technical safeguards to restrain the soldiers, sailors, and airmen. Washington as well as Moscow had to rely on the sense of discipline of their commanders and their troops.

One incident was later much debated by historians. Oleg Penkovsky, the Soviet military intelligence officer working for the British, had been given a procedure by his British and American handlers to warn them if he 'learned for a fact that the Soviet Union had decided to attack'. He was to ring them, blow three times into the telephone, wait one minute, then do it again.* He was then to leave more detailed information at a dead letter box. Penkovsky was arrested on 22 October, the day Kennedy imposed the quarantine. Ten days later his handlers received the warning signal. Gervase Cowell, the

---

* This was a bizarre instruction, hardly adequate as a warning of nuclear war. The Moscow telephone system was notoriously unreliable and it was a common experience to hear heavy breathing when you picked up the phone.

British handler, decided it was a fake, and suppressed it. The CIA took a risk and sent their man to the dead letter box: he was arrested when he turned up. The CIA told Kennedy that Penkovsky 'in all probability had been compromised and in an effort to save himself he had exposed this prearranged plan of the transmission of information'. The incident had no effect on the course of the crisis, which was already over. No one explained why the KGB would want to warn the West that a Soviet attack was imminent.

Arkhipov, who blew the whistle on Savitsky, died in 1998. He became something of a folk hero in the West and to some extent in Russia too for – perhaps – saving the world from nuclear catastrophe. Gervase Cowell was later also added to the list.[27]

In the end Khrushchev agreed to withdraw his missiles and troops from Cuba. Kennedy promised in return that the Americans would not invade Cuba, and gave a private assurance that they would withdraw their Thor and Jupiter missiles from Turkey.

Khrushchev had gambled extravagantly and dangerously. A British observer commentated later 'that he achieved what he set out to do, though not quite in the manner he intended'.[28] Not all Khrushchev's colleagues were so tolerant; they brought the failure in Cuba into the balance when they forced him out of office two years later.

Not everyone on the American side was happy either. Curtis LeMay never wavered in his belief that the Americans should have struck Cuba and destroyed the Soviet missiles there.

The British role in these excitements was modest but illuminating.

Prime Minister Macmillan's initial inclination was to play the crisis down. He reminded Kennedy that the Europeans had already been facing Soviet missiles for several years. The Russians were merely evening the score: after all, there were American missiles on the Soviet border with Turkey.

Kennedy replied that the political and psychological effect was quite different. 'What is essential at this moment of highest test,' said Kennedy, 'is that Khrushchev should discover that if he is counting on weakness or irresolution, he has miscalculated.'

Macmillan was nevertheless determined to do nothing which the

Russians might see as provocative. He gave no orders to evacuate the government or to activate its underground crisis headquarters. The V-bombers were not dispersed to the airfields from which they would launch their attacks.

But at the height of the crisis on 27 October Air Marshal Cross, who commanded the British bombers, nevertheless ordered that they be armed and ready to take off. One pilot, sitting in his Vulcan at four minutes' notice to scramble, remembered, 'We knew with certainty that should the policy of deterrence fail, not only would we almost certainly not survive (our chances of getting back in one piece were assessed at only twenty per cent) but more importantly our wives and children would also be dead, as the airfields were high priority targets for Soviet attack.'

Cross, like Curtis LeMay, thought his political boss was feeble. Afterwards he complained, 'From me downwards, everything worked perfectly. From me upwards, nothing worked at all.' These speculations were not only improper. They were wrong. Macmillan was operating well within the limits laid down by the War Book, which said that 'the primary purpose of government in an international crisis must be to avert war, and they must take account of the danger that premature resort to dramatic preparatory measures … would appear threatening to a potential enemy, might be misinterpreted, and so precipitate the outbreak of war'.[29]

The American and the Soviet governments had thoroughly frightened themselves as well as one another. Anatoli Dobrynin, the Soviet ambassador in Washington, later wrote, 'I cannot overemphasize the vast significance of the Cuban crisis for the subsequent development of Soviet–American relations.'[30] Oleg Troyanovsky, Khrushchev's foreign policy adviser, believed that the crisis 'had a tremendous educational value for both sides and both leaders', who now realised 'not in theory, but in practical terms, that nuclear annihilation was a real possibility and consequently, that brinkmanship had to be ruled out and a safer and more constructive relationship between the two superpowers had to be designed and pursued'.[31]

Communication between the Kremlin and the White House had been bedevilled by absurd technical difficulties during the Cuban crisis. In June 1963 the Russians and the Americans agreed to set up a 'hotline' between them. Though it was popularly thought to be a telephone, it was originally a secure teletype link between the Pentagon and the headquarters of the Soviet Communist Party, later upgraded to email carried by satellite link.*

In October 1963 Gromyko and Secretary Rusk met for lunch in the Soviet Embassy in Washington. Rusk suggested that the two sides might consider cutting their bomber fleets. Gromyko added that they might look also at their armoury of missiles. They agreed to talk further.[32] It was only ten days before Kennedy was assassinated in Dallas, and the hotline was used for the first time.

But the Soviet government drew an additional conclusion. If they were to confront the Americans again, they needed more sophisticated weapons in much larger numbers. As Deputy Foreign Minister Vasili Kuznetsov told a senior American official, 'You got away with it this time, but you will never get away with it again.'[33]

The lesson of Cuba faded as the Russians began a massive development of their nuclear forces and the Americans responded. The arms race heated up, and became even more dangerous.[34]

The Mad President

Richard Nixon was President between 1969 and 1974. He left a mixed reputation behind him. He was a notorious Red-baiter in the McCarthy period. He was forced from the presidency because of his unsavoury political methods in the Watergate scandal.[†] He was the sophisticated architect of détente with the Soviet Union and the opening to China. And he developed the disconcerting 'Mad President' theory of deterrence.

Nixon believed that the Korean War ended because Eisenhower issued a discreet nuclear threat. The evidence is unclear, though when

---

* The hotline was used at times of crisis, such as the Six Day War in 1967, the Yom Kippur War in 1973, the Turkish invasion of Cyprus in 1974, and the Soviet invasion of Afghanistan in 1979. China, Britain, and France also set up hotlines with Moscow. The Americans later set up other hotlines with China and India.
† Nixon's minions had broken into the campaign headquarters of his Democrat rivals. The 'Watergate scandal' was named after the hotel where the Democrats had their base.

Truman, Eisenhower's predecessor, hinted that he was considering the idea, the British Prime Minister, Clement Attlee, was worried enough to rush over to Washington to dissuade him.

Nixon's thought was that 'If the adversary feels that you are unpredictable, even rash, he will be deterred from pressing you too far. The odds that he will fold will increase and the unpredictable president will win another hand.' As the Vietnam War went increasingly badly, he remarked to his aide, Bob Haldeman, 'I want the North Vietnamese to believe that I've reached the point that I might do anything to stop the war. We'll just slip the word to them that "for God's sake, you know Nixon is obsessed about Communism. We can't restrain him when he is angry – and he has his hand on the nuclear button."'

In October 1969 Nixon put his theory into practice. His aim was to get the Russians to exert pressure on Hanoi to negotiate. US forces were ordered on to heightened alert. American bombers in Europe and in the United States itself were placed at readiness. Nuclear armed B-52s flew close to Soviet airspace. Nixon believed that the Russians would make the link with Vietnam without seeing a direct threat to themselves.

This would have been at best a delicate operation, with much scope for misunderstanding and confusion. Nixon's advisers were unhappy with the tactic. But there were no disasters. The Russians did not react. And the North Vietnamese seemed no more ready to negotiate than before.

Four years later the Russians hinted that they might send troops to support the Egyptians during the Yom Kippur War between Israel and Egypt in 1973. In the hope of deterring them, Nixon rattled the nuclear sabre again. American strategic forces were put on DEFCON 3 for the first time since 1963. The Americans alerted their bombers and missile launchers. Their missile submarines put to sea from Holy Loch in Scotland.

The Russians were unmoved. Anatoli Chernyaev, then working in the International Department of the Central Committee, said that 'Brezhnev had already decided that the Soviet Union would not intervene'.[35] When it was over, Henry Kissinger, by now Nixon's Secretary of State, told colleagues that the Russians 'have tried to be fairly reasonable all across the board. Even in the Middle East where our political strategy put them in an awful bind, they haven't really tried to screw us.'[36]

The Superpowers Negotiate

By then both sides had understood that they needed to get their confrontation under some sort of control. They rose to the challenge fitfully, in a swirl of domestic political controversy, but with a degree of solid success.

In both capitals conservative opinion was convinced of the need to achieve and maintain numerical superiority over the other: in America there was a public outcry whenever the Russians looked like drawing ahead. But common sense did prevail after a fashion. As General Viktor Starodubov, a Soviet General Staff expert on arms control, put it, 'It was logical for both countries that at some point the leaders came to the conclusion that it was impossible to continue increasing armaments any longer. The US saw ... that the Soviet Union was capable of achieving parity and sustaining it, and that made any further arms race unwinnable. We in the Soviet Union understood it too, but we also understood that for us trying to catch up with the United States would be too costly. That is why we came to the conclusion about the need for negotiating limits on, and later reducing, strategic weapons.'[37]

Agreement was complicated by contentious differences over definitions, and over the technical characteristics of individual weapons systems, which were dissimilar and often hard to compare. General Nikolai Detinov, one of the Soviet negotiators, pointed out that, in addition to all the tricky political questions, there were also 'a lot of very technical issues, very specific technical issues. Only very few people understood those issues. And those technical questions were very hard to formulate, and to find satisfactory solutions to.' The negotiators spent months trying, for example, to agree on the definition of a cruise missile. But the result was a cumulation of agreed definitions which simplified further negotiation.

From time to time each side exaggerated the numbers and capacity of the other's armoury, either because their intelligence was flawed or ambiguous, or to gain an advantage in the negotiating process. But with the passage of time and improvements in their capacity to gather technical intelligence through reconnaissance satellites and electronic surveillance, both sides became better at counting the weapons of the other and establishing their technical characteristics. But both sides continued to suffer serious intelligence failures from time to time.

But there was still plenty of scope for misinformation, misinterpretation, and disagreement. An exaggerated fear that the Russians' SS-18 missiles could destroy the American Minutemen fuelled a fevered controversy in Washington over 'missile vulnerability'. The Russians feared that American submarines could operate undetected close enough to the Soviet heartland to launch a bolt from the blue with little warning. The Americans maintained, though the Russians denied it, that later versions of the Soviet TU-22 'Backfire' bomber could hit the United States. The Russians believed that American Pershing II missiles could hit the Soviet Union. The Americans denied it in their turn.[38]

The negotiations were therefore intellectually, technically, and politically hideously difficult for both sides. They were surrounded by an atmosphere of deep mutual suspicion close to paranoia. Neither side had a real perception of the fears, motives, and intentions of the other. Each feared that the other was cheating; or that it was on the verge of a technical breakthrough which would transform the strategic balance in its favour. Each feared that the other sought the ability to mount a first strike that would wipe out its strategic forces. Neither could conceive that the other might fear the same. Each regularly put forward proposals designed to protect its existing military arrangements and allow for the development of new ones. Each tried to limit the other's ability to so. Each accused the other of deviousness or outright deceit. The Americans assumed that the Russians would cheat if they thought they could get away with it. The Russians believed the same of the Americans. Each was plagued with internal disagreements between its domestic hawks and doves which made it harder to devise negotiable positions to carry the business forward.

The negotiations often fell hostage to extraneous political events: the Soviet invasion of Czechoslovakia in 1968 and Afghanistan in 1979, Soviet interference in local conflicts in Africa, and the more strident policies of the first Reagan years in the early 1980s. Kissinger tried

Warheads

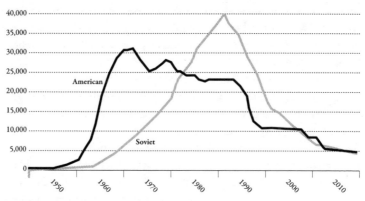

Source: 'Notebook: Arsenals of the World', *Bulletin of the Atomic Scientists*

to link progress on SALT with a change in Soviet behaviour abroad. President Ford banned the use of the word 'détente', even though a majority of the American population supported détente because they feared a nuclear confrontation.[39] American conservatives picked on the surge in Soviet production of warheads and rockets, which began to spike in the mid-1970s in ways which it was domestically impossible for a president to ignore (see the chart above).[40]

American presidents were always under domestic pressure to demand that the Russians modify their domestic behaviour and give more scope to the freedoms to which they had formally committed themselves at the Helsinki Conference in 1975. The Russians were incensed when Carter began to take what they considered an intolerable interest in the way the Soviet Union ran its domestic affairs.*

But both sides knew that the stakes were as high as it was possible to get: failure could lead to the ultimate catastrophe. They

---

*The Conference on Security and Cooperation in Europe was held in Helsinki in the summer of 1975. It was attended by the United States, Canada, and all the European states except Albania and Andorra. It agreed on measures to lessen the military confrontation and improve economic relations in Europe, and on a number of provisions on human rights which were subsequently exploited by Soviet dissidents against their government.

managed to forge a fragile, unwilling trust on which they eventually built a kind of understanding. Neither side was entirely happy: strong lobbies in each believed that their negotiators were giving far too much away. But the potentially lethal competition was brought under a kind of control. As the process stumbled on into the years that followed the ending of the Cold War, it continued to produce agreements which mitigated, though they did not abolish, the nuclear confrontation.

Thus over the years that followed the Cuban missile crisis, the two governments reached several agreements intended to limit the size of their armouries. The first was the Partial Test Ban Treaty of 1963. Thereafter the process was given a new impetus, paradoxically enough, by Richard Nixon, the former Red-baiter, and his tough-minded adviser Henry Kissinger, even though they were simultaneously waging a brutally devious campaign to extricate themselves from America's war with the Russians' allies in Vietnam. The two sides signed an agreement on strategic arms limitation and an Anti-Ballistic Missile (ABM) Treaty in 1972, and a vague Agreement on the Prevention of Nuclear War in 1973. There followed SALT II (1979), and the first agreements which actually reduced, rather than limited, the number of nuclear weapons: the Intermediate-range Nuclear Forces Treaty (INF, 1987) and a Strategic Arms Reduction Treaty (START I, 1991).

Kissinger proceeded from a simple proposition, which the politicians and negotiators on both sides (though not always the military) tended to accept implicitly, though they rarely voiced it aloud: '[W]hat in the name of God is strategic superiority?' he asked. 'What is the significance of it, politically, militarily, operationally, at these levels of numbers? What do you do with it?'[41]

The negotiations with the Russians that began in November 1969 – the Strategic Arms Limitation Talks (SALT I) – were designed to get a preliminary handle on that problem. Formal negotiations took place in Helsinki and Vienna. A secret back-channel negotiation took place in parallel between Kissinger and the Soviet ambassador in Washington, Anatoli Dobrynin. The back-channel exchanges managed to overcome some difficult blockages. They also infuriated

William Rogers, Nixon's Secretary of State, the foreign ministries in both capitals, and the officials in both negotiating teams: all were often left ignorant of quite what was going on.

The Soviet delegation laboured under the additional disadvantage that its military members refused to reveal figures for Soviet weapons even to their colleagues from the Foreign Ministry. Until the end, the negotiation had to take place on the basis of figures supplied by the Americans. To demonstrate back home that no secrets had been given away, the Russians kept a stenographic record of the talks – a boon to future historians.[42]

The SALT I agreement was signed by Nixon and Brezhnev at a summit meeting in Moscow in May 1972.* It did not reduce the armouries. But it did place limits on the number of missiles and missile submarines each side could hold, and on their freedom to modernise and replace their existing systems. These arrangements allowed the Russians to retain their 'heavy' SS-9 single-warhead intercontinental missiles. These were larger and more powerful than the American Minutemen. The Russians saw this as an implied compensation for the American refusal to include the British and French deterrents and US 'forward-based systems'. But American conservatives were outraged at what they saw as a dangerous concession, especially when the SS-9s were succeeded by 'heavy' SS-18s capable of carrying ten or more individually targettable re-entry vehicles (MIRVs) and thus, so they thought, able to destroy the American missile force in a first strike. There was no provision for inspection: each side would continue to use its own 'national technical means of verification' – reconnaissance satellites and radio interception – to check that the other was not cheating. Since these could not count the number of warheads hidden inside each missile, no limit was placed on the number of warheads held by either side. Given the rate at which both sides were now developing MIRVs, this was a serious

---

* The 'T' in 'SALT' meant 'Talks'. It was a measure of their domestic political problems that the Americans negotiators preferred to call the final text an agreement rather than a treaty: a treaty would have to be ratified by the Senate and might fail there. For various reasons SALT II was indeed a treaty, and the politics of the time meant that it could not be ratified.

weakness. But SALT I was nevertheless a significant breakthrough, and a promise of more agreements to come.

The agreement to limit defences against missiles – the Anti-Ballistic Missile Treaty – was equally significant, and in many ways counter-intuitive. Both sides had been developing anti-ballistic missile defences since the 1950s. In 1958 the US Army started work on the Nike-Zeus ABM system to protect US cities, although Kennedy doubted that it would be up to the job. The Russians were also developing an ABM system, which Khrushchev boasted in public could 'hit a fly in outer space'. He was much more sceptical in private. To hit a missile in space was much harder than swatting a fly: it was like using a bullet to hit another bullet.

But sophisticated strategic theorists feared that a missile defence system, if it could be made to work, would undermine Mutually Assured Destruction. MAD implied, after all, that each side was willing to accept a degree of vulnerability to reassure the other that it did not expect to survive the devastation that both were trying to deter. The fear that your enemy could hit you even after he had hit you was the surest deterrent against firing first.

This led to the counterintuitive idea that, to preserve MAD and maintain the balance of terror, both sides should limit or abandon their plans for missile defence. The Russians found this hard to swallow. When the Americans presented the idea to a Pugwash meeting in India in January 1964, Mikhail Millionshchikov, the chairman of the Soviet Pugwash Committee, thought the translator must have got it wrong. How could one be opposed to *defensive* weapons? He eventually conceded that the American arguments had a peculiar logic to them, but added that 'no government would survive if it told its people it opposed building defences'.*

The Russians held out for several years. Aleksei Kosygin, the sensible and phlegmatic Prime Minister, strongly argued the case for building missile defences when his opposite number Harold Wilson

---

* The Pugwash movement, which brought scientists and experts from both sides together for comparatively informal discussions, is described more fully in Chapter 15.

visited Moscow in 1966. McNamara formally put the idea of ABM limitation to him again when they met in June 1967 in Glassboro, New Jersey. Kosygin remained adamant, and came uncharacteristically close to losing his temper: 'Defence is moral, aggression is immoral!'[43]

But the Russians began to come round when the Americans started to develop their ideas as part of the talks on arms limitation. Brezhnev and Nixon signed an Anti-Ballistic Missile Treaty at the same time as they signed SALT I. This allowed each country two sites at which it could base a defensive system, one for the capital and one for an ICBM rocket base. The Americans did not bother to protect Washington, but built a system to protect their Minuteman base in North Dakota. They dismantled it in 1975 because it was expensive and ineffective. The Russians built a system to protect Moscow. Whether it was effective or not, the Moscow ABM system thereafter figured largely in British and American calculations about their ability to destroy the Soviet capital.*

The Russians came to regard the Anti-Ballistic Missile Treaty as a cornerstone of the network of agreements they had negotiated with the Americans. They were correspondingly furious when Ronald Reagan proposed his Strategic Defense Initiative in 1982, and the Americans began to argue that they were legally entitled to proceed at least with research into the possibilities. The Anti-Ballistic Missile Treaty nevertheless remained in force until 2001, when President G. W. Bush denounced it on the grounds that America needed to defend itself against missiles from rogue states.

In 1974 Nixon was forced from office in a welter of scandal. His successor, Gerald Ford, met Leonid Brezhnev in Vladivostok that November to work out the basis of an agreement to succeed SALT I, which was due to expire in October 1977. Brezhnev had just suffered his first stroke. But he was well enough to argue passionately that the process had not yet gone far enough: both sides were spending huge sums on weapons which would be better devoted to improving the lives of ordinary people. He and Ford agreed that each side should

---

*On the inadequacies of the Soviet ABM system see Chapter 8.

be allowed an equal number of strategic missile delivery vehicles. Unlike SALT I, this would include bombers. There would be limits on the number of warheads (MIRVs) each side's missiles were permitted to carry. The Russians would again be allowed to retain their SS-18 missiles.

For a while the Soviet Defence Minister, Marshal Andrei Grechko, held out against the agreement. He had always believed that disarmament talks were a trap designed by the Americans to gain unilateral advantage. Now he objected to the continued failure to take into account the American 'forward-based systems' and the British and French nuclear forces. At one point he said that the General Staff would refuse to accept responsibility for the nation's security if the negotiating position was not changed. Brezhnev faced him down in a late night exchange of telephone calls. 'If we make no concessions, the nuclear arms race will go further. Can you give me, the Commander-in-Chief of the Armed Forces, a firm guarantee that in such a situation we will get superiority over the United States and the correlation of forces will become more advantageous to us?' Grechko was unable to answer the question and was brought into line by his colleagues in the Politburo.[44]

For Soviet officials the Vladivostok agreement was a benchmark for subsequent disarmament talks.[45] But the political high-water mark had been passed. Brezhnev never recovered his health or his energy. Ford and Kissinger were heavily criticised on their return to Washington. Ronald Reagan, already on his way into national politics, accused them of having given too much away. Ford tried to build support by moving towards the right, but lost the election nevertheless. Jimmy Carter, a liberal full of goodwill but with no experience of international affairs, succeeded him in January 1977.

At first it seemed a hopeful moment. That January, in a deliberate gesture to Carter on the eve of his inauguration, Brezhnev said in Tula, south of Moscow, that the goal of Soviet military policy was defensive and designed only to deter an aggressor. 'We are prepared jointly with the new administration in the United States to accomplish a major advance in relations between our two countries.'[46] Three days later, in his inaugural speech, Carter announced, 'We will move this year a step towards the ultimate goal – the elimination of all nuclear weapons from the face of the earth': an aspiration he was neither the first nor the last to voice.

The hope was frustrated almost immediately. Carter was determined to put his own stamp on arms control, even though his advisers warned him that the Russians would hardly move further until the Vladivostok agreements had been formalised. He sent his new Secretary of State, Cyrus Vance, to Moscow in March 1977 with two proposals. The first was modestly based on the Vladivostok understanding, though it failed to mention it. But Carter had pinned his ambitions to a proposal for major cuts in the American and Soviet nuclear arsenals, a first stage towards their total abolition. The ceiling on warheads should be cut to above the level agreed at Vladivostok. There should, for the first time, be cuts in the Soviet 'heavy' missiles. In return the Americans would accept a ban on all new strategic missiles, including their own heavy missile, the MX. The proposal was unbalanced, in the view of one American observer, a 'wrenching departure' which called for 'substantial reductions in existing Soviet systems in exchange for marginal cuts in future American ones'. There was no chance that the Russians would accept it.

Previous arms control suggestions had been explored discreetly. But Carter publicised his ideas before they had been put to the Russians. He publicly insisted that the Soviets treat their people better, and the KGB picked up the letter he wrote on the subject to Andrei Sakharov, now in increasingly open opposition to the Soviet government. Asked by the press whether this linkage might not jeopardise the chances of SALT, he firmly replied that he doubted 'whether there is any connection between the two in the minds of the Soviets'.[47]

For that he had no evidence and he was of course quite wrong. The Russians concluded that he was more interested in propaganda than substance. Brezhnev took it very personally. The Americans were ignoring the progress he had achieved in Vladivostok. Human rights had nothing to do with arms control. Carter's remarks were an intolerable interference in Soviet affairs, as if the Soviet Union were a banana republic. He therefore ordered Gromyko to rebuff the American ideas publicly. Gromyko did so in such vicious language that Vance felt in turn as if he had been 'slapped in the face with a wet rag'. The trust which had been lost was never fully recovered while Carter was President. When some of the protagonists from both sides met two decades later at a conference in Musgrove Plantation, Georgia, they still could not quite understand how they had managed to mishandle what had seemed such a promising opportunity.[48]

But both the Russians and the Americans realised that things could not be left there. They gritted their teeth and surprisingly soon they managed to get talks going again. In 1979 Carter and Brezhnev signed SALT II, the first agreement which provided for some reduction of strategic weapons. The Russians had more launchers than the Americans, but the Americans had more warheads. The treaty required the Russians to reduce the total number of their missiles, though they were allowed to keep their SS-18s. Each side was allowed to place up to ten warheads on one missile: that restricted the Russians, since the SS-18 was capable of carrying more. The United States had no heavy missiles to cut: their proposed MX missile was too light to qualify. But the MX could do all the things that the SS-18 could do: it too could carry ten warheads, it was more accurate, and it was less vulnerable. The cuts were not substantial. But on the whole the Americans, once again, came out ahead.

Brezhnev had been able to face down the opposition of his Defence Minister. Carter was less able to silence those in Washington who criticised SALT II. They were particularly angry at the failure to reduce the number of SS-18 missiles. Senator Scoop Jackson, a vigorous campaigner on Soviet human rights abuses and the plight of Soviet Jewry, accused the Administration of caving in. Richard Perle, Jackson's assistant, believed that the Administration had 'given away the store ... arms control negotiations with the Soviet Union essentially were disadvantageous to the United States: ... they had the effect of disarming the American public, of creating a false impression that things were better than they were, and of reducing support for necessary military appropriations'.* Paul Nitze said that the SALT

---

*Two decades later Richard Perle was a strong advocate of the invasion of Iraq. He was ruthless, charming, and a very good cook. Paul Nitze turned out to be a conscientious partner when he departed from theory and actually got down to negotiating with the Russians for the Intermediate-Range Nuclear Forces

II agreement would leave the Russians with the ability to destroy 90 per cent of the US Minuteman force in a preemptive strike. He leaked the secret details of the negotiations, which had 'the effect, if not the intention, of sabotaging SALT'. Jackson denied that he had stimulated the leak.

Each side now increasingly accused the other of cheating. In December 1977 former Defense Secretary Melvin Laird declared in an article in *Reader's Digest* that the Russians had 'repeatedly, flagrantly and indeed contemptuously' violated the SALT I and ABM agreements.[49] Two years later the Russians began to build a massive radar near Krasnoyarsk, deep inside the Soviet Union. This was prohibited by the ABM Treaty but the Russians believed that, like Topsy's baby, the sin was only a small one. In July 1983, however, the Americans raised the matter: for hardliners it became a prime example of Soviet perfidy. The site was never completed. Under Gorbachev the Russians dismantled the buildings: the Ministry of Internal Affairs rejected a suggestion that they might be used to house prisoners, on the grounds that the housing would be too comfortable.[50]

When the Russians invaded Afghanistan at the end of 1979. Carter told his cabinet (with unpardonable exaggeration) that the invasion was 'the greatest threat to world peace since the Second World War'. He asked the Senate to shelve ratification of SALT II. He and Brezhnev nevertheless declared that their countries would meanwhile comply with its provisions.[51]

Things were about to get worse.

Treaty in 1981–4. Perle called his attempt to reach a deal with the Russians – the so-called 'walk in the woods' with his opposite number, Yuli Kvitsinsky – 'an act of intellectual and political cowardice' (S. Talbott, *The Master of the Game*, New York, 1989, p. 176).

FOURTEEN

THE SECOND COLD WAR

'WE WILL SEE A NUCLEAR WAR IN THIS DECADE.'

Timothy Garton Ash, diary entry, New Year's Eve 1980[1]

Ronald Reagan had called détente a satanic device to blunt America's sword.[2] Now, with his arrival in power at the beginning of 1981, the stage was set for the last major confrontation of the Cold War.

He began by reviving the language of Godless Communism. In January 1981 he accused the Soviets of 'reserving unto themselves the right to commit any crime, to lie, to cheat' in order to achieve their goal of 'world revolution and a one-world socialist or Communist state'. In March 1983 he announced that the Soviet Union was 'the focus of evil in the modern world ... an evil empire'.[3] He joked to the sound technicians just before making his weekly broadcast: 'My fellow Americans, I'm pleased to tell you today that I've signed legislation that will outlaw Russia forever. We begin bombing in five minutes.' Unfortunately the Soviet government lacked a sense of humour, publicly condemned 'this unprecedented and hostile attack by the US President', and went on, 'this kind of behavior is incompatible with the great responsibility borne by heads of nuclear states for the destinies of their own people and mankind.'[4] It was very far from the conciliatory tone that John Kennedy had adopted twenty years earlier at American University.

Reagan had sneered at Carter for not facing up to the Soviets. But it was Carter's arms build-up that he continued and accelerated. In October 1981 Congress approved a five-year programme of defence expenditure, costing $1.5 trillion, to match the great spurt in Soviet arms production which began in the 1970s.[5] Reagan's admirers later claimed that he won the Cold War by forcing the Russians to compete with America's massive arms expenditure, thus bankrupting their economy.* But by the time the American arms build-up got going, the Russians had already concluded that the Soviet economy had little more to give. As Andrei Grachev, one of Gorbachev's shrewdest advisers, later put it, 'After launching the first man into space, it was increasingly obvious that the USSR was losing the technological competition with the West. Having destroyed its own agriculture, the most powerful agricultural nation in the world was having to feed its population by spending its oil revenues on imported food.'[6]

There were many reasons for the Soviet collapse. Excessive spending on arms was certainly one of them. But the intrinsic political and economic weaknesses of the Soviet system, combined with an imprudent imperial overstretch, and Gorbachev's aversion to bloodshed, were more important.

Provocation

Almost Reagan's first act, in March 1981, was to authorise a highly secret series of PsyOps (psychological operations) to test Soviet defences and unsettle Soviet nerves. American bombers flew directly towards Soviet airspace, peeling away at the last minute. American naval vessels probed the sea borders of the Soviet Union. American attack submarines penetrated the protected areas ('bastions') in the northern seas where Soviet ballistic missile submarines were stationed.

In May 1981 Leonid Brezhnev and Yuri Andropov, the Chairman of the KGB, told a meeting of Soviet intelligence officers that the United States was preparing for a surprise nuclear attack. They ordered the Soviet military and civilian intelligence agencies to combine forces – an attempt at collaboration between sworn rivals – to pick up any indications that nuclear war was imminent. The operation was code-named RYaN (the Russian acronym for *Raketno-Yadernoe Napadenie*, Rocket Nuclear Attack). In 1982 Soviet television showed a film, *Who Threatens Peace?*, portraying the United States as a dangerous militaristic power. The Soviet intelligence effort was intensified as the events of 1983 unfolded.[†]

---

* The theory finds a noisy expression in P. Schweitzer, *Victory*, New York, 1996.
† The last head of the Soviet KGB, Vadim Bakatin, abolished the RYaN programme in 1991 on the grounds that it was an ineffective and atavistic

In spring 1983 three US carrier battle groups mounted a massive exercise in the north-west Pacific. One carrier deliberately flew aircraft over the Soviet island of Zeliony in the Kurile Archipelago. The aim, said John Lehman, the US Secretary of the Navy, was to keep 'the Soviets concerned with threats all around their periphery'.

Jerry Whitworth, the chief radio man on the carrier *Enterprise*, had been spying for the Russians for many years. He passed most of the messages about the exercise to the KGB. Four days later Yuri Andropov, who had recently succeeded Brezhnev, told the Central Committee that there had been an 'unprecedented sharpening of the struggle' between East and West.

All this activity exposed gaping holes in the Soviet defences. The Russians were 'as naked as a jaybird', one official told Congress. 'It really got to them,' another remarked.[7]

The Russians had always been obsessed with what they called 'the correlation of forces' between them and the West.* KGB analysts had been using an ingenious computer program which they hoped would establish the correlation on a scientific basis. They now concluded that the correlation was turning against the Soviet Union. Ronald Reagan was accelerating his predecessor's arms build-up to the accompaniment of some very inflammatory rhetoric. 'Throughout the mid-1970s and through the mid-1980s,' said General Varfolomei Korobushin, a former Deputy Chief of the General Staff of the Strategic Rocket Forces, in 1992, 'I firmly believed that the U.S. was willing and capable of a first strike against us.' NATO's official positions, the Americans' new weapons programmes, 'only affirmed my belief that this was possible ... All U.S. actions pointed in this direction.'[8]

The Americans were no less prone to panic. Reagan's first years

hangover from the Cold War (V. Bakatin, *Izbavlenie ot KGB*, Moscow, 1991, p. 89). Some of the indicators the Soviet agents were asked to look at were trivial, and they attracted much derision among Western commentators. But others were not. The British and Americans had their own lists of indicators of impending war. They were not particularly convincing either.

* Western analysts used to argue that 'correlation of forces' was a peculiarly Soviet, and rather sinister, term of art. In fact it meant much the same as the common Western term 'balance of power'.

were dominated by the noisy debate over Minuteman vulnerability which had boiled up during the Carter years. The argument went like this: the latest Russian SS-18 missiles with their multiple warheads were now so accurate that they could wipe the Minutemen out with a single bolt from the blue. The airborne and submarine legs of the American deterrent would survive. But – so the story went – the Soviet leader might then issue an ultimatum to a President contemplating the ruin of his country. 'Mr President, do you want to continue up the ladder of escalation? Or will you submit to our demands?'

This scenario was based on three dubious premises: that the Soviet missiles would function impeccably; that the Soviets were confident enough of their technology to launch a pre-emptive strike which would nevertheless leave the other two legs of the American triad untouched; and that the Soviet leader would not be restrained by his colleagues. Paul Warnke, the chief arms control negotiator under Carter, thought that it might all have been avoided had the Americans been willing to negotiate a ban on multiple warheads in the late 1960s, when the technology was still little more than a gleam in the eye on both sides. But by the end of the 1970s the matter had ceased to be a hypothetical military problem. It had become a very real political problem, and a good example of the way strategic thinking could be derailed by technological development driven by misjudged intelligence distorted by bureaucratic infighting.[9]

In January 1983 Ronald Reagan commissioned Ford's former National Security Advisor, General Brent Scowcroft, to sort it out. Scowcroft's Commission reported four months later that the Russians did not have the capacity to wipe out the Minutemen. The Americans had overestimated the accuracy of the SS-18 missile by more than a third. The window of vulnerability, like its predecessors the Bomber Gap and the Missile Gap, did not exist. Another scary scenario had been knocked on the head.[10]

Star Wars
The Russians were further taken aback by Reagan's plan, announced in March 1983, for a Strategic Defense Initiative (SDI), an exotic combination of radar, space lasers and missiles which he hoped would form an impenetrable astrodome to ward off Soviet missiles.

The public promptly nicknamed it 'Star Wars'. Many of Reagan's own scientists and advisers agreed that no conceivable system could provide 100 per cent protection. Weinberger, Perle, and other American hardliners believed however that, whether the scheme worked or not, any Russian attempt to match it would be so expensive that it would further cripple the Soviet economy.

Many Russians, especially the scientists, were as sceptical as their American counterparts, and saw no reason to go down the same track. Vitali Kataev, who knew what he was talking about, drew on American sources to calculate that if the system were 99 per cent reliable, enough Soviet missiles would still get through to kill 20 million Americans. At 90 per cent reliability, the figure would go up to between 75 and 90 million.[11] There were plenty of ways the Soviets could deal with it: the simplest was to swamp it with an increased fusillade of their own offensive missiles.

But the Soviet military inevitably judged the matter in standard worst-case terms. The risk that the Americans could devise a technology that would catch Soviet missiles in mid-flight was too great for them to ignore. Maybe it would not work. But if it did, it would make the Soviet Union vulnerable to an American first strike: the Americans could hit the Soviet rockets with impunity, relying on their astrodome to ward off retaliation. The military and the defence industry demanded that research on countermeasures begin, despite the scientists' firm view that it would be a gross waste of money. The Russians believed in addition that Reagan's scheme was contrary to the letter as well as the spirit of the Anti Ballistic Missile Treaty of 1972, one of the main achievements of the Cold War arms control regime. They rejected the American claim that preliminary work on Star Wars, if not deployment, was permitted on a broad interpretation of the Treaty. None of them was convinced by Reagan's offer to share the research at some later point. Even if he were sincere, there could be no guarantee that his successor would honour the promise.

Mrs Thatcher had similar worries: Star Wars could reduce the effectiveness of the British deterrent too. But she went along with the idea once she realised how much it meant to Reagan – and once he offered British companies a share in the production of components for the scheme.

In the end the Russians avoided the trap prepared for them by Weinberger and Perle, and countered SDI by playing to their existing strengths: the development of more advanced missiles and anti-satellites. There is no sound evidence that, as some Americans later claimed, the Soviet economy was indeed crippled by the attempt to match SDI: it was already in serious trouble for quite separate reasons.*

But there was perhaps a more subtle threat. The research for SDI might bring about a technological revolution in military affairs, even if it produced no viable system of defence. Marshal Ogarkov, the Soviet Chief of Staff, lamented with remarkable frankness to Leslie Gelb, a former American arms control official, 'We cannot equal the quality of US arms for a generation or two. Modern military power is based on technology ... We will never be able to catch up with you in modern arms until we have an economic revolution. And the question is whether we have an economic revolution without a political revolution.'[12] He argued that the military budget should be reoriented away from costly weapons projects which aped the US to no useful purpose. In May 1984, in the army newspaper *Krasnaya Zvezda*, he publicly criticised the idea that a limited nuclear war could be fought and won: 'Any so-called limited use of nuclear weapons will immediately lead to the immediate use of the whole nuclear arsenals of both sides. This is the terrible logic of war.' Ogarkov's independence of mind did not make him popular. In September 1984 he was sacked by Defence Minister Ustinov for his pains, and replaced by Sergei Akhromeyev.[13]

Despite his aggressive rhetoric, Reagan was not the unthinking cowboy portrayed by his critics in the Soviet Union, Europe, and even his own country. His moral aversion to nuclear war was deeply rooted and sincere. Worried about where the bad relationship between America and the Soviet Union might lead, in June 1983 he sent the wartime American ambassador in Moscow, the 91-year-old Averell Harriman, to talk to Brezhnev's successor as General Secretary, Yuri Andropov, to see if there was scope for something better.

---

* The arguments are complex. They are analysed by Pavel Podvig, among others, in his article 'Did Star Wars Help End the Cold War? Soviet Response to the SDI Program', *Science & Global Security* 25, no. 1 (2017): 3–27, p. 21

Andropov was frank. He told Harriman that he saw real grounds for alarm: 'Nuclear war could occur not through evil intent, but could happen through miscalculation. Then nothing could save mankind ... statesmen of both countries [should] exercise restraint and seek mutual understanding to strengthen confidence, to avoid the irreparable. However, I must say that I do not see it on the part of the current administration and they may be moving toward the dangerous "red line".' The two countries 'cannot afford the luxury of destructive rivalry in interaction between them'. Harriman judged that Andropov had 'a real worry that we could come into conflict through miscalculation'.[14]

Reagan did not follow up, and meanwhile the Americans continued their probes into Soviet airspace. There was a tragic, almost inevitable, consequence. The Russians were tired of being naked as a jaybird. They put their air defences on permanent alert. On 1 September 1983 a Soviet fighter shot down an aircraft which had strayed into Soviet airspace in the Far East, in the belief that it was yet another American spy plane. It was in fact a Korean airliner, KAL 007, and 269 people were killed.*

The Russians expressed regret over the loss of life. But they argued that an American RC-135 reconnaissance aircraft had been flying in the area at the time, and blamed the CIA for this 'criminal, provocative act'. In private, Andropov lambasted the Soviet military for shooting the aircraft down instead of forcing it to land. The generals themselves were dismayed: the latest incident revealed yet another flaw in their air defences.

Reagan's public reaction was blistering. 'This was the Soviet Union against the world and the moral precepts which guide human relations among people everywhere,' he said on 5 September. 'It was an act of barbarism born of a society which wantonly disregards

---

* It was not the first such incident. In 1978 a Korean airliner managed to get so comprehensively lost that it flew over the sensitive area around the naval and submarine base at Murmansk. It was fired on by a Soviet fighter and landed on a frozen lake. Two passengers were killed (M. Herman and G. Hughes (eds), *Intelligence in the Cold War*, Abingdon, 2013, p. 42 n.).

individual rights and the value of human life and seeks constantly to expand and dominate other nations.'[15] This unmeasured rhetoric far outran the facts as known to the administration. And it was two-edged: five years later an American warship shot down an Iranian airliner over Iranian territorial waters and 290 people were killed.*

Andropov responded with equal fury: 'If anyone had any illusions about the possibility of an evolution for the better in the policy of the present American administration, recent events have dispelled them completely.'

Anatoli Dobrynin, the Soviet ambassador in Washington, remarked that 'Both sides went slightly crazy.' The Soviet press, for almost the first time, started to abuse the US President personally, and repeated that the danger of nuclear war was higher than at any time since the Second World War. People in Moscow practised shelter drills once a week, and were told that they would only have eleven minutes to get there before the bomb arrived.[16]

Able Archer

It was against this disturbed background that NATO conducted its annual Autumn Forge exercises in Europe, under which the Americans deployed a division or more of troops from the United States to West Germany to demonstrate their capacity to reinforce Europe in a crisis.

The exercises began in September, and culminated in Able Archer from 7 to 11 November. Able Archer simulated an 'initial limited use of nuclear weapons against pre-selected fixed targets' to repel a Soviet conventional attack. For the first time the exercise involved high-level officials, including the Chairman of the American Joint Chiefs of Staff and the American Defense Secretary. Reagan was originally intended to play his real-life role; but his National Security Advisor advised him to pull out, because the Americans were already beginning to pick up Soviet worries.

Both the Russians and NATO had always feared that a surprise

---

*The US government did not formally apologise or admit liability. But in 1996 the Americans settled with Iran at the International Court of Justice, and paid $61.8 million in compensation to the families of the passengers and crew.

attack, 'a bolt from the blue', might be launched under cover of an elaborate exercise: Soviet plans for a conventional assault on Western Europe had included just such a possibility. Able Archer could almost have been designed to persuade the Russians that this was what was now happening.[17] The General Staff were reasonably sure that NATO was only engaged in an exercise. But for safety's sake they stepped up intelligence flights, alerted air units in Poland and East Germany, and moved their mobile SS-20s to camouflaged firing positions. Marshal Ogarkov, the Chief of the General Staff, went discreetly to his command bunker deep under Moscow.[18]

After it was over, CIA analysts tried to work out whether they had underestimated the danger of a violent Soviet reaction. They admitted that they had 'inadequate information about ... the Soviet reading of our own military operations [and] current reconnaissance and exercises'. Some analysts argued that the Russians knew from their spies in NATO and elsewhere that the West had no plans to attack. The Russian rhetoric was mere propaganda, designed to increase European opposition to the deployment of American missiles or divert attention from Soviet moves outside Europe. The analysts concluded, 'We believe strongly that Soviet actions are not inspired by, and Soviet leaders do not perceive, a genuine danger of imminent conflict or confrontation with the United States.'[19]

The British were less complacent. The Russian reaction to Able Archer seemed to them unprecedented. Drawing on the insights provided by their agent Oleg Gordievsky, they concluded that the Russians might indeed have thought that Able Archer posed a real threat.[20] Mrs Thatcher told the British ambassador, Sir Oliver Wright, to convey her concerns. He was met with scepticism: some Americans suspected that the British were 'simply capitalizing on a good political occasion to force President Reagan to tone down his rhetoric'.

People nevertheless continued to pick away at the story. In 1990 President George H. W. Bush's Foreign Intelligence Advisory Board produced a critical report. Little hard intelligence, it said, was available about Soviet motives and intentions. But the Russians had taken measures during Able Archer that were previously only seen in actual crises. The CIA analysts had failed to take into account the possibility that the Russians were indeed worried. They had committed the 'especially grave error to assume that since we know the US is not going to start World War III, the next leaders of the Kremlin will also believe that'. The report concluded that, by 1983, 'The Soviets had concern that the West might decide to attack the USSR without warning during a time of vulnerability ... thus compelling the Soviets to consider a preemptive strike at the first sign of US preparations for a nuclear strike ... we may inadvertently have placed our relations with the Soviet Union on a hair trigger.'[21] The report was not finally released until October 2015.

Robert Gates, the CIA's Deputy Director of Intelligence at the time, believed that it had indeed been a moment of great risk. He wondered if there had nearly been a terrible miscalculation: 'To what degree was our skepticism about the war scare prompted by the fact that our military didn't want to admit that one of its exercises might have been dangerously if inadvertently provocative, or because our intelligence experts didn't want to admit that we had badly misread the state of mind of the Soviet leadership?'[22]

Some said that the Able Archer crisis was second in danger only to the Cuba crisis. That was an exaggeration. But Fritz Ermarth, a veteran CIA analyst, continued to maintain that the Russians never thought the Americans were about to attack.[23] Michael Quinlan, a British defence official, argued that since NATO had no aggressive intentions, and moved no 'major' nuclear weapons in 'abnormal ways' at the time of Able Archer, there was nothing that could 'credibly have triggered Soviet nuclear response'.[24]

It was not quite that simple: the Russians might have frightened themselves into making an 'incredible' response. Marshal Akhromeyev, Ogarkov's deputy at the time, did not remember Able Archer as such; but he did believe that 'the most dangerous military exercises [were] Autumn Forge ... the NATO exercise in Europe'. Even Caspar Weinberger, Reagan's hawkish Defense Secretary, later admitted that there was scope for the Russians to misjudge what was happening: '[T]he difference between a realistic exercise or manoeuvre and what could be preparations for an attack, that line is sometimes quite blurred.'[25] In 1999 the veteran American analyst Ray Garthoff asked Vladimir Kryuchkov, who was in charge of the KGB's foreign intelligence at the time, whether he had meant what he said in 1984 that 'the threat of an outbreak of a nuclear war has reached dangerous proportions'. Kryuchkov replied that, though he had never expected an American nuclear strike, '1983 was the most alarming time'.[26]

The Soviet leadership may well have been paranoid; but their paranoia was fuelled by events in the real world. The paranoia was in any case matched on the other side: the distinguished right-wing strategist Colin Gray announced as the New Cold War got under way, 'We will be fortunate if we survive the 1980s.'[27]

The crisis neatly illustrated the paradox of deterrence: you intend to terrify your enemy into behaving properly; but you risk frightening him into doing something silly.

Reagan Sees the Light

Reagan drew a lesson from the events of 1983 rather more quickly than some of his advisers. He now began to give more weight to that strain in his attitude towards the Russians which looked for agreement.

His attitude towards arms control was ambiguous. He wavered between the idea of ignoring Carter's unratified SALT II agreement and affirming that it was in the American interest to maintain a framework of mutual restraint.

But he was more open-minded towards radical agreements with the Russians than some of his advisers realised or wanted. On the whole he was determined to push the process forward. In May 1982 he announced at his alma mater, Eureka College, that he was proposing a new treaty to Brezhnev which would reduce strategic nuclear weapons instead of merely stabilising them at existing levels. A month later American officials presented their ideas to the Russians in Geneva. In a first phase, strategic nuclear warheads would be reduced to a common ceiling, and the number of intercontinental missiles would be cut. There would be particular cuts in the number of heavy missiles to get a grip on the Russians' SS-18s. The second phase would reduce the number of heavy bombers, where the Americans had a considerable advantage. The Russians considered, with some justification, that the proposals were front-loaded in the Americans' favour.

Reagan's attitudes continued to evolve. In November 1983, just before the beginning of Exercise Able Archer, American and British television showed a full-length docudrama called *The Day After*, about the effects of a nuclear strike on a medium-sized American town. Before it was shown the British and American governments issued soothing statements: the events depicted were much exaggerated. Psychological counselling was nevertheless arranged for children in American schools. The normal commercial breaks were replaced with evangelists calling for the sinful viewer to repent before it was too late.*

One of those viewers was Ronald Reagan. He wrote in his diary that the film was 'very effective and left me greatly depressed', though it did not shift him from his view that the right way forward was deterrence. A few days later he was briefed on the Single Integrated Operational Plan. '[S]imply put, it was a scenario for a sequence of events that could lead to the end of civilization as we knew it. In several ways the events described in the briefings paralleled those in the ABC movie,' he later wrote. 'Yet there were still some people in the Pentagon who claimed that a nuclear war was "winnable". I thought they were crazy.'

He now began to understand a central truth about the confrontation. '[T]he Soviets are so defense-minded, so paranoid about being attacked, that ... we ought to tell them that no one here has any intention of doing anything like that,' he wrote in his diary. 'Maybe they are scared of us and think we are a threat.' It was hard for him to grasp. After all, 'it must be clear to anyone', he later wrote in his memoirs, that Americans were a moral people who 'had always used our power only as a force for good in the world'. But, more perceptive

---

* The 1980s saw a spate of films about nuclear accidents and war. Among the most striking were the BBC film *Threads* (1984), about the effects in Sheffield of a Soviet nuclear strike on Britain, including the collapse of authority, industry, and agriculture, and the genetic impact on the population; and a Soviet film, *Pisma Mertvogo Cheloveka* (Letters of a Dead Man, 1986), also about life after a nuclear war. Both films portrayed the effect of nuclear winter. The possibility of nuclear winter, caused by atmospheric pollution after a nuclear exchange, became a matter of wide interest and scientific controversy in the 1980s. Conspiracy theorists thought that it might be a KGB plot to strengthen the anti-nuclear movement in the West.

than some of his officials, he added, 'I began to realize that many Soviet officials fear us not only as adversaries but as potential aggressors who might hurl nuclear weapons at them in a first strike.'[28]

On 16 January 1984, in a television address, Reagan set out to repair some of the damage caused by his previous rhetoric. The main interest of both America and the Soviet Union, he said, was 'to avoid war and reduce the level of arms'. They should cooperate to find ways to cut back on the vast stockpiles of armaments in the world, and to reduce, and eventually to eliminate, the threat and use of force in international affairs. He repeated his criticism of the Soviet system, and his belief in the need for American strength. But his language was more measured and he avoided the accusation of evil that had so upset the Russians. And he ended with a folksy story, which he himself had drafted, about how Russian Ivan and Anya, American Jim and Sally, would all get on with one another perfectly well if they were only given the chance.[29]

The Arrival of Gorbachev

Reagan's new insight was fortuitously matched by the arrival in Moscow of a new Soviet leader.

The old men running the Soviet Union already knew that their country was in an increasing mess. When Andropov's successor, Konstantin Chernenko, died in March 1985, they chose Mikhail Gorbachev to succeed him as Secretary General. Gorbachev was young, intelligent, energetic, imaginative, experienced, and – they thought – orthodox. They hoped that he would bring energy, imagination, and decisiveness to solve what was rapidly becoming a hideous mix of international, economic, and domestic political problems. Neither they nor he suspected that he would be the last man to hold the office.

Gorbachev began a whirlwind of change. He proclaimed in public that there would be neither victor nor vanquished in a nuclear war: world civilisation would inevitably perish. Genuine security could be achieved only at a lower level of confrontation, from which nuclear weapons were entirely excluded. Even in the Soviet military, many of his listeners agreed with him. Of course they saw the problems. The Americans would have to accept that arms reductions would be mutual, and Soviet military strength would have to be kept at a level roughly equivalent to that of the West. But in Gorbachev's first months they were prepared to accommodate him.[30]

Unlike his predecessors, Gorbachev had no direct military service, even as a conscript soldier: a serious disadvantage in the eyes of the military. But it meant that he was willing to listen to other people who knew what they were talking about. Vitali Kataev, a senior official in the Central Committee's Defence Department, remarked, 'For the first time in the history of the Soviet Union, the highest skilled professionals were summoned to prepare decisions on complicated military-political issues ... A narrow military approach gave way to a broad unbiased approach. This step should be registered in the positive column of Gorbachev's record.'[31]

Gorbachev saw the discrepancy between Soviet disarmament proposals and the high levels of Soviet conventional forces in Europe. He had learned, from talks with Mrs Thatcher and others, that the West was genuinely afraid of the Soviet Union. He concluded that the level of confrontation was absurdly high and absurdly expensive. The Soviet Union needed just enough weapons to convince an opponent that it could respond effectively if attacked.[32]

He began by releasing the figures of Soviet military expenditure to create a public mood in favour of arms reductions.[33] Most of the Soviet leadership were themselves unaware of the true figures: they were bamboozled by the determination of the military to keep defence costs secret, by their inability to keep track of their own weapons stocks, and indeed by the ingrained failure of the Soviet system to produce reliable estimates of economic costs on any subject at all. Calculations of the proportion of the Soviet economy that was devoted directly or indirectly to defence, whether by the CIA or the Russians themselves, varied wildly from 20 per cent to 50 per cent or more.[34]

The result was that unnecessary weapons were produced at crippling expense. The Soviet Union spent about 70 per cent more on its ballistic missile submarines than the Americans. The Russians fielded eight types of submarine-launched ballistic missile, compared to the Americans' three. From 1979 to 1989 they produced 2,400 intercontinental ballistic missiles, compared to the Americans' 280.[35] There was no serious military rationale for these excesses. The Sorcerer's Apprentice had lost control.

It became increasingly clear even to the military, as well as to Gorbachev and his fellow reformers, that Soviet defence expenditure was unsustainable as a proportion of the Soviet economy, even though in absolute figures it lagged well behind American defence expenditure. In May 1987, when the Chief of Staff, Marshal Akhromeyev, reported on the figures, Gorbachev blew his top: 'Everyone knows everything about each other. What do we think we are saying with our publicity? The whole world is laughing. The United States is spending 300 billion whereas we spend seventeen. And that's how we're supposed to ensure parity!' Akhromeyev admitted that the position was hard to sustain in the light of the economic realities.[36]

Gorbachev's priorities for action imposed themselves. First, get out of Afghanistan; second, eliminate the dangerous stand-off over missiles in Europe; third, bring the seemingly endless talk about strategic nuclear weapons to a successful conclusion. In April 1985 he proposed a moratorium on nuclear tests. The Americans rejected it and continued their underground tests in Nevada.[37] In May 1987 he took advantage of a bizarre incident to purge the military when a young German, Matthias Rust, evaded the Soviet defences and flew his private plane to Red Square. He sacked the Defence Minister, Marshal Sokolov, and a host of other officers on a scale, some claimed, even more far-reaching than Stalin's bloody purges in the late 1930s – though this time no one went to the Gulag and no one was shot.[38] In May 1988 he finally negotiated an arrangement for the withdrawal of Soviet troops from Afghanistan. In December 1988, in a sensational speech to the United Nations, he announced that the Soviet Union would unilaterally withdraw substantial forces from Germany.

At first Western cynics took all this as simply another Communist trick: the talk of peace, the calls to end the arms race, were simply a veil behind which to strengthen the Soviet Union's military muscle. CIA analysts said that Gorbachev and his entourage were not liberalisers either at home or abroad. Before his first meeting with Gorbachev, Reagan was firmly briefed that 'the Soviet Union would not change no matter how bad their internal economic and social problems were'.[39]

The scepticism persisted almost to the end. In December 1987, Robert Gates told Reagan that 'all evidence points to continuity in

the Soviet Union's military policy ... It is hard to detect fundamental changes currently or in prospect, in the way the Soviets govern
at home or in their principal objectives abroad ... A sober – even
somber – reminder of the enduring features of the regime and the
still long competition and struggle ahead will be needed.' Reagan's
successor, George H. W. Bush, declared in the middle of his election
campaign in autumn 1988, just as Gorbachev's reforms began to reach
their peak, 'The Cold War is not over.' The new President's National
Security Advisor, Brent Scowcroft, 'feared that Gorbachev was trying
to rope the United States into another period of détente in order to
gain some advantage'. As late as April 1989 the intelligence analysts
were still predicting that 'for the foreseeable future the Soviet Union
will remain the West's principal adversary'.[40]

The sceptics failed to notice that Gorbachev, unlike his predecessors – and indeed many Americans – was determined to change the
language as well as the substance, to get away from the habit of seeing
the world in black and white – or Red and Black.

A Radical Solution?

Surprisingly, it was Gorbachev's military who gave him an opening.

In the spring of 1985 – coinciding with Gorbachev's assumption
of power but before he had made his mark – Akhromeyev told two
of his colleagues in the General Staff, General Nikolai Chervov and
General Victor Starodubov, both veterans of the SALT negotiations,
to begin work on a packet of proposals for the complete elimination
of nuclear weapons within fifteen years.* To avoid going off at half-
cock, the work was to be tightly restricted even inside the Ministry
of Defence. The arms controllers in the Foreign Ministry were to
be kept in the dark, except for Deputy Minister Georgi Kornienko,
Akhromeyev's crony. Neither the Defence Minister nor Gorbachev
and his Foreign Minister were to be informed at that stage.[41]

---

*Later historians debated his motives with varying degrees of scepticism. In his
memoirs (*Ot Razoruzhenia k Kapituliatsii*, Moscow, 2007), Starodubov gives
a cool account of how all these matters looked to the professional military.
Akhromeyev's own memoirs were unclear about his motives. Perhaps the answer
was in his diary, which his family refused to release after his death.

Akhromeyev's purpose was not clear. The negotiating process had broken down when the Russians had pulled out of the talks in Geneva in November 1983 in protest against the Americans' deployment of missiles in Europe: he may have hoped to jolt it back into life. He told Chervov and Starodubov that his main aim was to remove the threat of nuclear war. The Americans, he said, would recognise that both superpowers shared a common interest. Abolishing nuclear weapons would not damage the security of the Soviet Union, which had ample conventional means of defending itself. His ideas, he claimed, were different from those that had been previously negotiated. Unlike them, they looked to a genuine reduction in the armouries of both sides in a comparatively short period of time. To preserve a balance the Americans would have to limit their ambitions for Star Wars; something would have to be done about American 'forward-based systems' and the French and British deterrents; and nuclear testing would have to be stopped. But even if nuclear weapons could not be eliminated entirely, a radical but balanced reduction would reduce the danger.

Akhromeyev's military colleagues were divided. Some thought the packet would indeed damage national security. Others thought that the West would never agree to abandon deterrence. Still others feared that the idea would merely fizzle. Starodubov later admitted that many people thought the proposal was just propaganda. But he insisted, 'We were ready to go for a total elimination of nuclear weapons, even though, frankly, we thought that our opponents would not agree with us. We thought that it would probably be impossible to reach a total zero – complete nuclear disarmament. Maybe we will never be able to achieve it. But we were not afraid and we were ready to go down to a very low, agreed-upon minimum.'[42]

All agreed that the idea had one advantage. If the Americans rejected it, their lack of interest in serious arms control would be publicly demonstrated to the world.

The Geneva Summit
Gorbachev and Reagan did not meet until November 1985, when they came together in Geneva.

By then both the Americans and the Russians were beginning to conclude that they had more weapons than they needed for effective deterrence. Gorbachev and Reagan had both suggested in various contexts that their two countries should cut their nuclear weapons by 50 per cent. This broad figure concealed many problems of definition. The advisers on both sides suspected, with some justification, that the other had skewed his proposals in his own favour. Any progress would require arduous negotiation.

Both men claimed, no doubt sincerely, to look forward to a world in which nuclear weapons were abolished entirely. But the obstacles were overwhelming: all governments would have to agree and there would have to be a completely reliable and worldwide system of inspection to ensure that no one was cheating. There was not much reason to think such conditions could be achieved.

At Geneva the two men struck up a friendly working relationship. After the poisonous exchanges of the early Reagan years, all were relieved. The Soviet delegates were delighted to see their new leader performing in public so fluently and with such authority, unlike his sclerotic predecessors.

But behind the façade of friendship little was achieved. Reagan repeated his proposals. There should be a 50 per cent cut in strategic weapons. Intermediate-range missiles in Europe should be eliminated. For good measure he laid into Gorbachev about the Soviet human rights record and Russian meddling in the Third World.* And he remained uncompromisingly attached to his idea of Star Wars, into which the Americans were determined to continue limited research.

Gorbachev had floated the idea of a 50 per cent cut during his visit to President Mitterrand in Paris a month earlier. He broadly accepted Reagan's proposal on condition that missiles carried by the French and British deterrents and American 'forward-based systems' were included in the numbers. Recognising Reagan's determination, he was prepared to offer a compromise on Star Wars. The Americans might continue research in the laboratory. But they should not deploy the results, or exercise their right to leave the ABM Treaty, for the next ten years.

---

* Gorbachev countered with some boilerplate phrases about the treatment of coloured people and women in the United States.

Reagan rejected both conditions.

In private Gorbachev called Reagan a dinosaur, a pleasant neighbour in the countryside perhaps, but depressing as a political interlocutor. Reagan concluded that Gorbachev was still ideologically set in the old ways: if he wanted a deal on arms control, it was merely to reduce the burden of Soviet military expenditure.[43]

In their final communiqué the two men agreed that 'nuclear war cannot be won and should never be fought'. This was widely hailed as a breakthrough, though the aspiration had, after all, figured in the rhetoric of all their predecessors.

Akhromeyev and his colleagues waited to see how Gorbachev got on with Reagan at Geneva before putting their packet forward. They then submitted it to the Defence Minister, Marshal Sokolov. At the beginning of January 1986 Sokolov ordered General Chervov to take it urgently to the Black Sea resort where Gorbachev was on holiday.[44]

Gorbachev liked the idea of a Soviet initiative. But he pointed out that proposals for the complete elimination of nuclear weapons had been the stuff of Soviet propaganda since 1945. What was new? Chervov explained that previous Soviet 'initiatives' had consisted of words without content. This packet contained concrete proposals. Gorbachev was not immediately convinced. The West believed that security had to be based on deterrence. Perhaps they were right? Chervov countered that Mrs Thatcher and others did indeed think like that. But such ideas were dangerous unless, perhaps, they were based on nuclear parity and a low level of weapons on both sides. The packet was based on that principle. Gorbachev was won over.

The arms negotiators were meeting in the Ministry of Defence the following day when Akhromeyev burst in and announced without ceremony that the Defence Ministry had been working for nearly a year in secret on a disarmament packet. Now Gorbachev had approved it, so there was nothing more to discuss.

The diplomats were furious to have been kept in the dark. Akhromeyev's scheme reeked of propaganda, they thought. It contained no convincing detail, and ignored all the bitter experience which Soviet negotiating teams had acquired over the years about what was and was not negotiable. In a series of bad-tempered meetings the diplomats and the military men hammered out a three-stage plan for eliminating nuclear weapons and ballistic missiles. The first stage was not too different from what had been discussed in Geneva. The Soviet Union and America would cut their strategic weapons by half; they would remove their medium-range missiles from Europe; and they would cease nuclear testing. In the second, the superpowers would liquidate their medium-range systems. But they would be joined by the British, French, and Chinese, who would also cease testing. Once the 50 per cent cut was complete, a start would be made on eliminating nuclear weapons entirely. The process would be completed by the year 2000.

The military reluctantly accepted that the negotiations would remain stuck unless they modified their long-standing position on the British and French nuclear forces. These could, they now agreed, be left out of the count until the second stage – but only if plans to modernise them were abandoned, and the Russians were meanwhile allowed to keep medium-range missiles to balance them.

They remained adamant that the Americans should abandon Star Wars, or at least severely limit it. They were not prepared to accept even a remote risk that Star Wars might degrade the Soviet deterrent. It was a typical piece of military worst-case thinking.

Gorbachev wrote to Reagan on 14 January 1986 to set out these ideas. He went public with them the next day. The Americans were furious that he had upstaged them with what Secretary of State George Shultz called a 'blockbuster'. But Shultz believed that this was more than another Soviet propaganda stunt. Reagan agreed: had he not proposed something similar when he met Gorbachev in Geneva? Why wait until the year 2000? he asked.

Reagan and Shultz wanted to send a positive response quickly. But hardliners among Reagan's advisers – Caspar Weinberger, his Defense Secretary, Kenneth Adelman, the Director of the Arms Control Agency, and Richard Perle, now Assistant Secretary in the Defense Department – believed Gorbachev's move to be a dangerous propaganda ploy or worse. Allies had to be consulted. Mrs Thatcher was highly suspicious. Mitterrand and the German Chancellor reasserted their belief that nuclear weapons had preserved the peace. It took a month for Reagan to prepare his response: not a long time by bureaucratic standards, given the importance of the issues. But the delay irritated and upset Gorbachev.

Reagan finally replied on 22 February. A world free of nuclear weapons had been America's objective for many years, he pointed out. He praised Gorbachev's proposals as a significant and positive step forward. He agreed with many of his broad points. But he reminded him that the West relied on nuclear weapons to offset the Soviet Union's conventional superiority. Progress would depend on tackling that issue as well, and it would have to be backed by stringent inspection. To restore trust between the two countries, the Russians would have to do something about their intrigues in the Third World and their human rights record at home. He concluded, 'Neither of us has illusions about the major problems which remain between our two countries, but I want to assure you that I am determined to work with you energetically in finding practical solutions to those problems.'[45]

Gorbachev was no more ready than Reagan to abandon the principle of deterrence unless a satisfactory and mutually agreed alternative had been nailed down. But he shared the view that both sides had a vast superfluity of nuclear weapons. They could be cut substantially without undermining deterrence, provided both sides did so in a rough balance.[46]

On his holiday that summer, egged on by Anatoli Chernyaev, now his foreign policy adviser, Gorbachev decided that there would be no progress without a dramatic concession. The military and many of the diplomats were unnecessarily cautious, he thought, steeped in the conservatism of their professions, incapable of realising that great prizes could only be achieved by daring and unorthodoxy. He concluded that the British and French forces should be left out of the count. He instructed the Foreign Ministry to sound out the Americans about a possible summit meeting with Reagan in the autumn. He suggested that Reykjavik would be a good place for a meeting: politically neutral and geographically halfway between the two capitals. Through Chernyaev, he instructed the diplomats to prepare the material, concentrating especially on disarmament and aiming 'not at the specialists who know all about modern weapons, but at people and at states, at the world community'.[47] Initially the Ministry of Defence was kept out of the discussion.

The diplomats grumbled, as professional civil servants do, that once again the politicians were being misled by their special advisers. But the military were aghast. Gorbachev had abandoned essential conditions without consulting them. They began to wonder if he really had the country's best interests at heart. Perhaps he was pursuing a will-o'-the-wisp of universal peace out of naivety or, worse, out of personal vanity and a desire to 'go down to history'. Akhromeyev considered resignation.[*]

In the end the Soviet military did their duty and supported their civilian masters in preparing and conducting the negotiations. They were able to reassert the notion of deterrence, and inject what they saw as a more realistic and responsible approach to the nation's security. But they did so through gritted teeth. The growing tensions culminated five years later in the abortive coup of August 1991.

Most of the arms controllers in the Foreign Ministry had some sympathy with them. They recognised that, however obstructive and irritating the soldiers might be, it was their professional duty to judge what was necessary for the national security. Increasingly the diplomats too wondered if Gorbachev's 'new thinking' paid sufficient attention to the harsh realities of international life.

Chernobyl

The need to do something about the nuclear confrontation was dramatised in April 1986 by the accident at the nuclear power station at Chernobyl in Ukraine, which was wrecked by a major explosion and fire in one of its four reactors. It was the worst technological disaster of the twentieth century. Gorbachev remarked, 'In one moment we all felt what nuclear war is.'[48] With hindsight many saw this as the moment which symbolised the beginning of the end of the Soviet Union.[49]

Large amounts of radioactive fallout – far more than was generated by the Hiroshima bomb because the explosion had taken place

---

[*] Akhromeyev finally resigned after Gorbachev's speech to the United Nations in December 1988, although Gorbachev kept him on as his military adviser (W. Odom, *The Collapse of the Soviet Military*, Yale, 1998, p. 144).

at ground level and involved many tons of nuclear material – entered the atmosphere and travelled for hundreds of miles. The Prime Minister, Nikolai Ryzhkov, and his group of senior minsters worked night and day to limit the effects of the disaster. The army mobilised over 30,000 men. General Varennikov, the senior general in Afghanistan, was brought back to take over the military operation on the spot. Men fought heroically, but with inadequate equipment and expertise, to bring the conflagration under control. Thirty-one people died immediately. Tens of thousands were evacuated.

Vladimir Gubarev, the science correspondent of *Pravda*, was one of the first journalists to visit the scene. A year later he wrote a play called *Sarcophagus*, after the immense concrete structure in which the stricken reactor was entombed. It played successfully across the world. It was set in a small radiology clinic outside Moscow which received some of the victims. In a sign that people were already seeking comfort in an older tradition, the three young doctors were called Vera, Nadezhda, and Liubov – Faith, Hope, and Charity. Overwhelmed by the scale of the disaster, Faith left first, followed by Hope. Only Charity remained until the end.

The initial estimates of those who were expected to die in the aftermath were very high. In 2005 the United Nations reported that 'The total number of deaths already attributable to Chernobyl or expected in the future over the lifetime of emergency workers and local residents in the most contaminated areas is estimated to be about 4,000. This includes some 50 emergency workers who died of acute radiation syndrome and nine children who died of thyroid cancer, and an estimated total of 3,940 deaths from radiation-induced cancer and leukemia among the 200,000 emergency workers from 1986–1987, 116,000 evacuees and 270,000 residents of the most contaminated areas (total about 600,000).' The long-term effects of the accident, said the United Nations, were psychological and economic, rather than medical.[50]*

---

* Sunichi Yamashita was a Japanese expert on radiation professionally involved in following up the Chernobyl and Fukushima accidents. In both, he believed, the long-term effects were psychological rather than physical. Sixty people died in Fukushima in the early days: but these were old people and others overwhelmed

The figures in the UN report have also been challenged. But the effect of the Chernobyl accident on Soviet policymakers and the local population was profound. Gorbachev's confidence in those responsible for the nuclear industry, the Military Industrial Commission (the VPK) and the Ministry of Medium Machine Building, was reduced still further.[51] The military were forced to look again at their way of thinking about nuclear war. Akhromeyev called the accident a tragedy on the level of the German invasion of 22 June 1941: both brought about a revolution in the hearts and minds of the Soviet people. 'After Chernobyl,' he later wrote, 'the nuclear danger for our people ceased to be an abstraction. It became a palpable reality.'[52] The Deputy Defence Minister, General Shabanov, warned that even a conventional war in Europe could lead to the accidental or deliberate destruction of nuclear power stations, with incalculable consequences. The effect could be 'similar to that of a nuclear attack, and the after-effects more serious than those of Chernobyl'.[53] When they met in June 1990, Marshal Yazov, the Soviet Defence Minister, used the same argument in an attempt to persuade Mrs Thatcher out of her enthusiasm for nuclear weapons. She was unmoved.[54]

Reykjavik: A Lost Opportunity?

When they met in October 1986 in Reykjavik, Reagan and Gorbachev began by putting forward their prepared schemes for substantial cuts in strategic offensive arms. Gorbachev proposed that they should be reduced by half. There should be deep cuts in the heavy Soviet missiles, which remained a particular American worry. Medium-range missiles in Europe should be eliminated. The British and French deterrents and American 'forward-based systems' could be left out of the reckoning, but modernising them should be prohibited. So should all nuclear testing. He posed the usual limitations on Star Wars. No scheme of reduction could be equitable unless all these conditions were met.

---

by the disorganisation and stress of the emergency. Later there were eighty suicides linked to the accident, but no deaths or sickness from direct exposure to radiation. (Sunichi Yamashita, 'An Epidemic of Fear', *New Scientist*, 13 May 2017, pp. 40–41.)

The Americans came straight back with a version of their earlier proposals for reductions to fixed ceilings rather than percentage cuts. The two sets of proposals were referred to a working group of officials. Before the meeting the CIA had predicted that the military members of the Soviet delegation would be opposed root and branch to any concessions that Gorbachev might make. In fact, as George Shultz, who was never impressed by CIA predictions, sourly observed, Akhromeyev was particularly helpful.[55] Overnight two groups of officials, led by Akhromeyev and Paul Nitze, agreed on large and equitable reductions in ballistic missiles and the outline of an agreement on medium-range missiles in Europe. It had the makings of a major breakthrough.

The two leaders then met without their teams. Perhaps carried away by the occasion, each went far beyond their brief. Why should they not go straight away for a programme to eliminate all nuclear weapons within ten years? When they heard what their leaders had been up to, the advisers on both sides were aghast.

They need not have worried. The idea foundered on the issue of Star Wars. Reagan insisted that he could only accept a radical solution if Star Wars went ahead. He repeated his offer to share the American technology. Gorbachev was unconvinced. But he was willing to look at a deal: Star Wars research should be confined to the laboratory; both sides should remain in the ABM Treaty for a decade. Reagan feared these conditions would kill his favourite project. Attempts to bridge the gap by ingenious drafting failed. Reagan blamed Gorbachev for turning down 'a historic opportunity because of a single word'. But he had been just as intransigent. The summit ended in massive disappointment and a degree of mutual anger.

The world's press, and some historians, presented the outcome as a tragically missed opportunity to end the nuclear confrontation. Hardliners on both sides heaved a sigh of relief. Mrs Thatcher, the British Prime Minister, was appalled to hear that her friend Ronald Reagan had gone for a nuclear-free world without consulting her: she thought he had gone crazy. She lambasted the President on the telephone, and was only marginally consoled by his soothing response. General Rogers, the NATO Supreme Commander, said that the worst outcome at Reykjavik would have been a successful outcome.[56]

Of course there was never a realistic chance. Decades later the two sides still showed no sign of eliminating their nuclear weapons entirely. In so far as Reagan and Gorbachev genuinely hoped for a different result they were being naive. In any case, both imposed conditions at Reykjavik which ensured failure.

Aftermath

But despite the disappointments the two men had been gripped by a common, if impractical, passion for a nuclear-free world. George Shultz never lost the feeling that Reykjavik had been a uniquely important moment in history: twenty years later it inspired him to resume the search for a nuclear-free world.[57] And the meeting had established a new degree of trust. The halting process of negotiation resumed. Reagan and Gorbachev signed the Intermediate-range Nuclear Forces (INF) Treaty in Washington in 1987. This eliminated missiles with ranges between 500 and 5,500 kilometres – the Soviet SS-20s and the American Pershing IIs and cruise missiles which had been such a bone of contention in Europe for so long. There were provisions for strict verification of a kind the Soviet military had hitherto resisted. It was the first treaty that eliminated an entire class of weapons, rather than simply limiting their numbers. But to reach the agreement Shevardnadze included in the list of Soviet missiles to be eliminated one of the very latest, the SS-23 'Oka'. He did not consult the military. Once again the soldiers were incensed.[58]

As negotiations developed, the Russians found themselves surrendering one long-standing objective after another: on the number of accurate heavy missiles they should be allowed to keep; on the inclusion of the British and French nuclear deterrents and American 'forward-based systems'; and of course on Star Wars.

Critics inside the Soviet Union accused Gorbachev, and his Foreign Minister Shevardnadze, of cutting and running in the face of American pressure, of culpable incompetence, or even of treachery. Some of those intimately involved nevertheless understood that the Soviet Union, with its weaker economy and its technology still playing catch-up with the Americans, could not indefinitely sustain the nuclear confrontation. A reasonable if imperfect deal was the better outcome, and in the best interests of the country. More generous than many of his colleagues, General Detinov thought the accusations against Gorbachev and Shevardnadze were 'absolutely groundless and unfair'.[59]

It was another illustration of a general truth. Throughout the Cold War, in negotiation as on the ground, when the Russians came up against superior American power they were stopped in their tracks. After all, even Stalin had failed to get his way over Berlin in 1948.

FIFTEEN

ARMAGEDDON AVERTED?

'My guess is that nuclear weapons will be used in the next hundred years, but that their use will be much more likely to be small and limited than widespread and unconstrained. Deterrence would then have failed – but not totally.'

Herman Kahn, American strategist[1]

'It'll be a long time before humanity gives up the nuclear weapon – after all it is a very big club! It's true that no one knows how to use it: but it exists, and that's the reality.'

Boris Litvinov, senior Russian weapons designer[2]

Sensible people, in and out of power, concluded after the bombing of Hiroshima that mankind could either destroy itself entirely or, as Prime Minister Attlee said, go for a system of effective control or world government, 'the essential condition,' he said, 'of the survival of civilisation and possibly of life in this planet'.[3] The more ambitious believed that these things could be achieved, but only if human nature itself were transformed.

Through all these decades, there were citizens who distrusted the ability of their governments to manage the confrontation. Some organised very large protest movements across much of the Western world. They had little measurable influence on the making of policy. Successive governments in London and Washington denounced them as extreme, irresponsible, ignorant of realities which were too secret to be revealed, dupes, or even agents of the Communist adversary.

Moscow was under no pressure from home-grown protesters. Instead the Soviet government actively exploited Western protest movements to try to put a spoke in the military plans of Western governments. The Stockholm Peace Appeal, proposed by Frédéric ·

Joliot-Curie and set up in 1960 by the Soviet-sponsored World Peace Council, claimed to gather nearly 3 million signatures against the bomb. Soviet front organisations launched a fierce campaign of propaganda against the American deployment of missiles in the 1980s. They too had little effect.

Governments were at least as well aware as the protesters of the terrible destruction that could be wreaked by nuclear weapons. The protests perhaps helped to ensure that they did not forget it.

Quiet Advocacy

There were plenty of people who were not prepared to leave it at that.

Even before the bombs had been dropped on Japan, scientists involved in the Manhattan Project warned against the long-term consequences. In November 1944 and again in June 1945, the Nobel Prize winner James Franck and several of his colleagues warned the government that 'improper post-war policies might prove to be very damaging, or even disastrous, to the United States and to the fate of mankind'. All of us, they said, 'live with the vision before our eyes of sudden destruction visited on our own country, of Pearl Harbor disaster, repeated in thousandfold magnification, in every one of our major cities'. Other countries – particularly the Russians – would certainly soon work out the principles behind this 'secret weapon' for themselves. The result would be a new arms race. A new enemy might be tempted to strike 'a sudden unprovoked blow' against America, which could lead to 'the loss of tens of millions of lives and destruction of our largest cities'.[4] The government ignored their reports.

In November 1945 the Federation of Atomic Scientists was set up to educate the public about nuclear weapons, and to promote nuclear disarmament.[5] It too predicted that the American monopoly over atomic technology would be fleeting, and that it would be replaced by a global arms race. That autumn it successfully blocked a bill backed by General Groves and the Pentagon which would effectively have handed the development of atomic energy to the military. It promoted an alternative, which became the McMahon Act, created the Atomic Energy Commission, and put civilians in charge.[6] In 1946 the Atomic Scientists of Chicago, a group which had worked on the Manhattan Project, began publishing the *Bulletin of the Atomic*

Scientists, which kept invaluable track of what was going on. The *Bulletin* carried on its masthead a 'Doomsday Clock', which showed how many minutes remained before nuclear catastrophe. As international tension waxed and waned over the years, the minute hand on the clock moved towards and away from midnight.

Another scientist, Joseph Rotblat, succeeded in constructing a campaign which had a discreet but genuine influence on the thinking of governments.[7] Born in Warsaw, where he studied physics, he spent spring 1939 at Liverpool University, where he demonstrated that explosive nuclear fission was possible and drew up a rough paper on a fission bomb. If Hitler had such a bomb, he argued, he would be unstoppable unless confronted with an opponent equally armed. That summer his wife, Tola, was in Warsaw with appendicitis, and was unable to join him. She was trapped when the Germans invaded and died in the Holocaust. He never married again.

Convinced that all ideals would be at an end if Hitler got the bomb, he overcame his scruples about working on a weapon of mass destruction and joined the Manhattan Project early in 1944.[8] As he later remembered it, General Groves, the overall director of the Project, told him shortly after he arrived at Los Alamos, 'You realize of course that the main purpose of this project is to subdue the Russkies.'[9]

When Strasbourg fell to the Americans that September, they found documents confirming that the Germans had abandoned their nuclear programme. Rotblat was convinced that the moral basis for his participation in the Project had been undermined. He left it in December 1944. Clumsy efforts by the FBI to show that he was a Soviet spy got nowhere. He abandoned nuclear physics with its military associations, and turned to the medical uses of radiation, becoming Professor of Physics at St Bartholomew's Hospital in London.

In July 1955 Rotblat helped Bertrand Russell, the British philosopher, draft 'The Russell–Einstein Manifesto'. The eleven signatories included Albert Einstein; ten of them were Nobel Prize winners. They warned of nuclear apocalypse and proposed a conference to examine the dangers. Cyrus Eaton, a Canadian businessman, paid for it to be held in his birthplace in Pugwash, Nova Scotia, in 1957. Rotblat was one of the leading organisers.

The Pugwash conferences aimed to bring together scientists from East and West in a discreet and politically neutral context. The first was attended by scientists from the US, the Soviet Union, Japan, Britain, Canada, Australia, Austria, China, France, and Poland. By the end of the Cold War in 1991, forty-one Pugwash conferences had been held in various parts of the world, including the Soviet Union.

The Russian team at the first conference was led by Alexander Topchiev, an organic chemist. He and the other Soviet scientists were senior members of the Soviet Academy of Sciences, closely linked with senior policymakers and well placed to convey official views and report what they heard back to Moscow. Later conferences were attended by Tamm, Kapitsa, and others who had worked on the Soviet bomb. Of course there were attempts to promote the official Soviet line: at the first meeting a Soviet colleague translated Topchiev's opening remarks with some additional bits of propaganda. He was promptly corrected by Eugene Rabinowitch, an American participant who was also a native Russian speaker.

Many of the Western participants also had official connections: they would otherwise have had little practical influence, as Rotblat recognised. On the American side there were scientists who had worked on the Manhattan Project, such as Rabinowitch, Szilard, and Rotblat himself. There were also establishment figures, such as Walt Rostow, later a member of Kennedy's national security team, and Jerome Wiesner, Kennedy's chief scientific adviser. Among the Britons were Lord Zuckerman, the government's scientific adviser, William Penney, adviser to the UK Atomic Energy Authority and later its chairman, and John Cockcroft, the head of the Atomic Energy Research Establishment. The Foreign Office welcomed their participation, but with some concern, since they did not want 'to see the importance of the Pugwash meetings unduly inflated'.

Rotblat himself was determined to remain independent. He never accepted an official brief and resisted official attempts to take over his conferences. In October 1963 a Foreign Office official wearily complained that 'the difficulty is to get Prof Rotblat to pay any attention to what we think. He is no doubt jealous of his independence and scientific integrity.' But for his efforts to bring nuclear weapons under control, he was awarded the Nobel Peace Prize in 1995. And the British gave him a knighthood in 1998.

The first meeting had little difficulty in finding a common language: Topchiev said, 'We have an overriding interest to survive and to avoid nuclear war. We must draw back from the brink.' All agreed on the danger of radiation and fallout, singling out strontium-90: there was no safe threshold. They announced that 'the prompt suspension of nuclear bomb tests could be a good first step', a conclusion eventually accepted by their governments. They were less successful in suggesting practical ways of bringing the weapons under control, concluding feebly that 'war must be eliminated, not merely regulated by limiting the weapons to be used'.

Rabinowitch concluded from the first meeting that scientists could address intractable problems 'thoughtfully and without the discussion degenerating into an exchange of tiresome clichés'. Otto Frisch, the co-author of the seminal 1940 memorandum 'On the Construction of a "Superbomb"', told the Foreign Office that the Russians were naive but sincere: 'all our proposals are tentative, so we can roam where diplomats fear to tread. I think those of the participants who have the ear of their government will help to make the public performance a success.' Zuckerman believed that the Russians were 'genuine in their fears that the West was ready and anxious to launch a war against the Soviet Union'. At a later meeting Tamm pointed out that 'both sides harboured fears and suspicions that the other side dismissed as make-believe'.

Governments remained sceptical. Khrushchev complained that those who talked were not those who decided. An American senator denounced Pugwash on television: the Soviet scientists were all political tools of an international conspiracy, he said, and the Americans who met with them were deceived and misled.

On the whole, however, governments found Pugwash a useful channel for exchanging ideas when relations between them were strained and more formal channels clogged. Thanks in part to these contacts, American and Russian officials began to meet secretly to hammer out their own bilateral agreements. The eventual result was a series of significant arms control agreements, starting with the Partial Test Ban Treaty of 1963. By then Pugwash had made its main contribution to history, though it continued to meet.

Popular Protest

Popular protests were, of course, more dramatic than the quiet exchanges between experts. One British organisation, the Campaign for Nuclear Disarmament (CND) and its characteristic logo came to symbolise the anti-nuclear movement worldwide. The Aldermaston Marches, which it organised every Easter from 1958, were a model for protest everywhere.*

CND was set up in 1957 by people who hoped to persuade the British Labour Party to renounce nuclear weapons, end nuclear testing, and negotiate an international convention on general disarmament. They chose as their president Bertrand Russell, co-author of 'The Russell–Einstein Manifesto'. Russell was a colourful figure from one of England's oldest political families, a mathematician with a worldwide reputation, and a recipient of the British Order of Merit and the Nobel Prize in Literature. He was married four times, had many affairs, and was pronounced 'morally unfit' to teach at the City College of New York in 1940. Vocal, apocalyptic, inconsistent, at various times a liberal, a socialist, and a pacifist, he went to prison for opposing the First World War but in 1948 gave a speech which seemed to call for a pre-emptive nuclear strike against the Soviet Union. In 1961, at the age of eighty-nine, he was briefly imprisoned once more for his part in an anti-nuclear demonstration in London. In his last years his ferocious criticism of American policy was rarely balanced by criticism of Soviet policy.

Despite the hopes of its founders, CND was unable to get its ideas adopted in mainstream British politics. So Russell turned to more direct action. His Committee of 100 demonstrated against the arrival of American nuclear submarines in Scotland, against the Ministry of Defence, and against the American and Soviet embassies in

---

*In the late 1960s the British Security Service, MI5, designated CND as 'communist-controlled', but in 1985 downgraded it to 'communist-penetrated', and eventually lost interest.

London. It then moved on from demonstrations to action against military bases. Some of its officers were imprisoned. But its disruptive tactics increasingly lost public sympathy. With the signature of the Partial Nuclear Test Ban Treaty in 1963, public concern about nuclear weapons declined. Russell resigned in 1963 and the Committee of 100 was wound up in 1968.

But CND remained in being. It got a new lease of life with the 'Second Cold War'. Its membership jumped to 15,000 in 1981–2 and to 50,000 in 1983. In August 1981 a group of women set up a 'peace camp' at the American cruise missile base at Greenham Common in Berkshire. In October 1981 and June 1982 about a quarter of a million people marched through London in support of unilateral nuclear disarmament. Around 300,000 people demonstrated in London in October 1983. In 1982 the Ministry of Defence was forced to cancel a planned civil defence exercise when numerous Labour councils declared their areas 'nuclear-free zones' and refused to cooperate.

The demonstrations against cruise missiles in Britain were matched on the European continent and in America.[10] But these impressive protests did not change policy. The American missiles were deployed in Europe as planned. Neither the British government nor any other adopted the policy of unilateral nuclear disarmament. With the rise of Gorbachev and the end of the Cold War the steam ran out of CND. It lingered into the new century, campaigning against the nuclear power industry, and British and American policy in the Middle East. It was still firmly lodged in one wing of the Labour Party. But it had lost focus, and no longer had much broad appeal or political influence.* The British decided in 2016 to renew their force of Trident submarines with very little protest from voters or even the Labour Party itself.

In the United States anti-nuclear protests were directed against the nuclear power industry and against nuclear weapons and the places where they were designed and tested. They had one particularly American characteristic: in addition to demonstrations and sit-ins,

---

* The late John Ainslie of Scottish CND nevertheless continued to produce measured articles on various aspects of nuclear policy until his death in 2016.

activists lobbied and occasionally sued government in an attempt to change policy.

In November 1961 the National Committee for a Sane Nuclear Policy mobilised some 50,000 women to march against nuclear weapons in sixty cities across the United States. From the mid-1980s there were demonstrations and arrests every Good Friday outside the Lawrence Livermore Laboratory. In 1987 there were demonstrations at the Nevada test site: among those arrested were the actors Martin Sheen and Kris Kristofferson, an 84-year-old priest, and a Catholic nun.

In 1976 four nuclear engineers resigned from the Nuclear Regulatory Commission in protest against inadequate safety measures. They testified to the Joint Committee on Atomic Energy that 'the cumulative effect of all design defects and deficiencies in the design, construction and operations of nuclear power plants makes a nuclear power plant accident, in our opinion, a certain event. The only question is when, and where.' The accident duly took place at Three Mile Island in March 1979, when a partial reactor meltdown released radioactive products into the atmosphere in amounts that remained disputed. That September 200,000 people demonstrated in New York. They were addressed by celebrities such as Jane Fonda and Ralph Nader. Nearly twenty plants were shut down and the building of new plants stopped.[11]

The protests intensified as Ronald Reagan's rhetoric began to take hold and the 'Second Cold War' reached its height. Roger Molander, a nuclear engineer, contributed to nuclear policymaking in the National Security Council under Nixon, Ford, and Carter. He left in disgust in 1981 when a naval captain told him that 'only' 500 or 600 million people would be killed in a nuclear war. That April he set up 'Ground Zero', which a year later organised a nationwide protest of up to a million people across 800 cities and towns. Students at Columbia University organised a 'die-in'.[12] In June 1981 a million people demonstrated in New York City's Central Park, the largest political demonstration in American history. An International Day of Nuclear Disarmament was held two years later at fifty sites across the United States. Thousands of women set up a peace camp outside the Seneca Army Depot in New York State to prevent cruise and Pershing II missiles being shipped to Europe: like their sisters in Europe, they failed. In August 1985 a service for peace and nuclear disarmament was held in Washington Cathedral. In 1986 hundreds walked from Los Angeles to Washington in the Great Peace March for Global Nuclear Disarmament.

Like the British protests, these devoted efforts had very little direct impact on policy.

By the mid-1980s the Americans and Russians had begun to realise that they could preserve their security with far fewer weapons.

In October 1981 Frank Miller, Deputy Director in the Office of the Secretary of Defense under Caspar Weinberger, launched a determined and largely successful campaign to tackle the many irrationalities in American targeting policy. He concluded that the United States could cut its armoury substantially without undermining its strategic capacity.* Curtis LeMay and his immediate successors had planned for an all-or-nothing strategic attack which would have embraced the Soviet Union, China, and Eastern Europe without discrimination. The result was a nightmare of duplication, in which the same target would have been hit more than once, and American bombers would be sent to fight their way through the Soviet defences to attack targets which had already been destroyed by missiles. Miller and his team demonstrated that the United States could destroy the same range of targets (and thus supposedly achieve the same deterrent effect) while reducing warhead numbers by 40 per cent from the 10,000 warheads the Americans were entitled to deploy under the START I Treaty signed in 1991. Moving back from MIRVed missiles to missiles with a single warhead could restore the comparative stability lost when the Americans first deployed MIRVs on their Minutemen in the early 1970s.[13] The Russians were also cutting back their nuclear weapons, above all under the pressure of economic necessity.

It was thus independently of any negotiations that warhead numbers tumbled from 40,000 at the end of the 1980s to something less than 15,000 in 2010.[14] But the trend greatly simplified the negotiation of new treaties: START II in 1993 and SORT (Strategic

---

* Frank (Franklin) Miller was closely involved in US–UK collaboration over Trident, and received a British knighthood.

Offensive Reductions) in 2002. In 2010 Putin and Obama agreed to halve their strategic launchers and limit the number of deployed warheads in what they called New START (New Strategic Arms Reduction Treaty). The tension between the two superpowers greatly diminished. It seemed improbable that they would now visit a final orgy of destruction upon the world. The threat of Armageddon appeared to recede.

Geopolitical Catastrophe?

That appearance was reinforced by the collapse of the Soviet Union. As his country was falling apart in the spring of 1991 Anatoli Chernyaev, Gorbachev's foreign policy adviser, remarked with a rueful grin to Michael Alexander, by then British ambassador to NATO, that it was only because the Soviet Union had nuclear weapons that the West was still taking it seriously. Marshal Akhromeyev admitted to Alexander that the Soviet Union was no longer able to sustain the confrontation. Military parity with the United States was now beyond its grasp. He assured Alexander that, despite all the difficulties, the Soviet armed forces were mature, loyal, and would never act against the President.[15]

Four months later they did just that. Senior figures in the army, the KGB, the Party and the military-industrial establishment were increasingly appalled at the way Gorbachev's policies seemed to be leading to a collapse in the authority of the government, accelerating economic chaos, and the disintegration of the Soviet Union itself as the Balts, the Georgians, and the Ukrainians began to demand control of their own affairs, if not outright independence. In August 1991 Marshal Yazov, the Minister of Defence, Vladimir Kryuchkov, the head of the KGB, and some of their colleagues tried to do something about it. They sequestered Gorbachev in his holiday villa in the Crimea, flooded Moscow with troops and tanks, and declared a return to the old ways.

It was a dismal failure. The people of Moscow and Leningrad refused to bend to the plotters' will. Yazov, appalled at the idea of bloodshed on the streets of the capital, sent the tanks back to their bases. Gorbachev was rescued from the Crimea and returned to Moscow. But his authority, too, had been destroyed. Instead of restoring Soviet power, the plot opened the way for Boris Yeltsin, an ambitious and popular politician from the Russian provinces, to oust Gorbachev as the leader of the country. In December 1991 Yeltsin declared that the Soviet Union had ceased to exist and the country disintegrated into fifteen separate independent states.

Russia was of course by far the largest of the successor states and, under Yeltsin, its relationships with the West continued to improve. Yeltsin embarked on a series of reforms intended to strengthen Russian democracy and transform the economic system into something resembling the liberal economies of the capitalist world. His success was distinctly mixed. The collapse of Soviet power brought economic chaos in its wake. In places people were close to famine: the West provided food aid, a gesture that was seen by many Russians as a humiliation. Inflation ran out of control. Corruption mounted as some people got extremely rich while many of their compatriots became distinctly poorer as salaries and wages went unpaid for months at a time. In 1998 Russia was forced to default on its debts.

Meanwhile the politicians and generals of the new Russia never lost sight of the thought that their country still disposed of nuclear forces of devastating power, and that for a while at least this alone would give it status on the world scene.[16]

The collapse had made it harder to manage this arsenal. Military spending was drastically cut from around $246 billion in 1988 to $14 billion in 1994. Weapons production tailed off. Much military equipment had been produced, and many bases and testing grounds were situated, in parts of the Soviet Union that were now independent countries. There were few spares available for maintenance. Defective equipment was not replaced. There was no money for training and exercises. In the period 1991–5 the navy got less than a third of the money it needed. By 1998 only twenty-three of their missile submarines were operational and the number continued to decline: submarine patrols halved between 1991 and 1996. The bomber force continued to rely on an updated version of the veteran TU-95, first introduced in the 1950s, but had no money for the stealth cruise missile that might have enabled it to penetrate modern American air defences. By the late 1990s funds for the rocket forces had been cut by more than half. Rocket bases could not pay for their electricity supplies, and some had to take over local power stations to ensure that they could function.[17] Tens of thousands of officers were sacked or resigned. Many of the rest went without their salaries for months at a time. Some had to live with their families in converted containers or even in tents. Two American senators, Sam Nunn and Richard Lugar, pushed through the Cooperative Threat Reduction Program, a very generous scheme of funding and expert advice to help the Russians dismantle their weapons and store their nuclear materials securely. The Russians accepted with a mixture of gratitude and resentment.

The scientists and weapons designers were in trouble too. As the Soviet Union collapsed they were roundly abused as immoral by some of their fellow countrymen for the catastrophically destructive weapons they had designed and built. Now the funding for Arzamas-16 and Chelyabinsk-70 was drastically cut.* There, too, salaries went unpaid. Some scientists left to seek jobs abroad. Others set up specialist businesses in an attempt to turn their knowledge into commercial profit: one group offered to destroy waste of all kinds by incinerating it with thermonuclear blasts 2,000 feet underground. A shortage loomed of qualified people to service the weapons that remained or dismantle those that were withdrawn from service. In 1989 the distinguished scientist Valery Nechai became Director of Chelyabinsk-70. By the mid-1990s he was having to borrow money from the new commercial banks to pay his staff a miserable $50 a month. On 1 October 1996 he shot himself in despair. No one from the government bothered to go to his funeral.[18]

For most people outside the Soviet Union – the peoples of Eastern Europe who had had Communist governments foisted on them after 1945, the peoples of Western Europe who had lived with the fear of Soviet invasion, people everywhere who feared a nuclear catastrophe – the end of the Cold War and the collapse of the Soviet Union were an unmitigated blessing.

Some people inside the Soviet Union saw it the same way,

---

*Now known respectively as the All-Russian Institute of Experimental Physics (VNIIEF) and the All-Russian Institute of Technical Physics (VNIITF).

especially of course the Balts, Ukrainians, Georgians, and others for whom it was the key to national independence. Russians, too, were glad to see the end of the nuclear confrontation, and at first many of them were glad to see the back of Communism and the end of empire.

And so when in 2005 Vladimir Putin, Yeltsin's successor as President, called the Soviet collapse 'the greatest geopolitical catastrophe of the twentieth century', most people in the West could not understand what he was talking about: it was surely beyond doubt that the world was better off without the Soviet Union.[19]

Neither Putin nor the many ordinary Russians who had thought of themselves as patriotic Soviet citizens wanted a return to Stalin and the Gulag. But to them the collapse had indeed come to feel like a catastrophe. Even those who had hated Communism, who knew perfectly well what crimes had been committed in its name, were appalled by the humiliation, confusion, poverty, and hardship which now engulfed their country. One of the two arbiters of world history had been destroyed almost overnight – some said by treachery. Paranoia, never far below the surface, began to bubble up again.

And for the Soviet – now Russian – military the extent of the catastrophe was beyond doubt. At a blow they saw their profession, the institution they had worked for, the country they had served with patriotic dedication, all brought to their knees, perhaps beyond redemption: General Danilevich's Shakespearean tragedy.

For one man it was too much. Marshal Akhromeyev had tried to serve Gorbachev loyally. But he lost faith in the direction in which Gorbachev was leading the country. He offered his assistance to those who tried to turn the clock back in August 1991. When the plot failed, he hanged himself in his office. He was buried on 1 September. That night his grave was vandalised and his uniform and medals stolen.

Modernisation

The fragile Cold War system of nuclear constraint became perversely harder to maintain as the old pressures diminished and the number of nuclear weapons states slowly rose. Despite the cuts, the world still kept a large number of nuclear warheads. Of these 93 per cent were in the arsenals of Russia and America. There were still nearly 200 nuclear bombs at six American bases in Europe.[20] The US Congress refused to ratify the Comprehensive Test Ban Treaty of 1996 on the grounds that America needed to retain the right to test its existing stock of nuclear weapons for reliability.[21] Russia and America still kept half their strategic forces on high alert.

Before too long Akhromeyev's successors set out to rebuild Russian military power, encouraged by a President who shared their views, and supported by many Russian politicians, and indeed by many ordinary Russian people, who felt that Russian military might had declined far below what a great country needed for its defence and for its self-respect.

Conservatives in the military still hankered after the massive armoured formations of the past. But reformers wanted something slimmer, more nimble, better equipped – and fully affordable. The debate was more or less resolved in favour of the latter. After the poor performance of the Russian military in the brief war with Georgia in 2008, Russia embarked on a major programme of defence modernisation which was expected to cost some $700 billion by 2020. The plan was to build and deploy 400 new intercontinental ballistic missiles, eight nuclear missile submarines, and a new heavy bomber armed with a long-range cruise missile. This was an ambitious programme, but by 2016, according to one observer, 'for all its weaknesses, the Russian defense industry is now second only to that of the United States in its ability to produce large quantities of relatively high-quality weapon systems across the full spectrum of defense-industrial products'. The government was determined to keep a firm grip on military expenditure this time round. But the continuing fragility of the economy left a question mark.[22]

The Americans kept their qualified teams of scientists, weapons designers, and manufacturers together to service and modernise the nuclear weapons which they still possessed. They put surplus warheads into store in case they might be needed in future. And in 2011 the Obama administration announced its intention to 'modernize or replace the triad of strategic nuclear delivery systems'. The programme foresaw the construction of 100 new strategic bombers, twelve new ballistic missile submarines, 400 new ICBMs, and at least

1,000 new cruise missiles capable of carrying nuclear warheads. It was expected to start in 2020, and to cost $350 billion in the first ten years and about $1 trillion over the thirty years it would take to complete.[23]

Other very destructive weapons were beginning to emerge: highly accurate hypersonic cruise missiles designed to carry a conventional or nuclear warhead halfway round the globe in a matter of minutes, to kill terrorists, evade missile defences, and wipe out foreign governments and their command-and-control systems. The Americans had plans to build over 1,000 of these weapons, and to bring them into service in 2025. They were also looking at another device capable of remaining in orbit for a year and being brought down on to a target at any time.[24] They called their programme 'Prompt Global Strike'. Because they could launch a surprise 'bolt from the blue' with almost no warning, such exotic weapons could disrupt the comparative strategic stability that had been negotiated so painfully over five decades of arms control. The Russians took note, and were deeply worried.

By 2015 the United States was spending nearly $600 billion a year on defence. China was next, its military expenditure variously estimated at somewhere between $145 and $215 billion. Despite its burgeoning military programmes, Russia was still only spending around $65 billion, less than Saudi Arabia, though more than Britain or France.[25] Meanwhile the British and the French were also planning to modernise their nuclear forces. China, India, Pakistan, and North Korea were doing the same. Only Iran, under immense diplomatic and economic pressure, agreed to abandon the nuclear weapons programme it had always denied having.

The Return of Confrontation?

In 1994 Presidents Clinton and Yeltsin agreed that their missiles would no longer be targeted against one another. When George W. Bush was running for president in May 2000, he declared that 'the United States should remove as many weapons as possible from high-alert, hair-trigger status … keeping so many weapons on high alert may create unacceptable risks of accidental or unauthorized launch.' Barack Obama repeated the promise during his election campaign in 2007.

There turned out to be less to this than met the eye. It would in any case have been easy enough to re-target the missiles. De-alerting also fell by the wayside. A review commissioned by President Obama in 2010 concluded that it 'could reduce crisis stability by giving an adversary the incentive to attack before "re-alerting" was complete'.[26]

The nuclear confrontation between America and the Soviet Union had been given its particular venom by the ideological conflict between Godless Communism and Capitalist Imperialism, and the mutual hatreds, the demonisation, and the paranoia which these generated. After the Soviet collapse the threat of Armageddon did indeed recede for the time being: there was no other pair of superpowers, no other pair of scorpions, who might have locked themselves into a similar bottle. The new ideological or religious divide was between a humiliated and vengeful Islam and a 'West', secular but still partly Christian. This lacked the underpinning of great power, though it too generated paranoia, fear, and hatred in plenty.

In 2009, speaking in Prague, President Obama pledged America to seek a world without nuclear weapons. His pious aspiration was no more prophetic than those of his predecessors. The bilateral confrontation, its viciousness underpinned by ideological conflict, might have ended, but the scope for great power rivalry of a more old-fashioned kind, the kind that had spawned plenty of major wars in the past, had not gone away. As the new century advanced, few people talked any more about eliminating nuclear weapons entirely.

The American military continued to argue that the United States needed to be able to deter an adversary, or, if that failed, to fight a variety of nuclear wars. The Russians, British, and French still spoke of the need to retain an adequate deterrent in a dangerous world. After the fragile honeymoon of the first post-Soviet years, the relationship between Russia and America began to deteriorate in a welter of accusation, counter-accusation, and military adventure on both sides.

With the collapse in their conventional forces after 1992, the Russians abandoned their doctrine of 'No First Use' of nuclear weapons, and began to look again at the possibility of using them on the battlefield or in a regional conflict to compensate for their conventional weakness. This evolution in their thinking was accelerated by the massive Western bombing campaign against Serbia in 1999, which the Russians regarded as an act of aggression against a small sovereign country. An expanding NATO, they thought, brought the threat ever closer to their own borders. Their immediate response was to practise the limited use of nuclear weapons in a major exercise, Zapad 1999. Their sense of threat was reinforced by American military action in Afghanistan, Iraq, and elsewhere in the Middle East after the terrorist attack in New York in September 2001. The idea that you could use 'non-strategic' nuclear weapons to 'de-escalate' a conventional conflict figured increasingly in their thinking.[27]

In 2008 the Russians defeated Georgia in a short war which each accused the other of provoking. In 2014 they took Crimea from Ukraine, in whose eastern provinces they encouraged a rebellion. In response to Western sanctions, they demonstratively moved Iskander short-range (up to 500 kilometres) nuclear-capable missiles to the borders of Eastern Europe. In 2016 NATO sent token contingents of troops and aircraft into the Baltic States and Poland to reassure its nervous eastern members. The Russians conducted massive exercises of their emergency and civil defence services in ways which had not been seen for many years: it was implausibly claimed in the West that 40 million people were involved.[28] The Americans accused the Russians of violating the INF Treaty, while in return the Russians accused the Americans of undermining nuclear stability by pressing ahead with their plans for anti-missile defence. Establishment figures in Moscow made bombastic statements about nuclear war. Western reactions were often ill-informed and exaggerated. A sensible discussion of strategic matters nevertheless continued in Russia and America; but it was often drowned out by the noise.*

It was not a return to the hair-trigger confrontation of the Cold

---

*A noisy flurry was stirred up in March 2014 by Dmitry Kiselev, a Russian TV anchorman, who said, 'Russia is the only nation capable of turning the United States into radioactive ash.' He was speaking about Russia's ability to retaliate even after a massive first strike by the Americans, but in the West his remarks were taken out of context and interpreted as a threat. In February 2016 the BBC ran a sensational programme entitled *World War Three: Inside the War Room*, which envisaged a Russian nuclear strike against a British aircraft carrier, and left open the possibility that the British would then fire off their Trident missiles in retaliation.

War. But mutual vituperation reached levels unseen since then. Attempts to get informal discussions going between Russia and America, along the lines successfully pioneered by Pugwash, ran into the sands in the new atmosphere of hostility.[29]

In 2016 the Russians and the Americans still had comparable, and very large, stocks of warheads, far exceeding those of all the other nuclear powers.

The logic of nuclear confrontation – if the other guy's got it, we have to have it – did not go away just because the Soviet Union had ceased to exist. In 1963 Kennedy predicted that by 1970 twenty-five nations might have nuclear weapons, which he regarded as 'the greatest possible danger and hazard'.[30] That did not happen. A number of countries capable of acquiring the necessary skills renounced them – Canada, South Africa, Argentina, Brazil. By 2015 there were far fewer nuclear weapons states than originally feared. But in addition to America, Russia, China, Britain, and France, India and Pakistan now had effective nuclear arsenals, Israel was assumed to have one, and North Korea was on the way to getting one too.

In 1999 the long-standing antagonism between India and Pakistan erupted yet again in the 'Kargil War' over the disputed province of Kashmir. There was further fighting in 2001–2 after terrorists

Estimated Nuclear Warhead Inventories

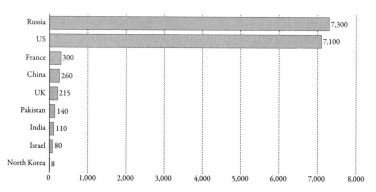

murdered a number of people in the Indian Parliament and in 2008 after terrorist attacks in Mumbai: the Indians claimed that the terrorists came from Pakistan and were perhaps sponsored by the Pakistani intelligence services. Pakistan refused to rule out the use of nuclear weapons if the conflicts escalated. The Indians threatened to retaliate in kind. Some speculated that if it came to a nuclear exchange, India might suffer 100 million deaths; but Pakistan would be wiped off the map. Both pulled back after heavy pressure from America, Britain, and others – and no doubt after considering the likely consequences of nuclear war, which sobers people up when they contemplate it closely. A later unofficial American study claimed that in addition to the large numbers of people in India and Pakistan that would be killed by a nuclear exchange, up to 2 billion more might die of starvation as a result of climate change and failed harvests: a high figure whose plausibility the layman could not judge. The incidents dented the theory that nuclear-armed states do not go to war with one another for fear of the consequences.[31]

Much excitement was generated by the possibility that an irresponsible 'rogue government' might be so fanatical, so lost to reason, that it would be undeterred by the risk of immediate nuclear punishment: an Iranian leader might lob a missile at Israel, or a North Korean at South Korea (or America) just for the hell of it. The American government called Iran 'one of the greatest global concerns we face. A nuclear-armed Iran would pose a threat to the region, to the world, and to the future of the global nuclear proliferation regime.'[32] Less official sources used more extreme language.

But launching a nuclear strike is a complicated business: it is not just a question of one man pressing a button in isolation. No one examined how likely it was that the mad dictator's entourage and his generals would allow him to impose destruction on himself, on them, and on their country. Even during the Cold War governments said and did some foolish and provocative things; but the possession of nuclear weapons sobered them up. There was no obvious reason why rogue states under mad dictators should be all that different.

There was a further worry. The old-established nuclear powers had systems of command and control, 'Permissive Action Links', and sophisticated technology which they hoped were reliable. These required much experience and a technical sophistication which the johnny-come-latelies may well have lacked. Even the established nuclear states continued to have problems with military and civilian nuclear safety. There was no reason to assume that the new arrivals would do better. However remote, none could rule out the possibility of accident.

One new and frightening scenario remained: the possibility of terrorist attack. The idea that a great city might be destroyed by a 'suitcase bomb' surfaced in the press immediately after Hiroshima. The prospects for nuclear terrorism were insistently canvassed after the destruction of the Twin Towers in New York in 2001. Sober analysts argued that it would be hard for even the most sophisticated and best-financed terrorist to obtain the nuclear material, assemble it into an explosive device, and transport it undiscovered to its target. Even a rogue government would be unlikely to risk retaliation by supporting such an enterprise. But a lesser disaster was more plausible. Terrorists could let off a simple 'dirty' bomb, made from fissile material and conventional explosive, thus generating lethal radiation within a limited area. Neither such an attack, nor even the destruction of one city, would be a catastrophe on the scale of nuclear war. But it would still be a terrifying tragedy.*

The Road to Damascus

Endlessly determined and necessarily optimistic people continued to seek a solution. George Shultz and Henry Kissinger, both former Republican Secretaries of State, Senator Sam Nunn, Bill Perry, Clinton's former Defense Secretary, and Sidney Drell, a theoretical physicist, had all been at the heart of American nuclear policymaking. In their time they believed that deterrence and the multiplication of nuclear weapons were a necessary and patriotic response to the dangers their country faced. But when the Cold War ended, they warned that tremendous risks and dangers remained. The number of

---

*William Perry, US Defense Secretary under President Clinton, speculated that a fifteen-kiloton terrorist bomb in Washington could kill 80,000 people outright, wiping out the President, Congress, and the administration (W. Perry, *My Journey at the Nuclear Brink*, Stanford, 2015, p. xiii).

nuclear powers was increasing. Nuclear weapons could fall into the hands of terrorists. They wondered if the world would be as fortunate in the next fifty years as it had been during the Cold War. They launched a Nuclear Security Project, which proposed concrete steps to reduce the threat.[33]

It was not quite a conversion on the road to Damascus. The five men still insisted that nuclear deterrence had preserved the peace. Their remedies were not very original: the number of existing weapons should be slashed; stocks of uranium worldwide should be secured; the production of weapons-grade material should be stopped; dangerous international conflicts should be brought under control.

By 2015 George Shultz had abandoned the idea that nuclear weapons could keep the peace: he now believed that they 'were, and are, the gravest threat to humanity's survival. Their effect in preventing wars has been overrated and reports of the damage they cause tend to be brushed aside.' He compared his crusade to climbing an arduous mountain. At the bottom was a slew of nuclear weapons and nuclear-armed states, and a high probability that a weapon would eventually be detonated with unimaginable consequences. At the mountain's peak was a world free of nuclear weapons.[34]

People blamed the politicians for failing to muster the will to take decisive action. But you cannot generate political will in the abstract: it is the reflection of a wider will among ordinary people. And most ordinary people in most nuclear weapons states still agreed that if the other guy had the bomb, you had to have it too.

In the State of the Union speech he delivered in January 1992, just after the Soviet Union had ceased to exist, President George H. W. Bush said, 'By the grace of God, America won the cold war … A world once divided into two armed camps now recognizes one sole and preeminent power, the United States of America. And they regard this with no dread. For the world trusts us with power, and the world is right. They trust us to be fair and restrained. They trust us to be on the side of decency. They trust us to do what's right.'

Twenty-five years later that certainty had been dissipated, and the age of American pre-eminence seemed to be over. Leaders in Russia, China, and India, and radicals across the Muslim world were no longer willing to accept American tutelage. They substituted their own ideas for the Western liberal values that had seemed triumphant in the last decade of the twentieth century. At the end of 2016 Britain voted to leave the European Union, and the European dream of civilised unity was under increasing attack from within. As the year ended America elected a new and untried President in the shape of Donald Trump. The future became as unpredictable as it has ever been.

But the nuclear weapons remained. No one listened to the sensible and experienced people like George Shultz and Joseph Rotblat who tried to move things forward by reasoned criticism, patient education, and persuasion. The optimists among them had to comfort themselves with the thought that with enough hard work reason would prevail: 'Things that have never happened before happen often.'[35]

RUSSIAN ROULETTE

'God is alive and well and working on a less ambitious project.'

Graffito in men's lavatory, London School of Economics[1]

Why Didn't It End with a Bang?

Murphy's law states that if something can go wrong, it will.

And yet, despite the hair-trigger fragility of the nuclear confrontation, the ultimate catastrophe did not occur. People suggested several reasons.

The first was that 'the long peace' after 1945, when there was no war between the two superpowers, was maintained by the universal fear of nuclear weapons, by deterrence, by what Churchill called 'the sturdy child of terror'.

Another theory was that the long peace was a product not of nuclear terror but of a general determination that the conventional horrors of the Second World War should not be repeated.

A third view was even more optimistic: that what Abraham Lincoln had called 'the better angels of our nature' were now generating a progressive and, in the long run, irreversible decline in human violence.

A fourth was that we were all just very lucky.

For much of the world, of course, there was no long peace. Violent wars, hugely destructive of human life and property, continued after 1945 in China, South-East Asia, Afghanistan, and across large swathes of the Middle East and Africa. The two superpowers were directly or indirectly involved in many of them.

The Burden of Responsibility

How did the world get itself into such a long-running mess? Who was to blame? Was it the scientists? The soldiers and the officials? The politicians?

It was easy enough to blame the scientists. President Eisenhower said in his Inaugural Address: 'Science seems ready to confer upon us, as its final gift, the power to erase human life from this planet.'[2]

That was not quite fair. Scientists such as Leo Szilard spent much of their lives warning passionately against nuclear weapons and their use. The Nobel Prize winner James Franck argued against dropping the bomb on a Japanese city. Isidor Rabi and Enrico Fermi called the hydrogen bomb 'an evil thing considered in any light'. In 1995 Hans Bethe appealed to 'all scientists in all countries to cease and desist from work creating, developing, improving, manufacturing further nuclear weapons', though few responded to his call.[3]

And yet, when war loomed, most scientists swallowed their scruples and joined their countries' weapons projects, moved by a sense of patriotic duty. Fermi and Bethe both returned to Los Alamos as the Cold War got under way. Only Lise Meitner, who had confirmed Hahn's discovery of the nuclear chain reaction, refused to join the Manhattan Project, saying, 'I will have nothing to do with a bomb!' She remained a pacifist to the end of her life. She is buried in Hampshire in England. Her gravestone reads: 'Lise Meitner: a physicist who never lost her humanity'.*

Soviet scientists had much the same scruples as their American colleagues, though they felt that for them the moral issue was less stark. It was not they who had opened Pandora's box; nor was it their country that had used the weapon in war. Some felt that Truman was guilty of a major war crime. Others accepted that his responsibility for the lives of America's fighting men left him no option. Either way the greater part of the moral burden fell on the Americans.[4]

---

* Meitner never got the Nobel Prize for her work on nuclear fission, though her colleague Otto Hahn got it in 1945. Some believed that this was a further manifestation of the prejudice against women scientists which had hampered her career, as it had hampered that of Marie Curie (R. Sime, *Lise Meitner*, Berkeley/ Los Angeles, 1996, pp. 305–6). There has been only one other Nobel Prize-winning woman in physics – Maria Goeppert-Mayer – in 1963.

But for the most part the Soviet scientists too were haunted. Evgeny Zavoisky, who worked at Arzamas-16 in the early years, was flummoxed when his daughter eventually asked him, 'How could you do it?' He could only reply, 'I've been waiting the whole of my life for you to ask that question. All I can say is that I fell right into the soup.' We do not know if his daughter was satisfied with this unilluminating response.[5]

Yuli Khariton, Oppenheimer's nearest opposite number in the Soviet nuclear project, born in the same year, briefly a contemporary at Cambridge, sent a message to the ceremony held to honour Oppenheimer's memory at Los Alamos in 1995. 'I too was involved in the remarkable scientific and engineering achievements which enabled humanity to master a practically inexhaustible source of energy,' he wrote. 'But I am no longer certain that humanity has matured enough to manage that energy. We have contributed to the terrible death of people, and done monstrous damage to Nature, to our home the Earth. Words of regret will change nothing. May God grant that those who follow us find the way, the strength of spirit and determination in themselves, to do nothing bad as they strive towards the good.'[6]

The military were inhibited by their profession from expressing doubt. British, American, and Russian officers all insisted that they were trained to go to nuclear war, and would have done so without hesitation if ordered. General Mikhail Milshtein told Solly Zuckerman, '[N]uclear weapons ... are not an instrument for waging war in any rational sense ... But if we are forced to use them, in reply to their first use by an aggressor, we shall use them, with all their consequences.' Field Marshal Montgomery was brutally clear: 'They will be used, if we are attacked.'[7]

A steady trickle of military men nevertheless made their worries known once they had retired. General Omar Bradley, an American wartime hero, said on Armistice Day 1948, 'We live in an age of nuclear giants and ethical infants, in a world that has achieved brilliance without wisdom, power without conscience.'[8] General George Lee Butler, the last commander of the Strategic Air Command, was a devout Christian. He became a leading figure in the nuclear disarmament movement when he retired in 1994. More than twenty years later he published a lengthy memoir, a blistering attack on the way in which the US military had mismanaged the deterrent and bamboozled their political masters.[9] He came to consider the Single Integrated Operational Plan, the SIOP, the most 'absurd and irresponsible document I had ever reviewed in my life'.* He was much criticised by his former colleagues and his influence did not long survive in his old profession.

General LeMay would have turned in his grave.

In the end it was the politicians who had to make the final judgements. Denis Healey, the most formidable post-war British Defence Minister, was firmly of the opinion that 'This is not, after all, to do with technology; this is to do with how likely you think a certain contingency, how you think the other side will react to their knowledge that you have certain capabilities. That's what it's all about. It's nothing whatsoever to do with scientists or, with respect, with generals.'[10]

Whatever their nationality, the politicians were trapped in a web of inexorable logic. The nuclear weapon could not be uninvented. If their opponent had it, or was getting it, they too had to have it if they were not to fail in their patriotic duty. And they had to devise effective ways of using it if they were not to be seen as toothless. They made mistakes, and sometimes they were swept away by emotion and said and did foolish or aggressive things.

But they had little doubt that nuclear war made no sense. They were not cynical, stupid, or ignorant. When Khrushchev became First Party Secretary and was briefed about the nuclear weapon, he was unable to sleep for days. Reagan wondered in public how much sense there was in mutual threats to kill tens of millions of your

---

* Butler said that the Soviet target plan was even more irrational than SIOP, though it is unlikely that he ever saw it. In 1993 the Strategic Air Command was replaced by US Strategic Command. This was intended to bring the naval and the air force elements in the US deterrent under a single command and targeting authority. SIOP was replaced by plans which were allegedly designed for more flexible use against rogue states.

opponent's people. British Prime Ministers sometimes hinted that they would have difficulty in pressing the button.[11]

Every leader of a nuclear power recognised that he had to convince his opponent that he would go up to the brink and beyond. But none could be sure how the other side would behave when faced by the ultimate crisis. Deterrence worked not because your enemy was certain that you would press the button, but because he could never be certain that you would not. And he could not afford to guess wrong.

McGeorge Bundy, Kennedy's National Security Advisor, made the point with persuasive force: 'There is an enormous gulf between what political leaders really think about nuclear weapons and what is assumed in complicated calculations ... [by] Think Tank analysts ... In the real world of real political leaders – whether here or in the Soviet Union – a decision that would bring even one hydrogen bomb on one city of one's own country would be recognised in advance as a catastrophic blunder.'[12]

The stakes were very high, but for the most part the politicians did what they could to ensure that the risks were very low. They had little choice but to believe or hope that the gamble would somehow pay off.

What Would God Have Thought About It?

Colin Gray, a hawkish adviser to the Reagan administration, believed that nuclear wars were there to be won. He once remarked, 'As a general rule, strategists do not spend their days debating moral issues.'[13] And for many officials working on the British deterrent, morality was indeed not an issue. 'Effective deterrence thinking was what was morally required from us as British civil servants,' one remarked.[14]

But for some people the prospect of all-out nuclear war was so dreadful that they turned to the language of religion. Time and again politicians, officers, and scientists in Russia as well as the West quoted the Book of Revelation and spoke as if apocalypse had been averted only by divine intervention. As he descended into old age, Winston Churchill increasingly seemed to fear that mankind had been abandoned by God.[15]

Some devout Christians comforted themselves with the thought that a nuclear cataclysm might herald the second coming of Christ. It was a view held not only by eccentrics, but by people in the American military and by President George W. Bush. Ronald Reagan used to chat with his closest friends about 'Armageddon theology', the idea that a final confrontation was inevitable.[16] 'I swear I believe Armageddon is near,' he wrote in his diary in 1981.

Others saw a diabolical hand at work.[17] Robert Oppenheimer said, 'The physicists have known sin; and this is a knowledge which they cannot lose.' Vladimir Shapiro, a scientist in the Kurchatov Institute in Moscow, concluded harshly that those who had worked on the bomb, men he personally admired, had all to some extent sold their souls to the Devil.

Some of those involved in the business of preparing for nuclear war nevertheless did attempt to construct an orderly ethic.

One was Michael Quinlan, a leading British official on matters of nuclear deterrence, a man of intellectual force, courteous but ruthless in argument. Profoundly religious, educated by Jesuits, he devoted much effort to combating the views of his own Catholic hierarchy, whose moral concerns about nuclear warfare he regarded as muddle-headed and dangerous.*

Quinlan had an understated but philosophical, moral, patriotic, and visceral dislike of Soviet Communism. To those who spoke of nuclear war as a 'unique moral horror', he responded that the same might be said of 'global conquest by an atheistic totalitarianism possessed of super-power force and modern technology of repression'. 'In extremis', according to his editor, he argued that 'it would be a *moral obligation* for the West to launch a nuclear attack on the Soviet Union in order to maintain international peace and stability' (emphasis in the original).[18]

Thus, at the limit, death was better than submission to an intolerable evil. But, Quinlan argued, that was a false choice. There was a

---

* Michael Quinlan was much loved and admired by all who knew him. His memorial service in Westminster Cathedral was conducted by the Cardinal Archbishop and attended by a galaxy of senior public figures, colleagues, and friends.

third way between being dead or being Red, and it was called deterrence. For that to work, it must not be a bluff. We had to perfect our weapons, train and motivate our fighting men to use them, and make it clear beyond doubt that we would indeed make an enemy pay the price of his aggression.

A moral justification for all this could be found, Quinlan thought, in the 'Just War' theory of St Thomas Aquinas and others. This proposed two main principles.

The first was that – as a last resort, and if there was a reasonable prospect of victory – a properly constituted government (but not a dictatorship like Hitler's or Stalin's) might rightly go to war to attain a just end.

The second was that, once war had begun, the combatants must be 'proportionate' in their use of violence. Put crudely, that meant they might kill civilians as a by-product of military action, provided they did not deliberately target them.

Alas, these principles gave no clear guide to action. They left the combatants to decide for themselves whether their cause was just and their actions proportionate. The fine distinctions of moral philosophy had a habit of fading once war was engaged. As the British and American bombing campaigns against Germany and Japan mounted to a climax, 'proportionate' became whatever secured victory.

And the Just War theory did not meet the test of universality. When Catholic theologians first elaborated it, they assumed that God would judge whose cause was just. Later theorists suggested that a royal sovereign ruling by divine right could judge in God's place. But once we abandoned the idea of divine right, we all became judges in our own case. The British Chiefs of Staff believed that their country had an inalienable right to develop its own bomb.[19] Unfortunately Russians, Frenchmen, Chinese, Indians, Pakistanis, Israelis, Iranians, and North Koreans all felt the same. They too believed that it was their patriotic, indeed their moral, duty to arm themselves in their own defence.*

---

* This lack of universality was criticised by Arthur Hockaday, Quinlan's equally devout colleague in the Ministry of Defence (T. Ogilvie-White (ed.), *On Nuclear Deterrence*, London, 2011, p. 181).

The counterargument was well put by a British soldier. Lt General Sir John Cowley asked, 'Is it right for a government of a country to choose complete destruction of the population rather than some other alternative, however unpleasant ... that may be? Should we in any circumstances be morally right to choose not only the termination of our own existence as a nation, but also the existence of future generations of our own countrymen and even of the whole civilised world? ... The human race can recover from almost anything but it cannot recover from universal death.'[20]

An individual, and perhaps a community – the Jews besieged by the Roman army at Masada, for example – were entitled to prefer suicide to surrender. But no one had the right to take that decision on behalf of the millions of people who would be killed in a strategic nuclear exchange.

And indeed, while there was life there was hope. Unpleasant regimes eventually passed because people got sick of them. Godless Communism was eventually seen off without a war, rejected by the mass of ordinary people, including ordinary Russians, disappointed or angered by its failures and crimes. But that could not happen if there were no people left.*

In later years Quinlan himself had moments of doubt. He once remarked to a correspondent that 'it would unquestionably be directly awkward for me to find myself driven to a conviction that having these weapons was ethically intolerable.' After the Soviet collapse he no longer found the arguments for a British deterrent quite so absolute. He had perhaps, he once remarked ruefully, been stuck in 'obvious adversary patterns of thinking'.

In the end Quinlan's solution was the same as that of so many other optimists: 'We have to aim ... at a world in which major states recognise that they simply must not go to war.'[21] But neither he nor anyone else managed to suggest how this admirable objective should be achieved. In brutal practice, governments would continue to go ahead with the meticulous planning of the unthinkable and the unimaginable.

---

*Whether the system that continued in China after the Soviet collapse could meaningfully be called 'Communism' is a matter of debate.

Perhaps Curtis LeMay was right when he remarked sarcastically, 'Anyone who seeks an absolute end to the possibility of war might as well resign from the human race.'[22]

Stop Worrying and Love the Bomb: The Cheerful Alternative?

Serious people tried to put a figure on the probability of disaster. The British science writer C. P. Snow, speaking in 1961 'as responsibly as I can', thought it certain that 'within, at the most, ten years, some of those bombs are going off'. The irrepressible Leo Szilard made similar predictions from time to time. The American scholar Graham Allison wrote in 2004 that 'on the current path a nuclear terrorist attack on America in the next decade is more likely than not.'[23] The United States Senate Foreign Relations Committee echoed him with unconvincing precision: there was a 29 per cent probability, they said, of a nuclear strike occurring within the next ten years.[24] The Federation of American Scientists continued to keep close track of the spread and number of nuclear weapons. The Doomsday Clock moved half a minute closer to midnight on the arrival of President Trump.

One particularly gloomy expert argued, '[W]e might argue whether the probability of nuclear war per year was high or low. But it would make no real difference. If the probability is 10 percent per year, then we expect the holocaust to come in about 10 years. If it is 1 percent per year, then we expect it in about 100 years. The lower probability per year changes the time frame until we expect civilization to be destroyed, but it does not change the inevitability of the ruin. In either scenario, nuclear war is 100 percent certain to occur.'[25]

The problem with all such estimates was that none of these things had happened since Hiroshima. There was insufficient evidence to calculate a plausible figure. Accidents were as inherent in the nuclear enterprise as in all others. Even the optimists did not argue that the risk that a bomb would eventually go off was zero. One American expert called it a game of Russian roulette.

There were those who nevertheless believed that the whole thing was overblown. Nuclear war would be bad, of course, but it would not be *that* bad. Society would survive: 'The ants eventually build another ant hill.'[26]

Steven Pinker, an American scholar who believed in the better angels of our being, offered an even more optimistic vision. Mankind was undergoing a secular change – perhaps even a genetic change – away from savagery; organised violence between and within states was clearly declining. Pinker backed this thesis with a mind-numbing array of apparently scientific evidence which the sceptical layman was ill placed to judge. His ideas attracted many people because they seemed to offer the hope of eventual release from the nightly slaughter on television.

John Mueller, an American political scientist, cheerfully asserted that 'if all the people who could start one hold major war to be undesirable, and if in addition they remain rational and in control, no major war will take place' – a daring assertion of belief in the power of human rationality and the improbability of accident.* Policymakers and protesters alike should stop worrying, he said, and sleep well at night.[27]

There was not much policymakers could usefully draw from such ideas. They believed, feared, spoke, and acted as if the nuclear weapon did indeed present an existential threat. Whatever the optimists said, that was not a thought to encourage sleep.

The raw material for new confrontations continued to accumulate. Those who had the bomb showed no sign of giving it up. Those who wanted to abolish it had no effective influence on their governments or their people. The likelihood that the nations would agree to effective and all-embracing international control, let alone 'world government', remained vanishingly small.

Humanity had got itself into a fix from which it seemed incapable of extricating itself. People would have to go on living on the volcano, relying as best they could on luck, helped perhaps by some good management. The sword of Damocles remained suspended, though by a stouter thread.

---

*Mueller added that the deterrent was not even good at its job. It had not stopped Stalin causing trouble in Berlin, North Korea invading the South, Egypt invading Israel, or Argentina from invading the Falklands.

TIMELINE

Scientists marked * are Nobel Prize winners

1898	The Polish scientist Marie Skłodowska* (1867–1934) and her French husband, Pierre Curie* (1859–1906), discover radium. H. G. Wells (1866–1946) publishes his prophetic and influential novel *The War of the Worlds*.
1905	The German scientist Albert Einstein* (1879–1955) proposes his theory of special relativity, which he elaborates ten years later into his general theory.
1913–28	The Danish scientist Niels Bohr* (1885–1962) writes his first papers on quantum theory. His ideas are elaborated by the German Werner Heisenberg* (1901–76), the Austrian Erwin Schrödinger* (1887–1961), and the Englishman Paul Dirac* (1902–84). Together with Einstein's propositions, these efforts would provide the essential theoretical backbone for the later understanding of nuclear technology.
1919	The New Zealander Ernest Rutherford* (1871–1937) becomes head of the Cavendish Laboratory in Cambridge. Several scientists later involved on their national bomb projects work or study there, including the British James Chadwick* (1891–1974), John Cockcroft* (1897–1967), and Patrick (P. M. S.) Blackett* (1897–1974), the American Robert Oppenheimer (1904–67), and the Russians Piotr Kapitsa* (1894–1984) and Yuli Khariton (1904–96).
1931	Ernest Lawrence* (1901–58) of Berkeley University, California, invents the cyclotron particle accelerator, a basic tool for exploring the atom.
1932	The *annus mirabilis* for the Cavendish Laboratory. Chadwick discovers the neutron, Cockcroft and Ernest Walton* (1903–95) split the lithium nucleus, and Blackett demonstrates the existence of the positron.
1936	As Stalin's terror gets under way, eleven members of the Ukrainian Institute of Physics and Technology are arrested. Five are shot.

December 1938	Otto Hahn* (1879–1968) and Fritz Strassmann (1902–80) of the Kaiser Wilhelm Institute for Chemistry in Berlin split uranium nuclei by bombarding it with neutrons. Within weeks two Austrian physicists in exile from Hitler's anti-Semitic laws, Lise Meitner (1878–1968) and her nephew Otto Frisch (1904–79) provide a theoretical explanation of Hahn's findings and find a name for the phenomenon – fission.
1939	Lev Landau* (1908–68), the Soviet Union's most brilliant and rebellious physicist, is imprisoned for a year but survives.
	Einstein warns US President Roosevelt (1882–1945) about the danger that the Germans might develop an atom bomb.
March 1940	Rudolf Peierls (1907–95) and Frisch suggest a practical way of developing an atomic bomb to the British government.
October 1940	Two Soviet researchers, Viktor Maslov and Vladimir Shpinel, propose the elements of an atom bomb, on lines similar to those set out by Frisch and Peierls.
22 June 1941	The Germans invade the Soviet Union.
30 August 1941	Winston Churchill (1874–1965) authorises work on a British bomb.
September 1941	The Russians acquire the first secret intelligence on the British project from their agents Klaus Fuchs (1911–88), a refugee German scientist, and John Cairncross (1913–95), a senior civil servant.
	Heisenberg visits Bohr in German-occupied Copenhagen, perhaps to gather ideas for a German nuclear project. He learns nothing. Four years later the Russians send their own man to Bohr, with equally little effect.
October 1941	Roosevelt proposes to Churchill that their two countries cooperate on the bomb. Churchill's response is dilatory and lukewarm.
7 December 1941	The Japanese attack Pearl Harbor.
December 1941	The Russian scientist Georgi Flerov (1913–90) sets out his proposal for an experimental bomb. This too is similar to the Peierls–Frisch proposal, though Flerov has not seen the intelligence.

June 1942	Churchill and Roosevelt meet in Washington and discuss cooperation face to face for the first time. By the end of the year collaboration had faltered and nearly died. It is resumed, with the British clearly in a junior role, when the two men meet in August and September 1943.
September 1942	General Leslie Groves (1896–1970) is appointed to direct the Manhattan Project tasked with producing an atom bomb for use in the war. Oppenheimer heads the scientific side of the project at Los Alamos.
December 1942	The Italian scientist Enrico Fermi* (1901–54) and his team build an 'atomic pile' (nuclear reactor) in Chicago to generate a sustained nuclear chain reaction: a major step towards a bomb.
February 1943	Joseph Stalin (1878–1953) appoints Igor Kurchatov (1903–60) to manage a Soviet bomb project, but gives priority to defeating the Germans.
12 April 1945	Roosevelt dies and is succeeded by his Vice President, Harry Truman (1884–1972).
9 May 1945	Germany surrenders.
16 July 1945	The Americans successfully test a nuclear device (the Trinity Test) at Alamogordo in the New Mexican desert.
	Truman hints as much to Stalin at their meeting in Potsdam.
6 August 1945	The *Enola Gay* drops a uranium bomb, 'Little Boy', on Hiroshima.
9 August 1945	The plutonium bomb 'Fat Man' is dropped on Nagasaki. Soviet forces attack the Japanese in Manchuria.
14 August 1945	Japan surrenders.
20 August 1945	Stalin orders the Soviet bomb project to be given the greatest priority. Lavrenti Beria (1899–1953), the head of the secret police, is put in charge.
April 1946	Khariton is appointed to run Design Bureau No. II, the Soviet weapons laboratory in Sarov (Arzamas-16) on the Volga, the equivalent of Los Alamos.
June 1946	The Americans propose a United Nations scheme for the international control of nuclear power and weapons (the Baruch Plan). The Russians propose a counter-scheme. Neither is accepted.

December 1946	Kurchatov's experimental nuclear reactor, the first in Europe, goes critical in Moscow.
1947	Prime Minister Clement Attlee (1883–1967) decides to resume work on an independent British nuclear weapon project.
1948–9	The Anglo-American airlift breaks Stalin's blockade of Berlin.
29 August 1949	The Russians successfully test an atomic device, to American dismay.
1 October 1949	The People's Republic of China is proclaimed in Peking.
February 1950	Klaus Fuchs, a German scientist who has worked on the Manhattan Project, is arrested and later convicted in London as a Soviet spy.
June 1950	The Korean War begins when the North attacks the South. It lasts for three years.
October 1952	Britain tests its first atomic bomb.
November 1952	The Americans test their first experimental hydrogen bomb.
January 1953	Dwight Eisenhower (1890–1969) succeeds Truman as US President.
5 March 1953	Stalin dies. In the course of the subsequent power struggle Beria is shot in December, and by the following spring Nikita Khrushchev (1894–1971) has become Soviet leader.
June 1953	Julius and Ethel Rosenberg (1917–53 and 1916–53) are executed in America as Soviet spies.
August 1953	The Russians test a thermonuclear device. The team responsible includes three future Nobel Prize winners: Igor Tamm* (1895–1971), Vitali Ginzburg* (1916–2009), and Andrei Sakharov* (1921–89).
December 1953	Eisenhower proposes 'Atoms for Peace' to the United Nations.
March 1954	The Americans test their first hydrogen bombs.
April 1954	Kurchatov and Vyacheslav Malyshev (1902–57), Beria's replacement, warn Khrushchev that atomic weapons pose 'a huge threat which could obliterate all life on Earth'.
May 1954	Oppenheimer is stripped of his security clearance because of earlier associations with American Communists.

1955	The B-52 Stratofortress intercontinental bomber, the star of the film *Dr Strangelove,* enters service in the US Air Force. It is still there sixty years later.
November 1955	The Soviets test their first multimegaton hydrogen bomb
Autumn 1956	The British and French invade Egypt (the Suez Crisis). The Russians suppress an uprising in Hungary.
4 October 1957	The Russians launch the first artificial satellite, the Sputnik.
November 1957	The UK tests its first successful thermonuclear weapon.
1960	France tests its first nuclear fission device.
	The Americans launch the first of forty-one nuclear-powered submarines armed with Polaris nuclear missiles.
January 1961	John Kennedy (1917–63) succeeds Eisenhower as US President.
12 April 1961	Yuri Gagarin (1934–68), a Soviet airman, becomes the first man to journey into space.
14 August 1961	The East Germans erect a dividing wall in Berlin, which provokes a face-off between American and Soviet tanks in the city. The Wall remains; but Western military contingents stay in the city.
October 1962	Khrushchev's attempt to install Soviet missiles on Cuba is frustrated by Kennedy's determined show of force. It is the closest the world has come to nuclear war.
December 1962	Prime Minister Harold Macmillan (1894–1986) persuades Kennedy to provide American Polaris missiles for British-built nuclear submarines to replace Britain's obsolescent nuclear V-bombers. This effectively ends British pretensions to have a genuinely independent nuclear deterrent.
5 August 1963	Test Ban Treaty is signed in Moscow by Britain, the Soviet Union, and the United States.
22 November 1963	Kennedy is assassinated. He is succeeded by his Vice President, Lyndon Johnson (1908–73).
14 October 1964	Khrushchev is replaced in a coup by Leonid Brezhnev (1906–82).
16 October 1964	The Chinese explode their first nuclear fission device.
17 June 1967	The Chinese test their first thermonuclear device.
1 July 1968	Non-Proliferation Treaty (NPT) is signed by Britain, the Soviet Union, and the United States. In due course a

	substantial number of non-weapons states also sign. France and China do not do so until 1992.
24 August 1968	The French test their first thermonuclear device.
January 1969	Richard Nixon (1913–94) succeeds Johnson as US President.
December 1971	France's first ballistic submarine, *Le Redoubtable*, enters service.
3 June 1972	The four wartime allies (Britain, France, the United States, and the Soviet Union) agree a settlement on Berlin. Following Strategic Arms Limitation Talks (SALT I), Nixon and Brezhnev sign an Interim Agreement on limiting strategic offensive arms, and an Anti-Ballistic Missile (ABM) Treaty.
Autumn 1973	Nixon puts American strategic forces on heightened alert to deter the Russians from interfering in the Yom Kippur War between Israel and Egypt.
April 1974	Nixon is forced to resign and is succeeded by his Vice President, Gerald Ford (1913–2006).
18 May 1974	India carries out its first nuclear weapon test.
30 April 1975	Saigon falls to the North Vietnamese, ending twenty years of US military involvement in Vietnam.
1 August 1975	The countries of Europe, the Soviet Union, Canada, and the United States agree on the Helsinki Accords, which impose a moral (but not a legal) obligation not to use force to settle disputes, and to accord human rights to their citizens.
January 1977	Jimmy Carter (1924–) succeeds Ford as US President.
March 1979	Accident at Three Mile Island.
May 1979	Margaret Thatcher (1925–2013) becomes British Prime Minister.
18 June 1979	Brezhnev and Carter sign an agreement in a second round of Strategic Arms Limitation Talks (SALT II). Because of domestic opposition in the United States, neither side ratifies the treaty, but both say that they will abide by its provisions.
December 1979	The Soviet Union invades Afghanistan. Andrei Sakharov, formerly a leading scientist on the Soviet weapon project, publicly opposes the invasion and is exiled to the city of Gorki on the Volga.

1980	Carter agrees with Thatcher to supply Trident missiles for British nuclear submarines.
1981	Ronald Reagan (1911–2004) succeeds Carter as US President. He calls the Soviet Union an 'evil empire' and launches a series of secret psychological operations to unsettle the Russians. The 'Second Cold War' begins.
1 September 1983	The Russians shoot down a Korean airliner, KAL 007.
November 1983	NATO Exercise Able Archer leads the Russians to put some of their nuclear forces on alert. Some later speculate that this risked nuclear war.
March 1985	Mikhail Gorbachev (1931–) becomes Soviet leader.
April 1986	Accident at Chernobyl.
8 December 1987	Intermediate-Range Nuclear Forces (INF) Treaty, signed in Moscow by Gorbachev and Reagan, eliminates Soviet and American short- and medium-range missiles.
January 1989	George H. W. Bush (1924–) succeeds Reagan.
March 1989	The Soviet Union holds the first partially democratic elections in a Communist country since 1948.
9 November 1989	The Wall is torn down by the citizens of Berlin.
12 September 1990	The Soviet Union, the United States, Britain, and France sign the Treaty on the Final Settlement with Respect to Germany. Germany is reunited on 3 October.
31 July 1991	Following Strategic Arms Reduction Talks (START I), Gorbachev and Bush agree to reduce their countries' stocks of nuclear weapons.
August 1991	An unsuccessful coup in Moscow by military, party, and KGB leaders opens the way for Boris Yeltsin (1931–2007) to take over from Gorbachev.
25 December 1991	Yeltsin dissolves the Soviet Union, which disintegrates into its constituent republics. The Cold War ends.
3 January 1993	Outgoing President Bush and Yeltsin sign START II, which fails to come into effect when the Russians protest against American withdrawal from the ABM Treaty.
20 January 1993	Bill Clinton (1946–) becomes US President.
5 December 1994	Budapest Memorandum on Security Assurances: Ukraine, Kazakhstan, and Belarus agree to give up nuclear weapons inherited from the Soviet Union, in exchange for security guarantees from Britain, the United States, and Russia.

10 September 1996	The UN General Assembly adopts the Comprehensive Test Ban Treaty (CTBT), which prohibits all nuclear explosions. A number of countries, including the United States, sign but do not ratify it.
May 1998	Pakistan, which probably has usable but untested nuclear weapons, carries out its first tests in response to a round of tests by India.
1999	NATO bombs Serbia to protect the people of Kosovo from Serbian oppression. Kosovo declares independence. The Russians protest that this is illegal. NATO begins to enlarge its membership to the east.
	The 'Kargil War' between India and Pakistan erupts over Kashmir; both countries by then have usable nuclear weapons. There is further fighting in 2001–2 and 2008.
2000	Vladimir Putin (1952–) succeeds Yeltsin as President of Russia.
2001	George W. Bush (1946–) succeeds Clinton as US President.
11 September 2001	Terrorists destroy the Twin Towers in New York and damage the Pentagon in Washington. A month later the Americans invade Afghanistan, from where the attack was planned.
24 May 2002	The Strategic Offensive Reductions Treaty (SORT), signed by Putin and Bush in Moscow, envisages a substantial reduction of nuclear warheads.
March 2003	The Americans invade Iraq. A stunning initial victory is followed by years of civil war and terrorist violence.
9 October 2006	The North Koreans conduct their first underground nuclear test.
8 May 2008	Dmitri Medvedev (1965–) succeeds Putin as President.
August 2008	Russia wins a short war against Georgia, which shows up the weakness of its armed forces. It embarks on a major programme of defence modernisation expected to cost some $700 billion by 2020.
2009	Barack Obama (1961–) succeeds Bush as President.
5 April 2009	Obama calls in Prague for a nuclear-free world.
April 2010	Obama and Medvedev sign a New START Treaty, further reducing their nuclear weapons.
February 2011	The Obama administration includes in its budget proposals for 2012 a plan to modernise US nuclear forces, to start

	in 2020. It is expected to cost about $1 trillion over thirty years.
7 May 2012	Putin resumes the Russian presidency.
March 2014	Russia annexes the Ukrainian province of Crimea and supports rebels in eastern Ukraine against the government in Kiev. The EU and the United States impose sanctions on Russia. NATO eventually sends token reinforcements to Poland and the Baltic States.
September 2015	Russia begins providing military support to the Syrian regime in its war against domestic rebels.
14 July 2015	Iran, the five Permanent Members of the UN Security Council, Germany, and the EU reach a deal on Iran's nuclear programme.
19 July 2016	The British Parliament votes to renew Britain's submarine deterrent armed with American Trident missiles.
2017	Donald Trump (1946–) succeeds Obama as President. The *Bulletin of the Atomic Scientists* moves its Doomsday Clock half a minute closer to midnight.

NOTES

Prologue: The Sword of Damocles
1. President Kennedy, speech to the UN General Assembly on 25 September 1961.
2. F. Iklé, 'Can Nuclear Deterrence Last out the Century?', *Foreign Affairs*, Vol. 51, No. 2, January 1973.
3. Joint declaration by presidents Yeltsin and Clinton, 14 January 1994.

Chapter 1: The Destruction of Japan
1. Max Hastings, 'Human Smoke by Nicholson Baker' (review), *Sunday Times*, 4 May 2008.
2. The novels included Pierton Dooner's *Last Days of the Republic*, San Francisco, 1880, and Homer Lea's *The Valor of Ignorance*, New York, 1909. The latter was studied by Douglas MacArthur, the future victor in the Pacific. See also J. Tchen and D. Yeats, *Yellow Peril! An Archive of Anti-Asian Fear*, London, 2014, pp. 12, 91, 117, 246; J. Dower, *War without Mercy: Race and Power in the Pacific War*, New York, 1986, p. 95.
3. M. Macmillan, *Peacemakers: Six Months that Changed the World*, London, 2002, p. 327.
4. Dower, *War without Mercy*, p. 100.
5. J. Chappell, *Before the Bomb: How America Approached the End of the Pacific War*, Lexington, 1996, p. 30.
6. Examples in the previous two paragraphs are taken from Dower, *War without Mercy*, pp. 53, 55, 49, 71, 84.
7. Figures from Roper Center Data Services at Cornell University, which holds the Gallup Poll archives.

8. W. Hopkins, *The Pacific War: The Strategy, Politics, and Players that Won the War*, Minneapolis, 2010, p. 23.

9. E. May, 'The U.S., the S.U., and the Far Eastern War, 1941–45', *Pacific Historical Review*, Vol. 24, No. 2, May 1955, pp. 153–74.

10. A. Werth, *Russia at War 1941–1945*, London, 1964, p. 1041.

11. May, 'The U.S., the S.U., and the Far Eastern War, 1941–45'.

12. D. Holloway, *Stalin and the Bomb*, New Haven, 1994, p. 123.

13. W. Kozak, *LeMay: The Life and Wars of General Curtis LeMay*, New York, 2012, pp. 96–7.

14. M. Hastings, *Nemesis: The Battle for Japan, 1944–5*, London, 2008, p. 320.

15. The most common estimate of Japanese casualties from the raids is 333,000 killed and 473,000 wounded. There are other estimates, which range from 241,000 to 900,000. The Americans lost 414 aircraft and over 2,600 airmen (http://en.wikipedia.org/wiki/Air_Raids_on_Japan, accessed 5 March 2017); M. Gowing, *Britain and Atomic Energy 1939–45*, London, 1964, pp. 138–9, 158–63; G. Farmelo, *Churchill's Bomb*, London, 2013, p. 234.

16. P. Ham, *Hiroshima Nagasaki*, London, 2013, p. 158.

17. A facsimile of Churchill's note on this agreement is at http://www.atomicheritage.org/key-documents/hyde-park-aide-mémoire (accessed 5 March 2017).

18. G. Herken, *Brotherhood of the Bomb: The Tangled Lives and Loyalties of Robert Oppenheimer, Ernest Lawrence, and Edward Teller*, New York, 2002, pp. 131, 133.

19. Ham, *Hiroshima Nagasaki*, p. 222.

20. M. Bundy, *Danger and Survival: Choices about the Bomb in the First Fifty Years*, New York, 1988, p. 87.

21. Ham, *Hiroshima Nagasaki*, p. 229.

22. The figure of 1.7–4 million American casualties, including 400,000–800,000 fatalities, and five to ten million Japanese fatalities is based on the assumption that large numbers of Japanese civilians would participate in the defence comes in a study prepared for Stimson by his staff. (https://en.wikipedia.org/wiki/Operation_Downfall#Estimated_casualties).

23. Quoted in M. Hogan (ed.), *Hiroshima in History and Memory*, Cambridge, 1996, p. 73.

24. Truman papers at http://www.trumanlibrary.org/publicpapers/.

25. Ham, *Hiroshima Nagasaki*, p. 513.

26. Operational order for the mission at https://timedotcom.files.wordpress.com/2015/07/nagasaki-operations-order-aug-8–1945.jpg?quality=85 (accessed 28 November 2016).

27. Ham, *Hiroshima Nagasaki*, p. 329.

28. Text in Truman Library at http://wwwtrumanlibraryorg/calendar/viewpapersphp?pid=100.

29. Quoted in Boyer, *By the Bomb's Early Light*, p. 40.

30. Ham, *Hiroshima Nagasaki*, p. 349; Boyer, *By the Bomb's Early Light*, Chapter 1, note quoting 'The Atomic Age', *Life* magazine, 20 August 1945, p. 32.

31. Ham, *Hiroshima Nagasaki*, p. 357; https://en.wikipedia.org/wiki/Atomic_bombings_of_Hiroshima_and_Nagasaki#The_bombing.

32. H. Gusterson, *People of the Bomb*, Minneapolis, 2004, p. 68.

33. J. Hersey, *Hiroshima*, London, 2015, pp. 1, 32.

34. There is a full description of the Trinity test and the reactions of Truman and others in R. Monk, *Inside the Centre: The Life of J. Robert Oppenheimer*, London, 2012, pp. 437 et seq. Churchill's remark about the Second Coming was quoted by Henry Stimson in his diary: see J. Gaddis (ed.), *Cold War Statesmen Confront the Bomb: Nuclear Diplomacy since 1945*, Oxford, 1999, p. 1 and n. 3 on p. 284.

35. M. Dobbs, *Six Months in 1945: FDR, Stalin, Churchill, and Truman – from World War to Cold War*, London, 2012; W. Churchill, *The Second World War*, Vol. VI, London, 1954, p. 580.

36. Ham, *Hiroshima Nagasaki*, p. 280.

37. Ryabev (ed.), Atomny Proekt SSSR: Dokumenty i Materialy (The Atom Project of the USSR: Documents and Materials), Vol I, 1938–45, Part 2, Moscow 2002, Documents 367 and 371; Holloway, *Stalin and the Bomb*, p. 117.

38. Ham, *Hiroshima Nagasaki*, p. 391, quoting Harriman memorandum of 8–9 August 1945.

39. Soviet invasion of Manchuria: see Hastings, *Nemesis*, pp. 525 et seq. See also G. Krivosheev, *Rossia i SSSR v Voinakh XX Veka*, Moscow, 2001, p. 309.

40. The effect of the Russians' attack on Manchuria and their plans to invade Hokkaido on the Japanese decision to surrender has been much debated by historians. See, for example, Tsuyoshi Hasegawa, 'The Atomic Bombs and the Soviet Invasion: What Drove Japan's Decision to Surrender?', *Asia-Pacific Journal*, 1 August 2007 (accessed 14 September 2016).

41. Ham, *Hiroshima Nagasaki*, p. 436.

42. The text of the Japanese emperor's broadcast is at https://www.mtholyoke.edu/acad/intrel/hirohito.htm (accessed 24 December 2015).

43. M. Hogan, 'The Enola Gay Controversy: History, Memory, and the Politics of Presentation', in Hogan (ed.), *Hiroshima in History and Memory*, pp. 200–232.

44. H. Stimson, 'The Decision to Use the Atomic Bomb', Harper's, February 1947, p. 97.

45. Ham, *Hiroshima Nagasaki*, p. 513.

46. P. Fussell, 'Thank God for the Atom Bomb', *New Republic*, August 1981.

Chapter 2: Touching Infinity

1. C. Rovelli, *Seven Brief Lessons on Physics*, London, 2015, p. 10.
2. R. Rhodes, *The Making of the Atomic Bomb*, London, 2012, p. 28.
3. R. Stannard, *Relativity: A Very Short Introduction*, Oxford, 2008, p. ix.
4. R. Feynman, *The Character of Physical Law*, London, 1965, quoted in J. Polkinghorne, *Quantum Theory: A Very Short Introduction*, Oxford, 2002, p. v.
5. Letter to Max Born of 4 December 1926, *The Born–Einstein Letters*, translated by Irene Born, New York, 1971, quoted https://en.wikiquote.org/wiki/Albert_Einstein (accessed 5 March 2017).
6. A. Einstein, *Autobiographical Notes*, edited by P. Schlipp, Chicago, 1991, p. 43.
7. V. Gubarev, *Atomnaya Bomba: Khronika Velikikh Otkrytii*, Moscow, 2009, Chapter 'Obed v Dome Literatorov'.
8. US Atomic Energy Commission, *In the matter of J. Robert Oppenheimer*, Volume VIII, Washington, April 1954, p. 1541 at http://www.osti.gov/includes/opennet/includes/Oppenheimer%20hearings/Vol%20VIII%20Oppenheimer.pdf (accessed 11 April 2016).
9. K. Bird and M. Sherwin, *American Prometheus: The Triumph and Tragedy of J. Robert Oppenheimer*, New York, 2005, pp. 39, 42.
10. G. Herken, *Brotherhood of the Bomb: The Tangled Lives and Loyalties of Robert Oppenheimer, Ernest Lawrence, and Edward Teller*, New York, 2002, p. 92.
11. Feynman was the only American to appear on the top 10 list, and the only one who did his most important work in the second half of the twentieth century: http://www.caltech.edu/news/physics-world-poll-names-richard-feynman-one-10-greatest-physicists-all-time-368 (accessed 4 March 2016).
12. Conversation with Anna Kapitsa, 22 June 1989.
13. Igor Tamm, 'Oktiabr' i nauchnyi progres', in B. M. Bolotovskii and V. Ya. Frenkel (eds), *I. E. Tamm: Selected Papers*, Berlin, 1991, pp. 284–90, quoted in K. Hall, 'The Schooling of Lev Landau: The European Context of Post-Revolutionary Soviet Theoretical Physics', *Osiris*, Vol. 23, 2008, pp. 230–259.
14. The history of Russian nuclear physics and the Soviet weapons programme is told clearly and briefly in P. Podvig (ed.), *Russian Strategic Nuclear Forces*, Cambridge, MA, 2004, pp. 67–74.
15. L. Graham, *Science in Russia and the Soviet Union: A Short History*, Cambridge, 1994, p. 199.
16. A. Pervushin, *Atomny Proekt: Istoria Sverkhoruzhia*, Moscow, 2015, pp. 294, 300.
17. Gubarev, *Atomnaya Bomba*, Chapter 'Taina Sergeya Vavilova'.

18. N. Khrushchev, *Khrushchev Remembers*, London, 1971, pp. 402–3; Kurchatov biography at http://www.atomicarchive.com/Bios/Kurchatov.shtml (accessed 5 March 2017).

19. Gubarev, *Atomnaya Bomba*, Chapter 'Zvezda Kharitona'; biography in (Russian) Wikipedia, https://ru.wikipedia.org/wiki/Харитон,_Юлий_Борисович (accessed 13 September 2016).

20. A. Kojevnikov, *Stalin's Great Science: The Times and Adventures of Soviet Physicists*, London, 2004, pp. 65 et seq. on Tamm's career. Tamm's brush with death is described in a slightly different version in 'A Question of Life and Death – Radiation Caused by Atmospheric Testing and Jesuit Involvement', *Materials World Magazine*, 1 December 2007: http://www.iom3.org/materials-world-magazine/feature/2007/dec/01/question-life-or-death-radiation-caused-atmospheric?c=574 (accessed 27 September 2015). I have combined the two.

21. A. Sakharov, *Memoirs*, London, 1990, p. 128.

22. I. Hargittai, *Buried Glory: Portraits of Soviet Scientists*, Oxford, 2013, p. 103.

23. Details of Kapitsa's time in Cambridge and his correspondence with Soviet leaders are at Kojevnikov, *Stalin's Great Science*, pp.103–4, 110, 112.

24. Hargittai, *Buried Glory*, pp. 103–11.

25. M. Bundy, *Danger and Survival: Choices about the Bomb in the First Fifty Years*, New York, 1988, p. 5.

26. Pervushin, *Atomny Proekt*, p. 30; https://en.wikipedia.org/wiki/Simon_Newcomb (accessed 16 September 2016).

27. A. France, *Penguin Island*, London, 1908, pp. 193 et seq.

28. Pervushin, *Atomny Proekt*. Nikolsky's novel is available at http://profilib.com/chtenie/33878/v-nikolskiy-cherez-tysyachu-let.php (accessed 4 March 2017).

29. J. Priestley, *The Doomsday Men*, London, 1938.

30. H. G. Wells, *The World Set Free*, London, 1914.

31. G. Farmelo, *Churchill's Bomb*, London, 2013, pp. 53, 71.

32. Churchill's articles in the *News of the World* are quoted in Farmelo, *Churchill's Bomb*, pp. 90, 93.

33. Wikipedia, 'German Strategic Bombing in World War I', at https://en.wikipedia.org/wiki/German_strategic_bombing_during_World_War_I#1916 (accessed 15 March 2017); J. Terraine, *The Right of the Line: The Royal Air Force in the European Air War 1939–1945*, London, 1985, p. 10; D. Lloyd George, *War Memoirs of David Lloyd George*, Vol. II (New Edition), London, 1938, pp. 1105, 1108. There is a succinct account of the development of the RAF's strategic doctrine in M. Hastings, *Bomber Command*, London, 1993, Chapter 1.

34. Quoted by Laurence Freedman, *The Evolution of Nuclear Strategy*, London, 2003, p. 8.

35. Farmelo, *Churchill's Bomb*, p. 81.
36. See https://en.wikipedia.org/wiki/The_bomber_will_always_get_through (accessed 5 March 2017).
37. Farmelo, *Churchill's Bomb*, p. 110, quoting D. Edgerton, *Warfare State*, Cambridge, 2006.
38. H. Macmillan, *Winds of Change, 1914–1939*, London, 1966, p. 575, quoted in Farmelo, Churchill's Bomb, p. 92.
39. L. Meitner and O. Frisch, 'Disintegration of Uranium by Neutrons: A New Type of Nuclear Reaction', *Nature*, Vol. 143, 11 February 1939, pp. 239–40; A. Brown, *Keeper of the Nuclear Conscience: The Life and Work of Joseph Rotblat*, Oxford, 2012, p. 25.
40. Rhodes, *The Making of the Atomic Bomb*, p. 292. Alex Wellerstein confirmed the date of this incident.
41. D. Holloway, *Stalin and the Bomb*, New Haven, 1994, p. 57.
42. C. P. Snow in *Discovery*, No. 2, September 1939, pp. 443–4, reproduced in C. Snow, *The Physicists*, London, 1981, pp. 167–7.
43. Transcript of surreptitiously taped conversations among German nuclear physicists at Farm Hall (6–7 August 1945), http://germanhistorydocs.ghi-dc.org/pdf/eng/English101.pdf (accessed 5 March 2017).
44. Three years later the Russians sent their own representative to Copenhagen to pump Bohr. He too failed. See page XXX.
45. The Wikipedia article on the Japanese nuclear weapons programme, https://en.wikipedia.org/wiki/Japanese_nuclear_weapon_program (accessed 4 March 2017), refers to an improbable story that the Japanese were preparing a nuclear test at the end of the war. See Charles Weiner, 'Retroactive Saber Rattling', *Bulletin of the Atomic Scientists*, April 1978, p. 9, https://books.google.co.uk/books? (accessed 17 January 2016).
46. Philip Bell expands on this thought in *Serving the Reich: The Struggle for the Soul of Physics under Hitler*, London, 2013, p. 261.

Chapter 3: Brighter Than a Thousand Suns

1. The title of this chapter is taken from the *Bhagavad Gita*, in the version used by Robert Junck for his pioneering *Brighter Than a Thousand Suns*, Orlando, 1958, p. 201.
2. V. Gubarev, *Yaderny Vek Bomba*, Moscow, 1995, p. 60.
3. 'The bomb that destroyed Hiroshima was equivalent to the load of some two hundred B-29 bombers', L. Freedman, *Strategy: A History*, London, 2013, p. 156.
4. R. Rhodes, *Dark Sun: The Making of the Hydrogen Bomb*, New York, 1996, p. 253.
5. P. Podvig, 'The Window of Vulnerability that Wasn't', http://russianforces.org/podvig/2008/06/the_window_of_vulnerability_that_wasnt.shtml;

Polmar N, Norris R, *US Nuclear Arsenal: A History of Weapons and Delivery Systems since 1945*, Washington 2009, pp.36–70.

6. R. Monk, *Inside the Centre: The Life of J. Robert Oppenheimer*, London, 2012, p. 263; R. Hewlett and O. Anderson, *A History of the United States Atomic Energy Commission: The New World, 1939–1946*, Philadelphia, 1962, p. 19.

7. A. Pervushin, *Atomny Proekt: Istoria Sverkhoruzhia*, Moscow, 2015, p. 192.

8. Texts of the Frisch–Peierls memorandum and of the MAUD Report are in P. Hennessy, *Cabinets and the Bomb*, Oxford, 2007.

9. The quotations in this and the previous three paragraphs are from G. Farmelo, *Churchill's Bomb*, London 2013, pp. 172, 188, 190, and footnote.

10. M. Gowing, *Britain and Atomic Energy 1939–45*, London, 1964, p. 123; Farmelo, *Churchill's Bomb*, pp. 203 et seq.

11. Gowing, *Britain and Atomic Energy 1939–45*, pp. 131, 145.

12. W. Churchill, *The Second World War: The Hinge of Fate*, London, 1951, p. 341.

13. Farmelo, *Churchill's Bomb*, p. 226.

14. Gowing, *Britain and Atomic Energy 1939–45*, pp. 147–77; Farmelo, *Churchill's Bomb*, pp. 224–33.

15. Gowing, *Britain and Atomic Energy 1939–45*, pp. 138–9, 158–63; Farmelo, *Churchill's Bomb*, p. 234.

16. Texts at http://www.atomicarchive.com/Docs/ManhattanProject/Quebec. shtml; and http://www.atomicarchive.com/Docs/ManhattanProject/ TubeAlloys.shtml (accessed 4 March 2017).

17. Pervushin, *Atomny Proekt*, p. 236.

18. M. Bundy, *Danger and Survival: Choices about the Bomb in the First Fifty Years*, New York, 1988, pp. 491, 183; L. Groves, *Now It Can Be Told*, New York, 1981, p. 408.

19. G. Herken, *Brotherhood of the Bomb: The Tangled Lives and Loyalties of Robert Oppenheimer, Ernest Lawrence, and Edward Teller*, New York, 2002, p. 49.

20. Junck, *Brighter than a Thousand Suns*, p. 126.

21. Herken, *Brotherhood of the Bomb*, p. 51; Monk, *Inside the Centre*, p. 313.

22. Ibid., p. 320.

23. The Berkeley discussions are described in K. Bird and M. Sherwin, *American Prometheus: The Triumph and Tragedy of J. Robert Oppenheimer*, New York, 2006, pp. 181 et seq.

24. Monk, *Inside the Centre*, p. 315; Bird and Sherwin, *American Prometheus*, p. 180.

25. Profile of Groves, Atomic Heritage Foundation, at http://www. atomicheritage.org/profile/leslie-r-groves (accessed 21 August 2016).

26. Herken, *Brotherhood of the Bomb*, p. 57.

27. Ibid., p. 71 n.

28. Bird and Sherwin, *American Prometheus*, pp. 185–7.

29. Monk, *Inside the Centre*, p. 363.
30. Groves, *Now It Can Be Told*, p. 63.
31. Figures kindly provided by Alex Wellerstein. See also the Los Alamos website at http://www.lanl.gov/about/facts-figures/index.php (accessed 24 June 2017).
32. Monk, *Inside the Centre*, p. 315.
33. Bird and Sherwin, *American Prometheus*, p. 210.
34. R. Serber, *The Los Alamos Primer*, Berkeley/Los Angeles, 1992.
35. R. Rhodes, *The Making of the Atomic Bomb*, London, 2012, p. 455; Herken, *Brotherhood of the Bomb*, p. 80.
36. P. Ham, *Hiroshima Nagasaki*, London, 2013, p. 257.
37. This description and the accompanying quotations are taken primarily from Monk, *Inside the Centre*, Bird and Sherwin, *American Prometheus*, and Junck, *Brighter than a Thousand Suns*.
38. According to Junck, ibid., p. 197, the successful punter was Robert Serber, who thought he should 'name a flatteringly high figure'.
39. Herken, *Brotherhood of the Bomb*, p. 151.
40. The discussion over the possibility of a 'Super' bomb are described ibid., pp. 67, 75, 127, 138–9, 151, 154, 171, 187 n.
41. The text of the report is at http://www.http://www.atomicarchive.com/Docs/Hydrogen/GACReport.shtml (accessed 19 January 2016).
42. I. Hargittai, *Judging Edward Teller: A Closer Look at One of the Most Influential Scientists of the Twentieth Century*, New York, 2010, p. 194.
43. A. Sakharov, *Memoirs*, London, 1990, p. 99.
44. Quoted G. DeGroot, *The Bomb: A Life*, London, 2004, p. 170.
45. Monk, *Inside the Centre*, p. 217.
46. D. Acheson, *Present at the Creation*, New York, 1969, p. 349.
47. G. Herken, *Brotherhood of the Bomb: The Tangled Lives and Loyalties of Robert Oppenheimer, Ernest Lawrence, and Edward Teller*, New York, 2002, p. 302.
48. Monk, *Inside the Centre*, p. 569.
49. The following account of the crushing of Robert Oppenheimer is described ibid., p. 222; interview by Barton Bernstein (Professor of History at Stanford University) on PBS film *The Race for the Superbomb*, January 1999, at http://www.pbs.org/wgbh/amex/bomb/filmmore/reference/interview/bernstein.html (accessed 4 March 2017).
50. H. Gusterson, *People of the Bomb*, Minneapolis, 2004, p. 54.
51. Herken, *Brotherhood of the Bomb*, pp. 169, 174.
52. Monk, *Inside the Centre*, pp. 539, 592, 576.
53. See http://www.colorado.edu/ReligiousStudies/chernus/4820-ColdWarCulture/Readings/PrayingGodBlessAmerica.pdf (accessed 4 March 2017).

54. US Atomic Energy Commission, *In the Matter of J. Robert Oppenheimer*, Vol. VII, Washington, DC, April 1954.

55. G. Herken, *Brotherhood of the Bomb*, pp. 280–81.

56. Monk, *Inside the Centre*, p. 534.

57. Bird and Sherwin, *American Prometheus*, p. 542.

58. Herken, *Brotherhood of the Bomb*, pp. 296, 331.

Chapter 4: A Flash of Lightning

1. A. Werth, *Russia at War 1941–1945*, London, 1964, p. 1037. This is still one of the most gripping accounts of the war in the East.

2. H. Smyth, *A General Account of the Development of Methods of Using Atomic Energy for Military Purposes*, at http://www.atomicarchive.com/Docs/ SmythReport/index.shtml (accessed 5 March 2017). Quoted in P. Boyer, *By the Bomb's Early Light*, New York, 1985, p. 40.

3. A. Solzhenitsyn, *The Gulag Archipelago 1918–1956: An Experiment in Literary Investigation*, Vols I–II, New York 1974, pp. 598–9, quoted by Alex Wellerstein, http://blog.nuclearsecrecy.com/2016/02/12/ solzhenitsyn-smyth-report/

4. The foregoing description of the Soviet Union after the war is taken from Vladislav Zubok, 'Stalin', in J. Gaddis (ed.), *Cold War Statesmen Confront the Bomb: Nuclear Diplomacy since 1945*, Oxford, 1999, p. 45; E. Zubkova, *Russia After the War: Hopes, Illusions, and Disappointments, 1945–1957*, Armonk, NY, 1998, p. 83; Frank Roberts, the British chargé d'affaires; A. Brown, *The Neutron and the Bomb: A Biography of Sir James Chadwick*, Oxford, 1997, pp. 318–19, quoted in N. Yegorova and A. Chubarian (eds), *Kholodnaya Voina 1945–1963*, Moscow, 2003, p. 283; Archibald Clark-Kerr, British ambassador, quoted in D. Holloway, *Stalin and the Bomb*, New Haven, 1994, p. 154; Wikipedia article GULAG, at https://en.wikipedia. org/wiki/Gulag#After_World_War_II (accessed 1 August 2016). See also O. Khlevniuk, *Stalin: New Biography of a Dictator*, New Haven, 2015, p. 261.

5. P. Ham, *Hiroshima Nagasaki*, London, 2012, p. 513.

6. Quoted in R. Rhodes, *Dark Sun: The Making of the Hydrogen Bomb*, New York, 1996, p. 211.

7. V. Gubarev, *Yaderny Vek Bomba*, Moscow, 1995, p. 51.

8. Zubkova, *Russia After the War*, p. 84.

9. Holloway, *Stalin and the Bomb*, p. 23.

10. The comparison of Landau with Einstein and Feynman is made by Feynman's biographer: see J. Gleick, *Genius: Richard Feynman and Modern Physics*, London, 1992, p. 130.

11. This account of Landau's early life is taken from A. Kojevnikov, *Stalin's Great Science: The Times and Adventures of Soviet Physicists*, London, 2004, pp. 75 et seq.

12. I. Hargittai, *Buried Glory: Portraits of Soviet Scientists*, Oxford, 2013, p. 117.

13. Kurchatov's recommendation is at V. Gubarev, *Atomnaya Bomba: Khronika Velikikh Otkrytii*, Moscow, 2009, Chapter 'Dialog s Raz'. Ivanov, a senior KGB official, listed Landau's blasphemies in a note for the politburo dated 19 December 1957: a photocopy is at http://psi.ece.jhu.edu/~kaplan/IRUSS/ BUK/GBARC/pdfs/sovter74/land-17.pdf (accessed 19 June 2016).

14. R. Sagdeev, *The Making of a Soviet Scientist*, New York, 1994, p. 94. Kapitsa's 1945 correspondence with Stalin and Khrushchev was published by the Soviet journal *Ogoenek* in June 1989 (No. 25, pp. 18–221, available at https:// yadi.sk/i/4JjjvCOWoRdbg, accessed 10 June 2017). See also the article by A. B. Kozhevnikov, Ucheny i Gosudarstvo: Fenomen Kapitsy [The Scientist and the State: The Kapitsa Phenomenon], Filosofskie Issledovania, Moscow 1993 at http://www.ihst.ru/projects/sohist/papers/koj93sp.htm, also accessed on 10 June 2017. There is an interesting analysis of the reasons why Kapitsa was able to take such an independent, and occasionally effective, line in his dealings with the Soviet leaders.

15. Much of the following is taken from the meticulously detailed account by Goncharov and Ryabev, 'O Sozdanii Pervoi Otechestvennoi Atomnoi Bomby', at https://ufn.ru/ufn01/ufn01_1/Russian/r011c.pdf (accessed 5 March 2017). Ryabev was a distinguished Soviet nuclear engineer and administrator. His article gives due weight to the way the intelligence reports from London encouraged the Soviet authorities to press ahead. See also Kojevnikov, *Stalin's Great Science*, passim.

16. Kojevnikov, ibid, p. 133; Holloway, *Stalin and the Bomb*, pp. 49–54, 58; Gubarev, *Atomnaya Bomba*, and L. Ryabev (ed.), *Atomny Proekt SSSR: Dokumenty i Materialy*, Vol. I, Part 1, Sarov, 1998, Document No. 16, p. 53.

17. Laurence's article is quoted in Holloway, *Stalin and the Bomb*, p. 60; see also A. Pervushin, *Atomny Proekt: Istoria Sverkhoruzhia*, Moscow, 2015, p. 328.

18. Holloway, *Stalin and the Bomb*, pp. 67, 62; Rhodes, *Dark Sun*, p. 53. The story of Maslov's patent application is in Gubarev, *Atomnaya Bomba*, Chapter 'Avtorskoe Svidetelstvo'. The text of the application is at Ryabev (ed.), *Atomny Proekt SSSR*, Vol. 1, Part 1, Document No. 75, p. 193. Maslov's letter to Timoshenko is Document No. 92, p. 224. Pervushin, *Atomny Proekt*, p. 325; Hargittai, *Buried Glory*, p. 148; Pervushin, *Atomny Proekt*, pp. 316 et seq.

19. Kapitsa's October 1941 speech and the story of Flerov's alleged appeal to Stalin are covered by Vladimir Gubarev. Earlier histories quoted the letter Flerov is supposed to have sent to Stalin, but the letter itself has not been found. Gubarev, *Atomnaya Bomba*, electronic version, Chapter 'Leitenant Uchit Stalina'. See also Holloway, *Stalin and the Bomb*, pp. 74–8.

20. The text of the GKO decision of 28 September 1942 to set up the laboratory is at Ryabev (ed.), *Atomny Proekt SSSR*, Vol. 1, Part 1, Document No. 128, p. 269.

21. For Kurchatov's note to Molotov see ibid., Document No. 133, p. 276.

22. Holloway, *Stalin and the Bomb*, p. 96.

23. Pervushin, *Atomny Proekt*, p. 388.

24. The creation and role of this important committee are described in Goncharov and Ryabev 'O Sozdanii Pervoi Otechestvennoi Atomnoi Bomby', at https://ufn.ru/ufn01/ufn01_1/Russian/r011c.pdf (accessed 5 March 2017).

25. A. Zubov, *Istoria Rossii XX-ogo Veka* [History of Twentieth Century Russia], Moscow, 2011, Vol. II, p. 202.

26. D. Holloway, *Stalin and the Bomb*, Yale 1994, p. 211; F. Thom, *Beria: Le Janus du Kremlin*, Paris, 2013, pp. 450–52.

27. Council of Ministers decision, Mo.2266, V. Gubarev, *Atomnaya Bomba: Khronika Velikikh Otkrytii* [The Atom Bomb: A Chronicle of Great Discoveries], Moscow, 2009, Chapter *Rozhdenie atomnogo Gulaga* [The birth of the atomic Gulag].

28. A. Sakharov, *Memoirs*, p. 146.

29. P. Podvig (ed), *Russian Strategic Nuclear Forces*, MIT, 2004, pp. 69, 110

30. Gubarev, *Atomnaya Bomba*, Chapter 'Gde zhe Kupit Uran?'.

31. Kojevnikov, *Stalin's Great Science*, p. 138; Podvig (ed.), *Russian Strategic Nuclear Forces*, p. 71.

32. Nuclear Weapons Archive at http://nuclearweaponarchive.org/Russia/ Russreac.html (accessed on 20 September 2016); Gubarev, *Atomnaya Bomba*, Chapter 'Taina Proekta', No. 1859; Pervushin, *Atomny Proekt*, p. 415.

33. Pervushin, *Atomny Proekt*, pp. 422 et seq.; Gubarev, *Yaderny Vek Bomba*, p. 137.

34. The views of some of the scientists are reported in Gubarev, *Yaderny Vek Bomba*, pp. 23, 161.

35. The remarks by Sakharov in this and the preceding paragraphs come from Sakharov, *Memoirs*, pp. 104, 164, 116.

36. Quoted in M. Bundy, *Danger and Survival: Choices about the Bomb in the First Fifty Years*, New York, 1988, p. 57.

37. Kurchatov's remarks are quoted in Pervushin, *Atomny Proekt*, pp. 417–18; for the accidents see A. Dyachenko, 'Vmesto Predislovia: Avaria ili Katastrofa?', in V. Mikhailov and A. Dyachenko (eds), *Opalennye v Borbe pri Sozdanii Yadernovo Shchita Rodiny*, Moscow, 2008, p. 92; Zh. Medvedev, *Nuclear Disaster in the Urals*, New York, 1979; https://en.wikipedia.org/wiki/ Kyshtym_disaster#References (accessed 16 November 2016).

38. Gubarev, *Yaderny Vek Bomba*, p. 235.

39. Gubarev, *Atomnaya Bomba*, Chapter 'Govorit li A-Bmba po Nemetski?'; Pervushin, *Atomny Proekt*, p. 411; Holloway, *Stalin and the Bomb*, p. 128.

40. Article on Sarov: https://ru.wikipedia.org/wiki/Саров.

41. Gubarev, *Yaderny Vek Bomba*, pp. 385 et seq.

42. Gubarev, *Atomnaya Bomba*, electronic version, Chapter 'Reaktivny Dvigatel S'.

43. Pervushin, *Atomny Proekt*, p. 433.

44. Text of statement at http://www.pbs.org/wgbh/amex/bomb/filmmore/reference/primary/trumanstatement.html (accessed 13 November 2015).

45. Podvig (ed.), *Russian Strategic Nuclear Forces*, pp. 72–3. See also article on RDS-1 at https://ru.wikipedia.org/wiki/РДС-1; article from Truman Presidential Library at http://www.prlib.ru/History/Pages/Item.aspx?itemid=653.

46. Nuclear Power Engineering: see http://m.com/NPRE%20402%20ME%20405%20Nuclear%20Power%20Engineering/index.htm (accessed 5 March 2017).

47. Extract from a report to Igor Kurchatov by Yakov Frenkel on a conversation with F. Joliot-Curie, 22 September 1945. Ryabev (ed.), *Atomny Proekt SSSR*, Vol. III, Part 1, Sarov, 2008, Document No. 2, p. 9.

48. See G. Goncharov, 'American and Soviet H-bomb Development Programmes: Historical Background', Uspekhi Fizicheskikh Nauk, Vol. 39, No. 10, 1996, available in translation at http://fas.org/nuke/guide/russia/nuke/goncharov-h-bomb.pdf (accessed 5 March 2017).

49. Sakharov, Memoirs, pp. 91, 95.

50. Ibid., pp. 172, 180; on Malyshev see https://ru.wikipedia.org/wiki/Малышев,_Вячеслав_Александрович (accessed 21 July 2016).

51. Ryabev (ed.), *Atomny Proekt SSSR*, Vol. III, Part 2, p. 189, Document No. 89; Goncharov, 'American and Soviet H-bomb Development Programmes: Historical Background', *Uspekhi Fizicheskikh Nauk*, Vol. 166, No. 10, 1996, pp. 1096–104.

52. A. Sakharov, *Memoirs*, London, 1990; Sidney Drell, 'Andrei Sakharov and the Nuclear Danger', *Hoover Digest*, No. 4, 30 October 2000, at http://www.hoover.org/research/andrei-sakharov-and-nuclear-danger (accessed 25 March 2016).

53. Gubarev, *Atomnaya Bomba*, electronic version, Chapter 'Ne Chudo a Chudishche'. Gubarev's Russian original makes a neater pun.

54. Gubarev, *Yaderny Vek Bomba*, pp. 109, 238.

55. Sakharov, *Memoirs*, p. 114. This is a common theme of the interviews which Vladimir Gubarev conducted with scientists in Arzamas-16 in the early 1990s: Gubarev, *Yaderny Vek Bomba*, p.128 and passim.

Chapter 5: The Charm of Strategy

1. S. Kull, *Minds at War: Nuclear Reality and the Inner Conflicts of Defense Policymakers*, New York, 1988, p. 228.

2. T. Pratchett, *Jingo*, London, 1997, n. 8.

3. This quotation (more fully rendered as 'No plan of operations extends with certainty beyond the first encounter with the enemy's main strength') and Moltke's other remark that 'Strategy is a system of expedients' originally come from his *Militarische Werke*, Vol. II, Part 2, pp. 33–40. See D. J. Hughes (ed.), *Moltke on the Art of War: Selected Writings*, New York, 1993, pp. 45–7, and https://en.wikipedia.org/wiki/Helmuth_von_Moltke_the_Elder#cite_note-moltke-3 (accessed 5 March 2017).

4. The campaign was called Operation Infektion. It is described at https://en.wikipedia.org/wiki/Operation_INFEKTION (accessed 5 March 2017).

5. In his encyclical *Quanta Cura* of 1864, Pope Pius IX condemned Communism and socialism as a 'most fatal error'.

6. Letter to Pope Pius XII, W. Inboden, *Religion and American Foreign Policy 1945–1960*, Cambridge, 2008, p. 112; President Truman, Navy Day Address, 17 October 1945, at http://www.ibiblio.org/pha/policy/post-war/451027a.html (accessed 8 March 2016).

7. See http://archiveorg/details/ThisGodlessCommunism.

8. S. Bates, '"Godless Communism" and Its Legacies', *Society*, Vol. 41, No. 3, March–April 2004, pp. 29–33.

9. V. I. Lenin, *Complete Works*, Vol. 35, p. 349, at Marxists Internet Archive, https://www.marxists.org/archive/lenin/works/1918/aug/09gff.htm (accessed 5 March 2017).

10. Central Committee document #148 of 1949, quoted in Wikipedia article 'Anti-American Sentiment in Russia', http://en.wikipedia.org/wiki/Anti-American_sentiment_in_Russia (accessed 5 March 2017).

11. The figure of 100,000 comes from R. Garthoff, *Soviet Leaders and Intelligence: Assessing the American Adversary during the Cold War*, Washington, DC, 2015, p. 6.

12. J. Baylis, *Ambiguity and Deterrence: British Nuclear Strategy 1945–1964*, Oxford, 1995, p. 63.

13. G. Kennan, *Memoirs: 1950–1963*, London, 1972, p. 547.

14. G. Kennan, 'America and the Russian Future', *Foreign Affairs*, Vol. 29, No.3, April 1951.

15. P. Ham, *Hiroshima Nagasaki*, London, 2013, p. 517.

16. Nikolai Novikov, Soviet Ambassador in Washington, telegram of 27 September 1946, https://www.mtholyoke.edu/acad/intrel/novikov.htm (accessed 22 April 2016).

17. Hansard, 10 November 1932, Vol. 270, cc. 525–641, at http://hansard. millbanksystems.com/commons/1932/nov/10/international-affairs (accessed 4 February 2017).

18. M. Hastings, *Bomber Command*, London, 1993, p. 46; B. Heuser, *The Bomb: Nuclear Weapons in the Historical, Strategic and Ethical Context*, London, 2000, pp. 38 et seq., 52.

19. L. Freedman, *The Evolution of Nuclear Strategy*, London, 2003, p. 90; R. Oppenheimer, 'Atomic Weapons and American Policy', *Foreign Affairs*, July 1953, p. 529.

20. These issues are succinctly set out in the introduction to D. Ball and J. Richelson, *Strategic Nuclear Targeting*, Ithaca, 1986.

21. The G. W. Bush National Strategy of 2002 is at https://georgewbush-whitehouse.archives.gov/nsc/nss/2002/ (accessed 29 May 2017).

22. Freedman, *The Evolution of Nuclear Strategy*, pp. 292, xix, 464.

23. H. Kahn, *Thinking about the Unthinkable in the 1980s*, Washington, DC, 1984, p. 41.

24. V. Gubarev, *Yaderny Vek Bomba*, Moscow, 1995, p. 81.

25. S. Zaloga, *The Kremlin's Nuclear Sword: The Rise and Fall of Russia's Strategic Nuclear Forces, 1945–2000*, Washington, DC, 2002, p. 59.

26. M. Herman and G. Hughes (eds), *Intelligence in the Cold War: What Difference Did It Make?*, Abingdon, 2013, p. 31.

27. The politics surrounding the Minuteman scare are ably dissected by David Dunn in his *The Politics of Threat: Minuteman Vulnerability in American National Security Policy*, London, 1987.

28. P. McCray, 'Project Vista, Caltech, and the Dilemmas of Lee DuBridge', *Historical Studies in the Physical and Biological Sciences*, Vol. 34, No. 2, 2004, pp. 339–70.

29. Private information.

30. Lockheed Martin, the company that built the Pershing II, says in a relevant brochure that by the time the missile was deployed to West Germany in 1983 its range had been increased to 1,500 miles (*The Pershing Missile: Peace Through Strength*. http://www.lockheedmartin.com/us/100years/stories/pershing.html). See also A. Savel'yev & N. Detinov, *The Big Five: Arms Control Decision-Making in the Soviet Union*, New York 1995, p. 57; G. Barrass, 'Able Archer 83: What Were the Soviets Thinking?' Mr Barrass kindly gave me an advance view of this article written for the Winter 2016 edition of *Survival* Magazine.

31. A joint Foreign Office/Defence Ministry paper on 'Nuclear Sufficiency' pointed out in 1958 that the Russians could now deliver a crippling strike on the United States. Quoting a recent speech by Vice President Nixon, it argued that there could be no certainty that the Americans would be willing to risk their cities for the sake of their allies (private information).

32. Chiefs of Staff Committee/Joint Planning Staff note of 15 August 1963, quoted in Baylis, *Ambiguity and Deterrence*, p. 439.

33. In 1955 NATO's exercise Carte Blanche simulated a limited war in Europe in which only the NATO side used tactical nuclear weapons. Over two days up to 1.7 million West Germans would have been killed, without allowing for the effects of radiation, and 3.5 million wounded: Freedman, *The Evolution of Nuclear Strategy*, p. 104. The German politician was quoted in the *New York Times*, 26 April 1990.

34. Kull, *Minds at War*, p. 13.

35. O. Grinevsky, *Perelom: Ot Brezhneva do Gorbacheva*, Moscow, 2004, pp. 11–12, Chapter 2, 'Kto Pobedit v Yadernoj Voine?'.

36. P. Goodchild, *Edward Teller: The Real Dr Strangelove*, London, 2004, p. xx.

37. H. Kissinger, *Nuclear Weapons and Foreign Policy*, New York, 1969, pp. 227 et seq.

38. Robert McNamara to President Kennedy, 20 February 1961: E. Schlosser, *Command and Control*, London, 2013, p. 271.

39. B. Blair, *The Logic of Accidental War*, Washington, DC, 1994, p. 49.

40. P. Feaver, *Armed Servants: Agency, Oversight, and Civil–Military Relations*, Cambridge, 2005, p. 151, quoted https://en.wikipedia.org/wiki/Permissive_Action_Link.

41. F. Kaplan, *Wizards of Armageddon*, New York, 1983, p. 246.

42. The Wikipedia article on PALs is substantial: https://en.wikipedia.org/wiki/Permissive_Action_Link (accessed 4 October 2016).

43. V. Yarynich, *C3: Nuclear Command, Control, Cooperation*, Washington, DC, 2003, pp. 140 et seq.; Blair, *The Logic of Accidental War*, pp.73, 208; B. Blair, 'Russia's Doomsday Machine', *New York Times*, 8 October 1993; Zaloga, *The Kremlin's Nuclear Sword*, p. 198; D. Hoffman, *The Dead Hand*, New York, 2009, pp. 146–50.

44. Both Marshal Akhromeyev, Gorbachev's military adviser and a former Chief of the General Staff, and General Batenin, a military adviser to the Soviet Foreign Ministry, said that Soviet missile submarines could launch their missiles without external authority: Blair, *The Logic of Accidental War*, pp. 81, 97. For incidents of poor morale in the US missile forces in the twenty-first century, see J. Doyle, 'Better Ways to Modernize the US Nuclear Arsenal', *Survival*, August–September 2016, pp. 27–50.

45. Hoffman, *The Dead Hand*, p. 148.

46. Yarynich, *C3*, p. 25.

47. Peter Hennessy, BBC Radio 4 documentary *The Human Button*, December 2008.

Chapter 6: Thinking about the Unthinkable

1. Ivan Selin, Head of Strategic Forces Division, Department of Defense, 1966, quoted in A. Cockburn, *The Threat: Inside the Soviet Military Machine*, New York, 1983, p. vii.

2. S. Ghamari-Tabrizi, *The Worlds of Herman Kahn*, Cambridge, MA, 2005, p. 40.

3. H. Kissinger, *Nuclear Weapons and Foreign Policy* (abridged edition), New York, 1969, p. 103.

4. P. Erickson et al., *How Reason Almost Lost Its Mind: The Strange Career of Cold War Rationality*, Chicago, 2013, pp. 10, 16, 24. On the games players, Erickson quotes Theodore H. White, 'The Action Intellectuals', *Life*, 9 June 1967. Erickson criticises game theory for 'its obsessive narrowing of vision, its mind-bogglingly implausible assumptions, its devotion to method above content, above all its towering ambitions'.

5. L. Freedman, *The Evolution of Nuclear Strategy*, London, 2003, p. 171.

6. *The Absolute Weapon: Atomic Power and World Order* was published by Yale in June 1946. General Eisenhower's copy, countersigned by General LeMay, is in the Eisenhower Library, at https://www.osti.gov/opennet/servlets/purl/16380564-wvLB09/16380564.pdf.

7. 'The Delicate Balance of Terror' is available at http://www.rand.org/about/history/wohlstetter/P1472/P1472.html

8. H. Kahn, *On Escalation: Metaphors and Scenarios*, New York, 2010, p. 41.

9. For a summary of Kahn's thinking see Freedman, *The Evolution of Nuclear Strategy*, pp. 203–6, which also contains the quotation from the review by the mathematician James Newman.

10. F. Kaplan, *The Wizards of Armageddon*, New York, 1983, pp. 390–91.

11. D. Engerman, *Know Your Enemy: The Rise and Fall of America's Soviet Experts*, Oxford, 2009, pp. 1, 44, 73, 330. These paragraphs draw heavily on Engerman's careful study.

12. Admiral Turner said at the Musgrove Plantation conference 'neither side gave adequate consideration to how the other side would interpret its actions': D. Watch and S. Savranskaya, *SALT II and the Growth of Mistrust: Transcript of Proceedings of Conference*, National Security Archive, Washington, DC, 1994, p. 220.

13. R. Garthoff, *Deterrence and the Revolution in Soviet Military Doctrine*, Washington, DC, 1990, p. 17, n. 11: 'Contrary to the common assumption, at peak wartime strength the Soviet Union had fewer personnel in uniform than did the United States. The Soviet armed forces in mid-1945 numbered some 11,565,000 – as compared with some 12,125,000 for the United States.' By 1947–8 the Soviet armed forces were down to 2,874,000 and the US armed forces to 1,446,000; see also E. Zubkova, *Russia After the War: Hopes, Illusions, and Disappointments, 1945–1957*, Armonk, NY, p. 22.

14. Freedman, *The Evolution of Nuclear Strategy*, p. 50.
15. 'The Evaluation of the Atomic Bomb as a Military Weapon', 30 June 1947. A redacted version of the report is held in the Truman Library: http://www.trumanlibrary.org/whistlestop/study_collections/bomb/large/documents/pdfs/81.pdf (accessed 28 September 2015).
16. Freedman, *The Evolution of Nuclear Strategy*, p. 52.
17. 'Nine – disassembled – bombs': R. Garthoff, *Soviet Leaders and Intelligence: Assessing the American Adversary during the Cold War*, Washington, DC, 2015, p. 110. Other sources say the Americans had eleven bombs at that time.
18. J. Correll, 'SAC's Half Century', *Air Force Magazine*, Vol. 96, No, 3, March 2013, pp. 74–9.
19. W. Kozak, *LeMay: The Life and Wars of General Curtis LeMay*, New York, 2012, electronic edition, Chapter 11.
20. S. Drew (ed.), *NSC-68: Forging the Strategy of Containment*, Washington, DC, 1994, p. 24. Texts reproduced in T. Etzold and J. Gaddis (eds), 'Containment: Documents on American Foreign Policy and Strategy, 1945–1950', New York, 1978, pp. 173–211.
21. V. Mikhailov and A. Dyachenko (eds), *Opalennye v Borbe pri Sozdanii Yadernovo Shchita Rodiny*, Moscow, 2008, p. 11. The mangled translation there of NSC 20/1 makes it seem even more hostile.
22. Drew (ed.), *NSC-68*, p. 24.
23. Text in Etzgold and Gaddis (eds), *Containment*, pp. 385–442.
24. B. Heuser, 'NSC 68 and the Soviet Threat: A New Perspective on Western Threat Perception and Policy Making', *Review of International Studies*, Vol. 17, 1991, p. 18.
25. J. Gaddis and P. Nitze, 'NSC 68 and the Soviet Threat Reconsidered', *International Security*, Vol. 4, No. 4, Spring 1980, pp. 164–76.
26. D. Acheson, *Present at the Creation*, New York, 1969, pp. 374–7.
27. M. Cox, 'Western Intelligence: The Soviet Threat and NSC-68: A Reply to Beatrice Heuser', *Review of International Studies*, Vol. 18, No. 1, January 1992, p. 82. Cox quotes two CIA reports from July 1948 entitled 'The Strategic Value to the Soviet Union of the Conquest of Western Europe and the Near East (to Cairo) prior to 1950'; J. Gaddis, *George F. Kennan: An American Life*, New York, 2011, p. 39; Freedman, *The Evolution of Nuclear Strategy*, p. 66.
28. There is a very critical account of NSC-68 in G. Kornienko, *Kholodnaya Voina: Svidetelstvo ee Uchastnika*, Moscow, 2001, Chapter 2, 'U Istokov "Kholodnoi Voiny": Glavny Dokument "Kholodnoi Voiny"'.
29. Freedman, *The Evolution of Nuclear Strategy*, pp. 65, 73.
30. M. Bundy, *Danger and Survival: Choices about the Bomb in the First Fifty Years*, New York, 1988, p. 335.
31. V. Zubok, *A Failed Empire*, Chapel Hill, 2007, p. 131.

32. Engerman, *Know Your Enemy*, pp. 115–17.
33. N. Thompson, *The Hawk and the Dove: Paul Nitze, George Kennan, and the History of the Cold War*, New York, 2009, pp. 164–6, 168.
34. Freedman, *The Evolution of Nuclear Strategy*, p. 284.
35. J. Dulles, 'A Policy of Boldness', *Life*, 19 May 1952, pp. 146 et seq.
36. NSC-162/2, of 30 October 1953, at https://fas.org/irp/offdocs/nsc-hst/nsc-162–2.pdf (accessed 7 August 2016); Freedman, *The Evolution of Nuclear Strategy*, pp. 77 et seq.; Wikipedia article NSC-162/2 at https://en.wikipedia.org/wiki/NSC_162/2 (accessed 24 May 2016). The text of NSC-162/2 is at http://fas.org/irp/offdocs/nsc-hst/nsc-162–2.pdf (accessed 24 May 2016).
37. Freedman, *The Evolution of Nuclear Strategy*, passim and p. 222; https://en.wikipedia.org/wiki/Single_Integrated_Operational_Plan (accessed 4 June 2016). Headquarters Strategic Air Command, History and Research Division, *History of the Joint Strategic Planning Staff: Preparation of SIOP-63*, at http://nsarchive.gwu.edu/nukevault/ebb285/sidebar/SIOP-63_history.pdf (accessed 15 November 2016); D. Ball and J. Richelson (eds), *Strategic Nuclear Targeting*, Ithaca, 1986, pp. 55, 62.
38. Freedman, *The Evolution of Nuclear Strategy*, p. 216.
39. Ibid., p. 220.
40. Ball and Richelson (eds), *Strategic Nuclear Targeting*, p. 63.
41. Freedman, *The Evolution of Nuclear Strategy*, p. 233.
42. Quoted by James Wood Forsyth Jr in 'The Common Sense of Small Nuclear Arsenals', *Strategic Studies Quarterly*, Summer 2012, p. 96.
43. President Nixon, Report to Congress, February 1970.
44. Freedman, *The Evolution of Nuclear Strategy*, pp. 235, 241; A. Dobrynin, *In Confidence*, New York, 1995, p. 307.
45. A. Cahn, *Killing Detente: The Right Attacks the CIA*, Pennsylvania, 1998, pp. 7, 15–16, 25, 188, 190, 191.
46. Kaplan, *Wizards of Armageddon*, p. 380.
47. Cahn, *Killing Detente*, pp. 31–2.
48. Presidential Directive, PD NSC18, Nuclear Targeting Policy Review, 1 November 1978, at http://nsarchive.gwu.edu/nukevault/ebb390/docs/11-1-78%20policy%20review%20summary.pdf (accessed 16 November 2015).
49. Ball and Richelson (eds), *Strategic Nuclear Targeting*, p. 242.
50. G. Barrass, *The Great Cold War*, Stanford, 2006, p. 235.
51. S. Kull, *Minds at War: Nuclear Reality and the Inner Conflicts of Defense Policymakers*, New York, 1988, p. 13; A. Enthoven, 'US Forces In Europe: How Many? Doing What?', *Foreign Affairs*, Vol. 53, No. 3, April 1975, pp. 513–32.
52. Ball and Richelson (eds), *Strategic Nuclear Targeting*, pp. 194 et seq., pp. 267 et seq.

53. J. Lebovic, *Flawed Logics: Strategic Nuclear Arms Control from Truman to Obama*, Baltimore, 2013, p. 102.

54. For Yuri Andropov's speech of 4 January 1983 see http://nsarchive.gwu.edu/NSAEBB/NSAEBB14/doc19.htm (accessed 16 July 2016).

55. Watch and Savranskaya, *SALT II and the Growth of Mistrust*, p. 220.

Chapter 7: Updating the Art of Victory

1. J. Hines et al., *Soviet Intentions 1965–1985, Vol. II*, Washington, DC, 1995, p. 27.

2. G. Wardak, G. Turbiville and R. Garthoff, *The Voroshilov Lectures: Materials from the Soviet Military Staff Academy*, Washington, DC, 1989, p. 72.

3. How all this looked from the Soviet point of view is described in A. Savel'yev and N. Detinov, *The Big Five: Arms Control Decision-Making in the Soviet Union*, New York, 1995, pp. 1–14; see also D. Watch and S. Savranskaya, *SALT II and the Growth of Mistrust: Transcript of Proceedings of Conference*, National Security Archive, Washington, DC, 1994, pp. 19, 204.

4. According to Ray Garthoff, 'the Soviet Armed Forces have the most extensive and intensive military staff in command training system of any major power' (Wardak, Turbiville and Garthoff, *The Voroshilov Lectures*, p. 6).

5. There is an excellent analysis of the state of the Soviet strategic debate in the early 1960s in the introduction to the RAND edition of Sokolovsky's book, published in April 1963 (R-416-PR) by H. Dinerstein, L. Goure and T. Wolfe. Khrushchev's remark is quoted in V. Zubok, *A Failed Empire*, Chapel Hill, 2007, p. 136.

6. A. Lebedinsky (ed.), *What Russian Scientists Say about Radiation*, London, 1962. The findings of Chazov and his colleagues were eventually published in 1984. A. Kokoshin, *Soviet Strategic Thought, 1917–91*, Cambridge, MA, 1998, p. 136, quoting E. Chazov, L. Ilyin and A. Gus'kova (eds), *Yadernaya Voina: Mediko-biologicheskie Posledstviya* (Nuclear War: The Medical and Biological Effects), Moscow, 1984.

7. See the vicious attack on Arbatov by the Heritage Foundation, 'Unmasking Moscow's Institute of the USA and Canada', 17 December 1982, at http://www.heritage.org/research/reports/1982/12/unmasking-moscows-institute-of-the-usa (accessed 5 February 2016).

8. See A. Arbatov, *Svidetelstvo Sovremennika*, p. 280, and the memoirs of the penultimate chairman of the KGB, Vladimir Kryuchkov (V. Kryuchkov, *Lichnoe Delo*, Moscow, 1996, Vol. I, p. 327).

9. G. Arbatov, *Svidetelstvo Sovremmenika*, Moscow, 1991, pp. 243, 369, 380.

10. J. Hines et al., *Soviet Intentions 1965–1985*, Vol. II, Washington, DC, 1995, pp. 37, 31.

11. Morton Kaplan, quoted in L. Freedman, *The Evolution of Nuclear Strategy*, London, 2003, p. 201; J. Stone, *Strategic Persuasion: Arms Limitation Through Dialogue*, New York, 1967, quoted by Friedman, ibid., p. 347; Warnke is quoted in R. Pipes, 'Why the Soviet Union Thinks It Could Fight and Win a Nuclear War', Commentary, New York, July 1977.

12. B. Blair, *The Logic of Accidental War*, Washington, DC, 1993, pp. 40, 60.

13. M. Dobbs, *Six Months in 1945: FDR, Stalin, Churchill, and Truman – from World War to Cold War*, London, 2012, p. 349.

14. A. Dobrynin, *In Confidence*, New York, 1995, p. 524.

15. See remarks by Generals Detinov and Starodubov at the Musgrove Conference, 7–9 May 1994; Watch and Savranskaya, *SALT II and the Growth of Mistrust*, pp. 14–15.

16. G. Kennan, *Memoirs: 1950–1963*, London, 1972, p. 328.

17. Vasilevsky in *Red Star*, 22 February 1954, quoted H. Dinerstein, 'The Revolution in Soviet Strategic Thinking', *Foreign Affairs*, January 1958.

18. Hines et al., *Soviet Intentions 1965–1985*, Vol. I, p. 9, Vol. II, p. 40.

19. Kokoshin, *Soviet Strategic Thought*, p. 115, drawing on A. Kiryan et al., *Istoriya Voennogo Isskustvtva*, Moscow, 1986.

20. Marshal Rotmistrov, 'The Role of Surprise in Contemporary War', February 1955; General Talensky, 'The Role of Surprise in Contemporary War', November 1955. Oleg Penkovsky, the Soviet military intelligence officer recruited as a spy by the British, supplied them with a valuable collection of copies of *Voennaya Mysl* in the early 1960s.

21. Zubok, *A Failed Empire*, p. 128.

22. The speeches by Malenkov and Mikoyan are quoted by R. Garthoff, *Deterrence and the Revolution in Soviet Military Doctrine*, Washington, DC, 1990, p. 33. The political manoeuvres are described in V. Zubok and H. Harrison, 'Nikita Khrushchev', in J. Gaddis (ed.), *Cold War Statesmen Confront the Bomb: Nuclear Diplomacy since 1945*, Oxford, 1999, p. 145.

23. The text is at http://www.atomicarchive.com/Docs/Deterrence/ Atomsforpeace.shtml (accessed 5 March 2017).

24. Note of 1 April 1954 from V. A. Malyshev to N. S. Khrushchev, with attached draft article 'The Dangers of Atomic War and President Eisenhower's Proposal', L. Ryabev (ed), *Atomny Proekt SSSR: Dokumenty i Materialy*, Vol. III, Part 2, Moscow-Sarov 2009, Document No. 75, p. 163 [my translation].

25. V. Adamski and Yu. Smirnov, 'Moralnaya Otvetsvennost Uchenykh i Politicheskikh Liderov v Yadernuyu Epokhu', in *Nauka i Obshchestvo: Istoria Sovietskogo Atomnogo Proekta (40–50 Gody)*, Moscow, 1997.

26. Zubok and Harrison, 'Nikita Khrushchev', in Gaddis (ed.), *Cold War Statesmen Confront the Bomb*, p. 147.

27. Molotov attacked Khrushchev for saying that the nuclear stalemate would eventually lead to an agreement between the Soviet Union and the United States; Garthoff, *Deterrence and the Revolution in Soviet Military Doctrine*, p. 32; Dinerstein, 'The Revolution in Soviet Strategic Thinking'.

28. A. Belyakov and F. Burlatsky, 'Lenin's Theory of the Socialist Revolution and the Present Day', *Kommunist*, No. 13, September 1960, pp. 15–16; quoted in Garthoff, *Deterrence and the Revolution in Soviet Military Doctrine*, p. 33.

29. Garthoff, ibid., p. 34.

30. Comment by Edward Crankshaw in N. Khrushchev, *Khrushchev Remembers*, London, 1971, p. 507.

31. Ibid., pp. 402–3; D. Holloway, *Stalin and the Bomb*, New Haven, 1994, pp. 360–62.

32. Zubok, *A Failed Empire*, p. 135.

33. Kokoshin, *Soviet Strategic Thought*, p. 117.

34. Ibid., p. 123, quoting N. Krylov, 'Raketno-yaderni Shchit Sovietskogo Gosudarstva', Voennaya Mysl, No. 2, 1967; Garthoff, *Deterrence and the Revolution in Soviet Military Doctrine*, pp. 45–6.

35. E. Chazov, *Zdorovie i Vlast*, Moscow, 1993, p. 11; Dobrynin, *In Confidence*, p. 313.

36. R. Garthoff, *Soviet Leaders and Intelligence: Assessing the American Adversary during the Cold War*, Washington, DC, 2015, p. 174; G. Krivosheev, *Rossia I SSSR v Voinakh XX Veka*, Moscow, 2001, pp. 521 et seq.

37. Arbatov, *Svidetelstvo Sovremennika*, p. 232.

38. Chernyaev, *Moya Zhizn i Moe Vremya*, Moscow, 1995, p. 305.

39. Zubok, *A Failed Empire*, p. 209.

40. Arbatov, *Svidetelstvo Sovremmenika*, pp. 282–97; Brezhnev's speech of 5 November 1967 is in L. Brezhnev, *Izbrannye proizvedenia*, Vol. I, Moscow, 1981, p, 198, quoted in Garthoff, *Deterrence and the Revolution in Soviet Military Doctrine*, p. 53.

41. Arbatov, *Svidetelstvo Sovremennika*, p. 191.

42. Zubok, *A Failed Empire*, pp. 209, 214.

43. Brezhnev was moved to tears by the speech these people drafted for him to make in support of détente at the Moscow Congress of Peaceloving Forces in October 1973. In his own eyes at least he was entirely sincere: Chernyaev, *Moya Zhizn i Moe Vremya*, pp. 292, 299, 304.

44. Sakharov's warning to Brezhnev is taken from G. Hosking, *The Awakening of the Soviet Union* (1988 Reith Lectures), London, 1988. See also M. Gorbachev, *Zhizn i Reformy*, Moscow, 1995, pp. 327 et seq.; L. Aron, *Boris Yeltsin: A Revolutionary Life*, London, 2000, pp. 90, 281–4, 295; R. Braithwaite, *Across the Moscow River: The World Turned Upside Down*, London, 2002, p. 285.

45. Chernyaev, *Moya Zhizn i Moe Vremya*, p. 306.

46. Zubok, *A Failed Empire*, p. 225.

47. Chernyaev, *Moya Zhizn i Moe Vremya*, pp. 292, 299.

48. Anatoli Chernyaev diary entry for 15 January 1977; for Russian text see http://nsarchive.gwu.edu/rus/text_files/Chernyaev/1977.pdf (accessed 15 July 2016); Dobrynin, *In Confidence*, New York, 1995, pp. 430–32.

49. In 1976 the Warsaw Pact formally proposed a draft treaty banning first use. *Pravda*, 28 November 1976, quoted in Garthoff, *Deterrence and the Revolution in Soviet Military Doctrine*, p. 85. In 1982 Brezhnev told the UN, 'The Soviet Union is assuming the obligation not to be the first to use nuclear weapons.' For one example of a suspicious Western reaction, see the remarks by General Brent Scowcroft to *New Perspectives Quarterly*, Vol. 1, No. 4, Fall–Winter 1984–5, at http://digitalnpq.org/archive/1984_85_fall_winter/general.html (accessed 11 February 2016).

50. Hines et al., *Soviet Intentions 1965–1985*, Vol. II, p. 10: interview with General Batenin; D. Hoffman, *The Dead Hand*, New York, 2009, p. 533.

51. G. Barrass, *The Great Cold War*, Stanford, 2006, p. 213.

52. Arbatov, *Svidetelstvo Sovremmenika*, p. 236.

53. Kokoshin, *Soviet Strategic Thought*, p. 133; D. Proektor, 'O Politike, Klausevitse, i Pobede v Yadernoj Voine', *Mezhdunarodnaya Zhizn*, No. 4, 1988, quoted in Kokoshin, *Soviet Strategic Thought*, p. 60.

54. Yuri Yartsev, *Literaturnaya Gazeta*, 27 October 1982, quoted in Garthoff, *Deterrence and the Revolution in Soviet Military Doctrine*, p. 89.

55. General Ogarkov, *Istoria Uchit Bditelnosti*, Moscow, 1985, quoted in Garthoff, *Deterrence and the Revolution in Soviet Military Doctrine*, p. 52.

56. Ibid., p. 69.

57. Kokoshin, *Soviet Strategic Thought*, pp. 134–5, quoting V. Zhurkin, 'Net – Kontseptyam Yadernoi Voiny', in *Novy Mirovoi Poryadok i Politicheskaya Obshchnost*, Moscow, 1983; and E. Velikhov, 'Nauka i Aktualnye Problemy Borby Protiv Ugrozy Yadernoi Voiny', *Vestnik Akademii Nauk SSSR*, No. 9, 1983.

58. Kokoshin, *Soviet Strategic Thought*, p. 145, quoting S. Blagovolin, 'Geopoliticheskie Aspekty Oboronitelnoj Dostatochnosti', *Kommunist*, No. 4, 1990. B. Lambeth, 'A Generation Too Late: Civilian Analysts and Soviet Military Thinking', in D. Leebaert, *Soviet Strategy and New Military Thinking*, Cambridge, 1992, p. 217.

59. A 'new thinker', speaking in 1985 to Ray Garthoff: see Garthoff, *Soviet Leaders and Intelligence*, p. 82.

60. S. Akhromeyev and G. Kornienko, *Glazami Marshala i Diplomata*, Moscow, 1992, pp. 122–6; Garthoff, *Soviet Leaders and Intelligence*, p. 79.

61. J. Hines et al., *Soviet Intentions 1965–1985*, Washington 1995, Vol II, p. 29.

Chapter 8: Strategy for a Small Island

1. P. Hennessy, *The Secret State: Preparing for the Worst 1945–2010*, London, 2010, p. 57; see also N. Wheeler, 'British Nuclear Weapons and Anglo-American Relations 1945–54'.

2. R. Braithwaite, unpublished Moscow diary, 30 January 1992.

3. The text of the MAUD Report is in P. Hennessy, *Cabinets and the Bomb*, Oxford, 2007, pp. 32–4.

4. I. Clark and N. Wheeler, *The British Origins of Nuclear Strategy 1945–1955*, Oxford, 1989, pp. 35, 44.

5. Text of Operation Unthinkable at https://web.archive.org/web/20101116152301/http://www.history.neu.edu/PR02/ (accessed 23 July 2015).

6. See https://en.wikipedia.org/wiki/Brien_McMahon; the text is at http://www.osti.gov/atomicenergyact.pdf (both accessed 22 July 2015).

7. Attlee's paper, GEN 79/1 of 29 August 1945, is reproduced in Hennessy, *Cabinets and the Bomb*, pp. 36–8.

8. H. Stimson, 'Memorandum of the Effects of Atomic Bomb', 11 September 1945, at http://www.nuclearfiles.org/menu/library/correspondence/stimson-henry/corr_stimson_1945–09–11.htm (accessed 30 July 2016).

9. Declaration on Atomic Bomb by President Truman and prime ministers Attlee and King, Washington, DC, 15 November 1945, http://nuclearfiles.org/menu/key-issues/nuclear-energy/history/dec-truma-atlee-king_1945–11–15.htm.

10. G. Farmelo, *Churchill's Bomb*, London, 2013, p. 315.

11. J. Baylis, *Ambiguity and Deterrence: British Nuclear Strategy 1945–1964*, Oxford, 1995, pp. 45–50, and Appendix 1.

12. Clark and Wheeler, *The British Origins of Nuclear Strategy 1945–1955*, p. 29.

13. Hansard, 21 August 1945, Vol. 413, cc. 441–4, oral answers.

14. J. Lewis, *Changing Direction: British Military Planning for Post-war Strategic Defence, 1942–1947*, London, 1988; Clark and Wheeler, *The British Origins of Nuclear Strategy 1945–1955*, p. 46.

15. Hennessy, *Cabinets and the Bomb*, p. 57.

16. Lord Zuckerman's paper on Comprehensive Test Ban of 3 October 1978 in D. Owen, *Nuclear Papers*, Liverpool, 2009, pp. 238–42.

17. Baylis, *Ambiguity and Deterrence*, p. 91.

18. Ibid., p. 135.

19. Ibid., p. 180.

20. N. Wheeler, 'British Nuclear Weapons and Anglo-American Relations 1945–54', *International Affairs (Royal Institute of International Affairs 1944–)*, Vol. 62, No. 1, pp. 71–86.

21. The Joint Intelligence Committee later reported that a nuclear attack on Britain would 'effectively disrupt the life of the country and make

normal activity completely impossible'. Hennessy, *Cabinets and the Bomb*, pp. 117–19; Hennessy, *The Secret State*, pp. 57–8, 153.

22. Hansard, House of Commons debate, 16 April 1957, Vol. 568, cc. 1758–878. The text of the White Paper is partially reproduced as Annex 10 in Baylis, *Ambiguity and Deterrence*, p. 427.

23. Ibid., p. 86.

24. M. Gowing, *Independence and Deterrence: Britain and Atomic Energy, 1945–52*, London, 1974, Vol. I, p. 169.

25. Clark and Wheeler, *The British Origins of Nuclear Strategy 1945–1955*, p. 46.

26. Hennessy, *The Secret State*, p. 278.

27. J. Wilson, *Britain on the Brink*, Barnsley, p. 127.

28. See http://en.wikipedia.org/wiki/Blue_Streak_(missile).

29. R. Neustadt, *Report to JFK: The Skybolt Crisis in Perspective*, New York, 1999; http://nuclearweaponarchive.org/Uk/UKArsenalDev.htm; http://en.wikipedia.org/wiki/GAM-87_Skybolt.

30. L. Freedman, *The Evolution of Nuclear Strategy*, London, 2003, p. 291.

31. The Nassau negotiations are described in P. Hennessy and J. Jinks, *The Silent Deep: The Royal Navy Submarine Service since 1945*, London, 2015, pp. 209–13. See also Hennessy, *The Secret State*, p. 65.

32. Cabinet Minutes, 21 December 1962, Hennessy, *Cabinets and the Bomb*, pp. 145–6.

33. Hennessy, *The Secret State*, pp. 71–2, 76–7.

34. Hennessy and Jinks, *The Silent Deep*, p. 506.

35. Hennessy and Jinks examined with great care allegations that a British missile submarine was deployed to the South Atlantic during the crisis and found them baseless: ibid., pp. 455 et seq.

36. Owen, *Nuclear Papers*, p. 6.

37. The Duff–Mason memorandum (TNA/DEFE/25/355, Mason to Hunt, 12 December 1978) is quoted extensively in Hennessy and Jinks, *The Silent Deep*, pp. 471 et seq.

38. The back history to the 'Moscow Criterion' is set out in J. Baylis and K. Stoddart, *The British Nuclear Experience: The Roles of Beliefs, Culture and Identity*, London, 2014, p. 101 and passim, and in J. Ainslie, 'Unacceptable Damage: Damage Criteria in British Nuclear Planning', Scottish CND, February 2013, at http://www.banthebomb.org/index.php/publications/reports/1419-unacceptable-damage (accessed 4 March 2017).

39. Owen, *Nuclear Papers*, pp. 136, 151.

40. Lawrence Freedman, a leading British scholar, summarises Quinlan's sometimes convoluted arguments in 'The Intellectual Legacy of Sir Michael Quinlan', in B. Tertrais (ed.), *Thinking about Strategy: A Tribute to Sir Michael Quinlan*, Paris, 2011, pp. 15–28.

41. Hennessy and Jinks, *The Silent Deep*, p. 483.

42. Wohlstetter suggested that the Russians were comparatively indifferent to casualties in his 1958 article 'The Delicate Balance of Terror'. Professor Richard Pipes, Chairman of Team B, echoed it in 'Why the Soviet Union Thinks It Could Fight and Win a Nuclear War', *Commentary*, New York, July 1977.

43. *Britain's Nuclear Deterrent Force: The Choice of a System to Succeed Polaris*, Defence Open Government Document 80/23, July 1980.

44. Hennessy and Jinks, *The Silent Deep*, p. 483.

45. *The Tablet*, 15 August 1981. Quoted in Lawrence Freedman, 'British Nuclear Targeting ', in D. Ball and J. Richelson (eds), *Strategic Nuclear Targeting*, Ithaca, 1986, p. 124.

46. T. Ogilvie-White (ed.), *On Nuclear Deterrence: The Correspondence of Sir Michael Quinlan*, London, 2011, p. 136.

47. J. Ainslie, 'If Britain Fired Trident: The Humanitarian Consequences of a Nuclear Attack by a Trident Submarine on Moscow', Scottish CND, February 2014, at http://www.ican.org/wp-content/uploads/2013/ifbritainfiredtrident.pdf (accessed 22 February 2016).

48. Minutes of ministerial meeting of 31 December 1962, Hennessy, *Cabinets and the Bomb*, pp. 149–53.

49. The French deterrent force and the thinking behind it are described in http://en.wikipedia.org/wiki/M5 1_(missile); https://en.wikipedia.org/wiki/Force_de_dissuasion; S. Gadal, *Forces aériennes stratégiques: histoire des deux premières composantes de la dissuasion nucléaire française*, Economica, 2009, p. 86; National Security Archive Electronic Briefing Book No. 346, 26 May 2011, http://nsarchive.gwu.edu/nukevault/ebb346/ (accessed 4 March 2017); R. H. Ullman, 'The Covert French Connection', *Foreign Policy*, Vol. 75, Summer 1989, pp. 3–33.

50. Robert Armstrong to Mrs Thatcher, 'Future of the Strategic Deterrent', 4 December 1979 TNA/PREM/19/159, quoted in Hennessy and Jinks, *The Silent Deep*, p. 468.

51. R. Woodman and D. Conley, *Cold War Command: The Dramatic Story of a Nuclear Submariner*, Barnsley, 2014, p. 263.

52. Text of Franco-British declaration of 2 November 2010 is at https://www.gov.uk/government/news/uk-france-summit-2010-declaration-on-defence-and-security-co-operation (accessed 4 March 2017).

Chapter 9: Know Your Enemy

1. C. Clausewitz, *On War*, edited by M. Howard and P. Paret, Princeton, 1976, Vol. I, Book I, Ch. VI, p. 117.

2. Report of the Oversight and Investigations Subcommittee of the Committee on Armed Services, House of Representatives, on 'Intelligence Successes and

Failures in Operations Desert Shield/Storm', 103rd Congress, First Session, 16 August 1993, p. 2, n. 2.

3. Bearden opposed the Russians in Afghanistan and was head of the CIA's Soviet/East European Division at the time of the Soviet collapse. Quoted in G. Barrass, *The Great Cold War*, Stanford, 2006, p. 379.

4. Clausewitz, *On War*, p. 117.

5. See https://en.wikipedia.org/wiki/United_States_Intelligence_Community (accessed 20 July 2015).

6. This account is taken from a report by the Joint Chiefs of Staff, 'Evaluation of the Atomic Bomb as a Military Weapon'. A redacted text is in the Truman Library: http://www.trumanlibrary.org/whistlestop/study_collections/bomb/large/documents/pdfs/81.pdf (accessed 29 November 2016).

7. 'Possibility of Direct Soviet Military Action during 1948–9', Report of Ad Hoc Committee Reviewing the Conclusions on ORE 22–48, https://www.cia.gov/library/center-for-the-study-of-intelligence/csi-publications/books-and-monographs/cias-analysis-of-the-soviet-union-1947–1991/ (accessed 4 March 2017).

8. D. Hoffman, *The Billion Dollar Spy*, London, 2015, quoting G. Haynes and R. Leggett, *The CIA's Analysis of the Soviet Union, 1947–1991: A Documentary Collection*, Washington, DC, 2001.

9. CIA website, News and Information, https://www.cia.gov/news-information/featured-story-archive/2011-featured-story-archive/pyotr-popov.html (accessed 28 September 2016).

10. Tolkachev's story is told in fully documented detail in Hoffman, *The Billion Dollar Spy*, 2015.

11. A. Pervushin, *Atomny Proekt: Istoria Sverkhoruzhia*, Moscow, 2015, p. 388; A. Shitov, 'Agent Delmar Makes Contact', *Rossiiskaya Gazeta*, 30 January 2008, at https://rg.ru/2008/01/30/delmar.html (accessed 24 September 2016).

12. D. Holloway, *Stalin and the Bomb*, New Haven, 1994, pp. 82–4.

13. Thus V. Gubarev, *Atomnaya Bomba: Khronika Velikikh Otkrytii*, Chapter 'Razvedka Nachinaet "Drobit Atom"'. Another version has it that Kurchatov was first shown the intelligence material by Molotov in March 1943.

14. L. Ryabev (ed.), *Atomny Proekt SSSR: Dokumenty i Materialy*, Sarov, 1998–2009, Vol. I, Part 1, Document No. 296, p. 194.

15. See A. Kojevnikov, *Stalin's Great Science: The Times and Adventures of Soviet Physicists*, London, 2004, p. 189; G. Herken, *Brotherhood of the Bomb: The Tangled Lives and Loyalties of Robert Oppenheimer, Ernest Lawrence, and Edward Teller*, New York, 2002, p. 91; Holloway, *Stalin and the Bomb*, pp. 82–4; P. and A. Sudoplatov, *Special Tasks*, New York, 1994; P. Dolgopolov, 'Kurchatov "Rozhal" Bombu, Razvedka Prinimal "Rody"'; interview with Vladimir Barkovsky in V. Mikhailov and A. Dyachenko

(eds), *Opalennye v Borbe pri Sozdanii Yadernovo Shchita Rodiny*, Moscow, 2008, p. 71. Yuri Kobeladze's article in *Literaturnaya Gazeta*, 26 July 1994, quoted in Jeremy Stone, 'Conscience, Arrogation and the Atomic Scientists', *Journal of the Federation of Atomic Scientists*, Vol. 47, No. 4, July/August 1994. See also article by Vladislav Zubok, 'Atomic Espionage and Soviet Witnesses'; Yu. Smirnov, 'The KGB Mission to Niels Bohr: Its Real "Success"', *Cold War International History Project Bulletin*, Fall 1994, p. 50, Woodrow Wilson Center, Washington, DC.

16. Ryabev (ed.), *Atomny Proekt SSSR*, Sarov, 1998–2009, Vol. I, Part 1, Document No. 175, p. 375.

17. See Yuli Khariton, 'The Nuclear Weapons of the USSR: Did It Come from America or Was It Built Independently?', in Mikhailov and Dyachenko (eds), *Opalennye v Borbe pri Sozdanii Yadernovo Shchita Rodiny*, pp. 32–5.

18. See https://en.wikipedia.org/wiki/John_Anthony_Walker (accessed 18 March 2016).

19. See https://en.wikipedia.org/wiki/Rainer_Rupp (accessed 18 March 2016).

20. Barrass, *The Great Cold War*, p. 90.

21. See https://en.wikipedia.org/wiki/Lockheed_U-2#Renewal_of_Eastern_Bloc_overflights (accessed 30 August 2016).

22. See https://en.wikipedia.org/wiki/Corona_(satellite) (accessed 20 July 2015).

23. M. Herman and G. Hughes (eds), *Intelligence in the Cold War: What Difference Did it Make?*, Abingdon, 2013, p. 45, quoting R. Garthoff, *Détente and Confrontation: US–Soviet Relations from Nixon to Reagan*, Washington, DC, pp. 719 n., 726.

24. See https://en.wikipedia.org/wiki/Project_Azorian; https://en.wikipedia.org/wiki/Operation_Ivy_Bells (both accessed 21 July 2015).

25. See https://en.wikipedia.org/wiki/Zenit_(satellite) (accessed 20 July 2015).

26. S. Talbott, *Endgame: The Inside Story of SALT II*, New York, 1979, p. 251.

27. Examples of such exaggeration are listed by Alain Enthoven in 'US Forces in Europe: How Many? Doing What?', *Foreign Affairs*, Vol. 53, No. 3, April 1975, pp. 513–32.

28. For the texts of the American strategic documents see T. Etzold and J. Gaddis, *Containment: Documents on American Foreign Policy and Strategy, 1945–1950*, New York, 1978. Some scholars claim that the American and British governments did have hard information about the prospects for Soviet aggression in Europe, but they do not elaborate: see B. Heuser, 'NSC 68 and the Soviet Threat: A New Perspective on Western Threat Perception and Policy Making', *Review of International Studies*, Vol. 17, 1991, pp. 17–40.

29. Leites's ideas are dissected in R. Robin, *The Making of the Cold War Enemy*, Princeton, 2001, pp. 131 et seq.

30. S. Drew (ed.), *NSC-68: Forging the Strategy of Containment*, Washington, DC, 1994, p. 24; Marshall Shulman to Secretary of State Muskie,

2 September 1980, at http://nsarchive.gwu.edu/nukevault/ebb390/docs/9–2-80%20Shulman%20critique.pdf (accessed 29 August 2016).

31. Reagan diary and memoirs quoted in D. Hoffman, *The Dead Hand*, New York, 2009, pp. 95–6.

32. Talbott, *Endgame*, p. 82.

33. M. Cox, 'Western Intelligence: The Soviet Threat and NSC-68: A Reply to Beatrice Heuser', *Review of International Studies*, Vol. 18, No. 1, January 1992, pp. 75–83.

34. A. Cahn, *Killing Detente: The Right Attacks the CIA*, Pennsylvania, 1998, pp. 1–2.

35. C. Clausewitz, *On War*, translated by J. Graham, Oxford, 1973, Chapter 6, Book 8.

36. See the discussion of Soviet attitudes to Clausewitz in Beatrice Heuser, *Reading Clausewitz*, Chapter 7.

37. T. Scheer, *With Enough Shovels: Reagan, Bush and Nuclear War*, New York, 1983, pp. 105–6.

38. Team B report, Part 2; K. Rose, *One Nation Underground: The Fallout Shelter in American Culture*, New York, 2001, p. 217; Barrass, *The Great Cold War*, p. 210.

39. R. Pipes, 'Why the Soviet Union Thinks It Could Fight and Win a Nuclear War', *Commentary*, New York, July 1977.

40. SNIE (Special National Intelligence Estimate) 80–82 of 17 January 1962, and SNIE 85–3-62 of 19 September 1962, quoted in A. Zegan, 'The Cuban Missile Crisis as Intelligence Failure', Hoover Institution Policy Review, 2 October 2012.

41. R. Garthoff, *Assessing the Adversary*, Washington, DC, 1991, p. 51; R. Neustadt and E. May, *Thinking in Time: The Uses of History for Decisionmakers*, New York, 1988, p. 12.

42. R. Garthoff, *Soviet Leaders and Intelligence: Assessing the American Adversary during the Cold War*, Washington, DC, 2015, p. 13.

43. This is a tangled history. This account is based on G. Kornienko, *Kholodnaya Voina: Svidetelstvo ee Uchastnika*, Moscow, 2001, and Garthoff, *Soviet Leaders and Intelligence*, p. 34.

44. V. Bakatin, *Izbavlenie ot KGB*, Moscow, 1991, p. 163.

45. R. Braithwaite, unpublished Moscow diary, 22 December 1990. The text of Kryuchkov's June 1991 speech is in V. Kryuchkov, *Lichnoe Delo*, Moscow, 1996, Vol. I, p. 414.

46. Garthoff, *Soviet Leaders and Intelligence*, p. 94, quoting General Vadim Kirpichenko, *Razvedka: Litsa i Lichnosti*, Moscow, 2001, p. 33.

47. P. Cradock, *Know Your Enemy*, London, 2002, p. 294.

48. B. Fischer (ed.), *At Cold War's End: US Intelligence on the Soviet Union and Eastern Europe, 1989–1991*, Washington, DC, 2001, Preface.

49. National Intelligence Council, 'Soviet Policy Toward the West: The Gorbachev Challenge', 1 April 1989, Cold War International History Project, Documents and Papers, at https://chnm.gmu.edu/1989/items/show/349 (accessed 9 August 2016).

50. Bakatin, *Izbavlenie ot KGB*, p. 85.

51. M. Alexander, *Managing the Cold War: A View from the Front Line*, London, 2005, pp. xi, 193; quoted in Herman and Hughes (eds), *Intelligence in the Cold War*, p. 143.

Chapter 10: Now Thrive the Armourers

1. S. Zuckerman, *Nuclear Illusion & Reality*, New York, 1982, p. 108.

2. Ya. Golovanov, *Korolev: Fakty i Mify*, Moscow, 1994, Chapter 49, 'Istoria o Tom, Kak Myshi seli Volkodav'; A. Beevor, *Stalingrad*, London, 1998, p. 231.

3. Zuckerman, *Nuclear Illusion & Reality*, p. 108.

4. These two paragraphs are drawn from Parts I and II of H. Gusterson, *People of the Bomb*, Minneapolis, 2004.

5. N. Polmar and R. Norris, *US Nuclear Arsenal: A History of Weapons and Delivery Systems since 1945*, Washington, DC, 2009, p. 254; H. Kissinger, *Nuclear Weapons and Foreign Policy* (abridged edition), New York, 1969, p. 20.

6. 'VPK Kommissia po Voenno-promyshlennym Voprosam pri SM SSSR', *Semeinye Istorii*, at http://www.famhist.ru/famhist/chertok/00422733.htm (accessed 18 October 2016).

7. V. Gubarev, *Yaderny Vek Bomba*, Moscow, 1995, pp. 82, 164.

8. A. Savel'yev and N. Detinov, *The Big Five: Arms Control Decision-Making in the Soviet Union*, New, York 1995, p. 19; V. Kataev, *A Memoir of the Missile Age: One Man's Journey*, Stanford, 2015, pp. 152–7.

9. Gubarev, *Yaderny Vek Bomba*, p. 163.

10. G. Kornienko, *Kholodnaya Voina: Svidetelstvo ee Uchastnika*, Moscow, 2001, Chapter 7, 'Razryadka i ee Ugasanie: OSV-1, Nachalny Etap'.

11. Kataev, *A Memoir of the Missile Age*, pp. 114–16.

12. Kissinger, *Nuclear Weapons and Foreign Policy*, p. 12.

13. These patrols had code names such as Head Start, Chrome Dome, Hard Head, Round Robin, and Giant Lance.

14. S. Zaloga, *The Kremlin's Nuclear Sword: The Rise and Fall of Russia's Strategic Nuclear Forces, 1945–2000*, Washington, DC, 2002, p. 12.

15. The characteristics of Soviet strategic bombers are comprehensively described in Ye. Gordon, *Soviet Strategic Aviation in the Cold War*, Manchester, 2013, pp. 16, 31; see also Zaloga, *The Kremlin's Nuclear Sword*, p. 16.

16. The adjective is Steven Zaloga's: *The Kremlin's Nuclear Sword*, p. 17.

17. Ibid., p. 30.

18. E. May, J. Steinbruner and T. Wolfe, *History of the Strategic Arms Competition, Part 1*, Washington, DC, 1981, p. 185–6.

19. National Intelligence Estimate 11-6-55, 1 July 55: Probable Intelligence Warning of Soviet Attack on the US through mid-1958 (US National Archive Catalogue at https://research.archives.gov/id/7326921).

20. J. Newhouse, *The Nuclear Age: From Hiroshima to Star Wars*, London, 1989, p. 111.

21. Zaloga, *The Kremlin's Nuclear Sword*, pp. 30, 175.

22. F. Kaplan, *Wizards of Armageddon*, New York, 1983, pp. 156–63; E. Schlosser, *Command and Control*, London, 2013, p. 150; https://en.wikipedia.org/wiki/Myasishchev_M-4; Zaloga, *The Kremlin's Nuclear Sword*, pp. 247–8.

23. The equation was first set out in 1813 in a pamphlet, 'A Treatise on the Motion of Rockets', by William Moore, a British mathematician, but it was not published and had no international influence.

24. Glushko's career is briefly described at https://en.wikipedia.org/wiki/Valentin_Glushko (accessed 27 September 2016).

25. D. Holloway, *Stalin and the Bomb*, New Haven, 1994, p. 147; Zaloga, *The Kremlin's Nuclear Sword*, pp. 36–7.

26. Ibid., pp. 38, 41, 48.

27. There is a detailed description of the accident and its causes in E. Chertok, *Rockets and People*, Washington, DC, 2005–11, Vol. II, p. 598. The casualty figures range from 74 to 180. Chertok settles on a figure of 101.

28. Kataev, *A Memoir of the Missile Age*, p. 48.

29. See https://en.wikipedia.org/wiki/Nedelin_catastrophe.

30. M. Herman and G. Hughes (eds), *Intelligence in the Cold War: What Difference Did it Make?*, Abingdon, 2013, p. 26.

31. May, Steinbruner and Wolfe, *History of the Strategic Arms Competition, Part 1*, p. 433.

32. Ibid., p. 436.

33. B. Blair, *Nuclear Recollections*, at http://web.archive.org/web/20100706211333/http://www.cdi.org/blair/nuclear-recollections.cfm.

34. Description of a visit to the site, R. Braithwaite, unpublished Moscow diary, 10 December 1990.

35. See http://www2.hn.psu.edu/faculty/jmanis/poldocs/uspressu/SUaddressDEisenhower.pdf.

36. J. Prados, *The Soviet Estimate*, New York, 1982, p. 120.

37. Kaplan, *Wizards of Armageddon*, pp. 286–9; Prados, *The Soviet Estimate*, p. 120.

38. May, Steinbruner and Wolfe, *History of the Strategic Arms Competition*, p. 439.

39. Zaloga, *The Kremlin's Nuclear Sword*, pp. 51–2, 74.

40. Herman and Hughes (eds), *Intelligence in the Cold War*, p. 44.

41. Zaloga, *The Kremlin's Nuclear Sword*, p. 179.

42. Figures are ibid., p. 77; Appendix 2: Soviet Strategic Forces, 1960–Present; R. Norris and H. Kristensen, 'Global Nuclear Weapons Inventories, 1945–2010', *Bulletin of the Atomic Scientists*, Vol. 66, No. 4, July 2010, pp. 77–83; Polmar and Norris, *US Nuclear Arsenal*, p. 258.

43. National Security Archive Electronic Briefing Book No. 371, nsarchiv@gwu.edu.

44. S. Sagan, *The Limits of Safety*, Princeton, 1993; R. Gates, *From the Shadows*, New York, 1996, p. 114. Gates mistakenly says that the error was caused by the insertion of the wrong tape – which is what had happened in the earlier false alert.

45. B. Blair, *The Logic of Accidental War*, Washington, DC, 1993, p. 194; *Guardian*, 26 May 2016.

46. There is a vivid account of this incident in David Hoffman's *The Dead Hand*, New York, 2009, pp. 6–11.

47. Michael Maggelet and James Oskins argue that the true number is nearly twice that in their book *Broken Arrows*, Vol. II, Raleigh, NC, 2010; 'How Many Broken Arrows?', 9 July 2014, at http://nuclearweaponsaccidents.blogspot.co.uk/2014/07/how-many-broken-arrows.html; see also Schlosser, *Command and Control*, p. 329; United States military nuclear incident terminology at https://en.wikipedia.org/wiki/United_States_military_nuclear_incident_terminology; '50 Facts about U.S. Nuclear Weapons Today', Brookings Institute, Washington, DC, 28 April 2014 at http://www.brookings.edu/research/articles/2014/04/28–50-nuclear-facts (accessed 12 May 2016).

48. Schlosser, *Command and Control*, p. 26.

49. Wikipedia, 'List of Military Nuclear Accidents'; Schlosser, *Command and Control*, p. 436.

50. Ibid., pp. 444, 475.

51. Ibid., p. 220.

52. Interview with Chief Designer Stanislav Voronin in Gubarev, *Yaderny Vek Bomba*, p. 31

53. Ibid., p. 79.

54. S. Vladimirovsky, 'K Istorii Realizatsii Sovietskogo Atomnogo Proekta', in V. Mikhailov and A. Dyachenko (eds), *Opalennye v Borbe pri Sozdanii Yadernovo Shchita Rodiny*, Moscow, 2008, pp. 35–9.

55. There is a daunting list of accidents involving Soviet submarines in P. Huchthausen, *K-19 The Widowmaker*, Washington, DC, 2002, pp. 214–21.

Chapter 11: A Very Pleasant Way to Die

1. T. Pratchett, *Sourcery*, at http://metro.co.uk/2015/03/12/
    rip-terry-pratchett-10-of-his-most-moving-quotes-about-life-and-death-
    5100810/#ixzz3hjsZdOvz.

2. P. Ham, *Hiroshima Nagasaki*, London, 2013, p. 184.

3. The story is told in *Fears of a German dirty bomb*, by Alex Wellerstein,
    6 September 2013 at http://blog.nuclearsecrecy.com/2013/09/06/fears-of-
    a-german-dirty-bomb/. The text of Oppenheimer's letter is at http://blog.
    nuclearsecrecy.com/wp-content/uploads/2013/09/1943-Oppenheimer-to-
    Fermi.pdf

4. Ham, *Hiroshima Nagasaki*, p. 320.

5. R. Monk, *Inside the Centre: The Life of J. Robert Oppenheimer*, London, 2012,
    p. 457.

6. US Strategic Bombing Survey, Washington, DC, July 1946, p. 23.

7. Ham, *Hiroshima Nagasaki*, p. 470.

8. Ibid., p. 258.

9. Burchett's story appeared in the London *Daily Express* on 5 September 1945.
    Monk, *Inside the Centre*, p. 463.

10. Ham, *Hiroshima Nagasaki*, p. 476; J. Dower, 'The Bombed: Hiroshimas and
    Nagasakis in Japanese Memory', in M. Hogan (ed.), *Hiroshima: History and
    Memory*, Cambridge, 1996.

11. There is a careful examination of the issues in S. Malloy, '"A Very Pleasant
    Way to Die": Radiation Effects and the Decision to Use the Atomic Bomb
    against Japan', Diplomatic History, Vol. 36, No. 3, June 2012.

12. R. Serber, *The Los Alamos Primer*, Berkeley/Los Angeles, 1992, p. 34;
    D. Listwa, 'Hiroshima and Nagasaki: The Long-Term Health Effects', July
    2012, at https://k1project.columbia.edu/news/hiroshima-and-nagasaki,
    updated 7/3/2014.

13. G. DeGroot, *The Bomb: A Life*, Cambridge, MA, 2005, p. 107.

14. Ham, *Hiroshima Nagasaki*, quoting Dr Henry Smyth's report on the
    technical history of the bomb, p. 469.

15. J. Rotblat, *Nuclear Radiation in Warfare*, London, 1981, p. 3.

16. The Foundation, which continually updated its research, concluded that
    the most deadly long-term effect was leukaemia, which increased about two
    years after the attacks and peaked around four to six years thereafter. Other
    cancers increased later: http://www.rerf.jp/index_e.html (accessed 3 August
    2015); Ham, *Hiroshima Nagasaki*, p. 487 n.; Rotblat, *Nuclear Radiation
    in Warfare*, pp. 3, 139, 79. In his deliberately provocative book *Atomic
    Obsession*, John Mueller quotes a number of alternative views (pp. 195–6 and
    passim).

17. P. Goodchild, *Edward Teller: The Real Dr Strangelove*, London, 2004,
    pp. 228–9; Rotblat, *Nuclear Radiation in Warfare*; Nishiwaki's letter

is displayed at the Atomic Testing Museum in Nevada, http://www.japantimes.co.jp/news/2012/01/11/national/scientist-immediately-sought-details-from-u-s-on-1954-bikini-h-bomb-test/#.WVjBhsaZPeQ.

18. R. Guyer, 'Radioactivity and Rights: Clashes at Bikini Atoll', American Journal of Public Health, Vol. 91, No. 9, September 2001, pp. 1371–6, at http://www.ncbi.nlm.nih.gov/pmc/articles/PMC1446783/ (accessed 9 March 2016). Details of testing programmes are at Preparatory Commission for the Comprehensive Test Ban Organization, http://www.ctbto.org/nuclear-testing/ (accessed 26 March 2016).

19. Details of US tests at http://en.wikipedia.org/wiki/List_of_nuclear_weapons_tests_of_the_United_States and http://en.wikipedia.org/wiki/Desert_Rock_exercises. Sandefuhr's own account is at https://www.myservicepride.com/content/pfc-curtis-sandefur/.

20. Western accounts of the Totsk exercise say that the soldiers had no protective gear. The contrary version comes from accounts by participants: 'Pravda Poligona Smerti', Moskovsky Komsomolets, 13 September 2004, at http://www.mk.ru/editions/daily/article/2004/09/13/104911-pravda-poligona-smerti.html.

21. A. Sakharov, Memoirs, London, 1990, p. 221; http://en.wikipedia.org/wiki/Tsar_Bomba.

22. See http://www.ctbto.org/nuclear-testing/the-effects-of-nuclear-testing/the-united-kingdomsnuclear-testing-programme/; P. Grabosky, Wayward Governance: Illegality and Its Control in the Public Sector, Chapter 16, 'A Toxic Legacy: British Nuclear Weapons Testing in Australia', Canberra, 1989.

23. See http://www.ctbto.org/nuclear-testing/the-effects-of-nuclear-testing/frances-nuclear-testing-programme/; http://en.wikipedia.org/wiki/List_of_nuclear_weapons_tests_of_France.

24. On Foreign Office guidance: private information; P. Ortmeyer and A. Makhijani, 'Let Them Drink Milk', at http://www.ieer.org/latest/iodnart.html (originally published as 'Worse Than We Knew', Bulletin of the Atomic Scientists, November/December 1997); Herken, Brotherhood of the Bomb, p. 303.

25. Sakharov, Memoirs, p. 160.

26. I. Hargittai, Buried Glory: Portraits of Soviet Scientists, Oxford, 2013, p. 75, quoting E. Teller and A. Brown, The Legacy of Hiroshima, New York, 1962, pp. 180–81.

27. Report of NSC Ad Hoc Working Group on the Technical Feasibility of a Cessation of Nuclear Testing, 27 March 1958, at http://nsarchiv.gwu.edu/NSAEBB/NSAEBB94/index2htm; Goodchild, Edward Teller, pp. 274–6.

28. J. Rotblat, 'The Hydrogen-Uranium Bomb', Bulletin of the Atomic Scientists, Vol. 11, May 1955, pp. 171–2, 177; Pugwash History Series Number One,

May 2005, at http://www.tandfonline.com/doi/abs/10.1080/00963402.1955.1 1453597?journalCode=rbul20.

29. Yu. Smirnov, '*Kholodnaya Voina* kak Yavlenie Yadernogo Veka', in N. Yegorova and A. Chubarian (eds), *Kholodnaya Voina 1945–1963*, Moscow, 2003, p. 605.

30. Ibid., pp. 605, 606. See also V. Zubok and H. Harrison, 'Nikita Khrushchev', in J. Gaddis (ed.), *Cold War Statesmen Confront the Bomb: Nuclear Diplomacy since 1945*, Oxford, 1999, p. 164.

31. A. Lebedinsky (ed.), *What Russian Scientists Say about Radiation*, London, 1962. Sakharov's contribution, 'Radioactive Carbon from Nuclear Explosions and Non-threshold Biological Effects', is on p. 54.

32. Zubok and Harrison, 'Nikita Khrushchev', in Gaddis (ed.), *Cold War Statesmen Confront the Bomb*, p. 164.

33. Herken, *Brotherhood of the Bomb*, p. 307.

34. W. Burr and H. Montford (eds), *The Making of the Limited Test Ban Treaty, 1958–1963*, at http://nsarchive.gwu.edu/NSAEBB/NSAEBB94/ (accessed 25 March 2016); B. Greene, *Eisenhower, Science Advice, and the Nuclear Test-Ban Debate, 1945–1963*, Stanford, 2003, pp. 68 et seq.

35. Goodchild, *Edward Teller*, pp. 260–61, 267.

36. 'Army Fails to Bar Bomb Testimony: Secret Hearing Told Millions Would Die in Many Lands If Soviet Were Attacked', *New York Times*, 29 June 1956; Goodchild, *Edward Teller*, pp. 267.

37. N. Shute, *On the Beach*, London, 1957.

38. Herken, *Brotherhood of the Bomb*, p. 309.

39. Eleanor Roosevelt, Interview with Nikita Khrushchev, 3 October 1957, *The Eleanor Roosevelt Papers Project*, at https://www2.gwu.edu/~erpapers/documents/columns/kruschev_interview.cfm (accessed 4 December 2016).

40. G. Herken, *Brotherhood of the Bomb: The Tangled Lives and Loyalties of Robert Oppenheimer, Ernest Lawrence, and Edward Teller*, New York, 2002, p. 314.

41. Burr and Montford (eds), *The Making of the Limited Test Ban Treaty, 1958–1963*, letter from Philip Farley, 28 March 1958, at http://nsarchive.gwu.edu/NSAEBB/NSAEBB94/ (accessed 25 March 2016).

42. Ibid., Document No. 4: Meeting with Disarmament Advisers, 26 April 1956.

43. Herken, *Brotherhood of the Bomb*, p. 305.

44. Burr and Montford (eds), *The Making of the Limited Test Ban Treaty, 1958–1963*, at http://nsarchive.gwu.edu/NSAEBB/NSAEBB94/ (accessed 25 March 2016).

45. Herken, *Brotherhood of the Bomb*, p. 164.

46. N. Khrushchev, *Khrushchev Remembers: The Last Testament*, London, 1974, p. 536.

47. M. Herman and G. Hughes (eds), *Intelligence in the Cold War: What Difference Did it Make?*, Abingdon, 2013, p. 49.

48. Goodchild, *Edward Teller*, p. xxiii.

49. A. Horne, *Macmillan 1957–1986*, London, 1989, pp. 221, 228. Macmillan diary entry for 23 March 1960.

50. Horne, *Macmillan 1957–1986*, p. 284.

51. Sakharov, *Memoirs*, p. 216.

52. Ibid., p. 217; Khrushchev, *Khrushchev Remembers*, p. 70.

53. Burr and Montford (eds), *The Making of the Limited Test Ban Treaty, 1958–1963*, at http://nsarchive.gwu.edu/NSAEBB/NSAEBB94/ (accessed 25 March 2016).

54. Ibid., August 2003: Document 37: Memorandum from Air Force Chief of Staff Curtis LeMay, 'USAF Briefing for Dr. Teller on Nuclear Testing', 31 October 1961, enclosing report on 'Priority of Nuclear Weapons Tests of Primary Interest to the Air Force', 25 October 1961.

55. Horne, *Macmillan 1957–1986*, pp. 322–3.

56. Ibid., p. 325.

57. Burr and Montford (eds), *The Making of the Limited Test Ban Treaty, 1958–1963*, at http://nsarchive.gwu.edu/NSAEBB/NSAEBB94/ (accessed 25 March 2016).

58. The following account is heavily based on Horne, *Macmillan 1957–1986*, pp. 502–12.

59. See http://www.presidency.ucsb.edu/ws/?pid=9266 (accessed 25 March 2016).

60. Burr and Montford (eds), *The Making of the Limited Test Ban Treaty, 1958–1963*, at http://nsarchive.gwu.edu/NSAEBB/NSAEBB94/ (accessed 25 March 2016).

61. J. Lebovic, *Flawed Logics: Strategic Nuclear Arms Control from Truman to Obama*, Baltimore, 2013, p. 61.

62. Horne, *Macmillan 1957–1986*, pp. 522–3.

63. L. Wittner, *Confronting the Bomb: A Short History of the World Nuclear Disarmament Movement*, Stanford, 2009, pp. 132–3.

64. See http://en.wikipedia.org/wiki/Neutron_bomb (accessed 4 March 2017).

Chapter 12: Living on the Volcano

1. Attlee letter to Truman, September 1945, M. Grant, *After the Bomb: Civil Defence and Nuclear War in Britain, 1945–68*, London, 2010, p. 18.

2. Harold Macmillan, diary entry for 4 November 1962, quoted in Grant, *After the Bomb*, p. 9.

3. F. Kaplan, *Wizards of Armageddon*, New York, 1983, p. 127.

4. Ralph Lapp in *Must We Hide?* (1949), quoted in P. Boyer, *By the Bomb's Early Light*, New York, 1985, p. 321.

5.   *Life*, 18 December 1950, quoted ibid., p. 312.

6.   P. Boyer, *By the Bomb's Early Light*, New York, 1985, p. 332.

7.   Ibid., pp. 330–33; the reference to goats is on p. 323.

8.   See http://library.uoregon.edu/ec/e-asia/read/atomicattack.pdf (accessed 15 August 2015).

9.   See https://www.youtube.com/watch?v=IKqXu-5jw6o (accessed 4 March 2017).

10. Boyer, *By the Bomb's Early Light*, p. 314.

11. *Our Cities Must Fight* at https://www.youtube.com/watch?v=m_noFER9AUA; *Let's Face It* is available at https://www.youtube.com/watch?v=NFK2PBD4_TE; *A Day Called X* at https://www.youtube.com/watch?v=ueE17A7KaHA; Robert Moser is quoted on p. 28 of K. Rose, *One Nation Underground, The Fallout Shelter in American Culture*, New York, 2001.

12. *Deterrence and Survival in the Nuclear Age*, published US Congress 1976, at https://archive.org/details/detevivoounit.

13. G. Oakes, *The Imaginary War: Civil Defense and American Cold War Culture*, Oxford, 1994, p. 166.

14. J. Galbraith, *Letters to Kennedy*, Cambridge, MA, 1998, p. 20.

15. *Life*, 15 September 1961, at http://conelrad.com/books/flyleaf.php?id=322_0_1_0_M7 (accessed 12 August 2015).

16. The Reverend McHugh and Edward Teller are quoted in Kaplan, *Wizards of Armageddon*, pp. 312–14.

17. Presidential Directive 41 of 29 September 1978 on Civil Defense, at https://www.jimmycarterlibrary.gov/documents/pddirectives/pd41.pdf (accessed 1 December 2016).

18. Quoted in 'President Reagan's Civil Defense Program', *Defense Monitor*, Vol. XI, No. 5, 1982.

19. T. K. Jones was Deputy Under Secretary of Defense for Research and Engineering, Strategic and Theater Nuclear Forces. T. Scheer, *With Enough Shovels: Reagan, Bush and Nuclear War*, New York, 1983, pp. 31 et seq. See also Kaplan, *The Wizards of Armageddon*, p. 388.

20. Air Raid Drill Protests: See http://www.lokashakti.org/encyclopedia/movements/97-air-raid-drill-protests.

21. D. Hoffman, *The Dead Hand*, New York, 2009, p. 45.

22. H. Kissinger, *Nuclear Weapons and Foreign Policy*, New York, 1969, p. 64.

23. *Grazhdanskaya Oborona v selskoi mestnosti*, at http://eradoks.com/epoha-sssr/27-grazhdanskaya-oborona-v-selskoy-mestnosti.html (accessed 15 August 2015). The 1962 edition of *Grazhdanskaya Oborona*, and the extract from *Voennye Znania* of May 1978 with its lament about those who fear nuclear death, are available in translation on the Internet Archive at

https://ia601609.us.archive.org/17/items/UssrCivilDefenseDocuments/
UssrCivilDefenseDocuments.pdf (accessed 25 August 2016).

24. These quotations come from R. Garthoff, *Deterrence and the Revolution in
Soviet Military Doctrine*, Washington, 1990; poll conducted by the Institute
of Sociological Research of the USSR Academy of Sciences, 'Muscovites on
War and Peace', and published in *Izvestia*, 14 February 1987, p. 110, n. 46; L.
Ptitsyna, 'Games People Play', *XX Vek i Mir*, Vol. 10, October 1987, p. 111;
Interview with General Vladimir Govorov, *Komsomolskaya Pravda*, 9 March
1987, p. 111.

25. His Majesty's Stationery Office, *The Effects of the Atomic Bombs at Hiroshima
and Nagasaki*, London, 1946.

26. The following description of the development of British civil defence policy
is heavily based on Grant, *After the Bomb*, pp. 21–91, passim.

27. J. Baylis, *Ambiguity and Deterrence: British Nuclear Strategy 1945–1964*,
Oxford, 1995.

28. Grant, *After the Bomb*, pp. 48–53.

29. Ibid., p. 78.

30. Ibid., pp. 78–9.

31. There is a description of the Strath Report in P. Hennessy, *The Secret State:
Preparing for the Worst 1945–2010*, London, 2010, pp. 163 et seq.

32. Ibid., pp. 183–6.

33. Grant, *After the Bomb*, pp. 126, 152.

34. The existence of Corsham was comprehensively documented by Duncan
Campbell in 1982, in his book *War Plan UK: The Truth about Civil Defence
in Britain*, London, 1982. By then, the government suspected, its position
was already well known to the Russians.

35. Grant, *After the Bomb*, p. 187.

36. See http://www.atomica.co.uk/cdwhy.htm (accessed 15 August 2015).

37. G. DeGroot, *The Bomb: A Life*, Cambridge, MA, 2008, p. 48.

Chapter 13: Skirting the Brink

1. Andropov in conversation with Ronald's Reagan's emissary, Averell
Harriman, quoted in N. Jones (ed.), *The 1983 War Scare: 'The Last Paroxysm'
of the Cold War*, Part I, Documents 12 and 14, National Security Archive, at
http://nsarchive.gwu.edu/NSAEBB/NSAEBB426/ (accessed 4 March 2017).

2. Memorandum of 11 September 1945 from Henry Stimson to President
Truman, at http://nuclearfiles.org/menu/library/correspondence/stimson-
henry/corr_stimson_1945-09-11.htm (accessed 13 June 2017).

3. D. Acheson, *Present at the Creation*, New York, 1969, p. 148.

4. G. Shultz and J. Goodby (eds), *The War That Must Never Be Fought*,
Stanford, 2015, p. 29.

5. T. Schelling, *Arms and Influence*, New Haven, p. 287.

6. R. Garthoff, *Soviet Leaders and Intelligence: Assessing the American Adversary during the Cold War*, Washington, DC, 2015, p. 29.

7. McGeorge Bundy memorandum of 7 July 1961, quoted in F. Kaplan, *The Wizards of Armageddon*, New York, 1983, p. 297.

8. D. Watch and S. Savranskaya, *SALT II and the Growth of Mistrust: Transcript of Proceedings of Conference*, National Security Archive, Washington, DC, 1994, p. 37.

9. Kaplan, *Wizards of Armageddon*, p. 294.

10. J. Galbraith and H. Purcell, 'Did the U.S. Military Plan a Nuclear First Strike for 1963?', *American Prospect*, Fall 1994, at http://prospect.org/article/did-us-military-plan-nuclear-first-strike-1963 (accessed 27 November 2016).

11. N. Khrushchev, *Khrushchev Remembers*, London, 1971, p. 460; F. Burlatsky, *Khrushchev and the First Russian Spring*, London, 1991, p. 167; Kaplan, *Wizards of Armageddon*, pp. 296–8.

12. The course of the Cuban missile crisis has been exhaustively described. The following account is taken from Khrushchev, *Khrushchev Remembers*, pp. 486 et seq.; A. Fursenko and T. Naftali, *One Hell of a Gamble: The Secret History of the Cuban Missile Crisis*, London, 1997 (this is particularly good on Khrushchev and the discussions in Moscow. There is also a full description of Kennedy's exchanges with his advisers from p. 200); M. Dobbs, *One Minute to Midnight*, New York, 2008, passim; G. Barrass, *The Great Cold War*, Stanford, 2006, p. 139. See also A. Dobrynin, *In Confidence*, New York, 1995, p. 75.

13. Missile figures from S. Zaloga, *The Kremlin's Nuclear Sword: The Rise and Fall of Russia's Strategic Nuclear Forces, 1945–2000*, Washington, DC, 2002, p. 84.

14. R. Neustadt & E. May, *Thinking in Time*, New York 1988, p.9; Bundy McGeorge, *Danger and Survival: Choices about the Bomb in the First Fifty Years*, New York 1988, pp. 438–9.

15. V. Zubok, *A Failed Empire*, Chapel Hill, 2007, p. 147.

16. J. Hines et al., *Soviet Intentions 1965–1985*, Vol. II, Washington, DC, 1995, p. 31.

17. D. Hoffman, *The Dead Hand*, New York, 2009, p. 147.

18. Zaloga, *The Kremlin's Nuclear Sword*, p. 87.

19. The story of Brigade 69 and its mission to Cuba began to emerge in documents and the fallible reminiscences of participants after the collapse of the Soviet Union. Gaps and inconsistencies remain. The following account is based on a meticulous review of the evidence by Svetlana Savranskaya, 'New Sources on the Role of Soviet Submarines in the Cuban Missile Crisis', National Security Archive; National Security Archive Briefing Book, *The Submarines of October*, at http://nsarchive.gwu.edu/NSAEBB/NSAEBB75/ (accessed 4 March 2017); Savranskaya quotes, among others,

A. Mozgovoi, *Kubinskaya Samba Kvarteta 'Fokstrotov'*, Moscow, 2002; P. Huchthausen, *October Fury*, Hoboken, 2002 (Huchthausen was on a US destroyer hunting the Soviet submarines during the crisis. His account is based on documents and personal accounts in a somewhat fictionalised style); J. Drent, 'Confrontation in the Sargasso Sea: Soviet Submarines during the Cuban Missile Crisis', *Northern Mariner/Le marin du nord*, Vol. XIII, No. 3, July 2003, pp. 1–19; G. Weir and W. Boyne, *Rising Tide: The Untold Story of the Russian Submarines That Fought the Cold War*, New York, 2003; Russian TV documentary *Russki 'Fokstrot'*, at https://www.youtube.com/watch?v=RZjUVxIBaTw (accessed 4 March 2017). Most witnesses say that the commanders were given vague oral instructions on the use of the nuclear torpedoes: Huchthausen gives what he says is the text of their sealed orders; Mozgovoi has a similar text. Riurik Ketov, one of the commanders, told an American TV film, *The Man Who Saved the World*, that he had written authority to use the weapon at discretion (http://www.pbs.org/wnet/secrets/the-man-who-saved-the-world-watch-the-full-episode/905/).

20. National Security Archive, Chronology of Submarine Contact During the Cuban Missile Crisis 1 October–14 November, 1962 at http://nsarchive.gwu.edu/NSAEBB/NSAEBB75/subchron.htm (accessed 31 May 2017).

21. Admiral Rybalko, commanding the group to which the four Foxtrots belonged, may have passed the American notice to them, in defiance of an explicit order from the Commander-in-Chief of the Navy that operational security would be violated thereby. P. Huchthausen, *October Fury*, Hoboken 2002, p. 153. See also E. May, J. Steinbruner and T. Wolfe, *History of the Strategic Arms Competition, Part 2*, Washington, DC, 1981, p. 615.

22. Dobrynin, *In Confidence*, p. 85.

23. 'About Participation of Submarines "B-4", "B-36", "B-59", "B-130" of the 69th Submarine Brigade of the Northern Fleet in Operation Anadyr during the Period October–December 1962', undated report, c. December 1962, prepared by the USSR Northern Fleet Headquarters, translated by Svetlana Savranskaya, at http://nsarchive.gwu.edu/NSAEBB/NSAEBB399/docs/Report%20of%20the%20submarine%20mission.pdf (accessed 14 November 2016).

24. R. Garthoff, *Reflections on the Cuban Missile Crisis*, Washington, DC, 1987, pp. 37–8.

25. The incidents with the Atlas missile, the errant U-2, and the bear have been often described. See, for example, S. Sagan, *The Limits of Safety*, Princeton, 1993, pp. 127, 142, 100. Kennedy's furious remark is quoted in Dobbs, *One Minute to Midnight*, p. 270.

26. Zubok, *A Failed Empire*, p. 147.

27. This incident has been variously described in Garthoff, *Reflections on the Cuban Missile Crisis*. J. Schecter and P. Deriabin, *The Spy Who Saved the*

World, New York, 1992, quotes McCone's note of 5 November 1962 to Kennedy on p. 346. Peter Hennessy in *The Secret State: Preparing for the Worst 1945–2010*, London, 2010, quotes Cowell directly on pp. 44–5.

28. Comment by Edward Crankshaw, in Khrushchev, *Khrushchev Remembers*, p. 488.

29. J. Wilson, *Britain on the Brink*, Barnsley, 2012, pp. 34, 50, 76, 119, 125, 145.

30. Dobrynin, *In Confidence*, p. 93.

31. Quoted In V. Zubok and H. Harrison, 'Nikita Khrushchev', in J. Gaddis (ed.), *Cold War Statesmen Confront the Bomb: Nuclear Diplomacy since 1945*, Oxford, 1999, p. 160.

32. G. Kornienko, *Kholodnaya Voina: Svidetelstvo ee Uchastnika*, Moscow, 2001.

33. Dobbs, *One Minute to Midnight*, p. 349.

34. Zubok and Harrison in Gaddis (ed.), *Cold War Statesmen Confront the Bomb*, p. 163.

35. Quoted in Barrass, *The Great Cold War*, p. 186.

36. This account draws on Scott D. Sagan and Jeremi Suri, 'The Madman Nuclear Alert: Secrecy, Signaling, and Safety in October 1969, *International Security*, Vol. 27, No. 4, Spring 2003, pp. 150–83. The Kissinger quotation is from Zubok, *A Failed Empire*, p. 239.

37. General Viktor Starodubov: Watch and Savranskaya, *SALT II and the Growth of Mistrust*, p. 24. His CV and that of General Detinov among the Conference documents, p. 94.

38. A. Savel'yev and N. Detinov, *The Big Five: Arms Control Decision-Making in the Soviet Union*, New York, 1995, p. 57; G. Barrass, 'Able Archer 83: What Were the Soviets Thinking?', *Survival*, Vol. 58, No. 6, Winter 2016, pp. 7–30.

39. So at least the Soviet ambassador Anatoli Dobrynin was told at the time by the pollster Lou Harris: Dobrynin, *In Confidence*, p. 366.

40. *Bulletin of the Atomic Scientists*, at http://thebulletin.org/nuclear-notebook-multimedia (accessed 2 October 2016).

41. L. Freedman, *The Evolution of Nuclear Strategy*, London, 2003, p. 346.

42. Grigori Kornienko, who was on the Soviet SALT team, gives some useful detail on the negotiations, including the Soviet attitude to the ABM Treaty and the story that the Americans agreed to a deal whereby the Russians retained their 'heavy' ICBMs in exchange for accepting that American forward based systems would not be counted. G, *Kholodnaya Voina: Svidetelstvo ee uchastnika .Glava 7: Razryadka i ee Ugasanie* [The Cold War: The evidence of an eyewitness. Chapter 7: Détente and its Decline], Moscow 2001. See also Talbott S, *Endgame: The Inside Story of SALT II*, New York 1979, p. 33; Zubok V, *A Failed Empire*, Chapel Hill 2007, p. 245

43. Dobrynin, *In Confidence*, pp. 153, 165.

44. Grechko strongly objected to the only formula for counting MIRVs which would have been acceptable to the Americans. A. Savel'yev & N. Detinov, *The Big Five: Arms Control Decision-Making in the Soviet Union*, New York 1995, p. 35; and Kornienko, op. cit.

45. There is a good summary of the SALT II issues ibid., p. 333. See also Kornienko, *Kholodnaya Voina*, Chapter 7, 'Razryadka i ee Ugasanie: K vladivostoksoi dogovorennosti'; S. Talbott, *Endgame: The Inside Story of SALT II*, New York, 1979, p. 33; Zubok, *A Failed Empire*, p. 245.

46. *Pravda*, 17 January 1976.

47. Barrass, *The Great Cold War*, p. 207. Andropov reported to the Politburo on the Carter–Sakharov correspondence on 6 February 1977, at www.memo.ru/history/diss/carter/files/21-eng.doc.

48. Protagonists from both sides met at a three day conference in 1994. See D. Watch, S. Savranskaya, *SALT II and the Growth of Mistrust*, Transcript of Proceedings at Conference, 1994, National Security Archive Washington; J. Blight and J. Lang, article 'Forum: When Empathy Failed', *Journal of Cold War Studies*, Vol. 12, No. 12, pp. 29–74 at http://nsarchive.gwu.edu/carterbrezhnev/ (accessed 15 February 2016).

49. Talbott S, *Endgame: The Inside Story of SALT II*, New York 1979, p. 142.

50. A. Savel'yev & N. Detinov, *The Big Five: Arms Control Decision-Making in the Soviet Union*, New York 1995, pp. 95–111.

51. The story of SALT II and the subsequent controversies in Washington is told in detail in Talbott S, *Endgame: The Inside Story of SALT II*, New York 1979, passim and pp. 44, 61–2, 120, 142; D. Watch, S. Savranskaya, *op.cit.* passim; J. Blight & J. Lang, *op. cit.*; V. Zubok, A Failed Empire, Chapel Hill 2007, p. 221; A. Savel'yev & N. Detinov, *The Big Five: Arms Control Decision-Making in the Soviet Union*, New York 1995, pp. 95–111; A. Aleksandrov-Agentov, Ot Kollontai do Gorbacheva [From Kollontai to Gorbachev], Moscow 1994 pp. 352, 390; S. Akhromeyev & G. Kornienko, *Glazami Marshala i Diplomata* [Through the Eyes of a Marshal and a Diplomat], Moscow 1992, p. 128; A. Dobrynin, *In Confidence*, New York 1995, p. 333.

Chapter 14: The Second Cold War

1. On New Year's Eve 1980 Timothy Garton Ash wrote this prediction in his diary – twice, the second time in capital letters for emphasis: T. Garton Ash, *The File*, London, 2009, p. 138.

2. 'Greatest threat' quoted in R. Braithwaite, *Afgantsy: The Russians in Afghanistan 1979–1989*, London, 2011, p. 113; 'Satanic device' quoted in G. Barrass, *The Great Cold War*, Stanford, 2006, p. 263.

3. Reagan press conference of 29 January 1991, at http://www.presidency.ucsb.edu/ws/?pid=44101 (accessed 2 August 2016); Reagan speech to the National

Association of Evangelicals, 8 March 1983, at http://voicesofdemocracy.umd.
edu/reagan-evil-empire-speech-text/ (accessed 25 July 2016).

4. For Reagan's incautious remarks about bombing the Soviet Union, see
    https://www.youtube.com/watch?v=kfwsgdWnQro. For the Soviet response,
    see https://en.wikipedia.org/wiki/We_begin_bombing_in_five_minutes
    (accessed 5 June 2016).

5. Barrass, *The Great Cold War*, p. 280.

6. A. Grachev, *Gibel Sovetskogo Titanika: Sudovoi Zhurnal*, Moscow, 2015, Part
    II, Section 1, 'A Voice from the Chorus'.

7. D. Hoffman, *The Dead Hand*, New York, 2009, pp. 64–7. The PsyOps
    operations are still under-researched; they are summarised in B. Fischer,
    A Cold War Conundrum: The 1983 Soviet War Scare, CIA, p. 4, at https://
    www.cia.gov/library/center-for-the-study-of-intelligence/c...publications/
    books-and-monographs/a-cold-war-conundrum/source.htm.

8. Interview with General Korobushin, In J. Hines et al., *Soviet Intentions
    1965–1985*, Vol. II, Washington, DC, 1995, p. 106–7.

9. S. Talbott, *Endgame: The Inside Story of SALT II*, New York, 1979, pp. 57, 99.

10. A. Cahn, *Killing Detente: The Right Attacks the CIA*, Pennsylvania, 1998,
    p. 141; P. Podvig, 'The Window of Vulnerability That Wasn't: Soviet Military
    Buildup in the 1970s – A Research Note', *International Security*, Vol. 33, No.
    1, Summer 2008, pp. 118–38.

11. R. Service, *The End of the Cold War*, London, 2015, p. 194.

12. Ogarkov was talking to Leslie Gelb, who is quoted in Fischer, *A Cold
    War Conundrum*. See also V. Zubok, *A Failed Empire*, Chapel Hill, 2007,
    pp. 277, 307.

13. Ogarkov's article in *Krasnaya Zvezda* of 9 May 1984 is quoted in Service, *The
    End of the Cold War*, p. 106.

14. N. Jones (ed.), The 1983 War Scare: 'The Last Paroxysm' of the Cold War,
    Part I, Documents 12 and 14, National Security Archive, at http://nsarchive.
    gwu.edu/NSAEBB/NSAEBB426/ (accessed 22 November 2016).

15. Reagan's speech of 5 September 1983 is at http://www.presidentialrhetoric.
    com/historicspeeches/reagan/ka1007.html.

16. Some of these details come from A. Dobrynin, *In Confidence*, New York,
    1995, pp. 535 et seq. See also Hoffman, *The Dead Hand*, p. 89; V. Zubok,
    A Failed Empire, Chapel, Hill 2007, p. 276; Barrass, T*he Great Cold War*,
    p. 296.

17. N. Jones, 'Countdown to Declassification: Finding Answers to a 1983
    Nuclear War Scare', *Bulletin of the Atomic Scientists*, Vol. 69, No. 6,
    1 November 2013. The motive for Reagan pulling out of the exercise is at
    Hoffman, *The Dead Hand*, p. 95.

18. Barrass, *The Great Cold War*, pp. 300–301.

19. 'Implications of Recent Soviet Military-Political Activities', 18 May 1984. The paper was largely drafted by Fritz Ermath. Jones (ed.), 'The 1983 War Scare', Part III, National Security Archive Electronic Briefing Book No. 428, Document 6.

20. Nuclear Information Service, 'Thirty Years Ago: The Nuclear Crisis Which Frightened Thatcher and Reagan into Ending the Cold War', at www.nuclearinfo.org.

21. N. Stewart et al., 'The Soviet War Scare: President's Foreign Intelligence Advisory Board', February 18, 1990. The report was declassified in October 2015 after eleven years of effort by the National Security Archive in Washington, DC: see http://nsarchive.gwu.edu/nukevault/ebb533-The-Able-Archer-War-Scare-Declassified-PFIAB-Report-Released/ (accessed 13 November 2015). See also D. Hoffman, 'In 1983 "war scare," Soviet leadership feared nuclear surprise attack by U.S.', *Washington Post*, 24 October 2014. I am grateful to David Hoffman and Marc Ambinder for drawing my attention to the report.

22. R. Gates, *From the Shadows*, New York, 1996, p. 273.

23. F. Ermarth, 'Observations on the "War Scare" of 1983 from an Intelligence Perch', Parallel History Project on NATO and the Warsaw Pact (PHP), 6 November 2003; Stasi Intelligence on NATO, at www.isn.ethz.ch/php.

24. M. Quinlan, *Thinking about Nuclear Weapons*, Oxford, 2009, p. 62 n.

25. Don Oberdorfer, unpublished interviews with Sergei Akhromeyev (10 January 1990) and Caspar Weinberger (18 October 1989). Jones (ed.), 'The 1983 War Scare', Part II, Documents 14 and 15, National Security Archive Electronic Briefing Book No. 427.

26. R. Garthoff, *Soviet Leaders and Intelligence: Assessing the American Adversary during the Cold War*, Washington, DC, 2015, p. 68.

27. D. Dunn, *The Politics of Threat: Minuteman Vulnerability in American National Security Policy*, London, 1987, p. 1.

28. R. Reagan, *The Reagan Diaries*, New York, 2007, pp. 186, 199; R. Reagan, *An American Life*, New York, 1992, pp. 588–9.

29. Reagan speech of 16 January 1984 at https://reaganlibrary.archives.gov/archives/speeches/1984/11684a.htm (accessed 19 July 2016).

30. M. Gorbachev, *Perestroika i Novoe Myshlenie dla Nashei Strany i Vsego Mira*, Moscow, 1987, Chapter IV, 'Zapad i Perestroika'; V. Starodubov, *Ot Razoruzhenia k Kapituliatsii*, Moscow, 2007, p. 251; W. Odom, *The Collapse of the Soviet Military*, New Haven, 1998, p. 225.

31. V. Kataev, *A Memoir of the Missile Age: One Man's Journey*, Stanford, 2015, p. 159.

32. Gorbachev's comments to the Politburo on 8 May 1987 are in A. Chernyaev et al., *V Politburo KPSS*, Moscow, 2006, p. 182.

33. Zubok, *A Failed Empire*, p. 285.

34. Estimates of Soviet defence expenditure were disputed both before and after the collapse of the Soviet Union. The higher estimate is taken from V. Mau, *The Political History of Economic Reform in Russia, 1985–1994*, London, 1996, p. 5. Vitaly Kataev reckoned that the military-industrial complex (i.e. excluding direct expenditure on the armed forces) accounted for 20 per cent of the Soviet Union's GDP: see *A Memoir of the Missile Age*, p. 119.

35. S. Zaloga, *The Kremlin's Nuclear Sword: The Rise and Fall of Russia's Strategic Nuclear Forces, 1945–2000*, Washington, DC, 2002, pp. 213–14.

36. Chernyaev et al., *V Politburo KPSS*, p. 152, my translation.

37. Hoffman, *The Dead Hand*, pp. 212, 243.

38. Odom, *The Collapse of the Soviet Military*, p. 110; O. Grinevsky, *Perelom: Ot Brezhneva do Gorbacheva*, Moscow, 2004, p. 155.

39. Hoffman, *The Dead Hand*, pp. 191, 225.

40. Ibid., pp. 294, 316; National Intelligence Council, 'Soviet Policy Toward the West: The Gorbachev Challenge', 1 April 1989, Cold War International History Project, Documents and Papers, at https://chnm.gmu.edu/1989/items/show/349 (accessed 9 August 2016).

41. V. Starodubov, *Ot Razoruzhenia k Kapituliatsii*, p. 261.

42. D. Watch and S. Savranskaya, *SALT II and the Growth of Mistrust: Transcript of Proceedings of Conference*, National Security Archive, Washington, DC, 1994, p. 103.

43. O. Grinevsky, *Perelom*, pp. 123–30.

44. This account of the General Staff's package draws on S. Akhromeyev and G. Kornienko, *Glazami Marshala i Diplomata*, Moscow, 1992, pp. 97, 108 et seq.; G. Kornienko, *Kholodnaya Voina: Svidetelstvo ee Uchastnika*, Moscow, 2001; N. Chervov, Yaderny Krugovorot: Shto Bylo, Shto Budet, Moscow, 2001; Grinevsky, *Perelom*; Service, *The End of the Cold War*; Hoffman, *The Dead Hand*, p. 236.

45. Facsimiles of Gorbachev's letter of 14 January and Reagan's of 22 February are at the Reagan Files, http://www.thereaganfiles.com/document-collections/letters-between-president.html (accessed 5 October 2016). Shultz's account is in G. Shultz, *Turmoil and Triumph: My Years as Secretary of State*, New York, 1993, pp. 699 et seq.

46. G. Wettig, 'Gorbachev's "Sufficient Deterrence"', *Journal à plusieurs voix*, No. 1, Summer 1988, at http://www.european-journal.org/archives/issues/old/n1/n1p62–75.pdf (accessed 7 February 2016).

47. A. Chernyaev, *Shest Let s Gorbachevym*, Moscow 1993, p. 106; Starodubov, *Ot Razoruzhenia k Kapituliatsii*, p. 267.

48. For the small former Soviet republic of Belarus, this was almost literally true. Belarus lost 619 villages during the war. One in four of its inhabitants died. After Chernobyl the country lost 485 villages and hamlets, and one in five of its people continued to live on contaminated territory: 2.1 million

people, of whom 700,000 were children (S. Aleksievich, *Chernobylskaya Molitva*, Moscow, 2015, Introduction, Historical Note).

49. V. Mikhailov and A. Dyachenko (eds), *Opalennye v Borbe pri Sozdanii Yadernovo Shchita Rodiny*, Moscow, 2008, pp. 11–12; Hoffman, *The Dead Hand*, p. 252.

50. Akhromeyev and Kornienko, *Glazami Marshala i Diplomata*, pp. 103–6; V. Varennikov, *Nepovtorimoe*, Vol. V, Moscow, 2001, pp. 501 et seq.; Joint Press Release by World Health Organization and two other UN agencies, 5 September 2005, at http://www.who.int/mediacentre/news/releases/2005/pr38/en/ (accessed 2 September 2016).

51. Odom, *The Collapse of the Soviet Military*, p. 129.

52. Akhromeyev and Kornienko, *Glazami Marshala i Diplomata*, p. 98; Zubok, *A Failed Empire*, p. 288.

53. A. Kokoshin, *Soviet Strategic Thought, 1917–91*, Cambridge, MA, 1998, p. 140, quoting V. Shabanov, 'Obychnaya Voina: Novye Opasnosti' (Conventional War, New Dangers), *Novoe Vremya*, 14 January 1986.

54. R. Braithwaite, unpublished Moscow diary, 8 June 1990.

55. Shultz's view of the CIA's performance at Reykjavik is at Shultz, *Turmoil and Triumph*, p. 780.

56. C. Moore, *Margaret Thatcher: The Authorised Biography, Vol. II*, London, 2015, p. 598. Rogers is quoted in Starodubov, *Ot Razoruzhenia k Kapituliatsii*, p. 279.

57. Shultz, *Turmoil and Triumph*, p. 780; W. Perry, *My Journey at the Nuclear Brink*, Stanford, 2015, p. 180.

58. There is a succinct description of these negotiations in Odom, *The Collapse of the Soviet Military*, pp. 133–5, and a fuller one from the Russian point of view in Starodubov, *Ot Razoruzhenia k Kapituliatsii*, pp. 288 et seq., 296.

59. A. Savel'yev and N. Detinov, *The Big Five: Arms Control Decision-Making in the Soviet Union*, New York, 1995. pp. 121, 161.

Chapter 15: Armageddon Averted?

1. H. Kahn, *Thinking about the Unthinkable in the 1980s*, Washington, DC, 1984, p. 28.

2. V. Gubarev, *Yaderny Vek Bomba*, Moscow, 1995, p. 343.

3. Attlee's paper, GEN 79/1 of 29 August 1945, is reproduced in P. Hennessy, *Cabinets and the Bomb*, Oxford, 2007, pp. 36–8.

4. The text of the first report, the Prospectus on Nucleonics, is at http://marshallfoundation.org/library/digital-archive/xerox-1482–045-compton-report-prospectus-on-nucleonics/ (accessed 6 July 2016). The second, known to history as the Franck Report, was declassified and released to the public in early 1946, after officials had censored some passages. The text is at http://fas.org/sgp/eprint/franck.html (accessed 9 April 2016).

5. See https://en.wikipedia.org/wiki/
Federation_of_American_Scientists#History.

6. Dr Harold Urey, a Nobel Prize winner, called it 'the first totalitarian bill ever written by Congress. You can call it a Communist bill or a Nazi bill, whichever you think is worse': 'Dr. Urey Excoriates Atom Bill', *New York Times*, 31 October 1945.

7. The following details of Rotblat's career and the rise of the Pugwash Conferences, except where otherwise indicated, are taken from A. Brown, *Keeper of the Nuclear Conscience: The Life and Work of Joseph Rotblat*, Oxford, 2012, pp. 25, 27, 54, 71, 137–42, 156, 174, 196–7.

8. A. Pervushin, *Atomny Proekt: Istoria Sverkhoruzhia*, Moscow, 2015, p. 197.

9. R. Monk, *Inside the Centre: The Life of J. Robert Oppenheimer*, London, 2012, p. 403.

10. T. Ogilvie-White (ed.), *On Nuclear Deterrence: The Correspondence of Sir Michael Quinlan*, London, 2011, pp. 319, 340.

11. The foregoing account is drawn from Wikipedia articles 'Anti-nuclear movement in the United States' at https://en.wikipedia.org/wiki/Anti-nuclear_movement_in_the_United_States (accessed 7 June 2017); *The Mercury News*, 17 April 2014, http://www.mercurynews.com/2014/04/17/livermore-lab-security-arrests-40-in-annual-good-friday-anti-nuke-protest/ (accessed 7 June 2017); *New York Times*, 6 February 1987, http://www.nytimes.com/1987/02/06/us/438-protesters-are-arrested-at-nevada-nuclear-test-site.html (accessed 7 June 2017).

12. See Molander's obituaries in the *Washington Post*, 27 March 2012, at https://www.washingtonpost.com/national/national-security/roger-c-molander-arms-control-strategist-who-led-movement-on-nuclear-threat-dies-at-71/2012/03/27/gIQAQndNfS_story.html (accessed 25 July 2016) and the *New York Times*, 31 March 2012, at http://www.nytimes.com/2012/04/01/us/roger-c-molander-dies-at-71-stirred-nuclear-protests.html?_r=0 (accessed 18 August 2015); S. Talbott, *Endgame: The Inside Story of SALT II*, New York, 1979, p. 43.

13. G. Butler, *Uncommon Cause: A Life at Odds with Convention*, Vol. II, Parker, CO, 2016, Part II: Frank Miller's narrative.

14. N. Polmar and R. Norris, *US Nuclear Arsenal: A History of Weapons and Delivery Systems since 1945*, Washington, DC, 2009, pp. 258–9.

15. R. Braithwaite, unpublished Moscow diary, 5 May 1991; private information.

16. In addition Russia retained – illegally, under the relevant international agreements to which it was committed – substantial stocks of chemical and biological weapons. See D. Hoffman, *The Dead Hand*, New York, 2009, passim.

17. D. Trenin, 'The Revival of the Russian Military', *Foreign Affairs*, May/June 2016.

18. Hoffman, *The Dead Hand*, p. 391; G. Yavlinsky, 'Death of a Scientist', *New York Times*, 13 November 1996, at http://www.nytimes.com/1996/11/15/opinion/death-of-a-scientist.html (accessed 20 July 2016).

19. Putin made this remark in an address to the Federal Assembly on 20 April 2005, at http://kremlin.ru/events/president/transcripts/22931 (accessed 18 October 2016).

20. Status of World Nuclear Forces, Federation of Atomic Scientists, at https://fas.org/issues/nuclear-weapons/status-world-nuclear-forces/ (accessed 24 October 2016).

21. W. Burr and H. Montford (eds), *The Making of the Limited Test Ban Treaty, 1958–1963*, at http://nsarchive.gwu.edu/NSAEBB/NSAEBB94/ (accessed 25 March 2016).

22. A. Arbatov, 'Rossia i Yadernoe Oruzhie', *Federal'nyi spravochnik. Natsional'naya bezopasnost' Rossii*, No. 2, 2015, at http://federalbook.ru/files/BEZOPASNOST/soderghanie/NB_2/NB2–2015-Arbatov.pdf (accessed 4 December 2015); R. Connolly and C. Sendstad, 'Russian Rearmament: An Assessment of Defense-Industrial Performance', *Problems of Post Communism*, published online 19 October 2016, at http://www.tandfonline.com/doi/full/10.1080/10758216.2016.1236668 (accessed 21 October 2016).

23. J. Doyle, 'Better Ways to Modernise the US Nuclear Arsenal', *Survival*, August–September 2016, pp. 27–50.

24. A. Arbatov, 'Rossia i Gonka Vooruzhenia', *Nezavisimaya Gazeta NG Tsenarii*, 26 April 2016, at http://www.ng.ru/scenario/2016–04–26/13_race.html (accessed 29 June 2016); Message to the Senate on the New START Treaty, 2 February 2011, at https://www.whitehouse.gov/the-press-office/2011/02/02/message-president-new-start-treaty-0 (accessed 30 June 2016).

25. Figures for military expenditure are notoriously difficult to establish and compare. They are usually calculated in terms of US dollars, but because of exchange rate fluctuations expenditure figures and rankings between countries can vary from year to year. The figures given here for 2015 are based on reports by two internationally respected bodies, the Stockholm International Peace Institute (SIPRI) and the London-based Institute of Strategic Studies (IISS).

	SIPRI	IISS
USA	596 (3.3%)	597
China	215 (1.9%)	145
Saudi Arabia	87.2 (13.7%)	81.9
Russia	66.4 (5.4)	65.6
UK	55.5 (2%)	56.2
India	51.3 (2.3%)	48
France	50.9 (2.1)	46.8

Billions of dollars at constant or current exchange rates, also expressed in the SIPRI report as % of GNP

Source: Wikipedia, 'List of Countries by Military Expenditure'

26. Joint declaration by Presidents Yeltsin and Clinton, 14 January 1994; W. Burr (ed.), *Launch on Warning: The Development of U.S. Capabilities, 1959–1979*, National Security Archive Electronic Briefing Book No. 43, April 2001, at http://nsarchive.gwu.edu/NSAEBB/NSAEBB43/ (accessed 4 October 2016); B. Blair (Study Director), *De-Alerting and Stabilizing the World's Nuclear Force Postures*, Global Zero, 2015; A. Gill (Rapporteur), *Reframing Nuclear De-Alert: Decreasing the Operational Readiness of U.S. and Russian Arsenals*, New York, 2009, and H. Kristensen and M. McKinzie, *Reducing Alert Rates of Nuclear Weapons*, Geneva, 2012.

27. Pavel Podvig discusses the evolution in Russian thinking about nuclear weapons in Chapter 5, 'Russia, Strategic Stability, and Nuclear Weapons', G. Shultz and J. Goodby (eds), *The War That Must Never Be Fought*, Stanford, 2015, pp. 143–74.

28. Statement on 2 October 2016, 'Emergencies Ministry to Organize All-Russian Civil Defence', by the Ministry of the Russian Federation for Civil Defence, Emergencies and Elimination of Consequences of Natural Disasters, at http://en.mchs.ru/mass_media/news/item/32914206/ (accessed 21 October 2016).

29. Sensible Russian experts such as Aleksei Arbatov, Vladimir Dvorkin, Fedor Lukyanov, and Dmitri Trenin continued, meanwhile, to publish well-informed pieces stressing the need for moderation on both sides. Kristin van Bruusgaard analysed the measured discussion among Russian strategic professionals in 'Russian Strategic Deterrence', *Survival*, August–September 2016, pp. 7–25. The irrepressible Fred Kaplan discussed these matters in a typically acerbic article, 'Taking Stock of the Stockpile', *Foreign Affairs*, September/October 2016.

30. Kennedy's warning is quoted by Robert Gard in 'JFK's Nuclear Proliferation Warnings: Up to 25 Countries with Nuclear Weapons' of 11 May 2012, at http://livableworld.org/jfks-nuclear-proliferation-warnings-up-to-25-countries-with-nuclear-weapons/ (accessed 14 December 2016).

31. I. Helland, 'Two Billion People at Risk: Global Impacts of Limited Nuclear War on Agriculture, Food Supplies, and Human Nutrition', International Physicians for the Prevention of Nuclear War & Physicians for Social Responsibility, Washington, DC, 2015.

32. Wendy Sherman, US Under Secretary for Political Affairs, Written Statement to Senate Foreign Relations Committee, 15 May 2013.

33. G. Shultz, W. Perry, H. Kissinger, and S. Nunn, 'A World Free of Nuclear Weapons', *Wall Street Journal*, 4 January 2007; P. Taubman, *The Partnership: Five Cold Warriors and the Quest to Ban the Bomb*, New York, 2013.

34. Shultz and Goodby (eds), *The War That Must Never Be Fought*, p. xv; W. Perry, *My Journey at the Nuclear Brink*, Stanford, 2015, p. x.

35. Shultz and Goodby (eds), *The War That Must Never Be Fought*, p. 55.

Epilogue: Russian Roulette

1. The provenance and text of this graffito is obscure and contested. This is how I remember it.

2. See http://www.bartleby.com/124/pres54.html (accessed 15 July 2016).

3. S. Schweber, *In the Shadow of the Bomb: Oppenheimer, Bethe, and the Moral Responsibility of the Scientist*, Princeton, 2000, pp. 160–62, 171.

4. V. Shapiro, *Moral i Bomba: O Moralnoi Otevetstvennosti Uchenykh i Politikov v Yadernuyu Epokhu*, Moscow, 2007, p. 8.

5. V. Adamski and Yu. Smirnov, 'Moralnaya Otvetsvennost Uchenykh i Politicheskikh Liderov v Yadernuyu Epokhu', *Nauka i Obshchestvo: Istoria Sovietskogo Atomnogo Proekta* (40–50 Gody), Moscow, 1997.

6. Memorial address by Yuli Khariton, July 1995, J. Robert Oppenheimer Memorial Committee, at osoboe-vystuplenie-akademika-yuliya-borisovicha-haritona.pdf.

7. S. Zuckerman, *Nuclear Illusion & Reality*, New York, 1982, pp. 73–5.

8. General Bradley is widely quoted. This reference comes from an article by D. Ellsberg, 'Hiroshima Day: America Has Been Asleep at the Wheel for 64 Years', posted 5 August 2009 on Truthdig, at http://www.truthdig.com/report/item/20090805_hiroshima_day_america_has_been_asleep_at_the_wheel_for_64_years? (accessed 22 August 2015).

9. G. Butler, *Uncommon Cause: A Life at Odds with Convention*, Vols I and II, Parker, CO, 2016, passim.

10. P. Hennessy, *Muddling Through: Power, Politics, and the Quality of Government in Post-War Britain*, London, 1997, p. 124, quoted in K. Stoddart, 'Maintaining the "Moscow Criterion": British Strategic Nuclear Targeting 1974–1979', *Journal of Strategic Studies*, Vol. 31, No. 6, December 2008, pp. 897–924.

11. Khrushchev quoted in V. Zubok, *A Failed Empire*, Chapel Hill, 2007, p. 127. Some very broad details of the top-secret 'Last Resort' letters issued by successive prime ministers to British nuclear submarine commanders are in P. Hennessy, *The Secret State: Preparing for the Worst 1945–2010*, London, 2010, pp. 311–13. The letters give instructions on how the commanders are to act if government in Britain is destroyed by a nuclear attack. They are destroyed unopened when a prime minister leaves office.

12. M. Bundy, 'To Cap the Volcano', *Foreign Affairs*, Vol. 48, No. 1, October 1969, quoted in L. Freedman, *The Evolution of Nuclear Strategy*, London, 2003, p. 344.

13. C. Gray, *Nuclear Strategy and National Style*, London, 1986, p. 9.

14. Private information.

15. In his declining years, Winston Churchill returned to his pessimistic fear that mankind was incapable of mastering the forces that his science had unleashed. 'If I were God Almighty, and humanity blew itself to bits, as it

most certainly could, I don't think I'd start again in case they got me too next time': G. Farmelo, *Churchill's Bomb*, London, 2013, p. 446, quoting J. Lees-Milne, *A Mingled Measure*, London, 1994, p. 54.

16. William Walker in B. Tertrais (ed.), *Thinking about Strategy: A Tribute to Sir Michael Quinlan*, Paris, 2011, p. 90.

17. Robert Oppenheimer, 'Physics in the Contemporary World', Arthur D. Little Memorial Lecture at MIT, 25 November 1947; Shapiro, *Moral i Bombaepokhu*, p. 8.

18. T. Ogilvie-White (ed.), *On Nuclear Deterrence: The Correspondence of Sir Michael Quinlan*, London, 2011, pp. 129, 65. Quinlan's ideas are set out in his *Thinking about Nuclear Weapons*, Oxford, 2009, and C. Guthrie and M. Quinlan, *Just War: The Just War Tradition – Ethics in Modern Warfare*, London, 2010; see also Tetrais (ed.), *Thinking About Strategy*.

19. J. Baylis, *Ambiguity and Deterrence: British Nuclear Strategy 1945–1964*, Oxford, 1995, p. 101.

20. Lt General Sir John Cowley, quoted in P. Blackett, *Studies in War: Nuclear and Conventional*, New York, 1962, p. 96.

21. This and other direct quotations by Michael Quinlan come from Ogilvie-White (ed.), *On Nuclear Deterrence*, pp. 54, 144. Quinlan set out his ideas in *Thinking About Nuclear Weapons*; see also Tertrais (ed.), *Thinking About Strategy*.

22. Quoted in W. Kozak, *LeMay: The Life and Wars of General Curtis LeMay*, New York, 2012, p. 363.

23. J. Mueller, *Atomic Obsession: Nuclear Alarmism from Hiroshima to Al-Qaeda*, Oxford, 2010, p. 182.

24. J. Siracusa, *Nuclear Weapons: A Very Short Introduction*, Oxford, 2008, introduction.

25. M. Hellman, 'On the Probability of Nuclear War', at https://www-ee.stanford.edu/~hellman/opinion/inevitability.html (accessed 29 June 2016).

26. T. Scheer, *With Enough Shovels: Reagan, Bush and Nuclear War*, New York, 1983, p. 3, quoting one of Reagan's civil defence officials.

27. S. Pinker, *The Better Angels of Our Nature: Why Violence Has Declined*, New York, 2011; J. Mueller, 'Duelling Counterfactuals', in J. Gaddis (ed.), *Cold War Statesmen Confront the Bomb: Nuclear Diplomacy since 1945*, Oxford, 1999, and *Atomic Obsession*. See also W. Wilson, *Five Myths about Nuclear Weapons*, New York, 2013.

SOURCES

Writing in English on nuclear affairs – scholarly works, memoirs, polemics – must rival in volume all that has been written on the lives of Christ, Hitler, Stalin, and Richard Wagner combined. Some of it is scholarly and illuminating. Some of it is superficial and biased. It is impossible to address it other than selectively.

Much British and American documentation has been released and much continues to emerge. We owe a particular debt to the National Security Archive in Washington for their decades-long campaign to extract documents from an often reluctant US government, and in Britain especially to Peter Hennessy for the skill, charm, and cunning with which he has persuaded the unforthcoming British official system to disgorge some of its secrets. An excellent school of younger British historians has much to thank him for.

Although Russian sources are more limited, much material has emerged over the past twenty-five years. *Atomny Proekt*, a major collection of documents about the Soviet weapons project, was systematically published between 1998 and 2009. Other documents continue to emerge from time to time. There are many frank memoirs and interviews with former Soviet politicians, diplomats, senior officers, scientists, and weapons designers. Much has been gleaned by Russian scholars from the internet: some have been imprisoned for allegedly violating national security. But no Soviet intelligence assessments or strategic planning papers have yet been published to match what is available on the Western side: there is no equivalent to the British Duff–Mason memorandum of 1978 about Trident.

Some of the Russian sources, in particular, are readily available only in electronic versions. This makes giving precise references harder. But I hope the assiduous will nevertheless be able to track down any references they need.

Those who wish to read further might start with the two early classics, John Hersey's *Hiroshima*, and Robert Junck's *Brighter Than a Thousand Suns*. Gerard DeGroot's *The Bomb: A Life* is an excellent one-volume history of the nuclear weapon. A short cut is Joseph Siracusa's *Nuclear Weapons: A Very Short Introduction*.

The complexities of nuclear strategy are tackled comprehensibly in Lawrence Freedman's *The Evolution of Nuclear Strategy*. One gets a sense of the American debate from Henry Kissinger's *Nuclear Weapons and Foreign Policy*. Michael Howard deals briskly with one of the classics in *Clausewitz: A Very Short Introduction*.

The science is covered briefly in Russell Stannard's *Relativity: A Very Short Introduction* and John Polkinghorne's *Quantum Theory: A Very Short Introduction*. You can get a sense of the personality of one of the twentieth century's great scientists from Richard Feynman's *Surely You're Joking Mr Feynman!* and of another from Andrei Sakharov's *Memoirs*.

Gordon Barrass gives an overview of *The Great Cold War*. McGeorge Bundy describes what it was like to be in the centre of the decision-making process in *Danger and Survival*. Paul Ham describes the end of the war against Japan in *Hiroshima Nagasaki*. Michael Dobbs gives a detailed description of the Cuban missile crisis in *One Minute to Midnight*.

There is a very detailed account of the American bomb project in Richard Rhodes's *The Making of the Atomic Bomb*. David Holloway's account of the Soviet project in *Stalin and the Bomb* has become the standard work in Russia as well. David Hoffman covers some worrying intricacies of the last stage of the Cold War confrontation in *The Dead Hand*. Peter Hennessy gives a characteristically ebullient account of some of the most secret corners of the British government in *The Secret State*.

Michael Frayn's play *Copenhagen* goes with great sensitivity into the moral issues faced by those who helped to design the bomb. Masuji Ibuse's novel *Black Rain* describes what it was like to survive Hiroshima. Neville Shute's *On the Beach*, and the film version, imagine how life would gutter out after a massive nuclear war. Peter Bryant was an RAF bomber pilot: his *Red Alert* was the novel on which *Dr Strangelove* was based. There is a brilliant fictional recreation of the moral problems of scientists working under Stalin in Vasily Grossman's great novel, *Life and Fate*.

The films listed below are mostly available on YouTube. *Dr Strangelove or: How I Learned to Stop Worrying and Love the Bomb* is of course definitive; *Failsafe* is a pale reflection. Two excellent docudramas, *Oppenheimer* and *Hiroshima*, convincingly cover the American bomb project and the end of the Pacific War; the second also gives an excellent idea of how it looked to the Japanese. *Crimson Tide* shows (convincingly, despite the disclaimer from the US Navy) how a communications failure on an American submarine could risk disaster. *Thirteen Days* is a gripping account of the Cuban missile crisis from the point of view of Kennedy and his colleagues: it takes a few liberties with history which can safely be ignored. *The War Game* (BBC TV), *The Day After* (US TV), and *Threads* (BBC TV) show in distressing detail what a nuclear attack and its aftermath might be like. Two Russian films, *Devyat Dnei Odnogo Goda* (Nine Days in One Year) and *Vybor Tseli* (Choosing the Target) give an idea of how the moral issue looked from the other side. (I have not found a subtitled version of *Vybor Tseli*.) *I Was a Communist for the FBI, My Son John*, and *Big Jim McLain* are curiosities which illustrate the hysteria of the McCarthy era. *Strategic Air Command* starring James Stewart is propaganda for the US Air Force, its climax based on a real incident.

Bibliography

The following bibliography lists printed books and collections of documents only. The provenance of individual documents and articles which I have consulted is given in the Notes.

Acheson, D., *Present at the Creation*, New York, 1969

Akhromeyev, S. and Kornienko, G., *Glazami Marshala i Diplomata* (Through the Eyes of a Marshal and a Diplomat), Moscow, 1992

Aldous, R., *Reagan and Thatcher*, London, 2013

Aleksandrov-Agentov, A., *Ot Kollontai do Gorbacheva* (From Kollontai to Gorbachev), Moscow, 1994

Aleksievich, S., *Chernobylskaya Molitva: Khronika Budushchego* (Chernobyl Prayer: A Chronicle of the Future), Moscow, 2015

Alexander, M., *Managing the Cold War: A View from the Front Line*, London, 2005

Applebaum, A., *Iron Curtain: The Crushing of Eastern Europe 1944–56*, London, 2012

Arbatov, A. and Dvorkin, V., *Beyond Nuclear Deterrence*, Washington, DC, 2006

Arbatov, G., *Svidetelstvo Sovremennika* (Testimony of a Contemporary Man), Moscow, 1991; published in English as *The System: An Insider's Life in Soviet Politics*, New York, 1992

Aron, L., *Boris Yeltsin: A Revolutionary Life*, London, 2000

Bakatin, V., *Izbavlenie ot KGB* (Getting Rid of the KGB), Moscow, 1991

Ball, D. and Richelson, J. (eds), *Strategic Nuclear Targeting*, Ithaca, 1986

Ball, P., *Serving the Reich: The Struggle for the Soul of Physics under Hitler*, London, 2013

Barrass, G., *The Great Cold War*, Stanford, 2006

Baylis, J., *Ambiguity and Deterrence: British Nuclear Strategy 1945–1964*, Oxford, 1995

Beevor, A., *Stalingrad*, London, 1998

Beria, S., *My Father: Inside Stalin's Kremlin*, London, 2001

Bird, K. and Sherwin, M., *American Prometheus: The Triumph and Tragedy of J. Robert Oppenheimer*, New York, 2006

Blackett, P. M. S., *Studies in War: Nuclear and Conventional*, New York, 1962

Boyer, P., *By the Bomb's Early Light: American Thought and Culture at the Dawn of the Atomic Age*, New York, 1985

Braithwaite, R., *Across the Moscow River: The World Turned Upside Down*, London, 2002

Braithwaite, R., *Afgantsy: The Russians in Afghanistan 1979–1989*, London, 2011

Braithwaite, R., unpublished Moscow diary, 1988–92

Briggs, R., *When the Wind Blows*, London, 1996

Brodie, B. (ed.), *The Absolute Weapon: Atomic Power and World Order*, New Haven, 1946

Brown, A., *The Neutron and the Bomb: A Biography of Sir James Chadwick*, Oxford, 1997

Brown, A., *Keeper of the Nuclear Conscience: The Life and Times of Joseph Rotblat*, Oxford, 2012

Bryant, P., *Red Alert*, London, 1958 (e-book)

Bundy, M., *Danger and Survival: Choices about the Bomb in the First Fifty Years*, New York, 1988

Burlatsky, F., *Khrushchev and the First Russian Spring*, London, 1991

Butler, G., *Uncommon Cause: A Life at Odds with Convention*, Vols I and II, Parker, CO, 2016

Butler, R. (ed.), *Review of Intelligence on Weapons of Mass Destruction: Report of a Committee of Privy Counsellors*, London, July 2004

Cahn, A., *Killing Detente: The Right Attacks the CIA*, Pennsylvania, 1998

Campbell, D., *War Plan UK: The Truth about Civil Defence in Britain*, London, 1982

Campbell, D., *The Unsinkable Aircraft Carrier*, London, 1986

Chappell, J., *Before the Bomb: How America Approached the End of the Pacific War*, Lexington, 1996

Chazov, E., *Zdorovie i Vlast* (Health and Power), Moscow, 1993

Cherkashin, N., *Vozmutiteli Glubin* (Disturbers of the Ocean Depths), Moscow, 2009

Chernyaev, A., *Shest Let s Gorbachevym* (Six Years with Gorbachev), Moscow, 1993

Chernyaev, A., *Moya Zhizn i Moe Vremya* (My Life and Times), Moscow, 1995

Chernyaev, A. et al., *V Politburo KPSS* (In the Politburo of the Communist Party), Moscow, 2006

Chernyaev A, *Sovmestny Iskhod* (Joint Outcome), Moscow, 2008

Chertok, E., *Rockets and People*, Vols I–IV, NASA, Washington, DC, 2005–11

Chervov, N., *Yaderny Krugovorot: Shto Bylo, Shto Budet* (The Nuclear Roundabout: What Was, What Will Be), Moscow, 2001

Churchill, W., *The Second World War: The Hinge of Fate*, London, 1951

Churchill, W., *Thoughts and Adventures*, Washington, DC, 2009

Clark, I. and Wheeler, N., *The British Origins of Nuclear Strategy 1945–1955*, Oxford, 1989

Clausewitz, C., *On War*, edited by M. Howard and P. Paret, Princeton, 1976

Cockburn, A., *The Threat: Inside the Soviet Military Machine*, New York, 1983

Cox, B. and Forshaw, J., *Why Does E=mc²?*, London, 2009

Cradock, P., *Know Your Enemy*, London, 2002

DeGroot, G., *The Bomb: A Life*, Cambridge, MA, 2008

Dobbs, M., *One Minute to Midnight*, New York, 2008

Dobbs, M., *Six Months in 1945: FDR, Stalin, Churchill, and Truman – from World War to Cold War*, London, 2012

Dobrynin, A., *In Confidence*, New York, 1995

Dooner, P., *Last Days of the Republic*, San Francisco, 1880

Dower, J., *War without Mercy: Race and Power in the Pacific War*, New York, 1986

Drew, S. (ed.), *NSC-68: Forging the Strategy of Containment* (analyses by Paul H. Nitze), Washington, DC, 1994

Dunn, D., *The Politics of Threat: Minuteman Vulnerability in American National Security Policy*, London, 1987

Engerman, D., *Know Your Enemy: The Rise and Fall of America's Soviet Experts*, Oxford, 2009

Erickson, P. et al., *How Reason Almost Lost Its Mind: The Strange Career of Rationality*, Chicago, 2013

Etzold, T. and Gaddis, J. (eds), *Containment: Documents on American Foreign Policy and Strategy, 1945–1950*, New York, 1978

Farmelo, G., *Churchill's Bomb*, London, 2013

Feynman, R., *Surely You're Joking Mr Feynman!*, New York, 1997

Fischer, B. (ed.), *At Cold War's End: US Intelligence on the Soviet Union and Eastern Europe, 1989–1991*, Washington, DC, 2001

FitzGerald, F., *Way Out There in the Blue*, New York, 2000

Forward, N., *The Field of Nations*, London, 1971

France, A., *Penguin Island*, London, 1908 (University of Adelaide e-book)

Frayn, M., *Copenhagen*, London, 2014

Freedman, L., *The Evolution of Nuclear Strategy*, London, 2003

Freedman, L., *Strategy*, London, 2013

Fursenko, A. and Naftali, T., *One Hell of a Gamble: The Secret History of the Cuban Missile Crisis*, London, 1997

Gaddis, J., *Strategies of Containment*, Oxford, 1982

Gaddis, J., *George F. Kennan: An American Life*, New York, 2011

Gaddis J. (ed.), *Statesmen Confront the Bomb: Nuclear Diplomacy since 1945*, Oxford, 1999

Galbraith, J., *Letters to Kennedy*, Cambridge, MA, 1998

Garthoff, R., *Reflections on the Cuban Missile Crisis*, Washington, DC, 1987

Garthoff, R., *Deterrence and the Revolution in Soviet Military Doctrine*, Washington, DC, 1990

Garthoff, R., *Assessing the Adversary*, Washington, DC, 1991

Garthoff, R., *Soviet Leaders and Intelligence: Assessing the American Adversary during the Cold War*, Washington, DC, 2015

Gates, R., *From the Shadows*, New York, 1996

Ghamari-Tabrizi, S., *The Worlds of Herman Kahn*, Cambridge, MA, 2005

Gleick, J., *Genius: Richard Feynman and Modern Physics*, London, 1992

Golovanov, Ya., *Korolev: Fakty i Mify* (Korolev: Facts and Myths), Moscow, 1994

Goodchild, P., *Edward Teller: The Real Dr Strangelove*, London, 2004

Goodwin, G. (ed.), *Ethics and Nuclear Deterrence*, London, 1982

Gorbachev, M., *Perestroika i Novoe Myshlenie dla Nashei Strany i Vsego Mira* (Perestroika and New Thinking for Our Country and the Whole World), Moscow, 1987

Gorbachev, M., *Zhizn i Reformy* (Life and Reforms), Moscow, 1995

Gorbachev, M., *Memoirs*, London, 1996

Gordon, Ye., *Soviet Strategic Aviation in the Cold War*, Manchester, 2013

Goure, L., *War Survival in Soviet Strategy: USSR Civil Defense*, Center for Advanced International Studies, University of Miami, 1976

Gowing, M., *Britain and Atomic Energy 1939–45*, London, 1964

Gowing, M., *Independence and Deterrence: Britain and Atomic Energy, 1945–52*, London, 1974

Grachev, A., *Gorbachev's Gamble: Soviet Foreign Policy and the End of the Cold War*, Cambridge, 2008

Grachev, A., *Gibel Sovetskogo 'Titanika': Sudovoi Zhurnal* (The Wreck of the Soviet 'Titanic': A Log Book), Moscow, 2015

Graham, L., *Science in the Soviet Union*, Cambridge, 1994

Grant, M., *After the Bomb: Civil Defence and Nuclear War in Britain, 1945–68*, London, 2010

Gray, C., *Nuclear Strategy and National Style*, London, 1986

Grayling, A., *Among the Dead Cities*, London, 2006

Greene, B., *Eisenhower, Science Advice, and the Nuclear Test-Ban Debate, 1945–1963*, Stanford, 2003

Gribbin, J., *In Search of Schrodinger's Cat*, London, 1984

Grinevsky, O., *Perelom: Ot Brezhneva do Gorbacheva* (Turning Point: From Brezhnev to Gorbachev), Moscow, 2004

Grossman, V., *Life and Fate*, London, 2006

Groves, L., *Now It Can Be Told*, New York, 1981

Grushin, B., *Chetyre Zhizni Rossii. Zhizn Vtoraya: Epokha Brezhneva – Chast 1* (Four Lives of Russia. Second Life: The Brezhnev Epoch – Part 1), Moscow, 2003

Gubarev, V., *Sarcophagus*, London, 1987

Gubarev, V., *Yaderny Vek Bomba* (The Nuclear Age: The Bomb), Moscow, 1995

Gubarev, V., *Atomnaya Bomba: Khronika Velikikh Otkrytii* (The Atom Bomb: A Chronicle of Great Discoveries), Moscow, 2009

Gusterson, H., *People of the Bomb*, Minneapolis, 2004

Guthrie, C. and Quinlan, M., *Just War: The Just War Tradition – Ethics in Modern Warfare*, London, 2010

Ham, P., *Hiroshima Nagasaki*, London, 2013

Hargittai, I., *Judging Edward Teller: A Closer Look at One of the Most Influential Scientists of the Twentieth Century*, New York, 2010

Hargittai, I., *Buried Glory: Portraits of Soviet Scientists*, Oxford, 2013

Hastings, M., *Bomber Command*, London, 1993

Hastings, M., *Nemesis: The Battle for Japan, 1944–5*, London, 2008

Healey, D., *The Time of My Life*, London, 1990

Hennessy, P., *Cabinets and the Bomb*, Oxford, 2007

Hennessy, P., *The Secret State: Preparing for the Worst 1945–2010*, London, 2010

Hennessy, P. and Jinks, J., *The Silent Deep: The Royal Navy Submarine Service since 1945*, London, 2015

Herken, G., *Brotherhood of the Bomb: The Tangled Lives and Loyalties of Robert Oppenheimer, Ernest Lawrence, and Edward Teller*, New York, 2002

Herman, M. and Hughes, G. (eds), *Intelligence in the Cold War: What Difference Did it Make?*, Abingdon, 2013

Hersey, J., *Hiroshima*, London, 2015

Heuser, B., *The Bomb: Nuclear Weapons in the Historical, Strategic and Ethical Context*, London, 2000

Heuser, B., *Reading Clausewitz*, New York, 2002

Hewlett, R. and Anderson, O., *A History of the United States Atomic Energy Commission: The New World, 1939–1946*, Philadelphia, 1962

Hines, J. et al., *Soviet Intentions 1965–1985*, Vols I and II, Washington, DC, 1995

HMSO, *Advising the Householder on Protection against Nuclear Attack*, London, 1963

Hoffenaar, J. and Findlay, C. (eds), *Military Planning for European Theatre Conflict during the Cold War: An Oral History Roundtable Stockholm, 24 – 25 April 2006*, Zürcher Beiträge Zur Sicherheitspolitik, 79, Zurich, 2006

Hoffman, D., *The Dead Hand*, New York, 2009

Hoffman, D., *The Billion Dollar Spy: A True Story of Cold War Espionage and Betrayal*, London, 2015

Hogan, M. (ed.), *Hiroshima: History and Memory*, Cambridge, 1996

Holloway, D., *Stalin and the Bomb*, New Haven, 1994

Hopkins, W., *The Pacific War: The Strategy, Politics, and Players That Won the War*, Minneapolis, 2010

Horne, A., *Macmillan 1957–1986*, London, 1989

Hosking, G., *The Awakening of the Soviet Union* (1988 Reith Lectures), London, 1988

Howard, M., *Clausewitz: A Very Short Introduction*, Oxford, 2002

Huchthausen, P., *K-19 The Widowmaker*, Washington, DC, 2002

Huchthausen, P., *October Fury*, Hoboken, 2002

Ibuse, M., *Black Rain*, serialised in *Shincho* magazine in Japan from 1965; American edition, New York, 2012

Inboden, W., *Religion and American Foreign Policy 1945–1960*, Cambridge, 2008

Jones, N., *Able Archer 83*, New York, 2016

Junck, R., *Brighter Than a Thousand Suns*, Orlando, 1958

Kahn, H., *Thinking about the Unthinkable in the 1980s*, Washington, DC, 1984

Kaplan, F., *The Wizards of Armageddon*, New York, 1983

Kataev, V., *A Memoir of the Missile Age: One Man's Journey*, Stanford, 2015

Kennan, G., *Memoirs: 1950–1963*, London, 1972

Khlevniuk, O., *Stalin: New Biography of a Dictator*, New Haven, 2015

Khrushchev, N., *Khrushchev Remembers*, London, 1971

Khrushchev, N., *Khrushchev Remembers: The Last Testament*, London, 1974

Kissinger, H., *Nuclear Weapons and Foreign Policy*, abridged edition, New York, 1969

Kojevnikov, A., *Stalin's Great Science: The Times and Adventures of Soviet Physicists*, London, 2004

Kokoshin, A., *Soviet Strategic Thought, 1917–91*, Cambridge, MA, 1998

Kokoshin, A., *O Strategicheskom Planirovanii v Politike* (On Strategic Planning in Politics), Moscow, 2007

Kornienko, G., *Kholodnaya Voina: Svidetelstvo ee Uchastnika* (The Cold War: The Evidence of an Eyewitness), Moscow, 2001

Kozak, W., *LeMay: The Life and Wars of General Curtis LeMay*, New York, 2012

Krivosheev, G., *Rossia i SSSR v Voinakh XX Veka* (Russia and the USSR in the Wars of the 20th Century), Moscow, 2001

Kryuchkov, V., *Lichnoe Delo* (Personal File), Moscow, 1996

Kull, S., *Minds at War: Nuclear Reality and the Inner Conflicts of Defense Policymakers*, New York, 1988

Lebedinsky, A., *What Russian Scientists Say about Fallout*, London, 1962

Lebovic, J., *Flawed Logics: Strategic Nuclear Arms Control from Truman to Obama*, Baltimore, 2013

Leebaert, D., *Soviet Strategy and New Military Thinking*, London, 1992

Leffler, M., *For the Soul of Mankind*, New York, 2007

Leites, N., *Operational Code of the Kremlin*, Santa Monica, 1951

LeMay, C., *America is in Danger*, New York, 1968

Lewis, J., *Changing Direction: British Military Planning for Post-war Strategic Defence, 1942–1947*, London, 1988

Lloyd George, D., *War Memoirs of David Lloyd George,* Vol. II (New Edition), London, 1938

Macmillan, M., *Peacemakers: Six Months That Changed the World*, London, 2002

Maggelet, M. and Oskins, J., *Broken Arrow*, Vol. II, *A Disclosure of Significant US, Soviet, and British Nuclear Weapons Incidents and Accidents, 1945–2008*, Raleigh, NC, 2010

Matlock, J., *Reagan and Gorbachev: How the Cold War Ended*, New York, 2004

Mau, V., *The Political History of Economic Reform in Russia, 1985–1994*, London, 1996

May, E., Steinbruner, J. and Wolfe, T., *History of the Strategic Arms Competition, Parts 1 and 2*, Washington, DC, 1981

Medvedev, Zh., *Nuclear Disaster in the Urals*, New York, 1979

Mikhailov, V. and Dyachenko, A. (eds), *Opalennye v Borbe pri Sozdanii Yadernogo Shchita Rodiny* (Scorched in the Battle to Build the Motherland's Nuclear Shield), Moscow, 2008

Monk, R., *Inside the Centre: The Life of J. Robert Oppenheimer*, London, 2012

Moore, C., *Margaret Thatcher: The Authorised Biography, Vol. II*, London, 2015

Mueller, J., *Atomic Obsession: Nuclear Alarmism from Hiroshima to Al-Qaeda*, Oxford, 2010

Neustadt, R., *Report to JFK: The Skybolt Crisis in Perspective*, New York, 1999

Neustadt R. and May E., *Thinking in Time: The Uses of History for Decisionmakers*, New York 1988

Newhouse, J., *The Nuclear Age: From Hiroshima to Star Wars*, London, 1989

Oakes, G., *The Imaginary War: Civil Defense and American Cold War Culture*, Oxford, 1994

Odom, W., *The Collapse of the Soviet Military*, New Haven, 1998

Office of Technology Assessment, *The Effects of Nuclear War*, Washington, DC, 1979

Ogilvie-White, T. (ed.,) *On Nuclear Deterrence: The Correspondence of Sir Michael Quinlan*, London, 2011

Owen, D., *Nuclear Papers*, Liverpool, 2009

Perry, W., *My Journey at the Nuclear Brink*, Stanford, 2015

Pervushin, A., *Atomny Proekt: SSSR: Dokumenty i Materialy* (The Atom Project of the USSR: Documents and Materials) Vols. 1–3, Moscow-Sarov, 1998–2009

Pinker, S., *The Better Angels of Our Nature: Why Violence Has Declined*, New York, 2011

Podvig, P. (ed.), *Russian Strategic Nuclear Forces*, Cambridge, MA, 2004

Pokrovsky, G. and Garthoff, R., *Science and Technology in Contemporary War*, New York, 1959

Polkinghorne, J., *Quantum Theory: A Very Short Introduction*, Oxford, 2002

Polmar, N. and Norris, R., *US Nuclear Arsenal: A History of Weapons and Delivery Systems since 1945*, Washington, DC, 2009

Prados, J., *The Soviet Estimate*, New York, 1982

Pratchett, T., *Jingo*, London, 1997

Pratchett, T., *Sourcery*, London, 2004

Priestley, J., *The Doomsday Men*, London, 1938; Richmond, VA, 2014

Quinlan, M., *Thinking about Nuclear Weapons*, Oxford, 2009

Reagan, R., *The Reagan Diaries*, New York, 2007

Rhodes, R., *Dark Sun: The Making of the Hydrogen Bomb*, New York, 1996

Rhodes, R., *The Making of the Atomic Bomb*, London, 2012

Robin, R., *The Making of the Cold War Enemy*, Princeton, 2001

Rose, K., *One Nation Underground: The Fallout Shelter in American Culture*, New York, 2001

Rotblat, J., *Nuclear Radiation in Warfare*, London, 1981

Ryabev, L. (ed.), *Atomny Proekt SSSR: Dokumenty i Materialy* (The Atom Project of the USSR: Documents and Materials), Vols I–III, Sarov, 1998–2009

Rybas, S., *Gromyko: Voina, Mir i Diplomatia* (Gromyko: War, Peace, and Diplomacy), Moscow, 2011

Sagan, S., *The Limits of Safety*, Princeton, 1993

Sagdeev, R., *The Making of a Soviet Scientist*, New York, 1994

Sakharov, A., *Memoirs*, London, 1990

Savel'yev, A. and Detinov, N., *The Big Five: Arms Control Decision-Making in the Soviet Union*, New York, 1995

Scheer, T., *With Enough Shovels: Reagan, Bush and Nuclear War*, New York, 1983

Schelling, T., *Arms and Influence*, New Haven, 2008

Schlosser, E., *Command and Control*, London, 2013

Schweber, S., *In the Shadow of the Bomb: Oppenheimer, Bethe, and the Moral Responsibility of the Scientist*, Princeton, 2000

Schweitzer, P., *Victory: The Reagan Administration's Secret Strategy That Hastened the Collapse of the Soviet Union*, New York, 1996

Serber, R., *The Los Alamos Primer*, Berkeley/Los Angeles, 1992

Service, R., *The End of the Cold War*, London, 2015

Shahnazarov, G., *Tsena Svobody* (The Price of Freedom), Moscow, 1995

Shapiro, V., *Moral i Bomba: O Moralnoi Otevetstvennosti Uchenykh i Politikov v Yadernuyu Epokhu* (Morality and the Bomb: The Moral Responsibility of Scientists and Politicians in the Nuclear Age), Moscow, 2007

Shultz, G., *Turmoil and Triumph: My Years as Secretary of State*, New York, 1993

Shultz, G. and Goodby, J. (eds), *The War That Must Never Be Fought*, Stanford, 2015

Shute, N., *On the Beach*, London, 1966

Sime, R., *Lise Meitner: A Life in Physics*, Berkeley/Los Angeles, 1996

Siracusa, J., *Nuclear Weapons: A Very Short Introduction*, Oxford, 2008

Snow, C., *The Physicists*, London, 1981

Sokolovsky, V., *Military Strategy: Soviet Doctrine and Concepts*, Introduction by H. Dinerstein, L. Goure, and T. Wolfe, Santa Monica, 1963

Sokolski, H. (ed.), *Getting MAD: Nuclear Mutual Assured Destruction, Its Origins and Practice*, Carlisle, PA, 2004

Stannard, R., *Relativity: A Very Short Introduction,* Oxford, 2008

Starodubov, V., *Superderzhavy XX Veka* (Superpowers of the Twentieth Century), Moscow, 2001

Starodubov, V., *Ot Razoruzhenia k Kapituliatsii* (From Disarmament to Capitulation), Moscow, 2007

Stewart, N. et al., 'The Soviet War Scare', Washington, DC, 1990

Sudoplatov, P. and A., *Special Tasks*, New York, 1994

Szilard, L., *Voice of the Dolphins*, London, 1967

Talbott, S., *Endgame: The Inside Story of SALT II*, New York, 1979

Talbott, S., *The Master of the Game: Paul Nitze and the Nuclear Peace*, New York, 1989

Taubman, P., *The Partnership: Five Cold Warriors and Their Quest to Ban the Bomb*, London, 2012

Taubman, W., *Khrushchev: The Man and His Era*, London, 2003

Tchen, J. and Yeats, D., *Yellow Peril! An Archive of Anti-Asian Fear*, London, 2014

Terraine, J., *The Right of the Line: The Royal Air Force in the European Air War 1939–1945*, London, 1985

Tertrais, B. (ed.), *Thinking about Strategy: A Tribute to Sir Michael Quinlan*, Paris, 2011

Thom, F., *Beria: Le Janus du Kremlin*, Paris, 2013

Thompson, N., *The Hawk and the Dove: Paul Nitze, George Kennan, and the History of the Cold War*, New York, 2009

Thomson, W. et al., *The Effects of the Atomic Bombs at Hiroshima and Nagasaki*, London, 1946

US Congress, *Deterrence and Survival in the Nuclear Age*, Washington, DC, 1976

US Atomic Energy Commission, *In the Matter of J. Robert Oppenheimer*, Vol. VII, Washington, DC, 1954

Varennikov, V., *Nepovtorimoe* (Unrepeatable), Vols I–VII, Moscow, 2001

Vucinich, A., *Einstein and Soviet Ideology*, Stanford, 2001

Wainstein, L. et al., *The Evolution of U.S. Strategic Command and Control and Warning, 1945–1972*, Arlington, VA, 1975

Wardak, G., Turbiville, G. and Garthoff, R., *The Voroshilov Lectures: Materials from the Soviet Military Staff Academy*, Washington, DC, 1989

Watch, D. and Savranskaya, S., *SALT II and the Growth of Mistrust: Transcript of Proceedings of Conference*, National Security Archive, Washington, DC, 1994

Weir, G. and Boyne, W., *Rising Tide: The Untold Story of the Russian Submarines That Fought the Cold War*, New York, 2003

Wells, H. G., *The War of the Worlds*, London, 1898

Wells, H. G., *The World Set Free*, London, 1914

Werth, A., *Russia at War 1941–1945*, London, 1964

Whitfield, S., *The Culture of the Cold War*, Baltimore, 2006

Wilson, J., *Britain on the Brink*, Barnsley, 2012

Wilson, W., *Five Myths about Nuclear Weapons*, New York, 2013

Wittner, L., *Confronting the Bomb: A Short History of the World Nuclear Disarmament Movement*, Stanford, 2009

Woodman, R. and Conley, D., *Cold War Command: The Dramatic Story of a Nuclear Submariner*, Barnsley, 2014

Wynne, H., *RAF Nuclear Deterrent Forces*, London, 1994

Yarynich, V., *C3: Nuclear Command, Control, Cooperation*, Washington, DC, 2003

Yegorova, N. and Chubarian, A. (eds), *Kholodnaya Voina 1945–1963* (The Cold War 1945–1963), Moscow, 2003

Zaloga, S., *The Kremlin's Nuclear Sword: The Rise and Fall of Russia's Strategic Nuclear Forces, 1945–2000*, Washington, DC, 2002

Zubkova, E., *Russia After the War: Hopes, Illusions, and Disappointments, 1945–1957*, Armonk, NY, 1998

Zubok, V., *A Failed Empire*, Chapel Hill, NJ, 2007

Zubov, A., *Istoria Rossii XX-ogo Veka* (History of 20th-century Russia), Vols I and II, Moscow, 2011

Zuckerman, S., *Nuclear Illusion & Reality*, New York, 1982

Filmography

Films, whether documentary or fictional, give a good idea of prevailing attitudes to nuclear war and the surrounding politics. There is a plethora in English, Russian, Japanese, and other languages. Some, such as the French prize-winning film *Hiroshima Mon Amour* (1959), are unpleasantly exploitative. Others, such as *Dr Strangelove*, *On the Beach*, and *The Day After*, helped to set the debate. Most of those listed are available on the internet and YouTube.

Films about nuclear accidents and nuclear warfare became particularly popular in the last decade of the Cold War. These included *The China Syndrome* (1979), *The Chain Reaction* (1980), *Silkwood* (1983), *Testament* (1983), *WarGames* (1983), *Ground Zero* (1987), and *Rules of Engagement* (1989).

Feature Films

English language
I Married a Communist (1949)
Seven Days to Noon (1950), British feature film
I Was a Communist for the FBI (1951)
My Son John (1952)
Strategic Air Command (1955)
Big Jim McLain (1956)
On the Beach (1959)
Dr Strangelove (1964)
Fail Safe (1964)
The War Game (1965), BBC drama
Oppenheimer (1980), BBC docudrama
The Day After (1983)

Threads (1984), BBC drama
When the Wind Blows (1986)
By Dawn's Early Light (1990), US TV drama
The Hunt for Red October (1990)
Crimson Tide (1995)
Hiroshima (1995), Japanese-Canadian docudrama
Thirteen Days (2000)
K-19 The Widowmaker (2002)

Russian language
Devyat Dnei Odnogo Goda (Nine Days in One Year, 1962)
Ukroshchnie Ognya (Mastering the Fire, 1972)
Vybor Tseli (Choosing the Target, 1975)
Pisma Mertvogo Cheloveka (Letters of a Dead Man, 1986)

Japanese language
Barefoot Gen (1983)
Black Rain (1989)

Documentary and Official Films

English language
Duck and Cover (1951)
Survival under Atomic Attack (1951)
Let's Face It (1954), US Air Force
The Air Force Missile Mission (1957), Strategic Air Command (with James Stewart)
Protect and Survive (1975)
The Price of Peace and Freedom (1976)
The Atomic Café (1982)
Nuclear War in Britain: Home Front Civil Defence Films, 1951–1987
Space Race (2005), BBC docudrama

Russian language
Grazhdanskaya oborona v selskoi mestnosti (Civil Defence in the Countryside, 1962)
Strasti po Atomu (Passions about the Atom) http://russia.tv/brand/show/brand_id/22125 (2012)
Khariton i Oppengeimer: Genii i Zlodei (Khariton and Oppenheimer: Geniuses and Villains) https://www.youtube.com/watch?v=VL_qvI4IcGM (2014)

LIST OF ILLUSTRATIONS
AND PHOTO CREDITS

13. John F. Kennedy and Harold Macmillan at the Key West Naval Station, 1961 (Don Pinder/Florida Keys Public Library)

14. Peggy Pond Church residence, Los Alamos, 1925–42 by T. Harmon Parkhurst (courtesy Palace of the Governors Photo Archives (NMHM/DCA, neg. 001288)

15. The Russian royal family visiting Sarov Monastery, Russia, 1903 (Heritage Image Partnership/Alamy)

16. Peter Sellers in *Dr Strangelove*, 1964 (Granger/TopFoto)

17. Herman Khan, New York, 1968 (John Loengard/The *LIFE* Picture Collection/Getty Images)

18. Edward Teller, Stanford, 1968 (STF/AFP/Getty Images)

19. 'This Godless Communism', 1961, illustration by R. Crandall from *Treasure Chest*, comic book issued by the Catholic Guild, vol.17, no. 20, p. 9 (Private collection)

20. Poster for *I Was a Communist for the F.B.I.*, 1951 (Paul Faherty/Warner Bros/Kobal/Rex Shutterstock)

21. 'Capitalists from all countries, unite!', poster by Viktor Deni, satirising the League of Nations, *c*.1917–20 (akg-images)

22. Cartoon showing a Pentagon official and US scientist with vial of the AIDS virus, from *Pravda*, 31 October 1986

23. Albert Einstein and Niels Bohr, *c*.1920 (Science & Society Picture Library/Getty Images)

24. General Leslie R. Groves (left) and Dr J. Robert Oppenhiemer during the Manhattan Project, *c*.1945 (Science History Images/Alamy)

25. Igor Vasilyevich Kurchatov (left) and Yulii Borisovich Khariton at the Kremlin (courtesy Kurchatov Museum, Kurchatov, Kursk)

26. Pyotr Kapitsa and Nikolay Semyonov, 1921, portrait by Boris Kustodiev. Private Collection (Fine Art Images/Heritage Images/Getty Images)

27. NKVD mugshots of Lev Davidovich Landau, 1938

28. Gen. Curtis LeMay, 1954 (A. Y. Owen/The *LIFE* Picture Collection/Getty Images)

29. US Air Force Staff Sergeant Billy Davis, Strategic Air Command security guard, on sentry duty at the entrance to Offutt Air Force Base, Nebraska, early 1960s (National Archives & Records Administration, Still Pictures Division, RG 342B/Box 434)

30. B-52 bomber, 1960 (akg-images/NASA)

31. Nuclear submarine HMS Vanguard in the Clyde estuary, Scotland (Defence Images)

32. SS-18 'Satan' missile test at Baikonur, Kazakhstan, 2014 (TASS/TopFoto)

33. Bertrand Russell with anti-nuclear demonstrators in front of the Ministry of Defence, Whitehall, London, 18 February 1961 (Sally & Richard Greenhill/Alamy)

34. 'No Room for them to Land', *c.*1947, poster by Mark Aleksandrovich Abramov (CCI/Rex Shutterstock) © DACS, London, 2017
35. Sir Joseph Rotblat, 2002 (Rossano B. Maniscalch/Alinari Archives/Getty Images)
36. Nuclear test site at Semipalatinsk, Kazakhstan, 1991 (Alain Nogues/Sygma/ Getty Images)

Every effort has been made to contact all copyright holders. The publishers will be pleased to make good in future editions any error or omission brought to their attention.

ACKNOWLEDGEMENTS

My daughter Kate grew up in the age of nuclear anxiety. Wanting to understand, she gave the initial impulse.

Many people enlightened my ignorance, challenged my judgements, and pointed out my mistakes. Pavel Podvig and Alex Wellerstein read the draft at a very late stage with scrupulous care: their detailed comments and suggestions saved me from gross error. David Hoffman, the prizewinning author of *The Dead Hand,* was particularly generous from the beginning with ideas, references and textual comments. Richard Mottram drew for me on his decades of professional experience of British defence policy. Igor Maskaev commented helpfully on the draft, and tracked down relevant books in Russian which were unavailable here. Frank Kelly and Richard Batley corrected my science. Greg Herken gave an encouraging assessment of the final draft. Alexander Bessmertnykh, Michael Herman, Mervyn Jones, and Kris Stoddart commented on the evolving text. My former colleagues David Logan and Mark Pellew contributed more than they realised. The final judgements remain my own, of course. So do the errors I have failed to identify.

This is the fourth book I have worked on with my editor Penny Daniel, a constant pleasure and a laugh. Lesley Levene was again an eagle-eyed copy editor, and Cecilia Mackay dug out some striking pictures. Andrew Franklin, Penny's boss at Profile Books, presided over all with acerbic wit and encyclopaedic knowledge.

I owe a special debt of gratitude to Sue McLaren, who brought light and love into the darkness which followed the deaths of Robin and Jill, and gave me continual support as I wrote this book.

INDEX